Ontario Civil Practice 2011 Forms and Other Materials

by

PROFESSOR GARRY D. WATSON, Q.C.

and

MICHAEL McGOWAN
of the Ontario Bar

CARSWELL®

This work reproduces official English language versions of federal statutes and regulations. As this material also exists in official French language form, the reader is advised that reference to the official French language version may be warranted in appropriate circumstances.

♾ The paper used in this publication meets the minimum requirements of American National Standard for Information Sciences — Permanence of Paper for Printed Library Materials, ANSI Z39.48-1984.

A cataloguing record for this publication is available from Library and Archives Canada.

ISSN 1184-7433

ISBN 978-0-7798-2703-9 (bound: 2011 ed.)

ISBN 978-0-7798-2704-6 (pbk.: 2011 ed.)

Printed in the United States by Thomson Reuters.

THOMSON REUTERS

CARSWELL, A DIVISION OF THOMSON REUTERS CANADA LIMITED

One Corporate Plaza
2075 Kennedy Road
Toronto, Ontario
M1T 3V4

Customer Relations
Toronto 1-416-609-3800
Elsewhere in Canada/U.S. 1-800-387-5164
Fax 1-416-298-5082
www.carswell.com
E-mail www.carswell.com/email

TABLE OF CONTENTS

TABLE OF CASES

References to the Courts of Justice Act, Judicial Review Procedure Act and Statutory Powers Procedure Act are preceded by the appropriate abbreviation and "s." All other references are to the Rules of Civil Procedure.

T. OF C.

TABLE OF CASES

TABLE OF CASES

TABLE OF CASES

FORMS

TABLE OF FORMS

FORMS

TABLE OF FORMS

FORMS

TABLE OF FORMS

FORMS

TABLE OF FORMS

FORMS

Made under the *Courts of Justice Act*

R.R.O. 1990, Reg. 194

as am. R.R.O. 1990, Reg. 194, r. 13.1.02(12), 24.01(2), 37.03(3), 78.14; O. Reg. 219/91; 396/91; 73/92; 175/92; 535/92; 770/92; 212/93; 465/93; 466/93; 766/93; 351/94; 484/94; 739/94; 740/94; 69/95; 70/95; 377/95; 533/95; 534/95; 60/96; 61/96; 175/96; 332/96; 333/96; 536/96; 554/96; 555/96; 118/97; 348/97; 427/97; 442/97; 171/98; 214/98; 217/98; 292/98; 452/98; 453/98 [s. 2(2) revoked O. Reg. 244/01, s. 7.]; 570/98; 627/98; 288/99; 290/99; 292/99; 484/99; 488/99; 583/99; 24/00; 25/00; 504/00; 652/00; 653/00; 654/00; 113/01; 243/01; 244/01; 284/01; 427/01 [ss. 1(2), 4(2), 5(2), 6(2), (5) not in force at date of publication. Revoked O. Reg. 308/02, ss. 1(2), 2(2), 3(2), 4(3), (5).]; 447/01; 457/01; 206/02; 308/02; 336/02; 19/03; 54/03; 263/03; 419/03; 14/04; 131/04; 132/04, ss. 1–10, 11 (Fr.), 12–24; 219/04; 42/05; 168/05; 198/05; 260/05 [Corrected Ont. Gaz. 9/7/05, Vol. 138:28; 4/3/2006, Vol. 139:9.]; 77/06; 8/07; 573/07; 575/07, ss. 1–4, 5 (Fr.), 6–24, 25(1) (Fr.), (2), 26–38; 55/08; 438/08, ss. 1–12, 13(1)–(3), (4) (Fr.), 14–65, 66 (Fr.), 67; 394/09; 453/09; 186/10, ss. 1–5 (Fr.), 6.

FORM 4A — GENERAL HEADING OF DOCUMENTS — ACTIONS

Courts of Justice Act

[Repealed O. Reg. 77/06, s. 3.]

[Editor's Note: Forms 4A to 78A of the Rules of Civil Procedure have been repealed by O. Reg. 77/06, effective July 1, 2006. Pursuant to Rule of Civil Procedure 1.06, when a form is referred to by number, the reference is to the form with that number that is described in the Table of Forms at the end of these rules and which is available on the Internet through www.ontariocourtforms.on.ca. For your convenience, the government form as published on this website is reproduced below.]

ONTARIO (*Court file no.*)

SUPERIOR COURT OF JUSTICE

BETWEEN:

(*name*)

Plaintiff

and

(*name*)

Defendant

(Title of document)

(Text of document)

(For the title of the proceeding in the case of a,

(a) counterclaim against a person who is not already a party to the main action, follow Form 27B;

(b) third or subsequent party claim in an action, follow Form 29A in all documents in the main action and the third or subsequent party action;

(c) garnishment, follow Form 60H; or

(d) mortgage action in which defendants are added on a reference, follow Form 64N;

(For the general heading in a proceeding in an appellate court, follow Form B.)

November 1, 2005

FORM 4B — GENERAL HEADING OF DOCUMENTS — APPLICATIONS

Courts of Justice Act

[Repealed O. Reg. 77/06, s. 3.]

[Editor's Note: Forms 4A to 78A of the Rules of Civil Procedure have been repealed by O. Reg. 77/06, effective July 1, 2006. Pursuant to Rule of Civil Procedure 1.06, when a form is referred to by number, the reference is to the form with that number that is described in the Table of Forms at the end of these rules and which is available on the Internet through www.ontariocourtforms.on.ca. For your convenience, the government form as published on this website is reproduced below.]

ONTARIO *(Court file no.)*
SUPERIOR COURT OF JUSTICE

BETWEEN:

(name)

Applicant

and

(name)

Respondent

APPLICATION UNDER *(statutory provision or rule under which the application is made)*

(Title of document)
(Text of document)

(In a proceeding in an appellate court, follow Form 61B; in an appeal from the Ontario Court of Justice, follow Form 70A.)

November 1, 2005

FORM 4C — BACKSHEET

Courts of Justice Act

[Repealed O. Reg. 77/06, s. 3.]

[Editor's Note: Forms 4A to 78A of the Rules of Civil Procedure have been repealed by O. Reg. 77/06, effective July 1, 2006. Pursuant to Rule of Civil Procedure 1.06, when a form is referred to by number, the reference is to the form with that number that is described in the Table of Forms at the end of these rules and which is available on the Internet through www.ontariocourtforms.on.ca. For your convenience, the government form as published on this website is reproduced below.]

(Short title of proceeding)	*(Court file no.)*
	(Name of Court) PROCEEDING COMMENCED AT *(place)* *(Title of document)* *(if affidavit, indicate name of deponent and date sworn)* *(Name, address, telephone number and fax number of lawyer or party)* *(Law society registration number of lawyer)* *(Fax number, if known, of person on whom document is to be served)*

July 1, 2007

FORM 4D — AFFIDAVIT

Courts of Justice Act

[Repealed O. Reg. 77/06, s. 3.]

[Editor's Note: Forms 4A to 78A of the Rules of Civil Procedure have been repealed by O. Reg. 77/06, effective July 1, 2006. Pursuant to Rule of Civil Procedure 1.06, when a form is referred to by number, the reference is to the form with that number that is described in the Table of Forms at the end of these rules and which is available on the Internet through www.ontariocourtforms.on.ca. For your convenience, the government form as published on this website is reproduced below.]

(*General heading*)

AFFIDAVIT OF (NAME)

I, (*full name of deponent*), of the (City, Town, *etc.*) of ...., in the (County, Regional Municipality, *etc.*) of ...., (*where the deponent is a party or the lawyer, officer, director, member or employee of a party, set out the deponent's capacity*), MAKE OATH AND SAY (*or* AFFIRM):

1. (*Set out the statements of fact in consecutively numbered paragraphs, with each paragraph being confined as far as possible to a particular statement of fact.*)

Sworn (*or* Affirmed) before me at the (City, Town, *etc.*) of .... in the (County, Regional Municipality, *etc.*) of ...., on (*date*).	
.... Commissioner for Taking Affidavits (*or as may be*)	.... (*Signature of deponent*)

July 1, 2007

FORM 4E — REQUISITION

Courts of Justice Act

[Repealed O. Reg. 77/06, s. 3.]

[Editor's Note: Forms 4A to 78A of the Rules of Civil Procedure have been repealed by O. Reg. 77/06, effective July 1, 2006. Pursuant to Rule of Civil Procedure 1.06, when a form is referred to by number, the reference is to the form with that number that is described in the Table of Forms at the end of these rules and which is available on the Internet through www.ontariocourtforms.on.ca. For your convenience, the government form as published on this website is reproduced below.]

(*General heading*)

REQUISITION

TO THE LOCAL REGISTRAR at (*place*)

I REQUIRE (*Set out a concise statement of what is sought and include all particulars necessary for the registrar to act. Where what is sought is authorized by an order, refer to the order in the requisition and attach a copy of the entered order. Where an affidavit or other document must be filed with the requisition, refer to it in the requisition and attach it.*)

(*Date*) (*Name, address and telephone number of lawyer or person filing requisition*)

(*The following are examples of different kinds of requisition.*)

(*Simple requisition*)

I REQUIRE a certified copy of the (*identify document by nature and date*).

(*Order attached*)

I REQUIRE, in accordance with the order dated (*date*), a copy of which is attached, a commission authorizing the taking of evidence before the commissioner named in the order and a letter of request.

I REQUIRE, in accordance with the order dated (*date*), a copy of which is attached, a certificate of pending litigation in respect of the land described in the statement of claim.

(*Affidavit attached*)

I REQUIRE an order to continue this action with (*name*) as plaintiff and (*name*) as defendants. An affidavit stating that the defendant (*name*) has reached the age of majority is attached.

July 1, 2007

FORM 4F — NOTICE OF CONSTITUTIONAL QUESTION

Courts of Justice Act

[Repealed O. Reg. 77/06, s. 3.]

[Editor's Note: Forms 4A to 78A of the Rules of Civil Procedure have been repealed by O. Reg. 77/06, effective July 1, 2006. Pursuant to Rule of Civil Procedure 1.06, when a form is referred to by number, the reference is to the form with that number that is described in the Table of Forms at the end of these rules and which is available on the Internet through www.ontariocourtforms.on.ca. For your convenience, the government form as published on this website is reproduced below.]

(General heading)

NOTICE OF CONSTITUTIONAL QUESTION

The .... *(identify party)* intends to question the constitutional validity *(or* applicability) of .... *(identify the particular legislative provisions or the particular rule of common law) (or* to claim a remedy under subsection 24(1) of the *Cana-*

dian Charter of Rights and Freedoms in relation to an act or omission of the Government of Canada *(or* Ontario)).

The question is to be argued on .... *(day)*, ... *(date)*, at .... *(time)*, at .... *(address of court house)*.

The following are the material facts giving rise to the constitutional question: .... *(Set out concisely the material facts that relate to the constitutional question. Where appropriate, attach pleadings or reasons for decision.)*

The following is the legal basis for the constitutional question: .... *(Set out concisely the legal basis for each question, identifying the nature of the constitutional principles to be argued.)*

(Date) *(Name, address and telephone number of lawyer or party)*

TO

The Attorney General of Ontario *(as required by section 109 of the Courts of Justice Act)*

Constitutional Law Branch

4th floor

720 Bay Street

Toronto, Ontario M5G 2K1

fax: (416) 326-4015

The Attorney General of Canada *(as required by section 109 of the Courts of Justice Act)*

Suite 3400, Exchange Tower

Box 36, First Canadian Place

Toronto, Ontario M5X 1K6

fax: (416) 973-3004

(or Justice Building

239 Wellington Street

Ottawa, Ontario K1A 0H8

fax: (613) 954-1920)

(Names and addresses of lawyers for all other parties and of all other parties acting in person) ....

(This notice must be served as soon as the circumstances requiring it become known and, in any event, at least 15 days before the question is to be argued, unless the court orders otherwise.)

July 1, 2007

FORM 7A — REQUEST FOR APPOINTMENT OF LITIGATION GUARDIAN

Courts of Justice Act

[Repealed O. Reg. 77/06, s. 3.]

[Editor's Note: Forms 4A to 78A of the Rules of Civil Procedure have been repealed by O. Reg. 77/06, effective July 1, 2006. Pursuant to Rule of Civil Procedure 1.06, when a form is referred to by number, the reference is to the form with that number that is described in the Table of Forms at the end of these rules and which is available on the Internet through www.ontariocourtforms.on.ca. For your convenience, the government form as published on this website is reproduced below.]

(*General heading*)

REQUEST FOR APPOINTMENT OF LITIGATION GUARDIAN

THE PLAINTIFF (*or as may be*) BELIEVES THAT YOU ARE UNDER A LEGAL DISABILITY. As a party under disability, you must have a litigation guardian appointed by the court to act on your behalf in defending this proceeding.

YOU ARE REQUIRED to have some proper person make a motion to this court forthwith to be appointed as your litigation guardian.

IF YOU FAIL TO DO SO WITHIN TEN DAYS after service of this request, the plaintiff (*or as may be*) may move without further notice to have the court appoint a litigation guardian to act on your behalf.

(*Date*)	(*Name, address and telephone number of lawyer or party*)

TO: (*Name and address of party under disability*)

July 1, 2007

FORM 7B — ORDER TO CONTINUE (MINOR REACHING AGE OF MAJORITY)

Courts of Justice Act

[Repealed O. Reg. 77/06, s. 3.]

[Editor's Note: Forms 4A to 78A of the Rules of Civil Procedure have been repealed by O. Reg. 77/06, effective July 1, 2006. Pursuant to Rule of Civil Procedure 1.06, when a form is referred to by number, the reference is to the form with that number that is described in the Table of Forms at the end of these rules and which is available on the Internet through

www.ontariocourtforms.on.ca. For your convenience, the government form as published on this website is reproduced below.]

(*General heading*)

(*Court seal*)

ORDER TO CONTINUE

On the requisition of (*identify party*) and on reading the affidavit of (*name*), filed, which states that the minor (*name of party*) reached the age of majority on (*date*),

IT IS ORDERED that this proceeding continue by (*or* against) (*name of party*) without a litigation guardian and that the title of the proceeding be amended accordingly in all documents issued, served or filed after the date of this order.

Date .... Signed by ....
Local registrar

Address of court office ....
....

November 1, 2005

FORM 8A — NOTICE TO ALLEGED PARTNER

Courts of Justice Act

[Repealed O. Reg. 77/06, s. 3.]

[Editor's Note: Forms 4A to 78A of the Rules of Civil Procedure have been repealed by O. Reg. 77/06, effective July 1, 2006. Pursuant to Rule of Civil Procedure 1.06, when a form is referred to by number, the reference is to the form with that number that is described in the Table of Forms at the end of these rules and which is available on the Internet through www.ontariocourtforms.on.ca. For your convenience, the government form as published on this website is reproduced below.]

(*General heading*)

NOTICE TO ALLEGED PARTNER

YOU ARE ALLEGED TO HAVE BEEN A PARTNER on (*date*) (*or* during (*period*)) in the partnership of (*firm name*) named as a party to this proceeding.

IF YOU WISH TO DENY THAT YOU WERE A PARTNER at any material time, you must defend this proceeding separately from the partnership, denying that you were a partner at the material time. If you fail to do so, you will be deemed to have been a partner on the date (*or* during the period) set out above.

AN ORDER AGAINST THE PARTNERSHIP MAY BE ENFORCED AGAINST YOU PERSONALLY if you are deemed to have been a partner, if you admit that you were a partner or if the court finds that you were a partner at the material time.

(*Date*) (*Name, address and telephone number of plaintiff's lawyer or plaintiff*)

TO (*Name and address of alleged partner*)

July 1, 2007

FORM 11A — ORDER TO CONTINUE (TRANSFER OR TRANSMISSION OF INTEREST)

Courts of Justice Act

[Repealed O. Reg. 77/06, s. 3.]

[Editor's Note: Forms 4A to 78A of the Rules of Civil Procedure have been repealed by O. Reg. 77/06, effective July 1, 2006. Pursuant to Rule of Civil Procedure 1.06, when a form is referred to by number, the reference is to the form with that number that is described in the Table of Forms at the end of these rules and which is available on the Internet through www.ontariocourtforms.on.ca. For your convenience, the government form as published on this website is reproduced below.]

(*General heading*)

(*Court seal*)

ORDER TO CONTINUE

On the requisition of (*identify party or person*) and on reading the affidavit of (*name*), filed, which indicates that on (*date*), (*recite the details of the transfer or transmission of interest or liability*),

IT IS ORDERED that this proceeding continue and that the title of the proceeding in all documents issued, served or filed after the date of this order be as follows: (*Set out new title of proceeding, deleting name of party whose interest is transferred or transmitted and showing name of new party.*)

Date .... Signed by ....

Local registrar

Address of court office ....

....

A party who wishes to set aside or vary this order must make a motion to do so forthwith after the order comes to the party's attention.

Where a transmission of interest occurs by reason of bankruptcy, leave of the bankruptcy court may be required under section 69.4 of the *Bankruptcy and Insolvency Act* (Canada) before the proceeding may continue.

November 1, 2005

FORM 14A — STATEMENT OF CLAIM (GENERAL)

Courts of Justice Act

[Repealed O. Reg. 77/06, s. 3.]

[Editor's Note: Forms 4A to 78A of the Rules of Civil Procedure have been repealed by O. Reg. 77/06, effective July 1, 2006. Pursuant to Rule of Civil Procedure 1.06, when a form is referred to by number, the reference is to the form with that number that is described in the Table of Forms at the end of these rules and which is available on the Internet through www.ontariocourtforms.on.ca. For your convenience, the government form as published on this website is reproduced below.]

(*General heading*)

(*Court seal*)

STATEMENT OF CLAIM

TO THE DEFENDANT

A LEGAL PROCEEDING HAS BEEN COMMENCED AGAINST YOU by the plaintiff. The claim made against you is set out in the following pages.

IF YOU WISH TO DEFEND THIS PROCEEDING, you or an Ontario lawyer acting for you must prepare a statement of defence in Form 18A prescribed by the *Rules of Civil Procedure*, serve it on the plaintiff's lawyer or, where the plaintiff does not have a lawyer, serve it on the plaintiff, and file it, with proof of service in this court office, WITHIN TWENTY DAYS after this statement of claim is served on you, if you are served in Ontario.

If you are served in another province or territory of Canada or in the United States of America, the period for serving and filing your statement of defence is forty days. If you are served outside Canada and the United States of America, the period is sixty days.

Instead of serving and filing a statement of defence, you may serve and file a notice of intent to defend in Form 18B prescribed by the Rules of Civil Procedure. This will entitle you to ten more days within which to serve and file your statement of defence.

IF YOU FAIL TO DEFEND THIS PROCEEDING, JUDGMENT MAY BE GIVEN AGAINST YOU IN YOUR ABSENCE AND WITHOUT FURTHER NOTICE TO YOU. IF YOU WISH TO DEFEND THIS PROCEEDING BUT ARE UNABLE TO PAY LEGAL FEES, LEGAL AID MAY BE AVAILABLE TO YOU BY CONTACTING A LOCAL LEGAL AID OFFICE.

(*Where the claim made is for money only, include the following:*)

IF YOU PAY THE PLAINTIFF'S CLAIM, and $ .... for costs, within the time for serving and filing your statement of defence you may move to have this proceeding dismissed by the court. If you believe the amount claimed for costs is excessive, you may pay the plaintiff's claim and $400 for costs and have the costs assessed by the court.

Date .... Issued by ....
Local registrar

Address of court office ....
....

TO (*Name and address of each defendant*)

(In an action under the simplified procedure provided in Rule 76, add:)

THIS ACTION IS BROUGHT AGAINST YOU UNDER THE SIMPLIFIED PROCEDURE PROVIDED IN RULE 76 OF THE RULES OF CIVIL PROCEDURE.

CLAIM

1. The plaintiff claims: (*State here the precise relief claimed.*)

(*Then set out in separate, consecutively numbered paragraphs each allegation of material fact relied on to substantiate the claim.*)

(*Where the statement of claim is to be served outside Ontario without a court order, set out the facts and the specific provisions of Rule 17 relied on in support of such service.*)

(*Date of issue*) (*Name, address and telephone number of lawyer or plaintiff*)

July 1, 2007

FORM 14B — STATEMENT OF CLAIM (MORTGAGE ACTION — FORECLOSURE)

Courts of Justice Act

[Repealed O. Reg. 77/06, s. 3.]

[Editor's Note: Forms 4A to 78A of the Rules of Civil Procedure have been repealed by O. Reg. 77/06, effective July 1, 2006. Pursuant to Rule of Civil Procedure 1.06, when a form is referred to by number, the reference is to the form with that number that is described in the Table of Forms at the end of these rules and which is available on the Internet through www.ontariocourtforms.on.ca. For your convenience, the government form as published on this website is reproduced below.]

(*General heading*)

(*Court seal*)

STATEMENT OF CLAIM (MORTGAGE ACTION — FORECLOSURE)

TO THE DEFENDANT

A LEGAL PROCEEDING HAS BEEN COMMENCED AGAINST YOU by the plaintiff. The claim made against you is set out in the following pages.

IF YOU WISH TO DEFEND THIS PROCEEDING, you or an Ontario lawyer acting for you must prepare a statement of defence in Form 18A prescribed by the *Rules of Civil Procedure*, serve it on the plaintiff's lawyer or, where the plaintiff does not have a lawyer, serve it on the plaintiff, and file it, with proof of service, in this court office, WITHIN 20 DAYS after this statement of claim is served on you, if you are served in Ontario.

If you are served in another province or territory of Canada or in the United States of America, the period for serving and filing your statement of defence is 40 days. If you are served outside Canada and the United States of America, the period is 60 days.

Instead of serving and filing a statement of defence, you may serve and file a notice of intent to defend in Form 18B prescribed by the *Rules of Civil Procedure*. This will entitle you to 10 more days within which to serve and file your statement of defence.

(*Where payment of the mortgage debt is claimed, add:*)

IF YOU PAY THE PLAINTIFF'S CLAIM, and $ .... for costs, within the time for serving and filing your statement of defence, you may move to have this proceeding dismissed by the court. If you believe the amount claimed for costs is excessive, you may pay the plaintiff's claim and $400 for costs and have the costs assessed by the court.

REQUEST TO REDEEM

Whether or not you serve and file a statement of defence, you may request the right to redeem the mortgaged property by serving a request to redeem (Form 64A) on the plaintiff and filing it in this court office within the time for serving and filing your statement of defence or at any time before being noted in default. If you do so, you will be entitled to seven days notice of the taking of the account of the amount due to the plaintiff, and to 60 days from the taking of the account within which to redeem the mortgaged property.

If you hold a lien, charge or encumbrance on the mortgaged property subsequent to the mortgage in question, you may file a request to redeem, which must contain particulars of your claim verified by an affidavit, and you will be entitled to redeem only if your claim is not disputed or, if disputed, is proved on a reference.

REQUEST FOR SALE

If you do not serve and file a statement of defence, you may request a sale of the mortgaged property by serving a request for sale (Form 64F) on the plaintiff and filing it in this court office within the time for serving and filing your statement of defence, or at any time before being noted in default. If you do so, the plaintiff will be entitled to obtain a judgment for a sale with a reference and you will be entitled to notice of the reference.

If you hold a lien, charge or encumbrance on the mortgaged property subsequent to the mortgage in question and you do not serve and file a request to redeem, you may file a request for sale which must contain particulars of your claim verified by an affidavit, and must be accompanied by a receipt showing that $250 has been paid into court as security for the costs of the plaintiff(s) and of any other party having carriage of the sale.

DEFAULT JUDGMENT

IF YOU FAIL TO SERVE AND FILE A STATEMENT OF DEFENCE, JUDGMENT MAY BE GIVEN AGAINST YOU WITHOUT FURTHER NOTICE. IF YOU WISH TO DEFEND THIS PROCEEDING BUT ARE UNABLE TO PAY LEGAL FEES, LEGAL

AID MAY BE AVAILABLE TO YOU BY CONTACTING A LOCAL LEGAL AID OFFICE.

Date .... Issued by ....
Local Registrar

Address of
court office ....
....

TO: (*Name and address of each defendant*)

(sale action)

REQUEST TO REDEEM

Whether or not you serve and file a statement of defence, you may request the right to redeem the mortgaged property by serving a request to redeem (Form 64A) on the plaintiff and filing it in this court office within the time for serving and filing your statement of defence, or at any time, before being noted in default. If you do so, you will be entitled to seven days notice of the taking of the account of the amount due to the plaintiff, and to 60 days from the taking of the account within which to redeem the mortgaged property.

DEFAULT JUDGMENT

IF YOU FAIL TO SERVE AND FILE A STATEMENT OF DEFENCE, JUDGMENT MAY BE GIVEN AGAINST YOU WITHOUT FURTHER NOTICE. IF YOU WISH TO DEFEND THIS PROCEEDING BUT ARE UNABLE TO PAY LEGAL FEES, LEGAL AID MAY BE AVAILABLE TO YOU BY CONTACTING A LOCAL LEGAL AID OFFICE.

Date .... Issued by ....
Local Registrar

Address of
court office ....
....

TO: (*Name and address of each defendant*)

(*Subsequent encumbrancers are not to be named as defendants in this statement of claim in a sale action.*)

(*In an action under the simplified procedure provided in Rule 76, add:*)

THIS ACTION IS BROUGHT AGAINST YOU UNDER THE SIMPLIFIED PROCEDURE PROVIDED IN RULE 76 OF THE RULES OF CIVIL PROCEDURE.

CLAIM

1. The plaintiff claims:

(*foreclosure*)

(a) that the equity of redemption in the property secured by the mortgage mentioned below be foreclosed;

(*or*)

(*sale*)

(a) that the property secured by the mortgage mentioned below be sold and proceeds of sale applied towards the amount due under the mortgage, and payment to the plaintiff by the defendant (*name of defendant against whom payment of any deficiency is claimed*) personally of any deficiency if the sale proceeds are not sufficient to pay the amount found due to the plaintiff;

(*possession*)

(b) possession of the mortgaged property;

(*payment of mortgage debt*)

(c) payment by the defendant (*name of defendant against whom payment of mortgage debt is claimed*) of the sum of $ .... (*from paragraph 6 below*) now due under the mortgage together with interest at the rate of (*mortgage rate*) per cent per year until judgment;

(*interest*)

(d) post-judgment interest in accordance with the *Courts of Justice Act* (*or where the mortgage provides for interest after judgment at the mortgage rate, substitute:* post-judgment interest at the rate of (*mortgage rate*) per cent per year in accordance with the mortgage); and

(*costs*)

(e) the costs of this action (on a substantial indemnity basis *if the mortgage so provides, or if it provides for costs on a solicitor and client basis*).

2. The plaintiff's claim is on a mortgage dated (*date*), made between (*name of mortgagor*) and (*name of mortgagee*), and registered (*give particulars of registration and of any assignment of the mortgage*), under which the defendant (*or as may be*) mortgaged the property described below for a term of .... years securing the sum of $ .... and interest on that sum at the rate of .... per cent per year. The mortgage provides for the payment of principal and interest as follows: (*Set out terms of payment. Add a reference to provisions in the mortgage for solicitor and client costs and post-judgment interest if applicable*).

3. The mortgage provides that on default of payment of any sum required to be paid under the mortgage, the principal becomes due and payable and the plaintiff is entitled to possession of the mortgaged property and to foreclosure of the equity of redemption in the mortgaged property (*or* sale of the mortgaged property or *as may be*).

4. (*Where a claim for payment is made under section 20 of the* Mortgages Act *against a person other than the original mortgagor, add:*) The defendant (name) became liable under section 20 of the *Mortgages Act* to pay the amount of the mortgage debt to the plaintiff by reason of (*set out particulars of the transfer of the mortgaged property from the original mortgagor to this defendant*).

5. Default in payment of principal and interest (*or as may be*) occurred on (*date*), and still continues.

6. There is now due the terms of the mortgage:

(a)	for principal	$ ....
(b)	for taxes paid	$ ....
(c)	for premiums of insurance paid	$ ....
(d)	for maintenance costs paid	$ ....
(e)	for heating costs paid	$ ....
(f)	for utility costs paid	$ ....
	(add any other costs in similar fashion)	$ ....
(g)	for interest (set out particulars)	$ ....

Total now due: $ . . . .

The defendant (*name*) is liable to pay these sums and subsequent interest at the rate of .... per cent per year.

7. The following is a description of the mortgaged property: (*Set out a description sufficient for registration. For Land Titles land, include the parcel number.*)

(*In a foreclosure action where one or more subsequent encumbrancers are named as defendants, add:*)

8. The defendant (*name*) has been made a party to this action as a subsequent encumbrancer.

(*Where the statement of claim is to be served outside Ontario without a court order, set out the facts and the specific provisions of Rule 17 relied on in support of the service.*)

(*Date*) (*Name, address and telephone number of plaintiff's lawyer or plaintiff*)

July 1, 2007

FORM 14C — NOTICE OF ACTION

Courts of Justice Act

[Repealed O. Reg. 77/06, s. 3.]

[Editor's Note: Forms 4A to 78A of the Rules of Civil Procedure have been repealed by O. Reg. 77/06, effective July 1, 2006. Pursuant to Rule of Civil Procedure 1.06, when a form is referred to by number, the reference is to the form with that number that is described in the Table of Forms at the end of these rules and which is available on the Internet through www.ontariocourtforms.on.ca. For your convenience, the government form as published on this website is reproduced below.]

(*General heading*)

(*Court seal*)

NOTICE OF ACTION

TO THE DEFENDANT

A LEGAL PROCEEDING HAS BEEN COMMENCED AGAINST YOU by the plaintiff. The claim made against you is set out in the statement of claim served with this notice of action.

IF YOU WISH TO DEFEND THIS PROCEEDING, you or an Ontario lawyer acting for you must prepare a statement of defence in Form 18A prescribed by the Rules of Civil Procedure, serve it on the plaintiff's lawyer or, where the plaintiff does not have a lawyer, serve it on the plaintiff, and file it, with proof of service, in this court office, WITHIN TWENTY DAYS after this notice of action is served on you, if you are served in Ontario.

If you are served in another province or territory of Canada or in the United States of America, the period for serving and filing your statement of defence is forty days. If you are served outside Canada and the United States of America, the period is sixty days.

Instead of serving and filing a statement of defence, you may serve and file a notice of intent to defend in Form 18B prescribed by the Rules of Civil Procedure. This will entitle you to ten more days within which to serve and file your statement of defence.

IF YOU FAIL TO DEFEND THIS PROCEEDING, JUDGMENT MAY BE GIVEN AGAINST YOU IN YOUR ABSENCE AND WITHOUT FURTHER NOTICE TO YOU. IF YOU WISH TO DEFEND THIS PROCEEDING BUT ARE UNABLE TO PAY LEGAL FEES, LEGAL AID MAY BE AVAILABLE TO YOU BY CONTACTING A LOCAL LEGAL AID OFFICE.

(Where the claim made is for money only, include the following:)

IF YOU PAY THE PLAINTIFF'S CLAIM, and $ .... for costs, within the time for serving and filing your statement of defence, you may move to have this proceeding dismissed by the court. If you believe the amount claimed for costs is excessive, you may pay the plaintiff's claim and $400 for costs and have the costs assessed by the court.

Date .... Issued by ....
Local registrar

Address of court office ....
....

TO: *(Name and address of each defendant)*

(In an action under the simplified procedure provided in Rule 76, add:)

THIS ACTION IS BROUGHT AGAINST YOU UNDER THE SIMPLIFIED PROCEDURE PROVIDED IN RULE 76 OF THE RULES OF CIVIL PROCEDURE.

CLAIM

The plaintiff's claim is for *(set out a short statement of the nature of the plaintiff's claim).*

(Date of issue) *(Name, address and telephone number of lawyer or plaintiff)*

July 1, 2007

FORM 14D — STATEMENT OF CLAIM (ACTION COMMENCED BY NOTICE OF ACTION)

Courts of Justice Act

[Repealed O. Reg. 77/06, s. 3.]

[Editor's Note: Forms 4A to 78A of the Rules of Civil Procedure have been repealed by O. Reg. 77/06, effective July 1, 2006. Pursuant to Rule of Civil Procedure 1.06, when a form is referred to by number, the reference is to the form with that number that is described in the Table of Forms at the end of these rules and which is available on the Internet through www.ontariocourtforms.on.ca. For your convenience, the government form as published on this website is reproduced below.]

(General heading)

STATEMENT OF CLAIM

Notice of action issued on *(date)*

(In an action under the simplified procedure provided in Rule 76, add:)

THIS ACTION IS BROUGHT AGAINST YOU UNDER THE SIMPLIFIED PROCEDURE PROVIDED IN RULE 76 OF THE RULES OF CIVIL PROCEDURE.

1. The plaintiff claims: (*State here the precise relief claimed*).

(Then set out in separate, consecutively numbered paragraphs each allegation of material fact relied on to substantiate the claim.)

(Where the statement of claim is to be served outside Ontario without a court order, set out the facts and the specific provisions of Rule 17 relied on in support of such service.)

(Date) *(Name, address and telephone number of lawyer or plaintiff)*

July 1, 2007

FORM 14E — NOTICE OF APPLICATION

Courts of Justice Act

[Repealed O. Reg. 77/06, s. 3.]

[Editor's Note: Forms 4A to 78A of the Rules of Civil Procedure have been repealed by O. Reg. 77/06, effective July 1, 2006. Pursuant to Rule of Civil Procedure 1.06, when a form is referred to by number, the reference is to the form with that number that is described in the Table of Forms at the end of these rules and which is available on the Internet through www.ontariocourtforms.on.ca. For your convenience, the government form as published on this website is reproduced below.]

(General heading)

(Court seal)

NOTICE OF APPLICATION

TO THE RESPONDENT

A LEGAL PROCEEDING HAS BEEN COMMENCED by the applicant. The claim made by the applicant appears on the following page.

THIS APPLICATION will come on for a hearing on *(day)*, *(date)*, at *(time)*, at *(address of court house)*.

IF YOU WISH TO OPPOSE THIS APPLICATION, to receive notice of any step in the application or to be served with any documents in the application, you or an Ontario lawyer acting for you must forthwith prepare a notice of appearance in Form 38A prescribed by the *Rules of Civil Procedure*, serve it on the applicant's lawyer or, where the applicant does not have a lawyer, serve it on the applicant, and file it, with proof of service, in this court office, and you or your lawyer must appear at the hearing.

IF YOU WISH TO PRESENT AFFIDAVIT OR OTHER DOCUMENTARY EVIDENCE TO THE COURT OR TO EXAMINE OR CROSS-EXAMINE WITNESSES ON THE APPLICATION, you or your lawyer must, in addition to serving your notice of appearance, serve a copy of the evidence on the applicant's lawyer or, where the applicant does not have a lawyer, serve it on the applicant, and file it, with proof of service, in the court office where the application is to be heard as soon as possible, but at least four days before the hearing.

IF YOU FAIL TO APPEAR AT THE HEARING, JUDGMENT MAY BE GIVEN IN YOUR ABSENCE AND WITHOUT FURTHER NOTICE TO YOU. IF YOU WISH TO OPPOSE THIS APPLICATION BUT ARE UNABLE TO PAY LEGAL FEES, LEGAL AID MAY BE AVAILABLE TO YOU BY CONTACTING A LOCAL LEGAL AID OFFICE.

Date .... Issued by ....

Local registrar

Address of court office ....

....

TO *(Name and address of each respondent)*

APPLICATION

1. The applicant makes application for: *(State here the precise relief claimed.)*

2. The grounds for the application are: *(Specify the grounds to be argued, including a reference to any statutory provision or rule to be relied on.)*

3. The following documentary evidence will be used at the hearing of the application: *(List the affidavits or other documentary evidence to be relied on.)*

(Where the notice of application is to be served outside Ontario without a court order, state the facts and the specific provisions of Rule 17 relied on in support of such service.)

(Date of issue) *(Name, address and telephone number of lawyer or applicant)*

March 31, 2010

FORM 14F — INFORMATION FOR COURT USE

Courts of Justice Act

[Repealed O. Reg. 77/06, s. 3.]

[Editor's Note: Forms 4A to 78A of the Rules of Civil Procedure have been repealed by O. Reg. 77/06, effective July 1, 2006. Pursuant to Rule of Civil Procedure 1.06, when a form is referred to by number, the reference is to the form with that number that is described in the Table of Forms at the end of these rules and which is available on the Internet through www.ontariocourtforms.on.ca. For your convenience, the government form as published on this website is reproduced below.]

Courts of Justice Act

ONTARIO

SUPERIOR COURT OF JUSTICE

(General heading)

INFORMATION FOR COURT USE

1. This proceeding is an:	❑ action	❑ application
2. Has it been commenced under the *Class Proceedings Act, 1992*?	❑ yes	❑ no

3. If the proceeding is an action, does Rule 76 (Simplified Procedure) apply? Note: *Subject to the exceptions found in subrule 76.01(1), it is MANDATORY to proceed under Rule 76 for all cases in which the money amount claimed or the value of real or personal property claimed is $100,000 or less.*	❑ yes	❑ no

4. The claim in this proceeding (action or application) is in respect of:

(Select the one item that best describes the nature of the main claim in the proceeding.)

Bankruptcy or insolvency law	❑	Motor vehicle accident	❑
Collection of liquidated debt	❑	Municipal law	❑
Constitutional law	❑	Partnership law	❑
Construction law (other than construction lien)	❑	Personal property security	❑
Construction lien	❑	Product liability	❑
Contract law	❑	Professional malpractice (other than medical)	❑
Corporate law	❑	Real property (including leases; excluding mortgage or charge)	❑

Defamation	❑	Tort: economic injury (other than from medical or professional malpractice)	❑
Employment or labour law	❑		
Intellectual property law	❑	Tort: personal injury (other than from motor vehicle accident)	❑
Judicial review	❑	Trusts, fiduciary duty	❑
Medical malpractice	❑	Wills, estates	❑
Mortgage or charge	❑		

CERTIFICATION

I certify that the above information is correct, to the best of my knowledge.

Date: ....

Signature of lawyer
(if no lawyer, party must sign)

November 1, 2008

FORM 15A — NOTICE OF CHANGE OF LAWYERS

Courts of Justice Act

[Repealed O. Reg. 77/06, s. 3.]

[Editor's Note: Forms 4A to 78A of the Rules of Civil Procedure have been repealed by O. Reg. 77/06, effective July 1, 2006. Pursuant to Rule of Civil Procedure 1.06, when a form is referred to by number, the reference is to the form with that number that is described in the Table of Forms at the end of these rules and which is available on the Internet through www.ontariocourtforms.on.ca. For your convenience, the government form as published on this website is reproduced below.]

(*General heading*)

NOTICE OF CHANGE OF LAWYER

The plaintiff (*or as may be*), formerly represented by (*name of former lawyer*), has appointed (*name of new lawyer*) as lawyer of record.

(*Date*) (*Name, address and telephone number of new lawyer*)

TO (*Name and address of former lawyer*)

AND TO (*Names and addresses of*

lawyers for all other parties, or names and addresses of all other parties)

July 1, 2007

FORM 15B — NOTICE OF APPOINTMENT OF LAWYER

Courts of Justice Act

[Repealed O. Reg. 77/06, s. 3.]

[Editor's Note: Forms 4A to 78A of the Rules of Civil Procedure have been repealed by O. Reg. 77/06, effective July 1, 2006. Pursuant to Rule of Civil Procedure 1.06, when a form is referred to by number, the reference is to the form with that number that is described in the Table of Forms at the end of these rules and which is available on the Internet through www.ontariocourtforms.on.ca. For your convenience, the government form as published on this website is reproduced below.]

(*General heading*)

NOTICE OF APPOINTMENT OF LAWYER

The plaintiff (*or as may be*) has appointed (*name*), as lawyer of record.

(*Date*) (*Name, address and telephone number of lawyer of record*)

TO (*Names and addresses of lawyers for all other parties, or names and addresses of all other parties*)

July 1, 2007

FORM 15C — NOTICE OF INTENTION TO ACT IN PERSON

Courts of Justice Act

[Repealed O. Reg. 77/06, s. 3.]

[Editor's Note: Forms 4A to 78A of the Rules of Civil Procedure have been repealed by O. Reg. 77/06, effective July 1, 2006. Pursuant to Rule of Civil Procedure 1.06, when a form is

referred to by number, the reference is to the form with that number that is described in the Table of Forms at the end of these rules and which is available on the Internet through www.ontariocourtforms.on.ca. For your convenience, the government form as published on this website is reproduced below.]

(*General heading*)

NOTICE OF INTENTION TO ACT IN PERSON

The plaintiff (*or as may be*), formerly represented by (*name*) as lawyer of record, intends to act in person.

(complete if filed by the lawyer of record) The plaintiff *(or as may be)* consents to the filing of this form by the lawyer of record on his/her behalf.

Date.................................. Signed by..................................

(print name of plaintiff (or as may be))

(complete if filed by the lawyer of record) I *(name of lawyer of record)* confirm that I have explained the purpose of this form to *(name of the plaintiff or as may be)* and have confirmed his/her intention to act in person in place of me. The plaintiff *(or as may be)* signed this form at the time he/she consented to act in person.

Date.................................. Signed by..................................

(print name of lawyer of record and Law Society registration number)

(Date)

(Name, address for service and telephone number of party intending to act in person)

TO *(Name and address of former lawyer of record)*

AND TO *(Name and addresses of lawyers for all other parties, or names and addresses of all other parties)*

July 1, 2007

FORM 16A — ACKNOWLEDGMENT OF RECEIPT CARD

Courts of Justice Act

[Repealed O. Reg. 77/06, s. 3.]

[Editor's Note: Forms 4A to 78A of the Rules of Civil Procedure have been repealed by O. Reg. 77/06, effective July 1, 2006. Pursuant to Rule of Civil Procedure 1.06, when a form is referred to by number, the reference is to the form with that number that is described in the Table of Forms at the end of these rules and which is available on the Internet through www.ontariocourtforms.on.ca. For your convenience, the government form as published on this website is reproduced below.]

(*General heading*)

TO (*full name*)

You are served by mail with the documents enclosed with this card in accordance with the *Rules of Civil Procedure.*

You are requested to sign the acknowledgment below and mail this card immediately after you receive it. If you fail to do so, the documents may be served on you in another manner and you may have to pay the costs of service.

ACKNOWLEDGMENT OF RECEIPT

I ACKNOWLEDGE that I have received a copy of the following documents: (*To be completed in advance by the sender of the documents. Include sufficient particulars to identify each document.*)

....

Signature of person served

(*The reverse side of this card must bear the name and address of the sender and the required postage.*)

November 1, 2005

FORM 16B — AFFIDAVIT OF SERVICE

Courts of Justice Act

[Repealed O. Reg. 77/06, s. 3.]

[Editor's Note: Forms 4A to 78A of the Rules of Civil Procedure have been repealed by O. Reg. 77/06, effective July 1, 2006. Pursuant to Rule of Civil Procedure 1.06, when a form is referred to by number, the reference is to the form with that number that is described in the Table of Forms at the end of these rules and which is available on the Internet through www.ontariocourtforms.on.ca. For your convenience, the government form as published on this website is reproduced below.]

(*If a separate document insert general heading*)

AFFIDAVIT OF SERVICE

I, (*full name*), of the (City, Town, *etc.*) of ...., in the (County, Regional Municipality, *etc.*) of ...., MAKE OATH AND SAY (*or* AFFIRM):

(*Personal service*)

1. On (*date*), at (time), I served (*identify person served*) with the (*identify documents served*) by leaving a copy with him (*or* her) at (*address where service was made*). (*Where the rules provide for personal service on a corporation, etc. by leaving a copy of the document with another person, substitute:* by leaving a copy with (*identify person by name and title*) at (*address where service was made*).)

2. I was able to identify the person by means of (*state the means by which the person's identity was ascertained.*)

(Service by leaving a copy with an adult person in the same household as an alternative to personal service)

1. I served (*identify person served*) with the (*identify documents served*) by leaving a copy on (*date*), at (*time*), with a person (*insert name if known*) who appeared to be an adult member of the same household in which (*identify person served*) is residing, at (*address where service was made*), and by sending a copy by regular lettermail (*or* registered mail) on (*date*) to (*identify person served*) at the same address.

2. I ascertained that the person was an adult member of the household by means of (*state how it was ascertained that the person was an adult member of the household*).

3. Before serving the documents in this way, I made an unsuccessful attempt to serve (*identify person*) personally at the same address on (*date*). (*If more than one attempt has been made, add:* and again on (*date*).)

(Service by mail as an alternative to personal service)

1. On (*date*), I sent to the (*identify person served*) by regular lettermail (*or* registered mail) a copy of the (*identify documents served*).

2. On (*date*), I received the attached acknowledgment of receipt card (*or* post office receipt) bearing a signature that purports to be the signature of (*identify person*).

(Service by mail on a lawyer)

1. I served (*identify party served*) with the (*identify documents served*) by sending a copy by regular lettermail (*or* registered mail) on (*date*) to (*name of lawyer*), the lawyer for the (*identify party*), at (*full mailing address*).

(Service on a lawyer by fax)

1. I served (*identify party served*) with the (*identify documents served*) by sending a copy by fax to (*fax number*) on (*date*) to (*name of lawyer*), the lawyer for the (*identify party*).

(Service on a lawyer by courier)

1. I served (*identify party served*) with the (*identify documents served*) by sending a copy by (*name of courier*), a courier, to (*name of lawyer*), the lawyer for the (*identify party*), at (*full address of place for delivery*).

2. The copy was given to the courier on (*date*).

(Service by mail on a party acting in person or a non-party)

1. I served (*identify party or person served*) with the (*identify documents served*) by sending a copy by regular lettermail (*or* registered mail) on (*date*) to (*full mailing address*), the last address for service provided by (*identify party or person*) (*or, where no such address has been provided*: the last known address of (*identify party or person*).)

(Service on a lawyer by e-mail)

1. I served *(identify party served)* with the *(identify documents served)* by sending a copy by e-mail to *(e-mail address)* on *(date)* to *(name of lawyer)*, the lawyer for the *(identify party)*.

2. On *(date)* I received the attached acceptance by e-mail from *(name of lawyer)*, the lawyer of the *(identify party)*.

SWORN *(etc.)*

January 1, 2008

FORM 16C — CERTIFICATE OF SERVICE BY SHERIFF

Courts of Justice Act

[Repealed O. Reg. 77/06, s. 3.]

[Editor's Note: Forms 4A to 78A of the Rules of Civil Procedure have been repealed by O. Reg. 77/06, effective July 1, 2006. Pursuant to Rule of Civil Procedure 1.06, when a form is referred to by number, the reference is to the form with that number that is described in the Table of Forms at the end of these rules and which is available on the Internet through www.ontariocourtforms.on.ca. For your convenience, the government form as published on this website is reproduced below.]

(*If a separate document insert general heading*)

CERTIFICATE OF SERVICE BY SHERIFF

(*Personal service*)

I, (*full name*), Sheriff (*or* Sheriff's Officer) of the (County, District, *etc.*) of ...., certify that on (*date*), at (*time*), I served (*identify person served*) with (*identify documents served*) by leaving a copy with him (*or* her) at (*address where service was made*). (*Where the rules provide for personal service on a corporation, etc., by leaving a copy of the document with another person, substitute:* by leaving a copy with (*identify person by name and title*) at (*address where service was made*).)

I was able to identify the person by means of (*state the means by which the person's identity was ascertained.*)

(*Service by leaving a copy with an adult person in the same household as an alternative to personal service*)

I, (*full name*), Sheriff (*or* Sheriff's Officer) of the (County, District, *etc.*) of ...., certify that I served (*identify person served*) with this document by leaving a copy in a sealed envelope addressed to him (*or* her) on (*date*), at (*time*), with a person (*insert name if known*) who appeared to be an adult member of the same household in which (*identify person served*) is residing at (*address where service was made*), and by sending a copy by regular lettermail (*or* registered mail) on (*date*) to (*identify person served*) at the same address.

I ascertained that the person was an adult member of the household by means of (*state how it was ascertained that the person was an adult member of the household*).

Before serving the document in this way, I made an unsuccessful attempt to serve (*identify person*) personally at the same address on (*date*). (*If more than one attempt has been made, add:* and again on (*date*).)

Date ....
(*Signature of sheriff or sheriff's officer*)

November 1, 2005

FORM 17A — REQUEST FOR SERVICE ABROAD OF JUDICIAL OR EXTRAJUDICIAL DOCUMENTS

Courts of Justice Act

[Repealed O. Reg. 77/06, s. 3.]

[Editor's Note: Forms 4A to 78A of the Rules of Civil Procedure have been repealed by O. Reg. 77/06, effective July 1, 2006. Pursuant to Rule of Civil Procedure 1.06, when a form is referred to by number, the reference is to the form with that number that is described in the Table of Forms at the end of these rules and which is available on the Internet through www.ontariocourtforms.on.ca. For your convenience, the government form as published on this website is reproduced below.]

Convention on the service abroad of judicial and extrajudicial documents in civil or commercial matters, signed at The Hague, November 15, 1965.

Identity and address of the applicant	Address of receiving Authority
______________________________	______________________________

The undersigned applicant has the honour to transmit — in duplicate — the documents listed below and, in conformity with article 5 of the above-mentioned Convention, requests prompt service of one copy thereof on the addressee, i.e.

(identity and address) ....

....

(a) in accordance with the provisions of sub-paragraph (a) of the first paragraph of article 5 of the Convention*;

(b) in accordance with the following particular method (sub-paragraph (b) of the first paragraph of article 5)*: ....

....

(c) by delivery to the addressee, if the addressee accepts it voluntarily (second paragraph of article 5)*.

The authority is requested to return or to have returned to the applicant a copy of the documents — and of the annexes* — with a certificate as provided on the reverse side.

(*List of Documents*) ....

....

....

....

....

....

....

Done at ...., the ....
Signature or stamp.

* Delete if inappropriate

CERTIFICATE

The undersigned authority has the honour to certify, in conformity with article 6 of the Convention,

(1) that the document has been served*

— the (date) . . . .

— at (place, street, number) . . . .

— in one of the following methods authorized by article 5 —

(a) in accordance with the provisions of sub-paragraph (a) of the first paragraph of article 5 of the Convention*;

(b) in accordance with the following particular method*:

. . . .

. . . .;

(c) by delivery to the addressee, who accepted it voluntarily.

The documents referred to in the request have been delivered to:

— (identity and description of person) . . . .

. . . .

— relationship to the addressee (family, business or other)

. . . .

(2) that the document has not been served, by reason of the following facts*:

. . . .

. . . .

. . . .

In conformity with the second paragraph of article 12 of the Convention, the applicant is requested to pay or reimburse the expenses detailed in the attached statement*.

Annexes

Documents returned: . . . .
. . . .
. . . .

In appropriate cases, documents establishing the service: . . . .
. . . .
. . . .
. . . .

Done at ...., the ....

Signature or stamp.

* Delete if inappropriate

November 1, 2005

FORM 17B — SUMMARY OF THE DOCUMENT TO BE SERVED

Courts of Justice Act

[Repealed O. Reg. 77/06, s. 3.]

[Editor's Note: Forms 4A to 78A of the Rules of Civil Procedure have been repealed by O. Reg. 77/06, effective July 1, 2006. Pursuant to Rule of Civil Procedure 1.06, when a form is referred to by number, the reference is to the form with that number that is described in the Table of Forms at the end of these rules and which is available on the Internet through www.ontariocourtforms.on.ca. For your convenience, the government form as published on this website is reproduced below.]

Convention on the service abroad of judicial and extrajudicial documents in civil or commercial matters, signed at The Hague, November 15, 1965.
(article 5, fourth paragraph)

Name and address of the requesting authority: . . . .

Particulars of the parties*: . . . .

. . . .

JUDICIAL DOCUMENT**

Nature and purpose of the document: . . . .

. . . .

Nature and purpose of the proceedings and, where appropriate, the amount in dispute:

. . . .

Date and place for entering appearance**: . . . .

. . . .

Court which has given judgment**: . . . .

. . . .

Date of judgment**: . . . .

. . . .

Time limits stated in the document**: . . . .

. . . .

EXTRAJUDICIAL DOCUMENT**

Nature and purpose of the document: . . . .

. . . .

Time limits stated in the document** . . . .

. . . .

* If appropriate, identity and address of the person interested in the transmission of the document.

** Delete if inappropriate

November 1, 2005

FORM 17C — NOTICE AND SUMMARY OF DOCUMENT

Courts of Justice Act

[Repealed O. Reg. 77/06, s. 3.]

[Editor's Note: Forms 4A to 78A of the Rules of Civil Procedure have been repealed by O. Reg. 77/06, effective July 1, 2006. Pursuant to Rule of Civil Procedure 1.06, when a form is referred to by number, the reference is to the form with that number that is described in the Table of Forms at the end of these rules and which is available on the Internet through www.ontariocourtforms.on.ca. For your convenience, the government form as published on this website is reproduced below.]

identity and address of the addressee

____

____

IMPORTANT

THE ENCLOSED DOCUMENT IS OF A LEGAL NATURE AND MAY AFFECT YOUR RIGHTS AND OBLIGATIONS. THE SUMMARY OF THE DOCUMENT TO BE SERVED WILL GIVE YOU SOME INFORMATION ABOUT ITS NATURE AND PURPOSE. YOU SHOULD HOWEVER READ THE DOCUMENT ITSELF CAREFULLY. IT MAY BE NECESSARY TO SEEK LEGAL ADVICE.

IF YOUR FINANCIAL RESOURCES ARE INSUFFICIENT YOU SHOULD SEEK INFORMATION ON THE POSSIBILITY OF OBTAINING LEGAL AID OR ADVICE EITHER IN THE COUNTRY WHERE YOU LIVE OR IN THE COUNTRY WHERE THE DOCUMENT WAS ISSUED.

ENQUIRIES ABOUT THE AVAILABILITY OF LEGAL AID OR ADVICE IN THE COUNTRY WHERE THE DOCUMENT WAS ISSUED MAY BE DIRECTED TO:

. . . .

(*It is recommended that the standard terms in the notice be written in English and French and where appropriate also in the official language, or in one of the official languages of the State in which the document originated. The blanks could be completed either in the language of the State to which the document is to be sent, or in English or French.*)

SUMMARY OF THE DOCUMENT TO BE SERVED: . . . .

Name and address of the requesting authority: . . . .

. . . .

*Particulars of the parties: . . . .

. . . .

**JUDICIAL DOCUMENT:

Nature and purpose of the document: . . . .

. . . .

Nature and purpose of the proceedings and where appropriate, the amount in dispute:

. . . .

**Date and place for entering appearance: . . . .

. . . .

**Court which has given judgment: . . . .

. . . .

**Date of judgment: . . . .

**Time limits stated in the document: . . . .

. . . .

**EXTRAJUDICIAL DOCUMENT . . . .

Nature and purpose of the document: . . . .

. . . .

Time limits stated in the document: . . . .

. . . .

* If appropriate, identity and address of the person interested in the transmission of the document

** Delete if inappropriate

November 1, 2005

FORM 18A — STATEMENT OF DEFENCE

Courts of Justice Act

[Repealed O. Reg. 77/06, s. 3.]

[Editor's Note: Forms 4A to 78A of the Rules of Civil Procedure have been repealed by O. Reg. 77/06, effective July 1, 2006. Pursuant to Rule of Civil Procedure 1.06, when a form is referred to by number, the reference is to the form with that number that is described in the Table of Forms at the end of these rules and which is available on the Internet through www.ontariocourtforms.on.ca. For your convenience, the government form as published on this website is reproduced below.]

(*General heading*)

STATEMENT OF DEFENCE

1. The defendant admits the allegations contained in paragraphs .... of the statement of claim.

2. The defendant denies the allegations contained in paragraphs .... of the statement of claim.

3. The defendant has no knowledge in respect of the allegations contained in paragraphs .... of the statement of claim.

4. (*Set out in separate, consecutively numbered paragraphs each allegation of material fact relied on by way of defence.*)

(*Date*) (*Name, address and telephone number of defendant's lawyer or defendant*)

TO (*Name and address of plaintiff's lawyer or plaintiff*)

July 1, 2007

FORM 18B — NOTICE OF INTENT TO DEFEND

Courts of Justice Act

[Repealed O. Reg. 77/06, s. 3.]

[Editor's Note: Forms 4A to 78A of the Rules of Civil Procedure have been repealed by O. Reg. 77/06, effective July 1, 2006. Pursuant to Rule of Civil Procedure 1.06, when a form is referred to by number, the reference is to the form with that number that is described in the Table of Forms at the end of these rules and which is available on the Internet through www.ontariocourtforms.on.ca. For your convenience, the government form as published on this website is reproduced below.]

(*General heading*)

NOTICE OF INTENT TO DEFEND

The defendant (*or* defendant added by counterclaim *or* third party) intends to defend this action.

(*Date*) (*Name, address and telephone number of lawyer or party serving notice*)

TO (*Name and address of lawyer or party on whom notice is served*)

July 1, 2007

FORM 19A — DEFAULT JUDGMENT (DEBT OR LIQUIDATED DEMAND)

Courts of Justice Act

[Repealed O. Reg. 77/06, s. 3.]

[Editor's Note: Forms 4A to 78A of the Rules of Civil Procedure have been repealed by O. Reg. 77/06, effective July 1, 2006. Pursuant to Rule of Civil Procedure 1.06, when a form is referred to by number, the reference is to the form with that number that is described in the Table of Forms at the end of these rules and which is available on the Internet through www.ontariocourtforms.on.ca. For your convenience, the government form as published on this website is reproduced below.]

(*General heading*)

(*Court seal*)

JUDGMENT

On reading the statement of claim in this action and the proof of service of the statement of claim on the defendant, filed, and the defendant having been noted in default,

1. IT IS ORDERED AND ADJUDGED that the defendant pay to the plaintiff the sum of $ .... and the sum of $ .... for the costs of this action. (*Where costs are to be assessed, substitute* the costs of this action as assessed by the court.)

This judgment bears interest at the rate of .... per cent per year from its date.

Date .... Signed by ....
Local registrar

Address of court office ....
....

November 1, 2005

FORM 19B — DEFAULT JUDGMENT (RECOVERY OF POSSESSION OF LAND)

Courts of Justice Act

[Repealed O. Reg. 77/06, s. 3.]

[Editor's Note: Forms 4A to 78A of the Rules of Civil Procedure have been repealed by O. Reg. 77/06, effective July 1, 2006. Pursuant to Rule of Civil Procedure 1.06, when a form is referred to by number, the reference is to the form with that number that is described in the Table of Forms at the end of these rules and which is available on the Internet through

www.ontariocourtforms.on.ca. For your convenience, the government form as published on this website is reproduced below.]

(*General heading*)

(*Court seal*)

JUDGMENT

On reading the statement of claim in this action and the proof of service of the statement of claim on the defendant, filed, and the defendant having been noted in default,

1. IT IS ORDERED AND ADJUDGED that the defendant deliver to the plaintiff possession of the following land: (*Where the description of the land is very lengthy, substitute* the land described in the attached schedule.)

2. IT IS ORDERED AND ADJUDGED that the defendant pay to the plaintiff the sum of $ .... for the costs of this action. (*Where costs are to be assessed, substitute* the costs of this action as assessed by the court.)

The costs fixed by and payable under this judgment bear interest at the rate of .... per cent per year from its date.

Date .... Signed by ....
Local registrar

Address of court office ....
....

November 1, 2005

FORM 19C — DEFAULT JUDGMENT (RECOVERY OF POSSESSION OF PERSONAL PROPERTY)

Courts of Justice Act

[Repealed O. Reg. 77/06, s. 3.]

[Editor's Note: Forms 4A to 78A of the Rules of Civil Procedure have been repealed by O. Reg. 77/06, effective July 1, 2006. Pursuant to Rule of Civil Procedure 1.06, when a form is referred to by number, the reference is to the form with that number that is described in the Table of Forms at the end of these rules and which is available on the Internet through www.ontariocourtforms.on.ca. For your convenience, the government form as published on this website is reproduced below.]

(*General heading*)

(*Court seal*)

JUDGMENT

On reading the statement of claim in this action and the proof of service of the statement of claim on the defendant, filed, and the defendant having been noted in default,

1. IT IS ORDERED AND ADJUDGED that the defendant deliver to the plaintiff possession of the following personal property: (*or* the personal property described in the attached schedule.)

2. IT IS ORDERED AND ADJUDGED that the defendant pay to the plaintiff the sum of $ .... for the costs of this action. (*Where costs are to be assessed, substitute* the costs of this action as assessed by the court.)

The costs fixed by and payable under this judgment bear interest at the rate of .... per cent per year from its date.

Date .... Signed by ....

Local registrar

Address of court office ....

....

November 1, 2005

FORM 19D — REQUISITION FOR DEFAULT JUDGMENT

Courts of Justice Act

[Repealed O. Reg. 77/06, s. 3.]

[Editor's Note: Forms 4A to 78A of the Rules of Civil Procedure have been repealed by O. Reg. 77/06, effective July 1, 2006. Pursuant to Rule of Civil Procedure 1.06, when a form is referred to by number, the reference is to the form with that number that is described in the Table of Forms at the end of these rules and which is available on the Internet through www.ontariocourtforms.on.ca. For your convenience, the government form as published on this website is reproduced below.]

(*General heading*)

REQUISITION FOR DEFAULT JUDGMENT

TO THE LOCAL REGISTRAR at (*place*)

(*Where the defendant has not been noted in default, begin with:* I REQUIRE you to note the defendant (*name*) in default in this action on the ground that (*state nature of default*).)

I REQUIRE default judgment to be signed against the defendant (*name*).

Default judgment may properly be signed in this action because the claim is for:

❑ a debt or liquidated demand in money

❑ recovery of possession of land

❑ recovery of possession of personal property

❑ foreclosure, sale or redemption of a mortgage

(Debt or liquidated demand)

❑ There has been no payment on account of the claim since the statement of claim was issued. *(Complete Parts B and C.)*

OR

❑ The following payments have been made on account of the claim since the statement of claim was issued. *(Complete Parts A and C.)*

PART A — PAYMENT(S) RECEIVED BY PLAINTIFF

(Complete this part only where part payment of the claim has been received. Where no payment has been received on account of the claim, omit this part and complete Part B.)

1. Principal

Principal sum claimed in statement of claim (without interest) $............

Date of Payment	Amount of Payment	Payment Amount Principal	Applied to Interest	Principal Sum Owing
TOTAL	$................	$...............	$...............	A $................

2. Prejudgment interest

(Under section 128 of the Courts of Justice Act, judgment may be obtained for prejudgment interest from the date the cause of action arose, if claimed in the statement of claim.)

Date on which statement of claim was issued ....

Date from which prejudgment interest is claimed ....

The plaintiff is entitled to prejudgment interest on the claim, calculated as follows:

(Calculate simple interest only unless an agreement relied on in the statement of claim specifies otherwise. Calculate interest on the principal sum owing from the date of the last payment. To calculate the interest amount, count the number of days since the last payment, multiply that number by the annual rate of interest, multiply the result by the principal sum owing and divide by 365.)

Principal Sum Owing	Start Date	End Date (Date of Payment)	Number of Days	Rate	Interest Amount

(The last End Date should be the date judgment is signed.)

	TOTAL B	$ ....
Principal Sum Owing (Total A above)		$ ....
Total Interest Amount (Total B above)		$ ....
SIGN JUDGMENT FOR		$ ....

PART B — NO PAYMENT RECEIVED BY PLAINTIFF

(*Complete this part only where no payment has been received on account of the claim.*)

1. Principal

Principal sum claimed in statement of claim (without interest) A $ ....

2. Prejudgment interest

(*Under section 128 of the Courts of Justice Act, judgment may be obtained for prejudgment interest from the date the cause of action arose, if claimed in the statement of claim.*)

Date on which statement of claim was issued ....

Date from which prejudgment interest is claimed ....

The plaintiff is entitled to prejudgment interest on the claim, calculated as follows:

(*Calculate simple interest only unless an agreement relied on in the statement of claim specifies otherwise. To calculate the interest amount, count the number of days and multiply that number by the annual rate of interest, multiply the result by the principal sum owing and divide by 365.*)

Principal Sum Owing	Start Date	End Date (Date of Payment)	Number of Days	Rate	Interest Amount
				TOTAL B	$ ....

Principal Sum Owing (Total A above)	$ ....
Total Interest Amount (Total B above)	$ ....
SIGN JUDGMENT FOR	$ ....

PART C — POSTJUDGMENT INTEREST AND COSTS

1. Postjudgment interest

The plaintiff is entitled to postjudgment interest at the rate of .... per cent per year,

❑ under the *Courts of Justice Act*, as claimed in the statement of claim.

OR

❑ in accordance with the claim made in the statement of claim.

2. Costs

The plaintiff wishes costs to be,

❑ fixed by the local registrar.

OR

❑ assessed by an assessment officer.

Date ....

(*Signature of plaintiff's lawyer or plaintiff*)

(*Name, address and telephone number of plaintiff's lawyer or plaintiff*)

July 1, 2007

FORM 22A — SPECIAL CASE

Courts of Justice Act

[Repealed O. Reg. 77/06, s. 3.]

[Editor's Note: Forms 4A to 78A of the Rules of Civil Procedure have been repealed by O. Reg. 77/06, effective July 1, 2006. Pursuant to Rule of Civil Procedure 1.06, when a form is referred to by number, the reference is to the form with that number that is described in the Table of Forms at the end of these rules and which is available on the Internet through www.ontariocourtforms.on.ca. For your convenience, the government form as published on this website is reproduced below.]

(*General heading*)

SPECIAL CASE

THE FOLLOWING CASE is stated for the opinion of the court:

1. (*Set out, in consecutively numbered paragraphs, the material facts of the case, as agreed on by the parties, that are necessary to enable the court to determine the questions stated. Refer to and include a copy of any relevant documents.*)

THE QUESTIONS for the opinion of the court are:

1. (*Set out the questions in consecutively numbered paragraphs.*)

THE RELIEF SOUGHT on the determination of the questions stated is:

1. (*Set out the relief sought, as agreed on by the parties, in respect of each possible answer to each of the questions stated, in a form that could readily be incorporated into an order.*)

(*Date*)

(*Signature of all lawyers or parties in the proceeding*)
(*Names, addresses and telephone numbers of all lawyers or parties in the proceeding*)

July 1, 2007

FORM 23A — NOTICE OF DISCONTINUANCE

Courts of Justice Act

[Repealed O. Reg. 77/06, s. 3.]

[Editor's Note: Forms 4A to 78A of the Rules of Civil Procedure have been repealed by O. Reg. 77/06, effective July 1, 2006. Pursuant to Rule of Civil Procedure 1.06, when a form is referred to by number, the reference is to the form with that number that is described in the Table of Forms at the end of these rules and which is available on the Internet through www.ontariocourtforms.on.ca. For your convenience, the government form as published on this website is reproduced below.]

(*General heading*)

NOTICE OF DISCONTINUANCE

The plaintiff wholly discontinues this action. (*Where applicable, add* against the defendant (*name*).)

(*Or* The plaintiff discontinues that part of this action relating to .... *Where applicable, add* against the defendant (*name*).)

(*Date*) (*Name, address and telephone number of plaintiff's lawyer or plaintiff*)

TO (*Name and address of defendant's lawyer or defendant*)

NOTE: If there is a counterclaim, the defendant should consider rule 23.02, under which the counterclaim may be deemed to be discontinued.

NOTE: If there is a crossclaim or third party claim, the defendant should consider rule 23.03, under which the crossclaim or third party claim may be deemed to be dismissed.

July 1, 2007

FORM 23B — NOTICE OF ELECTION TO PROCEED WITH COUNTERCLAIM

Courts of Justice Act

[Repealed O. Reg. 77/06, s. 3.]

[Editor's Note: Forms 4A to 78A of the Rules of Civil Procedure have been repealed by O. Reg. 77/06, effective July 1, 2006. Pursuant to Rule of Civil Procedure 1.06, when a form is referred to by number, the reference is to the form with that number that is described in the Table of Forms at the end of these rules and which is available on the Internet through

www.ontariocourtforms.on.ca. For your convenience, the government form as published on this website is reproduced below.]

(*General heading*)

NOTICE OF ELECTION

The defendant elects to proceed with the counterclaim in this action.

(*Date*) (*Name, address and telephone number of defendant's lawyer or defendant*)

TO (*Name and address of plaintiff's lawyer or plaintiff*)

July 1, 2007

FORM 23C — NOTICE OF WITHDRAWAL OF DEFENCE

Courts of Justice Act

[Repealed O. Reg. 77/06, s. 3.]

[Editor's Note: Forms 4A to 78A of the Rules of Civil Procedure have been repealed by O. Reg. 77/06, effective July 1, 2006. Pursuant to Rule of Civil Procedure 1.06, when a form is referred to by number, the reference is to the form with that number that is described in the Table of Forms at the end of these rules and which is available on the Internet through www.ontariocourtforms.on.ca. For your convenience, the government form as published on this website is reproduced below.]

(*General heading*)

NOTICE OF WITHDRAWAL

The defendant withdraws the statement of defence in this action.

(*Or* The defendant withdraws paragraphs .... of the statement of defence in this action.)

(*Date*) (*Name, address and telephone number of defendant's lawyer or defendant*)

TO (*Name and address of plaintiff's lawyer or plaintiff*)

July 1, 2007

FORM 24.1A — NOTICE OF NAME OF MEDIATOR AND DATE OF SESSION

Courts of Justice Act

[Repealed O. Reg. 77/06, s. 3.]

[Editor's Note: Forms 4A to 78A of the Rules of Civil Procedure have been repealed by O. Reg. 77/06, effective July 1, 2006. Pursuant to Rule of Civil Procedure 1.06, when a form is referred to by number, the reference is to the form with that number that is described in the Table of Forms at the end of these rules and which is available on the Internet through www.ontariocourtforms.on.ca. For your convenience, the government form as published on this website is reproduced below.]

(*General heading*)

NOTICE OF NAME OF MEDIATOR AND DATE OF SESSION

TO: MEDIATION CO-ORDINATOR

1. I certify that I have consulted with the parties and that the parties have chosen the following mediator for the mediation session required by Rule 24.1: (*name*)

2. The mediator is named in the list of mediators for (*name county*).

(*or*)

2. The mediator is not named in a list of mediators, but has been chosen by the parties under clause 24.1.08(2)(a) or (c).

3. The mediation session will take place on (*date*).

(*Date*) (*Name, address, telephone number and fax number of plaintiff's lawyer or of plaintiff*)

November 1, 2005

FORM 24.1B — NOTICE OF ASSIGNED MEDIATOR

Courts of Justice Act

[Repealed O. Reg. 77/06, s. 3.]

[Editor's Note: Forms 4A to 78A of the Rules of Civil Procedure have been repealed by O. Reg. 77/06, effective July 1, 2006. Pursuant to Rule of Civil Procedure 1.06, when a form is referred to by number, the reference is to the form with that number that is described in the Table of Forms at the end of these rules and which is available on the Internet through www.ontariocourtforms.on.ca. For your convenience, the government form as published on this website is reproduced below.]

(*General heading*)

NOTICE BY ASSIGNED MEDIATOR

TO:

AND TO:

The notice of name of mediator and date of session (Form 24.1A) required by rule 24.1.09 of the *Rules of Civil Procedure* has not been filed in this action. Accordingly, the mediation co-ordinator has assigned me to conduct the mediation session under Rule 24.1. I am a mediator named in the list of mediators for (*name county*).

The mediation session will take place on (*date*), from (*time*) to (*time*), at (*place*).

Unless the court orders otherwise, you are required to attend this mediation session. If you have a lawyer representing you in this action, he or she is also required to attend.

You are required to file a statement of issues (Form 24.1C) by (*date*) (seven days before the mediation session). A blank copy of the form is attached.

When you attend the mediation session, you should bring with you any documents that you consider of central importance in the action. You should plan to remain throughout the scheduled time. If you need another person's approval before agreeing to a settlement, you should make arrangements before the mediation session to ensure that you have ready telephone access to that person throughout the session, even outside regular business hours.

YOU MAY BE PENALIZED UNDER RULE 24.1.13 IF YOU FAIL TO FILE A STATEMENT OF ISSUES OR FAIL TO ATTEND THE MEDIATION SESSION.

(*Date*) (*Name, address, telephone number and fax number of mediator*)

cc. Mediation co-ordinator

November 1, 2005

FORM 24.1C — STATEMENT OF ISSUES

Courts of Justice Act

[Repealed O. Reg. 77/06, s. 3.]

[Editor's Note: Forms 4A to 78A of the Rules of Civil Procedure have been repealed by O. Reg. 77/06, effective July 1, 2006. Pursuant to Rule of Civil Procedure 1.06, when a form is referred to by number, the reference is to the form with that number that is described in the Table of Forms at the end of these rules and which is available on the Internet through www.ontariocourtforms.on.ca. For your convenience, the government form as published on this website is reproduced below.]

(*General heading*)

STATEMENT OF ISSUES

(*To be provided to mediator and parties at least seven days before the mediation session*)

1. Factual and legal issues in dispute

The plaintiff (or defendant) states that the following factual and legal issues are in dispute and remain to be resolved.

(*Issues should be stated briefly and numbered consecutively.*)

2. Party's position and interests (what the party hopes to achieve)

(*Brief summary.*)

3. Attached documents

Attached to this form are the following documents that the plaintiff (*or* defendant) considers of central importance in the action: (*list*)

(*date*) (*party's signature*)

(*Name, address, telephone number and fax number of lawyer of party filing statement of issues, or of party*)

NOTE: When the plaintiff provides a copy of this form to the mediator, a copy of the pleadings shall also be included.

NOTE: Rule 24.1.14 provides as follows:

> All communications at a mediation session and the mediator's notes and records shall be deemed to be without prejudice settlement discussions.

November 1, 2005

FORM 24.1D — CERTIFICATE OF NON-COMPLIANCE

Courts of Justice Act

[Repealed O. Reg. 77/06, s. 3.]

[Editor's Note: Forms 4A to 78A of the Rules of Civil Procedure have been repealed by O. Reg. 77/06, effective July 1, 2006. Pursuant to Rule of Civil Procedure 1.06, when a form is referred to by number, the reference is to the form with that number that is described in the Table of Forms at the end of these rules and which is available on the Internet through www.ontariocourtforms.on.ca. For your convenience, the government form as published on this website is reproduced below.]

(*General heading*)

CERTIFICATE OF NON-COMPLIANCE

TO: MEDIATION CO-ORDINATOR

I, (*name*), mediator, certify that this certificate of non-compliance is filed because:

> ( ) (*Identify party(ies)*) failed to provide a copy of a statement of issues to the mediator and the other parties (*or* to the mediator *or* to *party(ies)*).

(*Identify plaintiff*) failed to provide a copy of the pleadings to the mediator.

( ) (*Identify party(ies)*) failed to attend within the first 30 minutes of a scheduled mediation session.

(*Date*) (*Name, address, telephone number and fax number, if any, of mediator*)

November 1, 2005

FORM 25A — REPLY

Courts of Justice Act

[Repealed O. Reg. 77/06, s. 3.]

[Editor's Note: Forms 4A to 78A of the Rules of Civil Procedure have been repealed by O. Reg. 77/06, effective July 1, 2006. Pursuant to Rule of Civil Procedure 1.06, when a form is referred to by number, the reference is to the form with that number that is described in the Table of Forms at the end of these rules and which is available on the Internet through www.ontariocourtforms.on.ca. For your convenience, the government form as published on this website is reproduced below.]

(*General heading*)

REPLY

1. The plaintiff admits the allegations contained in paragraphs .... of the statement of defence.

2. The plaintiff denies the allegations contained in paragraphs .... of the statement of defence.

3. The plaintiff has no knowledge in respect of the allegations contained in paragraphs .... of the statement of defence.

4. (*Set out in separate, consecutively numbered paragraphs each allegation of material fact relied on by way of reply to the statement of defence.*)

(*Date*) (*Name, address and telephone number of plaintiff's lawyer or plaintiff*)

TO (*Name and address of defendant's lawyer or defendant*)

July 1, 2007

FORM 27A — COUNTERCLAIM (AGAINST PARTIES TO MAIN ACTION ONLY)

Courts of Justice Act

[Repealed O. Reg. 77/06, s. 3.]

[Editor's Note: Forms 4A to 78A of the Rules of Civil Procedure have been repealed by O. Reg. 77/06, effective July 1, 2006. Pursuant to Rule of Civil Procedure 1.06, when a form is referred to by number, the reference is to the form with that number that is described in the Table of Forms at the end of these rules and which is available on the Internet through www.ontariocourtforms.on.ca. For your convenience, the government form as published on this website is reproduced below.]

(*Where the counterclaim includes as a defendant to the counterclaim a person who is not already a party to the main action, use Form 27B.*)

(*Include the counterclaim in the same document as the statement of defence, and entitle the document* STATEMENT OF DEFENCE AND COUNTERCLAIM. *The counterclaim is to follow the last paragraph of the statement of defence. Number the paragraphs in sequence commencing with the number following the number of the last paragraph of the statement of defence.*)

COUNTERCLAIM

The defendant (*name if more than one defendant*) claims: (*State here the precise relief claimed.*)

(*Then set out in separate, consecutively numbered paragraphs each allegation of material fact relied on to substantiate the counterclaim.*)

(*Where the defendant to the counterclaim is sued in a capacity other than that in which the defendant is a party to the main action, set out the capacity.*)

(*Date*) (*Name, address and telephone number of plaintiff's lawyer or plaintiff*)

TO (*Name and address of lawyer for defendant to the counterclaim or of defendant to the counterclaim*)

July 1, 2007

FORM 27B — COUNTERCLAIM (AGAINST PLAINTIFF AND PERSON NOT ALREADY PARTY TO MAIN ACTION)

Courts of Justice Act

[Repealed O. Reg. 77/06, s. 3.]

[Editor's Note: Forms 4A to 78A of the Rules of Civil Procedure have been repealed by O. Reg. 77/06, effective July 1, 2006. Pursuant to Rule of Civil Procedure 1.06, when a form is referred to by number, the reference is to the form with that number that is described in the Table of Forms at the end of these rules and which is available on the Internet through www.ontariocourtforms.on.ca. For your convenience, the government form as published on this website is reproduced below.]

(*Where all defendants to the counterclaim are already parties to the main action, use Form 27A.*)

(*General heading*)

(*Add a second title of proceeding, as follows:*)

AND BETWEEN:

(*name*)

Plaintiff by counterclaim

(*Court seal*)

and

(*name*)

Defendants to the counterclaim

STATEMENT OF DEFENCE AND COUNTERCLAIM

TO THE DEFENDANTS TO THE COUNTERCLAIM

A LEGAL PROCEEDING has been commenced against you by way of a counterclaim in an action in this court. The claim made against you is set out in the following pages.

IF YOU WISH TO DEFEND THIS COUNTERCLAIM, you or an Ontario lawyer acting for you must prepare a defence to counterclaim in Form 27C prescribed by the *Rules of Civil Procedure*, serve it on the plaintiff by counterclaim's lawyer or, where the plaintiff by counterclaim does not have a lawyer, serve it on the plaintiff by counterclaim, and file it, with proof of service, in this court, WITHIN TWENTY DAYS after this statement of defence and counterclaim is served on you.

If you are not already a party to the main action and you are served in another province or territory of Canada or in the United States of America, the period for serving and filing your defence is forty days. If you are served outside Canada and the United States of America, the period is sixty days.

If you are not already a party to the main action, instead of serving and filing a defence to counterclaim, you may serve and file a notice of intent to defend in Form 18B prescribed by the *Rules of Civil Procedure*. This will entitle you to ten more days within which to serve and file your defence to counterclaim.

IF YOU FAIL TO DEFEND THIS COUNTERCLAIM, JUDGMENT MAY BE GIVEN AGAINST YOU IN YOUR ABSENCE AND WITHOUT FURTHER NOTICE TO YOU. IF YOU WISH TO DEFEND THIS PROCEEDING BUT ARE UNABLE TO PAY LEGAL FEES, LEGAL AID MAY BE AVAILABLE TO YOU BY CONTACTING A LOCAL LEGAL AID OFFICE.

(*Where the counterclaim is for money only, include the following:*)

IF YOU PAY THE AMOUNT OF THE COUNTERCLAIM AGAINST YOU, and $ .... for costs, within the time for serving and filing your defence to counterclaim, you may move to have the counterclaim against you dismissed by the court. If you believe the amount claimed for costs is excessive, you may pay the amount of the counterclaim and $400 for costs and have the costs assessed by the court.

Date .... Issued by ....
Local registrar

Address of court office ....
....

TO (*Name and address of defendant to the counterclaim who is not already a party to the main action*)

(*Name and address of lawyer for other defendant to the counterclaim or of other defendant to the counterclaim*)

(*The counterclaim is to follow the last paragraph of the statement of defence. Number the paragraphs in sequence commencing with the number following the number of the last paragraph of the statement of defence.*)

COUNTERCLAIM

The defendant (*name if more than one defendant*) claims: (*State here the precise relief claimed.*)

(*Then set out in separate, consecutively numbered paragraphs each allegation of material fact relied on to substantiate the counterclaim.*)

(*Where a defendant to the counterclaim who is not already a party to the main action is to be served outside Ontario without a court order, set out the facts and the specific provisions of Rule 17 relied on in support of such service.*)

(*Date of issue*) (*Name, address and telephone number of plaintiff by counterclaim's lawyer or plaintiff by counterclaim*)

July 1, 2007

FORM 27C — DEFENCE TO COUNTERCLAIM

Courts of Justice Act

[Repealed O. Reg. 77/06, s. 3.]

[Editor's Note: Forms 4A to 78A of the Rules of Civil Procedure have been repealed by O. Reg. 77/06, effective July 1, 2006. Pursuant to Rule of Civil Procedure 1.06, when a form is referred to by number, the reference is to the form with that number that is described in the Table of Forms at the end of these rules and which is available on the Internet through

www.ontariocourtforms.on.ca. For your convenience, the government form as published on this website is reproduced below.]

(*General heading, including second title of proceeding, if required*)

(*A plaintiff who delivers a reply in the main action must include the defence to counterclaim in the same document as the reply, and the document is to be entitled* REPLY AND DEFENCE TO COUNTERCLAIM. *The defence to counterclaim is to follow immediately after the last paragraph of the reply and the paragraphs are to be numbered in sequence commencing with the number following the number of the last paragraph of the reply.*)

DEFENCE TO COUNTERCLAIM

1. The defendant to the counterclaim admits the allegations contained in paragraphs .... of the counterclaim.

2. The defendant to the counterclaim denies the allegations contained in paragraphs .... of the counterclaim.

3. The defendant to the counterclaim has no knowledge in respect of the allegations contained in paragraphs .... of the counterclaim.

4. (*Set out in separate, consecutively numbered paragraphs each allegation of material fact relied on by way of defence to the counterclaim.*)

(*Date*) (*Name, address and telephone number of lawyer for defendant to the counterclaim or defendant to the counterclaim*)

TO (*Name and address of plaintiff by counterclaim's lawyer or of plaintiff by counterclaim*)

July 1, 2007

FORM 27D — REPLY TO DEFENCE TO COUNTERCLAIM

Courts of Justice Act

[Repealed O. Reg. 77/06, s. 3.]

[Editor's Note: Forms 4A to 78A of the Rules of Civil Procedure have been repealed by O. Reg. 77/06, effective July 1, 2006. Pursuant to Rule of Civil Procedure 1.06, when a form is referred to by number, the reference is to the form with that number that is described in the Table of Forms at the end of these rules and which is available on the Internet through www.ontariocourtforms.on.ca. For your convenience, the government form as published on this website is reproduced below.]

(*General heading, including second title of proceeding, if required*)

REPLY TO DEFENCE TO COUNTERCLAIM

1. The plaintiff by counterclaim admits the allegations contained in paragraphs .... of the defence to counterclaim.

2. The plaintiff by counterclaim denies the allegations contained in paragraphs .... of the defence to counterclaim.

3. The plaintiff by counterclaim has no knowledge in respect of the allegations contained in paragraphs .... of the defence to counterclaim.

4. (*Set out in separate, consecutively numbered paragraphs each allegation of material fact relied on by way of reply to the defence to counterclaim.*)

(*Date*) (*Name, address and telephone number of plaintiff by counterclaim's lawyer or plaintiff by counterclaim*)

TO (*Name and address of lawyer for the defendant to the counterclaim or defendant to the counterclaim*)

July 1, 2007

FORM 28A — CROSSCLAIM

Courts of Justice Act

[Repealed O. Reg. 77/06, s. 3.]

[Editor's Note: Forms 4A to 78A of the Rules of Civil Procedure have been repealed by O. Reg. 77/06, effective July 1, 2006. Pursuant to Rule of Civil Procedure 1.06, when a form is referred to by number, the reference is to the form with that number that is described in the Table of Forms at the end of these rules and which is available on the Internet through www.ontariocourtforms.on.ca. For your convenience, the government form as published on this website is reproduced below.]

(*Include the crossclaim in the same document as the statement of defence, and entitle the document* STATEMENT OF DEFENCE AND CROSSCLAIM. *The crossclaim is to follow the last paragraph of the statement of defence. Number the paragraphs in sequence commencing with the number following the number of the last paragraph of the statement of defence.*)

CROSSCLAIM

The defendant (*name*) claims against the defendant (*name*): (*State here the precise relief claimed.*)

(*Then set out in separate, consecutively numbered paragraphs each allegation of material fact relied on to substantiate the crossclaim.*)

(*Where a defendant to the crossclaim is sued in a capacity other than that in which the defendant is a party to the main action, set out the capacity. Where the statement of defence and crossclaim is to be served outside Ontario without a court order, include the facts and the specific provisions of Rule 17 relied on in support of such service.*)

(*Date*) (*Name, address and telephone number of crossclaiming defendant's lawyer or crossclaiming defendant*)

TO (*Name and address of defendant to crossclaim's lawyer or defendant to crossclaim*)

July 1, 2007

FORM 28B — DEFENCE TO CROSSCLAIM

Courts of Justice Act

[Repealed O. Reg. 77/06, s. 3.]

[Editor's Note: Forms 4A to 78A of the Rules of Civil Procedure have been repealed by O. Reg. 77/06, effective July 1, 2006. Pursuant to Rule of Civil Procedure 1.06, when a form is referred to by number, the reference is to the form with that number that is described in the Table of Forms at the end of these rules and which is available on the Internet through www.ontariocourtforms.on.ca. For your convenience, the government form as published on this website is reproduced below.]

(*General heading*)

DEFENCE TO CROSSCLAIM

1. The defendant (*name*) admits the allegations contained in paragraphs .... of the crossclaim.

2. The defendant (*name*) denies the allegations contained in paragraphs .... of the crossclaim.

3. The defendant (*name*) has no knowledge in respect of the allegations contained in paragraphs .... of the crossclaim.

4. (*Set out in separate, consecutively numbered paragraphs each allegation of material fact relied on by way of defence to the crossclaim.*)

(*Date*) (*Name, address and telephone number of defendant to crossclaim's lawyer or defendant to crossclaim*)

TO (*Name and address of crossclaiming defendant's lawyer or crossclaiming defendant*)

July 1, 2007

FORM 28C — REPLY TO DEFENCE TO CROSSCLAIM

Courts of Justice Act

[Repealed O. Reg. 77/06, s. 3.]

[Editor's Note: Forms 4A to 78A of the Rules of Civil Procedure have been repealed by O. Reg. 77/06, effective July 1, 2006. Pursuant to Rule of Civil Procedure 1.06, when a form is referred to by number, the reference is to the form with that number that is described in the Table of Forms at the end of these rules and which is available on the Internet through www.ontariocourtforms.on.ca. For your convenience, the government form as published on this website is reproduced below.]

(*General heading*)

REPLY TO DEFENCE TO CROSSCLAIM

1. The defendant (*name*) admits the allegations contained in paragraphs .... of the defence to crossclaim.

2. The defendant (*name*) denies the allegations contained in paragraphs .... of the defence to crossclaim.

3. The defendant (*name*) has no knowledge in respect of the allegations contained in paragraphs .... of the defence to crossclaim.

4. (*Set out in separate, consecutively numbered paragraphs each allegation of material fact relied on by way of reply to the defence to crossclaim.*)

(*Date*) (*Name, address and telephone number of crossclaiming defendant's lawyer or crossclaiming defendant*)

TO (*Name and address of defendant to crossclaim's lawyer or defendant to crossclaim*)

July 1, 2007

FORM 29A — THIRD PARTY CLAIM

Courts of Justice Act

[Repealed O. Reg. 77/06, s. 3.]

[Editor's Note: Forms 4A to 78A of the Rules of Civil Procedure have been repealed by O. Reg. 77/06, effective July 1, 2006. Pursuant to Rule of Civil Procedure 1.06, when a form is referred to by number, the reference is to the form with that number that is described in the Table of Forms at the end of these rules and which is available on the Internet through www.ontariocourtforms.on.ca. For your convenience, the government form as published on this website is reproduced below.]

ONTARIO (*Court file no.*)

SUPERIOR COURT OF JUSTICE

BETWEEN:

(*name*)

(*Court seal*) Plaintiff

and

(*name*)

Defendant

and

(*name*)

Third Party

THIRD PARTY CLAIM

TO THE THIRD PARTY

A LEGAL PROCEEDING HAS BEEN COMMENCED AGAINST YOU by way of a third party claim in an action in this court.

The action was commenced by the plaintiff against the defendant for the relief claimed in the statement of claim served with this third party claim. The defendant has defended the action on the grounds set out in the statement of defence served with this third party claim. The defendant's claim against you is set out in the following pages.

IF YOU WISH TO DEFEND THIS THIRD PARTY CLAIM, you or an Ontario lawyer acting for you must prepare a third party defence in Form 29B prescribed by the *Rules of Civil Procedure*, serve it on the lawyers for the other parties or, where a party does not have a lawyer, serve it on the party, and file it, with proof of service, WITHIN TWENTY DAYS after this third party claim is served on you, if you are served in Ontario.

If you are served in another province or territory of Canada or in the United States of America, the period for serving and filing your third party defence is forty days. If you are served outside Canada and the United States of America, the period is sixty days.

Instead of serving and filing a third party defence, you may serve and file a notice of intent to defend in Form 18B prescribed by the *Rules of Civil Procedure*. This will entitle you to ten more days within which to serve and file your third party defence.

YOU MAY ALSO DEFEND the action by the plaintiff against the defendant by serving and filing a statement of defence within the time for serving and filing your third party defence.

IF YOU FAIL TO DEFEND THIS THIRD PARTY CLAIM, JUDGMENT MAY BE GIVEN AGAINST YOU IN YOUR ABSENCE AND WITHOUT FURTHER NOTICE TO YOU. IF YOU WISH TO DEFEND THIS PROCEEDING BUT ARE UNABLE TO PAY LEGAL FEES, LEGAL AID MAY BE AVAILABLE TO YOU BY CONTACTING A LOCAL LEGAL AID OFFICE.

(*Where the third party claim is for money only, include the following:*)

IF YOU PAY THE AMOUNT OF THE THIRD PARTY CLAIM AGAINST YOU, and $ .... for costs, within the time for serving and filing your third party defence, you may move to have the third party claim dismissed by the court. If you believe the amount claimed for costs is excessive, you may pay the amount of the third party claim and $400 for costs and have the costs assessed by the court.

Date .... Issued by ....

Local registrar

Address of court office ....

....

TO (*Name and address of third party*)

CLAIM

1. The defendant claims against the third party: (*State here the precise relief claimed.*)

(*Then set out in separate, consecutively numbered paragraphs each allegation of material fact relied on to substantiate the third party claim.*)

(*Where the third party claim is to be served outside Ontario without a court order, set out the facts and the specific provisions of Rule 17 relied on in support of such service.*)

(*Date of issue*) (*Name, address and telephone number of defendant's lawyer or defendant*)

July 1, 2007

FORM 29B — THIRD PARTY DEFENCE

Courts of Justice Act

[Repealed O. Reg. 77/06, s. 3.]

[Editor's Note: Forms 4A to 78A of the Rules of Civil Procedure have been repealed by O. Reg. 77/06, effective July 1, 2006. Pursuant to Rule of Civil Procedure 1.06, when a form is referred to by number, the reference is to the form with that number that is described in the Table of Forms at the end of these rules and which is available on the Internet through

www.ontariocourtforms.on.ca. For your convenience, the government form as published on this website is reproduced below.]

(General heading, with title of proceeding in accordance with Form 29A)

THIRD PARTY DEFENCE

1. The third party admits the allegations contained in paragraphs .... of the third party claim.

2. The third party denies the allegations contained in paragraphs .... of the third party claim.

3. The third party has no knowledge in respect of the allegations contained in paragraphs .... of the third party claim.

4. (*Set out in separate, consecutively numbered paragraphs each allegation of material fact relied on by way of defence to the third party claim.*)

(*Date*) (*Name, address and telephone number of third party's lawyer or third party*)

TO (*Name and address of defendant's lawyer or defendant*)

July 1, 2007

FORM 29C — REPLY TO THIRD PARTY DEFENCE

Courts of Justice Act

[Repealed O. Reg. 77/06, s. 3.]

[Editor's Note: Forms 4A to 78A of the Rules of Civil Procedure have been repealed by O. Reg. 77/06, effective July 1, 2006. Pursuant to Rule of Civil Procedure 1.06, when a form is referred to by number, the reference is to the form with that number that is described in the Table of Forms at the end of these rules and which is available on the Internet through www.ontariocourtforms.on.ca. For your convenience, the government form as published on this website is reproduced below.]

(General heading, with title of proceeding in accordance with Form 29A)

REPLY TO THIRD PARTY DEFENCE

1. The defendant admits the allegations contained in paragraphs .... of the third party defence.

2. The defendant denies the allegations contained in paragraphs .... of the third party defence.

3. The defendant has no knowledge in respect of the allegations contained in paragraphs .... of the third party defence.

4. (*Set out in separate, consecutively numbered paragraphs each allegation of material fact relied on by way of reply to the third party defence.*)

(*Date*) (*Name, address and telephone number of defendant's lawyer or defendant*)

TO (*Name and address of third party's lawyer or third party*)

July 1, 2007

FORM 30A — AFFIDAVIT OF DOCUMENTS (INDIVIDUAL)

Courts of Justice Act

[Repealed O. Reg. 77/06, s. 3.]

[Editor's Note: Forms 4A to 78A of the Rules of Civil Procedure have been repealed by O. Reg. 77/06, effective July 1, 2006. Pursuant to Rule of Civil Procedure 1.06, when a form is referred to by number, the reference is to the form with that number that is described in the Table of Forms at the end of these rules and which is available on the Internet through www.ontariocourtforms.on.ca. For your convenience, the government form as published on this website is reproduced below.]

Courts of Justice Act

(General heading)

AFFIDAVIT OF DOCUMENTS

I, *(full name of deponent)*, of the *(*City, Town, *etc.)* of ...., in the *(*County, Regional Municipality, *etc.)* of ...., the plaintiff *(or as may be)* in this action, MAKE OATH AND SAY *(or* AFFIRM*)*:

1. I have conducted a diligent search of my records and have made appropriate enquiries of others to inform myself in order to make this affidavit. This affidavit discloses, to the full extent of my knowledge, information and belief, all documents relevant to any matter in issue in this action that are or have been in my possession, control or power.

2. I have listed in Schedule A those documents that are in my possession, control or power and that I do not object to producing for inspection.

3. I have listed in Schedule B those documents that are or were in my possession, control or power and that I object to producing because I claim they are privileged, and I have stated in Schedule B the grounds for each such claim.

4. I have listed in Schedule C those documents that were formerly in my possession, control or power but are no longer in my possession, control or power, and I have stated in Schedule C when and how I lost possession or control of or power over them and their present location.

5. I have never had in my possession, control or power any document relevant to any matter in issue in this action other than those listed in Schedules A, B and C.

6. I have listed in Schedule D the names and addresses of persons who might reasonably be expected to have knowledge of transactions or occurrences in issue. *(Strike out this paragraph if the action is not being brought under the simplified procedure.)*

SWORN *(etc.)*

....
(Signature of deponent)

LAWYER'S CERTIFICATE

I CERTIFY that I have explained to the deponent,

(a) the necessity of making full disclosure of all documents relevant to any matter in issue in the action;

(b) what kinds of documents are likely to be relevant to the allegations made in the pleadings; and

(c) if the action is brought under the simplified procedure, the necessity of providing the list required under rule 76.03.

Date ....
(Signature of lawyer)

SCHEDULE A

Documents in my possession, control or power that I do not object to producing for inspection.

(Number each document consecutively. Set out the nature and date of the document and other particulars sufficient to identify it.)

SCHEDULE B

Documents that are or were in my possession, control or power that I object to producing on the grounds of privilege.

(Number each document consecutively. Set out the nature and date of the document and other particulars sufficient to identify it. State the grounds for claiming privilege for each document.)

SCHEDULE C

Documents that were formerly in my possession, control or power but are no longer in my possession, control or power.

(Number each document consecutively. Set out the nature and date of the document and other particulars sufficient to identify it. State when and how possession or control of or power over each document was lost, and give the present location of each document.)

SCHEDULE D

(To be filled in only if the action is being brought under the simplified procedure.)

Names and addresses of persons who might reasonably be expected to have knowledge of transactions or occurrences in issue.

November 1, 2008

FORM 30B — AFFIDAVIT OF DOCUMENTS (CORPORATION OR PARTNERSHIP)

Courts of Justice Act

[Repealed O. Reg. 77/06, s. 3.]

[Editor's Note: Forms 4A to 78A of the Rules of Civil Procedure have been repealed by O. Reg. 77/06, effective July 1, 2006. Pursuant to Rule of Civil Procedure 1.06, when a form is referred to by number, the reference is to the form with that number that is described in the Table of Forms at the end of these rules and which is available on the Internet through www.ontariocourtforms.on.ca. For your convenience, the government form as published on this website is reproduced below.]

Courts of Justice Act

(General heading)

AFFIDAVIT OF DOCUMENTS

I, (*full name of deponent*), of the (City, Town, *etc.*) of ...., in the (County, Regional Municipality, *etc.*) of ...., MAKE OATH AND SAY (or AFFIRM):

1. I am the (*state the position held by the deponent in the corporation or partnership*) of the plaintiff (*or as may be*), which is a corporation (*or* partnership).

2. I have conducted a diligent search of the corporation's (*or* partnership's) records and made appropriate enquiries of others to inform myself in order to make this affidavit. This affidavit discloses, to the full extent of my knowledge, information and belief, all documents relevant to any matter in issue in this action that are or have been in the possession, control or power of the corporation (*or* partnership).

3. I have listed in Schedule A those documents that are in the possession, control or power of the corporation (*or* partnership) and that it does not object to producing for inspection.

4. I have listed in Schedule B those documents that are or were in the possession, control or power of the corporation (*or* partnership) and that it objects to producing because it claims they are privileged, and I have stated in Schedule B the grounds for each such claim.

5. I have listed in Schedule C those documents that were formerly in the possession, control or power of the corporation (*or* partnership) but are no longer in its possession, control or power and I have stated in Schedule C when and how it lost possession or control of or power over them and their present location.

6. The corporation (*or* partnership) has never had in its possession, control or power any documents relevant to any matter in issue in this action other than those listed in Schedules A, B and C.

7. I have listed in Schedule D the names and addresses of persons who might reasonably be expected to have knowledge of transactions or occurrences in issue. *(Strike out this paragraph if the action is not being brought under the simplified procedure.)*

SWORN *(etc.)*

....
(Signature of deponent)

LAWYER'S CERTIFICATE

I CERTIFY that I have explained to the deponent,

(a) the necessity of making full disclosure of all documents relevant to any matter in issue in the action;

(b) what kinds of documents are likely to be relevant to the allegations made in the pleadings; and

(c) if the action is brought under the simplified procedure, the necessity of providing the list required under rule 76.03.

Date ....
(Signature of lawyer)

SCHEDULE A

Documents in the corporation's *(or* partnership's*)* possession, control or power that it does not object to producing for inspection.

(Number each document consecutively. Set out the nature and date of the document and other particulars sufficient to identify it.)

SCHEDULE B

Documents that are or were in the corporation's *(or* partnership's*)* possession, control or power that it objects to producing on the grounds of privilege.

(Number each document consecutively. Set out the nature and date of the document and other particulars sufficient to identify it. State the grounds for claiming privilege for each document.)

SCHEDULE C

Documents that were formerly in the corporation's *(or* partnership's*)* possession, control or power but are no longer in its possession, control or power.

(Number each document consecutively. Set out the nature and date of the document and other particulars sufficient to identify it. State when and how possession or control of or power over each document was lost, and give the present location of each document.)

SCHEDULE D

(To be filled in only if the action is being brought under the simplified procedure.)

Names and addresses of persons who might reasonably be expected to have knowledge of transactions or occurrences in issue.

November 1, 2008

FORM 30C — REQUEST TO INSPECT DOCUMENTS

Courts of Justice Act

[Repealed O. Reg. 77/06, s. 3.]

[Editor's Note: Forms 4A to 78A of the Rules of Civil Procedure have been repealed by O. Reg. 77/06, effective July 1, 2006. Pursuant to Rule of Civil Procedure 1.06, when a form is referred to by number, the reference is to the form with that number that is described in the Table of Forms at the end of these rules and which is available on the Internet through www.ontariocourtforms.on.ca. For your convenience, the government form as published on this website is reproduced below.]

(*General heading)*

REQUEST TO INSPECT DOCUMENTS

You are requested to produce for inspection all the documents listed in Schedule A of your affidavit of documents (*or* the following documents referred to in your (*identify pleading or affidavit*):)

(*Date*) (*Name, address and telephone number of requesting lawyer or party*)

TO (*Name and address of lawyer or party requested to produce*)

July 1, 2007

FORM 34A — NOTICE OF EXAMINATION

Courts of Justice Act

[Repealed O. Reg. 77/06, s. 3.]

[Editor's Note: Forms 4A to 78A of the Rules of Civil Procedure have been repealed by O. Reg. 77/06, effective July 1, 2006. Pursuant to Rule of Civil Procedure 1.06, when a form is referred to by number, the reference is to the form with that number that is described in the Table of Forms at the end of these rules and which is available on the Internet through www.ontariocourtforms.on.ca. For your convenience, the government form as published on this website is reproduced below.]

(*To be used only for a party to the proceeding, a person to be examined for discovery or in aid of execution on behalf or in place of a party or a person to be cross-examined on an affidavit. For the examination of any other person, use a summons to witness (Form 34B).*)

(*General heading)*

NOTICE OF EXAMINATION

TO (*Name of person to be examined*)

YOU ARE REQUIRED TO ATTEND, on *(day)*, *(date)*, at *(time)*, at the office of *(name, address and telephone number of examiner)*, for *(choose one of the following)*:

[ ] Cross-examination on your affidavit dated *(date)*

[ ] Examination for discovery

[ ] Examination for discovery on behalf of or in place of *(identify party)*

[ ] Examination in aid of execution

[ ] Examination in aid of execution on behalf of or in place of *(identify party)*

(*Examination for discovery of a party or a person examined on behalf or in place of a party*)

YOU ARE REQUIRED TO BRING WITH YOU and produce at the examination the documents mentioned in subrule 30.04(4) of the *Rules of Civil Procedure*, and the following documents and things: (*Set out the nature and date of each document and give particulars sufficient to identify each document and thing.*)

(*Other examinations*)

YOU ARE REQUIRED TO BRING WITH YOU and produce at the examination the following documents and things: (*Set out the nature and date of each document and give particulars sufficient to identify each document and thing.*)

(*Date*) (*Name, address and telephone number of examining lawyer or party*)

TO (*Name and address of lawyer or of person to be examined*)

July 1, 2007

FORM 34B — SUMMONS TO WITNESS (EXAMINATION OUT OF COURT)

Courts of Justice Act

[Repealed O. Reg. 77/06, s. 3.]

[Editor's Note: Forms 4A to 78A of the Rules of Civil Procedure have been repealed by O. Reg. 77/06, effective July 1, 2006. Pursuant to Rule of Civil Procedure 1.06, when a form is referred to by number, the reference is to the form with that number that is described in the Table of Forms at the end of these rules and which is available on the Internet through www.ontariocourtforms.on.ca. For your convenience, the government form as published on this website is reproduced below.]

(*General heading)*

(*Court seal*)

SUMMONS TO WITNESS

TO (*Name and address of person to be examined)*

YOU ARE REQUIRED TO ATTEND, on *(day)*, *(date)*, at *(time)*, at the office of *(name, address and telephone number of examiner)*, for *(choose one of the following)*:

[ ] Cross-examination on your affidavit dated *(date)*

[ ] Examination for discovery with leave of the court

[ ] Examination out of court as witness before hearing

[ ] Examination in aid of execution

[ ] Taking evidence before trial

YOU ARE REQUIRED TO BRING WITH YOU and produce at the examination the following documents and things: (*Set out the nature and date of each document and give particulars sufficient to identify each document and thing.*)

ATTENDANCE MONEY for .... day(s) of attendance is served with this summons, calculated in accordance with Tariff A of the *Rules of Civil Procedure*, as follows:

Attendance allowance of $ .... daily	$ ....
Travel allowance	$ ....
Overnight accommodation and meal allowance	$ ....
	=========
TOTAL	$ ....

If further attendance is required, you will be entitled to additional attendance money.

IF YOU FAIL TO ATTEND OR REMAIN UNTIL THE END OF THIS EXAMINATION, YOU MAY BE COMPELLED TO ATTEND AT YOUR OWN EXPENSE AND YOU MAY BE FOUND IN CONTEMPT OF COURT.

Date .... Issued by ....

Local registrar

Address of court office ....
....

This summons was issued at the request of, and inquiries may be directed to:

(*Name, address and telephone number of examining lawyer or party*)

July 1, 2007

FORM 34C — COMMISSION

Courts of Justice Act

[Repealed O. Reg. 77/06, s. 3.]

[Editor's Note: Forms 4A to 78A of the Rules of Civil Procedure have been repealed by O. Reg. 77/06, effective July 1, 2006. Pursuant to Rule of Civil Procedure 1.06, when a form is referred to by number, the reference is to the form with that number that is described in the Table of Forms at the end of these rules and which is available on the Internet through www.ontariocourtforms.on.ca. For your convenience, the government form as published on this website is reproduced below.]

(*General heading*)

(*Court seal*)

COMMISSION

TO (*Name and address of commissioner*)

YOU HAVE BEEN APPOINTED A COMMISSIONER for the purpose of taking evidence in this proceeding now pending in this court by order of the court made on (*date*), a copy of which is attached.

YOU ARE GIVEN FULL AUTHORITY to do all things necessary for taking the evidence mentioned in the order authorizing this commission. (*Where the commission is issued under Rule 36, add:* You are also authorized, on consent of the parties, to take the evidence of any other witnesses who may be found in (*name of province, state or country*).)

You are to send to this court a transcript of the evidence taken, together with this commission, forthwith after the transcript is completed.

In carrying out this commission, you are to follow the terms of the attached order and the instructions contained in this commission.

THIS COMMISSION is signed and sealed by order of the court.

Date .... Issued by ....
Local registrar

Address of court office ....
....

The registrar is to attach to this commission a copy of Rules 34 and 36 and section 45 of the Evidence Act.

INSTRUCTIONS TO COMMISSIONER

1. This commission is to be conducted in accordance with Rules 34 and 36 of the Ontario Rules of Civil Procedure, a copy of which is attached, to the extent that it is possible to do so. The law of Ontario applies to the taking of the evidence.

2. Before acting on this commission, you must take the oath (*or* affirmation) set out below. You may do so before any person authorized by section 45 of the *Evidence Act* of Ontario, a copy of which is attached, to take affidavits or administer oaths or affirmations outside Ontario.

> I, ..., swear (*or* affirm) that I will, according to the best of my skill and knowledge, truly and faithfully and without partiality to any of the parties to this proceeding, take the evidence of every witness examined under this commission, and cause the evidence to be transcribed and forwarded to the court. (*In an oath, conclude:* So help me God.)
>
> Sworn (*or* Affirmed) before me at the (City, Town, *etc.*) of ...., in the (Province, State, *etc.*) of ...., on (*date*).

....
(*Signature of commissioner*)

....
(*Signature and office of person before whom oath or affirmation is taken*)

3. The examining party is required to give the person to be examined at least .... days notice of the examination and, where the order so provides, to pay attendance money to the person to be examined.

4. You must arrange to have the evidence before you recorded and transcribed. You are to administer the following oath (*or* affirmation) to the person who records and transcribes the evidence:

> You swear (*or* affirm) that you will truly and faithfully record and transcribe all questions put to all witnesses and their answers in accordance with the directions of the commissioner. (*In an oath, conclude:* So help you God.)

On consent of the parties, or where the order for this commission provides for it, the examination may be recorded by videotape or other similar means.

5. You are to administer the following oath (*or* affirmation) to each witness whose evidence is to be taken:

> You swear (*or* affirm) that the evidence to be given by you touching the matters in question between the parties to this proceeding shall be the truth, the whole truth, and nothing but the truth. (*In an oath, conclude:* So help you God.)

6. Where a witness does not understand the language or is deaf or mute, the evidence of the witness must be given through an interpreter. You are to administer the following oath (*or* affirmation) to the interpreter:

> You swear (*or* affirm) that you understand the .... language and the language in which the examination is to be conducted and that you will truly interpret the oath (*or* affirmation) to the witness, all questions put to the witness and the answers of the witness, to the best of your skill and understanding. (*In an oath, conclude:* So help you God.)

7. You are to attach to this commission the transcript of the evidence and the exhibits, and any videotape or other recording of the examination. You are to complete the certificate set out below, and mail this commission, the transcript, the exhibits and any videotape or other recording of the examination to the office of the court where the commission was issued. You are to keep a copy of the transcript and, where practicable, a copy of the exhibits until the court disposes of this proceeding. Forthwith after you mail this commission and the accompanying material to the court office, you are to notify the parties who appeared at the examination that you have done so.

CERTIFICATE OF COMMISSIONER

I, ..., certify that:

1. I administered the proper oath (*or* affirmation) to the person who recorded and transcribed the evidence, to the witness the transcript of whose evidence is attached and to any interpreter through whom the evidence was given.

2. The evidence of the witness was properly taken.

3. The evidence of the witness was accurately transcribed.

Date ....

....
(*Signature of commissioner*)

November 1, 2005

FORM 34D — LETTER OF REQUEST

Courts of Justice Act

[Repealed O. Reg. 77/06, s. 3.]

[Editor's Note: Forms 4A to 78A of the Rules of Civil Procedure have been repealed by O. Reg. 77/06, effective July 1, 2006. Pursuant to Rule of Civil Procedure 1.06, when a form is referred to by number, the reference is to the form with that number that is described in the Table of Forms at the end of these rules and which is available on the Internet through

www.ontariocourtforms.on.ca. For your convenience, the government form as published on this website is reproduced below.]

(General heading)

(Court seal)

LETTER OF REQUEST

TO THE JUDICIAL AUTHORITIES OF (*name of province, state or country*)

A PROCEEDING IS PENDING IN THIS COURT at the (City, Town, *etc.*) of ...., in the Province of Ontario, Canada, between (*name*), plaintiff (*or as may be*), and (*name*), defendant (*or as may be*).

IT HAS BEEN SHOWN TO THIS COURT that it appears necessary for the purpose of justice that a witness residing within your jurisdiction be examined there.

THIS COURT HAS ISSUED A COMMISSION to (*name of commissioner*) of (*address of commissioner*), providing for the examination of the witness (*name of witness*), of (*address of witness*).

YOU ARE REQUESTED, in furtherance of justice, to cause (*name of witness*) (*where the commission was issued under Rule 36, add* and, on consent of the parties, any other witnesses who may be found in your jurisdiction) to appear before the commissioner by the means ordinarily used in your jurisdiction, if necessary to secure attendance, and to answer questions under oath or affirmation (*where desired, add:*) and to bring to and produce at the examination the following documents and things: (*Set out the nature and date of each document and give particulars sufficient to identify each document and thing*).

YOU ARE ALSO REQUESTED to permit the commissioner to conduct the examination of the witness in accordance with the law of evidence and Rules of Civil Procedure of Ontario and the commission issued by this court.

AND WHEN YOU REQUEST IT, the courts of Ontario are ready and willing to do the same for you in a similar case.

THIS LETTER OF REQUEST is signed and sealed by order of the court made on (*date*).

Date	Issued by	.... Local registrar
	Address of court office	....

November 1, 2005

FORM 34E — ORDER FOR COMMISSION AND LETTER OF REQUEST

Courts of Justice Act

[Repealed O. Reg. 77/06, s. 3.]

[Editor's Note: Forms 4A to 78A of the Rules of Civil Procedure have been repealed by O. Reg. 77/06, effective July 1, 2006. Pursuant to Rule of Civil Procedure 1.06, when a form is referred to by number, the reference is to the form with that number that is described in the Table of Forms at the end of these rules and which is available on the Internet through www.ontariocourtforms.on.ca. For your convenience, the government form as published on this website is reproduced below.]

(*Court file no.*)

(*Court*)

(*Name of judge or officer*) (*Day and date order made*)

(*Court seal*) (*Title of proceeding*)

ORDER

(*Recitals in accordance with Form 59A*)

1. THIS COURT ORDERS (*give particulars of any directions given by the court under rule 34.07*).

2. THIS COURT ORDERS that the registrar prepare and issue a commission naming (*name*), of (*address*), as commissioner to take the evidence of the witness (*name of witness*) in (*name of province, state or country*) (*where the order is made under Rule 36, add* and, on consent of the parties, any other witness who may be found there) for use at trial (*or* on examination for discovery, *etc.*).

3. THIS COURT ORDERS that the registrar prepare and issue a letter of request addressed to the judicial authorities of (*name of province, state or country*), requesting the issuing of such process as is necessary to compel the witness (*or* witnesses) to attend and be examined before the commissioner.

(*Signature of judge, officer or registrar*)

November 1, 2005

FORM 35A — QUESTIONS ON WRITTEN EXAMINATION FOR DISCOVERY

Courts of Justice Act

[Repealed O. Reg. 77/06, s. 3.]

[Editor's Note: Forms 4A to 78A of the Rules of Civil Procedure have been repealed by O. Reg. 77/06, effective July 1, 2006. Pursuant to Rule of Civil Procedure 1.06, when a form is referred to by number, the reference is to the form with that number that is described in the Table of Forms at the end of these rules and which is available on the Internet through www.ontariocourtforms.on.ca. For your convenience, the government form as published on this website is reproduced below.]

(*General heading*)

QUESTIONS ON WRITTEN EXAMINATION FOR DISCOVERY

THE (*identify examining party*) has chosen to examine the (*identify person to be examined*) for discovery (*where the person is not a party, state whether the person is examined on behalf or in place of or in addition to a party or under a court order*) by written questions and requires that the following questions be answered by affidavit in Form 35B prescribed by the *Rules of Civil Procedure*, served within fifteen days after service of these questions.

(*Where a further list of questions is served under rule 35.04 substitute:*)

The (*identify examining party*) requires that the (*identify person to be examined*) answer the following further questions by affidavit in Form 35B prescribed by the *Rules of Civil Procedure*, served within fifteen days after service of these questions.

1. (*Number each question. Where the questions are a further list under rule 35.04, number the questions in sequence following the last question of the previous list.*)

(*Date*) (*Name, address and telephone number of examining party's lawyer or examining party*)

TO (*Name and address of lawyer for person to be examined or of person to be examined*)

July 1, 2007

FORM 35B — ANSWERS ON WRITTEN EXAMINATION FOR DISCOVERY

Courts of Justice Act

[Repealed O. Reg. 77/06, s. 3.]

[Editor's Note: Forms 4A to 78A of the Rules of Civil Procedure have been repealed by O. Reg. 77/06, effective July 1, 2006. Pursuant to Rule of Civil Procedure 1.06, when a form is referred to by number, the reference is to the form with that number that is described in the Table of Forms at the end of these rules and which is available on the Internet through www.ontariocourtforms.on.ca. For your convenience, the government form as published on this website is reproduced below.]

(*General heading*)

ANSWERS ON WRITTEN EXAMINATION FOR DISCOVERY

I, (*full name of deponent*), of the (City, Town, *etc.*) of ...., in the (County, Regional Municipality, *etc.*) of ...., the (*identify the capacity in which the deponent makes the affidavit*), MAKE OATH AND SAY (*or* AFFIRM) that the following answers to the questions dated (*date*) submitted by the (*identify examining party*) are true, to the best of my knowledge, information and belief:

1. (*Number each answer to correspond with the question. Where the deponent objects to answering a question, state:* I object to answering this question on the ground that it is irrelevant to the matters in issue *or* that the information sought is privileged because (*specify*) *or as may be.*)

SWORN (*etc.*)

November 1, 2005

FORM 37A — NOTICE OF MOTION

Courts of Justice Act

[Repealed O. Reg. 77/06, s. 3.]

[Editor's Note: Forms 4A to 78A of the Rules of Civil Procedure have been repealed by O. Reg. 77/06, effective July 1, 2006. Pursuant to Rule of Civil Procedure 1.06, when a form is referred to by number, the reference is to the form with that number that is described in the Table of Forms at the end of these rules and which is available on the Internet through www.ontariocourtforms.on.ca. For your convenience, the government form as published on this website is reproduced below.]

(*General heading*)

NOTICE OF MOTION

The (*identify moving party*) will make a motion to the court (*or* judge) on (*day*), (*date*), at (*time*), or soon after that time as the motion can be heard, at (*address of court house*).

PROPOSED METHOD OF HEARING: The motion is to be heard (*choose appropriate option*)

❑ in writing under subrule 37.12.1(1) because it is (*insert one of* on consent, unopposed *or* made without notice);

❑ in writing as an opposed motion under subrule 37.12.1(4);

❑ orally.

THE MOTION IS FOR (*state here the precise relief sought*).

THE GROUNDS FOR THE MOTION ARE (*specify the grounds to be argued, including a reference to any statutory provision or rule to be relied on*).

THE FOLLOWING DOCUMENTARY EVIDENCE will be used at the hearing of the motion: (*list the affidavits or other documentary evidence to be relied on*).

(*Date*) (*Name, address and telephone number of*

moving party's lawyer or moving party)

TO *(Name and address of responding party's lawyer or responding party)*

July 1, 2007

FORM 37B — CONFIRMATION OF MOTION

Courts of Justice Act

[Repealed O. Reg. 77/06, s. 3.]

[Editor's Note: Forms 4A to 78A of the Rules of Civil Procedure have been repealed by O. Reg. 77/06, effective July 1, 2006. Pursuant to Rule of Civil Procedure 1.06, when a form is referred to by number, the reference is to the form with that number that is described in the Table of Forms at the end of these rules and which is available on the Internet through www.ontariocourtforms.on.ca. For your convenience, the government form as published on this website is reproduced below.]

(General heading)

I, ... *(name)*, lawyer for the moving party, confirm that the moving party has conferred or attempted to confer with the other party and confirm that the motion to be heard on .... *(date)* will proceed on the following basis:

[ ] for an adjournment on consent to .... *(date)*

[ ] for a contested adjournment to .... *(date)*, for the following reason: *(specify who is requesting the adjournment and why, and who is opposing it and why)*

[ ] for a consent order

[ ] for a hearing of all the issues

[ ] for a hearing of the following issues only *(specify)*

The presiding judge will be referred to the following materials: *(please be specific)*

I estimate that the time required for the motion, including costs submissions, will be .... minutes for the moving party*(ies)* and .... minutes for the responding party*(ies)* for a total of .... minutes.

(Date) ....

TO *(Name and address of responding party's lawyer or responding party)*

July 1, 2007

FORM 37C — REFUSALS AND UNDERTAKINGS CHART

Courts of Justice Act

[Repealed O. Reg. 77/06, s. 3.]

[Editor's Note: Forms 4A to 78A of the Rules of Civil Procedure have been repealed by O. Reg. 77/06, effective July 1, 2006. Pursuant to Rule of Civil Procedure 1.06, when a form is referred to by number, the reference is to the form with that number that is described in the Table of Forms at the end of these rules and which is available on the Internet through www.ontariocourtforms.on.ca. For your convenience, the government form as published on this website is reproduced below.]

(General heading)

REFUSALS					
Refusals to answer questions on the examination of ...., dated					
Issue & relationship to pleadings or affidavit *(Group the questions by issues.)*	*Question No.*	*Page No.*	*Specific question*	*Answer or precise basis for refusal*	*Disposition by the Court*
1.					
2.					
3.					

UNDERTAKINGS					
Outstanding undertakings given on the examination of ...., dated					
Issue & relationship to pleadings or affidavit *(Group the undertakings by issues.)*	*Question No.*	*Page No.*	*Specific undertaking*	*Date answered or precise reason for not doing so*	*Disposition by the Court*
1.					
2.					
3.					

(Date) *(Name, address and telephone and fax numbers of the party filing the refusals and undertakings chart)*

(Date) .... *(Name, address and telephone and fax numbers of the party filing the refusals and undertakings chart)* ....

November 1, 2005

FORM 38A — NOTICE OF APPEARANCE

Courts of Justice Act

[Repealed O. Reg. 77/06, s. 3.]

[Editor's Note: Forms 4A to 78A of the Rules of Civil Procedure have been repealed by O. Reg. 77/06, effective July 1, 2006. Pursuant to Rule of Civil Procedure 1.06, when a form is referred to by number, the reference is to the form with that number that is described in the Table of Forms at the end of these rules and which is available on the Internet through www.ontariocourtforms.on.ca. For your convenience, the government form as published on this website is reproduced below.]

(*General heading*)

NOTICE OF APPEARANCE

The respondent intends to respond to this application.

(*Date*) (*Name, address and telephone number of respondent's lawyer or respondent*)

TO (*Name and address of applicant's lawyer or applicant*)

July 1, 2007

FORM 38B — CONFIRMATION OF APPLICATION

Courts of Justice Act

[Repealed O. Reg. 77/06, s. 3.]

[Editor's Note: Forms 4A to 78A of the Rules of Civil Procedure have been repealed by O. Reg. 77/06, effective July 1, 2006. Pursuant to Rule of Civil Procedure 1.06, when a form is referred to by number, the reference is to the form with that number that is described in the Table of Forms at the end of these rules and which is available on the Internet through www.ontariocourtforms.on.ca. For your convenience, the government form as published on this website is reproduced below.]

(*General heading*)

CONFIRMATION OF APPLICATION

I, ... *(name)*, lawyer for the applicant confirm that the application to be heard on .... *(date)* will proceed on the following basis:

[ ] for an adjournment on consent to .... *(date)*

[ ] for a contested adjournment to .... *(date)*, for the following reason: *(specify who is requesting the adjournment and why, and who is opposing it and why)*

[ ] for a consent order

[ ] for hearing of all the issues

[ ] for hearing of the following issues only *(specify)*

I estimate that the time required for the application will be: .... minutes for the applicant*(s)* and .... minutes for the respondent*(s)* for a total of .... minutes.

(Date)

TO *(Name and address of respondent's lawyer or respondent)*

July 1, 2007

FORM 42A — CERTIFICATE OF PENDING LITIGATION

Courts of Justice Act

[Repealed O. Reg. 77/06, s. 3.]

[Editor's Note: Forms 4A to 78A of the Rules of Civil Procedure have been repealed by O. Reg. 77/06, effective July 1, 2006. Pursuant to Rule of Civil Procedure 1.06, when a form is referred to by number, the reference is to the form with that number that is described in the Table of Forms at the end of these rules and which is available on the Internet through www.ontariocourtforms.on.ca. For your convenience, the government form as published on this website is reproduced below.]

(*General heading*)

(*Court seal*)

CERTIFICATE OF PENDING LITIGATION

I CERTIFY that in this proceeding an interest in the following land is in question:

> (*Set out a description of the land sufficient for registration. Where the land is registered under the* Land Titles Act, *include the parcel number. Attach a schedule if necessary.*)

This certificate is issued under an order of the court made on (*date*).

Date .... Issued by ....
Local registrar

Address of court office ....

....

November 1, 2005

FORM 43A — INTERPLEADER ORDER — GENERAL

Courts of Justice Act

[Repealed O. Reg. 77/06, s. 3.]

[Editor's Note: Forms 4A to 78A of the Rules of Civil Procedure have been repealed by O. Reg. 77/06, effective July 1, 2006. Pursuant to Rule of Civil Procedure 1.06, when a form is referred to by number, the reference is to the form with that number that is described in the Table of Forms at the end of these rules and which is available on the Internet through www.ontariocourtforms.on.ca. For your convenience, the government form as published on this website is reproduced below.]

(*Court file no.*)

(*Court*)

(*Name of judge or officer*) (*Day and date order made*)

(*Court seal*) (*Title of proceeding*)

INTERPLEADER ORDER

(*Where an interpleader application results in a judgment, amend the form accordingly.*)

(*Recitals in accordance with Form 59A or 59B*)

Payment of money into court

1. THIS COURT ORDERS that the (*identify party*) pay into court the sum of $ ...., less costs fixed at $ ...., to await the outcome of a proceeding in this court between (*identify parties*) (*or* to await the outcome of this proceeding).

2. THIS COURT DECLARES that on compliance with paragraph 1 of this order, the liability of (*identify party*) in respect of the above sum is extinguished.

3. THIS COURT ORDERS (*include any other order made by the court under rule 43.04*).

Sale of property and payment of proceeds into court

1. THIS COURT ORDERS that (*identify property*) be sold by (*method of sale*) and that the proceeds, less expenses of sale and the costs of (*identify party*) fixed at $ ...., be paid into court to await the outcome of a proceeding in this court between (*identify parties*) (*or* to await the outcome of this proceeding).

2. THIS COURT DECLARES that on compliance with paragraph 1 of this order, the liability of (*identify party*) in respect of the above sum is extinguished.

3. THIS COURT ORDERS (*include any other order made by the court under rule 43.04*).

Deposit of property with an officer of the court

1. THIS COURT ORDERS that (*identify property*) be deposited with the Sheriff of the (*county or district*) (*or as may be*) to await the outcome of a proceeding in this court between (*identify parties*) (*or* to await the outcome of this proceeding).

2. THIS COURT DECLARES that on compliance with paragraph 1 of this order, the liability of (*identify party*) in respect of the above property is extinguished.

3. THIS COURT ORDERS (*include any other order made by the court under rule 43.04*).

Trial of an issue

(*This paragraph will normally form part of an order for payment into court or deposit of property with an officer of the court.*)

4. THIS COURT ORDERS that there be a trial of the issue of (*give particulars of issue to be tried*), in which (*identify party*) shall be plaintiff and (*identify party*) shall be defendant.

5. THIS COURT ORDERS (*include any directions given by the court respecting pleadings, discovery and other matters*).

(*Signature of judge, officer or local registrar*)

November 1, 2005

FORM 44A — BOND — INTERIM RECOVERY OF PERSONAL PROPERTY

Courts of Justice Act

[Repealed O. Reg. 77/06, s. 3.]

[Editor's Note: Forms 4A to 78A of the Rules of Civil Procedure have been repealed by O. Reg. 77/06, effective July 1, 2006. Pursuant to Rule of Civil Procedure 1.06, when a form is referred to by number, the reference is to the form with that number that is described in the Table of Forms at the end of these rules and which is available on the Internet through www.ontariocourtforms.on.ca. For your convenience, the government form as published on this website is reproduced below.]

(*General heading*)

BOND

WE, (*identify party*) and (*name of surety*), jointly and severally bind ourselves and our successors to the Sheriff of the (*county or district*) in the sum of $ .... if (*identify party*) fails to return (*identify property*) to (*identify opposite party*) without delay when ordered to do so, and to pay any damages and costs that (*identify opposite party*) has sustained by reason of the interim order for recovery of possession of the property.

Date ....

.... (*seal*)

Witness .... *Signature of party*

.... (*seal*)

Witness .... *Signature of surety*

November 1, 2005

FORM 47A — JURY NOTICE

Courts of Justice Act

[Repealed O. Reg. 77/06, s. 3.]

[Editor's Note: Forms 4A to 78A of the Rules of Civil Procedure have been repealed by O. Reg. 77/06, effective July 1, 2006. Pursuant to Rule of Civil Procedure 1.06, when a form is referred to by number, the reference is to the form with that number that is described in the Table of Forms at the end of these rules and which is available on the Internet through www.ontariocourtforms.on.ca. For your convenience, the government form as published on this website is reproduced below.]

(*General heading*)

JURY NOTICE

THE (*identify party*) REQUIRES that this action be tried (*or* that the issues of fact *or* that the damages in this action be assessed) by a jury.

(*Date*) (*Name, address and telephone number of lawyer or party delivering notice*)

TO (*Name and address of lawyer or party receiving notice*)

July 1, 2007

FORM 48C — [REPEALED O. REG. 438/08, S. 67(1).]

[Repealed O. Reg. 438/08, s. 67(1).]

FORM 48C.1 — STATUS NOTICE: ACTION NOT ON A TRIAL LIST

Courts of Justice Act

(General heading)

STATUS NOTICE: ACTION NOT ON A TRIAL LIST

TO THE PARTIES AND THEIR LAWYERS

1. According to the records in the court office:

(a) more than 2 years have passed since a defence in this action was filed;

(b) this action has not been placed on a trial list; and

(c) this action has not been terminated by any means.

2. AS A RESULT, THIS ACTION SHALL BE DISMISSED FOR DELAY, with costs, unless within 90 days of service of this Notice,

(a) the action is set down for trial;

(b) the action is terminated by any means;

(c) documents have been filed in accordance with subrule 48.14(10); or

(d) a judge or case management master orders otherwise.

NOTE: A "defence" means a statement of defence, a notice of intent to defend, or a notice of motion in response to a proceeding, other than a motion challenging the court's jurisdiction.

NOTE: You may request that the registrar arrange a status hearing to show cause why the action should not be dismissed. Unless the presiding judge or case management master orders otherwise, a status hearing may be held in writing by filing, at least 7 days before the day of the hearing, a timetable signed by all the parties to the action that contains the information set out in subrule 48.14(11) and a draft order establishing the timetable.

NOTE: Unless the court orders otherwise, where the plaintiff is a party under a disability, an action may not be dismissed for delay under rule 48.14 unless the defendant gives notice to the Children's Lawyer or, if the Public Guardian and Trustee is litigation guardian of the plaintiff, to the Public Guardian and Trustee.

Date .... Signed by ....
Local registrar

Address of court office ....

....

TO *(Names and addresses of all lawyers and parties acting in person)*

July 30, 2009

FORM 48C.2 — STATUS NOTICE: ACTION STRUCK FROM TRIAL LIST

Courts of Justice Act

(General heading)

STATUS NOTICE: ACTION STRUCK FROM TRIAL LIST

TO THE PARTIES AND THEIR LAWYERS

1. According to the records in the court office:

(a) this action was placed on a trial list and was subsequently struck off; and

(b) this action was not restored to the trial list within 180 days after being struck off.

2. AS A RESULT, THIS ACTION SHALL BE DISMISSED FOR DELAY, with costs, unless within 90 days of service of this Notice,

(a) the action is restored to a trial list;

(b) the action is terminated by any means;

(c) documents have been filed in accordance with subrule 48.14(10); or

(d) a judge or case management master orders otherwise.

NOTE: You may request that the registrar arrange a status hearing to show cause why the action should not be dismissed. Unless the presiding judge or case management master orders otherwise, a status hearing may be held in writing by filing, at least 7 days before the day of the hearing, a timetable signed by all the parties to the action that contains the information set out in subrule 48.14(11) and a draft order establishing the timetable.

NOTE: Unless the court orders otherwise, where the plaintiff is a party under a disability, an action may not be dismissed for delay under rule 48.14 unless the defendant gives notice to the Children's Lawyer or, if the Public Guardian and Trustee is litigation guardian of the plaintiff, to the Public Guardian and Trustee.

Date .... Signed by ....

Local registrar

Address
of court
office ....
....

TO *(Names and addresses of all lawyers and parties acting in person)*

November 1, 2008

FORM 48D — ORDER DISMISSING ACTION FOR DELAY

Courts of Justice Act

[Repealed O. Reg. 77/06, s. 3.]

[Editor's Note: Forms 4A to 78A of the Rules of Civil Procedure have been repealed by O. Reg. 77/06, effective July 1, 2006. Pursuant to Rule of Civil Procedure 1.06, when a form is referred to by number, the reference is to the form with that number that is described in the Table of Forms at the end of these rules and which is available on the Internet through www.ontariocourtforms.on.ca. For your convenience, the government form as published on this website is reproduced below.]

(*General heading*)

ORDER DISMISSING ACTION

The plaintiff has not (*give particulars of plaintiff's default under rule 48.14*) and has not cured the default.

IT IS ORDERED that this action be dismissed for delay, with costs.

Date Signed by ....
Local registrar

(Address of
court office) ....
....

NOTE: An order under rule 48.14 dismissing an action may be set aside under rule 37.14.

November 1, 2005

FORM 48E — NOTICE THAT ACTION WILL BE DISMISSED

Courts of Justice Act

(General heading)

NOTICE THAT ACTION WILL BE DISMISSED

TO THE PARTIES AND THEIR LAWYERS

According to the records in the court office:

(a) 180 days have passed since the originating process was issued,

(b) no defence has been filed,

(c) the action has not been disposed of by final order or judgment, and

(d) the action has not been set down for trial.

Pursuant to subrule 48.15(1), THIS ACTION WILL BE DISMISSED AS ABANDONED unless, within 45 days of being served with this notice:

(a) a defence is filed,

(b) it is disposed of by final order or judgment, or

(c) it is set down for trial.

NOTE: A "defence" means a statement of defence, a notice of intent to defend, or a notice of motion in response to a proceeding, other than a motion challenging the court's jurisdiction.

Date .... Signed by ....

Local registrar

(Address of court office)

TO *(Names and addresses of all lawyers and parties acting in person)*

July 30, 2009

FORM 48F — ORDER DISMISSING ACTION AS ABANDONED

Courts of Justice Act

(General heading)

ORDER DISMISSING ACTION AS ABANDONED

According to the records in the court office, more than 180 days have passed since the originating process was issued, no defence has been filed, the action has not been disposed of by final order or judgment, the action has not been set down for trial, and the registrar has given 45 days notice that the action will be dismissed as abandoned.

IT IS ORDERED that pursuant to subrule 48.15(1) this action be dismissed as abandoned.

Date .... Signed by ....

Local registrar

(Address of court office)

NOTE: A "defence" means a statement of defence, a notice of intent to defend, or a notice of motion in response to a proceeding, other than a motion challenging the court's jurisdiction.

NOTE: An order under rule 48.15 dismissing an action may be set aside under rule 37.14.

TO *(Names and addresses of all lawyers and parties acting in person)*

July 30, 2009

FORM 49A — OFFER TO SETTLE

Courts of Justice Act

[Repealed O. Reg. 77/06, s. 3.]

[Editor's Note: Forms 4A to 78A of the Rules of Civil Procedure have been repealed by O. Reg. 77/06, effective July 1, 2006. Pursuant to Rule of Civil Procedure 1.06, when a form is referred to by number, the reference is to the form with that number that is described in the Table of Forms at the end of these rules and which is available on the Internet through www.ontariocourtforms.on.ca. For your convenience, the government form as published on this website is reproduced below.]

(*General heading*)

OFFER TO SETTLE

The (*identify party*) offers to settle this proceeding (*or* the following claims in this proceeding) on the following terms: (*Set out terms in consecutively numbered paragraphs.*)

(*Date*) (*Name, address and telephone number of*

lawyer or party making offer)

TO (*Name and address of lawyer or party to whom offer is made*)

July 1, 2007

FORM 49B — NOTICE OF WITHDRAWAL OF OFFER

Courts of Justice Act

[Repealed O. Reg. 77/06, s. 3.]

[Editor's Note: Forms 4A to 78A of the Rules of Civil Procedure have been repealed by O. Reg. 77/06, effective July 1, 2006. Pursuant to Rule of Civil Procedure 1.06, when a form is referred to by number, the reference is to the form with that number that is described in the Table of Forms at the end of these rules and which is available on the Internet through www.ontariocourtforms.on.ca. For your convenience, the government form as published on this website is reproduced below.]

(*General heading*)

NOTICE OF WITHDRAWAL OF OFFER

The (*identify party*) withdraws the offer to settle dated (*date*).

(*Date*) (*Name, address and telephone number of lawyer or party giving notice*)

TO (*Name and address of lawyer or party to whom notice is given*)

July 1, 2007

FORM 49C — ACCEPTANCE OF OFFER

Courts of Justice Act

[Repealed O. Reg. 77/06, s. 3.]

[Editor's Note: Forms 4A to 78A of the Rules of Civil Procedure have been repealed by O. Reg. 77/06, effective July 1, 2006. Pursuant to Rule of Civil Procedure 1.06, when a form is

referred to by number, the reference is to the form with that number that is described in the Table of Forms at the end of these rules and which is available on the Internet through www.ontariocourtforms.on.ca. For your convenience, the government form as published on this website is reproduced below.]

(*General heading*)

ACCEPTANCE OF OFFER

The (*identify party*) accepts your offer to settle dated (*date*).

(*Date*) (*Name, address and telephone number of lawyer or party accepting offer*)

TO (*Name and address of lawyer or party whose offer is accepted*)

July 1, 2007

FORM 49D — OFFER TO CONTRIBUTE

Courts of Justice Act

[Repealed O. Reg. 77/06, s. 3.]

[Editor's Note: Forms 4A to 78A of the Rules of Civil Procedure have been repealed by O. Reg. 77/06, effective July 1, 2006. Pursuant to Rule of Civil Procedure 1.06, when a form is referred to by number, the reference is to the form with that number that is described in the Table of Forms at the end of these rules and which is available on the Internet through www.ontariocourtforms.on.ca. For your convenience, the government form as published on this website is reproduced below.]

(*General heading*)

OFFER TO CONTRIBUTE

The defendant (*name of defendant making offer*) offers to contribute to a settlement of the plaintiff's claim on the following terms: (*Set out terms in consecutively numbered paragraphs.*)

(*Date*) (*Name, address and telephone number of lawyer or defendant making offer*)

TO (*Name and address of lawyer or*

defendant to whom offer is made)

July 1, 2007

FORM 51A — REQUEST TO ADMIT

Courts of Justice Act

[Repealed O. Reg. 77/06, s. 3.]

[Editor's Note: Forms 4A to 78A of the Rules of Civil Procedure have been repealed by O. Reg. 77/06, effective July 1, 2006. Pursuant to Rule of Civil Procedure 1.06, when a form is referred to by number, the reference is to the form with that number that is described in the Table of Forms at the end of these rules and which is available on the Internet through www.ontariocourtforms.on.ca. For your convenience, the government form as published on this website is reproduced below.]

(*General heading*)

REQUEST TO ADMIT

YOU ARE REQUESTED TO ADMIT, for the purposes of this proceeding only, the truth of the following facts: (*Set out facts in consecutively numbered paragraphs.*)

YOU ARE REQUESTED TO ADMIT, for the purposes of this proceeding only, the authenticity (see rule 51.01 of the *Rules of Civil Procedure*) of the following documents: (*Number each document and give particulars sufficient to identify each. Specify whether the document is an original or a copy and, where the document is a copy of a letter, telegram or telecommunication, state the nature of the document.*)

Attached to this request is a copy of each of the documents referred to above. (*Where it is not practicable to attach a copy or where the party already has a copy, state which documents are not attached and give the reason for not attaching them.*)

YOU MUST RESPOND TO THIS REQUEST by serving a response to request to admit in Form 51B prescribed by the *Rules of Civil Procedure* WITHIN TWENTY DAYS after this request is served on you. If you fail to do so, you will be deemed to admit, for the purposes of this proceeding only, the truth of the facts and the authenticity of the documents set out above.

(*Date*) (*Name, address and telephone number of lawyer or party serving request*)

TO (*Name and address of lawyer or party on whom request is served*)

July 1, 2007

FORM 51B — RESPONSE TO REQUEST TO ADMIT

Courts of Justice Act

[Repealed O. Reg. 77/06, s. 3.]

[Editor's Note: Forms 4A to 78A of the Rules of Civil Procedure have been repealed by O. Reg. 77/06, effective July 1, 2006. Pursuant to Rule of Civil Procedure 1.06, when a form is referred to by number, the reference is to the form with that number that is described in the Table of Forms at the end of these rules and which is available on the Internet through www.ontariocourtforms.on.ca. For your convenience, the government form as published on this website is reproduced below.]

(*General heading*)

RESPONSE TO REQUEST TO ADMIT

In response to your request to admit dated (*date*), the (*identify party responding to the request*):

1. Admits the truth of facts numbers ....

2. Admits the authenticity of documents numbers ....

3. Denies the truth of facts numbers ....

4. Denies the authenticity of documents numbers ....

5. Refuses to admit the truth of facts numbers .... for the following reasons: (*Set out reason for refusing to admit each fact.*)

6. Refuses to admit the authenticity of documents numbers .... for the following reasons: (*Set out reason for refusing to admit each document.*)

(*Date*) (*Name, address and telephone number of lawyer or party serving response*)

TO (*Name and address of lawyer or party on whom response is served*)

July 1, 2007

FORM 53 — ACKNOWLEDGMENT OF EXPERT'S DUTY

Courts of Justice Act

(General heading)

ACKNOWLEDGMENT OF EXPERT'S DUTY

1. My name is .... *(name)*. I live at .... *(city)*, in the .... *(province/state)* of .... *(name of province/state)*.

2. I have been engaged by or on behalf of .... *(name of party/parties)* to provide evidence in relation to the above-noted court proceeding.

3. I acknowledge that it is my duty to provide evidence in relation to this proceeding as follows:

(a) to provide opinion evidence that is fair, objective and non-partisan;

(b) to provide opinion evidence that is related only to matters that are within my area of expertise; and

(c) to provide such additional assistance as the court may reasonably require, to determine a matter in issue.

4. I acknowledge that the duty referred to above prevails over any obligation which I may owe to any party by whom or on whose behalf I am engaged.

Date ....
Signature

NOTE: This form must be attached to any report signed by the expert and provided for the purposes of subrule 53.03(1) or (2) of the *Rules of Civil Procedure*.

November 1, 2008

FORM 53A — SUMMONS TO WITNESS (AT HEARING)

Courts of Justice Act

[Repealed O. Reg. 77/06, s. 3.]

[Editor's Note: Forms 4A to 78A of the Rules of Civil Procedure have been repealed by O. Reg. 77/06, effective July 1, 2006. Pursuant to Rule of Civil Procedure 1.06, when a form is referred to by number, the reference is to the form with that number that is described in the Table of Forms at the end of these rules and which is available on the Internet through

www.ontariocourtforms.on.ca. For your convenience, the government form as published on this website is reproduced below.]

(*General heading*)

(*Court seal*)

SUMMONS TO WITNESS

TO (*Name and address of witness*)

YOU ARE REQUIRED TO ATTEND TO GIVE EVIDENCE IN COURT at the hearing of this proceeding on (*day*), (*date*), at (*time*), at (*address of court house*), and to remain until your attendance is no longer required.

YOU ARE REQUIRED TO BRING WITH YOU and produce at the hearing the following documents and things: (*Set out the nature and date of each document and give particulars sufficient to identify each document and thing.*)

ATTENDANCE MONEY for .... day(s) of attendance is served with this summons, calculated in accordance with Tariff A of the *Rules of Civil Procedure*, as follows:

Attendance allowance of $ .... daily	$ ....
Travel allowance	$ ....
Overnight accommodation and meal allowance	$ ....
	========
TOTAL	$ ....

If further attendance is required, you will be entitled to additional attendance money.

IF YOU FAIL TO ATTEND OR TO REMAIN IN ATTENDANCE AS REQUIRED BY THIS SUMMONS, A WARRANT MAY BE ISSUED FOR YOUR ARREST.

Date	Issued by	.... Local registrar
	Address of court office	....

This summons was issued at the request of, and inquiries may be directed to:

(*Name, address and telephone number of lawyer or party serving summons*)

July 1, 2007

FORM 53B — WARRANT FOR ARREST (DEFAULTING WITNESS)

Courts of Justice Act

[Repealed O. Reg. 77/06, s. 3.]

[Editor's Note: Forms 4A to 78A of the Rules of Civil Procedure have been repealed by O. Reg. 77/06, effective July 1, 2006. Pursuant to Rule of Civil Procedure 1.06, when a form is referred to by number, the reference is to the form with that number that is described in the Table of Forms at the end of these rules and which is available on the Internet through www.ontariocourtforms.on.ca. For your convenience, the government form as published on this website is reproduced below.]

(*Court file no.*)

(*Court*)

(*Name of judge*) (*Day and date*)

(*Court seal*) (*Title of Proceeding*)

WARRANT FOR ARREST

TO ALL POLICE OFFICERS in Ontario

AND TO the officers of all correctional institutions in Ontario

WHEREAS the witness (*name*), of (*address*), was served with a summons to witness to give evidence at the hearing of this proceeding, and the proper attendance money was paid or tendered,

AND WHEREAS the witness failed to obey the summons, and I am satisfied that the evidence of the witness is material to this proceeding,

YOU ARE ORDERED TO ARREST and bring the witness (*name of witness*) before the court to give evidence in this proceeding, and if the court is not then sitting or if the witness cannot be brought forthwith before the court, to deliver the witness to a provincial correctional institution or other secure facility, to be admitted and detained there until the witness can be brought before the court.

(*Signature of judge*)

November 1, 2005

FORM 53C — SUMMONS TO A WITNESS OUTSIDE ONTARIO

Courts of Justice Act

[Repealed O. Reg. 77/06, s. 3.]

[Editor's Note: Forms 4A to 78A of the Rules of Civil Procedure have been repealed by O. Reg. 77/06, effective July 1, 2006. Pursuant to Rule of Civil Procedure 1.06, when a form is referred to by number, the reference is to the form with that number that is described in the Table of Forms at the end of these rules and which is available on the Internet through www.ontariocourtforms.on.ca. For your convenience, the government form as published on this website is reproduced below.]

(*General heading*)

(*Court seal*)

SUMMONS TO A WITNESS OUTSIDE ONTARIO

TO (*Name and address of witness*)

YOU ARE REQUIRED TO ATTEND TO GIVE EVIDENCE (in court at the hearing of this proceeding, on an examination for discovery, on a cross-examination on your affidavit dated (*date*), *etc.*) on (*day*), (*date*), at (*address of court house*), and to remain until your attendance is no longer required.

YOU ARE REQUIRED TO BRING WITH YOU and produce at the hearing the following documents and things: (*Set out the nature and date of each document and give particulars sufficient to identify each document and thing.*)

ATTENDANCE MONEY for .... day(s) of attendance is served with this summons, calculated in accordance with the *Interprovincial Summonses Act* (Ontario), as follows:

Attendance allowance of $20 daily for each day of absence from your ordinary residence (not less than $60)	$ ....
Travel allowance	$ ....
Hotel accommodation allowance for not less than three days (not less than $60)	$ ....
Meal allowance for not less than three days (not less than $48)	$ ....
	========
TOTAL	$ ....

If further attendance is required, you will be entitled to additional attendance money.

OBEDIENCE TO THIS SUMMONS may be compelled by the courts of your province under the *Interprovincial Summonses Act*.

Date .... Issued by ....
Local registrar

Address of court office ....
....

This summons was issued at the request of, and inquiries may be directed to:

(*Name, address and telephone number of lawyer or party serving summons*)

Attach or endorse the judge's certificate under section 5 of the Interprovincial Summonses Act.

July 1, 2007

FORM 53D — ORDER FOR ATTENDANCE OF WITNESS IN CUSTODY

Courts of Justice Act

[Repealed O. Reg. 77/06, s. 3.]

[Editor's Note: Forms 4A to 78A of the Rules of Civil Procedure have been repealed by O. Reg. 77/06, effective July 1, 2006. Pursuant to Rule of Civil Procedure 1.06, when a form is referred to by number, the reference is to the form with that number that is described in the Table of Forms at the end of these rules and which is available on the Internet through www.ontariocourtforms.on.ca. For your convenience, the government form as published on this website is reproduced below.]

(*Court file no.*)

(*Court*)

(*Name of judge or master*) (*Day and date order made*)

(*Court seal*) (*Title of Proceeding*)

ORDER FOR ATTENDANCE OF WITNESS IN CUSTODY

TO THE OFFICERS OF (*name of correctional institution*)

AND TO ALL POLICE OFFICERS in Ontario

WHEREAS it appears that the evidence of the witness (*name*), who is detained in custody, is material to this proceeding,

1. THIS COURT ORDERS that the witness (*name*) be brought before this court (*or as may be*) on (*day*), (*date*), at (*time*), at (*address*), to give evidence on behalf of the (*identify party*), and that the witness be returned and readmitted immediately thereafter to the correctional institution or other facility from which the witness was brought.

(*Signature of judge, officer or registrar*)

November 1, 2005

FORM 55A — NOTICE OF HEARING FOR DIRECTIONS

Courts of Justice Act

[Repealed O. Reg. 77/06, s. 3.]

[Editor's Note: Forms 4A to 78A of the Rules of Civil Procedure have been repealed by O. Reg. 77/06, effective July 1, 2006. Pursuant to Rule of Civil Procedure 1.06, when a form is referred to by number, the reference is to the form with that number that is described in the Table of Forms at the end of these rules and which is available on the Internet through www.ontariocourtforms.on.ca. For your convenience, the government form as published on this website is reproduced below.]

(*General heading*)

NOTICE OF HEARING FOR DIRECTIONS

By order of the court, a copy of which is served with this notice, a reference was directed to (*person conducting reference*) for the purpose of (*set out purpose of reference*).

The (*identify party*) has obtained an appointment with (*name of person conducting reference*) on (*day*), (*date*), at (*time*), at (*address*) for a hearing to consider directions for the conduct of the reference in this proceeding.

IF YOU FAIL TO ATTEND, in person or by an Ontario lawyer acting for you, directions may be given and the reference may proceed in your absence and without further notice to you, and you will be bound by any order made in the proceeding.

(*Date*) (*Name, address and telephone number of lawyer or party serving notice*)

TO (*Name and address of lawyer or party receiving notice*)

July 1, 2007

FORM 55B — NOTICE TO PARTY ADDED ON REFERENCE

Courts of Justice Act

[Repealed O. Reg. 77/06, s. 3.]

[Editor's Note: Forms 4A to 78A of the Rules of Civil Procedure have been repealed by O. Reg. 77/06, effective July 1, 2006. Pursuant to Rule of Civil Procedure 1.06, when a form is referred to by number, the reference is to the form with that number that is described in the Table of Forms at the end of these rules and which is available on the Internet through

www.ontariocourtforms.on.ca. For your convenience, the government form as published on this website is reproduced below.]

(General heading)

NOTICE TO PARTY ADDED ON REFERENCE

TO *(Name of party added on reference)*

By order of the court, a copy of which is served with this notice, a reference was directed to (*person conducting reference*) for the purpose of (*set out purpose of reference*).

YOU HAVE BEEN MADE A PARTY TO THIS PROCEEDING by order of (*name of person conducting reference*), a copy of which is also served with this notice.

THE REFERENCE WILL PROCEED on (*day*), (*date*), at (*time*), at (*address*).

YOU MAKE A MOTION to a judge of this court WITHIN TEN DAYS (*or where the person is to be served outside Ontario, such further time as the referee directs*) after this notice is served on you to set aside or vary the order directing the reference or the order adding you as a party.

IF YOU FAIL TO DO SO OR IF YOU FAIL TO ATTEND ON THE REFERENCE, in person or by an Ontario lawyer acting for you, the reference may proceed in your absence and without further notice to you, and you will be bound by any order made in this proceeding.

(*Date*) (*Name, address and telephone number of lawyer or party serving notice*)

TO (*Name and address of party added on reference*)

July 1, 2007

FORM 55C — REPORT ON REFERENCE (ADMINISTRATION OF ESTATE)

Courts of Justice Act

[Repealed O. Reg. 77/06, s. 3.]

[Editor's Note: Forms 4A to 78A of the Rules of Civil Procedure have been repealed by O. Reg. 77/06, effective July 1, 2006. Pursuant to Rule of Civil Procedure 1.06, when a form is referred to by number, the reference is to the form with that number that is described in the Table of Forms at the end of these rules and which is available on the Internet through www.ontariocourtforms.on.ca. For your convenience, the government form as published on this website is reproduced below.]

(General heading)

REPORT ON REFERENCE

In accordance with the order directing a reference dated (*date*), I have disposed of the matters referred to me, and I report as follows:

1. The following parties were served with the order directing a reference and a notice of hearing for directions: (*Set out names*). (*Where applicable, add:* Service on the following parties was dispensed with: (*Set out names and the reason for dispensing with service*).) The following parties were added on the reference and were served with a notice to party added on reference: (*Set out names*).

2. The following parties did not attend on the reference: (*Set out names*).

3. The personal estate not specifically bequeathed by the testator received by the executors and for which they are chargeable amounts to $ ...., and they have paid or are entitled to be allowed the sum of $ ...., leaving a balance due from (*or* to) them of $ .... (*or, where applicable:* No personal estate has been received by the executors, nor are they chargeable with any.)

4. The creditors' claims received in response to the advertisement for creditors and which I have allowed are set out in Schedule A and amount altogether to $ .... (*or, where applicable:* No creditor has sent in a claim in response to the advertisement for creditors, nor has any such claim been proved before me.)

5. The funeral expenses of the testator amounting to $ .... have been paid by the executors and are allowed to them in the account of personal estate.

6. The legacies given by the testator are set out in Schedule B, and with the interest therein mentioned, remain due to the persons named (*or as the case may be*).

7. The personal estate of the testator outstanding or undisposed of is set out in Schedule C.

8. The real estate owned by the testator and the encumbrances affecting it are set out in Schedule D.

9. The rents and profits of the testator's real estate received by the executors and for which they are chargeable amount to $ .... and they have paid or are entitled to be allowed the sum of $ ...., leaving a balance due from (*or* to) them of $ .... (*or, where applicable:* No rents and profits have been received by the executors, nor are they chargeable with any).

10. I have allowed the executors the sum of $ .... as compensation for their services in the management of the estate.

11. I have caused the real estate, other than (*identify property*), which has specifically devised, to be sold and the purchasers have paid their purchase money into court.

12. In Schedule E, I have shown how the money in court is to be dealt with.

(*Date*) (*Signature of referee*)

(*All schedules should be as brief as possible. Only the general character of the things described should be shown. Land should be described without setting out a full legal description.*)

(*In Schedule C, the personal estate not specifically bequeathed should be set out separately from the other personal property outstanding or undisposed of. Where there is no specific bequest, the report should state that fact.*)

November 1, 2005

FORM 55D — NOTICE OF CONTESTED CLAIM

Courts of Justice Act

[Repealed O. Reg. 77/06, s. 3.]

[Editor's Note: Forms 4A to 78A of the Rules of Civil Procedure have been repealed by O. Reg. 77/06, effective July 1, 2006. Pursuant to Rule of Civil Procedure 1.06, when a form is referred to by number, the reference is to the form with that number that is described in the Table of Forms at the end of these rules and which is available on the Internet through www.ontariocourtforms.on.ca. For your convenience, the government form as published on this website is reproduced below.]

(*General heading*)

NOTICE OF CONTESTED CLAIM

YOUR CLAIM IN THIS PROCEEDING IS BEING CONTESTED. You are required to prove your claim before the referee on (*day*), (*date*), (*time*), at (*address*).

IF YOU FAIL TO ATTEND AND PROVE YOUR CLAIM, YOUR CLAIM MAY BE DISALLOWED.

(*Date*)	(*Name, address and telephone number of party or lawyer serving notice*)

TO (*Name and address of creditor*)

July 1, 2007

FORM 55E — NOTICE TO CREDITOR

Courts of Justice Act

[Repealed O. Reg. 77/06, s. 3.]

[Editor's Note: Forms 4A to 78A of the Rules of Civil Procedure have been repealed by O. Reg. 77/06, effective July 1, 2006. Pursuant to Rule of Civil Procedure 1.06, when a form is referred to by number, the reference is to the form with that number that is described in the Table of Forms at the end of these rules and which is available on the Internet through www.ontariocourtforms.on.ca. For your convenience, the government form as published on this website is reproduced below.]

(*General heading*)

NOTICE TO CREDITOR

YOU MAY OBTAIN PAYMENT of the amount allowed by the court in respect of your claim in this proceeding from the office of the Accountant of the Superior Court of Justice, 2nd floor, 123 Edward Street, Toronto, Ontario M5G 1E2 (*or* the local registrar of this court at (*address*)).

(*Date*) (*Name, address and telephone number of lawyer or party serving notice*)

TO (*Name and address of creditor*)

July 1, 2007

FORM 55F — CONDITIONS OF SALE

Courts of Justice Act

[Repealed O. Reg. 77/06, s. 3.]

[Editor's Note: Forms 4A to 78A of the Rules of Civil Procedure have been repealed by O. Reg. 77/06, effective July 1, 2006. Pursuant to Rule of Civil Procedure 1.06, when a form is referred to by number, the reference is to the form with that number that is described in the Table of Forms at the end of these rules and which is available on the Internet through www.ontariocourtforms.on.ca. For your convenience, the government form as published on this website is reproduced below.]

1. No person shall advance the bidding in an amount less than $10 at any bidding under $500 nor in an amount less than $20 at any bidding over $500. No person shall be allowed to retract a bid.

2. The property shall be sold to the highest bidder. Where any dispute arises as to who is the last or highest bidder, the property shall be put up again.

3. All parties to the proceeding may bid, except the party having carriage of the sale and any trustee or agent for the party or other person in a fiduciary relationship to the party.

4. The purchaser shall, at the time of sale, pay to the party having carriage of the sale or to the party's lawyer a deposit of ten per cent of the purchase price and shall pay the balance of the purchase price on completion of the sale. On payment of the balance, the purchaser shall be entitled to receive a transfer and to take possession. The purchaser shall, at the time of sale, sign an agreement for the completion of the sale.

5. The purchaser shall have the transfer prepared at the purchaser's own expense and tender it to the party having carriage of the sale for execution.

6. Where the purchaser fails to comply with any of these conditions, the deposit and all other payments made shall be forfeited and the property may be resold. Any deficiency on the resale, together with all expenses incurred on the resale or caused by the default, shall be paid by the defaulting purchaser.

July 1, 2007

FORM 55G — INTERIM REPORT ON SALE

Courts of Justice Act

[Repealed O. Reg. 77/06, s. 3.]

[Editor's Note: Forms 4A to 78A of the Rules of Civil Procedure have been repealed by O. Reg. 77/06, effective July 1, 2006. Pursuant to Rule of Civil Procedure 1.06, when a form is referred to by number, the reference is to the form with that number that is described in the Table of Forms at the end of these rules and which is available on the Internet through www.ontariocourtforms.on.ca. For your convenience, the government form as published on this website is reproduced below.]

(*General heading*)

INTERIM REPORT ON SALE

1. In accordance with the order in this proceeding dated (*date*), in the presence of (*or* after notice to) all parties concerned, I settled the form of an advertisement and the conditions of sale for the sale of the property referred to in the judgment.

2. The advertisement was published as directed, and the property was offered for sale by public auction by me (*or* by (*name*), an auctioneer appointed by me for that purpose) on (*date*).

3. The sale was conducted in a fair, open and proper manner and (*name*) was declared the highest bidder for and became the purchaser of the property at the price of $ ...., payable as follows: (*Set out briefly the conditions of sale for payment of the purchase money.*)

(*Date*) (*Signature of referee*)

November 1, 2005

FORM 56A — ORDER FOR SECURITY FOR COSTS

Courts of Justice Act

[Repealed O. Reg. 77/06, s. 3.]

[Editor's Note: Forms 4A to 78A of the Rules of Civil Procedure have been repealed by O. Reg. 77/06, effective July 1, 2006. Pursuant to Rule of Civil Procedure 1.06, when a form is referred to by number, the reference is to the form with that number that is described in the Table of Forms at the end of these rules and which is available on the Internet through

www.ontariocourtforms.on.ca. For your convenience, the government form as published on this website is reproduced below.]

(*Court file no.*)

(*Court*)

(*Name of judge or master*) (*Day and date order made*)

(*Court seal*) (*Title of Proceeding*)

ORDER FOR SECURITY FOR COSTS

(*Recitals in accordance with Form 59A*)

1. THIS COURT ORDERS that within .... days after this order is served on the plaintiff, (*or* applicant), the plaintiff (*or* applicant) shall pay into court (*or* to (*name*)) the sum of $ .... as security for the costs of this proceeding.

(*Where a plaintiff or applicant is ordered to give security for costs in some other form, give a description of the security required and vary the form of the order accordingly.*)

2. THIS COURT ORDERS that until the security required by this order has been given, the plaintiff (*or* applicant) may not take any step in this proceeding, except an appeal from this order (*or as otherwise ordered*).

(*Signature of judge, master or registrar*)

November 1, 2005

FORM 57A — BILL OF COSTS

Courts of Justice Act

[Repealed O. Reg. 77/06, s. 3.]

[Editor's Note: Forms 4A to 78A of the Rules of Civil Procedure have been repealed by O. Reg. 77/06, effective July 1, 2006. Pursuant to Rule of Civil Procedure 1.06, when a form is referred to by number, the reference is to the form with that number that is described in the Table of Forms at the end of these rules and which is available on the Internet through www.ontariocourtforms.on.ca. For your convenience, the government form as published on this website is reproduced below.]

(*General heading*)
Bill of Costs

AMOUNTS CLAIMED FOR FEES AND DISBURSEMENTS

(Following the items set out in Tariff A, itemize the claim for fees and disbursements. Indicate the names of the lawyers, students-at-law and law clerks who provided services in connection with each item.

In support of the claim for fees, attach copies of the dockets or other evidence.

In support of the claim for disbursements, attach copies of invoices or other evidence.)

STATEMENT OF EXPERIENCE

A claim for fees is being made with respect to the following lawyers:

Name of lawyer Years of experience

TO: *(name and address of lawyer or party)*

November 1, 2005

FORM 57B — COSTS OUTLINE

Courts of Justice Act

[Repealed O. Reg. 77/06, s. 3.]

[Editor's Note: Forms 4A to 78A of the Rules of Civil Procedure have been repealed by O. Reg. 77/06, effective July 1, 2006. Pursuant to Rule of Civil Procedure 1.06, when a form is referred to by number, the reference is to the form with that number that is described in the Table of Forms at the end of these rules and which is available on the Internet through www.ontariocourtforms.on.ca. For your convenience, the government form as published on this website is reproduced below.]

ONTARIO
SUPERIOR COURT OF JUSTICE
COSTS OUTLINE

The *(identify party)* provides the following outline of the submissions to be made at the hearing in support of the costs the party will seek if successful:

Fees (as detailed below)		$
Estimated lawyer's fee for appearance		$
Disbursements (as detailed in the attached appendix)		$ ....
	Total	$

The following points are made in support of the costs sought with reference to the factors set out in subrule 57.01(1):

- the amount claimed and the amount recovered in the proceeding
- the complexity of the proceeding
- the importance of the issues
- the conduct of any party that tended to shorten or lengthen unnecessarily the duration of the proceeding

ONTARIO
SUPERIOR COURT OF JUSTICE
COSTS OUTLINE

- whether any step in the proceeding was improper, vexatious or unnecessary or taken through negligence, mistake or excessive caution

- a party's denial of or refusal to admit anything that should have been admitted

- the experience of the party's lawyer

- the hours spent, the rates sought for costs and the rate actually charged by the party's lawyer

FEE ITEMS *(e.g. pleadings, affidavits, cross-examinations, preparation, hearing, etc.)*	PERSONS *(identify the lawyers, students, and law clerks who provided services in connection with each item together with their year of call, if applicable)*	HOURS *(specify the hours claimed for each person identified in column 2)*	PARTIAL INDEMNITY RATE *(specify the rate being sought for each person identified in column 2)*	ACTUAL RATE*

* Specify the rate being charged to the client for each person identified in column 2. If there is a contingency fee arrangement, state the rate that would have been charged absent such arrangement.

- any other matter relevant to the question of costs

LAWYER'S CERTIFICATE

I CERTIFY that the hours claimed have been spent, that the rates shown are correct and that each disbursement has been incurred as claimed.

Date: ....

Signature of lawyer

July 1, 2007

FORM 58A — NOTICE OF APPOINTMENT FOR ASSESSMENT OF COSTS

Courts of Justice Act

[Repealed O. Reg. 77/06, s. 3.]

[Editor's Note: Forms 4A to 78A of the Rules of Civil Procedure have been repealed by O. Reg. 77/06, effective July 1, 2006. Pursuant to Rule of Civil Procedure 1.06, when a form is referred to by number, the reference is to the form with that number that is described in the Table of Forms at the end of these rules and which is available on the Internet through www.ontariocourtforms.on.ca. For your convenience, the government form as published on this website is reproduced below.]

(*General heading*)

NOTICE OF APPOINTMENT FOR ASSESSMENT OF COSTS

TO THE PARTIES

I HAVE MADE AN APPOINTMENT to assess the costs of (*identify party*), a copy of whose bill of costs is attached to this notice, on (*day*), (*date*), at (*time*), at (*address*).

Date ....

Assessment officer

TO (*Name and address of lawyer or party on whom notice is served*)

July 1, 2007

FORM 58B — NOTICE TO DELIVER A BILL OF COSTS FOR ASSESSMENT

Courts of Justice Act

[Repealed O. Reg. 77/06, s. 3.]

[Editor's Note: Forms 4A to 78A of the Rules of Civil Procedure have been repealed by O. Reg. 77/06, effective July 1, 2006. Pursuant to Rule of Civil Procedure 1.06, when a form is referred to by number, the reference is to the form with that number that is described in the Table of Forms at the end of these rules and which is available on the Internet through www.ontariocourtforms.on.ca. For your convenience, the government form as published on this website is reproduced below.]

(*General heading*)

NOTICE TO DELIVER A BILL OF COSTS FOR ASSESSMENT

TO THE PARTIES

I HAVE MADE AN APPOINTMENT, at the request of (*identify party who obtained appointment*) to assess the costs of (*identify party entitled to costs and what costs are to be assessed*) on (*day*), (*date*), at (*time*), at (*address*).

TO (*identify party entitled to costs*)

YOU ARE REQUIRED to file your bill of costs with me and serve your bill of costs on every party interested in the assessment at least seven days before the above date.

Date ....

Assessment officer

TO (*Name and address of lawyer or party on whom notice is served*)

July 1, 2007

FORM 58C — CERTIFICATE OF ASSESSMENT OF COSTS

Courts of Justice Act

[Repealed O. Reg. 77/06, s. 3.]

[Editor's Note: Forms 4A to 78A of the Rules of Civil Procedure have been repealed by O. Reg. 77/06, effective July 1, 2006. Pursuant to Rule of Civil Procedure 1.06, when a form is referred to by number, the reference is to the form with that number that is described in the Table of Forms at the end of these rules and which is available on the Internet through www.ontariocourtforms.on.ca. For your convenience, the government form as published on this website is reproduced below.]

(*General heading*)

CERTIFICATE OF ASSESSMENT OF COSTS

I CERTIFY that I have assessed the costs of (*identify party*) in this proceeding (*or as may be*) under the authority of (*give particulars of order or specify rule or statutory provision*), and I ALLOW THE SUM OF $ ....

(Where postjudgment interest is payable, add:)

THE COSTS ALLOWED IN THIS ASSESSMENT BEAR INTEREST at the rate of ... per cent per year commencing on (*date*).

Date ....

Assessment officer

November 1, 2005

FORM 59A — ORDER

Courts of Justice Act

[Repealed O. Reg. 77/06, s. 3.]

[Editor's Note: Forms 4A to 78A of the Rules of Civil Procedure have been repealed by O. Reg. 77/06, effective July 1, 2006. Pursuant to Rule of Civil Procedure 1.06, when a form is referred to by number, the reference is to the form with that number that is described in the Table of Forms at the end of these rules and which is available on the Internet through www.ontariocourtforms.on.ca. For your convenience, the government form as published on this website is reproduced below.]

(*Court file no.*)

(*Court*)

(*Name of judge or officer*) (*Day and date order made*)

(*Court seal*) (*Title of proceeding*)

ORDER

THIS MOTION, made by (*identify moving party*) for (*state the relief sought in the notice of motion, except to the extent that it appears in the operative part of the order*), (*where applicable, add* made without notice,) was heard this day (*or* heard on (date)), at (*place*), (*recite any particulars necessary to understand the order*).

ON READING the (*give particulars of the material filed on the motion*) and on hearing the submissions of the lawyer(s) for (*identify parties*), (*where applicable, add (identify party)* appearing in person *or* no one appearing for (*identify party*), although properly served as appears from (*indicate proof of service*)),

1. THIS COURT ORDERS that ...

2. THIS COURT ORDERS that ...

(*In an order for the payment of money on which postjudgment interest is payable, add:*)

THIS ORDER BEARS INTEREST at the rate of .... per cent per year commencing on (*date*).

(*Signature of judge, officer or registrar*)

July 1, 2007

FORM 59B — JUDGMENT

Courts of Justice Act

[Repealed O. Reg. 77/06, s. 3.]

[Editor's Note: Forms 4A to 78A of the Rules of Civil Procedure have been repealed by O. Reg. 77/06, effective July 1, 2006. Pursuant to Rule of Civil Procedure 1.06, when a form is referred to by number, the reference is to the form with that number that is described in the Table of Forms at the end of these rules and which is available on the Internet through www.ontariocourtforms.on.ca. For your convenience, the government form as published on this website is reproduced below.]

(*Court file no.*)

(*Court*)

(*Name of judge or officer*) (*Day and date judgment given*)

(*Court seal*) (*Title of Proceeding*)

JUDGMENT

(*Judgment after trial or hearing of application*)

THIS ACTION (*or* APPLICATION) was heard this day (*or* heard on (*date*)) without (*or* with) a jury at (*place*) in the presence of the lawyers for all parties (*where applicable, add* (*identify party*) appearing in person, *or* no one appearing for (*identify party*) although properly served as appears from (*indicate proof of service*)),

(*Action*) ON READING THE PLEADINGS AND HEARING THE EVIDENCE and the submissions of the lawyers for the parties,

(*Application*) ON READING THE NOTICE OF APPLICATION AND THE EVIDENCE FILED BY THE PARTIES, (*where applicable, add* on hearing the oral evidence presented by the parties,) and on hearing the submissions of the lawyers for the parties.

(*Judgment on motion*)

THIS MOTION, made by (*identify moving party*), for (*state the relief sought in the notice of motion, except to the extent that it appears in the operative part of the judgment*), (*where applicable, add* made without notice,) was heard this day (*or* heard on (*date*)), at (*place*), (*recite any particulars necessary to understand the judgment*).

ON READING THE (*give particulars of the material filed on the motion*) and on hearing the submissions of the lawyer(s) for (*identify parties*), (*where applicable, add (identify party)* appearing in person *or* no one appearing for (*identify party*), although properly served as appears from (*indicate proof of service*)),

1. THIS COURT ORDERS (*or* DECLARES, *if applicable*) (*where applicable, add:* AND ADJUDGES) that ....

2. THIS COURT ORDERS (*or as may be*) that ....

(*In a judgment for the payment of money on which postjudgment interest is payable add:*)

THIS JUDGMENT BEARS INTEREST at the rate of .... per cent per year commencing on (*date*).

(*Signature of judge, officer or registrar*)

July 1, 2007

FORM 59C — ORDER ON APPEAL

Courts of Justice Act

[Repealed O. Reg. 77/06, s. 3.]

[Editor's Note: Forms 4A to 78A of the Rules of Civil Procedure have been repealed by O. Reg. 77/06, effective July 1, 2006. Pursuant to Rule of Civil Procedure 1.06, when a form is referred to by number, the reference is to the form with that number that is described in the Table of Forms at the end of these rules and which is available on the Internet through www.ontariocourtforms.on.ca. For your convenience, the government form as published on this website is reproduced below.]

(*Court file no.*)

(*Court*)

(*Name(s) of judge(s)*) (*Day and date order made*)

(*Court seal*) (*Title of Proceeding*)

ORDER

THIS APPEAL by (*identify appellant*) for (*state the relief sought in the notice of appeal, except to the extent that it is stated in the operative part of the order*) was heard this day (*or* heard on (*date*)), at (*place*), (*recite any particulars necessary to understand the order*).

ON READING the (*give particulars of the material filed on the appeal*), and on hearing the submissions of the lawyer(s) for (*identify parties*), (*where applicable, add (identify party)* appearing in person *or* no one appearing for (*identify party*) although properly served as appears from (*indicate proof of service*)),

THIS COURT ORDERS (*or* CERTIFIES, *if applicable*) that ...

THIS ORDER BEARS INTEREST at the rate of .... per cent per year commencing

on ....
(*date*)

(*Signature of judge or registrar*)

July 1, 2007

FORM 60A — WRIT OF SEIZURE AND SALE

Courts of Justice Act

[Repealed O. Reg. 77/06, s. 3.]

[Editor's Note: Forms 4A to 78A of the Rules of Civil Procedure have been repealed by O. Reg. 77/06, effective July 1, 2006. Pursuant to Rule of Civil Procedure 1.06, when a form is

referred to by number, the reference is to the form with that number that is described in the Table of Forms at the end of these rules and which is available on the Internet through www.ontariocourtforms.on.ca. For your convenience, the government form as published on this website is reproduced below.]

(Court file no.)

ONTARIO
SUPERIOR COURT OF JUSTICE

BETWEEN

AND

WRIT OF SEIZURE AND SALE

TO: the Sheriff of the *(name of county or district)*

Under an order of this court made on *(date)*, in favour of *(name of creditor)*, YOU ARE DIRECTED to seize and sell the real and personal property within your county or district of

Surname of individual or name of corporation/firm, etc.		
First given name (individual only)	*Second given name (individual only) (if applicable)*	*Third given name (individual only) (if applicable)*

and to realize from the seizure and sale the following sums:

(a) $ .... and interest at .... per cent per year commencing on *(date)*

(Where the writ is for two or more periodic or instalment payments, substitute:)

Amount of payment . . . . Due Date

(b) $ .... and interest at .... per cent per year on the payments in default commencing on the date of default;

(c) $ .... for costs together with interest at .... per cent per year commencing on *(date)*; and

(d) your fees and expenses in enforcing this writ.

YOU ARE DIRECTED to pay out the proceeds according to law and to report on the execution of this writ if required by the party or lawyer who filed it.

Dated at .... Issued by ....
Registrar

on ....

Address of court office
....
....
....

FORM 60A WRIT OF SEIZURE AND SALE, BACKSHEET

(Short title of proceeding) *(Court file no.)*

(Name of court)

FEES

PROCEEDING COMMENCED AT
(place)

Fee	Item	Officer

	Paid for this writ	
$50	Lawyer's fee for issuing a writ	
	First renewal	
	Second renewal	
	Third renewal	

RENEWAL

Date	Officer

WRIT OF SEIZURE AND SALE

Creditor's name ....

Creditor's address ....

....

....

....

Lawyer's name ....

....

....

Lawyer's address and telephone no.

....

....

....

July 1, 2007

FORM 60B — WRIT OF SEQUESTRATION

Courts of Justice Act

[Repealed O. Reg. 77/06, s. 3.]

[Editor's Note: Forms 4A to 78A of the Rules of Civil Procedure have been repealed by O. Reg. 77/06, effective July 1, 2006. Pursuant to Rule of Civil Procedure 1.06, when a form is referred to by number, the reference is to the form with that number that is described in the Table of Forms at the end of these rules and which is available on the Internet through www.ontariocourtforms.on.ca. For your convenience, the government form as published on this website is reproduced below.]

(*General heading*)

(*Court seal*)

TO the Sheriff of the (*name of county or district*)

Under an order of this court made on (*date*) on motion of (*name of moving party*), YOU ARE DIRECTED to take possession of and hold the following property within your county or district of (*name of person against whom order was made*): (*Set out a description of the property to be taken and held.*)

AND YOU ARE DIRECTED to collect and hold any income from the property until further order of this court.

Date	Issued by	.... Local registrar
	Address of court office	....

November 1, 2005

FORM 60C — WRIT OF POSSESSION

Courts of Justice Act

[Repealed O. Reg. 77/06, s. 3.]

[Editor's Note: Forms 4A to 78A of the Rules of Civil Procedure have been repealed by O. Reg. 77/06, effective July 1, 2006. Pursuant to Rule of Civil Procedure 1.06, when a form is referred to by number, the reference is to the form with that number that is described in the Table of Forms at the end of these rules and which is available on the Internet through www.ontariocourtforms.on.ca. For your convenience, the government form as published on this website is reproduced below.]

(*General heading*)

(*Court seal*)

WRIT OF POSSESSION

To the Sheriff of the (*name of county or district*)

Under an order of this court made on (*date*) in favour of (*name of party who obtained order*), YOU ARE DIRECTED to enter and take possession of the following land and premises in your county or district: (*Set out a description of the land and premises.*)

AND YOU ARE DIRECTED to give possession of the above land and premises without delay to (*name of party who obtained order*).

Date	Issued by	.... Local registrar
	Address of court office	....

Renewed by order made on (*date*).

....
Local registrar

November 1, 2005

FORM 60D — WRIT OF DELIVERY

Courts of Justice Act

[Repealed O. Reg. 77/06, s. 3.]

[Editor's Note: Forms 4A to 78A of the Rules of Civil Procedure have been repealed by O. Reg. 77/06, effective July 1, 2006. Pursuant to Rule of Civil Procedure 1.06, when a form is referred to by number, the reference is to the form with that number that is described in the Table of Forms at the end of these rules and which is available on the Internet through www.ontariocourtforms.on.ca. For your convenience, the government form as published on this website is reproduced below.]

(*General heading*)

(*Court seal*)

WRIT OF DELIVERY

TO the Sheriff of the (*name of county or district*)

Under an order of this court made on (*date*), YOU ARE DIRECTED to seize from (*name of party*) and to deliver without delay to (*name of party who obtained order*) possession of the following personal property: (*Set out a description of the property to be delivered.*)

Date .... Issued by ....
Local registrar

Address of court office ....
....

November 1, 2005

FORM 60E — REQUEST TO RENEW

Courts of Justice Act

[Repealed O. Reg. 77/06, s. 3.]

[Editor's Note: Forms 4A to 78A of the Rules of Civil Procedure have been repealed by O. Reg. 77/06, effective July 1, 2006. Pursuant to Rule of Civil Procedure 1.06, when a form is referred to by number, the reference is to the form with that number that is described in the Table of Forms at the end of these rules and which is available on the Internet through www.ontariocourtforms.on.ca. For your convenience, the government form as published on this website is reproduced below.]

(*General heading*)

REQUEST TO RENEW

TO the Sheriff of the (*name of county or district*)

YOU ARE REQUESTED TO RENEW the writ of seizure and sale issued on (*date*) in this proceeding and filed in your office for a period of six years from the date of renewal.

(*Date*) (*Signature of party or lawyer*)

(*Name, address and telephone number of party or lawyer*)

July 1, 2007

FORM 60F — DIRECTION TO ENFORCE WRIT OF SEIZURE AND SALE

Courts of Justice Act

[Repealed O. Reg. 77/06, s. 3.]

[Editor's Note: Forms 4A to 78A of the Rules of Civil Procedure have been repealed by O. Reg. 77/06, effective July 1, 2006. Pursuant to Rule of Civil Procedure 1.06, when a form is referred to by number, the reference is to the form with that number that is described in the Table of Forms at the end of these rules and which is available on the Internet through www.ontariocourtforms.on.ca. For your convenience, the government form as published on this website is reproduced below.]

(Sheriff's file no.)

(Court)

between:

(name)

Creditor(s)

and

(name)

Debtor(s)

DIRECTION TO ENFORCE WRIT

TO: the Sheriff of the *(name of county or district)*

Under an order of this court in favour of *(name of creditor)* made on *(date)*, *(name of debtor)* was ordered to pay the sum of $ .... *(where applicable, add each month or as may be)* with interest at the rate of .... per cent per year commencing on *(date)* and costs of $.......... *(as fixed or assessed)* with interest at the rate of .... per cent per year commencing on *(date)*. Since the order was made, the creditor has received the following payments:

Date of payment . . . . Amount of payment

Under rule 60.19 of the *Rules of Civil Procedure*, the creditor is entitled to costs in the amount of,

(a) $50 for the preparation of documents in connection with issuing, renewing and filing with the sheriff the writ of execution or notice of garnishment;

(b) $ .... for disbursements paid to a sheriff, registrar, official examiner, court reporter or other public officer and to which the creditor is entitled under subrule 60.19(1); *(Attach copy of all receipts.)*

(c) $ .... for an amount determined in accordance with Tariff A for conducting an examination in aid of execution; *(Attach affidavit confirming that examination was conducted, and a bill of costs.)*

(d) $ .... for any other costs to which the creditor is entitled under subrule 60.19(1). *(Attach certificate of assessment.)*

YOU ARE DIRECTED to enforce the writ of seizure and sale issued on *(date)* and filed in your office for a sum sufficient to satisfy the total of the amounts set out above, together with subsequent interest, and your fees and expenses.

Date ....

(Signature of party or lawyer)
(Name, address and telephone number of party or lawyer)

November 1, 2005

FORM 60G — REQUISITION FOR GARNISHMENT

Courts of Justice Act

[Repealed O. Reg. 77/06, s. 3.]

[Editor's Note: Forms 4A to 78A of the Rules of Civil Procedure have been repealed by O. Reg. 77/06, effective July 1, 2006. Pursuant to Rule of Civil Procedure 1.06, when a form is referred to by number, the reference is to the form with that number that is described in the Table of Forms at the end of these rules and which is available on the Internet through www.ontariocourtforms.on.ca. For your convenience, the government form as published on this website is reproduced below.]

(General heading)

REQUISITION FOR GARNISHMENT

TO: the local registrar at *(place)*

I REQUIRE a notice of garnishment to be issued in this proceeding, in accordance with the attached draft Form 60H. The total amount to be shown in the notice of garnishment is $ ...., made up as follows:

1. $ .... for principal owing under the judgment or order, including prejudgment interest.

2. $ .... for the costs of the action.

3. $50 for the preparation of documents in connection with issuing, renewing and filing with the sheriff a writ of execution or notice of garnishment.

4. $ .... for disbursements paid to a sheriff, registrar, official examiner, court reporter or other public officer and to which the creditor is entitled under subrule 60.19(1). *(Attach copies of all receipts.)*

5. $ .... for an amount determined in accordance with Tariff A for conducting an examination in aid of execution. *(Attach affidavit confirming that examination was conducted, and a bill of costs.)*

6. $ .... for any other costs to which the creditor is entitled under subrule 60.19(1). *(Attach certificate of assessment.)*

7. $ .... for postjudgment interest to today's date. *(Calculate by counting the number of days that the principal sum has been owing, multiplying that number by the annual rate of interest, then multiplying by the principal sum owing and dividing by 365.)*

Date ....

____

(Signature of creditor or creditor's lawyer)

(Name, address and telephone number of creditor or creditor's lawyer)

November 1, 2005

FORM 60G.1 — REQUISITION FOR RENEWAL OF GARNISHMENT

Courts of Justice Act

[Repealed O. Reg. 77/06, s. 3.]

[Editor's Note: Forms 4A to 78A of the Rules of Civil Procedure have been repealed by O. Reg. 77/06, effective July 1, 2006. Pursuant to Rule of Civil Procedure 1.06, when a form is referred to by number, the reference is to the form with that number that is described in the Table of Forms at the end of these rules and which is available on the Internet through

www.ontariocourtforms.on.ca. For your convenience, the government form as published on this website is reproduced below.]

ONTARIO
SUPERIOR COURT OF JUSTICE
(General heading)

REQUISITION FOR RENEWAL OF GARNISHMENT

TO: the local registrar at *(place)*

I REQUIRE a notice of renewal of garnishment to be issued in this proceeding, in accordance with the attached draft Form 60H.1. The total amount to be shown in the notice of renewal of garnishment is $ ...., made up as follows:

1. $ .... for principal owing under the judgment or order, including prejudgment interest.

2. $ .... for the costs of the action.

3. $50 for the preparation of documents in connection with issuing, renewing and filing with the sheriff a writ of execution or notice of garnishment.

4. $ .... for disbursements paid to a sheriff, registrar, official examiner, court reporter or other public officer and to which the creditor is entitled under subrule 60.19(1). *(Attach copies of all receipts.)*

5. $ .... for an amount determined in accordance with Tariff A for conducting an examination in aid of execution. *(Attach affidavit confirming that examination was conducted, and a bill of costs.)*

6. $ .... for any other costs to which the creditor is entitled under subrule 60.19(1). *(Attach certificate of assessment.)*

7. $ .... for postjudgment interest to today's date. *(Calculate by counting the number of days that the principal sum has been owing, multiplying that number by the annual rate of interest, then multiplying by the principal sum owing and dividing by 365.)*

Date ....

(Signature of creditor or creditor's lawyer)
(Name, address and telephone number of creditor or creditor's lawyer)

November 1, 2005

FORM 60H — NOTICE OF GARNISHMENT

Courts of Justice Act

[Repealed O. Reg. 77/06, s. 3.]

[Editor's Note: Forms 4A to 78A of the Rules of Civil Procedure have been repealed by O. Reg. 77/06, effective July 1, 2006. Pursuant to Rule of Civil Procedure 1.06, when a form is

referred to by number, the reference is to the form with that number that is described in the Table of Forms at the end of these rules and which is available on the Internet through www.ontariocourtforms.on.ca. For your convenience, the government form as published on this website is reproduced below.]

(*Court file no.*)

(*Court*)

BETWEEN

(*name*)

Creditor

(*Court seal*)

(and)

(*name*)

Debtor

(and)

(*name*)

Garnishee

NOTICE OF GARNISHMENT

To (*name and address of garnishee*)

A LEGAL PROCEEDING in this court between the creditor and the debtor has resulted in an order that the debtor pay a sum of money to the creditor. The creditor claims that you owe a debt to the debtor. A debt to the debtor includes both a debt payable to the debtor and a debt payable to the debtor and one or more co-owners. The creditor has had this notice of garnishment directed to you as garnishee in order to seize any debt that you owe or will owe to the debtor. Where the debt is payable to the debtor and to one or more co-owners, you must pay one-half of the indebtedness or the greater or lesser amount specified in an order made under subrule 60.08(16).

YOU ARE REQUIRED TO PAY to the Sheriff of the (*name of county or district*),

(a) within 10 days after this notice is served on you, all debts now payable by you to the debtor; and

(b) within 10 days after they become payable, all debts that become payable by you to the debtor within 6 years after this notice is served on you,

subject to the exemptions provided by section 7 of the *Wages Act*. The total amount of all your payments to the sheriff is not to exceed $ .... less $10 for your costs of making each payment.

EACH PAYMENT MUST BE SENT with a copy of the attached garnishee's payment notice to the sheriff at the address shown below.

IF YOU DO NOT PAY THE TOTAL AMOUNT OF $ .... LESS $10 FOR YOUR COSTS OF MAKING EACH PAYMENT WITHIN 10 DAYS after this notice is served on you, because the debt is owed to the debtor and to one or more co-owners or for any other reason, you must within that time serve on the creditor and the debtor and file with the court a garnishee's statement in Form 60I attached to this notice.

IF YOU FAIL TO OBEY THIS NOTICE, THE COURT MAY MAKE AND ENFORCE AN ORDER AGAINST YOU for payment of the amount set out above and the costs of the creditor.

IF YOU MAKE PAYMENT TO ANYONE OTHER THAN THE SHERIFF, YOU MAY BE LIABLE TO PAY AGAIN.

TO THE CREDITOR, THE DEBTOR AND THE GARNISHEE

Any party may make a motion to the court to determine any matter in relation to this notice of garnishment.

Date .... Issued by ....
Local registrar

Address of court office ....
....

Creditor's address	Debtor's address	Sheriff's address
....	....	....
....	....	....
telephone no.		

....

(*The top portion of the garnishee's payment notice is to be completed by the creditor before the notice of garnishment is issued. Where it is anticipated that more than one payment will be made by the garnishee, the creditor should provide extra copies of the payment notice.*)

GARNISHEE PAYMENT NOTICE

Make payment by cheque or money order payable to the Sheriff of the (*the name of county or district*) and send it, along with a copy of this payment notice, to the (*address*).

Court .... File no. ....
Office at ....
Creditor ....
Debtor ....
Garnishee ....

TO BE COMPLETED BY GARNISHEE FOR EACH PAYMENT

Date of Payment ....
Amount enclosed $ ....

November 1, 2005

FORM 60H.1 — NOTICE OF RENEWAL OF GARNISHMENT

Courts of Justice Act

[Repealed O. Reg. 77/06, s. 3.]

[Editor's Note: Forms 4A to 78A of the Rules of Civil Procedure have been repealed by O. Reg. 77/06, effective July 1, 2006. Pursuant to Rule of Civil Procedure 1.06, when a form is referred to by number, the reference is to the form with that number that is described in the Table of Forms at the end of these rules and which is available on the Internet through www.ontariocourtforms.on.ca. For your convenience, the government form as published on this website is reproduced below.]

(Court file no.)

(Court)

BETWEEN *(name)*

Creditor

(Court seal) *(and)*

(name)

Debtor

(and)

(name)

Garnishee

NOTICE OF RENEWAL OF GARNISHMENT

TO *(name and address of garnishee)*

A LEGAL PROCEEDING in this court between the creditor and the debtor has resulted in an order that the debtor pay a sum of money to the creditor. The creditor claims that you owe a debt to the debtor. A debt to the debtor includes both a debt payable to the debtor and a debt payable to the debtor and one or more co-owners. The creditor has had this notice of renewal of garnishment directed to you as garnishee in order to seize any debt that you owe or will owe to the debtor. Where the debt is payable to the debtor and to one or more co-owners, you must pay one-half of the indebtedness or the greater or lesser amount specified in an order made under subrule 60.08(16).

(Where appropriate, add: This notice of renewal of garnishment enforces an order for support.)

YOU ARE REQUIRED TO PAY to the Sheriff of the *(name of county or district)*,

(a) within 10 days after this notice is served on you, all debts now payable by you to the debtor; and

(b) within 10 days after they become payable, all debts that become payable by you to the debtor within 6 years after this notice is served on you,

subject to the exemptions provided by section 7 of the *Wages Act*. The total amount of all your payments to the sheriff is not to exceed \$.......... less \$10 for your costs of making each payment.

EACH PAYMENT MUST BE SENT with a copy of the attached garnishee's payment notice to the sheriff at the address shown below.

IF YOU DO NOT PAY THE TOTAL AMOUNT OF \$.......... LESS \$10 FOR YOUR COSTS OF MAKING EACH PAYMENT WITHIN 10 DAYS after this notice is served on you, because the debt is owed to the debtor and to one or more co-owners or for any other reason, you must within that time serve on the creditor and the debtor and file with the court a garnishee's statement in Form 601 attached to this notice.

IF YOU FAIL TO OBEY THIS NOTICE, THE COURT MAY MAKE AND ENFORCE AN ORDER AGAINST YOU for payment of the amount set out above and the costs of the creditor.

IF YOU MAKE PAYMENT TO ANYONE OTHER THAN THE SHERIFF, YOU MAY BE LIABLE TO PAY AGAIN.

TO THE CREDITOR, THE DEBTOR AND THE GARNISHEE.

Any party may make a motion to the court to determine any matter in relation to this notice of renewal of garnishment.

Date .... Issued by ....

Local registrar

Address of court office ....

....

Creditor's address	Debtor's address	Sheriff's address
....	....	....
....	....	....

telephone no. ....

....

(The top portion of the garnishee's payment notice is to be completed by the creditor before the notice of renewal of garnishment is issued. Where it is anticipated that more than one payment will be made by the garnishee, the creditor should provide extra copies of the payment notice.)

GARNISHEE PAYMENT NOTICE

Make payment by cheque or money order payable to the Sheriff of the *(the name of county or district)* and send it, along with a copy of this payment notice, to the *(address)*.

Court .... File no. ....

Office at ....

Creditor ....

Debtor ....

Garnishee ....

TO BE COMPLETED BY GARNISHEE FOR EACH PAYMENT

Date of payment ....

Amount enclosed $ ....

November 1, 2005

FORM 60I — GARNISHEE'S STATEMENT

Courts of Justice Act

[Repealed O. Reg. 77/06, s. 3.]

[Editor's Note: Forms 4A to 78A of the Rules of Civil Procedure have been repealed by O. Reg. 77/06, effective July 1, 2006. Pursuant to Rule of Civil Procedure 1.06, when a form is

referred to by number, the reference is to the form with that number that is described in the Table of Forms at the end of these rules and which is available on the Internet through www.ontariocourtforms.on.ca. For your convenience, the government form as published on this website is reproduced below.]

(*The general heading on this form is to be completed by the creditor and the form is to be attached to the notice of garnishment to be served on the garnishee before the notice of garnishment is issued.*)

(*General heading as in Form 60H*)

GARNISHEE'S STATEMENT

1. I/We acknowledge that I/we owe or will owe the debtor or the debtor and one or more co-owners the sum of $ ...., payable on (*date*) because (*Give reasons why you owe the debtor or the debtor and one or more co-owners money. If you are making payment of less than the amount stated in line 2 of this paragraph because the debt is owed to the debtor and to one or more co-owners or for any other reason, give a full explanation of the reason. If you owe the debtor wages, state how often the debtor is paid. State the gross amount of the debtor's wages before any deductions and the net amount after all deductions and attach a copy of a pay slip.*)

1.1 (*If debt owed to debtor and one or more co-owners, check here ❑ and complete the following:*)

Co-owner(s) of the Debt (name, address) ....

2. (*If you do not owe the debtor money, explain why. Give any other information that will explain your financial relationship with the debtor.*)

3. (*If you have been served with any other notice of garnishment or a writ of execution against the debtor, give particulars.*)

Name of creditor	Location of Sheriff	Date of notice or writ	Date of service on you

4. (*If you have been served outside Ontario and you wish to object on the ground that service outside Ontario was improper, give particulars of your objection.*)

Date ....

Signature of or for garnishee ....
Name of garnishee ....
Address ....
....
Telephone number ....

November 1, 2005

FORM 60I.1 — NOTICE TO CO-OWNER OF THE DEBT

Courts of Justice Act

[Repealed O. Reg. 77/06, s. 3.]

[Editor's Note: Forms 4A to 78A of the Rules of Civil Procedure have been repealed by O. Reg. 77/06, effective July 1, 2006. Pursuant to Rule of Civil Procedure 1.06, when a form is referred to by number, the reference is to the form with that number that is described in the Table of Forms at the end of these rules and which is available on the Internet through www.ontariocourtforms.on.ca. For your convenience, the government form as published on this website is reproduced below.]

(*General heading as in Form 60H*)

TO (*name and address of co-owner of the debt*)

A LEGAL PROCEEDING in this court between the creditor and the debtor has resulted in an order that the debtor pay a sum of money to the creditor. The creditor has given a notice of garnishment to (*name of garnishee*) claiming that the garnishee owes a debt to the debtor. A debt to the debtor includes both a debt payable to the debtor and a debt payable to the debtor and one or more other co-owners. The garnishee has indicated in the attached garnishee's statement that you are a co-owner. Under the notice of garnishment the garnishee has paid the greater of the debtor's ownership interest, as known to the garnishee, or one-half of the indebtedness to the sheriff.

IF YOU HAVE A CLAIM to the money being paid to the sheriff by the garnishee, you have 30 days from service of this notice to make a motion to the court for a garnishment hearing. If you fail to do so, you may not hereafter dispute the enforcement of the creditor's order for the payment of recovery of money under the *Rules of Civil Procedure* and the funds may be paid out in accordance with the *Creditor's Relief Act.*

Date ....

November 1, 2005

FORM 60J — NOTICE OF TERMINATION OF GARNISHMENT

Courts of Justice Act

[Repealed O. Reg. 77/06, s. 3.]

[Editor's Note: Forms 4A to 78A of the Rules of Civil Procedure have been repealed by O. Reg. 77/06, effective July 1, 2006. Pursuant to Rule of Civil Procedure 1.06, when a form is referred to by number, the reference is to the form with that number that is described in the Table of Forms at the end of these rules and which is available on the Internet through www.ontariocourtforms.on.ca. For your convenience, the government form as published on this website is reproduced below.]

(*General heading as in Form 60H*)

NOTICE OF TERMINATION OF GARNISHMENT

TO (*name of garnishee*)

AND TO the Sheriff of the (*name of county or district*)

THE NOTICE OF GARNISHMENT DATED (*date*) SERVED ON YOU IS TERMINATED and you are not to make any further payments under it.

(*Date*)

(*Signature of creditor or lawyer*)

(*Name, address and telephone number of creditor or lawyer*)

July 1, 2007

FORM 60K — WARRANT FOR ARREST (CONTEMPT)

Courts of Justice Act

[Repealed O. Reg. 77/06, s. 3.]

[Editor's Note: Forms 4A to 78A of the Rules of Civil Procedure have been repealed by O. Reg. 77/06, effective July 1, 2006. Pursuant to Rule of Civil Procedure 1.06, when a form is referred to by number, the reference is to the form with that number that is described in the Table of Forms at the end of these rules and which is available on the Internet through www.ontariocourtforms.on.ca. For your convenience, the government form as published on this website is reproduced below.]

(*Court file no.*)

(*Court*)

(*Name of judge*) (*Day and date*)

(*Court seal*) (*Title of proceeding*)

WARRANT FOR ARREST

TO ALL POLICE OFFICERS in Ontario

AND TO the officers of all correctional institutions in Ontario

WHEREAS it appears that (*name*), of (*address*) may be in contempt of this court,

AND WHEREAS I am of the opinion that attendance of (*name*) at the hearing of the motion for a contempt order is necessary in the interest of justice and it appears that he (*or* she) is not likely to attend voluntarily,

YOU ARE ORDERED TO ARREST and bring (*name*) before the court for the hearing of the motion for a contempt order, and if the court is not then sitting or if he (*or* she) cannot be brought forthwith before the court, you are ordered to deliver him (or her) to a provincial correctional institution or other secure facility, to be admitted and detained there until he (*or* she) can be brought before the court.

(*Signature of judge*)

November 1, 2005

FORM 60L — WARRANT OF COMMITTAL

Courts of Justice Act

[Repealed O. Reg. 77/06, s. 3.]

[Editor's Note: Forms 4A to 78A of the Rules of Civil Procedure have been repealed by O. Reg. 77/06, effective July 1, 2006. Pursuant to Rule of Civil Procedure 1.06, when a form is referred to by number, the reference is to the form with that number that is described in the Table of Forms at the end of these rules and which is available on the Internet through www.ontariocourtforms.on.ca. For your convenience, the government form as published on this website is reproduced below.]

(*Court file no.*)

(*Court*)

(*Name of judge*) (*Day and date*)

(*Court seal*) (*Title of proceeding*)

WARRANT OF COMMITTAL

TO ALL POLICE OFFICERS in Ontario

AND TO THE OFFICERS OF (*name of correctional institution*)

WHEREAS I have found that (*name*) is in contempt of this court and have ordered imprisonment as punishment for the contempt,

YOU ARE ORDERED TO ARREST (*name*) and deliver him (*or her*) to a provincial correctional institution, to be detained there for (*or* until) (*give particulars of sentence*).

(*Signature of judge*)

November 1, 2005

FORM 60M — NOTICE OF CLAIM

Courts of Justice Act

[Repealed O. Reg. 77/06, s. 3.]

[Editor's Note: Forms 4A to 78A of the Rules of Civil Procedure have been repealed by O. Reg. 77/06, effective July 1, 2006. Pursuant to Rule of Civil Procedure 1.06, when a form is referred to by number, the reference is to the form with that number that is described in the Table of Forms at the end of these rules and which is available on the Internet through www.ontariocourtforms.on.ca. For your convenience, the government form as published on this website is reproduced below.]

(*General heading*)

TO THE CREDITORS OF (*name of debtor*)

I have received notice of a claim by (*name*), of (*address*), in respect of property or the proceeds of property taken or intended to be taken in execution against the debtor. Particulars of the claim are as follows: (*Give particulars.*)

You are required to give me notice in writing, within seven days after receiving this notice, stating whether you admit or dispute the claim.

(*Date*) (*Name, address and telephone number of sheriff*)

TO (*Name and address of each creditor or lawyer*)

July 1, 2007

FORM 60N — SHERIFF'S REPORT

Courts of Justice Act

[Repealed O. Reg. 77/06, s. 3.]

[Editor's Note: Forms 4A to 78A of the Rules of Civil Procedure have been repealed by O. Reg. 77/06, effective July 1, 2006. Pursuant to Rule of Civil Procedure 1.06, when a form is referred to by number, the reference is to the form with that number that is described in the Table of Forms at the end of these rules and which is available on the Internet through www.ontariocourtforms.on.ca. For your convenience, the government form as published on this website is reproduced below.]

(*General heading*)

SHERIFF'S REPORT

In response to your request of (*date*) concerning the execution of the writ of seizure and sale (*or* possession, delivery *or* sequestration) against (*name of party*) filed with me, I report that I have taken the following action, with the following results: (*Give particulars.*)

(*Date*) (*Signature of sheriff*)

TO (*Name and address of creditor or lawyer*)

July 1, 2007

FORM 60O — REQUEST TO WITHDRAW A WRIT

Courts of Justice Act

[Repealed O. Reg. 77/06, s. 3.]

[Editor's Note: Forms 4A to 78A of the Rules of Civil Procedure have been repealed by O. Reg. 77/06, effective July 1, 2006. Pursuant to Rule of Civil Procedure 1.06, when a form is referred to by number, the reference is to the form with that number that is described in the Table of Forms at the end of these rules and which is available on the Internet through www.ontariocourtforms.on.ca. For your convenience, the government form as published on this website is reproduced below.]

ONTARIO
SUPERIOR COURT OF JUSTICE
(General heading)

REQUEST TO WITHDRAW A WRIT

TO: the Sheriff of the *(name of county or district)*

Under an order of this court in the favour of *(name of creditor)* made on *(date)*, *(name of debtor)* was ordered to pay the sum of $ .... (*where applicable, add* each month *or* as may be) with interest at the rate of .... per cent per year commencing on *(date)* and costs of $ .... *(as fixed or assessed)* with interest at the rate of .... per cent per year commencing on *(date)*.

(name of debtor) states as follows:

Order of Discharge

1. The order has been released by an order of discharge under the *Bankruptcy and Insolvency Act* (Canada). A certified copy of the order is attached.

2. The debtor has no debts under section 178 of that Act.

OR

Certificate of Full Performance

1. The order has been released by a certificate of full performance under the *Bankruptcy and Insolvency Act* (Canada). A copy of the certificate is attached.

2. The debtor has no debts under section 178 of that Act.

(name of debtor) requests that the writ of seizure and sale issued with respect to the order be withdrawn under rule 60.15 of the *Rules of Civil Procedure*.

Date ....

(Signature of debtor)
(Name, address and telephone number of debtor or debtor's lawyer)

November 1, 2005

FORM 61A — NOTICE OF APPEAL TO AN APPELLATE COURT

Courts of Justice Act

[Repealed O. Reg. 77/06, s. 3.]

[Editor's Note: Forms 4A to 78A of the Rules of Civil Procedure have been repealed by O. Reg. 77/06, effective July 1, 2006. Pursuant to Rule of Civil Procedure 1.06, when a form is referred to by number, the reference is to the form with that number that is described in the Table of Forms at the end of these rules and which is available on the Internet through www.ontariocourtforms.on.ca. For your convenience, the government form as published on this website is reproduced below.]

(*General heading in accordance with Form 61B*)

NOTICE OF APPEAL

THE (*identify party*) APPEALS to the Court of Appeal (*or* Divisional Court) from the judgment (*or* order) of (*name of judge, officer or tribunal*) dated (*date*) made at (*place*).

THE APPELLANT ASKS that the judgment be set aside and a judgment be granted as follows (*or* that the judgment be varied as follows, *or as may be*): (*Set out briefly the relief sought.*)

THE GROUNDS OF APPEAL are as follows: (*Set out briefly the grounds of appeal.*)

THE BASIS OF THE APPELLATE COURT'S JURISDICTION IS: *(State the basis for the appellate court's jurisdiction, including (i) any provision of a statute or regulation establishing jurisdiction, (ii) whether the order appealed from is final or interlocutory, (iii) whether leave to appeal is required and if so whether it has been granted, and (iv) any other facts relevant to establishing jurisdiction.)*

(*Divisional Court appeals*) The appellant requests that this appeal be heard at (*place*).

(*Date*) (*Name, address and telephone and fax numbers of appellant's lawyer or of appellant*)

TO (*Name and address of respondent's lawyer or of respondent*)

November 1, 2005

FORM 61B — GENERAL HEADING IN PROCEEDINGS IN APPELLATE COURTS

Courts of Justice Act

[Repealed O. Reg. 77/06, s. 3.]

[Editor's Note: Forms 4A to 78A of the Rules of Civil Procedure have been repealed by O. Reg. 77/06, effective July 1, 2006. Pursuant to Rule of Civil Procedure 1.06, when a form is referred to by number, the reference is to the form with that number that is described in the Table of Forms at the end of these rules and which is available on the Internet through www.ontariocourtforms.on.ca. For your convenience, the government form as published on this website is reproduced below.]

COURT OF APPEAL FOR ONTARIO (OR DIVISIONAL COURT, SUPERIOR COURT OF JUSTICE)

(*Appeal in an action*)

BETWEEN:

(*name*)

Plaintiff
(Appellant) (*or* (Respondent))

and

(*name*)

Defendant
(Respondent) (*or* (Appellant))

(*Appeal in an application*)

BETWEEN: (*name*)

Applicant
(Appellant) (*or* (Respondent in appeal))

and

(*name*)

Respondent
(Respondent in appeal) (*or* (Appellant))

APPLICATION UNDER (*statutory provision or rule under which the application is made*)

(*Where there are multiple parties in the proceeding at first instance and only some of them are parties to the appeal, include the names of all of the parties at first instance and underline the names of the parties to the appeal.*)

November 1, 2005

FORM 61C — APPELLANT'S CERTIFICATE RESPECTING EVIDENCE

Courts of Justice Act

[Repealed O. Reg. 77/06, s. 3.]

[Editor's Note: Forms 4A to 78A of the Rules of Civil Procedure have been repealed by O. Reg. 77/06, effective July 1, 2006. Pursuant to Rule of Civil Procedure 1.06, when a form is referred to by number, the reference is to the form with that number that is described in the Table of Forms at the end of these rules and which is available on the Internet through www.ontariocourtforms.on.ca. For your convenience, the government form as published on this website is reproduced below.]

(*General heading in accordance with Form 61B*)

APPELLANT'S CERTIFICATE

The appellant certifies that the following evidence is required for the appeal, in the appellant's opinion:

1. Exhibits numbers ....
2. The affidavit evidence of (*names of deponents*)
3. The oral evidence of (*names of witnesses*)

(*Date*) (*Name, address and telephone and fax numbers of appellant's lawyer or appellant*)

TO (*Name and address of respondent's lawyer or respondent*)

November 1, 2005

FORM 61D — RESPONDENT'S CERTIFICATE RESPECTING EVIDENCE

Courts of Justice Act

[Repealed O. Reg. 77/06, s. 3.]

[Editor's Note: Forms 4A to 78A of the Rules of Civil Procedure have been repealed by O. Reg. 77/06, effective July 1, 2006. Pursuant to Rule of Civil Procedure 1.06, when a form is referred to by number, the reference is to the form with that number that is described in the Table of Forms at the end of these rules and which is available on the Internet through www.ontariocourtforms.on.ca. For your convenience, the government form as published on this website is reproduced below.]

(*General heading in accordance with Form 61B*)

RESPONDENT'S CERTIFICATE

The respondent confirms the appellant's certificate (*where necessary, add* except for the following:)

ADDITIONS

1. Exhibits numbers are required for the appeal.
2. The affidavit evidence of (*names of deponents*) is required for the appeal.
3. The oral evidence of (*names of witnesses*) is required for the appeal.

DELETIONS

4. Exhibits numbers are not required for the appeal.
5. The affidavit evidence of (*names of deponents*) is not required for the appeal.
6. The oral evidence of (*names of witnesses*) is not required for the appeal.

(*Date*) (*Name, address and telephone and fax numbers of respondent's lawyer or respondent*)

TO (*Name and address of appellant's lawyer or appellant*)

November 1, 2005

FORM 61E — NOTICE OF CROSS-APPEAL

Courts of Justice Act

[Repealed O. Reg. 77/06, s. 3.]

[Editor's Note: Forms 4A to 78A of the Rules of Civil Procedure have been repealed by O. Reg. 77/06, effective July 1, 2006. Pursuant to Rule of Civil Procedure 1.06, when a form is referred to by number, the reference is to the form with that number that is described in the Table of Forms at the end of these rules and which is available on the Internet through www.ontariocourtforms.on.ca. For your convenience, the government form as published on this website is reproduced below.]

(*General heading in accordance with Form 61B*)

NOTICE OF CROSS-APPEAL

THE RESPONDENT CROSS-APPEALS in this appeal and asks that the judgment be set aside and judgment be granted as follows: (*or* that the judgment be varied as follows, *or as may be*): (*Set out briefly the relief sought.*)

THE GROUNDS FOR THIS CROSS-APPEAL are as follows: (*Set out briefly the grounds of cross-appeal.*)

(*Date*) (*Name, address and telephone and fax numbers of*
respondent's lawyer or respondent)

TO (*Name and address of appellant's*

lawyer or appellant)

July 1, 2007

FORM 61F — SUPPLEMENTARY NOTICE OF APPEAL OR CROSS-APPEAL

Courts of Justice Act

[Repealed O. Reg. 77/06, s. 3.]

[Editor's Note: Forms 4A to 78A of the Rules of Civil Procedure have been repealed by O. Reg. 77/06, effective July 1, 2006. Pursuant to Rule of Civil Procedure 1.06, when a form is referred to by number, the reference is to the form with that number that is described in the Table of Forms at the end of these rules and which is available on the Internet through www.ontariocourtforms.on.ca. For your convenience, the government form as published on this website is reproduced below.]

(*General heading in accordance with Form 61B*)

SUPPLEMENTARY NOTICE OF APPEAL (OR CROSS-APPEAL)

The appellant (*or* respondent) amends the notice of appeal (*or* cross-appeal) dated (*date*) in the following manner: (*Give particulars of the amendment.*)

(*Date*) (*Name, address and telephone number of lawyer or party serving notice*)

TO (*Name and address of lawyer or party on whom notice is served*)

July 1, 2007

FORM 61G — NOTICE OF LISTING FOR HEARING (APPEAL)

Courts of Justice Act

[Repealed O. Reg. 77/06, s. 3.]

[Editor's Note: Forms 4A to 78A of the Rules of Civil Procedure have been repealed by O. Reg. 77/06, effective July 1, 2006. Pursuant to Rule of Civil Procedure 1.06, when a form is referred to by number, the reference is to the form with that number that is described in the Table of Forms at the end of these rules and which is available on the Internet through

www.ontariocourtforms.on.ca. For your convenience, the government form as published on this website is reproduced below.]

(*General heading in accordance with Form 61B*)

NOTICE OF LISTING FOR HEARING

THIS APPEAL HAS BEEN PERFECTED and has been listed for hearing at (*place*). You may ascertain from my office the approximate date of hearing.

Date .... Signed by ....
Registrar of the Court of Appeal
(*or* Divisional Court)
(*Address of court office*)

TO (*Name and address of every person listed in the certificate of perfection*)

November 1, 2005

FORM 61H — CERTIFICATE OF COMPLETENESS OF APPEAL BOOK AND COMPENDIUM

Courts of Justice Act

[Repealed O. Reg. 77/06, s. 3.]

[Editor's Note: Forms 4A to 78A of the Rules of Civil Procedure have been repealed by O. Reg. 77/06, effective July 1, 2006. Pursuant to Rule of Civil Procedure 1.06, when a form is referred to by number, the reference is to the form with that number that is described in the Table of Forms at the end of these rules and which is available on the Internet through www.ontariocourtforms.on.ca. For your convenience, the government form as published on this website is reproduced below.]

(*General heading in accordance with Form 61B*)

CERTIFICATE OF COMPLETENESS

I, (*name*), lawyer for the appellant (*or* appellant), certify that the appeal book and compendium in this appeal is complete and legible.

(*Date*) (*Signature of appellant's lawyer or appellant*)
(*Name, address and telephone number of appellant's lawyer or appellant*)

July 1, 2007

FORM 61I — ORDER DISMISSING APPEAL OR CROSS-APPEAL FOR DELAY

Courts of Justice Act

[Repealed O. Reg. 77/06, s. 3.]

[Editor's Note: Forms 4A to 78A of the Rules of Civil Procedure have been repealed by O. Reg. 77/06, effective July 1, 2006. Pursuant to Rule of Civil Procedure 1.06, when a form is referred to by number, the reference is to the form with that number that is described in the Table of Forms at the end of these rules and which is available on the Internet through www.ontariocourtforms.on.ca. For your convenience, the government form as published on this website is reproduced below.]

Courts of Justice Act

(General heading in accordance with Form 61B)

ORDER DISMISSING APPEAL (OR CROSS-APPEAL)

The appellant *(or* respondent*)* has not *(give particulars of appellant's or respondent's default under rule 61.13)* and has not cured the default, although given notice under rule 61.13 to do so.

IT IS ORDERED that this appeal *(or* cross-appeal) be dismissed for delay, with costs fixed at $750, despite rule 58.13.

Date .... Signed by ....

Registrar of the Court of Appeal (or Divisional Court)

NOTE: If there is a cross-appeal, the appellant by cross-appeal should consider rule 61.15, under which the cross-appeal may be deemed to be abandoned.

July 30, 2009

FORM 61J — ORDER DISMISSING MOTION FOR LEAVE TO APPEAL FOR DELAY

Courts of Justice Act

[Repealed O. Reg. 77/06, s. 3.]

[Editor's Note: Forms 4A to 78A of the Rules of Civil Procedure have been repealed by O. Reg. 77/06, effective July 1, 2006. Pursuant to Rule of Civil Procedure 1.06, when a form is referred to by number, the reference is to the form with that number that is described in the Table of Forms at the end of these rules and which is available on the Internet through

www.ontariocourtforms.on.ca. For your convenience, the government form as published on this website is reproduced below.]

Courts of Justice Act

(General heading in accordance with Form 61B)

ORDER DISMISSING MOTION FOR LEAVE

The moving party on this motion for leave to appeal from the order (*or as may be*) of *(name of court or tribunal*) dated (*date*) has not served and filed the motion record, factum and (*if necessary*) transcripts in accordance with clause 61.13(8)(a) (motion by responding party) (*or* clause 61.13(8)(b) (Registrar's notice)) of the *Rules of Civil Procedure*.

IT IS ORDERED that this motion be dismissed for delay, with costs fixed at $750, despite rule 58.13.

Date .... Signed by ....

Registrar of the Court of Appeal (or Divisional Court)

July 30, 2009

FORM 61J.1 — ORDER DISMISSING MOTION FOR DELAY

Courts of Justice Act

[Repealed O. Reg. 77/06, s. 3.]

[Editor's Note: Forms 4A to 78A of the Rules of Civil Procedure have been repealed by O. Reg. 77/06, effective July 1, 2006. Pursuant to Rule of Civil Procedure 1.06, when a form is referred to by number, the reference is to the form with that number that is described in the Table of Forms at the end of these rules and which is available on the Internet through www.ontariocourtforms.on.ca. For your convenience, the government form as published on this website is reproduced below.]

Courts of Justice Act

(General heading in accordance with Form 61B)

ORDER DISMISSING MOTION FOR DELAY

The moving party on this motion has not served and filed the motion record, factum and other material in accordance with subrule 61.16(4) of the *Rules of Civil Procedure*.

IT IS ORDERED that this motion be dismissed for delay, with costs fixed at $750, despite rule 58.13.

Date .... Signed by ....

Registrar of the Court of Appeal *(or* Divisional Court*)*

July 30, 2009

FORM 61K — NOTICE OF ABANDONMENT OF APPEAL OR CROSS-APPEAL

Courts of Justice Act

[Repealed O. Reg. 77/06, s. 3.]

[Editor's Note: Forms 4A to 78A of the Rules of Civil Procedure have been repealed by O. Reg. 77/06, effective July 1, 2006. Pursuant to Rule of Civil Procedure 1.06, when a form is referred to by number, the reference is to the form with that number that is described in the Table of Forms at the end of these rules and which is available on the Internet through www.ontariocourtforms.on.ca. For your convenience, the government form as published on this website is reproduced below.]

(*General heading in accordance with Form 61B*)

NOTICE OF ABANDONMENT

The appellant (*or* respondent) abandons this appeal (*or* cross-appeal).

(*Date*) (*Name, address and telephone number of lawyer or party serving notice*)

TO (*Name and address of lawyer or party on whom notice is served*)

NOTE: If there is a cross-appeal, the appellant by cross-appeal should consider rule 61.15, under which the cross-appeal may be deemed to be abandoned.

July 1, 2007

FORM 61L — NOTICE OF ELECTION TO PROCEED WITH CROSS-APPEAL

Courts of Justice Act

[Repealed O. Reg. 77/06, s. 3.]

[Editor's Note: Forms 4A to 78A of the Rules of Civil Procedure have been repealed by O. Reg. 77/06, effective July 1, 2006. Pursuant to Rule of Civil Procedure 1.06, when a form is referred to by number, the reference is to the form with that number that is described in the Table of Forms at the end of these rules and which is available on the Internet through www.ontariocourtforms.on.ca. For your convenience, the government form as published on this website is reproduced below.]

(*General heading in accordance with Form 61B*)

NOTICE OF ELECTION

The respondent elects to proceed with the cross-appeal.

(*Date*) (*Name, address and telephone number of respondent's lawyer or respondent*)

TO (*Name and address of appellant's lawyer or appellant*)

July 1, 2007

FORM 62A — NOTICE OF APPEAL TO A JUDGE

Courts of Justice Act

[Repealed O. Reg. 77/06, s. 3.]

[Editor's Note: Forms 4A to 78A of the Rules of Civil Procedure have been repealed by O. Reg. 77/06, effective July 1, 2006. Pursuant to Rule of Civil Procedure 1.06, when a form is referred to by number, the reference is to the form with that number that is described in the Table of Forms at the end of these rules and which is available on the Internet through www.ontariocourtforms.on.ca. For your convenience, the government form as published on this website is reproduced below.]

(*General heading*)

NOTICE OF APPEAL

THE (*identify party*) APPEALS to a judge from the order (*or* certificate) of (*name of judge or officers*) dated (*date*).

THE APPEAL WILL BE HEARD ON (*day*), (*date*), at (*time*) at (*address of court house*).

THE (*identify party*) ASKS (*state the precise relief sought*).

THE GROUNDS OF APPEAL are as follows: (*Set out briefly the grounds of appeal*).

(*Date*) (*Name, address and telephone number of lawyer or party serving notice*)

TO (*Name and address of lawyer or party on whom notice is served*)

July 1, 2007

FORM 63A — CERTIFICATE OF STAY

Courts of Justice Act

[Repealed O. Reg. 77/06, s. 3.]

[Editor's Note: Forms 4A to 78A of the Rules of Civil Procedure have been repealed by O. Reg. 77/06, effective July 1, 2006. Pursuant to Rule of Civil Procedure 1.06, when a form is referred to by number, the reference is to the form with that number that is described in the Table of Forms at the end of these rules and which is available on the Internet through www.ontariocourtforms.on.ca. For your convenience, the government form as published on this website is reproduced below.]

(*General heading*)

(*Court seal*)

CERTIFICATE OF STAY

The Registrar of the Court of Appeal (*or* Divisional Court) (*or* the local registrar of this court at (*place*)) certifies that the order (*or* judgment) of (*name of judge or officer*) dated (*date*) have been stayed by the delivery of a notice of appeal from the order (*or* judgment) (*or* by order of (*name of judge*) dated (*date*)). (*Where an order is made under Rule 63 limiting the stay, give particulars.*)

Date .... Issued by ....
Registrar

Address of court office ....
....

November 1, 2005

FORM 63B — CERTIFICATE OF STAY

Courts of Justice Act

[Repealed O. Reg. 77/06, s. 3.]

[Editor's Note: Forms 4A to 78A of the Rules of Civil Procedure have been repealed by O. Reg. 77/06, effective July 1, 2006. Pursuant to Rule of Civil Procedure 1.06, when a form is referred to by number, the reference is to the form with that number that is described in the Table of Forms at the end of these rules and which is available on the Internet through www.ontariocourtforms.on.ca. For your convenience, the government form as published on this website is reproduced below.]

(*General heading*)

(*Court Seal*)

CERTIFICATE OF STAY

The Registrar of the Divisional Court certifies that, under subsection 25(1) of the *Statutory Powers Procedure Act*, the order of the Ontario Rental Housing Tribunal dated (*date*) has been stayed by an appeal to this court.

Date .... Issued by ....
Registrar

November 1, 2005

FORM 64A — REQUEST TO REDEEM

Courts of Justice Act

[Repealed O. Reg. 77/06, s. 3.]

[Editor's Note: Forms 4A to 78A of the Rules of Civil Procedure have been repealed by O. Reg. 77/06, effective July 1, 2006. Pursuant to Rule of Civil Procedure 1.06, when a form is referred to by number, the reference is to the form with that number that is described in the Table of Forms at the end of these rules and which is available on the Internet through www.ontariocourtforms.on.ca. For your convenience, the government form as published on this website is reproduced below.]

(*General Heading*)

REQUEST TO REDEEM

The defendant (*name*) requests an opportunity to redeem the mortgaged property.

(*Date*) (*Name, address and telephone number of*

defendant's lawyer or defendant)

(*Where the defendant is a subsequent encumbrancer, add:*)

AFFIDAVIT VERIFYING CLAIM

I, (*full name of deponent*), of the (City, Town, *etc.*) of ...., in the (County, Regional Municipality, *etc.*) of ...., (*where the deponent is a party or the lawyer, officer, director, member or employee of a party, set out the deponent's capacity*), MAKE OATH AND SAY (*or* AFFIRM):

1. There is now due to me under a mortgage on (*or* an execution against *or* a construction lien registered against *or as may be*) the mortgaged property,

(a) for principal	$ ....
(b) for interest (*set out particulars*)	$ ....
(c) (*set out particulars of any other amounts due*)	$ ....
Total now due	$ ....

Sworn (*etc.*)

July 1, 2007

FORM 64B — DEFAULT JUDGMENT FOR FORECLOSURE WITH A REFERENCE

Courts of Justice Act

[Repealed O. Reg. 77/06, s. 3.]

[Editor's Note: Forms 4A to 78A of the Rules of Civil Procedure have been repealed by O. Reg. 77/06, effective July 1, 2006. Pursuant to Rule of Civil Procedure 1.06, when a form is referred to by number, the reference is to the form with that number that is described in the Table of Forms at the end of these rules and which is available on the Internet through www.ontariocourtforms.on.ca. For your convenience, the government form as published on this website is reproduced below.]

(*General heading*)

(*Court seal*)

JUDGMENT

On reading the statement of claim in this action and the proof of service of the statement of claim on the defendant(s), filed, no request to redeem or request for sale having been served and filed (*or* the defendant(s) (*name(s)*) having served and filed a request to redeem) and the defendant(s) having been noted in default, and the plaintiff wishing a reference (*or* the registrar having decided to sign judgment with a reference),

1. IT IS ORDERED AND ADJUDGED that all necessary inquiries be made, accounts taken, costs fixed or assessed and steps taken for redemption or foreclosure of the equity of re-

demption in the mortgaged property described in the attached schedule, and that for these purposes this action be referred to the master (*or as may be*) at (*place*). The mortgage is dated and made between (*name of mortgagor*) and (*name of mortgagee*), and registered (*give particulars of registration and of any assignment of the mortgage*).

(*Where judgment is for possession, add:*)

2. IT IS ORDERED AND ADJUDGED that the defendant (*name*) deliver to the plaintiff or as the plaintiff directs possession of the mortgaged property or of such part of it as is in the possession of the defendants.

(*Where judgment is for payment of the mortgage debt and the registrar is to take the account, and the following two paragraphs:*)

3. IT IS ORDERED AND ADJUDGED that the defendant (*name*) forthwith pay to the plaintiff the sum of $ ...., being the amount due to the plaintiff (s) today for principal, interest and costs; and on payment of the amount due to the plaintiff, the plaintiff convey the mortgaged property to the defendant or as the defendants directs, in accordance with section 2 of the *Mortgages Act*, and deliver up all documents relating to the mortgaged property.

THIS JUDGMENT BEARS INTEREST at the rate of (*rate claimed in the statement of claim*) per cent per year from its date.

(*Where judgment is for payment of the mortgage debt and the plaintiff wishes the account to be taken on the reference or the registrar refers the taking of the account, substitute the following two paragraphs:*)

> 3. IT IS ORDERED AND ADJUDGED that the defendant (*name*) pay to the plaintiff, forthwith after confirmation of the report on the reference, the amount found due for principal, interest and costs in accordance with the report, and on payment of the amount due to the plaintiff, the plaintiff convey the mortgaged property to the defendant or as the defendant directs, in accordance with section 2 of the *Mortgages Act*, and deliver up all documents relating to the mortgaged property.

THIS JUDGMENT BEARS INTEREST at the rate set out in the report on the reference from the date of confirmation of the report.

Date .... Signed by ....

Local registrar

Address of court office ....

....

(*The description of the mortgaged property in the attached schedule must be the same as in the statement of claim.*)

November 1, 2005

FORM 64C — DEFAULT JUDGMENT FOR IMMEDIATE FORECLOSURE

Courts of Justice Act

[Repealed O. Reg. 77/06, s. 3.]

[Editor's Note: Forms 4A to 78A of the Rules of Civil Procedure have been repealed by O. Reg. 77/06, effective July 1, 2006. Pursuant to Rule of Civil Procedure 1.06, when a form is referred to by number, the reference is to the form with that number that is described in the Table of Forms at the end of these rules and which is available on the Internet through www.ontariocourtforms.on.ca. For your convenience, the government form as published on this website is reproduced below.]

(*General heading*)

(*Court seal*)

JUDGMENT

On reading the statement of claim in this action and the proof of service of the statement of claim on the defendant(s), filed, no request to redeem or request for sale having been served and filed, the defendant(s) having been noted in default, and the plaintiff not wishing a reference,

1. IT IS ORDERED AND ADJUDGED that the right, title and equity of redemption of the defendant(s) (*name(s)*) to and in the mortgaged property described in the attached schedule are foreclosed. The mortgage is dated . . . . and made between (*name of mortgagor*) and (*name of mortgagee*), and registered (*give particulars of registration and of any assignment of the mortgage*).

(*Where judgment is for possession, add:*)

2. IT IS ORDERED AND ADJUDGED that the defendant (*name*) forthwith deliver to the plaintiff or as the plaintiff directs possession of the mortgaged property or of such part of it as is in the possession of the defendant.

(*Where judgment is for payment of the mortgage debt, add the following two paragraphs:*)

3. IT IS ORDERED AND ADJUDGED that the defendant (*name*) forthwith pay to the plaintiff the sum of $ ...., being the amount due to the plaintiff today for principal, interest and costs.

THIS JUDGMENT BEARS INTEREST at the rate of (*rate claimed in the statement of claim*) per cent per year from its date.

Date .... Signed by ....

Local registrar

Address of court office ....
....

(*The description of the mortgaged property in the attached schedule must be the same as in the statement of claim.*)

November 1, 2005

FORM 64D — DEFAULT JUDGMENT FOR FORECLOSURE WITHOUT A REFERENCE

Courts of Justice Act

[Repealed O. Reg. 77/06, s. 3.]

[Editor's Note: Forms 4A to 78A of the Rules of Civil Procedure have been repealed by O. Reg. 77/06, effective July 1, 2006. Pursuant to Rule of Civil Procedure 1.06, when a form is referred to by number, the reference is to the form with that number that is described in the Table of Forms at the end of these rules and which is available on the Internet through www.ontariocourtforms.on.ca. For your convenience, the government form as published on this website is reproduced below.]

(*General heading*)

(*Court seal*)

JUDGMENT

On reading the statement of claim in this action and the proof of service of the statement of claim on the defendant(s), filed, no request for sale having been served and filed the defendant(s) (*name(s)*) having served and filed a request to redeem and the defendant(s) having been noted in default, and the account having been taken in the presence of the lawyer(s) for the plaintiff(s) (*or* the plaintiff) and the lawyer(s) for the defendant(s) (*where applicable, add* (*identify party*) appearing in person *or* no one appearing for the defendant (*name*) although served with notice of the taking of the account as appears from the affidavit of (*name*), filed),

1. I FIND that the following sums are due to the plaintiff from the defendant (*name of owner of equity of redemption*) on (*redemption date*), the day I have fixed for payment under the mortgage in question in this action:

(a) for principal	$ ....
(b) for taxes paid	$ ....
(c) for premiums of insurance paid	$ ....
(d) for maintenance costs paid	$ ....
(e) for heating costs paid	$ ....
(f) for utility costs paid	$ ....
(*add any other costs in similar fashion*)	
(g) for interest up to (*date of judgment*)	$ ....
(h) for costs of this action	$ ....
(i) for subsequent interest on the principal at the rate of .... per cent per year up to the day fixed for payment	$ ....
making a total amount due on (*redemption date*) of	

2. IT IS ORDERED AND ADJUDGED that:

(a) on payment of the sum of $ (*total amount due from paragraph 1*) into the (*name of financial institution*) at (*address*), to the joint credit of the plaintiff and the Accountant of the Superior Court of Justice (*or* the local registrar); or

(b) on recovery by the plaintiff of the amount due under paragraph 6 of this judgment, together with post-judgment interest, on or before (*redemption date*), the plaintiff shall convey the mortgaged property described in the attached schedule to the defendant (*name*) or as the defendant(s) direct(s), in accordance with section 2 of the *Mortgages Act*, and deliver up all documents relating to the mortgaged property. The mortgage is dated and made between (*name of mortgagor*) and (*name of mortgagee*), and registered (*give particulars of registration and of any assignment of the mortgage*).

(*Delete clause (b) where the judgment does not order payment of the mortgage debt.*)

(*Where more than one party is entitled to redeem, add:*)

3. IT IS ORDERED AND ADJUDGED that the defendant (*name of encumbrancer*) is entitled to the first right to redeem and the defendant (*name*) is entitled to the second right to redeem (*and so on*) and the defendant (*name of owner of equity of redemption*) is entitled to the last right to redeem.

(*Foreclosure on default in payment*)

4. IT IS ORDERED AND ADJUDGED that, on default in payment as required by paragraph 2, the right, title and equity of redemption of the defendant(s) to and in the mortgaged property described in the attached schedule are foreclosed.

(*Where judgment is for possession, add:*)

5. IT IS ORDERED AND ADJUDGED that the defendant (*name*) forthwith deliver to the plaintiff or as the plaintiff directs, possession of the mortgaged property, or of such part of it as is in the possession of the defendant.

(*Where judgment is for payment of the mortgage debt, add the following two paragraphs:*)

6. IT IS ORDERED AND ADJUDGED that the defendant (*name*) forthwith pay to the plaintiff(s) the sum of $ ...., being the amount due to the plaintiff today for principal, interest and costs.

THIS JUDGMENT BEARS INTEREST at the rate of (*rate claimed in statement of claim*) per cent per year from its date.

Date .... Issued by ....
Local registrar

Address of court office ....
....

(*The description of the mortgaged property in the attached schedule must be the same as in the statement of claim.*)

July 1, 2007

FORM 64E — FINAL ORDER OF FORECLOSURE

Courts of Justice Act

[Repealed O. Reg. 77/06, s. 3.]

[Editor's Note: Forms 4A to 78A of the Rules of Civil Procedure have been repealed by O. Reg. 77/06, effective July 1, 2006. Pursuant to Rule of Civil Procedure 1.06, when a form is referred to by number, the reference is to the form with that number that is described in the Table of Forms at the end of these rules and which is available on the Internet through www.ontariocourtforms.on.ca. For your convenience, the government form as published on this website is reproduced below.]

(*Court*)

(*Court file no.*)

(*Name of judge or officer*) (*Day and date*)

(*Court seal*) (*Title of proceeding*)

FINAL ORDER OF FORECLOSURE

THIS MOTION made by (*identify moving party*), without notice, was heard this day.

(*Order following judgment granting redemption period*)

ON READING the judgment in this action dated (*date*), (*where there is an order fixing a new day for payment, add:* the order for a new day for payment dated (*date*)), (*where a notice of change of account has been delivered, add:* the notice of change of account, with proof of service,) and the certificate of the (*title*) of the (*financial institution*) at (*place*), with affidavit of execution, and the affidavit of the plaintiff, and on hearing the submissions of the lawyer for the plaintiff, and since the defendant(s) entitled to redeem has (have) not redeemed the mortgaged property,

1. IT IS ORDERED that the right, title and equity of redemption of the defendant(s) (*names of those who failed to serve and file a request to redeem, to attend and prove a claim on the taking of account or to redeem the mortgaged property*) to and in the mortgaged property described in the attached schedule and foreclosed. The mortgage is dated .... and made between (*name of mortgagor*) and (*name of mortgagee*), and registered (*give particulars of registration and of any assignment of the mortgage*).

(*Order following report granting no redemption period*)

ON READING the judgment in this action dated (*date*), and the report in this action dated (*date*) and confirmed on (*date*), with proof of service, (*where there is an order fixing a new day for payment, add:* the order for a new day for payment dated (*date*), with proof of service,) (*where a notice of change of account has been delivered, add:* the notice of change of account, with proof of service, and the certificate of the (*title*) of the (*financial institution*) at (*place*), with affidavit of execution,) and the affidavit of the plaintiff, and on hearing the submissions of the lawyer for the plaintiff, and since the defendant(s) entitled to redeem has (have) not redeemed the mortgaged property,

1. IT IS ORDERED that the right, title and equity of redemption of the defendant(s) (*names of those who failed to serve and file a request to redeem, to attend and prove a claim on the reference or to redeem the mortgaged property*) to and in the mortgaged property described in the attached schedule are foreclosed. The mortgage is dated and made between (*name of mortgagor*) and (*name of mortgagee*), and registered (*give particulars of registration and of any assignment of the mortgage*).

(*Order following report granting no redemption period*)

ON READING the judgment in this action dated (*date*) and the report in this action dated (*date*) and confirmed on (*date*), with proof of service, and the affidavit of the plaintiff, and on hearing the submissions of the lawyer for the plaintiff, and since no defendant is entitled to redeem,

1. IT IS ORDERED that the right, title and equity of redemption of the defendant(s) (*names*) to and in the mortgaged property described in the attached schedule are foreclosed. The mortgage is dated .... and made between (*name of mortgagor*) and (*name of mortgagee*), and registered (*give particulars of registration and of any assignment of the mortgage*).

(*Order following redemption of plaintiff by encumbrancer*)

ON READING the judgment in this action dated (*date*), (*where there is a report, add:* the report on the reference in this action dated (*date*) and confirmed on (*date*), with proof of service), the certificate of the (*title*) of the (*financial institution*) at (*place*), with affidavit of execution, and the affidavit of the defendant (*name of defendant who has redeemed*), on hearing the submissions of the lawyer for the defendant, and since the defendant has redeemed the plaintiff, and has obtained an assignment of the judgment and the mortgage and has registered the latter, and since the defendants (*names*) are in default,

1. IT IS ORDERED that the right, title and equity of redemption of the defendant(s) (*names of those who failed to serve and file a request to redeem, to attend and prove a claim on the reference or to redeem the mortgaged property*) to and in the mortgaged property described in the attached schedule and foreclosed. The mortgage is dated .... and made between (*name of mortgagor*) and (*name of mortgagee*), and registered (*give particulars of registration and of any assignment of the mortgage*).

(*Note: the preceding types of order in this form, which are for use in a foreclosure action, may be adapted for a redemption action by substituting "defendant" for "plaintiff" and "plaintiff" for "defendant", whenever those words appear.*)

(*Order following report in redemption action, where necessary to refer back to the master (or as may be) to complete redemption.*)

ON READING the judgment in this action dated (*date*), the report on the reference in this action dated (*date*) and confirmed on (*date*), with proof of service, the certificate of the (*title*) of the (*financial institution*) at (*place*), with affidavit of execution, and the affidavit of the defendant (*name*), and on hearing the submissions of the lawyer for the defendant, and since the plaintiff has failed to redeem (*where there are subsequent encumbrancers and the defendant wishes to foreclose them, add:* and it is necessary to take accounts between the defendants),

1. IT IS ORDERED that the right, title and equity of redemption of the plaintiff to and in the mortgaged property described in the attached schedule are foreclosed. The mortgage is dated .... and made between (*name of mortgagor*) and (*name of mortgagee*), and registered (*give particulars of registration and of any assignment of the mortgage*).

(*Where subsequent encumbrancers are to be foreclosed*)

2. IT IS ORDERED that all necessary inquiries be made, accounts taken, costs fixed or assessed and steps taken for redemption by or foreclosure against any subsequent encumbrancers, and that for these purposes this action be referred to the master (*or as may be*) at (*place*).

(*Where accounts are to be taken*)

3. IT IS ORDERED that all necessary inquiries be made, accounts taken, costs fixed or assessed and steps taken for the adjustment of the respective rights and liabilities of the original defendants.

(*Signature of judge, master or registrar*)

(*The description of the mortgaged property in the attached schedule must be the same as in the statement of claim.*)

July 1, 2007

FORM 64F — REQUEST FOR SALE

Courts of Justice Act

[Repealed O. Reg. 77/06, s. 3.]

[Editor's Note: Forms 4A to 78A of the Rules of Civil Procedure have been repealed by O. Reg. 77/06, effective July 1, 2006. Pursuant to Rule of Civil Procedure 1.06, when a form is referred to by number, the reference is to the form with that number that is described in the Table of Forms at the end of these rules and which is available on the Internet through www.ontariocourtforms.on.ca. For your convenience, the government form as published on this website is reproduced below.]

(*General heading*)

REQUEST FOR SALE

The defendant (*name*) requests a sale of the mortgaged property.

(Where the defendant is a subsequent encumbrancer, add:)

Attached is a certificate of the Accountant of the Superior Court of Justice (*or* the local registrar of the court at (*place*)) stating that the defendant has paid into court the sum of $250 as security for the costs of the plaintiff and of any other party having carriage of the sale.

(*Date*) (*Name, address and telephone number of defendant's lawyer or defendant*)

(*Where the defendant is a subsequent encumbrancer, add:*)

AFFIDAVIT VERIFYING CLAIM

I, (*full name of deponent*), of the (City, Town, *etc.*) of ...., in the (County Regional Municipality, *etc.*) of ...., (*where the deponent if a party or the lawyer, officer, director, member or employee of a party, set out the deponent's capacity*), MAKE OATH AND SAY (*or* AFFIRM):

1. There is now due to me under a mortgage on (*or* an execution against *or* a construction lien registered against *or as may be*) the mortgaged property,

   (a) for principal $..........

   (b) for interest (*set out particulars*) $..........

   (c) (*set out particulars of any other amounts due*) $..........

Total now due $..........

Sworn (*etc.*)

July 1, 2007

FORM 64G — DEFAULT JUDGMENT FOR SALE WITH A REDEMPTION PERIOD (ACTION CONVERTED FROM FORECLOSURE TO SALE)

Courts of Justice Act

[Repealed O. Reg. 77/06, s. 3.]

[Editor's Note: Forms 4A to 78A of the Rules of Civil Procedure have been repealed by O. Reg. 77/06, effective July 1, 2006. Pursuant to Rule of Civil Procedure 1.06, when a form is referred to by number, the reference is to the form with that number that is described in the Table of Forms at the end of these rules and which is available on the Internet through www.ontariocourtforms.on.ca. For your convenience, the government form as published on this website is reproduced below.]

(*General heading*)

(*Court seal*)

JUDGMENT

On reading the statement of claim in this action and the proof of service of the statement of claim on the defendant(s), filed, the defendant (*name*) having served and filed a request for sale, the defendant(s) having been noted in default and the defendant(s) (*name(s)*) having served and filed a request to redeem,

1. IT IS ORDERED AND ADJUDGED that all necessary inquiries be made, accounts taken, costs fixed or assessed and steps taken for redemption or sale of the mortgaged property described in the attached schedule, and that for these purposes this action be referred to the master (*or as may be*) at (*place*).

(*Where judgment is for possession, add:*)

2. IT IS ORDERED AND ADJUDGED that the defendant (*name*) deliver to the plaintiff or as the plaintiff directs possession of the mortgaged property or of such part of it as is in the possession of the defendant.

(*Where judgment is for payment of the mortgage debt and the registrar is to take the account, add the following two paragraphs:*)

3. IT IS ORDERED AND ADJUDGED that the defendant (*name*) forthwith pay to the plaintiff the sum of $ ...., being the amount due to the plaintiff today for principal, interest and costs; and that, on payment of the amount due to the plaintiff before the sale takes place, the plaintiff convey the mortgaged property to the defendant or as the defendant directs, in accordance with section 2 of the *Mortgages Act*, and deliver up all documents relating to the mortgage property.

THIS JUDGMENT BEARS INTEREST at the rate of (*rate claimed in statement of claim*) per cent per year from its date.

(*Where judgment is for payment of the mortgage debt and the plaintiff wishes the account to be taken on reference or the registrar refers the taking of the account, substitute the following two paragraphs:*)

3. IT IS ORDERED AND ADJUDGED that the defendant (*name*) pay to the plaintiff, forthwith after the confirmation of the report on the reference, the amount found due for principal, interest and costs in accordance with the report; and that on payment of the amount due to the plaintiff before the sale takes place, the plaintiff convey the mortgaged property to the defendant or as the defendant directs, in accordance with section 2 of the *Mortgages Act,* and deliver up all documents relating to the mortgage property.

THIS JUDGMENT BEARS INTEREST at the rate set out in the report on the reference from the date of confirmation of the report.

Date .... Signed by ....

Local registrar

Address of court office ....

....

(*The description of the mortgaged property in the attached schedule must be the same as in the statement of claim.*)

November 1, 2005

FORM 64H — DEFAULT JUDGMENT FOR IMMEDIATE SALE (ACTION CONVERTED FROM FORECLOSURE TO SALE)

Courts of Justice Act

[Repealed O. Reg. 77/06, s. 3.]

[Editor's Note: Forms 4A to 78A of the Rules of Civil Procedure have been repealed by O. Reg. 77/06, effective July 1, 2006. Pursuant to Rule of Civil Procedure 1.06, when a form is referred to by number, the reference is to the form with that number that is described in the Table of Forms at the end of these rules and which is available on the Internet through www.ontariocourtforms.on.ca. For your convenience, the government form as published on this website is reproduced below.]

(*General heading*)

(*Court seal*)

JUDGMENT

On reading the statement of claim in this action and the proof of service of the statement of claim on the defendant(s), filed, the defendant (*name*) having served and filed a request for sale, the defendant(s) having been noted in default and no request to redeem having been served and filed (*or* a request to redeem having been served and filed by the defendant (*name of subsequent encumbrancer*)),

1. IT IS ORDERED AND ADJUDGED that all necessary inquiries be made, accounts taken, costs fixed or assessed and steps taken for the immediate sale of the mortgaged property described in the attached schedule without a redemption period, and that for these purposes this action be referred to the master (*or as may be*) at (*place*).

2. IT IS ORDERED AND ADJUDGED that the purchasers pay the purchase money into court to the credit of this action and that the purchase money be applied in payment of what is found due to the plaintiff, together with subsequent interest and subsequent costs to be computed and fixed or assessed by the master (*or as may be*) and that the master (*or as may be*) also determine those parties or persons entitled to the balance of the money and the amounts to which they are entitled.

(*Where judgment is for possession, add:*)

3. IT IS ORDERED AND ADJUDGED that the defendant (*name*) forthwith deliver to the plaintiff or as the plaintiff directs possession of the mortgaged property, or of such part of it as is in the possession of the defendant.

(*Where judgment is for payment of the mortgage debt and the registrar is to take the account, add the following two paragraphs:*)

4. IT IS ORDERED AND ADJUDGED that the defendant (*name*) forthwith pay to the plaintiff the sum of $ ...., being the amount due to the plaintiff today for principal, interest and costs; and that on payment of the amount due to the plaintiff before the sale takes place, the plaintiff convey the mortgaged property to the defendant or as the defendant directs, in accordance with section 2 of the *Mortgages Act*, and deliver up all documents relating to the mortgaged property.

THIS JUDGMENT BEARS INTEREST at the rate of (*rate claimed in the statement of claim*) per cent per year from its date.

(*Where judgment is for payment of the mortgage debt and the plaintiff wishes the account to be taken on the reference or the registrar refers the taking of account, substitute the following two paragraphs:*)

4. IT IS ORDERED AND ADJUDGED that the defendant (*name*) pay to the plaintiff, forthwith after the confirmation of the report on the reference, the amount found due for principal, interest and costs in accordance with the report, and on payment of the amount due to the plaintiff before the sale takes place, the plaintiff convey the mortgaged property to the defendant or as the defendant directs, in accordance with section 2 of the *Mortgages Act,* and deliver up all documents relating to the mortgaged property.

THIS JUDGMENT BEARS INTEREST at the rate set out in the report on the reference from the date of confirmation of the report.

Date .... Signed by ....
Local registrar

Address of court office ....
....

(*The description of the mortgaged property in the attached schedule must be the same as in the statement of claim.*)

November 1, 2005

FORM 64I — DEFAULT JUDGMENT FOR SALE CONDITIONAL ON PROOF OF CLAIM (ACTION CONVERTED FROM FORECLOSURE TO SALE)

Courts of Justice Act

[Repealed O. Reg. 77/06, s. 3.]

[Editor's Note: Forms 4A to 78A of the Rules of Civil Procedure have been repealed by O. Reg. 77/06, effective July 1, 2006. Pursuant to Rule of Civil Procedure 1.06, when a form is referred to by number, the reference is to the form with that number that is described in the Table of Forms at the end of these rules and which is available on the Internet through www.ontariocourtforms.on.ca. For your convenience, the government form as published on this website is reproduced below.]

(*General heading*)

(*Court seal*)

JUDGMENT

On reading the statement of claim in this action and the proof of service of the statement of claim on the defendant(s), filed, no request to redeem having been served and filed (or the defendant (*name*) having served and filed a request to redeem), the defendant(s) having been noted in default, and the defendant (*name of subsequent encumbrancer*) having served and filed a request for sale and having paid into court the sum of $250 as security for costs,

1. IT IS ORDERED AND ADJUDGED that all necessary inquiries be made, accounts taken, costs fixed or assessed and steps taken for redemption or sale of the mortgaged property described in the attached schedule and that for these purposes this action be referred to the master (*or as may be*) at (*place*).

2. IT IS ORDERED AND ADJUDGED that, if the defendant (*name of subsequent encumbrancer*) fails to prove a claim on the reference for sale, the master (*or as may be*) shall proceed as on a reference for redemption or foreclosure.

(*Where judgment is for possession, add:*)

3. IT IS ORDERED AND ADJUDGED that the defendant (*name*) deliver to the plaintiff or as the plaintiff directs possession of the mortgaged property or of such part of it as is in the possession of the defendant.

(*Where judgment is for payment of the mortgage debt and the registrar is to take the account, add the following two paragraphs:*)

4. IT IS ORDERED AND ADJUDGED that the defendant (*name*) forthwith pay to the plaintiff the sum of $ ...., being the amount due to the plaintiff today for principal, interest and costs; and that on payment of the amount due to the plaintiff, the plaintiff convey the mortgaged property to the defendant or as the defendant directs, in accordance with section 2 of the *Mortgages Act,* and deliver up all documents relating to the mortgaged property.

THIS JUDGMENT BEARS INTEREST at the rate of (*rate claimed in statement of claim*) per cent per year from its date.

(*Where judgment is for payment of the mortgage debt and the plaintiff wishes the account to be taken on the reference or the registrar refers the taking of the account, substitute the following two paragraphs:*)

4. IT IS ORDERED AND ADJUDGED that the defendant (*name*) pay to the plaintiff, forthwith after the confirmation of the report on the reference, the amount found due for principal, interest and costs in accordance with the report, and on payment of the amount due to the plaintiff before the sale takes place, the plaintiff convey the mortgaged property to the defendant or as the defendant directs, in accordance with section 2 of the *Mortgages Act,* and deliver up all documents relating to the mortgaged property.

THIS JUDGMENT BEARS INTEREST at the rate set out in the report on the reference from the date of confirmation of the report.

Date .... Signed by ....
Local registrar

Address of court office ....
....

(*The description of the mortgaged property in the attached schedule must be the same as in the statement of claim.*)

November 1, 2005

FORM 64J — DEFAULT JUDGMENT FOR IMMEDIATE SALE

Courts of Justice Act

[Repealed O. Reg. 77/06, s. 3.]

[Editor's Note: Forms 4A to 78A of the Rules of Civil Procedure have been repealed by O. Reg. 77/06, effective July 1, 2006. Pursuant to Rule of Civil Procedure 1.06, when a form is referred to by number, the reference is to the form with that number that is described in the Table of Forms at the end of these rules and which is available on the Internet through www.ontariocourtforms.on.ca. For your convenience, the government form as published on this website is reproduced below.]

(*General heading*)

(*Court seal*)

JUDGMENT

On reading the statement of claim in this action and the proof of service of the statement of claim on the defendant(s), filed, no request to redeem having been served and filed and the defendant(s) having been noted in default,

1. IT IS ORDERED AND ADJUDGED that all necessary inquiries be made, accounts taken, costs fixed or assessed and steps taken for the immediate sale of the mortgaged property described in the attached schedule without a redemption period, and that for these purposes this action be referred to the master (*or as may be*) at (*place*).

2. IT IS ORDERED AND ADJUDGED that the purchasers pay the purchase money into court to the credit of this action and that the purchase money be applied in payment of what

is found due to the plaintiff, together with subsequent interest and subsequent costs to be computed and fixed or assessed by the master (*or as may be*) and that the master (*or as may be*) also determine those parties or persons entitled to the balance of the money and the amounts to which they are entitled.

(*Where judgment is for possession, add:*)

3. IT IS ORDERED AND ADJUDGED that the defendant (*name*) forthwith deliver to the plaintiff or as the plaintiff directs possession of the mortgaged property, or of such part of it as is in the possession of the defendant.

(*Where judgment is for payment of the mortgage debt and the registrar is to take the account, add the following two paragraphs:*)

4. IT IS ORDERED AND ADJUDGED that the defendant (*name*) forthwith pay to the plaintiff the sum of $ ...., being the amount due to the plaintiff today for principal, interest and costs; and that on payment of the amount due to the plaintiff before the sale takes place, the plaintiff convey the mortgaged property to the defendant or as the defendant directs, in accordance with section 2 of the *Mortgages Act*, and deliver up all documents relating to the mortgaged property.

THIS JUDGMENT BEARS INTEREST at the rate of (*rate claimed in statement of claim*) per cent per year from its date.

(*Where judgment is for payment of the mortgage debt and the plaintiff wishes the account to be taken on the reference or the registrar refers the taking of the account, substitute the following two paragraphs:*)

4. IT IS ORDERED AND ADJUDGED that the defendant (*name*) pay to the plaintiff, forthwith after the confirmation of the report on the reference, the amount found due for principal, interest and costs in accordance with the report, and on payment of the amount due to the plaintiff before the sale takes place, the plaintiff convey the mortgaged property to the defendant or as the defendant directs, in accordance with section 2 of the *Mortgages Act*, and deliver up all documents relating to the mortgaged property.

THIS JUDGMENT BEARS INTEREST at the rate set out in the report on the reference from the date of confirmation of the report.

Date .... Signed by ....
Local registrar

Address of court office ....
....

(*The description of the mortgaged property in the attached schedule must be the same as in the statement of claim.*)

November 1, 2005

FORM 64K — DEFAULT JUDGMENT FOR SALE WITH A REDEMPTION PERIOD

Courts of Justice Act

[Repealed O. Reg. 77/06, s. 3.]

[Editor's Note: Forms 4A to 78A of the Rules of Civil Procedure have been repealed by O. Reg. 77/06, effective July 1, 2006. Pursuant to Rule of Civil Procedure 1.06, when a form is referred to by number, the reference is to the form with that number that is described in the Table of Forms at the end of these rules and which is available on the Internet through www.ontariocourtforms.on.ca. For your convenience, the government form as published on this website is reproduced below.]

(*General heading*)

(*Court seal*)

JUDGMENT

On reading the statement of claim in this action and the proof of service of the statement of claim on the defendant(s), filed, the defendant(s) having been noted in default and the defendant (*name*) having served and filed a request to redeem,

1. IT IS ORDERED AND ADJUDGED that all necessary inquiries be made, accounts taken, costs fixed or assessed and steps taken for redemption or sale of the mortgaged property described in the attached schedule, and that for these purposes this action be referred to the master (*or as may be*) at (*place*).

(*Where judgment is for possession, add:*)

2. IT IS ORDERED AND ADJUDGED that the defendant (*name*) deliver to the plaintiff or as the plaintiff directs possession of the mortgaged property or of such part of it as is in the possession of the defendant.

(*Where judgment is for payment of the mortgage debt and the registrar is to take the account, add the following two paragraphs:*)

3. IT IS ORDERED AND ADJUDGED that the defendant (*name*) forthwith pay to the plaintiff the sum of $ ...., being the amount due to the plaintiff today for principal, interest and costs; and on payment of the amount due to the plaintiff before the sale takes place, the plaintiff convey the mortgaged property to the defendant(s) or as the defendant directs, in accordance with section 2 of the *Mortgages Act*, and deliver up all documents relating to the mortgaged property.

THIS JUDGMENT BEARS INTEREST at the rate of (*rate claimed in statement of claim*) per cent per year from its date.

(*Where judgment is for payment of the mortgage debt and the plaintiff wishes the account to be taken on the reference or the registrar refers the taking of the account, substitute the following two paragraphs:*)

3. IT IS ORDERED AND ADJUDGED that the defendant (*name*) pay to the plaintiff(s), forthwith after confirmation of the report on the reference, the amount found due for principal, interest and costs in accordance with the report; and that on payment of the amount due to the plaintiff before the sale takes place, the plaintiff convey the mortgaged property to the defendant or as the defendant directs, in accordance with section 2 of the *Mortgages Act*, and deliver up all documents relating to the mortgaged property.

THIS JUDGMENT BEARS INTEREST at the rate set out in the report on the reference from the date of confirmation of the report.

Date .... Signed by ....

Local registrar

Address of court office ....

....

(*The description of the mortgaged property in the attached schedule must be the same as in the statement of claim.*)

November 1, 2005

FORM 64L — FINAL ORDER FOR SALE

Courts of Justice Act

[Repealed O. Reg. 77/06, s. 3.]

[Editor's Note: Forms 4A to 78A of the Rules of Civil Procedure have been repealed by O. Reg. 77/06, effective July 1, 2006. Pursuant to Rule of Civil Procedure 1.06, when a form is referred to by number, the reference is to the form with that number that is described in the Table of Forms at the end of these rules and which is available on the Internet through www.ontariocourtforms.on.ca. For your convenience, the government form as published on this website is reproduced below.]

(*Court*)

(*Court file no.*)

(*Name of judge or officer*) (*Day and date*)

(*Court seal*) (*Title of proceeding*)

FINAL ORDER FOR SALE

THIS MOTION made by the plaintiff, without notice, was heard this day.

ON READING the judgment in this action dated (*date*), and the report in this action dated (*date*) and confirmed on (*date*), with proof of service, the certificate of the (*title*) of the (*financial institution*) at (*place*), with affidavit of execution, and the affidavit of the plaintiff, and on hearing the submissions of the lawyer for the plaintiff, and since the defendant(s) entitled to redeem has (have) not redeemed the mortgaged property,

1. IT IS ORDERED that the mortgaged property described in the attached schedule be sold forthwith as directed by the judgment in this action under the direction of the master (*or as may be*) at (*place*).

(*Where appropriate, add:*)

2. IT IS ORDERED that the right, title and equity of redemption of the defendants (*names of subsequent encumbrancers who failed to attend and prove a claim on the reference*) to and in the mortgaged property described in the attached schedule are foreclosed.

(*Signature of judge, master or registrar*)

(*The description of the mortgaged property in the attached schedule must be the same as in the statement of claim.*)

July 1, 2007

FORM 64M — DEFAULT JUDGMENT FOR REDEMPTION

Courts of Justice Act

[Repealed O. Reg. 77/06, s. 3.]

[Editor's Note: Forms 4A to 78A of the Rules of Civil Procedure have been repealed by O. Reg. 77/06, effective July 1, 2006. Pursuant to Rule of Civil Procedure 1.06, when a form is referred to by number, the reference is to the form with that number that is described in the Table of Forms at the end of these rules and which is available on the Internet through www.ontariocourtforms.on.ca. For your convenience, the government form as published on this website is reproduced below.]

(*General heading*)

(*Court seal*)

JUDGMENT

On reading the statement of claim in this action and the proof of service of the statement of claim on the defendant(s), filed, and the defendant(s) having been noted in default,

1. IT IS ORDERED AND ADJUDGED that all necessary inquiries be made, accounts taken, costs fixed or assessed and steps taken for the redemption of the mortgaged property described in the attached schedule, and that for this purpose this action be referred to the master (*or as may be*) at (*place*).

2. IT IS ORDERED AND ADJUDGED that, on the plaintiff paying to the defendant (*name of mortgagee*) the amount found due on the mortgage in question, or, if nothing is found due, then forthwith after the confirmation of the report on the reference, the defendant convey the mortgaged property to the plaintiff or as the plaintiff directs, in accordance with section 2 of the *Mortgages Act*, and deliver up all documents relating to the mortgaged property.

3. IT IS ORDERED AND ADJUDGED that if the plaintiff defaults in payment of the amount found due to the defendant (*name of mortgagee*), the defendant is entitled, on motion without notice, to a final order of foreclosure against the plaintiff or to an order dismissing the action with costs.

4. IT IS ORDERED AND ADJUDGED that if nothing is found due to the defendant (*name of mortgagee*), the defendant pay the plaintiff's costs of this action and, if any balance is found due from the defendant (*name of mortgagee*) to the plaintiff, that the defendant pay the balance to the plaintiff forthwith after confirmation of the report on the reference.

THIS JUDGMENT BEARS INTEREST at the rate set out in the report on the reference from the date of confirmation of the report.

Date .... Signed by ....

Local registrar

Address of court office ....

....

(*The description of the mortgaged property in the attached schedule must be the same as in the statement of claim.*)

November 1, 2005

FORM 64N — NOTICE OF REFERENCE TO SUBSEQUENT ENCUMBRANCER ADDED ON REFERENCE

Courts of Justice Act

[Repealed O. Reg. 77/06, s. 3.]

[Editor's Note: Forms 4A to 78A of the Rules of Civil Procedure have been repealed by O. Reg. 77/06, effective July 1, 2006. Pursuant to Rule of Civil Procedure 1.06, when a form is referred to by number, the reference is to the form with that number that is described in the Table of Forms at the end of these rules and which is available on the Internet through www.ontariocourtforms.on.ca. For your convenience, the government form as published on this website is reproduced below.]

ONTARIO (*Court file no.*)

SUPERIOR COURT OF JUSTICE

BETWEEN:

(*name*)

Plaintiff

and

(*name(s)*)

Defendant(s)

and

(*name(s)*)

Defendant(s) added on the reference

NOTICE OF REFERENCE

An action has been commenced by the plaintiff for the foreclosure (*or* sale) of the mortgaged property described in the attached schedule. I have been directed by the judgment in this action dated (*date*) (*where the judgment is for sale, insert:* to conduct a sale of the property and) to inquire whether any person other than the plaintiff has a lien, charge or encumbrance on the property subsequent to the plaintiff's claim. It appears that you may have a lien, charge or encumbrance on the property. I have therefore added you as a defendant in this action.

YOU ARE REQUIRED TO APPEAR before me and prove your claim, either in person or by an Ontario lawyer acting for you, on (*day*), (*date*), at (*time*), at (*address*). At that time, I shall determine the amount of the claim of the plaintiff, and of the encumbrancers who prove their claims before me. (*Where the judgment is for sale without a redemption period, add:* At the same time, I shall settle the conditions of sale and advertisement and make any other necessary preparations for the sale of the property.)

If you wish to set aside or vary my order adding you as a defendant or the judgment in this action, you must make a motion to the court within ten days after service on you of this notice (*or where the person is to be served outside Ontario, such further time as the referee directs*). If you fail to do so, you will be bound by the judgment and the subsequent steps in this action.

IF YOU FAIL TO ATTEND AND PROVE YOUR CLAIM at the time and place set out above, you will be treated as disclaiming all interest in the property and the action will proceed in your absence and without further notice to you. The property may be dealt with as if you had no claim, and your claim may be foreclosed.

(*Date*) (*Signature of referee*)

TO (*Names and addresses of defendants added on reference who appear to be subsequent encumbrancers*)

(*The description of the mortgaged property in the attached schedule must be the same as in the statement of claim.*)

November 1, 2005

FORM 64O — NOTICE OF REFERENCE TO SUBSEQUENT ENCUMBRANCER NAMED AS ORIGINAL PARTY

Courts of Justice Act

[Repealed O. Reg. 77/06, s. 3.]

[Editor's Note: Forms 4A to 78A of the Rules of Civil Procedure have been repealed by O. Reg. 77/06, effective July 1, 2006. Pursuant to Rule of Civil Procedure 1.06, when a form is referred to by number, the reference is to the form with that number that is described in the Table of Forms at the end of these rules and which is available on the Internet through www.ontariocourtforms.on.ca. For your convenience, the government form as published on this website is reproduced below.]

ONTARIO (*Court file no.*)
SUPERIOR COURT OF JUSTICE

BETWEEN:

(*name*)

Plaintiff

and

(*name*)

Defendant(*s*)

and

(*name(s)*)

Defendant(*s*) added on the reference

NOTICE OF REFERENCE

The judgment in this action directs me (*where the judgment is for sale, insert:* to conduct a sale of the mortgaged property and) to inquire whether any person other than the plaintiff has a lien, charge or encumbrance on the mortgaged property in question in this action subsequent to the plaintiff's claim, and to take an account of the amount due to the plaintiff and any such person. It appears that you may have a lien, charge or encumbrance on the property.

YOU ARE REQUIRED TO APPEAR before me and prove your claim, either in person or by an Ontario lawyer acting for you, on (*day*), (*date*), at (*time*), at (*address*). At that time, I shall determine the amount of the claim of the plaintiff, and of the encumbrancers who prove their claims before me. (*Where the judgment is for sale without redemption period, add:* At the same time, I shall settle the conditions of sale and advertisement and make any other necessary preparations for the sale of the property.)

IF YOU FAIL TO ATTEND AND PROVE YOUR CLAIM at the time and place set out above, you will be treated as disclaiming any lien, charged or encumbrance on the property and the action will proceed in your absence and without further notice to you. The property may be dealt with as if you had no such claim and your claim may be foreclosed.

(*Date*) (*Signature of referee*)

TO (*Names and addresses of defendants named in statement of claim who appear to be subsequent encumbrancers*)

November 1, 2005

FORM 64P — NOTICE OF REFERENCE TO ORIGINAL DEFENDANTS

Courts of Justice Act

[Repealed O. Reg. 77/06, s. 3.]

[Editor's Note: Forms 4A to 78A of the Rules of Civil Procedure have been repealed by O. Reg. 77/06, effective July 1, 2006. Pursuant to Rule of Civil Procedure 1.06, when a form is referred to by number, the reference is to the form with that number that is described in the Table of Forms at the end of these rules and which is available on the Internet through www.ontariocourtforms.on.ca. For your convenience, the government form as published on this website is reproduced below.]

ONTARIO (*Court file no.*)
SUPERIOR COURT OF JUSTICE

BETWEEN:

(*name*)

Plaintiff

and

(*name(s)*)

Defendant(*s*)

and
(*name(s)*)

Defendant(*s*) added
on the reference

NOTICE OF REFERENCE

The judgment in this action directs me (*where the judgment is for sale, insert:* to conduct a sale of the mortgaged property and) to inquire whether any person other than the plaintiff has a lien, charge or encumbrance on the mortgaged property in question in this action subsequent to the plaintiff's claim, and to take an account due to the plaintiff and any such person.

It appears that the persons named in the attached schedule may have a lien, charge or encumbrance on the property (*where the judgment directs the referee to add encumbrancers, add:* and I have therefore added as defendants those persons who were not already parties to this action).

YOU ARE REQUIRED TO APPEAR before me and prove your claim, either in person or by an Ontario lawyer acting for you, on (*day*), (*date*), at (*time*), at (*address*). At that time, I shall determine whether any of the parties have a lien, charge or encumbrance on the property and ascertain the amount of those claims and of the plaintiff's claim. (*Where the judgment is for sale without a redemption period, add:* At the same time, I shall settle the conditions of sale and advertisement and make any other necessary arrangements for the sale.)

(*Where the judgment is for sale conditional on proof of a claim by a subsequent encumbrancer, add:* The defendant (*name of subsequent encumbrancer*) has requested a sale of the property. If the defendant fails to attend and prove a claim before me, there will not be a sale of the property, and the claims of those who fail to appear before me may be foreclosed.)

IF YOU FAIL TO ATTEND at the time and place set out above, the action will proceed in your absence without further notice to you and your rights in the property may be foreclosed.

If you are a subsequent encumbrancer and fail to attend and prove your claim at the time and place set out above, you will be treated as disclaiming any lien, charge or encumbrance on the property, the property may be dealt with as if you had no such claim and your claim may be foreclosed.

(*Date*) (*Signature of referee*)

TO (*Names and addresses of defendants named in statement of claim*)

SCHEDULE OF ENCUMBRANCERS

Name of encumbrancer	Nature of encumbrance	Instrument no.	Date of instrument	Date of registration

November 1, 2005

FORM 64Q — NOTICE TO ADDED DEFENDANT HAVING INTEREST IN EQUITY

Courts of Justice Act

[Repealed O. Reg. 77/06, s. 3.]

[Editor's Note: Forms 4A to 78A of the Rules of Civil Procedure have been repealed by O. Reg. 77/06, effective July 1, 2006. Pursuant to Rule of Civil Procedure 1.06, when a form is referred to by number, the reference is to the form with that number that is described in the Table of Forms at the end of these rules and which is available on the Internet through www.ontariocourtforms.on.ca. For your convenience, the government form as published on this website is reproduced below.]

ONTARIO (*Court file no.*)
SUPERIOR COURT OF JUSTICE

BETWEEN:

(*name*)

Plaintiff

and

(*name(s)*)

Defendant(s)

and

(*name(s)*)

Defendant(s) added
on the reference

NOTICE TO ADDED DEFENDANT

An action has been commenced by the plaintiff for the foreclosure (*or* sale) of the mortgaged property described in the attached schedule. I have been directed by the judgment in this action dated (*date*) (*where the judgment is for sale, insert:* to conduct a sale of the property and) to inquire whether any person other than the plaintiff has a lien, charge or encumbrance on the property subsequent to the plaintiff's claim or whether any other person has an interest in the property. It appears that you may have an interest in the property. I have therefore added you as a defendant in this action. A copy of my order and the judgment in the action are attached to this notice.

If you wish to set aside or vary my order adding you as a defendant or the judgment in this action, you must make a motion to the court within ten days after service on you of this notice (*or where the defendant is to be served outside Ontario, such further time as the referee directs*). If you fail to do so, you will be bound by the judgment and the subsequent steps in this action.

IF YOU WISH AN OPPORTUNITY TO REDEEM the property, you are required to appear before me, either in person or by an Ontario lawyer acting for you, on (*day*), (*date*), at (*time*), at (*address*).

IF YOU FAIL TO ATTEND at the time and place set out above, you may be deemed to submit to an immediate foreclosure of your interest (*or* an immediate sale of the property) and the action may proceed in your absence and without further notice to you.

(*Date*) (*Signature of referee*)

TO *(Names and addresses of defendants added on reference who appear to be interested in equity of redemption)*

(The description of the mortgaged property in the attached schedule must be the same as in the statement of claim.)

November 1, 2005

FORM 65A — JUDGMENT FOR ADMINISTRATION OF ESTATE

Courts of Justice Act

[Repealed O. Reg. 77/06, s. 3.]

[Editor's Note: Forms 4A to 78A of the Rules of Civil Procedure have been repealed by O. Reg. 77/06, effective July 1, 2006. Pursuant to Rule of Civil Procedure 1.06, when a form is referred to by number, the reference is to the form with that number that is described in the Table of Forms at the end of these rules and which is available on the Internet through www.ontariocourtforms.on.ca. For your convenience, the government form as published on this website is reproduced below.]

(Court)

(Court file no.)

(Name of judge or officer) *(Day and date judgment given)*

(Court seal) *(Title of proceeding)*

JUDGMENT

(Recitals in accordance with Form 59B)

1. THIS COURT ORDERS AND ADJUDGES that all necessary inquiries be made, accounts taken, costs assessed and steps taken by the master (*or as may be*) at (*place*) for the administration and final winding up of the estate of (*name of deceased*) and for the adjustment of the rights of all parties interested in the property.

2. THIS COURT ORDERS AND ADJUDGES that any balance found due from the applicant or the respondent(s) to the estate be paid into court to the credit of this proceeding, subject to further order of the court.

3. THIS COURT ORDERS AND ADJUDGES that the property of the estate or such parts of it as the referee directs be sold as the referee directs and that the purchasers pay the purchase money into court to the credit of this proceeding, subject to the order of the court.

4. THIS COURT ORDERS AND ADJUDGES that the referee execute transfers for any party who is a minor.

(*Signature of judge or registrar*)

November 1, 2005

FORM 66A — JUDGMENT FOR PARTITION OR SALE

Courts of Justice Act

[Repealed O. Reg. 77/06, s. 3.]

[Editor's Note: Forms 4A to 78A of the Rules of Civil Procedure have been repealed by O. Reg. 77/06, effective July 1, 2006. Pursuant to Rule of Civil Procedure 1.06, when a form is referred to by number, the reference is to the form with that number that is described in the Table of Forms at the end of these rules and which is available on the Internet through www.ontariocourtforms.on.ca. For your convenience, the government form as published on this website is reproduced below.]

(*Court*)

(*Court file no.*)

(*Name of judge or officer*) (*Day and date judgment given*)

(*Court seal*) (*Title of proceeding*)

JUDGMENT

(*Recitals in accordance with Form 59B*)

1. THIS COURT ORDERS AND ADJUDGES that all necessary inquiries be made, accounts taken, costs assessed and steps taken by the master (*or as may be*) at (*place*) for the partition or sale, or for the partition of part and sale of the remainder, of the land described in the attached schedule in accordance with the interests of the parties entitled to share in it.

2. THIS COURT ORDERS AND ADJUDGES that the land, or such part of it as the referee thinks fit, be sold under the direction of the referee, free of the claims of encumbrancers, if any, who have consented to the sale, and subject to the claims of encumbrancers who have not consented to the sale, and that the purchaser pay the purchase money into court to the credit of this proceeding, subject to the order of the court.

3. THIS COURT ORDERS AND ADJUDGES that the referee execute a transfer for any party who is a minor.

4. THIS COURT ORDERS AND ADJUDGES that, if the land is partitioned or if part of the land is partitioned and the proceeds of the sale of the remainder are insufficient to pay the costs in full, the unpaid costs be paid by the parties according to their interests in the land (*where there are parties who are minors, add:* and that the portion of the costs payable by the parties who are minors be a lien on their respective shares, and that the plaintiff (*or*

applicant) pay the costs of their litigation guardian and that those costs be added to the plaintiff's (*or* applicant's) costs.)

(*Signature of judge, officer or registrar*)

November 1, 2005

FORM 68A — NOTICE OF APPLICATION TO DIVISIONAL COURT FOR JUDICIAL REVIEW

Courts of Justice Act

[Repealed O. Reg. 77/06, s. 3.]

[Editor's Note: Forms 4A to 78A of the Rules of Civil Procedure have been repealed by O. Reg. 77/06, effective July 1, 2006. Pursuant to Rule of Civil Procedure 1.06, when a form is referred to by number, the reference is to the form with that number that is described in the Table of Forms at the end of these rules and which is available on the Internet through www.ontariocourtforms.on.ca. For your convenience, the government form as published on this website is reproduced below.]

(General heading)

(Court seal)

NOTICE OF APPLICATION TO DIVISIONAL COURT FOR JUDICIAL REVIEW

TO THE RESPONDENT

A LEGAL PROCEEDING HAS BEEN COMMENCED by the applicant. The claim made by the applicant appears on the following page.

THIS APPLICATION for judicial review will come on for a hearing before the Divisional Court on a date to be fixed by the registrar at the place of hearing requested by the applicant. The applicant requests that this application be heard at .... *(place where a Divisional Court sitting is scheduled).*

IF YOU WISH TO OPPOSE THIS APPLICATION, to receive notice of any step in the application or to be served with any documents in the application, you or an Ontario lawyer acting for you must forthwith prepare a notice of appearance in Form 38A prescribed by the *Rules of Civil Procedure*, serve it on the applicant's lawyer or, where the applicant does not have a lawyer, serve it on the applicant, and file it, with proof of service, in the office of the Divisional Court, and you or your lawyer must appear at the hearing.

IF YOU WISH TO PRESENT AFFIDAVIT OR OTHER DOCUMENTARY EVIDENCE TO THE COURT OR TO EXAMINE OR CROSS-EXAMINE WITNESSES ON THE APPLICATION, you or your lawyer must, in addition to serving your notice of appearance, serve a copy of the evidence on the applicant's lawyer or, where the applicant does not have a lawyer, serve it on the applicant, and file it, with proof of service, in the office of the

Divisional Court within thirty days after service on you of the applicant's application record, or not later than 2 p.m. on the day before the hearing, whichever is earlier.

IF YOU FAIL TO APPEAR AT THE HEARING, JUDGMENT MAY BE GIVEN IN YOUR ABSENCE AND WITHOUT FURTHER NOTICE TO YOU. IF YOU WISH TO DEFEND THIS PROCEEDING BUT ARE UNABLE TO PAY LEGAL FEES, LEGAL AID MAY BE AVAILABLE TO YOU BY CONTACTING A LOCAL LEGAL AID OFFICE.

Date ....

Issued by ....
Registrar ....
Address of court office
....

TO *(Name and address of each respondent)* ....

AND TO

Attorney General of Ontario *(as required by subsection 9(4) of the Judicial Review Procedure Act)*

Crown Law Office — Civil

720 Bay Street

8th Floor

Toronto, Ontario M5G 2K1

APPLICATION

1. The applicant makes application for: *(State here the precise relief claimed.)* ....

2. The grounds for the application are: *(Specify the grounds to be argued, including a reference to any statutory provision to be relied on.)* ....

(Where the notice of application is to be served outside Ontario without a court order, state the facts and the specific provisions of Rule 17 relied on in support of such service.) ....

3. The following documentary evidence will be used at the hearing of the application: *(List the affidavits or other documentary evidence to be relied on.)* ....

(Date) .... *(Name, address and telephone number of applicant's lawyer or applicant)* ....

July 1, 2007

FORM 68B — NOTICE OF LISTING FOR HEARING (JUDICIAL REVIEW)

Courts of Justice Act

[Repealed O. Reg. 77/06, s. 3.]

[Editor's Note: Forms 4A to 78A of the Rules of Civil Procedure have been repealed by O. Reg. 77/06, effective July 1, 2006. Pursuant to Rule of Civil Procedure 1.06, when a form is referred to by number, the reference is to the form with that number that is described in the Table of Forms at the end of these rules and which is available on the Internet through www.ontariocourtforms.on.ca. For your convenience, the government form as published on this website is reproduced below.]

(*General heading*)

NOTICE OF LISTING FOR HEARING

THIS APPLICATION FOR JUDICIAL REVIEW HAS BEEN PERFECTED and has been listed for hearing at (*place*). You may ascertain from my office the approximate date of hearing.

Date . . . . Signed by . . . .

Registrar of the Divisional Court
(*Address of court office*)

TO (*Name and address of every person listed in the certificate of perfection*)

November 1, 2005

FORM 68C — ORDER DISMISSING APPLICATION FOR JUDICIAL REVIEW

Courts of Justice Act

[Repealed O. Reg. 77/06, s. 3.]

[Editor's Note: Forms 4A to 78A of the Rules of Civil Procedure have been repealed by O. Reg. 77/06, effective July 1, 2006. Pursuant to Rule of Civil Procedure 1.06, when a form is referred to by number, the reference is to the form with that number that is described in the Table of Forms at the end of these rules and which is available on the Internet through www.ontariocourtforms.on.ca. For your convenience, the government form as published on this website is reproduced below.]

Courts of Justice Act

(*General heading*)

(*Court seal*)

ORDER DISMISSING APPLICATION FOR JUDICIAL REVIEW

The applicant has not *(give particulars of applicant's default under rule 68.06)* and has not cured the default, although given notice under rule 68.06 to do so.

1. IT IS ORDERED that this application be dismissed for delay, with costs fixed at $750, despite rule 58.13.

Date .... Signed by ....

Registrar of the Divisional Court

(Address of court office)

July 30, 2009

FORM 72A — NOTICE OF PAYMENT INTO COURT

Courts of Justice Act

[Repealed O. Reg. 77/06, s. 3.]

[Editor's Note: Forms 4A to 78A of the Rules of Civil Procedure have been repealed by O. Reg. 77/06, effective July 1, 2006. Pursuant to Rule of Civil Procedure 1.06, when a form is referred to by number, the reference is to the form with that number that is described in the Table of Forms at the end of these rules and which is available on the Internet through www.ontariocourtforms.on.ca. For your convenience, the government form as published on this website is reproduced below.]

(*General heading*)

NOTICE OF PAYMENT INTO COURT

The (*identify party*) paid into court on (*date*) the sum of $ .... under the offer to settle (*or acceptance of offer*) dated (*date*).

(*Date*) (*Name, address and telephone number of lawyer or party giving notice*)

TO (*Name and address of lawyer or party receiving notice*)

July 1, 2007

FORM 72B — AFFIDAVIT (MOTION FOR PAYMENT OUT OF COURT)

Courts of Justice Act

[Repealed O. Reg. 77/06, s. 3.]

[Editor's Note: Forms 4A to 78A of the Rules of Civil Procedure have been repealed by O. Reg. 77/06, effective July 1, 2006. Pursuant to Rule of Civil Procedure 1.06, when a form is referred to by number, the reference is to the form with that number that is described in the Table of Forms at the end of these rules and which is available on the Internet through www.ontariocourtforms.on.ca. For your convenience, the government form as published on this website is reproduced below.]

(*General heading*)

AFFIDAVIT

I, (*full name of deponent*) of the (City, Town, *etc.*) of ...., in the (County, Regional Municipality, *etc.*) of ...., (*where the deponent is a party or the lawyer, officer, director, member or employee of a party, set out the deponent's capacity*), MAKE OATH AND SAY (*or* AFFIRM):

1. This affidavit is filed in support of a motion for payment out of court of money belonging to (*name of person under disability*), of (*address*), who is (*state the nature of the disability*) and who was born on (*date*).

2. I am (*state the deponent's connection with the person under disability*).

3. The Accountant (*or* local registrar at (*place*)) has informed me that the sum of $ ...., including interest accrued to (*date*), is in court. There has been previously paid out the sum of $ .... on (*date*) (*or as may be*).

4. It is proposed that the sum of $ .... be paid out of court to (*name*) for the following purpose: (*Give particulars.*)

5. I believe that this expenditure is justified for the following reasons: (*Give particulars.*)

Sworn, etc.

July 1, 2007

FORM 72C — STOP ORDER

Courts of Justice Act

[Repealed O. Reg. 77/06, s. 3.]

[Editor's Note: Forms 4A to 78A of the Rules of Civil Procedure have been repealed by O. Reg. 77/06, effective July 1, 2006. Pursuant to Rule of Civil Procedure 1.06, when a form is referred to by number, the reference is to the form with that number that is described in the

Table of Forms at the end of these rules and which is available on the Internet through www.ontariocourtforms.on.ca. For your convenience, the government form as published on this website is reproduced below.]

(*Court file no.*)

(*Court*)

(*Name of judge or officer*) (*Day and date order made*)

(*Court seal*) (*Title of Proceeding*)

ORDER

(*Recitals in accordance with Form 59A or 59B, followed by:*) the (*identify applicant or moving party*) having undertaken through their lawyer to be bound by any order this court makes in respect of costs or damages caused by this order,

1. THIS COURT ORDERS that all money and securities held by the Accountant (*or* local registrar at (*place*)) in this proceeding now or in the future, together with any interest, to which (*identify party*) is or becomes entitled shall not be dealt with except on notice to (*identify applicant or moving party*).

(*Signature of judge or officer*)

July 1, 2007

FORM 73A — NOTICE OF APPLICATION FOR REGISTRATION OF UNITED KINGDOM JUDGMENT

Courts of Justice Act

[Repealed O. Reg. 77/06, s. 3.]

[Editor's Note: Forms 4A to 78A of the Rules of Civil Procedure have been repealed by O. Reg. 77/06, effective July 1, 2006. Pursuant to Rule of Civil Procedure 1.06, when a form is referred to by number, the reference is to the form with that number that is described in the Table of Forms at the end of these rules and which is available on the Internet through www.ontariocourtforms.on.ca. For your convenience, the government form as published on this website is reproduced below.]

(*General heading*)

(*Court seal*)

NOTICE OF APPLICATION

To the Respondent

A LEGAL PROCEEDING HAS BEEN COMMENCED by the applicant for registration and enforcement in Ontario of a judgment granted against you by a court in the United Kingdom. The claim made by the applicant appears on the following pages.

THIS APPLICATION will come on for a hearing on (*day*), (*date*), at (*time*), at (*address of court house*).

IF YOU WISH TO OPPOSE THIS APPLICATION, to receive notice of any step in the application or to be served with any documents in the application, you or an Ontario lawyer acting for you must forthwith prepare a notice of appearance in Form 38A prescribed by the Rules of Civil Procedure, serve it on the applicant's lawyer or, where the applicant does not have a lawyer, serve it on the applicant, and file it, with proof of service, in this court office, and you or your lawyer must appear at the hearing.

IF YOU WISH TO PRESENT AFFIDAVIT OR OTHER DOCUMENTARY EVIDENCE TO THE COURT OR TO EXAMINE OR CROSS-EXAMINE WITNESSES ON THE APPLICATION, you or your lawyer must, in addition to serving your notice of appearance, serve a copy of the evidence on the applicant's lawyer or, where the applicant does not have a lawyer, serve it on the applicant, and file it, with proof of service, in the court office where the application is to be heard, as soon as possible, but not later than 2 p.m. on the day before the hearing.

IF YOU FAIL TO APPEAR AT THE HEARING, THE UNITED KINGDOM JUDGMENT MAY BE REGISTERED AND ENFORCED AGAINST YOU WITHOUT FURTHER NOTICE.

Date .... Issued by ....

Local registrar

Address of court office ....

....

TO (*Name and address of each respondent*)

APPLICATION

1. The applicant applies under the *Reciprocal Enforcement of Judgments (U.K.) Act* for registration of the following judgment of a court in the United Kingdom:

(a) Name of court ....

(b) Plaintiff (*or* applicant) ....

....

(c) Defendant (*or* respondent) ....

....

(d) Date of judgment ....

(e) Amount awarded, in the currency of the judgment, in favour of each plaintiff (*or* applicant) and against each defendant (*or* respondent)

Judgment in favour of	Judgment against	Amount of judgment	Amount awarded for costs

. . . .

(f) Post judgment interest

Rate . . . . per year

Commencing on (*date*) . . . .

Payable on (*principal amount*) . . . .

(g) Amount unpaid, in the currency of the judgment, to each plaintiff (*or* applicant) and by each defendant (*or* respondent)

Payable to	Payable by	Amount unpaid on judgment, including interest	Amount unpaid on award of costs, including interest

. . . .

. . . .

2. The grounds for the application are:

(a) The judgment is one to which the Act and the Convention appearing as a schedule to the Act apply.

(b) The Act and the Convention do not preclude registration of the judgment.

(c) The defendant (*or* respondent) ( ) appeared

( ) did not appear

before the United Kingdom court that granted the judgment.

(*If the defendant (or respondent) did not appear, explain in detail why registration is nevertheless permitted under the Reciprocal Enforcement of Judgments (U.K.) Act.*)

(d) The applicant is entitled to register and enforce the judgment as,

( ) a plaintiff (*or* applicant) named in the judgment

( ) an assignee of the judgment

( ) other (*specify*) . . . .

. . . .

3. The following documentary evidence is relied on in support of the application:

(a) the original or a certified copy of the judgment;

(b) the affidavit of . . . .

(c) the original or a certified copy of proof of service of the originating process of the United Kingdom court.

4. The respondent in this application resides at:

. . . .

(*Date of issue*) (*Name, address and telephone number of lawyer or applicant*)

July 1, 2007

FORM 74.1 — NOTICE TO ESTATE REGISTRAR OF DEPOSIT OF WILL OR CODICIL

Courts of Justice Act

[Repealed O. Reg. 77/06, s. 3.]

[Editor's Note: Forms 4A to 78A of the Rules of Civil Procedure have been repealed by O. Reg. 77/06, effective July 1, 2006. Pursuant to Rule of Civil Procedure 1.06, when a form is referred to by number, the reference is to the form with that number that is described in the Table of Forms at the end of these rules and which is available on the Internet through www.ontariocourtforms.on.ca. For your convenience, the government form as published on this website is reproduced below.]

ONTARIO

SUPERIOR COURT OF JUSTICE

NOTICE

TO THE ESTATE REGISTRAR FOR ONTARIO:

A will or codicil has been deposited in this office. Particulars of the document follow.

DETAILS ABOUT THE TESTATOR

Complete in full as applicable

First given name	Second given name	Third given name	Surname

And if the testator is known by any other name(s), state below the full name(s) used including surname.

First given name	Second given name	Third given name	Surname

Birth date of testator: ______________ ______________ ______________
day *month* *year*

Date of will or codicil: ______________ ______________ ______________
day *month* *year*

Estate trustees named in will or codicil:

Name Address

Date of deposit: ______________ ______________ ______________
day *month* *year*

Office of deposit: ____

DATE: ______________ ______________ ______________
day *month* *year*

____
Registrar
Address of court office

November 1, 2005

FORM 74.2 — NOTICE TO ESTATE REGISTRAR OF WITHDRAWAL OF WILL OR CODICIL

Courts of Justice Act

[Repealed O. Reg. 77/06, s. 3.]

[Editor's Note: Forms 4A to 78A of the Rules of Civil Procedure have been repealed by O. Reg. 77/06, effective July 1, 2006. Pursuant to Rule of Civil Procedure 1.06, when a form is referred to by number, the reference is to the form with that number that is described in the Table of Forms at the end of these rules and which is available on the Internet through www.ontariocourtforms.on.ca. For your convenience, the government form as published on this website is reproduced below.]

ONTARIO

SUPERIOR COURT OF JUSTICE

NOTICE

TO THE ESTATE REGISTRAR FOR ONTARIO:

A will or codicil has been withdrawn from this office. Particulars of the document follow.

DETAILS ABOUT THE TESTATOR

Complete in full as applicable

First given name	Second given name	Third given name	Surname

And if the testator is known by any other name(s), state below the full name(s) used including surname.

First given name	Second given name	Third given name	Surname

Birth date of testator: __________ __________ __________
day *month* *year*

Date of will or codicil: __________ __________ __________
day *month* *year*

Date of deposit: __________ __________ __________
day *month* *year*

Date of withdrawal: __________ __________ __________
day *month* *year*

Office of deposit: ______________________________

DATE: ________________ ____________ ____________
day *month* *year*

____
Registrar
Address of court office

November 1, 2005

FORM 74.3 — REQUEST FOR NOTICE OF COMMENCEMENT OF PROCEEDING

Courts of Justice Act

[Repealed O. Reg. 77/06, s. 3.]

[Editor's Note: Forms 4A to 78A of the Rules of Civil Procedure have been repealed by O. Reg. 77/06, effective July 1, 2006. Pursuant to Rule of Civil Procedure 1.06, when a form is referred to by number, the reference is to the form with that number that is described in the Table of Forms at the end of these rules and which is available on the Internet through www.ontariocourtforms.on.ca. For your convenience, the government form as published on this website is reproduced below.]

ONTARIO

SUPERIOR COURT OF JUSTICE

In the Estate of the deceased person described below:

DETAILS ABOUT THE DECEASED PERSON

Complete in full as applicable

First given name	Second given name	Third given name	Surname

And if the deceased was known by any other name(s), state below the full name(s) used including surname.

First given name	Second given name	Third given name	Surname

REQUEST FOR NOTICE OF COMMENCEMENT OF PROCEEDING

I have or appear to have a financial interest in the estate and desire to be informed of the commencement of any proceeding in the estate.

Notice of the commencement of any proceeding may be mailed to me at the address shown below.

DATE ______________ ______________ ______________

day *month* *year*

NAME OF INTERESTED PARTY: ADDRESS:

November 1, 2005

FORM 74.4 — APPLICATION FOR CERTIFICATE OF APPOINTMENT OF ESTATE TRUSTEE WITH A WILL (INDIVIDUAL APPLICANT)

Courts of Justice Act

[Repealed O. Reg. 77/06, s. 3.]

[Editor's Note: Forms 4A to 78A of the Rules of Civil Procedure have been repealed by O. Reg. 77/06, effective July 1, 2006. Pursuant to Rule of Civil Procedure 1.06, when a form is referred to by number, the reference is to the form with that number that is described in the Table of Forms at the end of these rules and which is available on the Internet through www.ontariocourtforms.on.ca. For your convenience, the government form as published on this website is reproduced below.]

APPLICATION FOR CERTIFICATE OF APPOINTMENT OF ESTATE TRUSTEE WITH A WILL (INDIVIDUAL APPLICANT)

ONTARIO

SUPERIOR COURT OF JUSTICE

(Form 74.4 Under the Rules)

at

This application is filed by (*insert name and address*)

DETAILS ABOUT THE DECEASED PERSON

Complete in full as applicable

First given name	Second given name	Third given name	Surname

And if the deceased was known by any other name(s), state below the full name(s) used including surname.

First given name	Second given name	Third given name	Surname

Address of fixed place of abode (*street or postal address*) (*city or town*)	(*county or district*)
If the deceased person had no fixed place of abode in Ontario, did he or she have property in Ontario? ❑ No ❑ Yes	Last occupation of deceased person

Place of death *(city or town; county or district)*	Date of death (*day, month, year*)	Date of last will (*marked as Exhibit "A"*) (*day, month, year*)

Was the deceased person 18 years of age or older at the date of the will (or 21 years of age or older if the will is dated earlier than September 1, 1971)?	❑ No	❑ Yes
If not, explain why certificate is being sought. Give details in an attached schedule.		

Date of codicil (marked as Exhibit "B") (*day, month, year*)	Date of codicil (marked as Exhibit "C") (*day, month, year*)

Marital Status	❑ Unmarried	❑ Married	❑ Widowed	❑ Divorced

Did the deceased person marry after the date of the will? If yes, explain why certificate is being sought. Give details in an attached schedule.	❑ No	❑ Yes
Was a marriage of the deceased person terminated by a judgment absolute of divorce, or declared a nullity, after the date of the will? If yes, give details in an attached schedule.	❑ No	❑ Yes
Is any person who signed the will or a codicil as witness or for the testator, or the spouse of such person, a beneficiary under the will? If yes, give details in an attached schedule.	❑ No	❑ Yes

VALUE OF ASSETS OF ESTATE

Do not include in the total amount: insurance payable to a named beneficiary or assigned for value, property held jointly and passing by survivorship, or real estate outside Ontario.

Personal Property	**Real estate, net of encumbrances**	**Total**
$	$	$

Is there any person entitled to an interest in the estate who is not an applicant?	❑ No	❑ Yes
If a person named in the will or a codicil as estate trustee is not an applicant, explain.		
If a person not named in the will or a codicil as estate trustee is an applicant, explain why that person is entitled to apply.		
If the spouse of the deceased is an applicant, has the spouse elected to receive the entitlement under section 5 of the *Family Law Act*? If yes, explain why the spouse is entitled to apply.	❑ No	❑ Yes

AFFIDAVIT(S) OF APPLICANT(S)

(*Attach a separate sheet for additional affidavits, if necessary*)

I, an applicant named in this application, make oath and say/affirm:

1. I am 18 years of age or older.

2. The exhibit(s) referred to in this application are the last will and each codicil (where applicable) of the deceased person and I do not know of any later will or codicil.

3. I will faithfully administer the deceased person's property according to law and render a complete and true account of my administration when lawfully required.

4. If I am not named as estate trustee in the will or codicil, consents of persons who together have a majority interest in the value of the assets of the estate at the date of death are attached.

5. The information contained in this application and in any attached schedules is true, to the best of my knowledge and belief.

Name (*surname and forename(s)*)	Occupation

Address (*street or postal address*) (*city or town*) (*province*) (*postal code*)

Sworn/Affirmed before me at the . . . .
of . . . .
in the . . . .
of . . . .

Signature of applicant

this . . . . day of , 20. . . . . .

A Commissioner for taking Affidavits (*or as may be*)

Name (*surname and forename(s)*)	Occupation

Address (*street or postal address*) (*city or town*) (*province*) (*postal code*)

Sworn/Affirmed before me at the . . . .
of . . . .
in the . . . .
of . . . .

Signature of applicant

this . . . . day of , ...20. . . . .

A Commissioner for taking Affidavits (*or as may be*)

November 1, 2005

FORM 74.4.1 — APPLICATION FOR CERTIFICATE OF APPOINTMENT OF ESTATE TRUSTEE WITH A WILL (INDIVIDUAL APPLICANT) LIMITED TO ASSETS REFERRED TO IN THE WILL

Courts of Justice Act

[Repealed O. Reg. 77/06, s. 3.]

[Editor's Note: Forms 4A to 78A of the Rules of Civil Procedure have been repealed by O. Reg. 77/06, effective July 1, 2006. Pursuant to Rule of Civil Procedure 1.06, when a form is referred to by number, the reference is to the form with that number that is described in the Table of Forms at the end of these rules and which is available on the Internet through www.ontariocourtforms.on.ca. For your convenience, the government form as published on this website is reproduced below.]

APPLICATION FOR CERTIFICATE OF APPOINTMENT OF ESTATE TRUSTEE WITH A WILL (INDIVIDUAL APPLICANT) LIMITED TO ASSETS REFERRED TO IN THE WILL

ONTARIO

SUPERIOR COURT OF JUSTICE

(Form 74.4.1 Under the Rules)

at

This application is filed by *(insert name and address)*

DETAILS ABOUT THE DECEASED PERSON

Complete in full as applicable

First given name	Second given name	Third given name	Surname

And if the deceased was known by any other name(s), state below the full name(s) used including surname.

First given name	Second given name	Third given name	Surname

Address of fixed place of abode*(street or postal address) (city or town)*	*(county or district)*

If the deceased person had no fixed place of abode in Ontario, did he or she have property in Ontario? ❑ No ❑ Yes	Last occupation of deceased person

Place of death *(city or town; county or district)*	Date of death *(day, month, year)*	Date of last will (marked as Exhibit "A") *(day, month, year)*

Was the deceased person 18 years of age or older at the date of the will (or 21 years of age or older if the will is dated earlier than September 1, 1971)? If not, explain why certificate is being sought. Give details in an attached schedule.	❑ No	❑ Yes

Date of codicil (marked as Exhibit "B") *(day, month, year)*	Date of codicil (marked as Exhibit "C") *(day, month, year)*

Marital Status	❑ Unmarried	❑ Married	❑ Widowed	❑ Divorced

Did the deceased person marry after the date of the will? If yes, explain why certificate is being sought. Give details in an attached schedule.	❑ No	❑ Yes
Was a marriage of the deceased person terminated by a judgment absolute of divorce, or declared a nullity, after the date of the will? If yes, give details in an attached schedule.	❑ No	❑ Yes
Is any person who signed the will or a codicil as witness or for the testator, or the spouse of such person, a beneficiary under the will? If yes, give details in an attached schedule.	❑ No	❑ Yes

VALUE OF ASSETS REFERRED TO IN ATTACHED WILL (MARKED AS EXHIBIT "A" TO THIS APPLICATION)

Do not include in the total amount: insurance payable to a named beneficiary or assigned for value, property held jointly and passing by survivorship, or real estate outside Ontario.

Personal Property	*Real estate, net of encumbrances*	*Total*
$	$	$

Is there any person entitled to an interest in the estate who is not an applicant?	❑ No	❑ Yes
If a person named in the will or a codicil as estate trustee is not an applicant, explain.		
If a person not named in the will or a codicil as estate trustee is an applicant, explain why that person is entitled to apply.		
If the spouse of the deceased is an applicant, has the spouse elected to receive the entitlement under section 5 of the *Family Law Act*? If yes, explain why the spouse is entitled to apply.	❑ No	❑ Yes

AFFIDAVIT(S) OF APPLICANT(S)

(Attach a separate sheet for additional affidavits, if necessary)

I, an applicant named in this application, make oath and say/affirm:

1. I am 18 years of age or older.

2. The exhibit(s) referred to in this application are the last will and each codicil (where applicable) of the deceased person relating to the assets referred to in the will and I do not know of any later will or codicil affecting those assets.

3. I will faithfully administer the deceased person's property according to law and render a complete and true account of my administration when lawfully required.

4. If I am not named as estate trustee in the will or codicil, consents of persons who together have a majority interest in the value of the assets of the estate at the date of death are attached.

5. The information contained in this application and in any attached schedules is true, to the best of my knowledge and belief.

Name *(surname and forename(s))*	Occupation
Address*(city or town) (street or postal address)(province)(postal code)*	

Sworn/Affirmed before me at the . . . .
of . . . .
in the . . . .
of . . . .

Signature of applicant

this . . . . day of . . . ., 20 . . . .

A Commissioner for taking Affidavits *(or as may be)*

Name *(surname and forename(s))*	Occupation
Address*(city or town) (street or postal address)(province)(postal code)*	

Sworn/Affirmed before me at the . . . .
of . . . .
in the . . . .
of . . . .

Signature of applicant

this . . . . day of . . . ., 20 . . . .

A Commissioner for taking Affidavits *(or as may be)*

FORM 74.5 — APPLICATION FOR CERTIFICATE OF APPOINTMENT OF ESTATE TRUSTEE WITH A WILL (CORPORATE APPLICANT)

Courts of Justice Act

[Repealed O. Reg. 77/06, s. 3.]

[Editor's Note: Forms 4A to 78A of the Rules of Civil Procedure have been repealed by O. Reg. 77/06, effective July 1, 2006. Pursuant to Rule of Civil Procedure 1.06, when a form is referred to by number, the reference is to the form with that number that is described in the Table of Forms at the end of these rules and which is available on the Internet through www.ontariocourtforms.on.ca. For your convenience, the government form as published on this website is reproduced below.]

APPLICATION FOR CERTIFICATE OF APPOINTMENT OF ESTATE TRUSTEE WITH A WILL (CORPORATE APPLICANT)

ONTARIO

SUPERIOR COURT OF JUSTICE

(Form 74.5 Under the Rules)

at

This application is filed by *(insert name and address)*

DETAILS ABOUT THE DECEASED PERSON

Complete in full as applicable

First given name	Second given name	Third given name	Surname

And if the deceased was known by any other name(s), state below the full name(s) used including surname.

First given name	Second given name	Third given name	Surname

Address of fixed place of abode*(street or postal address) (city or town)*	*(county or district)*

If the deceased person had no fixed place of abode in Ontario, did he or she have property in Ontario? ❑ No ❑ Yes	Last occupation of deceased person

Place of death *(city or town; county or district)*	Date of death *(day, month, year)*	Date of last will (marked as Exhibit "A") *(day, month, year)*

Was the deceased person 18 years of age or older at the date of the will (or 21 years of age or older if the will is dated earlier than September 1, 1971)? If not, explain why certificate is being sought. Give details in an attached schedule.	❑ No	❑ Yes

Date of codicil (marked as Exhibit "B") *(day, month, year)*	Date of codicil (marked as Exhibit "C") *(day, month, year)*

Marital Status	❑ Unmarried	❑ Married	❑ Widowed	❑ Divorced

Did the deceased person marry after the date of the will? If yes, explain why certificate is being sought. Give details in an attached schedule.	❑ No	❑ Yes
Was a marriage of the deceased person terminated by a judgment absolute of divorce, or declared a nullity, after the date of the will? If yes, give details in an attached schedule.	❑ No	❑ Yes
Is any person who signed the will or a codicil as witness or for the testator, or the spouse of such person, a beneficiary under the will? If yes, give details in an attached schedule.	❑ No	❑ Yes

VALUE OF ASSETS OF ESTATE

Do not include in the total amount: insurance payable to a named beneficiary or assigned for value, property held jointly and passing by survivorship, or real estate outside Ontario.

Personal property	**Real estate, net of encumbrances**	**Total**
$	$	$

Is there any person interested in the estate who is not an applicant?	❑ No	❑ Yes
If a person named in the will or a codicil a estate trustee is not an applicant, explain.		
If a person not named in the will or a codicil as estate trustee is an applicant, explain why that person is entitled to apply.		
If the spouse of the deceased is an applicant, has the spouse elected to receive the entitlement under section 5 of the *Family Law Act*? If yes, explain why the spouse is entitled to apply	❑ No	❑ Yes

AFFIDAVIT(S) OF APPLICANT(S)

(*Attach a separate sheet for additional affidavits, if necessary*)

I, a trust officer named in this application, make oath and say/affirm:

1. I am a trust officer of the corporate applicant.
2. I am 18 years of age or older.

3. The exhibit(s) referred to in this application are the last will and each codicil (where applicable) of the deceased person and I do not know of any later will or codicil.

4. The corporate applicant will faithfully administer the deceased person's property according to law and render a complete and true account of its administration when lawfully required.

5. If the corporate applicant is not named as estate trustee in the will or codicil, consents of persons who together have a majority interest in the value of the assets of the estate at the date of death are attached.

6. The information contained in this application and in any attached schedules is true, to the best of my knowledge and belief.

Name of corporate applicant	Name of trust officer

Address of corporate applicant *(street or postal address)* *(city or town)* *(province)* *(postal code)*

Sworn/Affirmed before me at the . . . .
of . . . .
in the . . . .
of . . . .

____
Signature of trust officer

this . . . . day of . . . ., 20 . . . . . .

____
A Commissioner for taking Affidavits *(or as may be)*

I, an applicant named in this application, make oath and say/affirm:

1. I am 18 years of age or older.

2. The exhibit(s) referred to in this application are the last will and each codicil (where applicable) of the deceased person and I do not know of any later will or codicil.

3. I will faithfully administer the deceased person's property according to law and render a complete and true account of my administration when lawfully required.

4. If I am not named as estate trustee in the will or codicil, consents of persons who together have a majority interest in the value of the assets of the estate at the date of death are attached.

5. The information contained in this application and in any attached schedules is true, to the best of my knowledge and belief.

Name *(surname and forename(s))*	Occupation

Address*(street or postal address)* *(city or town)* *(province)* *(postal code)*

Sworn/Affirmed before me at the . . . .
of . . . .
in the . . . .
of . . . .

____
Signature of applicant

this . . . . day of . . . ., 20 . . . . . .

____

A Commissioner for taking Affidavits *(or as may be)*

November 1, 2005

FORM 74.5.1 — APPLICATION FOR CERTIFICATE OF APPOINTMENT OF ESTATE TRUSTEE WITH A WILL (CORPORATE APPLICANT) LIMITED TO ASSETS REFERRED TO IN THE WILL

Courts of Justice Act

[Repealed O. Reg. 77/06, s. 3.]

[Editor's Note: Forms 4A to 78A of the Rules of Civil Procedure have been repealed by O. Reg. 77/06, effective July 1, 2006. Pursuant to Rule of Civil Procedure 1.06, when a form is referred to by number, the reference is to the form with that number that is described in the Table of Forms at the end of these rules and which is available on the Internet through www.ontariocourtforms.on.ca. For your convenience, the government form as published on this website is reproduced below.]

ONTARIO

APPLICATION FOR CERTIFICATE OF APPOINTMENT OF ESTATE TRUSTEE WITH A WILL (CORPORATE APPLICANT) LIMITED TO ASSETS REFERRED TO IN THE WILL

SUPERIOR COURT OF JUSTICE

(Form 74.5.1 Under the Rules)

at ____

This application is filed by *(insert name and address)*

____

DETAILS ABOUT THE DECEASED PERSON

Complete in full as applicable

First given name	Second given name	Third given name	Surname

And if the deceased was known by any other name(s), state below the full name(s) used including surname.

First given name	Second given name	Third given name	Surname

Address of fixed place of abode*(street or postal address) (city or town)*	*(county or district)*

If the deceased person had no fixed place of abode in Ontario, did he or she have property in Ontario? ❑ No ❑ Yes	Last occupation of deceased person

Place of death *(city or town; county or district)*	Date of death *(day, month, year)*	Date of last will (marked as Exhibit "A") *(day, month, year)*

Was the deceased person 18 years of age or older at the date of the will (or 21 years of age or older if the will is dated earlier than September 1, 1971)?	❑ No	❑ Yes

If not, explain why certificate is being sought. Give details in an attached schedule.

Date of codicil (marked as Exhibit "B") *(day, month, year)*	Date of codicil (marked as Exhibit "C") *(day, month, year)*

Marital Status	❑ Unmarried	❑ Married	❑ Widowed	❑ Divorced

Did the deceased person marry after the date of the will? If yes, explain why certificate is being sought. Give details in an attached schedule.	❑ No	❑ Yes
Was a marriage of the deceased person terminated by a judgment absolute of divorce, or declared a nullity, after the date of the will? If yes, give details in an attached schedule.	❑ No	❑ Yes
Is any person who signed the will or a codicil as witness or for the testator, or the spouse of such person, a beneficiary under the will? If yes, give details in an attached schedule.	❑ No	❑ Yes

VALUE OF ASSETS REFERRED TO IN ATTACHED WILL
(MARKED AS EXHIBIT "A" TO THIS APPLICATION)

Do not include in the total amount: insurance payable to a named beneficiary or assigned for value, property held jointly and passing by survivorship, or real estate outside Ontario.

Personal Property	Real estate, net of encumbrances	Total
$	$	$

Is there any person interested in the estate who is not an applicant?	❑ No	❑ Yes

If a person named in the will or a codicil as estate trustee is not an applicant, explain.

If a person not named in the will or a codicil as estate trustee is an applicant, explain why that person is entitled to apply.

If the spouse of the deceased is an applicant, has the spouse elected to receive the entitlement under section 5 of the *Family Law Act*?	❑ No	❑ Yes
If yes, explain why the spouse is entitled to apply.		

AFFIDAVIT(S) OF APPLICANT(S)

(*Attach a separate sheet for additional affidavits, if necessary*)

I, a trust officer named in this application, make oath and say/affirm:

1. I am a trust officer of the corporate applicant.

2. I am 18 years of age or older.

3. The exhibit(s) referred to in this application are the last will and each codicil (where applicable) of the deceased person relating to the assets referred to in the will and I do not know of any later will or codicil affecting those assets.

4. The corporate applicant wilt faithfully administer the deceased person's property according to law and render a complete and true account of its administration when lawfully required.

5. If the corporate applicant is not named as estate trustee in the will or codicil, consents of persons who together have a majority interest in the value of the assets of the estate at the date of death are attached.

6. The information contained in this application and in any attached schedules is true, to the best of my knowledge and belief.

Name of corporate applicant	Name of trust officer
Address of corporate applicant *(street or postal address)* *(city or town)*	*(province)* *(postal code)*

Sworn/Affirmed before me at the . . . .
of . . . .
in the . . . .
of . . . .

Signature of trust officer

this . . . . day of . . . ., 20 . . . .

A Commissioner for taking Affidavits
(or as may be)

I, an applicant named in this application, make oath and say/affirm:

1. I am 18 years of age or older.

2. The exhibit(s) referred to in this application are the last will and each codicil (where applicable) of the deceased person relating to the assets referred to in the will and I do not know of any later will or codicil affecting those assets.

3. I will faithfully administer the deceased person's property according to law and render a complete and true account of my administration when lawfully required.

4. If I am not named as estate trustee in the will or codicil, consents of persons who together have a majority interest in the value of the assets of the estate at the date of death are attached.

5. The information contained in this application and in any attached schedules is true, to the best of my knowledge and belief.

Name *(surname and forename(s))*	Occupation		
Address*(street or postal address)*	*(city or town)*	*(province)*	*(postal code)*

Sworn/Affirmed before me at the ....
of ....
in the ....
of .... ______________________

Signature of applicant

this .... day of ...., 20 .....

____

A Commissioner for taking Affidavits
(or as may be)

November 1, 2005

FORM 74.6 — AFFIDAVIT OF SERVICE OF NOTICE

Courts of Justice Act

[Repealed O. Reg. 77/06, s. 3.]

[Editor's Note: Forms 4A to 78A of the Rules of Civil Procedure have been repealed by O. Reg. 77/06, effective July 1, 2006. Pursuant to Rule of Civil Procedure 1.06, when a form is referred to by number, the reference is to the form with that number that is described in the Table of Forms at the end of these rules and which is available on the Internet through www.ontariocourtforms.on.ca. For your convenience, the government form as published on this website is reproduced below.]

ONTARIO

SUPERIOR COURT OF JUSTICE

IN THE ESTATE OF *(insert name)* , deceased.

AFFIDAVIT OF SERVICE OF NOTICE

I, *(insert name)* , of *(insert city or town and county or district of residence)* , make oath and say/affirm:

1. I am an applicant for a certificate of appointment of estate trustee with a will in the estate.

2. I have sent or caused to be sent a notice in Form 74.7, a copy of which is marked as Exhibit "A" to this affidavit, to all adult persons and charities named in the notice (except to an applicant who is entitled to share in the distribution of the estate), to the Public Guardian and Trustee if paragraph 6 of the notice applies, to a parent or guardian of the minor and to the Children's Lawyer if paragraph 4 applies, to the guardian or attorney if paragraph 5 applies, and to the Children's Lawyer if paragraph 7 applies, all by regular lettermail sent to the person's last known address.

3. I have attached or caused to be attached to each notice the following:

(A) In the case of a notice sent to or in respect of a person entitled only to a specified item of property or stated amount of money, an extract of the part or parts of the will or codicil relating to the gift, or a copy of the will (and codicil(s), if any).

(B) In the case of a notice sent to or in respect of any other beneficiary, a copy of the will (and codicil(s), if any).

(C) In the case of a notice sent to the Children's Lawyer or the Public Guardian and Trustee, a copy of the will (and codicil(s), if any) and a statement of the estimated value of the interest of the person represented.

4. The following persons and charities specifically named in the Will are not entitled to be served for the reasons shown:

Name of person (as it appears in will, if applicable)	Reason not served

If paragraph 4 does not apply insert "Not Applicable."

5. The following persons named in the Will or being a member of a class of beneficiaries under the Will may be entitled to be served but have not been served for the reasons shown below:

Name of person (as it appears in will, if applicable)	Reason not served

If paragraph 5 does not apply insert "Not Applicable."

6. To the best of my knowledge and belief, subject to paragraph 5 (if applicable), the persons named in the notice are all the persons who are entitled to share in the distribution of the estate.

Sworn/Affirmed before me at the ......)
)
of ....)
)
in the ....)
)
of ....) ______________________________
) Signature of applicant

this . . . . day of . . . ., 20 . . .)
)
)
)

A Commissioner for taking Affidavits *(or as may be)*

November 1, 2005

FORM 74.7 — NOTICE OF AN APPLICATION FOR A CERTIFICATE OF APPOINTMENT OF ESTATE TRUSTEE WITH A WILL

Courts of Justice Act

[Repealed O. Reg. 77/06, s. 3.]

[Editor's Note: Forms 4A to 78A of the Rules of Civil Procedure have been repealed by O. Reg. 77/06, effective July 1, 2006. Pursuant to Rule of Civil Procedure 1.06, when a form is referred to by number, the reference is to the form with that number that is described in the Table of Forms at the end of these rules and which is available on the Internet through www.ontariocourtforms.on.ca. For your convenience, the government form as published on this website is reproduced below.]

ONTARIO

SUPERIOR COURT OF JUSTICE

IN THE ESTATE OF *(insert name)* , deceased.

NOTICE OF AN APPLICATION FOR A CERTIFICATE OF APPOINTMENT OF ESTATE TRUSTEE WITH A WILL

1. The deceased died on .... *(insert date).*

2. Attached to this notice are:

(A) If the notice is sent to or in respect of a person entitled only to a specified item of property or stated amount of money, an extract of the part or parts of the will or codicil relating to the gift, or a copy of the will (and codicil(s), if any).

(B) If the notice is sent to or in respect of any other beneficiary, a copy of the will (and codicil(s), if any).

(C) If the notice is sent to the Children's Lawyer or the Public Guardian and Trustee, a copy of the will (and codicil(s), if any), and if it is not included in the notice, a statement of the estimated value of the interest of the person represented.

3. The applicant named in this notice is applying for a certificate of appointment of estate trustee with a will.

APPLICANT

Name	**Address**

4. The following persons who are less than 18 years of age are entitled, whether their interest is contingent or vested, to share in the distribution of the estate:

Name	**Date of Birth *(day, month, year)***	**Name and Address of Parent or Guardian**	**Estimated Value of Interest to Estate***

Notes:

* Note: *The Estimated Value of Interest in Estate may be omitted in the form if it is included in a separate schedule attached to the notice sent to the Children's Lawyer.*

5. The following persons who are mentally incapable within the meaning of section 6 of the *Substitute Decisions Act, 1992* in respect of an issue in the proceeding, and who have guardians or attorneys acting under powers of attorney with authority to act in the proceeding, are entitled, whether their interest is contingent or vested, to share in the distribution of the estate:

Name and Address of Person	**Name and Address of Guardian or Attorney***

Notes:

* *Specify whether guardian or attorney*

6. The following persons who are mentally incapable within the meaning of section 6 of the *Substitute Decisions Act, 1992* in respect of an issue in the proceeding, and who do not have guardians or attorneys acting under powers of attorney with authority to act in the proceeding, are enti tled, whether their interest is contingent or vested, to share in the distribution of the estate:

Name and Address of Person	**Estimated Value of Interest in Estate***

Notes:

* Note: *The Estimated Value of Interest in Estate may be omitted in the form if it is included in a separate schedule attached to the notice sent to the Public Guardian and Trustee.*

7. Unborn or unascertained persons may be entitled to share in the distribution of the estate. *(Delete if not applicable)*

8. All other persons and charities entitled, whether their interest is contingent or vested, to share in the distribution of the estate are as follows:

Name	**Address**
	.

9. This notice is being sent, by regular lettermail, to all adult persons and charities named above in this notice (except to an applicant who is entitled to share in the distribution of the estate), to the Public Guardian and Trustee if paragraph 6 applies, to a parent or guardian of the minor a nd to the Children's Lawyer if paragraph 4 applies, to the guardian or attorney if paragraph 5 applies, and to the Children's Lawyer if paragraph 7 applies.

10. The following persons named in the Will or being a member of a class of beneficiaries under the Will may be entitled to be served but have not been served for the reasons shown below:

Name of person (as it appears in will, if applicable)	**Reason not served**

If paragraph 10 does not apply insert "Not Applicable."

DATE:

November 1, 2005

FORM 74.8 — AFFIDAVIT OF EXECUTION OF WILL OR CODICIL

Courts of Justice Act

[Repealed O. Reg. 77/06, s. 3.]

[Editor's Note: Forms 4A to 78A of the Rules of Civil Procedure have been repealed by O. Reg. 77/06, effective July 1, 2006. Pursuant to Rule of Civil Procedure 1.06, when a form is referred to by number, the reference is to the form with that number that is described in the Table of Forms at the end of these rules and which is available on the Internet through www.ontariocourtforms.on.ca. For your convenience, the government form as published on this website is reproduced below.]

ONTARIO
SUPERIOR COURT OF JUSTICE

In the matter of the execution of a will or codicil of (*insert name*)

AFFIDAVIT

I, (*insert name*), of (*insert city or town and county or district, metropolitan or regional municipality of residence*), make oath and say/affirm:

1. On (*date*), I was present and saw the document marked as Exhibit "A" to this affidavit executed by (*insert name*).

2. (*Insert name*) executed the document in the presence of myself and (*insert name of other witness and city or town, county or district, metropolitan or regional municipality of residence*). We were both present at the same time, and signed the document in the testator's presence as attesting witnesses.

SWORN/AFFIRMED BEFORE)
me at the of)
in the of)
this day of , 20 .) ....
)
)
)
)

....
A Commissioner for taking Affidavits
(or as may be)

NOTE: If the testator was blind or signed by making his or her mark, add the following paragraph:
3. Before its execution, the document was read over to the testator, who (was blind) (signed by making his or her mark). The testator appeared to understand the contents.

WARNING: A beneficiary or the spouse of a beneficiary should not be a witness.

November 1, 2005

FORM 74.9 — AFFIDAVIT ATTESTING TO THE HANDWRITING AND SIGNATURE OF A HOLOGRAPH WILL OR CODICIL

Courts of Justice Act

[Repealed O. Reg. 77/06, s. 3.]

[Editor's Note: Forms 4A to 78A of the Rules of Civil Procedure have been repealed by O. Reg. 77/06, effective July 1, 2006. Pursuant to Rule of Civil Procedure 1.06, when a form is referred to by number, the reference is to the form with that number that is described in the Table of Forms at the end of these rules and which is available on the Internet through www.ontariocourtforms.on.ca. For your convenience, the government form as published on this website is reproduced below.]

ONTARIO
SUPERIOR COURT OF JUSTICE

IN THE ESTATE OF (*insert name*), deceased.

AFFIDAVIT ATTESTING TO THE HANDWRITING AND SIGNATURE OF A HOLOGRAPH WILL OR CODICIL

I, (*insert name*), of (*insert city or town and county or district, metropolitan or regional municipality of residence*), make oath and say/affirm:

1. I was well acquainted with the deceased and have frequently seen the deceased's signature and handwriting.

2. I believe the whole of the document dated (*insert date*), now shown to me and marked as Exhibit "A" to this affidavit, including the signature, is in the handwriting of the deceased.

SWORN/AFFIRMED BEFORE	)	
me at the of	)	
in the of	)	
this day of , 20 .	)	....
	)	
	)	
	)	
	)	

....
A Commissioner for taking Affidavits
(or as may be)

November 1, 2005

FORM 74.10 — AFFIDAVIT OF CONDITION OF WILL OR CODICIL

Courts of Justice Act

[Repealed O. Reg. 77/06, s. 3.]

[Editor's Note: Forms 4A to 78A of the Rules of Civil Procedure have been repealed by O. Reg. 77/06, effective July 1, 2006. Pursuant to Rule of Civil Procedure 1.06, when a form is referred to by number, the reference is to the form with that number that is described in the Table of Forms at the end of these rules and which is available on the Internet through www.ontariocourtforms.on.ca. For your convenience, the government form as published on this website is reproduced below.]

ONTARIO
SUPERIOR COURT OF JUSTICE

IN THE ESTATE OF (*insert name*), deceased.

AFFIDAVIT OF CONDITION OF WILL OR CODICIL

I, (*insert name*), of (*insert cityor town and county or district, metropolitan or regional municipality of residence*), make oath and say/affirm:

1. On (*date*), I was present and saw the document marked as Exhibit "A" to this affidavit executed by the deceased, in the presence of myself and (*insert name of other witness*).

2. The following alterations, erasures, obliterations or interlineations that have not been attested appear in the document:

3. The document is now in the same condition as when it was executed.

SWORN/AFFIRMED BEFORE	)	
me at the of	)	
in the of	)	
this day of , 20 .	)	....
	)	
	)	
	)	
	)	

....
A Commissioner for taking Affidavits
(or as may be)

NOTE: If paragraph 3 is not correct, add the words "except that" and give details of the exceptions.

November 1, 2005

FORM 74.11 — RENUNCIATION OF RIGHT TO A CERTIFICATE OF APPOINTMENT OF ESTATE TRUSTEE (OR SUCCEEDING ESTATE TRUSTEE) WITH A WILL

Courts of Justice Act

[Repealed O. Reg. 77/06, s. 3.]

[Editor's Note: Forms 4A to 78A of the Rules of Civil Procedure have been repealed by O. Reg. 77/06, effective July 1, 2006. Pursuant to Rule of Civil Procedure 1.06, when a form is referred to by number, the reference is to the form with that number that is described in the Table of Forms at the end of these rules and which is available on the Internet through www.ontariocourtforms.on.ca. For your convenience, the government form as published on this website is reproduced below.]

ONTARIO
SUPERIOR COURT OF JUSTICE

IN THE ESTATE OF (*insert name*), deceased.

RENUNCIATION OF RIGHT TO A CERTIFICATE OF APPOINTMENT OF ESTATE TRUSTEE (OR SUCCEEDING ESTATE TRUSTEE) WITH A WILL

The deceased died on (*date*).

In that person's testamentary document dated (*date*), I, (*insert name*), was named an estate trustee.

I renounce my right to a certificate of appointment of estate trustee (or succeeding estate trustee) with a will.

DATE)
)
)
)
)
)
)
)

....
Signature of witness Signature of person renouncing

November 1, 2005

FORM 74.12 — CONSENT TO APPLICANT'S APPOINTMENT AS ESTATE TRUSTEE WITH A WILL

Courts of Justice Act

[Repealed O. Reg. 77/06, s. 3.]

[Editor's Note: Forms 4A to 78A of the Rules of Civil Procedure have been repealed by O. Reg. 77/06, effective July 1, 2006. Pursuant to Rule of Civil Procedure 1.06, when a form is referred to by number, the reference is to the form with that number that is described in the Table of Forms at the end of these rules and which is available on the Internet through www.ontariocourtforms.on.ca. For your convenience, the government form as published on this website is reproduced below.]

ONTARIO
SUPERIOR COURT OF JUSTICE

IN THE ESTATE OF (*insert name*), deceased.

CONSENT TO APPLICANT'S
APPOINTMENT AS ESTATE TRUSTEE WITH A WILL

The deceased died on (*date*).

No estate trustee named in a testamentary document of that person is applying for a certificate of appointment of estate trustee with a will.

I, (*insert name*), am entitled to share in the distribution of the estate.

I consent to the application by (*insert name*) for a certificate of appointment of estate trustee with a will.

I consent to an order dispensing with the filing of a bond by the applicant (*delete if inapplicable*).

DATE)
)
)
)
)
)
)
)

....
Signature of witness Signature of person consenting

November 1, 2005

FORM 74.13 — CERTIFICATE OF APPOINTMENT OF ESTATE TRUSTEE WITH A WILL

Courts of Justice Act

[Repealed O. Reg. 77/06, s. 3.]

[Editor's Note: Forms 4A to 78A of the Rules of Civil Procedure have been repealed by O. Reg. 77/06, effective July 1, 2006. Pursuant to Rule of Civil Procedure 1.06, when a form is referred to by number, the reference is to the form with that number that is described in the Table of Forms at the end of these rules and which is available on the Internet through www.ontariocourtforms.on.ca. For your convenience, the government form as published on this website is reproduced below.]

ONTARIO
SUPERIOR COURT OF JUSTICE

IN THE ESTATE OF , deceased,

late of

occupation

who died on

CERTIFICATE OF APPOINTMENT OF ESTATE TRUSTEE WITH A WILL

Applicant Address Occupation

This CERTIFICATE OF APPOINTMENT OF ESTATE TRUSTEE WITH A WILL is hereby issued under the seal of the court to the applicant named above. A copy of the deceased's last will (and codicil(s), if any) is attached.

DATE

. . . .
Registrar

Address of court office

November 1, 2005

FORM 74.13.1 — CERTIFICATE OF APPOINTMENT OF ESTATE TRUSTEE WITH A WILL LIMITED TO THE ASSETS REFERRED TO IN THE WILL

Courts of Justice Act

[Repealed O. Reg. 77/06, s. 3.]

[Editor's Note: Forms 4A to 78A of the Rules of Civil Procedure have been repealed by O. Reg. 77/06, effective July 1, 2006. Pursuant to Rule of Civil Procedure 1.06, when a form is referred to by number, the reference is to the form with that number that is described in the Table of Forms at the end of these rules and which is available on the Internet through www.ontariocourtforms.on.ca. For your convenience, the government form as published on this website is reproduced below.]

ONTARIO — SUPERIOR COURT OF JUSTICE

IN THE ESTATE OF , deceased,

late of

occupation

who died on

CERTIFICATE OF APPOINTMENT OF ESTATE TRUSTEE WITH A WILL LIMITED TO THE ASSETS REFERRED TO IN THE WILL

Applicant Address Occupation

By order of a judge of the Superior Court of Justice this grant of a certificate of appointment of estate trustee with a will is limited to the assets referred to in the will dated

.................................., a copy of which is attached. This will is the last will of the deceased dealing with those assets.

This CERTIFICATE OF APPOINTMENT OF ESTATE TRUSTEE WITH A WILL LIMITED TO THE ASSETS REFERRED TO IN THE WILL is hereby issued under the seal of the court to the applicant named above.

DATE . . . .

Registrar

Address of court office

November 1, 2005

FORM 74.14 — APPLICATION FOR CERTIFICATE OF APPOINTMENT OF ESTATE TRUSTEE WITHOUT A WILL (INDIVIDUAL APPLICANT)

Courts of Justice Act

[Repealed O. Reg. 77/06, s. 3.]

[Editor's Note: Forms 4A to 78A of the Rules of Civil Procedure have been repealed by O. Reg. 77/06, effective July 1, 2006. Pursuant to Rule of Civil Procedure 1.06, when a form is referred to by number, the reference is to the form with that number that is described in the Table of Forms at the end of these rules and which is available on the Internet through www.ontariocourtforms.on.ca. For your convenience, the government form as published on this website is reproduced below.]

ONTARIO

APPLICATION FOR CERTIFICATE OF APPOINTMENT OF ESTATE TRUSTEE WITHOUT A WILL (INDIVIDUAL APPLICANT)

SUPERIOR COURT OF JUSTICE

(Form 74.14 Under the Rules)

at ....

This application is filed by *(insert name and address)*

DETAILS ABOUT THE DECEASED PERSON

Complete in full as applicable

First given name	Second given name	Third given name	Surname

And if the deceased was known by any other name(s), state below the full name(s) used including surname.

First given name	Second given name	Third given name	Surname

Address of fixed place of abode (street or postal address) (city or town)	*(county or district)*
If the deceased person had no fixed place of abode in Ontario, did he or she have property in Ontario? ❑ No ❑ Yes	*Last occupation of deceased person*
Place of death (city or town; county or district)	*Date of death (day, month, year)*

Marital Status ❑ Unmarried ❑ Married ❑ Widowed ❑ Divorced

Was the deceased person's marriage terminated by a judgment absolute of divorce, or declared a nullity? ❑ No ❑ Yes
If yes, give details in an attached schedule.

Did the deceased person go through a form of marriage with a person where it appears uncertain whether an earlier marriage of the deceased person had been terminated by divorce or declared a nullity? ❑ No ❑ Yes
If yes, give the person's name and address, and the names and addresses of any children (including deceased children) of the marriage, in an attached schedule.

Was any earlier marriage of a person with whom the deceased person went through a form of marriage terminated by divorce or declared a nullity? ❑ No ❑ Yes
If yes, give details in an attached schedule.

Was the deceased person immediately before his or her death living with a person in a conjugal relationship outside marriage? ❑ No ❑ Yes
If yes, give the person's name and address in an attached schedule.

PERSONS ENTITLED TO SHARE IN THE ESTATE

(Attach a schedule if more space is needed. If a person entitled to share in the estate is not a spouse, child, parent, brother or sister of the deceased person, show how the relationship is traced.)

Name	*Address*	Relationship to deceased person	*Age (if under 18)*

VALUE OF ASSETS OF ESTATE

Do not include in the total amount: insurance payable to a named beneficiary or assigned for value, property held jointly and passing by survivorship, or real estate outside Ontario.

Personal property	*Real estate, net of encumbrances*	*Total*
$	$	$

Explain why the applicant is entitled to apply.

AFFIDAVIT(S) OF APPLICANT(S)

(Attach a separate sheet for additional affidavits, if necessary)

I, an applicant named in this application, make oath and say/affirm:

1. I am 18 years of age or older and a resident of Ontario.

5. The information contained in this application and in any attached schedules is true, to the best of my knowledge and belief.

2. I have made a careful search and inquiry for a will or other testamentary document of the deceased person, but none has been found. I believe that the person did not leave a will or other testamentary document.
3. I will faithfully administer the deceased person's property according to law and render a complete and true account of my administration when lawfully required.
4. Consents of persons who together have a majority interest in the value of the assets of the estate at the date of death are attached.

Name (surname and forename(s))	*Occupation*		
Address (street or postal address)	*(city or town)*	*(province)*	*(postal code)*

Sworn/Affirmed before me at the ....)
of ....)
in the ....)
of ....) ....
Signature of applicant

this .... day of ...., 20..........)

....
A Commissioner for taking Affidavits *(or as may be)*

Name (surname and forename(s))	*Occupation*		
Address (street or postal address)	*(city or town)*	*(province)*	*(postal code)*

Sworn/Affirmed before me at the ....)
of ....)
in the ....)
of ....) ....
Signature of applicant

this .... day of ...., 20..........)

....
A Commissioner for taking Affidavits (*or as may be*)

November 1, 2005

FORM 74.15 — APPLICATION FOR CERTIFICATE OF APPOINTMENT OF ESTATE TRUSTEE WITHOUT A WILL (CORPORATE APPLICANT)

Courts of Justice Act

[Repealed O. Reg. 77/06, s. 3.]

[Editor's Note: Forms 4A to 78A of the Rules of Civil Procedure have been repealed by O. Reg. 77/06, effective July 1, 2006. Pursuant to Rule of Civil Procedure 1.06, when a form is referred to by number, the reference is to the form with that number that is described in the Table of Forms at the end of these rules and which is available on the Internet through www.ontariocourtforms.on.ca. For your convenience, the government form as published on this website is reproduced below.]

ONTARIO

SUPERIOR COURT OF JUSTICE

APPLICATION FOR CERTIFICATE OF APPOINTMENT OF ESTATE TRUSTEE WITHOUT A WILL (CORPORATE APPLICANT)

(Form 74.15 Under the Rules)

at

This application is filed by *(insert name and address)*

DETAILS ABOUT THE DECEASED PERSON

Complete in full as applicable

First given name	Second given name	Third given name	Surname

And if the deceased was known by any other name(s), state below the full name(s) used including surname.

First given name	Second given name	Third given name	Surname

Address of fixed place of above (street or postal address)	*(county or district)*

If the deceased person had no fixed place of abode in Ontario, did he or she have property in Ontario? ❑ No ❑ Yes	*Last occupation of deceased person*

Place of death (city or town; county or district)	*Date of death (day, month, year)*

Marital Status ❑ Unmarried ❑ Married ❑ Widowed ❑ Divorced

Was the deceased person's marriage terminated by a judgment absolute of divorce, or declared a nullity? ❑ No ❑ Yes

If yes, give details in an attached schedule.

Did the deceased person go through a form of marriage with a person where it appears uncertain whether an earlier marriage of the deceased person had been terminated by divorce or declared a nullity? ❑ No ❑ Yes

If yes, give the person's name and address, and the names and addresses of any children (including deceased children) of the marriage, in an attached schedule.

Was any earlier marriage of a person with whom the deceased person went through a form of marriage terminated by divorce or declared a nullity? ❑ No ❑ Yes

If yes, give details in an attached schedule.

Was the deceased person immediately before his or her death living with a person in a conjugal relationship outside marriage? ❑ No ❑ Yes

If yes, give the person's name in an attached schedule.

PERSONS ENTITLED TO SHARE IN THE ESTATE

(Attach a schedule if more space is needed. If a person entitled to share in the estate is not a spouse, child, parent, brother or sister of the deceased person, show how the relationship is traced.)

Name	*Address*	*Relationship to deceased person*	*Age (if under 18)*

VALUE OF ASSETS OF ESTATE

Do not include in the total amount: insurance payable to a named beneficiary or assigned for value, property held jointly and passing by survivorship, or real estate outside Ontario.

Personal property	*Real estate, net of encumbrances*	*Total*
$	$	$

Explain why the applicant is entitled to apply.

AFFIDAVIT(S) OF APPLICANT(S)

(Attach a separate sheet for additional affidavits, if necessary)

I, a trust officer named in this application, make oath and say/affirm:

1. I am a trust officer of the corporate applicant.
2. I am 18 years of age or older.
3. I have made a careful search and inquiry for a will or other testamentary document of the deceased person, but none has been found. I believe that the person did not leave a will or other testamentary document.
4. The corporate applicant will faithfully administer the deceased person's property according to law and render a complete and true account of my administration when lawfully required.
5. Consents of persons who together have a majority interest in the value of the assets of the estate at the date of death are attached.
6. The information contained in this application and in any attached schedules is true, to the best of my knowledge and belief.

Name of corporate applicant	*Name of trust officer*

Address of corporate applicant (street or postal address)	*(city or town)*	*(province)*	*(postal code)*

Sworn/Affirmed before me at the ....
of ....
in the ....
of ....

....
Signature of trust officer

this .... day of ...., 20..........

....
A Commissioner for taking Affidavits *(or as may be)*

November 1, 2005

FORM 74.16 — AFFIDAVIT OF SERVICE OF NOTICE

Courts of Justice Act

[Repealed O. Reg. 77/06, s. 3.]

[Editor's Note: Forms 4A to 78A of the Rules of Civil Procedure have been repealed by O. Reg. 77/06, effective July 1, 2006. Pursuant to Rule of Civil Procedure 1.06, when a form is referred to by number, the reference is to the form with that number that is described in the Table of Forms at the end of these rules and which is available on the Internet through www.ontariocourtforms.on.ca. For your convenience, the government form as published on this website is reproduced below.]

ONTARIO

SUPERIOR COURT OF JUSTICE

IN THE ESTATE OF (insert name) , deceased.

AFFIDAVIT OF SERVICE OF NOTICE

I, *(insert name)* , of *(insert city or town and county or district of residence)* , make oath and say/affirm:

1. I am an applicant for a certificate of appointment of estate trustee without a will in the estate.

2. I have sent or caused to be sent a notice in Form 74.17, a copy of which is marked as Exhibit "A" to this affidavit, to all adult persons named in the notice (except to an applicant who is entitled to share in the distribution of the estate), to a parent or guardian of the minor an d to the Children's Lawyer if paragraph 3 of the notice applies, to the guardian or attorney

if paragraph 4 applies and to the Public Guardian and Trustee if paragraph 5 applies, all by regular lettermail sent to the person's last known address.

3. The following persons may be entitled to be served but have not been served for the reasons shown below:

Name of person (if applicable)	**Reason not served**

If paragraph 3 does not apply insert "Not Applicable."

4. To the best of my knowledge and belief, subject to paragraph 3 (if applicable), the persons named in the notice are all the persons who are entitled to share in the distribution of the estate.

Sworn/Affirmed before me at the	)	
	)	
of	)	
	)	
in the	)	
	)	
of	)	______________________________
	)	Signature of applicant
this .... day of ...., 20 ...	)	
	)	
	)	

____

A Commissioner for taking Affidavits
(or as may be)

November 1, 2005

FORM 74.17 — NOTICE OF AN APPLICATION FOR A CERTIFICATE OF APPOINTMENT OF ESTATE TRUSTEE WITHOUT A WILL

Courts of Justice Act

[Repealed O. Reg. 77/06, s. 3.]

[Editor's Note: Forms 4A to 78A of the Rules of Civil Procedure have been repealed by O. Reg. 77/06, effective July 1, 2006. Pursuant to Rule of Civil Procedure 1.06, when a form is referred to by number, the reference is to the form with that number that is described in the Table of Forms at the end of these rules and which is available on the Internet through www.ontariocourtforms.on.ca. For your convenience, the government form as published on this website is reproduced below.]

ONTARIO

SUPERIOR COURT OF JUSTICE

IN THE ESTATE OF *(insert name)* , deceased.

NOTICE OF AN APPLICATION FOR A CERTIFICATE OF APPOINTMENT OF ESTATE TRUSTEE WITHOUT A WILL

1. The deceased died on *(insert date)* , without a will.

2. The applicant named in this notice is applying for a certificate of appointment of estate trustee without a will.

APPLICANT

Name	**Address**

3. The following persons who are less than 18 years of age are entitled to share in the distribution of the estate:

Name	**Date of Birth** ***(day, month, year)***	**Name and Address of Parent or Guardian**	**Estimated Value of Interest in Estate**

Notes:

* Note: *The Estimated Value of Interest in Estate may be omitted in the form if it is included in a separate schedule attached to the notice sent to the Children's Lawyer.*

4. The following persons who are mentally incapable within the meaning of section 6 of the *Substitute Decisions Act, 1992* in respect of an issue in the proceeding, and who have guardians or attorneys acting under powers of attorney with authority to act in the proceeding, are entitled to share in the distribution of the estate:

Name and Address of Person	**Name and Address of Guardian or Attorney***

Notes:

* *Specify whether guardian or attorney.*

5. The following persons who are mentally incapable within the meaning of section 6 of the *Substitute Decisions Act, 1992* in respect of an issue in the proceeding, and who do not have guardians or attorneys acting under powers of attorney with authority to act in the proceeding, are enti tled to share in the distribution of the estate:

Name and Address of Person	**Estimated Value of Interest in Estate**

Notes:

* Note: *The Estimated Value of Interest in Estate may be omitted in the form if it is included in a separate schedule attached to the notice sent to the Public Guardian and Trustee.*

6. All other persons entitled to share in the distribution of the estate are as follows:

Name	**Address**

7. This notice is being sent, by regular lettermail, to all adult persons named above in this notice (except to an applicant who is entitled to share in the distribution of the estate), to a parent or guardian of the minor and to the Children's Lawyer if paragraph 3 applies, to the guardian or at torney if paragraph 4 applies, and to the Public Guardian and Trustee if paragraph 5 applies.

8. The following persons may be entitled to be served but have not been served for the reasons shown below:

Name of person	**Reason not served**

If paragraph 8 does not apply insert "Not Applicable."

DATE

November 1, 2005

FORM 74.18 — RENUNCIATION OF PRIOR RIGHT TO A CERTIFICATE OF APPOINTMENT OF ESTATE TRUSTEE WITHOUT A WILL

Courts of Justice Act

[Repealed O. Reg. 77/06, s. 3.]

[Editor's Note: Forms 4A to 78A of the Rules of Civil Procedure have been repealed by O. Reg. 77/06, effective July 1, 2006. Pursuant to Rule of Civil Procedure 1.06, when a form is referred to by number, the reference is to the form with that number that is described in the Table of Forms at the end of these rules and which is available on the Internet through www.ontariocourtforms.on.ca. For your convenience, the government form as published on this website is reproduced below.]

ONTARIO
SUPERIOR COURT OF JUSTICE

IN THE ESTATE OF (*insert name*) , deceased.

RENUNCIATION OF PRIOR RIGHT TO A CERTIFICATE OF APPOINTMENT OF ESTATE TRUSTEE WITHOUT A WILL

The deceased died on (*date*), without a will.

I, (*insert name*), am entitled to apply for a certificate of appointment of estate trustee without a will in priority to (*insert name*).

I renounce my right to a certificate of appointment of estate trustee without a will in priority to (*insert name*).

DATE	)	
	)	
	)	
	)	
	)	
	)	
....	)	....
Signature of witness	)	Signature of person renouncing

November 1, 2005

FORM 74.19 — CONSENT TO APPLICANT'S APPOINTMENT AS ESTATE TRUSTEE WITHOUT A WILL

Courts of Justice Act

[Repealed O. Reg. 77/06, s. 3.]

[Editor's Note: Forms 4A to 78A of the Rules of Civil Procedure have been repealed by O. Reg. 77/06, effective July 1, 2006. Pursuant to Rule of Civil Procedure 1.06, when a form is referred to by number, the reference is to the form with that number that is described in the Table of Forms at the end of these rules and which is available on the Internet through www.ontariocourtforms.on.ca. For your convenience, the government form as published on this website is reproduced below.]

ONTARIO
SUPERIOR COURT OF JUSTICE

IN THE ESTATE OF (*insert name*), deceased.

CONSENT TO APPLICANT'S APPOINTMENT AS ESTATE TRUSTEE WITHOUT A WILL

The deceased died on (*date*), without a will.

I, (*insert name*), am entitled to share in the distribution of the estate.

I consent to the application by (*insert name*) for a certificate of appointment of estate trustee without a will.

I consent to an order dispensing with the filing of a bond by the applicant (*delete if inapplicable*).

DATE	)	
	)	
	)	
	)	
	)	
	)	
....	)	....
Signature of witness	)	Signature of person consenting

November 1, 2005

FORM 74.20 — CERTIFICATE OF APPOINTMENT OF ESTATE TRUSTEE WITHOUT A WILL

Courts of Justice Act

[Repealed O. Reg. 77/06, s. 3.]

[Editor's Note: Forms 4A to 78A of the Rules of Civil Procedure have been repealed by O. Reg. 77/06, effective July 1, 2006. Pursuant to Rule of Civil Procedure 1.06, when a form is referred to by number, the reference is to the form with that number that is described in the Table of Forms at the end of these rules and which is available on the Internet through www.ontariocourtforms.on.ca. For your convenience, the government form as published on this website is reproduced below.]

Court file no.

ONTARIO
SUPERIOR COURT OF JUSTICE

IN THE ESTATE OF , deceased,

late of

occupation

who died on

CERTIFICATE OF APPOINTMENT
OF ESTATE TRUSTEE WITHOUT A WILL

Applicant	Address	Occupation

This CERTIFICATE OF APPOINTMENT OF ESTATE TRUSTEE WITHOUT A WILL is hereby issued under the seal of the court to the applicant named above.

DATE

. . . .
Registrar

Address of court office

November 1, 2005

FORM 74.20.1 — APPLICATION FOR CERTIFICATE OF APPOINTMENT OF A FOREIGN ESTATE TRUSTEE'S NOMINEE AS ESTATE TRUSTEE WITHOUT A WILL

Courts of Justice Act

[Repealed O. Reg. 77/06, s. 3.]

[Editor's Note: Forms 4A to 78A of the Rules of Civil Procedure have been repealed by O. Reg. 77/06, effective July 1, 2006. Pursuant to Rule of Civil Procedure 1.06, when a form is referred to by number, the reference is to the form with that number that is described in the Table of Forms at the end of these rules and which is available on the Internet through www.ontariocourtforms.on.ca. For your convenience, the government form as published on this website is reproduced below.]

ONTARIO

SUPERIOR COURT OF JUSTICE

APPLICATION FOR CERTIFICATE OF APPOINTMENT OF A FOREIGN ESTATE TRUSTEE'S NOMINEE AS ESTATE TRUSTEE WITHOUT A WILL

(Form 74.20.1 Under the Rules)

at

This application is filed by *(insert name)*

DETAILS ABOUT THE DECEASED PERSON

Complete in full as applicable

First given name	Second given name	Third given name	Surname

And if the deceased was known by any other name(s), state below the full name(s) used including surname.

First given name	Second given name	Third given name	Surname

Address*(street or postal address) (city or town) (province or state) (country)*

Place of death*(city or town; country)* Date of death *(day, month, year)*

Country of domicile

PARTICULARS OF FOREIGN CERTIFICATE

Country (and province or state if applicable) where issued	*Issuing court*	*Date issued(day, month, year)*
TOTAL VALUE OF ASSETS OF ESTATE		*Total* $

VALUE OF ASSETS LOCATED IN ONTARIO

Personal property	*Real estate, net of encumbrances*	*Total*
$	$	$

AFFIDAVIT(S) OF APPLICANT(S)

(*Attach a separate sheet for additional affidavits, if necessary.*)

I, an applicant named in this application, make oath and say/affirm:

1. I am the nominee of the foreign estate trustee appointed in the jurisdiction where the deceased was domiciled at the date of death.

2. A copy of the document appointing the foreign estate trustee, certified by the court that issued it, is marked as Exhibit "A" to this affidavit.

3. I am 18 years of age or older.

4. I will faithfully administer the deceased person's property according to law and render a complete and true account of my administration when lawfully required.

5. The information contained in this application and in any attached schedules is true, to the best of my knowledge and belief.

Name *(surname and forename(s))*	Occupation
Address*(street or postal address)* *(city or town)* *(province)* *(postal code)*	

Sworn/Affirmed before me at the . . . .
of . . . .
in the . . . .
of . . . .

this . . . . day of . . . ., 20 . . .

____
Signature of applicant

____
A Commissioner for taking Affidavits *(or as may be)*

Name *(surname and forename(s))*	Occupation
Address*(street or postal address)* *(city or town)* *(province)* *(postal code)*	

Sworn/Affirmed before me at the . . . .
of . . . .
in the . . . .
of . . . .

this . . . . day of . . . ., 20 . . .

____
Signature of applicant

____
A Commissioner for taking Affidavits *(or as may be)*

November 1, 2005

FORM 74.20.2 — NOMINATION OF APPLICANT BY FOREIGN ESTATE TRUSTEE

Courts of Justice Act

[Repealed O. Reg. 77/06, s. 3.]

[Editor's Note: Forms 4A to 78A of the Rules of Civil Procedure have been repealed by O. Reg. 77/06, effective July 1, 2006. Pursuant to Rule of Civil Procedure 1.06, when a form is referred to by number, the reference is to the form with that number that is described in the Table of Forms at the end of these rules and which is available on the Internet through www.ontariocourtforms.on.ca. For your convenience, the government form as published on this website is reproduced below.]

ONTARIO
SUPERIOR COURT OF JUSTICE

IN THE ESTATE OF.......................... (insert name), deceased.

NOMINATION OF APPLICANT BY FOREIGN ESTATE TRUSTEE

1. The deceased died on (*insert date*), without a will.

2. I, ... was appointed estate trustee by the ...., in the jurisdiction where the deceased was domiciled at the date of death, on the .... day of .... 20 .

3. I nominate .... to apply in Ontario for a certificate of estate trustee without a will.

DATE:

....	....
Signature of witness	Signature of person nominating

November 1, 2005

FORM 74.20.3 — CERTIFICATE OF APPOINTMENT OF FOREIGN ESTATE TRUSTEE'S NOMINEE AS ESTATE TRUSTEE WITHOUT A WILL

Courts of Justice Act

[Repealed O. Reg. 77/06, s. 3.]

[Editor's Note: Forms 4A to 78A of the Rules of Civil Procedure have been repealed by O. Reg. 77/06, effective July 1, 2006. Pursuant to Rule of Civil Procedure 1.06, when a form is referred to by number, the reference is to the form with that number that is described in the Table of Forms at the end of these rules and which is available on the Internet through www.ontariocourtforms.on.ca. For your convenience, the government form as published on this website is reproduced below.]

Court file no.

ONTARIO
SUPERIOR COURT OF JUSTICE

IN THE ESTATE OF , deceased,

late of

occupation

who died on

CERTIFICATE OF APPOINTMENT OF FOREIGN ESTATE TRUSTEE'S NOMINEE AS ESTATE TRUSTEE WITHOUT A WILL

Applicant	Address	Occupation

This CERTIFICATE OF APPOINTMENT OF FOREIGN ESTATE TRUSTEE'S NOMINEE AS ESTATE TRUSTEE WITHOUT A WILL is hereby issued under the seal of the court to the applicant named above.

DATE

. . . .
Registrar

Address of court office

November 1, 2005

FORM 74.21 — APPLICATION FOR CERTIFICATE OF APPOINTMENT AS SUCCEEDING ESTATE TRUSTEE WITH A WILL

Courts of Justice Act

[Repealed O. Reg. 77/06, s. 3.]

[Editor's Note: Forms 4A to 78A of the Rules of Civil Procedure have been repealed by O. Reg. 77/06, effective July 1, 2006. Pursuant to Rule of Civil Procedure 1.06, when a form is referred to by number, the reference is to the form with that number that is described in the Table of Forms at the end of these rules and which is available on the Internet through www.ontariocourtforms.on.ca. For your convenience, the government form as published on this website is reproduced below.]

ONTARIO

APPLICATION FOR CERTIFICATE OF APPOINTMENT AS SUCCEEDING ESTATE TRUSTEE WITH A WILL

SUPERIOR COURT OF JUSTICE

at

This application is filed by *(insert name and address)*

DETAILS ABOUT THE DECEASED PERSON

Complete in full as applicable

First given name	Second given name	Third given name	Surname

And if the deceased was known by any other name(s), state below the full name(s) used including surname.

First given name	Second given name	Third given name	Surname

PARTICULARS OF FIRST CERTIFICATE

Name(s) of estate trustee(s)	**Date issued** (*day, month, year*)

VALUE OF UNDISTRIBUTED ASSETS OF ESTATE

Personal property	Real estate, net of encumbrances	Total
$	$	$

Explain why the applicant is entitled to apply.

AFFIDAVIT(S) OF APPLICANT(S)

(*Attach a separate sheet for additional affidavits, if necessary.*)

I, a trust officer named in this application, make oath and say/affirm:

1. I am a trust officer of the corporate applicant.

2. I am 18 years of age or older.

3. The corporate applicant will faithfully administer the deceased person's property according to law and render a complete and true account of its administration when lawfully required.

4. If the corporate applicant is not named as estate trustee in the will or codicil, consents of persons who together have a majority interest in the value of the undistributed assets of the estate at the date of this application are attached.

5. The information contained in this application and in any attached schedules is true, to the best of my knowledge and belief.

Name of corporate applicant	Name of trust officer

Address of corporate applicant *(street or postal address) (city or town)* *(province)* *(postal code)*

Sworn/Affirmed before me at the . . .
of . . . .
in the . . . .
of . . . .

this . . . . day of . . . ., 20 . .
.

Signature of trust officer

A Commissioner for taking Affidavits
(or as may be)

I, an applicant named in this application, make oath and say/affirm:

1. I am 18 years of age or older.

2. I will faithfully administer the deceased person's property according to law and render a complete and true account of my administration when lawfully required.

3. If I am not named as estate trustee in the will or codicil, consents of persons who together have a majority interest in the value of the undistributed assets of the estate at the date of this application are attached.

4. The information contained in this application and in any attached schedules is true, to the best of my knowledge and belief.

Name *(surname and forename(s))*	Occupation

Address*(street or postal address) (city or town)* *(province)* *(postal code)*

Sworn/Affirmed before me at the . . . .
of . . . .
in the . . . .
of . . . .

this . . . . day of . . . ., 20 . . .

Signature of applicant

A Commissioner for taking Affidavits
(or as may be)

November 1, 2005

FORM 74.22 — CONSENT TO APPLICANT'S APPOINTMENT AS SUCCEEDING ESTATE TRUSTEE WITH A WILL

Courts of Justice Act

[Repealed O. Reg. 77/06, s. 3.]

[Editor's Note: Forms 4A to 78A of the Rules of Civil Procedure have been repealed by O. Reg. 77/06, effective July 1, 2006. Pursuant to Rule of Civil Procedure 1.06, when a form is referred to by number, the reference is to the form with that number that is described in the Table of Forms at the end of these rules and which is available on the Internet through www.ontariocourtforms.on.ca. For your convenience, the government form as published on this website is reproduced below.]

ONTARIO
SUPERIOR COURT OF JUSTICE

IN THE ESTATE OF (*insert name*), deceased.

CONSENT TO APPLICANT'S APPOINTMENT AS SUCCEEDING ESTATE TRUSTEE WITH A WILL

The deceased died on (*date*).

I, (*insert name*), am entitled to share in the distribution of the remaining estate.

I consent to the application by (*insert name*) for a certificate of appointment of succeeding estate trustee with a will.

I consent to an order dispensing with the filing of a bond by the applicant (*delete if inapplicable*).

DATE:	)	
	)	
	)	
	)	
	)	
....	)	....
Signature of witness	)	Signature of person consenting

November 1, 2005

FORM 74.23 — CERTIFICATE OF APPOINTMENT OF SUCCEEDING ESTATE TRUSTEE WITH A WILL

Courts of Justice Act

[Repealed O. Reg. 77/06, s. 3.]

[Editor's Note: Forms 4A to 78A of the Rules of Civil Procedure have been repealed by O. Reg. 77/06, effective July 1, 2006. Pursuant to Rule of Civil Procedure 1.06, when a form is referred to by number, the reference is to the form with that number that is described in the Table of Forms at the end of these rules and which is available on the Internet through www.ontariocourtforms.on.ca. For your convenience, the government form as published on this website is reproduced below.]

Court file no.

ONTARIO
SUPERIOR COURT OF JUSTICE

IN THE ESTATE OF , deceased,

late of

occupation

who died on

CERTIFICATE OF APPOINTMENT OF SUCCEEDING ESTATE TRUSTEE WITH A WILL

Applicant	Address	Occupation

This CERTIFICATE OF APPOINTMENT OF SUCCEEDING ESTATE TRUSTEE WITH A WILL is hereby issued under the seal of the court to the applicant named above. A copy of the deceased's last will (and codicil(s), if any) is attached.

DATE ....
Registrar
Address of court office

November 1, 2005

FORM 74.24 — APPLICATION FOR CERTIFICATE OF APPOINTMENT AS SUCCEEDING ESTATE TRUSTEE WITHOUT A WILL

Courts of Justice Act

[Repealed O. Reg. 77/06, s. 3.]

[Editor's Note: Forms 4A to 78A of the Rules of Civil Procedure have been repealed by O. Reg. 77/06, effective July 1, 2006. Pursuant to Rule of Civil Procedure 1.06, when a form is

referred to by number, the reference is to the form with that number that is described in the Table of Forms at the end of these rules and which is available on the Internet through www.ontariocourtforms.on.ca. For your convenience, the government form as published on this website is reproduced below.]

ONTARIO

APPLICATION FOR CERTIFICATE OF APPOINTMENT AS SUCCEEDING ESTATE TRUSTEE WITHOUT A WILL

SUPERIOR COURT OF JUSTICE

at

This application is filed by *(insert name and address)*

DETAILS ABOUT THE DECEASED PERSON

Complete in full as applicable

First given name	Second given name	Third given name	Surname

And if the deceased was known by any other name(s), state below the full name(s) used including surname.

First given name	Second given name	Third given name	Surname

PARTICULARS OF FIRST CERTIFICATE

Name(s) of estate trustee(s) or administrator(s)	Date issued *(day, month, year)*

PERSONS ENTITLED TO SHARE IN THE ESTATE (AT DATE OF THIS APPLICATION)

(Attach a schedule if more space is needed. If a person entitled to share in the estate is not a spouse, child, parent, brother or sister of the deceased person, show how the relationship is traced.)

Name	**Address**	**Relationship to deceased person**	**Age (if under 18)**

VALUE OF UNDISTRIBUTED ASSETS OF ESTATE

Personal property	**Real estate, net of encumbrances**	**Total**
$	$	$

Explain why the applicant is entitled to apply.

AFFIDAVIT(S) OF APPLICANT(S)

(*Attach a separate sheet for additional affidavits, if necessary.*)

I, a trust officer named in this application, make oath and say/affirm:

1. I am a trust officer of the corporate applicant.

2. I am 18 years of age or older.

3. The corporate applicant will faithfully administer the deceased person's property according to law and render a complete and true account of its administration when lawfully required.

4. Consents of persons who together have a majority interest in the value of the undistributed assets of the estate at the date of this application are attached.

5. The information contained in this application and in any attached schedules is true, to the best of my knowledge and belief.

Name of corporate applicant	Name of trust officer	
Address of corporate applicant *(street or postal address) (city or town)*	*(province)*	*(postal code)*

Sworn/Affirmed before me at the . . .
of . . . .
in the . . . .
of . . . .

this . . . . day of . . . ., 20 . . .

Signature of trust officer

A Commissioner for taking Affidavits
(or as may be)

I, an applicant named in this application, make oath and say/affirm:

1. I am 18 years of age or older and a resident of Ontario.

2. I will faithfully administer the deceased person's property according to law and render a complete and true account of my administration when lawfully required.

3. Consents of persons who together have a majority interest in the value of the undistributed assets of the estate at the date of this application are attached.

4. The information contained in this application and in any attached schedules is true, to the best of my knowledge and belief.

Name (surname and forename(s))	Occupation
Address*(street or postal address) (city or town)*	*(province)* *(postal code)*

Sworn/Affirmed before me at the ......
of ....
in the ....
of ....

____
Signature of applicant

this .... day of ...., 20 ...

____
A Commissioner for taking Affidavits
(or as may be)

November 1, 2005

FORM 74.25 — CONSENT TO APPLICANT'S APPOINTMENT AS SUCCEEDING ESTATE TRUSTEE WITHOUT A WILL

Courts of Justice Act

[Repealed O. Reg. 77/06, s. 3.]

[Editor's Note: Forms 4A to 78A of the Rules of Civil Procedure have been repealed by O. Reg. 77/06, effective July 1, 2006. Pursuant to Rule of Civil Procedure 1.06, when a form is referred to by number, the reference is to the form with that number that is described in the Table of Forms at the end of these rules and which is available on the Internet through www.ontariocourtforms.on.ca. For your convenience, the government form as published on this website is reproduced below.]

ONTARIO
SUPERIOR COURT OF JUSTICE

IN THE ESTATE OF (*insert name*), deceased.

CONSENT TO APPLICANT'S APPOINTMENT AS SUCCEEDING ESTATE TRUSTEE WITHOUT A WILL

The deceased died on (*date*), without a will.

I, (*insert name*), am entitled to share in the distribution of the estate.

I consent to the application by (*insert name*) for a certificate of appointment of succeeding estate trustee without a will.

I consent to an order dispensing with the filing of a bond by the applicant (*delete if inapplicable*).

DATE:)
)
)
)
)
. . . .) . . . .
Signature of witness) Signature of person consenting

November 1, 2005

FORM 74.26 — CERTIFICATE OF APPOINTMENT OF SUCCEEDING ESTATE TRUSTEE WITHOUT A WILL

Courts of Justice Act

[Repealed O. Reg. 77/06, s. 3.]

[Editor's Note: Forms 4A to 78A of the Rules of Civil Procedure have been repealed by O. Reg. 77/06, effective July 1, 2006. Pursuant to Rule of Civil Procedure 1.06, when a form is referred to by number, the reference is to the form with that number that is described in the Table of Forms at the end of these rules and which is available on the Internet through www.ontariocourtforms.on.ca. For your convenience, the government form as published on this website is reproduced below.]

Court file no.

ONTARIO
SUPERIOR COURT OF JUSTICE

IN THE ESTATE OF , deceased,

late of

occupation

who died on

CERTIFICATE OF APPOINTMENT
OF SUCCEEDING ESTATE TRUSTEE WITHOUT A WILL

Applicant	Address	Occupation

This CERTIFICATE OF APPOINTMENT OF SUCCEEDING ESTATE TRUSTEE WITHOUT A WILL is hereby issued under the seal of the court to the applicant named above.

DATE

. . . .
Registrar

Address of court office

November 1, 2005

FORM 74.27 — APPLICATION FOR CONFIRMATION BY RESEALING OF APPOINTMENT OR CERTIFICATE OF ANCILLARY APPOINTMENT OF ESTATE TRUSTEE

Courts of Justice Act

[Repealed O. Reg. 77/06, s. 3.]

[Editor's Note: Forms 4A to 78A of the Rules of Civil Procedure have been repealed by O. Reg. 77/06, effective July 1, 2006. Pursuant to Rule of Civil Procedure 1.06, when a form is referred to by number, the reference is to the form with that number that is described in the Table of Forms at the end of these rules and which is available on the Internet through www.ontariocourtforms.on.ca. For your convenience, the government form as published on this website is reproduced below.]

ONTARIO

APPLICATION FOR CONFIRMATION BY RESEALING OF APPOINTMENT OR CERTIFICATE OF ANCILLARY APPOINTMENT OF ESTATE TRUSTEE

SUPERIOR COURT OF JUSTICE

(Form 74.27 Under the Rules)

at

This is an application for *(check one)*

❑ confirmation by resealing of the appointment of an estate trustee with *(or without)* a will.

❑ a certificate of ancillary appointment of an estate trustee with a will.

This application is filed by *(insert name)*

DETAILS ABOUT THE DECEASED PERSON

Complete in full as applicable

First given name	Second given name	Third given name	Surname

And if the deceased was known by any other name(s), state below the full name(s) used including surname.

First given name	Second given name	Third given name	Surname

Address*(street or postal address) (city or town) (province or state) (country)*

Place of death *(city or town; country)*	Date of death *(day, month, year)*

PARTICULARS OF PRIMARY CERTIFICATE OR GRANT

Country*(and province or state if applicable) where issued*	Issuing court	Date issued*(day, month, year)*

VALUE OF ASSETS LOCATED IN ONTARIO

Personal property	**Real estate, net of encumbrances**	**Total**
$	$	$

AFFIDAVIT(S) OF APPLICANT(S)

(*Attach a separate sheet for additional affidavits, if necessary.*)

I, an applicant named in this application, make oath and say/affirm:

1. I am an estate trustee named in the primary certificate (*or* primary grant of letters probate *or* letters of administration), a copy of which, certified by the court that issued it, is Exhibit "A" to this affidavit.

2. I am 18 years of age or older.

3. I will faithfully administer the deceased person's property according to law and render a complete and true account of my administration when lawfully required.

4. The primary certificate (*or* primary grant of letters probate *or* letters of administration) is still effective.

5. The information contained in this application and in any attached schedules is true, to the best of my knowledge and belief.

Name*(surname and forename(s))*	Occupation		
Address*(street or postal address) (city or town)*		*(province)*	*(postal code)*

Sworn/Affirmed before me at the ......
of ....
in the ....
of ....

Signature of applicant

this .... day of ...., 20 ....

A Commissioner for taking Affidavits *(or as may be)*

November 1, 2005

FORM 74.28 — CONFIRMATION BY RESEALING OF APPOINTMENT OF ESTATE TRUSTEE

Courts of Justice Act

[Repealed O. Reg. 77/06, s. 3.]

[Editor's Note: Forms 4A to 78A of the Rules of Civil Procedure have been repealed by O. Reg. 77/06, effective July 1, 2006. Pursuant to Rule of Civil Procedure 1.06, when a form is referred to by number, the reference is to the form with that number that is described in the Table of Forms at the end of these rules and which is available on the Internet through www.ontariocourtforms.on.ca. For your convenience, the government form as published on this website is reproduced below.]

Sealed with the seal of the Superior Court of Justice by order of that court dated (*insert date*), under subsection 52(1) of the *Estates Act*.

DATE ....

Registrar

Address of court office

November 1, 2005

FORM 74.29 — CERTIFICATE OF ANCILLARY APPOINTMENT OF ESTATE TRUSTEE WITH A WILL

Courts of Justice Act

[Repealed O. Reg. 77/06, s. 3.]

[Editor's Note: Forms 4A to 78A of the Rules of Civil Procedure have been repealed by O. Reg. 77/06, effective July 1, 2006. Pursuant to Rule of Civil Procedure 1.06, when a form is referred to by number, the reference is to the form with that number that is described in the Table of Forms at the end of these rules and which is available on the Internet through www.ontariocourtforms.on.ca. For your convenience, the government form as published on this website is reproduced below.]

Court file no.

ONTARIO
SUPERIOR COURT OF JUSTICE

IN THE ESTATE OF , deceased,

late of

occupation

who died on

CERTIFICATE OF ANCILLARY APPOINTMENT
OF ESTATE TRUSTEE WITH A WILL

Applicant	Address	Occupation

Court of foreign grant

Date of foreign grant

This CERTIFICATE OF ANCILLARY APPOINTMENT OF ESTATE TRUSTEE WITH A WILL is hereby issued under the seal of the court to the applicant named above. A certified copy of the foreign grant, to which this certificate is ancillary, is attached.

DATE

. . . .
Registrar

Address of court office

November 1, 2005

FORM 74.30 — APPLICATION FOR CERTIFICATE OF APPOINTMENT OF ESTATE TRUSTEE DURING LITIGATION

Courts of Justice Act

[Repealed O. Reg. 77/06, s. 3.]

[Editor's Note: Forms 4A to 78A of the Rules of Civil Procedure have been repealed by O. Reg. 77/06, effective July 1, 2006. Pursuant to Rule of Civil Procedure 1.06, when a form is referred to by number, the reference is to the form with that number that is described in the Table of Forms at the end of these rules and which is available on the Internet through www.ontariocourtforms.on.ca. For your convenience, the government form as published on this website is reproduced below.]

ONTARIO

APPLICATION FOR CERTIFICATE OF APPOINTMENT OF ESTATE TRUSTEE DURING LITIGATION

SUPERIOR COURT OF JUSTICE

(Form 74.30 Under the Rules)

at

This application is filed by *(insert name)*

DETAILS ABOUT THE DECEASED PERSON

Complete in full as applicable

First given name	Second given name	Third given name	Surname

And if the deceased was known by any other name(s), state below the full name(s) used including surname.

First given name	Second given name	Third given name	Surname

Address of fixed place of abode *(street or postal address) (city or town)*	*(county or district)*

If the deceased person had no fixed place of abode in Ontario, did he or she have property in Ontario? ❑ No ❑ Yes	Last occupation of deceased person

Place of death *(city or town; county or district)*	Date of death *(day, month, year)*

VALUE OF ASSETS OF ESTATE

Do not include in the total amount: insurance payable to a named beneficiary or assigned for value, property held jointly and passing by survivorship, or real estate outside Ontario.

Personal property	Real estate, net of encumbrances	Total
$	$	$

This application is made pursuant to an order for the appointment of an estate trustee during litigation, made by

(name of judge)	*(day, month, year)*
	on

AFFIDAVIT(S) OF APPLICANT(S)

(*Attach a separate sheet for additional affidavits, if necessary*)

I, a trust officer named in this application, make oath and say/affirm:

1. I am a trust officer of the corporate applicant.

2. I am 18 years of age or older.

3. The corporate applicant will faithfully administer the deceased person's property according to law, make no distribution without a court order, and render a complete and true account of its administration when lawfully required.

4. The information contained in this application and in any attached schedules is true, to the best of my knowledge and belief.

Name of corporate applicant	Name of trust officer	
Address of corporate applicant *(street or postal address) (city or town)*	*(province)*	*(postal code)*

Sworn/Affirmed before me at the . . .
of . . . .
in the . . . .
of . . . .

this . . . . day of . . . ., 20 . .

Signature of trust officer

A Commissioner for taking Affidavits
(or as may be)

I, an applicant named in this application, make oath and say/affirm:

1. I am 18 years of age or older.

2. I will faithfully administer the deceased person's property according to law, make no distribution without a court order and render a complete and true account of my administration when lawfully required.

3. The information contained in this application and in any attached schedules is true, to the best of my knowledge and belief.

Name *(surname and forename(s))*	Occupation

Address*(street or postal address)* *(city or town)* *(province)* *(postal code)*

Sworn/Affirmed before me at the . . . .
of . . . .
in the . . . .
of . . . .

Signature of applicant

this . . . . day of . . . . . ., 20 ..

A Commissioner for taking Affidavits
(or as may be)

November 1, 2005

FORM 74.31 — CERTIFICATE OF APPOINTMENT OF ESTATE TRUSTEE DURING LITIGATION

Courts of Justice Act

[Repealed O. Reg. 77/06, s. 3.]

[Editor's Note: Forms 4A to 78A of the Rules of Civil Procedure have been repealed by O. Reg. 77/06, effective July 1, 2006. Pursuant to Rule of Civil Procedure 1.06, when a form is referred to by number, the reference is to the form with that number that is described in the Table of Forms at the end of these rules and which is available on the Internet through www.ontariocourtforms.on.ca. For your convenience, the government form as published on this website is reproduced below.]

Court file no.

ONTARIO
SUPERIOR COURT OF JUSTICE

IN THE ESTATE OF , deceased,

late of

occupation

who died on

CERTIFICATE OF APPOINTMENT
OF ESTATE TRUSTEE DURING LITIGATION

Applicant	Address	Occupation

By order of the Superior Court of Justice, this CERTIFICATE OF APPOINTMENT OF ESTATE TRUSTEE DURING LITIGATION to determine the validity of a testamentary document of the deceased is hereby issued under the seal of the court to the applicant named above.

DATE

. . . .
Registrar

Address of court office

November 1, 2005

FORM 74.32 — BOND — INSURANCE OR GUARANTEE COMPANY

Courts of Justice Act

[Repealed O. Reg. 77/06, s. 3.]

[Editor's Note: Forms 4A to 78A of the Rules of Civil Procedure have been repealed by O. Reg. 77/06, effective July 1, 2006. Pursuant to Rule of Civil Procedure 1.06, when a form is referred to by number, the reference is to the form with that number that is described in the Table of Forms at the end of these rules and which is available on the Internet through www.ontariocourtforms.on.ca. For your convenience, the government form as published on this website is reproduced below.]

ONTARIO
SUPERIOR COURT OF JUSTICE

BOND NO. AMOUNT: $

IN THE ESTATE OF (*insert name*), deceased.
The principal in this bond is (*insert name*)

The surety in this bond is (*insert name*), an insurer licensed under the *Insurance Act* to write surety and fidelity insurance in Ontario.

The obligee in this bond is the Accountant of the Superior Court of Justice acting for the benefit of creditors and persons entitled to share in the estate of the deceased.

The principal and the surety bind themselves, their heirs, executors, successors and assigns jointly and severally to the Accountant of the Superior Court of Justice in the amount of .... Dollars ($ ....).

The principal as an estate trustee is required to prepare a complete and true inventory of all the property of the deceased, collect the assets of the estate, pay the debts of the estate, distribute the property of the deceased according to law, and render a complete and true accounting of these activities when lawfully required.

The primary obligation under this bond belongs to the principal. The principal is liable under this bond for any amount found by the court to be owing to any creditors of the estate and persons entitled to share in the estate to whom proper payment has not been made.

The surety, provided it has been given reasonable notice of any proceeding in which judgment may be given against the principal for failure to perform the obligations of this bond shall, on order of the court, and on default of the principal to pay any final judgment made against the principal in the proceeding, pay to the obligee the amount of any deficiency in the payment by the principal, but the surety shall not be liable to pay more than the amount of the bond.

The amount of this bond shall be reduced by and to the extent of any payment made under the bond pursuant to an order of the court.

The surety is entitled to an assignment of the rights of any person who receives payment or benefit from the proceeds of this bond, to the extent of such payment or benefit received.

DATE

SIGNED, SEALED AND DELIVERED
in the presence of:

	.... Principal
....	.... Surety

November 1, 2005

FORM 74.33 — BOND — PERSONAL SURETIES

Courts of Justice Act

[Repealed O. Reg. 77/06, s. 3.]

[Editor's Note: Forms 4A to 78A of the Rules of Civil Procedure have been repealed by O. Reg. 77/06, effective July 1, 2006. Pursuant to Rule of Civil Procedure 1.06, when a form is referred to by number, the reference is to the form with that number that is described in the Table of Forms at the end of these rules and which is available on the Internet through www.ontariocourtforms.on.ca. For your convenience, the government form as published on this website is reproduced below.]

ONTARIO
SUPERIOR COURT OF JUSTICE

BOND NO. AMOUNT: $

IN THE ESTATE OF (*insert name*), deceased.

The principal in this bond is (*insert name*)

The sureties in this bond are (*insert names*)

The obligee in this bond is the Accountant of the Superior Court of Justice acting for the benefit of creditors and persons entitled to share in the estate of the deceased.

The principal and the sureties bind themselves, their heirs, executors, successors and assigns jointly and severally to the Accountant of the Superior Court of Justice in the amount of .... Dollars ($ ....).

The principal as an estate trustee is required to prepare a complete and true inventory of all the property of the deceased, collect the assets of the estate, pay the debts of the estate, distribute the property of the deceased according to law, and render a complete and true accounting of these activities when lawfully required.

The primary obligation under this bond belongs to the principal. The principal is liable under this bond for any amount found by the court to be owing to any creditors of the estate and persons entitled to share in the estate to whom proper payment has not been made.

The sureties, provided they have been given reasonable notice of any proceeding in which judgment may be given against the principal for failure to perform the obligations of this bond shall, on order of the court, and on default of the principal to pay any final judgment made against the principal in the proceeding, pay to the obligee the amount of any deficiency in the payment by the principal, but the sureties shall not be liable to pay more than the amount of the bond.

The amount of this bond shall be reduced by and to the extent of any payment made under the bond pursuant to an order of the court.

The sureties are entitled to an assignment of the rights of any person who receives payment or benefit from the proceeds of this bond, to the extent of such payment or benefit received.

DATE

SIGNED, SEALED AND DELIVERED
in the presence of:

. . . .
Principal

. . . .

. . . .
Surety

AFFIDAVIT OF SURETY

I, (*insert name*), of (*insert city or town and county or district, metropolitan or regional municipality of residence*), make oath and say/affirm:

I am a proposed surety on behalf of the intended estate trustees of the property of (*insert name*), deceased, named in the attached bond.

I am eighteen years of age or over and own property worth $ .... over and above all encumbrances, and over and above what will pay my just debts and every sum for which I am now bail or for which I am liable as surety or endorser or otherwise.

SWORN/AFFIRMED BEFORE me at the of in the of this day of , 20 .	)	....
.... A Commissioner for Taking Affidavits (*or as may be*)	)	

AFFIDAVIT OF SURETY

I, (*insert name*), of (*insert city or town and county or district, metropolitan or regional municipality of residence*), make oath and say/affirm:

I am a proposed surety on behalf of the intended estate trustees of the property of (*insert name*), deceased, named in the attached bond.

I am eighteen years of age or over and own property worth $ .... over and above all encumbrances, and over and above what will pay my just debts and every sum for which I am now bail or for which I am liable as surety or endorser or otherwise.

SWORN/AFFIRMED BEFORE the at the of in the of this day of , 20 .	)	....
.... A Commissioner for Taking Affidavits (*or as may be*)	)	

November 1, 2005

FORM 74.34 — REGISTRAR'S NOTICE TO ESTATE TRUSTEE NAMED IN A DEPOSITED WILL OF APPLICATION FOR CERTIFICATE OF APPOINTMENT OF ESTATE TRUSTEE WITH A WILL

Courts of Justice Act

[Repealed O. Reg. 77/06, s. 3.]

[Editor's Note: Forms 4A to 78A of the Rules of Civil Procedure have been repealed by O. Reg. 77/06, effective July 1, 2006. Pursuant to Rule of Civil Procedure 1.06, when a form is referred to by number, the reference is to the form with that number that is described in the Table of Forms at the end of these rules and which is available on the Internet through www.ontariocourtforms.on.ca. For your convenience, the government form as published on this website is reproduced below.]

ONTARIO
SUPERIOR COURT OF JUSTICE

NOTICE

Attached are a copy of an application for appointment of an estate trustee with a will in the estate of (*insert name*), deceased, and a copy of a certificate of the Estate Registrar indicating that you were named as an estate trustee in a later will or codicil of the deceased that is on deposit in the Superior Court of Justice.

DATE

. . . .
Registrar

Address of court office

TO:

November 1, 2005

FORM 74.35 — REGISTRAR'S NOTICE TO ESTATE TRUSTEE NAMED IN A DEPOSITED WILL OF APPLICATION FOR CERTIFICATE OF APPOINTMENT OF ESTATE TRUSTEE WITHOUT A WILL

Courts of Justice Act

[Repealed O. Reg. 77/06, s. 3.]

[Editor's Note: Forms 4A to 78A of the Rules of Civil Procedure have been repealed by O. Reg. 77/06, effective July 1, 2006. Pursuant to Rule of Civil Procedure 1.06, when a form is

referred to by number, the reference is to the form with that number that is described in the Table of Forms at the end of these rules and which is available on the Internet through www.ontariocourtforms.on.ca. For your convenience, the government form as published on this website is reproduced below.]

ONTARIO
SUPERIOR COURT OF JUSTICE

NOTICE

Attached are a copy of an application for appointment of an estate trustee without a will in the estate of (*insert name*), deceased, and a copy of a certificate of the Estate Registrar indicating that you were named as an estate trustee in a will or codicil of the deceased that is on deposit in the Superior Court of Justice.

DATE

. . . .
Registrar

Address of court office

TO:

November 1, 2005

FORM 74.36 — ORDER TO ACCEPT OR REFUSE APPOINTMENT AS ESTATE TRUSTEE WITH A WILL

Courts of Justice Act

[Repealed O. Reg. 77/06, s. 3.]

[Editor's Note: Forms 4A to 78A of the Rules of Civil Procedure have been repealed by O. Reg. 77/06, effective July 1, 2006. Pursuant to Rule of Civil Procedure 1.06, when a form is referred to by number, the reference is to the form with that number that is described in the Table of Forms at the end of these rules and which is available on the Internet through www.ontariocourtforms.on.ca. For your convenience, the government form as published on this website is reproduced below.]

(Heading in accordance with Form 59A)

IN THE ESTATE OF (*insert name*), deceased.

ORDER TO ACCEPT OR REFUSE APPOINTMENT AS ESTATE TRUSTEE WITH A WILL

A motion for this order has been made by (*insert name of moving party*). From an affidavit made by (*insert name of maker of affidavit*) that has been filed it appears that you are named as estate trustee in a will or codicil of the deceased dated (*insert date*).

1. THIS COURT ORDERS THAT you file an application for a certificate of appointment of estate trustee with a will in the court office within .... days after this order is served on you.

2. THIS COURT ORDERS THAT if you do not do so within that time, you shall be deemed to have renounced your right to be appointed.

....

Registrar

Address of court office

TO:

November 1, 2005

FORM 74.37 — ORDER TO ACCEPT OR REFUSE APPOINTMENT AS ESTATE TRUSTEE WITHOUT A WILL

Courts of Justice Act

[Repealed O. Reg. 77/06, s. 3.]

[Editor's Note: Forms 4A to 78A of the Rules of Civil Procedure have been repealed by O. Reg. 77/06, effective July 1, 2006. Pursuant to Rule of Civil Procedure 1.06, when a form is referred to by number, the reference is to the form with that number that is described in the Table of Forms at the end of these rules and which is available on the Internet through www.ontariocourtforms.on.ca. For your convenience, the government form as published on this website is reproduced below.]

(*Heading in accordance with Form 59A*)

IN THE ESTATE OF (*insert name*), deceased.

ORDER TO ACCEPT OR REFUSE APPOINTMENT AS ESTATE TRUSTEE WITHOUT A WILL

A motion for this order has been made by (*insert name of moving party*). From an affidavit made by (*insert name of maker of affidavit*) that has been filed it appears that you may have a prior right to be appointed estate trustee without a will in the deceased's estate.

1. THIS COURT ORDERS THAT you file an application for a certificate of appointment of estate trustee without a will in the court office within .... days after this order is served on you.

2. THIS COURT ORDERS THAT if you do not do so within that time, you shall be deemed to have renounced your right to be appointed.

. . . .
Registrar

Address of court office

TO:

November 1, 2005

FORM 74.38 — ORDER TO CONSENT OR OBJECT TO A PROPOSED APPOINTMENT OF AN ESTATE TRUSTEE WITH OR WITHOUT A WILL

Courts of Justice Act

[Repealed O. Reg. 77/06, s. 3.]

[Editor's Note: Forms 4A to 78A of the Rules of Civil Procedure have been repealed by O. Reg. 77/06, effective July 1, 2006. Pursuant to Rule of Civil Procedure 1.06, when a form is referred to by number, the reference is to the form with that number that is described in the Table of Forms at the end of these rules and which is available on the Internet through www.ontariocourtforms.on.ca. For your convenience, the government form as published on this website is reproduced below.]

(*Heading in accordance with Form 59A*)

IN THE ESTATE OF (*insert name*), deceased.

ORDER TO CONSENT OR OBJECT TO A PROPOSED APPOINTMENT OF AN ESTATE TRUSTEE WITH OR WITHOUT A WILL

A motion for this order has been made by (*insert name of moving party*). From an affidavit made by (*insert name of maker of affidavit*) that has been filed it appears that (*insert name*) is applying for a certificate of appointment as estate trustee with (*or* without) a will, that you are a person with a financial interest in the estate and that your consent to the appointment is being sought.

1. THIS COURT ORDERS THAT if you oppose that person's appointment as estate trustee, you must file a notice of objection to appointment of estate trustee, in the form attached as Schedule "A", in the court office within .... days after this order is served on you.

2. THIS COURT ORDERS THAT if you do not do so within that time, you shall be deemed to have consented to that person's appointment.

. . . .
Registrar

Address of court office

TO:

Schedule "A"

ONTARIO
SUPERIOR COURT OF JUSTICE

IN THE ESTATE OF (*insert name*), deceased.

NOTICE OF OBJECTION TO APPOINTMENT OF ESTATE TRUSTEE

I, (*insert name*), object to the appointment of (*insert name*) as estate trustee because (*indicate reason*).

DATE

....

(*Name, address and telephone number of objecting person or lawyer for objecting person*)

July 1, 2007

FORM 74.39 — ORDER TO FILE A STATEMENT OF ASSETS OF THE ESTATE

Courts of Justice Act

[Repealed O. Reg. 77/06, s. 3.]

[Editor's Note: Forms 4A to 78A of the Rules of Civil Procedure have been repealed by O. Reg. 77/06, effective July 1, 2006. Pursuant to Rule of Civil Procedure 1.06, when a form is referred to by number, the reference is to the form with that number that is described in the Table of Forms at the end of these rules and which is available on the Internet through www.ontariocourtforms.on.ca. For your convenience, the government form as published on this website is reproduced below.]

(*Heading in accordance with Form 59A*)

IN THE ESTATE OF (*insert name*), deceased.

ORDER TO FILE A STATEMENT OF ASSETS OF THE ESTATE

A motion for this order has been made by (*insert name of moving party*). From an affidavit made by (*insert name of maker of affidavit*) that has been filed it appears that you are an estate trustee of the estate and that you should provide further information about the assets of the estate.

THIS COURT ORDERS THAT you file a statement of the nature of each asset of the estate and its value at the date of death in the court office within .... days after this order is served on you.

....

Registrar

Address of court office

TO:

November 1, 2005

FORM 74.40 — ORDER TO BENEFICIARY WITNESS

Courts of Justice Act

[Repealed O. Reg. 77/06, s. 3.]

[Editor's Note: Forms 4A to 78A of the Rules of Civil Procedure have been repealed by O. Reg. 77/06, effective July 1, 2006. Pursuant to Rule of Civil Procedure 1.06, when a form is referred to by number, the reference is to the form with that number that is described in the Table of Forms at the end of these rules and which is available on the Internet through www.ontariocourtforms.on.ca. For your convenience, the government form as published on this website is reproduced below.]

(*Heading in accordance with Form 59A*)

IN THE ESTATE OF (*insert name*), deceased.

ORDER TO BENEFICIARY WITNESS

A motion for this order has been made by (*insert name of moving party*). From an affidavit made by (*insert name of maker of affidavit*), it appears that (insert name of moving party) has made an application for a certificate of appointment of estate trustee with a will, that you are a beneficiary under the will or codicil dated (*insert date*) and that you or your spouse witnessed the will or codicil or signed for the testator.

1. THIS COURT ORDERS THAT if you wish the court to find that neither you nor your spouse exercised any improper or undue influence on the testator, you must make a motion, within .... days after this order is served on you, asking the court to make that finding.

2. THIS COURT ORDERS THAT if you do not make such a motion within that time, the applicant may proceed to obtain a certificate of appointment of estate trustee with a will, bearing a note stating that your benefits under the will are void under section 12 of the *Succession Law Reform Act*.

....

Registrar

Address of court office

TO:

November 1, 2005

FORM 74.41 — ORDER TO FORMER SPOUSE

Courts of Justice Act

[Repealed O. Reg. 77/06, s. 3.]

[Editor's Note: Forms 4A to 78A of the Rules of Civil Procedure have been repealed by O. Reg. 77/06, effective July 1, 2006. Pursuant to Rule of Civil Procedure 1.06, when a form is referred to by number, the reference is to the form with that number that is described in the Table of Forms at the end of these rules and which is available on the Internet through www.ontariocourtforms.on.ca. For your convenience, the government form as published on this website is reproduced below.]

(*Heading in accordance with Form 59A*)

IN THE ESTATE OF (*insert name*), deceased.

ORDER TO FORMER SPOUSE

Subsection 17(2) of the *Succession Law Reform Act* provides as follows:

> "Except when a contrary intention appears by the will, where, after the testator makes a will, his or her marriage is terminated by a judgment absolute of divorce or is declared a nullity,
>
> > (a) a devise or bequest of a beneficial interest in property to his or her former spouse;
> >
> > (b) an appointment of his or her former spouse as executor or trustee; and
> >
> > (c) the conferring of a general or special power of appointment on his or her former spouse,
>
> are revoked and the will shall be construed as if the former spouse had predeceased the testator."

A motion for this order has been made by (*insert name of moving party*), who has also made an application for a certificate of appointment of estate trustee with a will. From the application it appears that the will is dated (*insert date*) (*and that the codicil(s) is (are) dated* ....), that you are a former spouse of the testator and that your marriage was terminated by a judgment absolute of divorce or declared a nullity after the date of the will (*or codicil*).

1. THIS COURT ORDERS THAT if you wish to take part in the determination of the question whether the provisions in the will that affect you are revoked under subsection 17(2) of the *Succession Law Reform Act*, you must enter an appearance in the office of the registrar of the court within .... days after this order is served on you.

2. THIS COURT ORDERS THAT if you do not do so within that time, the question will be determined in your absence and you will be bound by the result.

. . . .

Registrar

Address of court office

TO:

November 1, 2005

FORM 74.42 — ORDER TO PASS ACCOUNTS

Courts of Justice Act

[Repealed O. Reg. 77/06, s. 3.]

[Editor's Note: Forms 4A to 78A of the Rules of Civil Procedure have been repealed by O. Reg. 77/06, effective July 1, 2006. Pursuant to Rule of Civil Procedure 1.06, when a form is referred to by number, the reference is to the form with that number that is described in the Table of Forms at the end of these rules and which is available on the Internet through www.ontariocourtforms.on.ca. For your convenience, the government form as published on this website is reproduced below.]

(Heading in accordance with Form 59A)

IN THE ESTATE OF (*insert name*), deceased.

ORDER TO PASS ACCOUNTS

A motion for this order has been made by (*insert name of moving party*). From an affidavit made by (*insert name of maker of affidavit*) that has been filed it appears that you are an estate trustee of the estate and that you have made no accounting to the court of your dealings with the estate during the period from (*date*) to (*date*).

THIS COURT ORDERS THAT you file accounts of the estate and an application to pass accounts, in accordance with rules 74.17 and 74.18 of the Rules of Civil Procedure, in the court office within .... days after this order is served on you.

. . . .

Registrar

Address of court office

TO:

November 1, 2005

FORM 74.43 — AFFIDAVIT VERIFYING ESTATE ACCOUNTS

Courts of Justice Act

[Repealed O. Reg. 77/06, s. 3.]

[Editor's Note: Forms 4A to 78A of the Rules of Civil Procedure have been repealed by O. Reg. 77/06, effective July 1, 2006. Pursuant to Rule of Civil Procedure 1.06, when a form is referred to by number, the reference is to the form with that number that is described in the Table of Forms at the end of these rules and which is available on the Internet through www.ontariocourtforms.on.ca. For your convenience, the government form as published on this website is reproduced below.]

ONTARIO
SUPERIOR COURT OF JUSTICE

IN THE ESTATE OF (*insert name*), deceased.

AFFIDAVIT VERIFYING ESTATE ACCOUNTS

I, (*insert name*), of (*insert city or town and county or district, metropolitan or regional municipality of residence*), make oath and say/affirm:

1. I am an estate trustee for this estate.

2. The accounts marked as Exhibit "A" to this affidavit are complete and correct.

3. The information contained in the notice of application to pass accounts with respect to this estate is true.

4. All persons having a financial interest in the estate are named as respondents in the notice of application to pass accounts.

5. For any party with a disability, a representative has been identified in the notice of application.

SWORN/AFFIRMED BEFORE)
me at the of)
in the of)
this day of , 20 .)
)
)
) ....
)
....)
A Commissioner for Taking Affidavits
(*or as may be*)

November 1, 2005

FORM 74.44 — NOTICE OF APPLICATION TO PASS ACCOUNTS

Courts of Justice Act

[Repealed O. Reg. 77/06, s. 3.]

[Editor's Note: Forms 4A to 78A of the Rules of Civil Procedure have been repealed by O. Reg. 77/06, effective July 1, 2006. Pursuant to Rule of Civil Procedure 1.06, when a form is referred to by number, the reference is to the form with that number that is described in the Table of Forms at the end of these rules and which is available on the Internet through www.ontariocourtforms.on.ca. For your convenience, the government form as published on this website is reproduced below.]

ONTARIO
SUPERIOR COURT OF JUSTICE

IN THE ESTATE OF (*insert name*), deceased.

NOTICE OF APPLICATION TO PASS ACCOUNTS

This application to pass accounts will be heard on (*date*), at (*time*), at the court house at (*full address of court house*), if any person with a financial interest in the estate objects to the accounts or to the compensation claimed, or if a request for increased costs is served and filed.

The deceased died on (*date*).

A certificate of appointment of estate trustee was issued to (*insert name*) by this court on (*date*).

The accounts are for the period from (*date*) to (*date*).

The compensation claimed by the estate trustee, payable out of the estate, is (*insert amount*).

If there is no hearing, the costs of the application claimed by the estate trustee under Tariff C are (*amount*).

If there is no hearing, a person with a financial interest in the estate who retains a lawyer to review the accounts and makes no objection to them (or makes an objection and later withdraws it) but serves on the estate trustee and files with the court a request for costs (Form 74.49 under the *Rules of Civil Procedure*), will be allowed one-half of the costs allowed to the estate trustee. However, where two or more persons are represented by the same lawyer, they are entitled to receive only one person's costs. If the Children's Lawyer or the Public Guardian and Trustee makes no objection to the accounts (or makes an objection and later withdraws it) but serves on the estate trustee and files with the court a request for costs (Form 74.49.1), he or she will be allowed three-quarters of the costs allowed to the estate trustee.

If the estate trustee or any person with a financial interest in the estate seeks costs of the application greater than the amount allowed in Tariff C, the estate trustee or other person shall serve on every other party and file, with proof of service, a request for increased costs (Form 74.49.2 or 74.49.3 under the *Rules of Civil Procedure*), at least 10 days before the hearing date specified in this notice of application. In that case, the hearing shall proceed on the date specified.

Any person with a financial interest in the estate who wishes to object shall do so by serving upon the estate trustee, or the lawyer for the estate trustee, a notice of objection to accounts (Form 74.45 under the *Rules of Civil Procedure*, a copy of which is attached to this notice of application), and by filing a copy of the notice in the court office at least 20 days before the date fixed for the hearing.

At the hearing, the only issues upon which the court adjudicates are those raised in the notices of objection to accounts and requests for increased costs that have been filed, unless the court grants leave to a party to raise other issues.

If no notice of objection to accounts or request for increased costs is served and filed, the estate trustee may, without a hearing, obtain a judgment passing the accounts and allowing the compensation and costs claimed.

Any person may contact the estate trustee or the estate trustee's lawyer to find out whether there will be a hearing. A copy of the accounts may be obtained from the estate trustee or the estate trustee's lawyer, or may be inspected in the court office during regular business hours.

DATE ....
Registrar

(*Name, address and telephone number of estate trustee or lawyer for the estate trustee*)

TO: (*Name and address of each person with a financial interest in the estate*)

(*For a person under disability, also indicate name and address of personal representative*)

(*Attach a blank copy of Form 74.45 (notice of objection to accounts).*)

July 1, 2007

FORM 74.45 — NOTICE OF OBJECTION TO ACCOUNTS

Courts of Justice Act

[Repealed O. Reg. 77/06, s. 3.]

[Editor's Note: Forms 4A to 78A of the Rules of Civil Procedure have been repealed by O. Reg. 77/06, effective July 1, 2006. Pursuant to Rule of Civil Procedure 1.06, when a form is referred to by number, the reference is to the form with that number that is described in the Table of Forms at the end of these rules and which is available on the Internet through www.ontariocourtforms.on.ca. For your convenience, the government form as published on this website is reproduced below.]

ONTARIO
SUPERIOR COURT OF JUSTICE

IN THE ESTATE OF (*insert name*), deceased.

NOTICE OF OBJECTION TO ACCOUNTS

1. I, (*insert name*), object to the amount of compensation claimed by the estate trustee on the following grounds:

(*If applicable, set out each objection in separate consecutively numbered paragraphs. Attach separate sheet if necessary.*)

2. I, (*insert name*), object to the accounts of the estate trustee on the following grounds:

(*If applicable, set out each objection in separate consecutively numbered paragraphs. Attach separate sheet if necessary.*)

DATE

(*Name, address and telephone number of objecting person or lawyer for objecting person*)

TO: (*Name and address of estate trustee or lawyer for estate trustee*)

July 1, 2007

FORM 74.46 — NOTICE OF NO OBJECTION TO ACCOUNTS

Courts of Justice Act

[Repealed O. Reg. 77/06, s. 3.]

[Editor's Note: Forms 4A to 78A of the Rules of Civil Procedure have been repealed by O. Reg. 77/06, effective July 1, 2006. Pursuant to Rule of Civil Procedure 1.06, when a form is referred to by number, the reference is to the form with that number that is described in the Table of Forms at the end of these rules and which is available on the Internet through www.ontariocourtforms.on.ca. For your convenience, the government form as published on this website is reproduced below.]

ONTARIO
SUPERIOR COURT OF JUSTICE

IN THE ESTATE OF (*insert name*), deceased.

NOTICE OF NO OBJECTION TO ACCOUNTS

The (Public Guardian and Trustee) (Children's Lawyer) has no objection to the estate accounts and the claim for compensation by the estate trustee.

DATE

(Name, address and telephone number of Children's Lawyer or Public Guardian and Trustee, or lawyer for Children's Lawyer or Public Guardian and Trustee)

TO: *(Name and address of estate trustee or lawyer for estate trustee)*

July 1, 2007

FORM 74.46.1 — NOTICE OF NON-PARTICIPATION IN PASSING OF ACCOUNTS

Courts of Justice Act

[Repealed O. Reg. 77/06, s. 3.]

[Editor's Note: Forms 4A to 78A of the Rules of Civil Procedure have been repealed by O. Reg. 77/06, effective July 1, 2006. Pursuant to Rule of Civil Procedure 1.06, when a form is referred to by number, the reference is to the form with that number that is described in the Table of Forms at the end of these rules and which is available on the Internet through www.ontariocourtforms.on.ca. For your convenience, the government form as published on this website is reproduced below.]

ONTARIO
SUPERIOR COURT OF JUSTICE

IN THE ESTATE OF (*insert name*), deceased.

NOTICE OF NON-PARTICIPATION IN PASSING OF ACCOUNTS

The (Public Guardian and Trustee) (Children's Lawyer) does not intend to participate in the passing of accounts.

DATE

(Name, address and telephone number of Children's Lawyer or Public Guardian and Trustee, or lawyer for Children's Lawyer or Public Guardian and Trustee)

TO: (*Name and address of estate trustee
or lawyer for the estate trustee*)

July 1, 2007

FORM 74.47 — AFFIDAVIT IN SUPPORT OF UNOPPOSED JUDGMENT ON PASSING OF ACCOUNTS

Courts of Justice Act

[Repealed O. Reg. 77/06, s. 3.]

[Editor's Note: Forms 4A to 78A of the Rules of Civil Procedure have been repealed by O. Reg. 77/06, effective July 1, 2006. Pursuant to Rule of Civil Procedure 1.06, when a form is referred to by number, the reference is to the form with that number that is described in the Table of Forms at the end of these rules and which is available on the Internet through www.ontariocourtforms.on.ca. For your convenience, the government form as published on this website is reproduced below.]

ONTARIO
SUPERIOR COURT OF JUSTICE

IN THE ESTATE OF (*insert name*), deceased.

AFFIDAVIT SUPPORT OF UNOPPOSED JUDGMENT ON PASSING OF ACCOUNTS

I, (*insert name*), of (*insert city or town and county or district, metropolitan or regional municipality of residence*), make oath and say/affirm:

1. I am the applicant for an unopposed judgment on the passing of accounts in this estate with respect to estate accounts from (*date*) to (*date*).

2. A copy of the estate accounts has been provided to each person who was served with the notice of application and who requested a copy of the accounts.

3. The time for filing notices of objection to the estate accounts has expired.

4. No notice of objection has been received from any person served with the notice of application.

OR

4. Any notice of objection that was received has been withdrawn by the filing of a notice of withdrawal of objection.

SWORN/AFFIRMED BEFORE)
me at the of)
in the of)

this day of , 20 .)))) ....)

....
A Commissioner for Taking Affidavits
(*or as may be*)

NOTE: The two versions of paragraph 4 are in the alternative. Delete the one that does not apply.

November 1, 2005

FORM 74.48 — NOTICE OF WITHDRAWAL OF OBJECTION

Courts of Justice Act

[Repealed O. Reg. 77/06, s. 3.]

[Editor's Note: Forms 4A to 78A of the Rules of Civil Procedure have been repealed by O. Reg. 77/06, effective July 1, 2006. Pursuant to Rule of Civil Procedure 1.06, when a form is referred to by number, the reference is to the form with that number that is described in the Table of Forms at the end of these rules and which is available on the Internet through www.ontariocourtforms.on.ca. For your convenience, the government form as published on this website is reproduced below.]

ONTARIO
SUPERIOR COURT OF JUSTICE

IN THE ESTATE OF (*insert name*), deceased.

NOTICE OF WITHDRAWAL OF OBJECTION

I, (*insert name*), filed a notice of objection to accounts and hereby withdraw that notice of objection.

DATE

(*Name, address and telephone number of party or party's lawyer*)

TO: (*Name and address of estate trustee or lawyer for estate trustee*)

July 1, 2007

FORM 74.49 — REQUEST FOR COSTS (PERSON OTHER THAN CHILDREN'S LAWYER OR PUBLIC GUARDIAN AND TRUSTEE)

Courts of Justice Act

[Repealed O. Reg. 77/06, s. 3.]

[Editor's Note: Forms 4A to 78A of the Rules of Civil Procedure have been repealed by O. Reg. 77/06, effective July 1, 2006. Pursuant to Rule of Civil Procedure 1.06, when a form is referred to by number, the reference is to the form with that number that is described in the Table of Forms at the end of these rules and which is available on the Internet through www.ontariocourtforms.on.ca. For your convenience, the government form as published on this website is reproduced below.]

ONTARIO
SUPERIOR COURT OF JUSTICE

IN THE ESTATE OF (*insert name*), deceased.

REQUEST FOR COSTS (PERSON OTHER THAN CHILDREN'S LAWYER OR PUBLIC GUARDIAN AND TRUSTEE)

I, (*insert name*), have retained (*insert name*) as my lawyer to review the estate accounts. I have no objection to the estate accounts and the claim for compensation by the estate trustee.

I request that I be awarded costs payable out of the estate in the amount of $ ...., representing one-half of the amount payable to the estate solicitor under Tariff C.

DATE

(*Name, address and telephone number of party or party's lawyer*)

TO: (*Name and address of estate trustee or lawyer for estate trustee*)

July 1, 2007

FORM 74.49.1 — REQUEST FOR COSTS (CHILDREN'S LAWYER OR PUBLIC GUARDIAN AND TRUSTEE)

Courts of Justice Act

[Repealed O. Reg. 77/06, s. 3.]

[Editor's Note: Forms 4A to 78A of the Rules of Civil Procedure have been repealed by O. Reg. 77/06, effective July 1, 2006. Pursuant to Rule of Civil Procedure 1.06, when a form is referred to by number, the reference is to the form with that number that is described in the Table of Forms at the end of these rules and which is available on the Internet through www.ontariocourtforms.on.ca. For your convenience, the government form as published on this website is reproduced below.]

ONTARIO
SUPERIOR COURT OF JUSTICE

IN THE ESTATE OF (*insert name*), deceased.

REQUEST FOR COSTS (CHILDREN'S LAWYER OR PUBLIC GUARDIAN AND TRUSTEE)

The (Public Guardian and Trustee) (Children's Lawyer) has no objection to the estate accounts and the claim for compensation by the estate trustee.

The (Public Guardian and Trustee) (Children's Lawyer) requests that he or she be awarded costs payable out of the estate in the amount of $ ...., representing three-quarters of the amount payable to the estate solicitor under Tariff C.

DATE

(*Name, address and telephone number of Children's Lawyer or Public Guardian and Trustee, or lawyer for Children's Lawyer or Public Guardian and Trustee*)

TO: (*Name and address of estate trustee or lawyer for the estate trustee*)

July 1, 2007

FORM 74.49.2 — REQUEST FOR INCREASED COSTS (ESTATE TRUSTEE)

Courts of Justice Act

[Repealed O. Reg. 77/06, s. 3.]

[Editor's Note: Forms 4A to 78A of the Rules of Civil Procedure have been repealed by O. Reg. 77/06, effective July 1, 2006. Pursuant to Rule of Civil Procedure 1.06, when a form is referred to by number, the reference is to the form with that number that is described in the Table of Forms at the end of these rules and which is available on the Internet through www.ontariocourtforms.on.ca. For your convenience, the government form as published on this website is reproduced below.]

ONTARIO
SUPERIOR COURT OF JUSTICE

IN THE ESTATE OF (*insert name*), deceased.

REQUEST FOR INCREASED COSTS (ESTATE TRUSTEE)

I request that I be awarded costs payable out of the estate in the amount of $ ...., which is greater than the amount allowed under Tariff C. I understand that this necessitates a hearing on the date specified in the notice of application.

DATE

(*Name, address and telephone number of estate trustee or lawyer for estate trustee*)

TO: (*Name and address of each person with a financial interest in the estate*) (*For a person under disability, also indicate name and address of personal representative*)

July 1, 2007

FORM 74.49.3 — REQUEST FOR INCREASED COSTS (PERSON OTHER THAN ESTATE TRUSTEE)

Courts of Justice Act

[Repealed O. Reg. 77/06, s. 3.]

[Editor's Note: Forms 4A to 78A of the Rules of Civil Procedure have been repealed by O. Reg. 77/06, effective July 1, 2006. Pursuant to Rule of Civil Procedure 1.06, when a form is referred to by number, the reference is to the form with that number that is described in the Table of Forms at the end of these rules and which is available on the Internet through www.ontariocourtforms.on.ca. For your convenience, the government form as published on this website is reproduced below.]

ONTARIO
SUPERIOR COURT OF JUSTICE

IN THE ESTATE OF (*insert name*), deceased.

REQUEST FOR INCREASED COSTS
(PERSON OTHER THAN
ESTATE TRUSTEE)

1. I, (*insert name*), have retained (*insert name*) as my lawyer to review the estate accounts. I have no objection to the estate accounts and the claim for compensation by the estate trustee.

2. I request that I be awarded costs payable out of the estate in the amount of $ .... which is greater than one-half the amount payable to the estate trustee under Tariff C. I understand that this necessitates a hearing on the date specified in the notice of application.

DATE

(*Name, address and telephone number of person or person's lawyer*)

TO: (*Name and address of every other person with a financial interest in the estate*)

(*For a person under disability, also indicate name and address of personal representative*)

(*Name and address of estate trustee or lawyer for estate trustee*)

July 1, 2007

FORM 74.50 — JUDGMENT ON UNOPPOSED PASSING OF ACCOUNTS

Courts of Justice Act

[Repealed O. Reg. 77/06, s. 3.]

[Editor's Note: Forms 4A to 78A of the Rules of Civil Procedure have been repealed by O. Reg. 77/06, effective July 1, 2006. Pursuant to Rule of Civil Procedure 1.06, when a form is referred to by number, the reference is to the form with that number that is described in the Table of Forms at the end of these rules and which is available on the Internet through www.ontariocourtforms.on.ca. For your convenience, the government form as published on this website is reproduced below.]

(*Heading in accordance with Form 59B*)

IN THE ESTATE OF (*insert name*), deceased.

JUDGMENT ON PASSING OF ACCOUNTS

THIS APPLICATION was read on (*date*), at (*place*).

ON READING THE NOTICE OF APPLICATION TO PASS ACCOUNTS, the affidavit of service and the affidavit in support of an unopposed judgment on passing of accounts, as filed, and as there are no objections to the accounts or the claim for compensation by the estate trustee,

1. THIS COURT DECLARES that the estate accounts, as filed by the applicant for the period from (*date*) to (*date*), are hereby passed.

2. THIS COURT DECLARES that the capital receipts and capital disbursements of the applicant for the period are as follows:

CAPITAL ACCOUNT			
Credit balance forward (*if applicable*)	$		
Receipts	$	$	(total)
Debit balance forward (*if applicable*)	$		
Disbursements	$	$	(total)
Credit (or debit) balance		$	

3. THIS COURT DECLARES that the revenue receipts and revenue disbursements of the applicant for the period are as follows:

REVENUE ACCOUNT			
Credit balance forward (*if applicable*)	$		
Receipts	$	$	(total)
Debit balance forward (*if applicable*)	$		
Disbursements	$	$	(total)
Credit (or debit) balance		$	

4. THIS COURT ORDERS that the estate trustee shall be paid as fair and reasonable compensation for services as estate trustee of the estate and for disbursements expended in administering the affairs of the estate during the period the total amount of $ .... (including G.S.T.), of which $ .... shall be paid out of the capital of the estate and $ .... shall be paid out of the revenue of the estate.

5. THIS COURT ORDERS that the costs of the passing of the accounts allowed in accordance with Tariff C, and payable out of the capital of the estate, are as follows:

To the estate trustee $ ...., and G.S.T. of $ .... for a total of $ ....

To (*insert names and amounts, showing each person awarded costs on a separate line*)

6. THIS COURT DECLARES that the accounts show that there remain in the estate trustee's hands the original assets as set out in Schedule "A", attached.

November 1, 2005

FORM 74.51 — JUDGMENT ON CONTESTED PASSING OF ACCOUNTS

Courts of Justice Act

[Repealed O. Reg. 77/06, s. 3.]

[Editor's Note: Forms 4A to 78A of the Rules of Civil Procedure have been repealed by O. Reg. 77/06, effective July 1, 2006. Pursuant to Rule of Civil Procedure 1.06, when a form is

referred to by number, the reference is to the form with that number that is described in the Table of Forms at the end of these rules and which is available on the Internet through www.ontariocourtforms.on.ca. For your convenience, the government form as published on this website is reproduced below.]

(*Heading in accordance with Form 59B*)

IN THE ESTATE OF (*insert name*), deceased.

JUDGMENT ON PASSING OF ACCOUNTS

THIS APPLICATION was heard on (*date*), at (*place*) in the presence of the lawyer(s) for (*insert name*) (*where applicable add* and (*insert name*) appearing in person) (*where applicable add* and no one appearing for (*insert name*), although properly served as appears from the affidavit of service filed).

ON READING THE NOTICE OF APPLICATION TO PASS ACCOUNTS and on hearing the submissions made,

1. THIS COURT DECLARES that the estate accounts, as filed by the applicant for the period from (*date*) to (*date*), are hereby passed.

2. THIS COURT DECLARES that the capital receipts and capital disbursements of the applicant for the period are as follows:

CAPITAL ACCOUNT			
Credit balance forward (*if applicable*)	$		
Receipts	$	$	(total)
Debit balance forward (*if applicable*)	$		
Disbursements	$	$	(total)
Credit (or debit) balance		$	

3. THIS COURT DECLARES that the revenue receipts and revenue disbursements of the applicant for the period are as follows:

REVENUE ACCOUNT			
Credit balance forward (*if applicable*)	$		
Receipts	$	$	(total)
Debit balance forward (*if applicable*)	$		
Disbursements	$	$	(total)
Credit (or debit) balance		$	

4. THIS COURT ORDERS that the estate trustee shall be paid as fair and reasonable compensation for services as estate trustee of the estate and for disbursements expended in administering the affairs of the estate during the period the total amount of $ .... (including G.S.T.), of which $ .... shall be paid out of the capital of the estate and $ .... shall be paid out of the revenue of the estate.

5. THIS COURT ORDERS that the costs of the passing of the accounts allowed and payable out of the capital of the estate are as follows:

To the estate trustee $ ...., and G.S.T. of $ .... for a total of $ ....

To (*insert names and amounts, showing each person awarded costs on a separate line*)

6. THIS COURT DECLARES that the accounts show that there remain in the estate trustee's hands the original assets as set out in Schedule "A", attached.

July 1, 2007

FORM 75.1 — NOTICE OF OBJECTION

Courts of Justice Act

[Repealed O. Reg. 77/06, s. 3.]

[Editor's Note: Forms 4A to 78A of the Rules of Civil Procedure have been repealed by O. Reg. 77/06, effective July 1, 2006. Pursuant to Rule of Civil Procedure 1.06, when a form is referred to by number, the reference is to the form with that number that is described in the Table of Forms at the end of these rules and which is available on the Internet through www.ontariocourtforms.on.ca. For your convenience, the government form as published on this website is reproduced below.]

ONTARIO

SUPERIOR COURT OF JUSTICE

In the Estate of the deceased person described below:

DETAILS ABOUT THE DECEASED PERSON

Complete in full as applicable

First given name	Second given name	Third given name	Surname
And if the deceased was known by any other name(s), state below the full name(s) used including surname.			
First given name	Second given name	Third given name	Surname

IN THE MATTER OF an application for a certificate of appointment of estate trustee

NOTICE OF OBJECTION

I, ... *(insert name)*, object to the issuing of a certificate of appointment of estate trustee to .... *(insert name of applicant)* without notice to me because .... *(in-*

dicate reason, such as lack of testamentary capacity, undue influence or unfitness to act as estate trustee).

The nature of my interest in the estate is: *(state relationship to the deceased and whether a named beneficiary under the will, or other basis for financial interest).* ....

DATE ....

(Name, address and telephone number of objector or lawyer for objector) ....

July 1, 2007

FORM 75.1A — REQUEST FOR ASSIGNMENT OF MEDIATOR

Courts of Justice Act

[Repealed O. Reg. 77/06, s. 3.]

[Editor's Note: Forms 4A to 78A of the Rules of Civil Procedure have been repealed by O. Reg. 77/06, effective July 1, 2006. Pursuant to Rule of Civil Procedure 1.06, when a form is referred to by number, the reference is to the form with that number that is described in the Table of Forms at the end of these rules and which is available on the Internet through www.ontariocourtforms.on.ca. For your convenience, the government form as published on this website is reproduced below.]

ONTARIO (*Court file no.*)

SUPERIOR COURT OF JUSTICE

IN THE ESTATE OF deceased,

late of ,

occupation ,

who died on ,

REQUEST FOR ASSIGNMENT OF MEDIATOR

TO: Mediation co-ordinator for (*county*)

An order giving directions was made under rule 75.1.05 on (*date of order*). A copy of the order is attached to this request.

The designated parties have not chosen a mediator under subrule 75.1.06(1). The 30-day period mentioned in subrule 75.1.07(1) has expired.

This is a request that you assign a mediator from the list for the country.

(*Date*) (*Name, address, telephone number and fax number, if any, of lawyer of party filing request, or of party*)

November 1, 2005

FORM 75.1B — NOTICE BY MEDIATOR

Courts of Justice Act

[Repealed O. Reg. 77/06, s. 3.]

[Editor's Note: Forms 4A to 78A of the Rules of Civil Procedure have been repealed by O. Reg. 77/06, effective July 1, 2006. Pursuant to Rule of Civil Procedure 1.06, when a form is referred to by number, the reference is to the form with that number that is described in the Table of Forms at the end of these rules and which is available on the Internet through www.ontariocourtforms.on.ca. For your convenience, the government form as published on this website is reproduced below.]

ONTARIO (*Court file no.*)

SUPERIOR COURT OF JUSTICE

IN THE ESTATE OF deceased,

late of ,

occupation ,

who died on ,

NOTICE BY MEDIATOR

TO:

AND TO:

I am the mediator whom the mediation co-ordinator has appointed to conduct the mediation session under Rule 75.1. (*Delete this paragraph if mediator was chosen by designated parties under clause 75.1.06(1)(a) or (c).*)

The mediation session will take place on (*date*), from (*time*) to (*time*), at (*place*).

You are required to attend this mediation session. If you have a lawyer representing you in this proceeding, he or she is also required to attend.

You are required to file a statement of issues (Form 75.1C) by (*date*) (seven days before the mediation session). A blank copy of the form is attached.

When you attend the mediation session, you should bring with you any documents that you consider of central importance in the proceeding. You should plan to remain throughout the scheduled time. If you need another person's approval before agreeing to a settlement, you should make arrangements before the mediation session to ensure that you have ready telephone access to that person throughout the session, even outside regular business hours.

YOU MAY BE PENALIZED UNDER RULE 75.1.10 IF YOU FAIL TO FILE A STATEMENT OF ISSUES OR FAIL TO ATTEND THE MEDIATION SESSION.

(*Date*) (*Name, address, telephone number and fax number, if any, of mediator*)

November 1, 2005

FORM 75.1C — STATEMENT OF ISSUES

Courts of Justice Act

[Repealed O. Reg. 77/06, s. 3.]

[Editor's Note: Forms 4A to 78A of the Rules of Civil Procedure have been repealed by O. Reg. 77/06, effective July 1, 2006. Pursuant to Rule of Civil Procedure 1.06, when a form is referred to by number, the reference is to the form with that number that is described in the Table of Forms at the end of these rules and which is available on the Internet through www.ontariocourtforms.on.ca. For your convenience, the government form as published on this website is reproduced below.]

ONTARIO (*Court file no.*)

SUPERIOR COURT OF JUSTICE

IN THE ESTATE OF deceased,

late of ,

occupation ,

who died on ,

STATEMENT OF ISSUES

(*To be provided to mediator and designated parties at least seven days before the mediation session*)

1. *Factual and legal issues in dispute*

The undersigned designated party states that the following factual and legal issues are in dispute and remain to be resolved.

(*Issues should be stated briefly and numbered consecutively.*)

2. *Party's position and interests (what the party hopes to achieve)*

   (*Brief summary.*)

3. *Attached documents*

   Attached to this form are the following documents that the designated party considers of central importance in the proceeding: (*list*)

   (*Date*) (*party's signature*)

   (*Name, address, telephone number and fax number, if any, of lawyer of party filing statement of issues, or of party*)

NOTE: Rule 75.1.11 provides as follows:

All communications at a mediation session and the mediator's notes and records shall be deemed to be without prejudice settlement discussions.

November 1, 2005

FORM 75.1D — CERTIFICATE OF NON-COMPLIANCE

Courts of Justice Act

[Repealed O. Reg. 77/06, s. 3.]

[Editor's Note: Forms 4A to 78A of the Rules of Civil Procedure have been repealed by O. Reg. 77/06, effective July 1, 2006. Pursuant to Rule of Civil Procedure 1.06, when a form is referred to by number, the reference is to the form with that number that is described in the Table of Forms at the end of these rules and which is available on the Internet through www.ontariocourtforms.on.ca. For your convenience, the government form as published on this website is reproduced below.]

ONTARIO (*Court file no.*)

SUPERIOR COURT OF JUSTICE

IN THE ESTATE OF deceased,

late of ,

occupation ,

who died on ,

CERTIFICATE OF NON-COMPLIANCE

TO: (*court*)

1. (*name*), mediator, certify that this certificate of non-compliance is filed because:

( ) *Identify party(ies)*) failed to provide a copy of a statement of issues to the mediator and the other parties (*or* to the mediator *or* to *party*(ies)).

( ) (*Identify party*(ies)) failed to attend within the first 30 minutes of a scheduled mediation session.

(*Date*) (*Name, address, telephone number and fax number, if any, of mediator*)

November 1, 2005

FORM 75.2 — NOTICE THAT OBJECTION HAS BEEN FILED

Courts of Justice Act

[Repealed O. Reg. 77/06, s. 3.]

[Editor's Note: Forms 4A to 78A of the Rules of Civil Procedure have been repealed by O. Reg. 77/06, effective July 1, 2006. Pursuant to Rule of Civil Procedure 1.06, when a form is referred to by number, the reference is to the form with that number that is described in the Table of Forms at the end of these rules and which is available on the Internet through www.ontariocourtforms.on.ca. For your convenience, the government form as published on this website is reproduced below.]

ONTARIO
SUPERIOR COURT OF JUSTICE

IN THE ESTATE OF (*insert name*), deceased.

IN THE MATTER OF an application for a certificate of appointment of estate trustee

NOTICE THAT OBJECTION HAS BEEN FILED

A notice of objection, a copy of which is attached, has been filed with the court.

No further action regarding issuing a certificate of appointment to you will be taken until you have complied with subrule 75.03(4) of the *Rules of Civil Procedure*.

DATE ....
Registrar

Address of court office

TO: (*Name, address and telephone number of applicant or lawyer for the applicant*)

July 1, 2007

FORM 75.3 — NOTICE TO OBJECTOR

Courts of Justice Act

[Repealed O. Reg. 77/06, s. 3.]

[Editor's Note: Forms 4A to 78A of the Rules of Civil Procedure have been repealed by O. Reg. 77/06, effective July 1, 2006. Pursuant to Rule of Civil Procedure 1.06, when a form is referred to by number, the reference is to the form with that number that is described in the Table of Forms at the end of these rules and which is available on the Internet through www.ontariocourtforms.on.ca. For your convenience, the government form as published on this website is reproduced below.]

ONTARIO
SUPERIOR COURT OF JUSTICE

IN THE ESTATE OF (*insert name*), deceased.

IN THE MATTER OF an application for a certificate of appointment of estate trustee

NOTICE TO OBJECTOR

AN APPLICATION for a certificate of appointment of estate trustee in the estate has been made by (*name of applicant*).

IF YOU WISH TO OPPOSE this application, you or an Ontario lawyer acting for you must within 20 days of service on you of this notice to objector prepare a notice of appearance in Form 75.4 of the Rules of Civil Procedure, serve it on the applicant's lawyer, or where the applicant does not have a lawyer serve it on the applicant, and file it with proof of service in the court office at (*full court address where application for certificate of appointment was filed*).

IF YOU FAIL to serve and file a notice of appearance, the application for certificate of appointment of estate trustee shall proceed as if your notice of objection had not been filed.

DATE

(*Name, address and telephone number of applicant or lawyer for the applicant*)

TO: (*Name and address of the objector or lawyer for the objector*)

July 1, 2007

FORM 75.4 — NOTICE OF APPEARANCE

Courts of Justice Act

[Repealed O. Reg. 77/06, s. 3.]

[Editor's Note: Forms 4A to 78A of the Rules of Civil Procedure have been repealed by O. Reg. 77/06, effective July 1, 2006. Pursuant to Rule of Civil Procedure 1.06, when a form is referred to by number, the reference is to the form with that number that is described in the Table of Forms at the end of these rules and which is available on the Internet through www.ontariocourtforms.on.ca. For your convenience, the government form as published on this website is reproduced below.]

ONTARIO
SUPERIOR COURT OF JUSTICE

IN THE ESTATE OF (*insert name*), deceased.

IN THE MATTER OF an application for a certificate of appointment of estate trustee

NOTICE OF APPEARANCE

I desire to oppose the issuing of a certificate of appointment of estate trustee for the reasons set out in the notice of objection filed.

DATE

(*Name, address and telephone number of objector or lawyer for the objector*)

TO: (*Name, address and telephone number of applicant or lawyer for the applicant*)

July 1, 2007

FORM 75.5 — NOTICE OF APPLICATION FOR DIRECTIONS

Courts of Justice Act

[Repealed O. Reg. 77/06, s. 3.]

[Editor's Note: Forms 4A to 78A of the Rules of Civil Procedure have been repealed by O. Reg. 77/06, effective July 1, 2006. Pursuant to Rule of Civil Procedure 1.06, when a form is referred to by number, the reference is to the form with that number that is described in the Table of Forms at the end of these rules and which is available on the Internet through www.ontariocourtforms.on.ca. For your convenience, the government form as published on this website is reproduced below.]

ONTARIO
SUPERIOR COURT OF JUSTICE

IN THE ESTATE OF (*insert name*), deceased.

BETWEEN:

(*Name*)

Applicant

- and -

(*Name*)

Respondent

NOTICE OF APPLICATION FOR DIRECTIONS

TO THE RESPONDENT

A LEGAL PROCEEDING HAS BEEN COMMENCED by the applicant. The claim made by the applicant appears on the following page.

THIS APPLICATION will come on for a hearing before a judge on (*date*) at (*time*), at the Court House at (*place*).

IF YOU WISH TO OPPOSE THIS APPLICATION, you or an Ontario lawyer acting for you must forthwith prepare a notice of appearance in Form 38A prescribed by the *Rules of Civil Procedure*, serve it on the applicant's lawyer or, where the applicant does not have a lawyer, serve it on the applicant, and file it, with proof of service, in this court office, and you or your lawyer must appear at the hearing.

IF YOU WISH TO PRESENT AFFIDAVIT OR OTHER DOCUMENTARY EVIDENCE TO THE COURT OR TO EXAMINE OR CROSS-EXAMINE WITNESSES ON THE APPLICATION, you or your lawyer must, in addition to serving your notice of appearance, serve a copy of the evidence on the applicant's lawyer or, where the applicant does not have a lawyer, serve it on the applicant, and file it with proof of service, in the court office where the application is to be heard, as soon as possible, but not later than two days before the hearing.

IF YOU FAIL TO APPEAR AT THE HEARING, JUDGMENT MAY BE GIVEN IN YOUR ABSENCE AND WITHOUT FURTHER NOTICE TO YOU.

If you wish to oppose this application but are unable to pay legal fees, legal aid may be available to you by contacting a local Legal Aid office.

Date .... Issued by ....

Local registrar

Address of court office

TO: (*Name and address of respondent, or lawyer for respondent*)

1. The applicant makes application or directions from the court with respect to: (*state nature of proceeding*)

2. The grounds for the application are rule 75.06 and (*include a reference to any statutory provision or Rule to be relied on*).

3. The following documentary evidence will be used at the hearing of the application for directions: (*list the affidavits or other documentary evidence to be relied upon*).

July 1, 2007

FORM 75.6 — NOTICE OF MOTION FOR DIRECTIONS

Courts of Justice Act

[Repealed O. Reg. 77/06, s. 3.]

[Editor's Note: Forms 4A to 78A of the Rules of Civil Procedure have been repealed by O. Reg. 77/06, effective July 1, 2006. Pursuant to Rule of Civil Procedure 1.06, when a form is referred to by number, the reference is to the form with that number that is described in the Table of Forms at the end of these rules and which is available on the Internet through www.ontariocourtforms.on.ca. For your convenience, the government form as published on this website is reproduced below.]

ONTARIO
SUPERIOR COURT OF JUSTICE

IN THE ESTATE OF (*insert name*), deceased.

BETWEEN:

(*Name*)

Moving Party

- and -

(*Name*)

Respondent

NOTICE OF MOTION FOR DIRECTIONS

The moving party will make a motion to the court on (*date*), at (*time*), or so soon after that time as the motion can be heard at (*full address of Court House*).

The motion is for directions with respect to:

(*state nature of proceeding*)

The grounds for the motion are rule 75.06 and (*specify the further grounds to be argued, including a reference to any statutory provision or Rule*).

The following documentary evidence will be used at the hearing of the motion: (*list the affidavits or other documentary evidence to be relied on*).

DATE

(*Name, address and telephone number of applicant or lawyer for the applicant*)

TO: (*Name and address of respondent or lawyer for the respondent*)

July 1, 2007

FORM 75.7 — STATEMENT OF CLAIM PURSUANT TO ORDER GIVING DIRECTIONS

Courts of Justice Act

[Repealed O. Reg. 77/06, s. 3.]

[Editor's Note: Forms 4A to 78A of the Rules of Civil Procedure have been repealed by O. Reg. 77/06, effective July 1, 2006. Pursuant to Rule of Civil Procedure 1.06, when a form is referred to by number, the reference is to the form with that number that is described in the Table of Forms at the end of these rules and which is available on the Internet through www.ontariocourtforms.on.ca. For your convenience, the government form as published on this website is reproduced below.]

ONTARIO
SUPERIOR COURT OF JUSTICE

IN THE ESTATE OF (*insert name*), deceased.

BETWEEN:

(*Name*)

Plaintiff

- and -

(*Name*)

Defendant

- and -

(*Name*)

Persons Submitting
Rights to the Court

STATEMENT OF CLAIM PURSUANT TO ORDER GIVING DIRECTIONS

TO THE DEFENDANT

A LEGAL PROCEEDING HAS BEEN COMMENCED by the Plaintiff. The claim made is set out in the following pages.

IF YOU WISH TO DEFEND THIS PROCEEDING, you or an Ontario lawyer acting for you must prepare a statement of defence in Form 18A prescribed by the *Rules of Civil Procedure*, serve it on the plaintiff's lawyer, or, where the plaintiff does not have a lawyer, serve it on the plaintiff, and file it, with proof of service, in the court office, WITHIN 20 DAYS after this statement of claim is served upon you, if you are served in Ontario.

If you are served in another province or territory of Canada or in the United States of America, the period of serving and filing your statement of defence is 40 days. If you are served outside of Canada and the United States of America, the period is 60 days.

Instead of serving and filing a statement of defence, you may serve and file a Statement of Submission or Rights to the Court in Form 75.9 prescribed by the *Rules of Civil Procedure*.

IF YOU FAIL TO DEFEND THIS PROCEEDING, JUDGMENT MAY BE GIVEN AGAINST YOU IN YOUR ABSENCE AND WITHOUT FURTHER NOTICE TO YOU. IF YOU WISH TO DEFEND THIS PROCEEDING BUT ARE UNABLE TO PAY LEGAL FEES, LEGAL AID MAY BE AVAILABLE TO YOU BY CONTACTING A LOCAL LEGAL AID OFFICE.

1. The Plaintiff claims:

November 1, 2005

FORM 75.8 — ORDER GIVING DIRECTIONS WHERE PLEADINGS DIRECTED

Courts of Justice Act

[Repealed O. Reg. 77/06, s. 3.]

[Editor's Note: Forms 4A to 78A of the Rules of Civil Procedure have been repealed by O. Reg. 77/06, effective July 1, 2006. Pursuant to Rule of Civil Procedure 1.06, when a form is referred to by number, the reference is to the form with that number that is described in the Table of Forms at the end of these rules and which is available on the Internet through www.ontariocourtforms.on.ca. For your convenience, the government form as published on this website is reproduced below.]

(*Heading in accordance with Form 59A*)

IN THE ESTATE OF (*insert name*), deceased.

BETWEEN:

(*Name*)

Applicant
(Moving Party)

- and -

(*Name*)

Respondent
(Responding Party)

- and -

(*Name*)

Persons Submitting
Rights to the Court

ORDER GIVING DIRECTIONS

THIS APPLICATION (*or* MOTION) made by (*identify applicant or moving party*) for directions, was heard on (*date*), at (*place*), in the presence of the lawyer(s) for (*insert name*), and (*insert name*) appearing in person, and no one appearing for (*insert name*), although properly served as appears from the affidavit of service, filed.

ON READING the notice of application (*or* notice of motion) and on hearing the submissions made,

1. THIS COURT ORDERS that (*insert name*) shall be plaintiff and (*insert name*) shall be defendant, and that (*insert names*) are submitting their rights to the court.

2. THIS COURT ORDERS that the plaintiff(s) shall serve upon the defendant(s) and file with the court a statement of claim in Form 75.7 within .... days after this order is entered, after which pleadings shall be served and filed under rule 75.07 of the Rules of Civil Procedure.

2.1 THIS COURT ORDERS that (*insert directions relating to mandatory mediation under Rule 75.1*).

3. THIS COURT ORDERS that the applicant and respondent shall serve and file affidavits of documents and attend and submit to examinations for discovery in accordance with the *Rules of Civil Procedure.*

4. THIS COURT ORDERS that on filing the appropriate documents with the court, (*insert name*) shall be appointed as estate trustee during litigation.

5. THIS COURT ORDERS that this order giving directions shall be served by an alternative to personal service pursuant to rule 16.03 of the *Rules of Civil Procedure*, on the following persons: (*insert names*)

6. THIS COURT ORDERS that the issues be tried by a judge with (*or* without) a jury at (*place*) on a date to be fixed by the registrar.

7. THIS COURT ORDERS that the costs of this application (*or* motion) shall be (*insert amount*)

July 1, 2007

FORM 75.9 — ORDER GIVING DIRECTIONS WHERE TRIAL OF ISSUES DIRECTED

Courts of Justice Act

[Repealed O. Reg. 77/06, s. 3.]

[Editor's Note: Forms 4A to 78A of the Rules of Civil Procedure have been repealed by O. Reg. 77/06, effective July 1, 2006. Pursuant to Rule of Civil Procedure 1.06, when a form is referred to by number, the reference is to the form with that number that is described in the Table of Forms at the end of these rules and which is available on the Internet through www.ontariocourtforms.on.ca. For your convenience, the government form as published on this website is reproduced below.]

(*Heading in accordance with Form 59A*)

IN THE ESTATE OF (*insert name*), deceased.

BETWEEN:

(*Name*)

Applicant

- and - (Moving Party)

(*Name*)

Respondent
- and - (Responding Party)

(*Name*)

Persons Submitting
Rights to the Court

ORDER GIVING DIRECTIONS

THIS APPLICATION (*or* MOTION) made by (*identify applicant or moving party*) for directions, was heard on (*date*), at (*place*), in the presence of the lawyer(s) for (*insert name*), and (*insert name*) appearing in person, and no one appearing for (*insert name*), although properly served as appears from the affidavit of service, filed.

ON READING the notice of application (*or* notice of motion) and on hearing the submissions made,

1. THIS COURT ORDERS that the parties to the proceeding and the issues to be tried be as follows:

(a) (*insert name*) affirms and (*insert name*) denies that (*state nature of allegation*);

(b) (*list each issue in a separate paragraph, specifying which parties affirm and which deny*).

2. THIS COURT ORDERS that (*insert names*) are submitting their rights to the court.

2.1 THIS COURT ORDERS that (*insert directions relating to mandatory mediation under Rule 75.1*).

3. THIS COURT ORDERS that the applicant and respondent shall serve and file affidavits of documents and attend and submit to examinations for discovery in accordance with the Rules of Civil Procedure.

4. THIS COURT ORDERS that on filing the appropriate documents with the court, (*insert name*) shall be appointed as estate trustee during litigation.

5. THIS COURT ORDERS that this order giving directions shall be served by an alternative to personal service pursuant to rule 16.03 of the Rules of Civil Procedure, on the following persons (*insert names*)

6. THIS COURT ORDERS that the issues be tried by a judge with (*or* without) a jury at (*place*) on a date to be fixed by the registrar.

7. THIS COURT ORDERS that the costs of this application (*or* motion) shall be (*insert amount*)

July 1, 2007

FORM 75.10 — STATEMENT OF SUBMISSION OF RIGHTS TO THE COURT

Courts of Justice Act

[Repealed O. Reg. 77/06, s. 3.]

[Editor's Note: Forms 4A to 78A of the Rules of Civil Procedure have been repealed by O. Reg. 77/06, effective July 1, 2006. Pursuant to Rule of Civil Procedure 1.06, when a form is referred to by number, the reference is to the form with that number that is described in the Table of Forms at the end of these rules and which is available on the Internet through www.ontariocourtforms.on.ca. For your convenience, the government form as published on this website is reproduced below.]

ONTARIO
SUPERIOR COURT OF JUSTICE

IN THE ESTATE OF (*insert name*), deceased.

BETWEEN:

(*Name*)

Applicant

- and -

(*Name*)

Respondent

STATEMENT OF SUBMISSION OF RIGHTS TO THE COURT

I, (*insert name*), submit my rights to the court and understand that pursuant to rule 75.07.1 of the Rules of Civil Procedure, the following consequences apply to me:

(a) I shall not be entitled to receive any costs in the proceeding and shall not be liable to pay the costs of any party to the proceeding, except indirectly to the extent that costs are ordered by the court to be paid out of the estate;

(b) I shall not receive notice of any step taken in the proceeding except the notice of trial and a copy of the judgment disposing of the matter;

(c) If the proceeding is settled by agreement, a judgment on consent will not be given without notice to me.

DATE

(*Name, address and telephone number of the*)
person or lawyer acting for person)

TO: (*Name and address of plaintiff,*
or lawyer for plaintiff)

July 1, 2007

FORM 75.11 — NOTICE OF SETTLEMENT

Courts of Justice Act

[Repealed O. Reg. 77/06, s. 3.]

[Editor's Note: Forms 4A to 78A of the Rules of Civil Procedure have been repealed by O. Reg. 77/06, effective July 1, 2006. Pursuant to Rule of Civil Procedure 1.06, when a form is referred to by number, the reference is to the form with that number that is described in the Table of Forms at the end of these rules and which is available on the Internet through www.ontariocourtforms.on.ca. For your convenience, the government form as published on this website is reproduced below.]

ONTARIO
SUPERIOR COURT OF JUSTICE

IN THE ESTATE OF (*insert name*), deceased.

BETWEEN:

(*Name*)

Applicant

- and -

(*Name*)

Respondent

- and -

(*Name*)

Persons Submitting Rights to the Court

NOTICE OF SETTLEMENT

Pursuant to rule 75.07 of the *Rules of Civil Procedure*, attached as Schedule "A" is a copy of the settlement agreement that has been reached among the parties.

A judgment consistent with the settlement agreement will be sought. If you oppose that judgment, you or an Ontario lawyer acting for you must, within 10 days of service on you of this notice of settlement, serve a rejection of settlement in the form attached as Schedule "B" on the lawyer for the party serving this notice, or where the party serving this notice does not have a lawyer, serve it on the party serving this notice, and file it with proof of service in the court office at (*place*).

If you fail to serve and file a rejection of settlement, the court will consider the request for judgment without further notice to you.

DATE

(*Name, address and telephone number of party*) *or lawyer for the party*)

TO: (*Names and addresses of all persons who*

have submitted their rights to the court)

July 1, 2007

FORM 75.12 — REJECTION OF SETTLEMENT

Courts of Justice Act

[Repealed O. Reg. 77/06, s. 3.]

[Editor's Note: Forms 4A to 78A of the Rules of Civil Procedure have been repealed by O. Reg. 77/06, effective July 1, 2006. Pursuant to Rule of Civil Procedure 1.06, when a form is referred to by number, the reference is to the form with that number that is described in the Table of Forms at the end of these rules and which is available on the Internet through www.ontariocourtforms.on.ca. For your convenience, the government form as published on this website is reproduced below.]

ONTARIO
SUPERIOR COURT OF JUSTICE

IN THE ESTATE OF (*insert name*), deceased.

BETWEEN:

(*Name*)

Applicant
(Plaintiff)

- and -

(*Name*)

Respondent
(Defendant)

- and -

(*Name*)

Persons Submitting
Rights to the Court

REJECTION OF SETTLEMENT

I, (*insert name*), reject the settlement agreement attached to the notice of settlement dated (*insert date*), for the following reasons: (*state reasons*).

DATE

(*Name, address and telephone number of person or lawyer for person*)

TO: (*Name and address of party who served the notice of settlement or the lawyer for the party*)

July 1, 2007

FORM 75.13 — NOTICE OF CONTESTATION

Courts of Justice Act

[Repealed O. Reg. 77/06, s. 3.]

[Editor's Note: Forms 4A to 78A of the Rules of Civil Procedure have been repealed by O. Reg. 77/06, effective July 1, 2006. Pursuant to Rule of Civil Procedure 1.06, when a form is referred to by number, the reference is to the form with that number that is described in the Table of Forms at the end of these rules and which is available on the Internet through www.ontariocourtforms.on.ca. For your convenience, the government form as published on this website is reproduced below.]

ONTARIO
SUPERIOR COURT OF JUSTICE

IN THE ESTATE OF (*insert name*), deceased.

BETWEEN:

(*Name*)

Estate Trustee

- and -

(*Name*)

Claimant

NOTICE OF CONTESTATION

Pursuant to section 44 or 45 of the *Estates Act*, the estate trustee of the estate contests the claim made by you against the estate, on the following grounds:

(*state grounds*)

You may apply to this court at (*insert address of court office*) for an order allowing your claim and determining its amount. If you do not apply within 30 days after receiving this notice, or within 3 months after that date if the judge on application so allows, you shall be deemed to have abandoned your claim and your claim shall be forever barred.

DATE

(*Name, address and telephone number of estate trustee or lawyer for estate trustee*)

TO: (*Name and address of person submitting*

claim)

July 1, 2007

FORM 75.14 — CLAIM AGAINST ESTATE

Courts of Justice Act

[Repealed O. Reg. 77/06, s. 3.]

[Editor's Note: Forms 4A to 78A of the Rules of Civil Procedure have been repealed by O. Reg. 77/06, effective July 1, 2006. Pursuant to Rule of Civil Procedure 1.06, when a form is referred to by number, the reference is to the form with that number that is described in the Table of Forms at the end of these rules and which is available on the Internet through www.ontariocourtforms.on.ca. For your convenience, the government form as published on this website is reproduced below.]

ONTARIO
SUPERIOR COURT OF JUSTICE

IN THE ESTATE OF (*insert name*), deceased.

BETWEEN:

(*Name*)

Claimant

- and -

(*Name*)

Estate Trustee

CLAIM AGAINST ESTATE

1. The claim against the estate is for $ .... for (*state grounds for claim*).

AFFIDAVIT

I, (*name of claimant*), of (*insert city or town and country or district, metropolitan or regional municipality of residence*), MAKE OATH/AFFIRM AND SAY:

1. The grounds set out in this claim are true.

SWORN/AFFIRMED BEFORE)
me at the of)
in the of)
this day of , 20 .)
)

)
) ....

....
A Commissioner for Taking Affidavits
(*or as may be*)

November 1, 2005

FORM 76A — NOTICE WHETHER ACTION UNDER RULE 76

Courts of Justice Act

[Repealed O. Reg. 77/06, s. 3.]

[Editor's Note: Forms 4A to 78A of the Rules of Civil Procedure have been repealed by O. Reg. 77/06, effective July 1, 2006. Pursuant to Rule of Civil Procedure 1.06, when a form is referred to by number, the reference is to the form with that number that is described in the Table of Forms at the end of these rules and which is available on the Internet through www.ontariocourtforms.on.ca. For your convenience, the government form as published on this website is reproduced below.]

Courts of Justice Act

(General heading)

NOTICE WHETHER ACTION UNDER RULE 76

The plaintiff states that this action and any related proceedings are:

(select one of the following:)

( ) continuing under Rule 76

( ) continuing as an ordinary procedure.

(Name, address and telephone and fax numbers of lawyer or plaintiff)

November 1, 2008

FORM 76B — SIMPLIFIED PROCEDURE MOTION FORM

Courts of Justice Act

[Repealed O. Reg. 77/06, s. 3.]

[Editor's Note: Forms 4A to 78A of the Rules of Civil Procedure have been repealed by O. Reg. 77/06, effective July 1, 2006. Pursuant to Rule of Civil Procedure 1.06, when a form is referred to by number, the reference is to the form with that number that is described in the Table of Forms at the end of these rules and which is available on the Internet through www.ontariocourtforms.on.ca. For your convenience, the government form as published on this website is reproduced below.]

Court File No. ....

(*General heading*)

SIMPLIFIED PROCEDURE MOTION FORM

JURISDICTION
( ) Judge
( ) Master
( ) Registrar

THIS FORM IS FILED BY *(Check appropriate boxes to identify the party filing this form as a moving/responding party on this motion AND to identify this party as plaintiff, defendant, etc. in the action)*

[ ] moving party

[ ] plaintiff

. . . .

[ ] responding party

[ ] defendant

. . . .

[ ] Other — specify kind of party and name

MOTION MADE

[ ] on consent of all parties

[ ] on notice to all parties and unopposed

[ ] without notice

[ ] on notice to all parties and expected to be opposed

Notice of this motion was served on (date): . . . .

by means of:

. . . .

. . . .

METHOD OF HEARING REQUESTED

[ ] by attendance

[ ] in writing only, no attendance

[ ] by fax

[ ] by telephone conference under rule 1.08

[ ] by video conference under rule 1.08

Date, time and place for conference call, telephone call or appearances

..................................(date)..................................(time)..................................(place)

ORDER SOUGHT BY THIS PARTY (*Responding party is presumed to request dismissal of motion and costs*)

[ ] Extension of time — until *(give specific date)* . . . . :

[ ] serve claim

[ ] file or deliver statement of defence

[ ] Other relief — be specific

. . . .

. . . .

MATERIAL RELIED ON BY THIS PARTY

[ ] this form

[ ] pleadings

[ ] affidavits — specify

[ ] other — specify

. . . .

. . . .

GROUNDS IN SUPPORT OF/IN OPPOSITION TO MOTION (INCLUDING RULE AND STATUTORY PROVISIONS RELIED ON)

. . . .

. . . .

CERTIFICATION BY LAWYER

I certify that the above information is correct, to the best of my knowledge.

Signature of lawyer *(If no lawyer, party must sign)*

. . . .

Date

. . . .

THIS PARTY'S LAWYER *(If no lawyer, give party's name, address for service, telephone and fax number.)*

Name and firm:

Address:

Telephone:
Fax:

OTHER LAWYER *(If no lawyer, give other party's name, address for service, telephone and fax number.)*

Name and firm:

Address:

Telephone:
Fax:

THIS PARTY'S LAWYER *(If no lawyer, give party's name, address for service, telephone and fax number.)*
Name and firm:

Address:

Telephone:
Fax:

OTHER LAWYER *(If no lawyer, give other party's name, address for service, telephone and fax number.)*
Name and firm:

Address:

Telephone:
Fax:

DISPOSITION

[ ] order to go as asked

[ ] adjourned to

[ ] order refused

[ ] order to go as follows:

. . . .

. . . .

Hearing method.................................Hearing duration.................................min.

Heard in: [ ] courtroom [ ] office

[ ] Successful party MUST prepare formal order for signature

[ ] No copy of disposition to be sent to parties

[ ] Other directions — specify

. . . .

. . . .

Date . . . . Name . . . . Signature . . . .
Judge/Master/Registrar

November 1, 2005

FORM 76C — NOTICE OF READINESS FOR PRE-TRIAL CONFERENCE

Courts of Justice Act

[Repealed O. Reg. 77/06, s. 3.]

[Editor's Note: Forms 4A to 78A of the Rules of Civil Procedure have been repealed by O. Reg. 77/06, effective July 1, 2006. Pursuant to Rule of Civil Procedure 1.06, when a form is referred to by number, the reference is to the form with that number that is described in the Table of Forms at the end of these rules and which is available on the Internet through www.ontariocourtforms.on.ca. For your convenience, the government form as published on this website is reproduced below.]

(*General heading*)

NOTICE OF READINESS FOR PRE-TRIAL CONFERENCE

The *(identify party)* is ready for a pre-trial conference and is setting this action down for trial. A pre-trial conference in the action will proceed as scheduled and the trial will proceed when the action is reached on the trial list, unless the court orders otherwise.

CERTIFICATE

I CERTIFY that there was a settlement discussion under rule 76.08.

Date (*Signature*)
(Name, address and telephone and fax numbers of lawyers or party giving notice)

TO *(Name and address of lawyer or party receiving notice)*

November 1, 2005

FORM 76D — TRIAL MANAGEMENT CHECKLIST

Courts of Justice Act

[Repealed O. Reg. 77/06, s. 3.]

[Editor's Note: Forms 4A to 78A of the Rules of Civil Procedure have been repealed by O. Reg. 77/06, effective July 1, 2006. Pursuant to Rule of Civil Procedure 1.06, when a form is referred to by number, the reference is to the form with that number that is described in the Table of Forms at the end of these rules and which is available on the Internet through www.ontariocourtforms.on.ca. For your convenience, the government form as published on this website is reproduced below.]

(*General heading*)
(*Insert name of party filing this form*)

TRIAL MANAGEMENT CHECKLIST

Trial Lawyer — Plaintiff(s):

Trial Lawyer — Defendant(s):

Filed by Plaintiff

Filed by Defendant

Filed by Subsequent Party

1. Issues Outstanding

(a) liability:

. . . .

(b) damages:

. . . .

(c) other

. . . .

2. Names of Plaintiff's Witnesses

. . . .

3. Names of Defendant's Witnesses

. . . .

4. Admissions

. . . .

Are the parties prepared to admit any facts for the purposes of the trial or summary trial?

yes ❑ no❑

5. Document Brief

Will there be a document brief? yes ❑ no ❑

6. Request to Admit

Will there be a request to admit? yes ❑ no ❑

If so, have the parties agreed to a timetable? yes ❑ no ❑

7. Expert's Reports

Are any expert's reports anticipated? yes ❑ no ❑

8. Amendments to Pleadings

Are any amendments likely to be sought? yes ❑ no ❑

9. Mode of Trial

Have the parties agreed to a summary trial? yes ❑ no ❑

Have the parties agreed to an ordinary trial? yes ❑ no ❑

If the parties have not agreed about the mode of trial, what mode of trial is being requested by the party filing this checklist?

. . . .

10. Factum of Law

Will the parties be submitting factums of law? yes ❑ no ❑

November 1, 2005

FORM 77C — [REPEALED O. REG. 438/08, S. 67(4).]

[Repealed O. Reg. 438/08, s. 67(4).]

FORM 77D — [REPEALED O. REG. 438/08, S. 67(4).]

[Repealed O. Reg. 438/08, s. 67(4).]

FORM 78A — [REPEALED O. REG. 438/08, S. 67(4).]

[Repealed O. Reg. 438/08, s. 67(4).]

INDEX TO FORMS

S

T

TARIFFS

Tariff A — LAWYERS' FEES AND DISBURSEMENTS ALLOWABLE UNDER RULES 57.01 AND 58.05 [HEADING AMENDED O. REG. 42/05, S. 7(1).]

PART I — FEES [HEADING AMENDED O. REG. 42/05, S. 7(2).]

The fee for any step in a proceeding authorized by the *Rules of Civil Procedure* and the counsel fee for motions, applications, trials, references and appeals shall be determined in accordance with section 131 of the *Courts of Justice Act* and the factors set out in subrule 57.01(1).

Where students-at-law or law clerks have provided services of a nature that the Law Society of Upper Canada authorizes them to provide, fees for those services may be allowed.

PART II — DISBURSEMENTS

21.	Attendance money actually paid to a witness who is entitled to attendance money, to be calculated as follows:	
	1. Attendance allowance for each day of necessary attendance	$50
	2. Travel allowance, where the hearing or examination is held,	
	(a) in a city or town in which the witness resides, $3.00 for each day of necessary attendance;	
	(b) within 300 kilometres of where the witness resides, 24¢ a kilometre each way between his or her residence and the place of hearing or examination;	
	(c) more than 300 kilometres from where the witness resides, the minimum return air fare plus 24¢ a kilometre each way from his or her residence to the airport and from the airport to the place of hearing or examination.	
	3. Overnight accommodation and meal allowance, where the witness resides elsewhere than the place of hearing or examination and is required to remain overnight, for each overnight stay	$75
22.	Fees or expenses actually paid to a court, court reporter, official examiner or sheriff under the regulations under the *Administration of Justice Act*.	
23.	For service or attempted service of a document,	
	(a) in Ontario, the amount actually paid, not exceeding the fee payable to a sheriff under the regulations under the *Administration of Justice Act*;	
	(b) outside Ontario, a reasonable amount;	

(c) that was ordered to be served by publication, a reasonable amount.

23.1 Fees actually paid to a mediator in accordance with Ontario Regulation 451/98 made under the *Administration of Justice Act.*

23.2 Fees actually paid to a mediator in accordance with Ontario Regulation 291/99 made under the *Administration of Justice Act*

24. For an examination and transcript of evidence taken on the examination, the amount actually paid, not exceeding the fee payable to an official examiner under the regulations under the *Administration of Justice Act.*

25. For the preparation of a plan, model, videotape, film or photograph reasonably necessary for the conduct of the proceeding, a reasonable amount.

26. For experts' reports that were supplied to the other parties as required by the *Evidence Act* or these rules and that were reasonably necessary for the conduct of the proceeding, a reasonable amount.

27. The cost of the investigation and report of the Official Guardian.

28. For an expert who gives opinion evidence at the hearing or whose attendance was reasonably necessary at the hearing, a reasonable amount not exceeding $350 a day, subject to increase in the discretion of the assessment officer.

29. For an interpreter for services at the hearing or on an examination, a reasonable amount not exceeding $100 a day, subject to increase in the discretion of the assessment officer.

29.1 Where ordered by the presiding judge or officer, for translation into English or French of a document that has been filed, a reasonable amount.

30. Where ordered by the presiding judge or officer, such travelling and accommodation expenses incurred by a party as, in the discretion of the assessment officer, appear reasonable.

31. For copies of any documents or authorities prepared for or by a party for the use of the court and supplied to the opposite party, a reasonable amount.

32. For copies of records, appeal books and compendiums, and factums, a reasonable amount.

33. The cost of certified copies of documents such as orders, birth, marriage, and death certificates, abstracts of title, deeds, mortgages and other registered documents where reasonably necessary for the conduct of the proceeding.

34. The cost of transcripts of proceedings of courts or tribunals,

(a) where required by the court or the rules; or

(b) where reasonably necessary for the conduct of the proceeding.

35. Where ordered by the presiding judge or officer, for any other disbursement reasonably necessary for the conduct of the proceeding, a reasonable amount in the discretion of the assessment officer.

36. Goods and services tax actually paid or payable on the lawyer's fees and disbursements allowable under rule 58.05.

O. Reg. 219/91, s. 16; 351/94, s. 19; 533/95, s. 12; 453/98, s. 3; 290/99, s. 6; 24/00, s. 32; 652/00, s. 8; 113/01, s. 15; 243/01, s. 1; 244/01, ss. 5, 6; 284/01, s. 38; 457/01, s. 18; 19/03, s. 26; 131/04, s. 27; 42/05, s. 7; 575/07, s. 37

Tariff B — [REVOKED O. REG. 131/04, S. 28.]

[Revoked O. Reg. 131/04, s. 28.]

Tariff C — LAWYERS' COSTS ALLOWED ON PASSING OF ACCOUNTS WITHOUT A HEARING [HEADING AMENDED O. REG. 575/07, S. 38(1).]

(1) — Estate Trustee

Amount of receipts	Amount of costs
Less than $100,000	$ 800
$100,000 or more, but less than $300,000	1,750
$300,000 or more, but less than $500,000	2,000
$500,000 or more, but less than $1,000,000	2,500
$1,000,000 or more, but less than $1,500,000	3,000
$1,500,000 or more, but less than $3,000,000	4,000
$3,000,000 or more	5,000

(2) — Person With Financial Interest in Estate

If a person with a financial interest in an estate retains a lawyer to review the accounts, makes no objection to the accounts (or makes an objection and later withdraws it), and serves and files a request for costs, the person is entitled to one-half of the amount payable to the estate trustee.

(3) — Children's Lawyer or Public Guardian and Trustee

If the Children's Lawyer or the Public Guardian and Trustee makes no objection to the accounts (or makes an objection and later withdraws it) and serves and files a request for costs, he or she is entitled to three-quarters of the amount payable to the estate trustee.

Note: If two or more persons are represented by the same lawyer, they are entitled to receive only one person's costs.

Note: A person entitled to costs under this tariff is also entitled to the amount of G.S.T. on those costs.

O. Reg. 484/94, s. 14; 332/96, s. 10; 575/07, s. 38

COURT AND SHERIFFS' FEES

SUPERIOR COURT OF JUSTICE AND COURT OF APPEAL — FEES

Made under the *Administration of Justice Act*

O. Reg. 293/92

as am. O. Reg. 136/94 (Fr.); 272/94; 359/94; 802/94; 212/97; 248/97 (Fr.); 403/98; 329/99; 14/00; 136/04; 10/05; 272/05; 169/07.

[Note: The title of this Regulation was changed from "Ontario Court (General Division) and Court of Appeal — Fees" to "Superior Court of Justice and Court of Appeal — Fees" by O. Reg. 14/00, s. 1.]

1. The following fees are payable, except in respect of proceedings to which section 1.2 applies:

1.	On the issue of,	
	i. a statement of claim or notice of action	$181.00
	ii. a notice of application	181.00
	iii. a third or subsequent party claim	181.00
	iv. a statement of defence and counterclaim adding a party	181.00
	v. a summons to a witness	22.00
	vi. a certificate, other than a certificate of a search by the registrar required on an application for a certificate of appointment of estate trustee, and not more than five pages of copies of the Court document annexed	22.00
	for each additional page	2.00
	vii. a commission	44.00
	viii. a writ of execution	55.00
	ix. a notice of garnishment (including the filing of the notice with the sheriff)	115.00
2.	On the signing of,	
	i. an order directing a reference, except an order on requisition directing the assessment of a bill under the *Solicitors Act*	235.00

	ii. an order on requisition directing the assessment of a bill under the *Solicitors Act*	
	A. if obtained by a client	75.00
	B. if obtained by a solicitor	144.00
	iii. a notice of appointment for the assessment of costs under the Rules of Civil Procedure	104.00
3.	On the filing of,	
	i. a notice of intent to defend	144.00
	ii. if no notice of intent to defend has been filed by the same party, a statement of defence, a defence to counterclaim, a defence to crossclaim or a third party defence	144.00
	iii. a notice of appearance	102.00
	iv. a notice of motion served on another party, a notice of motion without notice, a notice of motion for a consent order or a notice of motion for leave to appeal, other than a notice of motion in a family law appeal	127.00
	v. a notice of return of motion, other than a notice of return of motion in a family law appeal	127.00
	vi. in a family law appeal, a notice of motion served on another party, a notice of motion without notice, a notice of motion for a consent order or a notice of return of motion	90.00
	vii. a notice of motion for leave to appeal in a family law case	90.00
	viii. a requisition for signing of default judgment by registrar	127.00
	ix. a trial record, for the first time only	337.00
	x. a notice of appeal or cross-appeal from an interlocutory order	181.00
	xi. a notice of appeal or cross-appeal to an appellate court of a final order of the Small Claims Court	104.00
	xii. a notice of appeal or cross-appeal to an appellate court of a final order of any court or tribunal, other than the Small Claims Court or the Consent and Capacity Board	259.00
	xiii. a request to redeem or request for sale	104.00
	xiv. an affidavit under section 11 of the *Bulk Sales Act*	75.00
	xv. a jury notice in a civil proceeding	104.00
4.	For obtaining an appointment with a registrar for settlement of an order	104.00
5.	For perfecting an appeal or judicial review application	201.00
6.	For the making up and forwarding of papers, documents and exhibits	75.00 and the transportation costs
7.	For making copies of documents,	
	i. not requiring certification, per page	1.00
	ii. requiring certification, per page	4.00
8.	For the inspection of a court file,	
	i. by a solicitor or party in the proceeding	No charge
	ii. by a person who has entered into an agreement with the Attorney General for the bulk inspection of court files, per file	4.00
	iii. by any other person, per file	10.00

9.	For the retrieval from storage of a court file	61.00
10.	For the taking of an affidavit or declaration by a commissioner for taking affidavits	13.00
11.	For a settlement conference under rule 77.14 of the Rules of Civil Procedure	127.00

O. Reg. 359/94, s. 1; 212/97, s. 1; 248/97, s. 1; 403/98, s. 1; 329/99, s. 1; 14/00, s. 2; 136/04, s. 1; 10/05, s. 1; 272/05, s. 1; 169/07, s. 1

1.1 (1) If a minor or other person under disability is entitled to receive a payment or payments under a multi-provincial/territorial assistance program agreement between Ontario and a person who has been infected with the human immunodeficiency virus through the receipt by transfusion of blood or a blood product, no fee is payable for the issue of a notice of application under Rule 7.08 of the Rules of Civil Procedure on behalf of the minor or other person under disability, and subparagraph ii of paragraph 1 of section 1 does not apply.

(2) Where before the coming into force of this Regulation an applicant on behalf of a minor or other person under disability has paid a fee for the issue of a notice of application referred to in subsection (1), the fee shall be refunded to the applicant.

O. Reg. 272/94; 136/04, s. 2

1.2 (1) The following fees are payable in respect of proceedings that are governed by Ontario Regulation 114/99 (Family Law Rules), except for proceedings under rule 38 (appeals), to which section 1 applies:

1. On the filing of an application $157.00

2. On the filing of an answer, other than an answer referred to in item 3 . . . . 125.00

3. On the filing of an answer where the answer includes a request for a divorce by a respondent 157.00

4. On the placing of an application on the list for hearing 280.00

5. On the issue of a summons to a witness 19.00

6. On the issue of a certificate with not more than five pages of copies of the Court document annexed 19.00

For each additional page 2.00

7. For making copies of documents,

i. not requiring certification, per page 1.00

ii. requiring certification, per page 3.50

8. For making up and forwarding papers, documents and exhibits 65.00 and the transportation costs

(2) Despite subsection (1), no fees are payable for the filing of an application, the filing of an answer or the placing of an application on the list for hearing in respect of,

(a) proceedings under the *Children's Law Reform Act*, the *Family Law Act* (except Parts I and II), the *Family Responsibility and Support Arrears Enforcement Act, 1996*, the *Marriage Act* or the *Interjurisdictional Support Orders Act, 2002*; or

(b) proceedings to enforce an order for support, custody or access made under any of these Acts.

O. Reg. 136/04, s. 3; 169/07, s. 2

2. (1) The following fees are payable in estate matters:

1.	For a certificate of succeeding estate trustee or a certificate of estate trustee during litigation	$75.00
2.	For an application of an estate trustee to pass accounts, including all services in connection with it	322.00
3.	For a notice of objection to accounts	69.00
4.	For an application other than an application to pass accounts, including an application for proof of lost or destroyed will, a revocation of a certificate of appointment, an application for directions or the filing of a claim and notice of contestation	173.00
5.	For a notice of objection other than a notice of objection to accounts, including the filing of a notice of appearance	69.00
6.	For a request for notice of commencement of proceedings	69.00
7.	For the deposit of a will or codicil for safekeeping	20.00
8.	For an assessment of costs, including the certificate	46.00

(2) The fees set out in section 1 are payable in estate matters in addition to the fees set out in subsection (1).

O. Reg. 293/92, s. 2; 802/94; 14/00, s. 3; 10/05, s. 2

3. (1) The following fees are payable in an action under the *Construction Lien Act*:

1.	Where the claim, crossclaim, counterclaim or third party claim does not exceed $6,000,	
	i. on the issuing of a statement of claim, crossclaim, counterclaim or third party claim	$75.00
2.	Where the claim, crossclaim, counterclaim or third party claim exceeds $6,000,	
	i. on the issuing of a statement of claim, crossclaim, counterclaim or third party claim	181.00
	ii. on the filing of a statement of defence	104.00
	iii. on the issuing of a certificate of action	104.00
	iv. on the filing of a trial record	339.00

(2) The fees set out in section 1, except those in paragraphs 1, 2 and 3 of that section, are payable in an action under the *Construction Lien Act* in addition to the fees set out in subsection (1).

O. Reg. 359/94, s. 2; 212/97, s. 2; 14/00, s. 4; 10/05, s. 3

4. (1) The following fees are payable in respect of an application under the *Repair and Storage Liens Act*:

1.	On the filing of,	
	i. an application	$184.00
	ii. a notice of objection	104.00
	iii. a waiver of further claim and a receipt	no charge
2.	On the issuing of,	
	i. an initial certificate	104.00
	ii. a final certificate	104.00
	iii. a writ of seizure	55.00

(2) The fees set out in section 1, except those in paragraphs 1, 2 and 3 of that section, are payable in an action under the *Repair and Storage Liens Act* in addition to the fees set out in subsection (1).

O. Reg. 359/94, s. 3; 212/97, s. 3; 14/00, s. 5; 10/05, s. 4

5. (1) The following fees are payable to an official examiner:

1. For the appointment, for each person examined $9.50

2. For the provision of facilities, for the first two hours or part 32.00

For each additional hour or part 16.00

3. For a reporter's attendance, for the first two hours or part 40.00

For each additional hour or part 20.00

4. For the transcript of an examination, per page, regardless of the party ordering,

i. for one copy of the first transcript ordered 4.00

ii. for one copy of each transcript ordered after the reporter has satisfied the order for a transcript described in subparagraph i 3.40

iii. for each additional copy ordered before the reporter has satisfied the order for a transcript described in subparagraph i or ii 0.80

5. For handling costs, per invoice 5.50

6. For cancellation of or failure to keep an appointment, with less than three working days notice,

i. for the cancellation or failure to attend 11.50

ii. for the first two hours or part reserved for the appointment 72.00

iii. for each additional hour or part reserved for the appointment 36.00

(2) The official examiner shall be paid, in addition to the fees set out in subsection (1), a travelling allowance in accordance with Ontario Regulation 283/82, for attendance out of the office.

(3) If a party requires a transcript within five working days of placing the order for the transcript, the party shall pay the official examiner 75 cents per page, in addition to the fee set out in paragraph iv of subsection (1).

(4) If a party requires a transcript within two working days of placing the order for the transcript, the party shall pay the official examiner $1.50 per page, in addition to the fee set out in paragraph iv of subsection (1).

(5) If more than one party requires a transcript as described in subsection (3) or (4), only the first party to place the order shall be required to pay the additional fee.

Note: A solicitor who is charged more than the amounts provided in section 5 of this Regulation or who receives a transcript that does not substantially conform with Rule 4.09 of the Rules of Civil Procedure should notify the Assistant Deputy Minister, Courts Administration Division, Ministry of the Attorney General, in writing

O. Reg. 359/94, s. 4; 212/97, s. 4

6. Ontario Regulations 158/83, 405/84, 605/85, 171/90 and 393/90 are revoked.

SHERIFFS — FEES

Made under the *Administration of Justice Act*

O. Reg. 294/92

as am. O. Reg. 431/93; 137/94 (Fr.); 358/94; 213/97; 404/98; 4/99; 330/99; 217/00.

1. (1) The following fees are payable to a sheriff:

1. For up to three attempts, whether or not successful, to serve a document, for each person to be served $100.00

2. For filing or renewing a writ of execution or order which a sheriff is liable or required to enforce and for delivering a copy of the writ or order or a renewal of it to the land registrar of a land titles division 100.00

3. For filing or renewing a writ of execution or order which a sheriff is liable or required to enforce and which is not required to be delivered to a land registrar of a land titles division 75.00

4. For filing a writ of seizure or a direction to seize under the *Repair and Storage Liens Act* 115.00

5. For each attempt, whether or not successful, to enforce,

i. a writ of delivery,

ii. a writ of sequestration,

iii. an order for interim recovery of personal property,

iv. an order for interim preservation of personal property, or

v. a writ of seizure or direction to seize under the *Repair and Storage Liens Act* 400.00

6. For each attempt, whether or not successful, to enforce a writ of seizure and sale or an order directing a sale 240.00

7. For each attempt, whether or not successful, to enforce any other writ of execution or order 240.00

8. For a search for writs, per name searched 11.00

9. For each report showing the details of a writ, lien or order . . . . 6.00 to a maximum of $60.00 for each name searched

10. For preparing a schedule of distribution under the *Creditors' Relief Act*, per writ or notice of garnishment listed on the schedule 45.00 to a maximum of an amount equal to 20 per cent of the money received

11. For a calculation for satisfaction of writs and garnishments, per writ or notice of garnishment 45.00

12. For any service or act ordered by a court for which no fee is provided, for each hour or part of an hour spent performing the service or doing the act 55.00

13. For making copies of documents (other than writs of execution, orders and certificates of lien),

i. not requiring certification, per page 2.00

ii. requiring certification, per page 3.50

(2) In addition to the fees set out in paragraphs 5, 6, 7 and 12 of subsection (1), the person who requests the service shall pay the sheriff his or her reasonable and necessary disbursements in carrying out the services described in those paragraphs.

O. Reg. 213/97, s. 1; 404/98, s. 1; 4/99, s. 1; 330/99, s. 1; 217/00, s. 1

2. In addition to the fees and disbursements set out in section 1, the person who requests the service shall pay the sheriff a travel allowance as set out in [R.R.O. 1990, Reg. 11] for the distance he or she necessarily travels, both ways, between the court house and the place where the sheriff,

(a) [Revoked O. Reg. 431/93, s. 2.]

(b) enforces or attempts to enforce a writ or order; or

(c) performs or attempts to perform any other service directed by a court.

O. Reg. 431/93, s. 2

3. Ontario Regulation 392/90 is revoked.

RULES OF THE SMALL CLAIMS COURT

Made under the *Courts of Justice Act*

O. Reg. 258/98

as am. O. Reg. 295/99; 461/01 [ss. 1(2), 4(2), 7(4), 8(2), (4), 9(2), 10(3), 12(2), (4), 13(5), 14(3), 17(2), 19(3), 20(3), 22(2), 23(2) revoked O. Reg. 330/02, ss. 1(2), 3(2), 4(2), 5(2), (4), 6(2), 7(2), 8(2), (4), 9(2), 10(2), 11(2), 12(2), 13(3), 14(3), 15(2), respectively.]; 330/02, ss. 1(1), 2, 3(1), 4(1), (3), 5(1), (3), 6(1), 7(1), 8(1), (3), 9(1), 10(1), 11(1), 12(1), 13(1), (2), 14(1), (2), 15(1); 440/03; 78/06; 574/07; 56/08; 393/09, ss. 1–13, 14(1)–(3), (4) (Fr.), (5) (Fr.), (6), 15 (Fr.), 16–25; 505/09.

Summary of Contents

RULE 1 — GENERAL [HEADING AMENDED O. REG. 78/06, S. 1.]

CITATION

1.01 These rules may be cited as the Small Claims Court Rules.

Definitions

1.02 (1) In these rules,

"court" means the Small Claims Court;

"disability", where used in respect of a person or party, means that the person or party is,

(a) a minor,

(b) mentally incapable within the meaning of section 6 or 45 of the *Substitute Decisions Act, 1992* in respect of an issue in the proceeding, whether the person or party has a guardian or not, or

(c) an absentee within the meaning of the *Absentees Act*;

"document" includes data and information in electronic form;

"electronic" includes created, recorded, transmitted or stored in digital form in other intangible form by electronic, magnetic or optical means or by any other means that has capabilities for creation, recording, transmission or storage similar to those means, and **"electronically"** has a corresponding meaning;

"holiday" means,

(a) any Saturday or Sunday,

(b) New Year's Day,

(b.1) Family Day,

(c) Good Friday,

(d) Easter Monday,

(e) Victoria Day,

(f) Canada Day,

(g) Civic Holiday,

(h) Labour Day,

(i) Thanksgiving Day,

(j) Remembrance Day,

(k) Christmas Day,

(l) Boxing Day, and

(m) any special holiday proclaimed by the Governor General or the Lieutenant Governor, and if New Year's Day, Canada Day or Remembrance Day falls on a Saturday or Sunday, the following Monday is a holiday, and if Christmas Day falls on a Saturday or Sunday, the following Monday and Tuesday are holidays, and if Christmas Day falls on a Friday, the following Monday is a holiday;

"information technology" [Repealed O. Reg. 78/06, s. 2(1).]

"self-represented", when used in reference to a person, means that the person is not represented by a lawyer, student-at-law or agent;

"order" includes a judgment;

"territorial division" means,

(a) a county, a district or a regional municipality, and

(b) each of the following, as they existed on December 31, 2002:

(i) The combined area of County of Brant and City of Brantford.

(ii) Municipality of Chatham-Kent.

(iii) Haldimand County.

(iv) City of Hamilton.

(v) City of Kawartha Lakes.

(vi) Norfolk County.

(vii) City of Ottawa.

(viii) County of Prince Edward.

(ix) City of Toronto.

(2) [Repealed O. Reg. 78/06, s. 2(3).]

O. Reg. 461/01, s. 1 [s. 1(2) revoked O. Reg. 330/02, s. 1(2).]; 330/02, s. 1(1); 440/03, s. 5, item 1; 78/06, s. 2; 574/07, s. 1; 393/09, s. 1

General Principle

1.03 (1) These rules shall be liberally construed to secure the just, most expeditious and least expensive determination of every proceeding on its merits in accordance with section 25 of the *Courts of Justice Act*.

Matters Not Covered in Rules

(2) If these rules do not cover a matter adequately, the court may give directions and make any order that is just, and the practice shall be decided by analogy to these rules, by reference to the *Courts of Justice Act* and the Act governing the action and, if the court considers it appropriate, by reference to the *Rules of Civil Procedure*.

O. Reg. 78/06, s. 3

ORDERS ON TERMS

1.04 When making an order under these rules, the court may impose such terms and give such directions as are just.

STANDARDS FOR DOCUMENTS

1.05 A document in a proceeding shall be printed, typewritten, written or reproduced legibly.

O. Reg. 78/06, s. 4

Forms

1.06 (1) The forms prescribed by these rules shall be used where applicable and with such variations as the circumstances require.

Table of Forms

(2) In these rules, when a form is referred to by number, the reference is to the form with that number that is described in the Table of Forms at the end of these rules and is available on the Internet through *www.ontariocourtforms.on.ca.*

Additional Parties

(3) If a form does not have sufficient space to list all of the parties to the action on the first page, the remaining parties shall be listed in Form 1A, which shall be appended to the form immediately following the first page.

Additional Debtors

(4) If any of the following forms do not have sufficient space to list all of the debtors in respect of which the form applies, the remaining debtors shall be listed in Form 1A.1, which shall be appended to the form:

1. Certificate of judgment (Form 20A).
2. Writ of seizure and sale of personal property (Form 20C).
3. Writ of seizure and sale of land (Form 20D).
4. Direction to enforce writ of seizure and sale of personal property (Form 20O).

Affidavit

(5) If these rules permit or require the use of an affidavit, Form 15B may be used for the purpose unless another form is specified.

(6) [Repealed O. Reg. 78/06, s. 4.]

(7) [Repealed O. Reg. 78/06, s. 4.]

(8) [Repealed O. Reg. 78/06, s. 4.]

(9) [Repealed O. Reg. 78/06, s. 4.]

(10) [Repealed O. Reg. 78/06, s. 4.]

(11) [Repealed O. Reg. 78/06, s. 4.]

(12) [Repealed O. Reg. 78/06, s. 4.]

(13) [Repealed O. Reg. 78/06, s. 4.]

(14) [Repealed O. Reg. 78/06, s. 4.]

(15) [Repealed O. Reg. 78/06, s. 4.]

(16) [Repealed O. Reg. 78/06, s. 4.]

(17) [Revoked O. Reg. 440/03, s. 1.]

(18) [Revoked O. Reg. 440/03, s. 1.]

(19) [Revoked O. Reg. 440/03, s. 1.]

O. Reg. 461/01, s. 2; 330/02, s. 2; 440/03, s. 1; 78/06, s. 4; 393/09, s. 2

Telephone and Video Conferences — Where Available

1.07 (1) If facilities for a telephone or video conference are available at the court, all or part of any of the following may be heard or conducted by telephone or video conference as permitted by subrules (2) and (3):

1. A settlement conference.

2. A motion.

(1.1) If facilities for a video conference are available at the court, all or part of an examination of a debtor or other person under rule 20.10 may be conducted by video conference as permitted by subrules (2) and (3).

Request to be Made

(2) A settlement conference or motion may be heard or conducted by telephone or video conference or all or part of an examination under rule 20.10 may be conducted by video conference if a party files a request for the conference (Form 1B), indicating the reasons for the request, and the court grants the request.

Balance of Convenience

(3) In deciding whether to direct a telephone or video conference, the judge shall consider,

(a) the balance of convenience between the party that wants the telephone or video conference and any party that opposes it; and

(b) any other relevant matter.

Arrangements for Conference

(4) If an order directing a telephone or video conference is made, the court shall make the necessary arrangements for the conference and notify the parties of them.

Setting Aside or Varying Order

(5) A judge presiding at a proceeding or step in a proceeding may set aside or vary an order directing a telephone or video conference.

O. Reg. 78/06, s. 4; 393/09, s. 3

RULE 2 — NON-COMPLIANCE WITH THE RULES

EFFECT OF NON-COMPLIANCE

2.01 A failure to comply with these rules is an irregularity and does not render a proceeding or a step, document or order in a proceeding a nullity, and the court may grant all necessary amendments or other relief, on such terms as are just, to secure the just determination of the real matters in dispute.

COURT MAY DISPENSE WITH COMPLIANCE

2.02 If necessary in the interest of justice, the court may dispense with compliance with any rule at any time.

RULE 3 — TIME

COMPUTATION

3.01 If these rules or an order of the court prescribe a period of time for the taking of a step in a proceeding, the time shall be counted by excluding the first day and including the last day of the period; if the last day of the period of time falls on a holiday, the period ends on the next day that is not a holiday.

Powers of Court

3.02 (1) The court may lengthen or shorten any time prescribed by these rules or an order, on such terms as are just.

Consent

(2) A time prescribed by these rules for serving or filing a document may be lengthened or shortened by filing the consent of the parties.

O. Reg. 461/01, s. 3

RULE 4 — PARTIES UNDER DISABILITY

Plaintiff's Litigation Guardian

4.01 (1) An action by a person under disability shall be commenced or continued by a litigation guardian, subject to subrule (2).

Exception

(2) A minor may sue for any sum not exceeding $500 as if he or she were of full age.

Consent

(3) A plaintiff's litigation guardian shall, at the time of filing a claim or as soon as possible afterwards, file with the clerk a consent (Form 4A) in which the litigation guardian,

(a) states the nature of the disability;

(b) in the case of a minor, states the minor's birth date;

(c) sets out his or her relationship, if any, to the person under disability;

(d) states that he or she has no interest in the proceeding contrary to that of the person under disability;

(e) acknowledges that he or she is aware of his or her liability to pay personally any costs awarded against him or her or against the person under disability; and

(f) states whether he or she is represented by a lawyer or agent and, if so, gives that person's name and confirms that the person has written authority to act in the proceeding.

Defendant's Litigation Guardian

4.02 (1) An action against a person under disability shall be defended by a litigation guardian.

(2) A defendant's litigation guardian shall file with the defence a consent (Form 4A) in which the litigation guardian,

(a) states the nature of the disability;

(b) in the case of a minor, states the minor's birth date;

(c) sets out his or her relationship, if any, to the person under disability;

(d) states that he or she has no interest in the proceeding contrary to that of the person under disability; and

(e) states whether he or she is represented by a lawyer or agent and, if so, gives that person's name and confirms that the person has written authority to act in the proceeding.

(3) If it appears to the court that a defendant is a person under disability and the defendant does not have a litigation guardian the court may, after notice to the proposed litigation guardian, appoint as litigation guardian for the defendant any person who has no interest in the action contrary to that of the defendant.

O. Reg. 78/06, s. 5

Who May Be Litigation Guardian

4.03 (1) Any person who is not under disability may be a plaintiff's or defendant's litigation guardian, subject to subrule (2).

(2) If the plaintiff or defendant,

(a) is a minor, in a proceeding to which subrule 4.01(2) does not apply,

(i) the parent or person with lawful custody or another suitable person shall be the litigation guardian, or

(ii) if no such person is available and able to act, the Children's Lawyer shall be the litigation guardian;

(b) is mentally incapable and has a guardian with authority to act as litigation guardian in the proceeding, the guardian shall be the litigation guardian;

(c) is mentally incapable and does not have a guardian with authority to act as litigation guardian in the proceeding, but has an attorney under a power of attorney with that authority, the attorney shall be the litigation guardian;

(d) is mentally incapable and has neither a guardian with authority to act as litigation guardian in the proceeding nor an attorney under a power of attorney with that power,

(i) a suitable person who has no interest contrary to that of the incapable person may be the litigation guardian, or

(ii) if no such person is available and able to act, the Public Guardian and Trustee shall be the litigation guardian;

(e) is an absentee,

(i) the committee of his or her estate appointed under the *Absentees Act* shall be the litigation guardian,

(ii) if there is no such committee, a suitable person who has no interest contrary to that of the absentee may be the litigation guardian, or

(iii) if no such person is available and able to act, the Public Guardian and Trustee shall be the litigation guardian;

(f) is a person in respect of whom an order was made under subsection 72(1) or (2) of the *Mental Health Act* as it read before April 3, 1995, the Public Guardian and Trustee shall be the litigation guardian.

Duties of Litigation Guardian

4.04 (1) A litigation guardian shall diligently attend to the interests of the person under disability and take all steps reasonably necessary for the protection of those interests, including the commencement and conduct of a defendant's claim.

Public Guardian and Trustee, Children's Lawyer

(2) The Public Guardian and Trustee or the Children's Lawyer may act as litigation guardian without filing the consent required by subrule 4.01(3) or 4.02(2).

POWER OF COURT

4.05 The court may remove or replace a litigation guardian at any time.

SETTING ASIDE JUDGMENT, ETC.

4.06 If an action has been brought against a person under disability and the action has not been defended by a litigation guardian, the court may set aside the noting of default or any judgment against the person under disability on such terms as are just, and may set aside any step that has been taken to enforce the judgment.

SETTLEMENT REQUIRES COURT'S APPROVAL

4.07 No settlement of a claim made by or against a person under disability is binding on the person without the approval of the court.

Money to be Paid into Court

4.08 (1) Any money payable to a person under disability under an order or a settlement shall be paid into court, unless the court orders otherwise, and shall afterwards be paid out or otherwise disposed of as ordered by the court.

(2) If money is payable to a person under disability under an order or settlement, the court may order that the money shall be paid directly to the person, and payment made under the order discharges the obligation to the extent of the amount paid.

RULE 5 — PARTNERSHIPS AND SOLE PROPRIETORSHIPS

PARTNERSHIPS

5.01 A proceeding by or against two or more persons as partners may be commenced using the firm name of the partnership.

5.02 If a proceeding is commenced against a partnership using the firm name, the partnership's defence shall be delivered in the firm name and no person who admits being a partner at any material time may defend the proceeding separately, except with leave of the court.

Notice to Alleged Partner

5.03 (1) In a proceeding against a partnership using the firm name, a plaintiff who seeks an order that would be enforceable personally against a person as a partner may serve the person with the claim, together with a notice to alleged partner (Form 5A).

(2) A person served as provided in subrule (1) is deemed to have been a partner at the material time, unless the person defends the proceeding separately denying having been a partner at the material time.

Disclosure of Partners

5.04 (1) If a proceeding is commenced by or against a partnership using the firm name, any other party may serve a notice requiring the partnership to disclose immediately in writing the names and addresses of all partners constituting the partnership at a time specified in the notice; if a partner's present address is unknown, the partnership shall disclose the last known address.

(1.1) [Repealed O. Reg. 78/06, s. 6.]

(1.1.1) [Repealed O. Reg. 78/06, s. 6.]

(2) If a partnership fails to comply with a notice under subrule (1), its claim may be dismissed or the proceeding stayed or its defence may be struck out.

O. Reg. 461/01, s. 4 [s. 4(2) revoked O. Reg. 330/02, s. 3(2).]; 330/02, s. 3(1); 440/03, s. 5, item 2; 78/06, s. 6

Enforcement of Order

5.05 (1) An order against a partnership using the firm name may be enforced against the partnership's property.

(2) An order against a partnership using the firm name may also be enforced, if the order or a subsequent order so provides, against any person who was served as provided in rule 5.03 and who,

(a) under that rule, is deemed to have been a partner at the material time;

(b) has admitted being a partner at that time; or

(c) has been adjudged to have been a partner at that time.

Against Person not Served as Alleged Partner

(3) If, after an order has been made against a partnership using the firm name, the party obtaining it claims to be entitled to enforce it against any person alleged to be a partner other than a person who was served as provided in rule 5.03, the party may make a motion for leave to do so; the judge may grant leave if the person's liability as a partner is not disputed or, if disputed, after the liability has been determined in such manner as the judge directs.

O. Reg. 78/06, s. 7

Sole Proprietorships

5.06 (1) If a person carries on business in a business name other than his or her own name, a proceeding may be commenced by or against the person using the business name.

(2) Rules 5.01 to 5.05 apply, with necessary modifications, to a proceeding by or against a sole proprietor using a business name, as though the sole proprietor were a partner and the business name were the firm name of a partnership.

RULE 6 — FORUM AND JURISDICTION

PLACE OF COMMENCEMENT AND TRIAL

6.01 (1) An action shall be commenced,

(a) in the territorial division,

(i) in which the cause of action arose, or

(ii) in which the defendant or, if there are several defendants, in which any one of them resides or carries on business; or

(b) at the court's place of sitting that is nearest to the place where the defendant or, if there are several defendants, where any one of them resides or carries on business.

(2) An action shall be tried in the place where it is commenced, but if the court is satisfied that the balance of convenience substantially favours holding the trial at another place than those described in subrule (1), the court may order that the action be tried at that other place.

(3) If, when an action is called for trial or settlement conference, the judge finds that the place where the action was commenced is not the proper place of trial, the court may order that the action be tried in any other place where it could have been commenced under this rule.

O. Reg. 78/06, s. 8(1)

6.02 A cause of action shall not be divided into two or more actions for the purpose of bringing it within the court's jurisdiction.

6.03 [Repealed O. Reg. 78/06, s. 8(2).]

RULE 7 — COMMENCEMENT OF PROCEEDINGS

Plaintiff's Claim

7.01 (1) An action shall be commenced by filing a plaintiff's claim (Form 7A) with the clerk, together with a copy of the claim for each defendant.

Contents of Claim, Attachments

(2) The following requirements apply to the claim:

1. It shall contain the following information, in concise and non-technical language:

i. The full names of the parties to the proceeding and, if relevant, the capacity in which they sue or are sued.

ii. The nature of the claim, with reasonable certainty and detail, including the date, place and nature of the occurences on which the claim is based.

iii. The amount of the claim and the relief requested.

iv. The name, address, telephone number, fax number if any, and Law Society of Upper Canada registration number if any, of the lawyer or agent representing the plaintiff or, if the plaintiff is self-represented, the plaintiff's address, telephone number and fax number if any.

v. The address where the plaintiff believes the defendant may be served.

2. If the plaintiff's claim is based in whole or in part on a document, a copy of the document shall be attached to each copy of the claim, unless it is unavailable, in which case the claim shall state the reason why the document is not attached.

(3) [Repealed O. Reg. 78/06, s. 9(2).]

O. Reg. 461/01, s. 5; 78/06, s. 9; 56/08, s. 1

7.02 [Revoked O. Reg. 461/01, s. 6.]

Issuing Claim

7.03 (1) On receiving the plaintiff's claim, the clerk shall immediately issue it by dating, signing and sealing it and assigning it a court file number.

(2) The original of the claim shall remain in the court file and the copies shall be given to the plaintiff for service on the defendant.

RULE 8 — SERVICE

Service of Particular Documents — Plaintiff's or Defendant's Claim

8.01 (1) A plaintiff's claim or defendant's claim (Form 7A or 10A) shall be served personally as provided in rule 8.02 or by an alternative to personal service as provided in rule 8.03.

Time for Service of Claim

(2) A claim shall be served within six months after the date it is issued, but the court may extend the time for service, before or after the six months has elapsed.

Defence

(3) A defence shall be served by the clerk, by mail or by fax.

(3.1) [Repealed O. Reg. 78/06, s. 10.]

Default Judgment

(4) A default judgment (Form 11B) shall be served by the clerk, by mail or by fax, on all parties named in the claim.

(4.1) [Repealed O. Reg. 78/06, s. 10.]

(4.1.1) [Repealed O. Reg. 78/06, s. 10.]

Assessment Order

(5) An order made on a motion in writing for an assessment of damages under subrule 11.03(2) shall be served by the clerk to the moving party if the party provides a stamped, self-addressed envelope with the notice of motion and supporting affidavit.

Settlement Conference Order

(6) An order made at a settlement conference shall be served by the clerk by mail or by fax, on all parties that did not attend the settlement conference.

Summons to Witness

(7) A summons to witness (Form 18A) shall be served personally by the party who requires the presence of the witness, or by the party's lawyer or agent, at least 10 days before the trial date; at the time of service, attendance money calculated in accordance with the regulations made under the *Administration of Justice Act* shall be paid or tendered to the witness.

Notice of Garnishment

(8) A notice of garnishment (Form 20E) shall be served by the creditor,

(a) together with a sworn affidavit for enforcement request (Form 20P), on the debtor, by mail, by courier, personally as provided in rule 8.02 or by an alternative to personal service as provided in rule 8.03; and

(b) together with a garnishee's statement (Form 20F), on the garnishee, by mail, by courier, personally as provided in rule 8.02 or by an alternative to personal service as provided in rule 8.03.

Notice of Garnishment Hearing

(9) A notice of garnishment hearing (Form 20Q) shall be served by the person requesting the hearing on the creditor, debtor, garnishee and co-owner of the debt, if any, and any other interested persons by mail, by courier, personally as provided in rule 8.02 or by an alternative to personal services as provided in rule 8.03.

Notice of Examination

(10) A notice of examination (Form 20H) shall be served by the creditor on the debtor or person to be examined, personally as provided in rule 8.02 or by an alternative to personal service as provided in rule 8.03.

Financial Statement

(11) If the person to be examined is the debtor and the debtor is an individual, the creditor shall serve the notice of examination on the debtor together with a blank financial information form (Form 20I).

(12) The notice of examination,

(a) shall be served, together with the financial information form if applicable, at least 30 days before the date fixed for the examination; and

(b) shall be filed, with proof of service, at least three days before the date fixed for the examination.

Notice of Contempt Hearing

(13) A notice of a contempt hearing shall be served by the creditor on the debtor or person to be examined personally as provided in rule 8.02.

Other Documents

(14) A document not referred to in subrules (1) to (13) may be served by mail, by courier, by fax, personally as provided in rule 8.02 or by an alternative to personal service as provided in rule 8.03, unless the court orders otherwise.

O. Reg. 461/01, s. 7 [s. 7(4) revoked O. Reg. 330/02, s. 4(2).]; 330/02, s. 4(1), (3); 440/03, s. 5, item 3; 78/06, s. 10; 393/09, s. 4

PERSONAL SERVICE

8.02 If a document is to be served personally, service shall be made,

(a) **Individual** — on an individual, other than a person under disability, by leaving a copy of the document with him or her;

(b) **Municipality** — on a municipal corporation, by leaving a copy of the document with the chair, mayor, warden or reeve of the municipality, with the clerk or deputy clerk of the municipality or with a lawyer for the municipality;

(c) **Corporation** — on any other corporation, by leaving a copy of the document with an officer, director or agent of the corporation, or with a person at any place of business of the corporation who appears to be in control or management of the place of business;

(d) **Board or Commission** — on a board or commission, by leaving a copy of the document with a member or officer of the board or commission;

(e) **Person Outside Ontario Carrying on Business in Ontario** — on a person outside Ontario who carries on business in Ontario, by leaving a copy of the document with anyone carrying on business in Ontario for the person;

(f) **Crown in Right of Canada** — on Her Majesty the Queen in right of Canada, in accordance with subsection 23(2) of the *Crown Liability and Proceedings Act* (Canada);

(g) **Crown in Right of Ontario** — on Her Majesty the Queen in right of Ontario, in accordance with section 10 of the *Proceedings Against the Crown Act*;

(h) **Absentee** — on an absentee, by leaving a copy of the document with the absentee's committee, if one has been appointed or, if not, with the Public Guardian and Trustee;

(i) **Minor** — on a minor, by leaving a copy of the document with the minor and, if the minor resides with a parent or other person having his or her care or lawful custody, by leaving another copy of the document with the parent or other person;

(j) **Mentally Incapable Person** — on a mentally incapable person,

(i) if there is a guardian or an attorney acting under a validated power of attorney for personal care with authority to act in the proceeding, by leaving a copy of the document with the guardian or attorney,

(ii) if there is no guardian or attorney acting under a validated power of attorney for personal care with authority to act in the proceeding but there is an attorney under a power of attorney with authority to act in the proceeding, by leaving a copy of the document with the attorney and leaving an additional copy with the person,

(iii) if there is neither a guardian nor an attorney with authority to act in the proceeding, by leaving a copy of the document bearing the person's name and address with the Public Guardian and Trustee and leaving an additional copy with the person;

(k) **Partnership** — on a partnership, by leaving a copy of the document with any one or more of the partners or with a person at the principal place of business of the partnership who appears to be in control or management of the place of business; and

(l) **Sole Proprietorship** — on a sole proprietorship, by leaving a copy of the document with the sole proprietor or with a person at the principal place of business of the sole proprietorship who appears to be in control or management of the place of business.

Alternatives to Personal Service

8.03 (1) If a document is to be served by an alternative to personal service, service shall be made in accordance with subrule (2), (3) or (5); in the case of a plaintiff's claim or defendant's claim served on an individual, service may also be made in accordance with subrule (7).

At Place of Residence

(2) If an attempt is made to effect personal service at an individual's place of residence and for any reason personal service cannot be effected, the document may be served by,

(a) leaving a copy in a sealed envelope addressed to the individual at the place of residence with anyone who appears to be an adult member of the same household; and

(b) on the same day or the following day, mailing or sending by courier another copy of the document to the individual at the place of residence.

Corporation

(3) If the head office or principal place of business of a corporation or, in the case of an extra-provincial corporation, the attorney for service in Ontario cannot be found at the last address recorded with the Ministry of Government Services, service may be made on the corporation,

(a) by mailing or sending by courier a copy of the document to the corporation or to the attorney for service in Ontario, as the case may be, at that address; and

(b) by mailing or sending by courier a copy of the document to each director of the corporation as recorded with the Ministry of Government Services, at the director's address as recorded with that Ministry.

When Effective

(4) Service made under subrule (2) or (3) is effective on the fifth day after the document is mailed or verified by courier that it was delivered.

Acceptance of Service by Lawyer

(5) Service on a party who is represented by a lawyer may be made by leaving a copy of the document with the lawyer or an employee in the lawyer's office, but service under this subrule is effective only if the lawyer or employee endorses on the document or a copy of it an acceptance of service and the date of the acceptance.

(6) By accepting service the lawyer is deemed to represent to the court that he or she has the client's authority to accept service.

Service of Claim

(7) Service of a plaintiff's claim or defendant's claim on an individual against whom the claim is made may be made by sending a copy of the claim by registered mail or by courier to the individual's place of residence, if the individual's signature verifying receipt of the copy is obtained.

(8) Service under subrule (7) is effective on the date on which the individual verifies receipt of the copy of the claim by signature, as shown in a delivery confirmation provided by or obtained from Canada Post or the commercial courier, as the case may be.

(9) [Repealed O. Reg. 393/09, s. 5(4).]

O. Reg. 78/06, s. 11; 393/09, s. 5

SUBSTITUTED SERVICE

8.04 If it is shown that it is impractical to effect prompt service of a claim personally or by an alternative to personal service, the court may allow substituted service.

SERVICE OUTSIDE ONTARIO

8.05 If the defendant is outside Ontario, the court may award as costs of the action the costs reasonably incurred in effecting service of the claim on the defendant there.

O. Reg. 78/06, s. 12

PROOF OF SERVICE

8.06 An affidavit of service (Form 8A) made by the person effecting the service constitutes proof of service of a document.

O. Reg. 461/01, s. 8 [s. 8(2) revoked O. Reg. 330/02, s. 5(2); s. 8(4) revoked 330/02, s. 5(4).]; 330/02, s. 5(1), (3); 440/03, s. 5, item 4; 78/06, s. 13

Service by Mail

8.07 (1) If a document is to be served by mail under these rules, it shall be sent, by regular lettermail or registered mail, to the last address of the person or of the person's lawyer or agent that is,

(a) on file with the court, if the document is to be served by the clerk;

(b) known to the sender, if the document is to be served by any other person.

When Effective

(2) Service of a document by mail is deemed to be effective on the fifth day following the date of mailing.

Exception

(3) This rule does not apply when a claim is served by registered mail under subrule 8.03(7).

O. Reg. 78/06, s. 14; 393/09, s. 6

Service by Courier

8.07.1 (1) If a document is to be served by courier under these rules, it shall be sent by means of a commercial courier to the last address of the person or of the person's lawyer or agent that is on file with the court or known to the sender.

When Effective

(2) Service of a document sent by courier is deemed to be effective on the fifth day following the date on which the courier verifies to the sender that the document was delivered.

Exception

(3) This rule does not apply when a claim is served by courier under subrule 8.03(7).

O. Reg. 78/06, s. 15; 393/09, s. 7

Service by Fax

8.08 (1) Service of a document by fax is deemed to be effective,

(a) on the day of transmission, if transmission takes place before 5 p.m. on a day that is not a holiday;

(b) on the next day that is not a holiday, in any other case.

(2) A document containing 16 or more pages, including the cover page, may be served by fax only between 5 p.m. and 8 a.m. the following day, unless the party to be served consents in advance.

O. Reg. 393/09, s. 8

NOTICE OF CHANGE OF ADDRESS

8.09 (1) A party whose address for service changes shall serve notice of the change on the court and other parties within seven days after the change takes place.

(2) Service of the notice may be proved by affidavit if the court orders that proof of service is required.

(3) [Repealed O. Reg. 78/06, s. 16.]

(4) [Repealed O. Reg. 78/06, s. 16.]

(5) [Repealed O. Reg. 78/06, s. 16.]

O. Reg. 461/01, s. 9 [s. 9(2) revoked O. Reg. 330/02, s. 6(2).]; 330/02, s. 6(1); 440/03, s. 5, item 5; 78/06, s. 16

FAILURE TO RECEIVE DOCUMENT

8.10 A person who has been served or who is deemed to have been served with a document in accordance with these rules is nevertheless entitled to show, on a motion to set aside the consequences of default, on a motion for an extension of time or in support of a request for an adjournment, that the document,

(a) did not come to the person's notice; or

(b) came to the person's notice only at some time later than when it was served or is deemed to have been served.

O. Reg. 461/01, s. 9(1)

RULE 9 — DEFENCE

Defence

9.01 (1) A defendant who wishes to dispute a plaintiff's claim shall file a defence (Form 9A), with a copy for every plaintiff, with the clerk within 20 days of being served with the claim.

(2) On receiving the defence, the clerk shall serve it as described in subrule 8.01(3).

(3) [Repealed O. Reg. 78/06, s. 17(3).]

O. Reg. 461/01, s. 10 [s. 10(3) revoked O. Reg. 330/02, s. 7(2).]; 330/02, s. 7(1); 440/03, ss. 2, 5, item 6; 78/06, s. 17

Contents of Defence, Attachments

9.02 (1) The following requirements apply to the defence:

1. It shall contain the following information:

   i. The reasons why the defendant disputes the plaintiff's claim, expressed in concise non-technical language with a reasonable amount of detail.

   ii. If the defendant is self-represented, the defendant's name, address and telephone number, and fax number if any.

   iii. If the defendant is represented by a lawyer or agent, that person's name, address and telephone number, and fax number if any.

2. If the defence is based in whole or in part on a document, a copy of the document shall be attached to each copy of the defence, unless it is unavailable, in which case the defence shall state the reason why the document is not attached.

(2) [Repealed O. Reg. 78/06, s. 19.]

O. Reg. 461/01, s. 11; 78/06, ss. 18, 19

Admission of Liability and Proposal of Terms of Payment

9.03 (1) A defendant who admits liability for all or part of the plaintiff's claim but wishes to arrange terms of payment may in the defence admit liability and propose terms of payment.

Where No Dispute

(2) If the plaintiff does not dispute the proposal within the 20-day period referred to in subsection (3),

(a) the defendant shall make payment in accordance with the proposal as if it were a court order;

(b) the plaintiff may serve a notice of default of payment (Form 20L) on the defendant if the defendant fails to make payment in accordance with the proposal; and

(c) the clerk shall sign judgment for the unpaid balance of the undisputed amount on the filing of an affidavit of default of payment (Form 20M) by the plaintiff swearing,

(i) that the defendant failed to make payment in accordance with the proposal,

(ii) to the amount paid by the defendant and the unpaid balance, and

(iii) that 15 days have passed since the defendant was served with a notice of default of payment.

Dispute

(3) The plaintiff may dispute the proposal within 20 days after service of the defence by filing with the clerk and serving on the defendant a request to clerk (Form 9B) for a terms of payment hearing before a referee or other person appointed by the court.

(4) The clerk shall fix a time for the hearing, allowing for a reasonable notice period after the date the request is served, and serve a notice of hearing on the parties.

Manner of Service

(4.1) The notice of hearing shall be served by mail or fax.

Financial Information Form, Defendant an Individual

(4.2) The clerk shall serve a financial information form (Form 20I) on the defendant, together with the notice of hearing, if the defendant is an individual.

(4.3) Where a defendant receives a financial information form under subrule (4.2), he or she shall complete it and serve it on the creditor before the hearing, but shall not file it with the court.

Order

(5) On the hearing, the referee or other person may make an order as to terms of payment by the defendant.

Failure to Appear, Default Judgment

(6) If the defendant does not appear at the hearing, the clerk may sign default judgment against the defendant for the part of the claim that has been admitted and shall serve a default judgment (Form 11B) on the defendant in accordance with subrule 8.01(4).

(6.1) [Repealed O. Reg. 78/06, s. 20(5).]

Failure to Make Payments

(7) Unless the referee or other person specifies otherwise in the order as to terms of payment, if the defendant fails to make payment in accordance with the order, the clerk shall sign judgment for the unpaid balance on the filing of an affidavit by the plaintiff swearing to the default and stating the amount paid and the unpaid balance.

O. Reg. 461/01, s. 12 [s. 12(2) revoked O. Reg. 330/02, s. 8(2); s. 12(4) revoked 330/02, s. 8(4).]; 330/02, s. 8(1), (3); 440/03, s. 5, item 7; 78/06, s. 20

RULE 10 — DEFENDANT'S CLAIM

Defendant's Claim

10.01 (1) A defendant may make a claim,

(a) against the plaintiff;

(b) against any other person,

(i) arising out of the transaction or occurrence relied upon by the plaintiff, or

(ii) related to the plaintiff's claim; or

(c) against the plaintiff and against another person in accordance with clause (b).

(2) The defendant's claim shall be in Form 10A and may be issued,

(a) within 20 days after the day on which the defence is filed; or

(b) after the time described in clause (a) but before trial or default judgment, with leave of the court.

Copies

(3) The defendant shall provide a copy of the defendant's claim to the court.

Contents of Defendant's Claim, Attachments

(4) The following requirements apply to the defendant's claim:

1. It shall contain the following information:

i. The full names of the parties to the defendant's claim and, if relevant, the capacity in which they sue or are sued.

ii. The nature of the claim, expressed in concise non-technical language with a reasonable amount of detail, including the date, place and nature of the occurrences on which the claim is based.

iii. The amount of the claim and the relief requested.

iv. If the defendant is self-represented, the defendant's name, address and telephone number, and fax number if any.

v. If the defendant is represented by a lawyer or agent, that person's name, address and telephone number, and fax number if any.

vi. The address where the defendant believes each person against whom the claim is made may be served.

vii. The court file number assigned to the plaintiff's claim.

2. If the defendant's claim is based in whole or in part on a document, a copy of the document shall be attached to each copy of the claim, unless it is unavailable, in which case the claim shall state the reason why the document is not attached.

(5) [Repealed O. Reg. 78/06, s. 21(4).]

Issuance

(6) On receiving the defendant's claim, the clerk shall immediately issue it by dating, signing and sealing it, shall assign it the same court file number as the plaintiff's claim and shall place the original in the court file.

(7) [Repealed O. Reg. 78/06, s. 21(4).]

(8) [Repealed O. Reg. 78/06, s. 21(4).]

O. Reg. 461/01, s. 13 [s. 13(5) revoked O. Reg. 330/02, s. 9(2).]; 330/02, s. 9(1); 440/03, s. 3; 78/06, s. 21

SERVICE

10.02 A defendant's claim shall be served by the defendant on every person against whom it is made, in accordance with subrules 8.01(1) and (2).

Defence

10.03 (1) A party who wishes to dispute the defendant's claim or a third party who wishes to dispute the plaintiff's claim may, within 20 days after service of the defendant's claim, file a defence (Form 9A) with the clerk, together with a copy for each of the other parties or persons against whom the defendant's or plaintiff's claim is made.

Service of Copy by Clerk

(2) On receiving a defence under subrule (1), the clerk shall retain the original in the court file and shall serve a copy on each party in accordance with subrule 8.01(3).

(3) [Repealed O. Reg. 78/06, s. 22.]

O. Reg. 461/01, s. 14 [s. 14(3) revoked O. Reg. 330/02, s. 10(2).]; 330/02, s. 10(1); 440/03, ss. 4, 5, item 8; 78/06, s. 22

Defendant's Claim to be Tried with Main Action

10.04 (1) A defendant's claim shall be tried and disposed of at the trial of the action, unless the court orders otherwise.

Exception

(2) If it appears that a defendant's claim may unduly complicate or delay the trial of the action or cause undue prejudice to a party, the court may order separate trials or direct that the defendant's claim proceed as a separate action.

Rights of Third Party

(3) If the defendant alleges, in a defendant's claim, that a third party is liable to the defendant for all or part of the plaintiff's claim in the action, the third party may at the trial contest the defendant's liability to the plaintiff but only if the third party has filed a defence in accordance with subrule 10.03(1).

O. Reg. 78/06, s. 23

Application of Rules to Defendant's Claim

10.05 (1) These rules apply, with necessary modifications, to a defendant's claim as if it were a plaintiff's claim, and to a defence to a defendant's claim as if it were a defence to a plaintiff's claim.

Exception

(2) However, when a person against whom a defendant's claim is made is noted in default, judgment against that person may be obtained only in accordance with rule 11.04.

O. Reg. 56/08, s. 2

RULE 11 — DEFAULT PROCEEDINGS

Noting Defendant in Default

11.01 (1) If a defendant to a plaintiff's claim or a defendant's claim fails to file a defence to all or part of the claim with the clerk within the prescribed time, the clerk may, when proof is filed that the claim was served within the territorial division, note the defendant in default.

Leave Required for Person under Disability

(2) A person under disability may not be noted in default under subrule (1), except with leave of the court.

Service Outside Territorial Division

(3) If all the defendants have been served outside the court's territorial division, the clerk shall not note any defendant in default until it is proved by an affidavit for jurisdiction

(Form 11A) submitted to the clerk, or by evidence presented before a judge, that the action was properly brought in that territorial division.

O. Reg. 78/06, s. 24

Default Judgment, Plaintiff's Claim, Debt or Liquidated Demand

11.02 (1) If a defendant has been noted in default, the clerk may sign default judgment (Form 11B) in respect of the claim or any part of the claim to which the default applies that is for a debt or liquidated demand in money, including interest if claimed.

(2) The fact that default judgment has been signed under subrule (1) does not affect the plaintiff's right to proceed on the remainder of the claim or against any other defendant for all or part of the claim.

Manner of Service of Default Judgment

(3) A default judgment (Form 11B) shall be served in accordance with subrule 8.01(4).

(4) [Repealed O. Reg. 78/06, s. 24.]

O. Reg. 78/06, s. 24

Default Judgment, Plaintiff's Claim, Unliquidated Demand

11.03 (1) If all defendants have been noted in default, the plaintiff may obtain judgment against a defendant noted in default with respect to any part of the claim to which rule 11.02 does not apply.

(2) To obtain judgment, the plaintiff may,

(a) file a notice of motion and supporting affidavit (Form 15A) requesting a motion in writing for an assessment of damages, setting out the reasons why the motion should be granted and attaching any relevant documents; or

(b) file a request to clerk (Form 9B) requesting that an assessment hearing be arranged.

Inadequate Supporting Affidavit

(3) On a motion in writing for an assessment of damages under clause (2)(a), a judge who finds the plaintiff's affidavit inadequate or unsatisfactory may order that,

(a) a further affidavit be provided; or

(b) an assessment hearing be held.

Assessment Hearing

(4) If an assessment hearing is to be held under clause (2)(b) or (3)(b), the clerk shall fix a date for the hearing and send a notice of hearing to the plaintiff, and the assessment hearing shall proceed as a trial in accordance with rule 17.

Matters to be Proved

(5) On a motion in writing for an assessment of damages or at an assessment hearing, the plaintiff is not required to prove liability against a defendant noted in default, but is required to prove the amount of the claim.

Service of Order

(6) An order made on a motion in writing for an assessment of damages shall be served by the clerk in accordance with subrule 8.01(5).

No Assessment where Defence Filed

(7) If one or more defendants have filed a defence, a plaintiff requiring an assessment of damages against a defendant noted in default shall proceed to a settlement conference under rule 13 and, if necessary, a trial in accordance with rule 17.

O. Reg. 78/06, s. 24; 393/09, s. 9

DEFAULT JUDGMENT, DEFENDANT'S CLAIM

11.04 If a party against whom a defendant's claim is made has been noted in default, judgment may be obtained against the party only at trial or on motion.

O. Reg. 78/06, s. 24

CONSEQUENCES OF NOTING IN DEFAULT

11.05 (1) A defendant who has been noted in default shall not file a defence or take any other step in the proceeding, except making a motion under rule 11.06, without leave of the court or the plaintiff's consent.

(2) Any step in the proceeding may be taken without the consent of a defendant who has been noted in default.

(3) A defendant who has been noted in default is not entitled to notice of any step in the proceeding and need not be served with any other document, except the following:

1. Subrule 11.02(3) (service of default judgment).
2. Rule 12.01 (amendment of claim or defence).
3. Subrule 15.01(6) (motion after judgment).
4. Postjudgment proceedings against a debtor under rule 20.

O. Reg. 78/06, s. 24

SETTING ASIDE NOTING OF DEFAULT BY COURT ON MOTION

11.06 The court may set aside the noting in default or default judgment against a party and any step that has been taken to enforce the judgment, on such terms as are just, if the party makes a motion to set aside and the court is satisfied that,

(a) the party has a meritorious defence and a reasonable explanation for the default; and

(b) the motion is made as soon as is reasonably possible in all the circumstances.

O. Reg. 461/01, s. 15; 78/06, s. 24

RULE 11.1 — DISMISSAL BY CLERK

Dismissal — Undefended Actions

11.1.01 (1) The clerk shall make an order dismissing an action as abandoned if the following conditions are satisfied, unless the court orders otherwise:

1. More than 180 days have passed since the date the claim was issued or an order was made extending the time for service of the claim under subrule 8.01(2).

2. No defence has been filed.

3. The action has not been disposed of by order and has not been set down for trial.

4. The clerk has given 45 days notice to the plaintiff that the action will be dismissed as abandoned.

Dismissal — Defended Actions

(2) The clerk shall make an order dismissing an action as abandoned if the following conditions are satisfied, unless the court orders otherwise:

1. More than 150 days have passed since the date the first defence was filed.

2. [Repealed O. Reg. 56/08, s. 3(2).]

3. The action has not been disposed of by order and has not been set down for trial.

4. The clerk has given 45 days notice to all parties to the action that the action will be dismissed as abandoned.

Transition

(3) If an action was started before July 1, 2006, the following applies:

1. The action or a step in the action shall be carried on under these rules on or after July 1, 2006.

2. Despite paragraph 1, if a step in the action is taken on or after July 1, 2006, the timetable set out in subrules (1) and (2) shall apply as if the action started on the date on which the step was taken.

Same

(4) If an action was commenced before July 1, 2006 and no step is taken in the action on or after that date, the clerk may make an order dismissing it as abandoned if,

(a) where an action is undefended, more than two years have passed since the date the claim was issued and the conditions set out in paragraphs 2, 3 and 4 of subrule (1) are satisfied; or

(b) more than two years have passed since the date the first defence was filed and the conditions set out in paragraphs 3 and 4 of subrule (2) are satisfied.

Exception Where Terms of Settlement Signed

(5) Subrules (1), (2) and (4) do not apply if terms of settlement (Form 14D) signed by all parties have been filed.

Exception Where Admission of Liability

(6) Subrule (2) and clause (4)(b) do not apply if the defence contains an admission of liability for the plaintiff's claim and a proposal of terms of payment under subrule 9.03(1).

Service of Orders

(7) The clerk shall serve a copy of an order made under subrule (1) or clause (4)(a) on the plaintiff and a copy of an order made under subrule (2) or clause (4)(b) on all parties to the action.

O. Reg. 78/06, s. 24; 56/08, s. 3; 393/09, s. 10

RULE 11.2 — REQUEST FOR CLERK'S ORDER ON CONSENT

Consent Order

11.2.01 (1) The clerk shall, on the filing of a request for clerk's order on consent (Form 11.2A), make an order granting the relief sought, including costs, if the following conditions are satisfied:

1. The relief sought is,

   i. amending a claim or defence less than 30 days before the originally scheduled trial date,

   ii. adding, deleting or substituting a party less than 30 days before the originally scheduled trial date,

   iii. setting aside the noting in default or default judgment against a party and any specified step to enforce the judgment that has not yet been completed,

   iv. restoring a matter that was dismissed under rule 11.1 to the list,

   v. noting that payment has been made in full satisfaction of a judgment or terms of settlement, or

   vi. dismissing an action.

2. The request is signed by all parties (including any party to be added, deleted or substituted) and states,

   i. that each party has received a copy of the request, and

   ii. that no party that would be affected by the order is under disability.

3. [Repealed O. Reg. 393/09, s. 11(3).]

4. [Repealed O. Reg. 393/09, s. 11(3).]

Service of order

(2) The clerk shall serve a copy of an order made under subrule (1) in accordance with subrule 8.01(14) on a party that requests it and provides a stamped, self-addressed envelope.

Same, Refusal to Make Order

(3) Where the clerk refuses to make an order, the clerk shall serve a copy of the request for clerk's order on consent (Form 11.2A), with reasons for the refusal, on all the parties.

Notice of Setting Aside of Enforcement Step

(4) Where an order is made setting aside a specified step to enforce a judgment under subparagraph 1 iii of subrule (1), a party shall file a copy of the order at each court location where the enforcement step has been requested.

O. Reg. 78/06, s. 24; 393/09, s. 11

RULE 11.3 — DISCONTINUANCE [HEADING ADDED O. REG. 393/09, S. 12.]

DISCONTINUANCE BY PLAINTIFF IN UNDEFENDED ACTION

11.3.01 (1) A plaintiff may discontinue his or her claim against a defendant who fails to file a defence to all or part of the claim with the clerk within the prescribed time by,

(a) serving a notice of discontinued claim (Form 11.3A) on all defendants who were served with the claim; and

(b) filing the notice with proof of service.

(2) A claim may not be discontinued by or against a person under disability, except with leave of the court.

O. Reg. 393/09, s. 12

EFFECT OF DISCONTINUANCE ON SUBSEQUENT ACTION

11.3.02 The discontinuance of a claim is not a defence to a subsequent action on the matter, unless an order granting leave to discontinue provides otherwise.

O. Reg. 393/09, s. 12

RULE 12 — AMENDMENT

Right to Amend

12.01 (1) A plaintiff's or defendant's claim and a defence to a plaintiff's or defendant's claim may be amended by filing with the clerk a copy that is marked "Amended", in which any additions are underlined and any other changes are identified.

Service

(2) The amended document shall be served by the party making the amendment on all parties, including any parties in default, in accordance with subrule 8.01(14).

Time

(3) Filing and service of the amended document shall take place at least 30 days before the originally scheduled trial date, unless,

(a) the court, on motion, allows a shorter notice period; or

(b) a clerk's order permitting the amendment is obtained under subrule 11.2.01(1).

Service on Added Party

(4) A person added as a party shall be served with the claim as amended, except that if the person is added as a party at trial, the court may dispense with service of the claim.

No Amendment Required in Response

(5) A party who is served with an amended document is not required to amend the party's defence or claim.

O. Reg. 78/06, s. 25; 393/09, s. 13

MOTION TO STRIKE OUT OR AMEND A DOCUMENT

12.02 (1) The court may, on motion, strike out or amend all or part of any document that,

(a) discloses no reasonable cause of action or defence;

(b) may delay or make it difficult to have a fair trial; or

(c) is inflammatory, a waste of time, a nuisance or an abuse of the court's process.

(2) In connection with an order striking out or amending a document under subrule (1), the court may do one or more of the following:

1. In the case of a claim, order that the action be stayed or dismissed.
2. In the case of a defence, strike out the defence and grant judgment.
3. Impose such terms as are just.

O. Reg. 78/06, s. 26

RULE 13 — SETTLEMENT CONFERENCES [HEADING AMENDED O. REG. 78/06, S. 27.]

Settlement Conference Required in Defended Action

13.01 (1) A settlement conference shall be held in every defended action.

Duty of Clerk

(2) The clerk shall fix a time, date and place for the settlement conference and serve a notice of settlement conference, together with a list of proposed witnesses (Form 13A), on the parties.

Timing

(3) The settlement conference shall be held within 90 days after the first defence is filed.

Exception

(4) Subrules (1) to (3) do not apply if the defence contains an admission of liability for all of the plaintiff's claim and a proposal of terms of payment under subrule 9.03(1).

(5) [Repealed O. Reg. 78/06, s. 27.]

(6) [Repealed O. Reg. 78/06, s. 27.]

(7) [Repealed O. Reg. 78/06, s. 27.]

O. Reg. 78/06, s. 27

Attendance

13.02 (1) A party and the party's lawyer or agent, if any, shall, unless the court orders otherwise, participate in the settlement conference,

(a) by personal attendance; or

(b) by telephone or video conference in accordance with rule 1.07.

Authority to Settle

(2) A party who requires another person's approval before agreeing to a settlement shall, before the settlement conference, arrange to have ready telephone access to the other person throughout the conference, whether it takes place during or after regular business hours.

Additional Settlement Conferences

(3) The court may order the parties to attend an additional settlement conference.

(4) The clerk shall fix a time and place for any additional settlement conference and serve a notice of settlement conference, together with a list of proposed witnesses (Form 13A) on the parties.

Failure to Attend

(5) If a party who has received a notice of settlement conference fails to attend the conference, the court may,

(a) impose appropriate sanctions, by way of costs or otherwise; and

(b) order that an additional settlement conference be held, if necessary.

(6) If a defendant fails to attend a first settlement conference, receives notice of an additional settlement conference and fails to attend the additional settlement conference, the court may,

(a) strike out the defence and dismiss the defendant's claim, if any, and allow the plaintiff to prove the plaintiff's claim; or

(b) make such other order as is just.

Inadequate Preparation, Failure to File Material

(7) The court may award costs against a person who attends a settlement conference if,

(a) in the opinion of the court, the person is so inadequately prepared as to frustrate the purposes of the conference;

(b) the person fails to file the material required by subrule 13.03(2).

O. Reg. 78/06, s. 27

Purposes of Settlement Conference

13.03 **(1)** The purposes of a settlement conference are,

(a) to resolve or narrow the issues in the action;

(b) to expedite the disposition of the action;

(c) to encourage settlement of the action;

(d) to assist the parties in effective preparation for trial; and

(e) to provide full disclosure between the parties of the relevant facts and evidence.

Disclosure

(2) At least 14 days before the date of the settlement conference, each party shall serve on every other party and file with the court,

(a) a copy of any document to be relied on at the trial, including an expert report, not attached to the party's claim or defence; and

(b) a list of proposed witnesses (Form 13A) and of other persons with knowledge of the matters in dispute in the action.

(3) At the settlement conference, the parties or their representatives shall openly and frankly discuss the issues involved in the action.

Further Disclosure Restricted

(4) Except as otherwise provided or with the consent of the parties (Form 13B), the matters discussed at the settlement conference shall not be disclosed to others until after the action has been disposed of.

(5) [Repealed O. Reg. 78/06, s. 27.]

(6) [Repealed O. Reg. 78/06, s. 27.]

O. Reg. 78/06, s. 27

RECOMMENDATIONS TO PARTIES

13.04 The court may make recommendations to the parties on any matter relating to the conduct of the action, in order to fulfil the purposes of a settlement conference, including recommendations as to,

(a) the clarification and simplification of issues in the action;

(b) the elimination of claims or defences that appear to be unsupported; and

(c) the admission of facts or documents without further proof.

O. Reg. 78/06, s. 27

Orders at Settlement Conference

13.05 (1) A judge conducting a settlement conference may make any order relating to the conduct of the action that the court could make.

(2) Without limiting the generality of subrule (1), the judge may,

(a) make an order,

(i) adding or deleting parties,

(ii) consolidating actions,

(iii) staying the action,

(iv) amending or striking out a claim or defence under rule 12.02,

(v) staying or dismissing a claim,

(vi) directing production of documents,

(vii) changing the place of trial under rule 6.01,

(viii) directing an additional settlement conference under subrule 13.02(3), and

(ix) ordering costs; and

(b) at an additional settlement conference, order judgment under subrule 13.02(6).

Recommendations to Judge

(3) If the settlement conference is conducted by a referee, a judge may, on the referee's recommendation, make any order that may be made under subrules (1) and (2).

Consent to Final Judgment

(4) A judge may order final judgment at a settlement conference where the matter in dispute is for an amount under the appealable limit and a party files a consent (Form 13B) signed by all parties before the settlement conference indicating that they wish to obtain final determination of the matter at the settlement conference if a mediated settlement is not reached.

Service of Order

(5) Within 10 days after the judge signs an order made at a settlement conference, the clerk shall serve the order on the parties that were not present at the settlement conference in accordance with subrule 8.01(6).

O. Reg. 78/06, s. 27

MEMORANDUM

13.06 (1) At the end of the settlement conference, the court shall prepare a memorandum summarizing,

(a) recommendations made under rule 13.04;

(b) the issues remaining in dispute;

(c) the matters agreed on by the parties;

(d) any evidentiary matters that are considered relevant; and

(e) information relating to the scheduling of the remaining steps in the proceeding.

(2) The memorandum shall be filed with the clerk, who shall give a copy to the trial judge.

O. Reg. 78/06, s. 27

NOTICE OF TRIAL

13.07 At or after the settlement conference, the clerk shall provide the parties with a notice stating that one of the parties must request a trial date if the action is not disposed of within 30 days after the settlement conference, and pay the fee required for setting the action down for trial.

O. Reg. 78/06, s. 27

JUDGE NOT TO PRESIDE AT TRIAL

13.08 A judge who conducts a settlement conference in an action shall not preside at the trial of the action.

O. Reg. 78/06, s. 27

WITHDRAWAL OF CLAIM

13.09 After a settlement conference has been held, a claim against a party who is not in default shall not be withdrawn or discontinued by the party who brought the claim without,

(a) the written consent of the party against whom the claim is brought; or

(b) leave of the court.

O. Reg. 78/06, s. 27

COSTS

13.10 The costs of a settlement conference, exclusive of disbursements, shall not exceed $100 unless the court orders otherwise because there are special circumstances.

O. Reg. 78/06, s. 27

RULE 14 — OFFER TO SETTLE

14.01 A party may serve on any other party an offer to settle a claim on the terms specified in the offer.

Written Documents

14.01.1 (1) An offer to settle, an acceptance of an offer to settle and a notice of withdrawal of an offer to settle shall be in writing.

Use of Forms

(2) An offer to settle may be in Form 14A, an acceptance of an offer to settle may be in Form 14B and a notice of withdrawal of an offer to settle may be in Form 14C.

Terms of Settlement

(3) The terms of an accepted offer to settle may be set out in terms of settlement (Form 14D).

O. Reg. 78/06, s. 28

Time for Making Offer

14.02 (1) An offer to settle may be made at any time.

Costs Consequences

(2) The costs consequences referred to in rule 14.07 apply only if the offer to settle is served on the party to whom it is made at least seven days before the trial commences.

O. Reg. 78/06, s. 29

Withdrawal

14.03 (1) An offer to settle may be withdrawn at any time before it is accepted, by serving a notice of withdrawal of an offer to settle on the party to whom it was made.

Deemed Withdrawal

(2) If an offer to settle specifies a date after which it is no longer available for acceptance, and has not been accepted on or before that date, the offer shall be deemed to have been withdrawn on the day after that date.

Expiry When Court Disposes of Claim

(3) An offer may not be accepted after the court disposes of the claim in respect of which the offer is made.

O. Reg. 461/01, s. 16; 78/06, s. 29

NO DISCLOSURE TO TRIAL JUDGE

14.04 If an offer to settle is not accepted, no communication about it or any related negotiations shall be made to the trial judge until all questions of liability and the relief to be granted, other than costs, have been determined.

O. Reg. 78/06, s. 29

Acceptance of an Offer to Settle

14.05 (1) An offer to settle may be accepted by serving an acceptance of an offer to settle on the party who made it, at any time before it is withdrawn or before the court disposes of the claim in respect of which it is made.

Payment Into Court As Condition

(2) An offer by a plaintiff to settle a claim in return for the payment of money by a defendant may include a term that the defendant pay the money into court; in that case, the defendant may accept the offer only by paying the money into court and notifying the plaintiff of the payment.

(3) If a defendant offers to pay money to a plaintiff in settlement of a claim, the plaintiff may accept the offer with the condition that the defendant pay the money into court; if the offer is so accepted and the defendant fails to pay the money into court, the plaintiff may proceed as provided in rule 14.06.

Costs

(4) If an accepted offer to settle does not deal with costs, the plaintiff is entitled,

(a) in the case of an offer made by the defendant, to the plaintiff's disbursements assessed to the date the plaintiff was served with the offer;

(b) in the case of an offer made by the plaintiff, to the plaintiff's disbursements assessed to the date that the notice of acceptance was served.

O. Reg. 78/06, s. 30

FAILURE TO COMPLY WITH ACCEPTED OFFER

14.06 If a party to an accepted offer to settle fails to comply with the terms of the offer, the other party may,

(a) make a motion to the court for judgment in the terms of the accepted offer; or

(b) continue the proceeding as if there had been no offer to settle.

Costs Consequences of Failure to Accept

14.07 (1) When a plaintiff makes an offer to settle that is not accepted by the defendant, the court may award the plaintiff an amount not exceeding twice the costs of the action, if the following conditions are met:

1. The plaintiff obtains a judgment as favourable as or more favourable than the terms of the offer.

2. The offer was made at least seven days before the trial.

3. The offer was not withdrawn and did not expire before the trial.

(2) When a defendant makes an offer to settle that is not accepted by the plaintiff, the court may award the defendant an amount not exceeding twice the costs awardable to a successful party, from the date the offer was served, if the following conditions are met:

1. The plaintiff obtains a judgment as favourable as or less favourable than the terms of the offer.

2. The offer was made at least seven days before the trial.

3. The offer was not withdrawn and did not expire before the trial.

(3) If an amount is awarded under subrule (1) or (2) to a self-represented party, the court may also award the party an amount not exceeding $500 as compensation for inconvenience and expense.

O. Reg. 78/06, s. 31

RULE 15 — MOTIONS

Notice of Motion and Supporting Affidavit

15.01 (1) A motion shall be made by a notice of motion and supporting affidavit (Form 15A).

(2) The moving party shall obtain a hearing date from the clerk before serving the notice of motion and supporting affidavit under subrule (3).

(3) The notice of motion and supporting affidavit,

(a) shall be served on every party who has filed a claim and any defendant who has not been noted in default, at least seven days before the hearing date; and

(b) shall be filed, with proof of service, at least three days before the hearing date.

Supporting Affidavit in Response

(4) A party who prepares an affidavit (Form 15B) in response to the moving party's notice of motion and supporting affidavit shall serve it on every party who has filed a claim or defence and file it, with proof of service, at least two days before the hearing date.

Supplementary Affidavit

(5) The moving party may serve a supplementary affidavit on every party who has filed a claim or defence and file it, with proof of service, at least two days before the hearing date.

Motion After Judgment Signed

(6) A motion that is made after judgment has been signed shall be served on all parties, including those who have been noted in default.

O. Reg. 78/06, s. 32; 393/09, s. 14(1)–(3), (6)

METHOD OF HEARING

15.02 (1) A motion may be heard,

(a) in person;

(b) by telephone or video conference in accordance with paragraph 2 of subrule 1.07(1);

(c) by a judge in writing under clause 11.03(2)(a);

(d) by any other method that the judge determines is fair and reasonable.

(2) The attendance of the parties is not required if the motion is in writing under clause (1)(c).

O. Reg. 78/06, s. 32

Motion Without Notice

15.03 (1) Despite rule 15.01, a motion may be made without notice if the nature or circumstances of the motion make notice unnecessary or not reasonably possible.

Service of Order

(2) A party who obtains an order on motion without notice shall serve it on every affected party, together with a copy of the notice of motion and supporting affidavit used on the motion, within five days after the order is signed.

Motion to Set Aside or Vary Motion Made Without Notice

(3) A party who is affected by an order obtained on motion without notice may make a motion to set aside or vary the order, within 30 days after being served with the order.

O. Reg. 78/06, s. 32

NO FURTHER MOTIONS WITHOUT LEAVE

15.04 If the court is satisfied that a party has tried to delay the action, add to its costs or otherwise abuse the court's process by making numerous motions without merit, the court may, on motion, make an order prohibiting the party from making any further motions in the action without leave of the court.

O. Reg. 78/06, s. 32

ADJOURNMENT OF MOTION

15.05 A motion shall not be adjourned at a party's request before the hearing date unless the written consent of all parties is filed when the request is made, unless the court orders otherwise.

O. Reg. 78/06, s. 32

WITHDRAWAL OF MOTION

15.06 A motion shall not be withdrawn without,

(a) the written consent of all the parties; or

(b) leave of the court.

O. Reg. 78/06, s. 32

COSTS

15.07 The costs of a motion, exclusive of disbursements, shall not exceed $100 unless the court orders otherwise because there are special circumstances.

O. Reg. 78/06, s. 32

RULE 16 — NOTICE OF TRIAL

Clerk Fixes Date and Serves Notice

16.01 (1) The clerk shall fix a date for trial and serve a notice of trial on each party who has filed a claim or defence if,

(a) a settlement conference has been held; and

(b) a party has requested that the clerk fix a date for trial and has paid the required fee.

(1.1) [Repealed O. Reg. 78/06, s. 32.]

(1.2) [Repealed O. Reg. 78/06, s. 32.]

(1.3) [Repealed O. Reg. 78/06, s. 32.]

Manner of Service

(2) The notice of trial shall be served by mail or fax.

O. Reg. 461/01, s. 17 [s. 17(2) revoked O. Reg. 330/02, s. 11(2).]; 330/02, s. 11(1); 440/03, s. 5, item 9; 78/06, s. 32

RULE 17 — TRIAL

Failure to Attend

17.01 (1) If an action is called for trial and all the parties fail to attend, the trial judge may strike the action off the trial list.

(2) If an action is called for trial and a party fails to attend, the trial judge may,

(a) proceed with the trial in the party's absence;

(b) if the plaintiff attends and the defendant fails to do so, strike out the defence and dismiss the defendant's claim, if any, and allow the plaintiff to prove the plaintiff's claim, subject to subrule (3);

(c) if the defendant attends and the plaintiff fails to do so, dismiss the action and allow the defendant to prove the defendant's claim, if any; or

(d) make such other order as is just.

(2.1) In the case described in clause (2)(b) or (c), the person with the claim is not required to prove liability against the party who has failed to attend but is required to prove the amount of the claim.

(3) In the case described in clause (2)(b), if an issue as to the proper place of trial under subrule 6.01(1) is raised in the defence, the trial judge shall consider it and make a finding.

Setting Aside or Variation of Judgment

(4) The court may set aside or vary, on such terms as are just, a judgment obtained against a party who failed to attend at the trial.

Conditions to Making of Order under Subrule (4)

(5) The court may make an order under subrule (4) only if,

(a) the party who failed to attend makes a motion for the order within 30 days after becoming aware of the judgment; or

(b) the party who failed to attend makes a motion for an extension of the 30-day period mentioned in clause (a) and the court is satisfied that there are special circumstances that justify the extension.

O. Reg. 78/06, s. 33

ADJOURNMENT

17.02 (1) The court may postpone or adjourn a trial on such terms as are just, including the payment by one party to another of an amount as compensation for inconvenience and expense.

(2) If the trial of an action has been adjourned two or more times, any further adjournment may be made only on motion with notice to all the parties who were served with the notice of trial, unless the court orders otherwise.

O. Reg. 78/06, s. 34

INSPECTION

17.03 The trial judge may, in the presence of the parties or their representatives, inspect any real or personal property concerning which a question arises in the action.

Motion for New Trial

17.04 (1) A party may make a motion for a new trial within 30 days after a final order is made.

Transcript

(2) In addition to serving and filing the notice of motion and supporting affidavit (Form 15A) required under rule 15.01, the moving party shall serve and file proof that a request has been made for a transcript of,

(a) the reasons for judgment; and

(b) any other portion of the proceeding that is relevant.

Service and Filing of Transcript

(3) If available, a copy of the transcript shall, at least three days before the hearing date,

(a) be served on all parties who were served with the original notice of trial; and

(b) be filed, with proof of service.

Powers of Court on Motion

(4) On the hearing of the motion, the court may,

(a) if the party demonstrates that a condition referred to in subrule (5) is satisfied,

(i) grant a new trial, or

(ii) pronounce the judgment that ought to have been given at trial and order judgment accordingly; or

(b) dismiss the motion.

Conditions

(5) The conditions referred to in clause (4)(a) are:

1. There was a purely arithmetical error in the determination of the amount of damages awarded.

2. There is relevant evidence that was not available to the party at the time of the original trial and could not reasonably have been expected to be available at that time.

O. Reg. 78/06, s. 35; 393/09, s. 16

RULE 18 — EVIDENCE AT TRIAL

AFFIDAVIT

18.01 At the trial of an undefended action, the plaintiff's case may be proved by affidavit, unless the trial judge orders otherwise.

Written Statements, Documents and Records

18.02 (1) A document or written statement or an audio or visual record that has been served, at least 30 days before the trial date, on all parties who were served with the notice of trial, shall be received in evidence, unless the trial judge orders otherwise.

(2) Subrule (1) applies to the following written statements and documents:

1. The signed written statement of any witness, including the written report of an expert, to the extent that the statement relates to facts and opinions to which the witness would be permitted to testify in person.

2. Any other document, including but not limited to a hospital record or medical report made in the course of care and treatment, a financial record, a receipt, a bill, documentary evidence of loss of income or property damage, and a repair estimate.

Details about Witness or Author

(3) A party who serves on another party a written statement or document described in subrule (2) shall append to or include in the statement or document,

(a) the name, telephone number and address for service of the witness or author; and

(b) if the witness or author is to give expert evidence, a summary of his or her qualifications.

(4) A party who has been served with a written statement or document described in subrule (2) and who wishes to cross-examine the witness or author may summon him or her as a witness under subrule 18.03(1).

Where Witness or Author is Summoned

(5) A party who serves a summons to witness on a witness or author referred to in subrule (3) shall, at the time the summons is served, serve a copy of the summons on every other party.

(6) Service of a summons and the payment or tender of attendance money under this rule may be proved by affidavit (Form 8A).

Adjournment

(7) A party who is not served with a copy of the summons in accordance with subrule (5) may request an adjournment of the trial, with costs.

O. Reg. 78/06, s. 36

Summons to Witness

18.03 (1) A party who requires the attendance of a person in Ontario as a witness at a trial may serve the person with a summons to witness (Form 18A) requiring him or her to attend the trial at the time and place stated in the summons.

(2) The summons may also require the witness to produce at the trial the documents or other things in his or her possession, control or power relating to the matters in question in the action that are specified in the summons.

(3) A summons to witness (Form 18A) shall be served in accordance with subrule 8.01(7).

(4) Service of a summons and the payment or tender of attendance money may be proved by affidavit (Form 8A).

(5) A summons to witness continues to have effect until the attendance of the witness is no longer required.

Interpreter

(5.1) If a party serves a summons on a witness who requires an interpreter, the party shall arrange for a qualified interpreter to attend at the trial unless the interpretation is from English to French or French to English and an interpreter is provided by the Ministry of the Attorney General.

(5.2) If a party does not comply with subrule (5.1), every other party is entitled to request an adjournment of the trial, with costs.

Failure to Attend or Remain in Attendance

(6) If a witness whose evidence is material to the conduct of an action fails to attend at the trial or to remain in attendance in accordance with the requirements of a summons to witness served on him or her, the trial judge may, by warrant (Form 18B) directed to all police officers in Ontario, cause the witness to be apprehended anywhere within Ontario and promptly brought before the court.

Identification Form

(6.1) The party who served the summons on the witness may file with the clerk an identification form (Form 20K) to assist the police in apprehending the witness.

(7) On being apprehended, the witness may be detained in custody until his or her presence is no longer required or released on such terms as are just, and may be ordered to pay the costs arising out of the failure to attend or remain in attendance.

Abuse of Power to Summon Witness

(8) If satisfied that a party has abused the power to summon a witness under this rule, the court may order that the party pay directly to the witness an amount as compensation for inconvenience and expense.

O. Reg. 78/06, s. 37

RULE 19 — COSTS

Disbursements

19.01 (1) A successful party is entitled to have the party's reasonable disbursements, including any costs of effecting service and expenses for travel, accommodation, photocopying and experts' reports, paid by the unsuccessful party, unless the court orders otherwise.

(2) The clerk shall assess the disbursements in accordance with the regulations made under the *Administration of Justice Act* and in accordance with subrule (3); the assessment is subject to review by the court.

(3) The amount of disbursements assessed for effecting service shall not exceed $20 for each person served unless the court is of the opinion that there are special circumstances that justify assessing a greater amount.

O. Reg. 78/06, s. 38

LIMIT

19.02 Any power under this rule to award costs is subject to section 29 of the *Courts of Justice Act*, which limits the amount of costs that may be awarded.

O. Reg. 78/06, s. 39

PREPARATION AND FILING

19.03 The court may award a successful party an amount not exceeding $50 for preparation and filing of pleadings.

O. Reg. 78/06, s. 39

REPRESENTATION FEE

19.04 (1) If the amount claimed in an action exceeds $500, exclusive of interest and costs, and the successful party is represented by a lawyer, student-at-law or agent, the court may award the party a reasonable representation fee at trial or at an assessment hearing.

(2) In the case of a student-at-law or an agent, the representation fee shall not exceed half of the maximum costs that may be awarded under section 29 of the *Courts of Justice Act*.

O. Reg. 78/06, s. 39

COMPENSATION FOR INCONVENIENCE AND EXPENSE

19.05 The court may order an unsuccessful party to pay to a successful party an amount not exceeding $500 as compensation for inconvenience and expense, if,

(a) the successful party is self-represented; and

(b) the amount claimed in the action exceeds $500, exclusive of interest and costs.

(c) [Repealed O. Reg. 78/06, s. 39.]

O. Reg. 78/06, s. 39

PENALTY

19.06 If the court is satisfied that a party has unduly complicated or prolonged an action or has otherwise acted unreasonably, the court may order the party to pay an amount as compensation to another party.

O. Reg. 78/06, s. 39

RULE 20 — ENFORCEMENT OF ORDERS

DEFINITIONS

20.01 In rules 20.02 to 20.12,

"creditor" means a person who is entitled to enforce an order for the payment or recovery of money;

"debtor" means a person against whom an order for the payment or recovery of money may be enforced.

O. Reg. 78/06, s. 40

Power of Court

20.02 (1) The court may,

(a) stay the enforcement of an order of the court, for such time and on such terms as are just; and

(b) vary the times and proportions in which money payable under an order of the court shall be paid, if it is satisfied that the debtor's circumstances have changed.

Enforcement Limited While Periodic Payment Order in Force

(2) While an order for periodic payment is in force, no step to enforce the judgment may be taken or continued against the debtor by a creditor named in the order, except issuing a writ of seizure and sale of land and filing it with the sheriff.

Service of Notice of Default of Payment

(3) The creditor may serve the debtor with a notice of default of payment (Form 20L) in accordance with subrule 8.01(14) and file a copy of it, together with an affidavit of default of payment (Form 20M), if the debtor fails to make payments under an order for periodic payment.

Termination on Default

(4) An order for periodic payment terminates on the day that is 15 days after the creditor serves the debtor with the notice of default of payment, unless a consent (Form 13B) in which the creditor waives the default is filed within the 15-day period.

O. Reg. 78/06, s. 41

GENERAL

20.03 In addition to any other method of enforcement provided by law,

(a) an order for the payment or recovery of money may be enforced by,

(i) a writ of seizure and sale of personal property (Form 20C) under rule 20.06;

(ii) a writ of seizure and sale of land (Form 20D) under rule 20.07; and

(iii) garnishment under rule 20.08; and,

(b) a further order as to payment may be made under subrule 20.10(7).

Certificate of Judgment

20.04 (1) If there is default under an order for the payment or recovery of money, the clerk shall, at the creditor's request, supported by an affidavit for enforcement request (Form 20P) stating the amount still owing, issue a certificate of judgment (Form 20A) to the clerk at the court location specified by the creditor.

(2) The certificate of judgment shall state,

(a) the date of the order and the amount awarded;

(b) the rate of postjudgment interest payable; and

(c) the amount owing, including postjudgment interest.

O. Reg. 393/09, s. 17

Delivery of Personal Property

20.05 (1) An order for the delivery of personal property may be enforced by a writ of delivery (Form 20B) issued by the clerk to a bailiff, on the request of the person in whose favour the order was made, supported by an affidavit of that person or the person's agent stating that the property has not been delivered.

Seizure of Other Personal Property

(2) If the property referred to in a writ of delivery cannot be found or taken by the bailiff, the person in whose favour the order was made may make a motion to the court for an order directing the bailiff to seize any other personal property of the person against whom the order was made.

(3) Unless the court orders otherwise the bailiff shall keep personal property seized under subrule (2) until the court makes a further order for its disposition.

Storage Costs

(4) The person in whose favour the order is made shall pay the bailiff's storage costs, in advance and from time to time; if the person fails to do so, the seizure shall be deemed to be abandoned.

O. Reg. 78/06, s. 42

Writ of Seizure and Sale of Personal Property

20.06 (1) If there is default under an order for the payment or recovery of money, the clerk shall, at the creditor's request, supported by an affidavit for enforcement request (Form 20P) stating the amount still owing, issue to a bailiff a writ of seizure and sale of personal property (Form 20C), and the bailiff shall enforce the writ for the amount owing, postjudgment interest and the bailiff's fees and expenses.

(1.1) If more than six years have passed since the order was made, a writ of seizure and sale of personal property may be issued only with leave of the court.

(1.2) If a writ of seizure and sale of personal property is not issued within one year after the date on which an order granting leave to issue it is made,

(a) the order granting leave ceases to have effect; and

(b) a writ of seizure and sale of personal property may be issued only with leave of the court on a subsequent motion.

(1.3) A writ of seizure and sale of personal property shall show the creditor's name, address and telephone number and the name, address and telephone number of the creditor's lawyer or agent, if any.

Duration of Writ

(2) A writ of seizure and sale of personal property remains in force for six years after the date of its issue and for a further six years after each renewal.

Renewal of Writ

(3) A writ of seizure and sale of personal property may be renewed before its expiration by filing a request to renew a writ of seizure and sale (Form 20N) with the bailiff.

Direction to Enforce

(4) The creditor may request enforcement of a writ of seizure and sale of personal property by filing a direction to enforce writ of seizure and sale of personal property (Form 20O) with the bailiff.

Inventory of Property Seized

(5) Within a reasonable time after a request is made by the debtor or debtor's agent, the bailiff shall deliver an inventory of personal property seized under a writ of seizure and sale of personal property.

Sale of Personal Property

(6) Personal property seized under a writ of seizure and sale of personal property shall not be sold by the bailiff unless notice of the time and place of sale has been,

(a) mailed, at least 10 days before the sale,

(i) to the creditor at the address shown on the writ, or to the creditor's lawyer or agent, and

(ii) to the debtor at the debtor's last known address; and

(b) advertised in a manner that is likely to bring it to the attention of the public.

O. Reg. 78/06, s. 43; 393/09, s. 18

Writ of Seizure and Sale of Land

20.07 (1) If an order for the payment or recovery of money is unsatisfied, the clerk shall at the creditor's request, supported by an affidavit for enforcement request (Form 20P) stating the amount still owing, issue to the sheriff specified by the creditor a writ of seizure and sale of land (Form 20D).

(1.1) If more than six years have passed since the order was made, a writ of seizure and sale of land may be issued only with leave of the court.

(1.2) If a writ of seizure and sale of land is not issued within one year after the date on which an order granting leave to issue it is made,

(a) the order granting leave ceases to have effect; and

(b) a writ of seizure and sale of land may be issued only with leave of the court on a subsequent motion.

(2) A writ of seizure and sale of land issued under subrule (1) has the same force and effect and may be renewed or withdrawn in the same manner as a writ of seizure and sale issued under Rule 60 of the *Rules of Civil Procedure*.

Duration of Writ

(3) A writ of seizure and sale of land remains in force for six years after the date of its issue and for a further six years after each renewal.

Renewal of Writ

(4) A writ of seizure and sale of land may be renewed before its expiration by filing a request to renew a writ of seizure and sale (Form 20N) with the sheriff.

O. Reg. 78/06, s. 44; 393/09, s. 19

Garnishment

20.08 (1) A creditor may enforce an order for the payment or recovery of money by garnishment of debts payable to the debtor by other persons.

Joint Debts Garnishable

(2) If a debt is payable to the debtor and to one or more co-owners, one-half of the indebtedness or a greater or lesser amount specified in an order made under subrule (15) may be garnished.

Where Leave Required

(2.1) If more than six years have passed since the order was made, or if its enforcement is subject to a condition, a notice of garnishment may be issued only with leave of the court.

(2.2) If a notice of garnishment is not issued within one year after the date on which an order granting leave to issue it is made,

(a) the order granting leave ceases to have effect; and

(b) a notice of garnishment may be issued only with leave of the court on a subsequent motion.

(2.3) A notice of renewal of garnishment may be issued under subrule (5.3) without leave of the court before the original notice of garnishment or any subsequent notice of renewal of garnishment expires.

Obtaining Notice of Garnishment

(3) A creditor who seeks to enforce an order by garnishment shall file with the clerk of a court in the territorial division in which the debtor resides or carries on business,

(a) an affidavit for enforcement request (Form 20P) naming one debtor and one garnishee and stating,

(i) the date of the order and the amount awarded,

(ii) the territorial division in which the order was made,

(iii) the rate of postjudgment interest payable,

(iv) the total amount of any payments received since the order was granted,

(v) the amount owing, including postjudgment interest,

(vi) the name and address of the named garnishee to whom a notice of garnishment is to be directed,

(vii) the creditor's belief that the named garnishee is or will become indebted to the debtor, and the grounds for the belief, and

(viii) any particulars of the debts that are known to the creditor; and

(b) a certificate of judgment (Form 20A), if the order was made in another territorial division.

(4) On the filing of the documents required by subrule (3), the clerk shall issue a notice of garnishment (Form 20E) naming as garnishee the person named in the affidavit.

(5) A notice of garnishment issued under subrule (4) shall name only one debtor and only one garnishee.

Duration and Renewal

(5.1) A notice of garnishment remains in force for six years from the date of its issue and for a further six years from each renewal.

(5.2) A notice of garnishment may be renewed before its expiration by filing with the clerk of the court in which the notice of garnishment was issued a notice of renewal of garnishment (Form 20E.1), together with an affidavit for enforcement request (Form 20P).

(5.3) On the filing of the notice and affidavit required by subrule (5.2), the clerk shall issue the notice of renewal of garnishment (Form 20E.1) naming as garnishee the person named in the affidavit.

(5.4) The provisions of these rules that apply with respect to notices of garnishment also apply with respect to notices of renewal of garnishment.

Service of Notice of Garnishment

(6) The notice of garnishment (Form 20E) shall be served by the creditor in accordance with subrule 8.01(8).

(6.1) The creditor shall serve the notice of garnishment on the debtor within five days of serving it on the garnishee.

Financial Institution

(6.2) If the garnishee is a financial institution, the notice of garnishment and all further notices required to be served under this rule shall be served at the branch at which the debt is payable.

Proof of Service

(6.3) Service of the notice of garnishment may be proved by affidavit.

Garnishee Liable From Time of Service

(7) The garnishee is liable to pay to the clerk any debt of the garnishee to the debtor, up to the amount shown in the notice of garnishment, within 10 days after service of the notice on the garnishee or 10 days after the debt becomes payable, whichever is later.

(8) For the purpose of subrule (7), a debt of the garnishee to the debtor includes,

(a) a debt payable at the time the notice of garnishment is served; and

(b) a debt payable (whether absolutely or on the fulfilment of a condition) after the notice is served and within six years after it is issued.

Payment by Garnishee

(9) A garnishee who admits owing a debt to the debtor shall pay it to the clerk in the manner prescribed by the notice of garnishment, and the amounts paid into court shall not exceed the portion of the debtor's wages that are subject to seizure or garnishment under section 7 of the *Wages Act*.

Equal Distribution Among Creditors

(10) If the clerk has issued notices of garnishment in respect of a debtor at the request of more than one creditor and receives payment under any of the notices of garnishment, he or she shall distribute the payment equally among the creditors who have filed a request for garnishment and have not been paid in full.

Disputing Garnishment

(11) A garnishee referred to in subrule (12) shall, within 10 days after service of the notice of garnishment, file with the court a statement (Form 20F) setting out the particulars.

(12) Subrule (11) applies to a garnishee who,

(a) wishes to dispute the garnishment for any reason; or

(b) pays to the clerk less than the amount set out in the notice of garnishment as owing by the garnishee to the debtor, because the debt is owed to the debtor and to one or more co-owners of the debt or for any other reason.

Service on Creditor and Debtor

(13) The garnishee shall serve a copy of the garnishee's statement on the creditor and the debtor.

Notice to Co-owner of Debt

(14) A creditor who is served with a garnishee's statement under subrule (13) shall forthwith send to any co-owners of the debt, in accordance with subrule 8.01(14), a notice to co-owner of debt (Form 20G) and a copy of the garnishee's statement.

Garnishment Hearing

(15) At the request of a creditor, debtor, garnishee, co-owner of the debt or any other interested person, the clerk shall fix a time and place for a garnishment hearing.

Service of Notice of Garnishment Hearing

(15.1) After having obtained a hearing date from the clerk, the party requesting the garnishment hearing shall serve the notice of garnishment hearing (Form 20Q) in accordance with subrule 8.01(9).

Powers of Court at Hearing

(15.2) At the garnishment hearing, the court may,

(a) if it is alleged that the garnishee's debt to the debtor has been assigned or encumbered, order the assignee or encumbrancer to appear and state the nature and particulars of the claim;

(b) determine the rights and liabilities of the garnishee, any co-owner of the debt, the debtor and any assignee or encumbrancer;

(c) vary or suspend periodic payments under a notice of garnishment; or

(d) determine any other matter in relation to a notice of garnishment.

Time to Request Hearing

(16) A person who has been served with a notice to co-owner of debt is not entitled to dispute the enforcement of the creditor's order for the payment or recovery of money or a payment made by the clerk unless the person requests a garnishment hearing within 30 days after the notice is sent.

Enforcement Against Garnishee

(17) If the garnishee does not pay to the clerk the amount set out in the notice of garnishment and does not send a garnishee's statement, the creditor is entitled to an order against the garnishee for payment of the amount set out in the notice, unless the court orders otherwise.

Payment to Person other than Clerk

(18) If, after service of a notice of garnishment, the garnishee pays a debt attached by the notice to a person other than the clerk, the garnishee remains liable to pay the debt in accordance with the notice.

Effect of Payment to Clerk

(19) Payment of a debt by a garnishee in accordance with a notice of garnishment is a valid discharge of the debt as between the garnishee and the debtor and any co-owner of the debt, to the extent of the payment.

Distribution of Payments

(20) When proof is filed that the notice of garnishment was served on the debtor, the clerk shall distribute a payment received under a notice of garnishment to a creditor in accordance with subrule (20.1), unless,

(a) a hearing has been requested under subrule (15);

(b) a notice of motion and supporting affidavit (Form 15A) has been filed under rule 8.10, 11.06 or 17.04; or

(c) a request for clerk's order on consent (Form 11.2A) has been filed seeking the relief described in subparagraph 1 iii of subrule 11.2.01(1).

(20.1) The clerk shall distribute the payment,

(a) in the case of the first payment under the notice of garnishment, 30 days after the date it is received; and

(b) in the case of every subsequent payment under the notice of garnishment, as they are received.

Notice Once Order Satisfied

(20.2) Once the amount owing under an order that is enforced by garnishment is paid, the creditor shall immediately serve a notice of termination of garnishment (Form 20R) on the garnishee and on the clerk.

Payment if Debt Jointly Owned

(21) If a payment of a debt owed to the debtor and one or more co-owners has been made to the clerk, no request for a garnishment hearing is made and the time for doing so under subrule (16) has expired, the creditor may file with the clerk, within 30 days after that expiry,

(a) proof of service of the notice to co-owner; and

(b) an affidavit stating that the creditor believes that no co-owner of the debt is a person under disability, and the grounds for the belief.

(22) The affidavit required by subrule (21) may contain statements of the deponent's information and belief, if the source of the information and the fact of the belief are specified in the affidavit.

(23) If the creditor does not file the material referred to in subrule (21) the clerk shall return the money to the garnishee.

O. Reg. 461/01, s. 18; 78/06, s. 45; 393/09, s. 20

Consolidation Order

20.09 (1) A debtor against whom there are two or more unsatisfied orders for the payment of money may make a motion to the court for a consolidation order.

(2) The debtor's notice of motion and supporting affidavit (Form 15A) shall set out, in the affidavit portion,

(a) the names and addresses of the creditors who have obtained an order for the payment of money against the debtor;

(b) the amount owed to each creditor;

(c) the amount of the debtor's income from all sources, identifying them; and

(d) the debtor's current financial obligations and any other relevant facts.

(3) For the purposes of clause 15.01(3)(a), the notice of motion and supporting affidavit shall be served on each of the creditors mentioned in it at least seven days before the hearing date.

Contents of Consolidation Order

(4) At the hearing of the motion, the court may make a consolidation order setting out,

(a) a list of unsatisfied orders for the payment of money against the debtor, indicating in each case the date, court and amount and the amount unpaid;

(b) the amounts to be paid into court by the debtor under the consolidation order; and

(c) the times of the payments.

(5) The total of the amounts to be paid into court by the debtor under a consolidation order shall not exceed the portion of the debtor's wages that are subject to seizure or garnishment under section 7 of the *Wages Act.*

Creditor May Make Submissions

(6) At the hearing of the motion, a creditor may make submissions as to the amount and times of payment.

Further Orders Obtained After Consolidation Order

(7) If an order for the payment of money is obtained against the debtor after the date of the consolidation order for a debt incurred before the date of the consolidation order, the creditor may file with the clerk a certified copy of the order; the creditor shall be added to the consolidation order and shall share in the distribution under it from that time.

(8) A consolidation order terminates immediately if an order for the payment of money is obtained against the debtor for a debt incurred after the date of the consolidation order.

Enforcement Limited While Consolidation Order in Force

(9) While the consolidation order is in force, no step to enforce the judgment may be taken or continued against the debtor by a creditor named in the order, except issuing a writ of seizure and sale of land and filing it with the sheriff.

Termination on Default

(10) A consolidation order terminates immediately if the debtor is in default under it for 21 days.

Effect of Termination

(11) If a consolidation order terminates under subrule (8) or (10), the clerk shall notify the creditors named in the consolidation order, and no further consolidation order shall be made in respect of the debtor for one year after the date of termination.

Manner of Sending Notice

(11.1) The notice that the consolidation order is terminated shall be served by mail or fax.

(11.2) [Repealed O. Reg. 78/06, s. 46(2).]

(11.3) [Repealed O. Reg. 78/06, s. 46(2).]

Equal Distribution Among Creditors

(12) All payments into a consolidation account belong to the creditors named in the consolidation order who shall share equally in the distribution of the money.

(13) The clerk shall distribute the money paid into the consolidation account at least once every six months.

O. Reg. 461/01, s. 19 [s. 19(3) revoked O. Reg. 330/02, s. 12(2).]; 330/02, s. 12(1); 440/03, s. 5, item 10; 78/06, s. 46; 393/09, s. 21

Examination of Debtor or Other Person

20.10 (1) If there is default under an order for the payment or recovery of money, the clerk of a court in the territorial division in which the debtor or other person to be examined resides or carries on business shall, at the creditor's request, issue a notice of examination (Form 20H) directed to the debtor or other person.

(2) The creditor's request shall be accompanied by,

(a) an affidavit for enforcement request (Form 20P) setting out,

(i) the date of the order and the amount awarded,

(ii) the territorial division in which the order was made,

(iii) the rate of postjudgment interest payable,

(iv) the total amount of any payments received since the order was granted, and

(v) the amount owing, including postjudgment interest; and

(b) a certificate of judgment (Form 20A), if the order was made in another territorial jurisdiction.

Service of Notice of Examination

(3) The notice of examination shall be served in accordance with subrules 8.01(10), (11) and (12).

(4) The debtor, any other persons to be examined and any witnesses whose evidence the court considers necessary may be examined in relation to,

(a) the reason for nonpayment;

(b) the debtor's income and property;

(c) the debts owed to and by the debtor;

(d) the disposal the debtor has made of any property either before or after the order was made;

(e) the debtor's present, past and future means to satisfy the order;

(f) whether the debtor intends to obey the order or has any reason for not doing so; and

(g) any other matter pertinent to the enforcement of the order.

Duties of Person to be Examined

(4.1) A person who is served with a notice of examination shall,

(a) inform himself or herself about the matters mentioned in subrule (4) and be prepared to answer questions about them; and

(b) in the case of an examination of a debtor who is an individual, complete a financial information form (Form 20I) and serve it on the creditor requesting the examination, but shall not file it with the court.

Who May Be Examined

(5) An officer or director of a corporate debtor, or, in the case of a debtor that is a partnership or sole proprietorship, the sole proprietor or any partner, may be examined on the debtor's behalf in relation to the matters set out in subrule (4).

Attendance

(5.1) A person required to attend an examination may attend,

(a) in person; or

(b) by video conference in accordance with rule 1.07.

Examinations Private, Under Oath and Recorded

(6) The examination shall be,

(a) held in the absence of the public, unless the court orders otherwise;

(b) conducted under oath; and

(c) recorded.

Order As To Payment

(7) After the examination or if the debtor's consent is filed, the court may make an order as to payment.

Enforcement Limited while Order as to Payment in Force

(8) While an order as to payment is in force, no step to enforce the judgment may be taken or continued against the debtor by a creditor named in the order, except issuing a writ of seizure and sale of land and filing it with the sheriff.

(9) [Repealed O. Reg. 78/06, s. 47(5).]

(10) [Repealed O. Reg. 78/06, s. 47(5).]

(10.1) [Repealed O. Reg. 78/06, s. 47(5).]

(11) [Repealed O. Reg. 78/06, s. 47(5).]

(12) [Repealed O. Reg. 78/06, s. 47(5).]

(13) [Repealed O. Reg. 78/06, s. 47(5).]

(14) [Repealed O. Reg. 78/06, s. 47(5).]

(15) [Repealed O. Reg. 78/06, s. 47(5).]

O. Reg. 461/01, s. 20 [s. 20(3) revoked O. Reg. 330/02, s. 13(3).]; 330/02, s. 13(1), (2); 440/03, s. 5, item 11; 78/06, s. 47; 393/09, s. 22

Contempt Hearing

20.11 (1) The court may order a person on whom a notice of examination has been served under rule 20.10 to attend before the court for a contempt hearing if the person attends the examination but refuses to answer questions or to produce documents or records.

Same

(2) The court may order a person on whom a notice of examination has been served under rule 20.10 to attend for a contempt hearing before a judge of the Superior Court of Justice if the person fails to attend the examination.

Notice of Contempt Hearing

(3) If an order for a contempt hearing is made under subrule (1) or (2),

(a) the clerk shall provide the creditor with a notice of contempt hearing setting out the time, date and place of the hearing; and

(b) the creditor shall serve the notice of contempt hearing on the debtor or other person in accordance with subrule 8.01(13) and file the affidavit of service at least seven days before the hearing.

Setting Aside Order for Contempt Hearing

(4) A person who has been ordered to attend a contempt hearing under subrule (2) may make a motion to set aside the order, before or after receiving the notice of contempt hearing but before the date of the hearing and, on the motion, the court may set aside the order and order that the person attend another examination under rule 20.10.

Finding of Contempt of Court

(5) At a contempt hearing held under subrule (1), the court may find the person to be in contempt of court if the person fails to show cause why the person should not be held in contempt for refusing to answer questions or produce records or documents.

Same

(6) At a contempt hearing held under subrule (2), a judge of the Superior Court of Justice may find the person to be in contempt of court if the judge is satisfied that the person failed to attend as required by the notice of examination and that the failure to attend was wilful.

Other Powers of Court at Contempt Hearing

(7) At a contempt hearing held under subrule (1) or (2), the court may order that the person,

(a) attend an examination under rule 20.10;

(b) be jailed for a period not exceeding 40 days;

(c) attend an additional contempt hearing; or

(d) comply with any other order that the judge considers necessary or just.

Warrant of Committal

(8) If a warrant of committal is ordered under clause (7)(b),

(a) the creditor may complete and file with the clerk an identification form (Form 20K) to assist the police in apprehending the person named in the warrant of committal; and

(b) the clerk shall issue a warrant of committal (Form 20J), accompanied by the identification form, if any, directed to all police officers in Ontario to apprehend the person named in the warrant anywhere in Ontario and promptly bring the person to the nearest correctional institution.

Discharge

(9) The person shall be discharged from custody on the order of the court or when the time prescribed in the warrant expires, whichever is earlier.

Duration and Renewal of Warrant of Committal

(10) The warrant remains in force for 12 months after the date of issue and may be renewed by order of the court on a motion made by the creditor for 12 months at each renewal, unless the court orders otherwise.

Orders under subrules (9) and (10)

(11) A warrant of committal issued pursuant to an order of a judge of the Superior Court of Justice under this rule may only be discharged or renewed by a judge of that court.

O. Reg. 78/06, s. 48

SATISFACTION OF ORDER

20.12 If payment is made in full satisfaction of an order,

(a) where all parties consent, a party may file a request for clerk's order on consent (Form 11.2A) indicating that payment has been made in full satisfaction of the order or terms of settlement; or

(b) the debtor may make a motion for an order confirming that payment has been made in full satisfaction of the order or terms of settlement.

O. Reg. 78/06, s. 48; 393/09, s. 23

RULE 21 — REFEREE

21.01 (1) A person assigned the powers and duties of a referee under subsection 73(2) of the *Courts of Justice Act* may, if directed by the regional senior justice or his or her designate,

(a) hear disputes of proposals of terms of payment under rule 9.03;

(b) conduct settlement conferences under rule 13;

(c) hear motions for consolidation orders under rule 20.09; and

(d) assess receipted disbursements for fees paid to the court, a court reporter or a sheriff under the regulations made under the *Administration of Justice Act*.

(2) Except under subrule 9.03(5) (order as to terms of payment), a referee shall not make a final decision in any matter referred to him or her but shall report his or her findings and recommendations to the court.

(3) [Repealed O. Reg. 78/06, s. 49.]

O. Reg. 78/06, s. 49; 393/09, s. 24

RULE 22

22. Regulation 201 of the Revised Regulations of Ontario, 1990 and Ontario Regulations 732/92, 66/95 and 132/96 are revoked.

RULE 23

23. This Regulation comes into force on September 1, 1998.

Table of Forms

1A	Additional Parties
1B	Request for Telephone or Video Conference
4A	Consent to Act as Litigation Guardian
5A	Notice to Alleged Partner
7A	Plaintiff's Claim
8A	Affidavit of Service
9A	Defence
9B	Request to Clerk
10A	Defendant's Claim
11A	Affidavit for Jurisdiction
11B	Default Judgment
11.2A	Request for Clerk's Order
11.2B	Consent for Clerk's Order
13A	Consent
13B	Offer to Settle
14A	Offer to Settle
14B	Acceptance of Offer to Settle
14C	Notice of Withdrawal of Offer to Settle
14D	Terms of Settlement
15A	Notice of Motion
15B	Affidavit
16A	Notice of Trial
18A	Summons to Witness

18B	Warrant for Arrest of Defaulting Witness
20A	Certificate of Judgment
20B	Writ of Delivery
20C	Writ of Seizure and Sale of Personal Property
20D	Writ of Seizure and Sale of Land
20E	Notice of Garnishment
20F	Garnishee's Statement
20G	Notice to Co-Owner of Debt
20H	Notice of Examination
22I	Financial Information Form
20J	Warrant of Committal
20K	Identification Form
20L	Notice of Default of Payment
20M	Affidavit of Default of Payment
20N	Request to Renew Writ of Seizure and Sale
20O	Affidavit for Writ of Seizure and Sale of Land
20P	Affidavit for Enforcement Request
20Q	Notice of Garnishment Hearing

FAMILY LAW RULES

O. Reg. 114/99

NOTICE TO THE PROFESSION AMENDMENTS TO FAMILY RULES (O.REG. 114/99)

A. Financial Statement amendments (O. Reg. 92/03)

Effective April 28, 2003, two new financial statements will replace Form 13: Financial Statement. Changes to Rule 13: Financial Statements and to the forms referred to below will also take effect.

Highlights of the amendments include:

- Two new financial statement forms:
    - Form 13: Financial Statement (Support Claims) will apply to cases where there is a claim for support, but no claim for property or exclusive possession of the matrimonial home and its contents.
    - Form 13.1: Financial Statement (Property and Support Claims) will apply to cases where there is a claim for property and/or exclusive possession of the matrimonial home, whether or not support is claimed.
- Streamlined requirements for simple child support claims:
    - Parties whose only claim for support is a child support claim in the table amount under the Child Support Guidelines, and who are not making a claim for property or exclusive possession of the matrimonial home and its contents, are not required to file a financial statement.
- Other amended forms:
    - Consequential changes have been made to Forms 8, 8A, 10, 10A and 17D to provide instructions as to which financial statement should be used.

B. Child protection amendments (O. Reg. 91/03)

Effective April 28, 2003, amendments affecting child protection cases will come into effect.

Highlights of the amendments include:

- New child protection timetable for cases commenced on or after April 28, 2003.

- Elimination of mandatory case conference in child protection cases.
- New Answer and Plan of Care form (Form 33B.1) for parties other than a Children's Aid Society.

These amendments will be published in the April 5th edition of the Ontario Gazette. The amendments can also be found at www.e-laws.gov.on.ca or www.ontariocourts.on.ca.

NOTICE TO THE PROFESSION AMENDMENTS TO FAMILY RULES

Family Law Rules (O. Reg. 114/99) Amendments to rules and forms will be effective on July 30, 2001. The amendments appear as O. Reg. 202/01 and will be published in the June 30th edition of the Ontario Gazette. The amendments can also be found at www.e-law.gov.on.ca or www.ontariocourts.on.ca as of July 23, 2001. Highlights of the amendments include:

- **Shorter, more streamlined conference brief**
- **New case and settlement conference briefs for child protection cases**
- **New timelines for serving and filing conference briefs and updated financial statements**
- **Confirmation form must now be served and filed no later than 2 p.m., 2 days before the date of the motion or conference**

FORMAL REQUIREMENTS OF THE CONTINUING RECORD UNDER THE FAMILY LAW RULES

I. — Introduction

The "Formal Requirements of the Continuing Record under the Family Law Rules" is published by the Family Rules Committee and available at the Ontario Court of Justice website at: www.ontariocourts.on.ca. These requirements must be followed in all cases governed by the Family Law Rules. The Family Rules Committee has the authority to make court rules for the practice and procedure in family cases, subject to the approval of the Lieutenant Governor in Council.

The Family Law Rules provide for a continuing record to be established and maintained by both parties in every case. The Family Rules Committee has approved the following changes to the continuing record to broaden its format and to permit it to be tailored to the case type:

> Separate records — The record may be separated into an Applicant's Record and Respondent's Record. Any party in a standard track case can elect, on filing their first document in the case, to have separate records. In all cases, a

party may request that the continuing record be separated, and the court may order that the continuing record by separated or that a separated record be combined.

Distinct records — There are distinct records for certain types of cases: child protection; status review; support enforcement; and a motion to change a final order. A party may request or the court may order at any time that a record in these cases be separated.

The substantive requirements of the continuing record are set out in Rule 9. There are provisions in Rules 13 and 17 that set out the types of documents that may be excluded from the record. The formal requirements for the preparation and maintenance of the continuing record, including separate and distinct records, are set out in this document, and in the following appendices:

Appendix A — Summary of Contents
Appendix B — Sample Cover
Appendix C — Sample Table of Contents

II. — Formal Requirements

1. — Contents of the record

Unless otherwise indicated, the continuing record consists of four sections, which comprise Part I of the record: table of contents, endorsements, pleadings (documents starting or answering a case), and financial statements.

Documents other than pleadings and financial statements must be filed in a second, separately bound part of the record (Part II). If a continuing record has been separated into an applicant's record and a respondent's record, the endorsements section must appear in the applicant's record only.

A child protection continuing record does not have a financial statements section.

A status review continuing record includes a table of contents, and a documents section only. There is no option to create a Part II.

A support enforcement continuing record includes a table of contents, an endorsements section and a documents section only. There is no option to create a Part II.

The formal requirements for a continuing record also apply to a new record made where there is a motion to change a final order.

If the Children's Lawyer prepares a separate record, the record will consist of a table of contents and documents section only.

A summary of the contents of each record is set out in a chart at Appendix A.

2. — Preparation of the Record

(a) — Record Cover

A sample record cover is attached at Appendix B. All elements of the sample cover must appear on a party's record cover. The title of the record (*e.g.* "Continuing Record") must appear in bold, font size 20, or an equivalent size, below the names of the parties to the case. The cover must identify the Part of the record and volume number, if applicable. Please see section (e), below, for additional information about further volumes.

(b) — Filing Documents

Documents must be filed in chronological order, with the most recently filed document at the back. All documents filed in the record must be punched in standard three-hole format.

Other than in a support enforcement continuing record, each document filed must be identified by a numbered tab. Tabs within sections must be in sequential order. A new section must start with a new tab sequence starting with tab 1. For example, if there are three documents in the pleadings section and three documents in the financial statements section, the tabs in the pleadings section must be labelled 1 to 3, and the tabs in the financial statements section must be labelled 1 to 3. If there is a Part II to the continuing record, it must start with a new tab sequence. For example, the first tab in Part II must be labelled 1.

Pages between numbered tabs shall be numbered consecutively. Page numbers are not required to appear in the table of contents.

(c) — Contents of sections

It is not necessary to create any of the sections referred to in Appendix A unless there is a document to be filed in it.

Each section, other than the table of contents, must be identified by a tab showing the name of the section.

(i) — Table of Contents

A sample table of contents is attached at Appendix C. The table of contents must list documents in the order in which they are filed, indicate the tab that locates the document, the kind of document, which party filed it, and the date it was filed. For an affidavit or transcript of evidence, the name of the person who gave the affidavit or the evidence must also be shown.

The table of contents must be updated every time a document is filed.

(ii) — Endorsements

The endorsements section must contain three (3) blank sheets (or more if necessary), on which the judge dealing with any step in the case will note the disposition of that step and the date. The court's file copy of each order made in the case must be put into the endorsement section after the endorsement pages.

(iii) — Pleadings

The pleadings section must contain all documents which start or answer the case.

(iv) — Financial Statements

The financial statements section must include all financial statements and documents that are required by the Family Law Rules to be attached to it (three years of notices of assessment and Form 13A: Directions to Canada Customs and Revenue Agency, if applicable).

(v) — Other Documents

If there are other documents filed in the case, they must be filed in Part II. This part will contain documents such as reports ordered by the court, motions documents (including motions to enforce orders other than a support order), documents to enforce a payment order other than a support order, and trial management conference briefs.

If there is an applicant's record and a respondent's record, a report ordered by the court must be filed in Part II of the applicant's record. A report requested by a party must be filed in the record of the party who requested it.

(d) — Affidavits of Service

Other than in a support enforcement record, affidavits of service must be filed in a separate section of the court file labelled "affidavits of service". However, in a support enforcement continuing record, affidavits of service are filed in the documents section.

(e) — Further volumes

If the clerk determines that a part of a continuing record needs to be continued in another volume, then the party filing the next document must create a new volume. A new volume of Part I consists of a table of contents, pleadings section and a financial statements section.

(f) — Separate or combined records

Where the court orders that the continuing record be separated, or that separate court records be combined,

- court staff must supervise the separation or the combination of separate records;
- the clerk must destroy the table of contents that existed just before the record is separated or combined;
- if the record is separated, each party must prepare and update a table of contents reflecting the contents of their record; and
- if separated records are combined, the party directed to combine the record shall prepare and update a table of contents that reflects the contents of the combined record.

3. — Additional requirements for distinct records

(a) — Child protection continuing record

The cover must identify the children who are the subject of the case. Below the title of the record state: "Child Protection Record with respect to the child(ren) ...."

Part II of the record must include documents other than pleadings, including plans of care (other than Form 33B.1: Answer and Plan of Care (Parties other than Children's Aid Society)), motions, reports, assessments, agreed statements of fact, and financial statements.

(b) — Status review continuing record

The cover must identify the children who are the subject of the status review and the relevant child protection order. Below the title of the record state: "Status Review Record with respect to the child(ren) .... and the order of Mr./Madam Justice .... dated.........."

The documents section of the record must contain each document filed in the case, including pleadings, plans of care (other than Form 33B.1: Answer and Plan of Care (Parties other than Children's Aid Society)), motions, reports, assessments, agreed statements of fact, and financial statements.

If the status review application is started at the court office where the child protection order was made, the endorsements in the status review application must be noted in the endorsements section of the child protection record. If not, the status review record must include an endorsements section.

(c) — Support enforcement continuing record

The documents section must be separated from the endorsements section by a labelled tab. The documents section must contain each document filed in the case, numbered consecutively and arranged in order, with the most recently filed document at the back. All affidavits of service must be filed in this section.

(d) — New record where motion to change made

The cover must identify the order that is the subject of the motion. Below the title of the record state: "Motion to Change Final Order of Mr./Madam Justice ...., dated ...., with respect to ...."

A motion for an order to refrain under s. 35(1) of the *Family Responsibility and Support Arrears Enforcement Act, 1996* must be filed in Part II of a motion to change final order record.

(e) — Children's Lawyer record

Documents filed in the documents section of a Children's Lawyer record will include Children's Lawyer reports and any Children's Lawyer motion documents.

Appendix A — Summary of Contents

CONTINUING RECORD SINGLE RECORD SEPARATE RECORDS			
SINGLE RECORD	**SEPARATE RECORDS**		
Continuing Record	**Applicant's Record**	**Respondent's Record**	**Children's Lawyer Record**
- red cover	- red cover	- blue cover	- red cover
Part I - Table of contents	Part I - Table of contents	Part I - Table of contents	Part I - Table of contents

CONTINUING RECORD SINGLE RECORD SEPARATE RECORDS			
SINGLE RECORD	**SEPARATE RECORDS**		
Continuing Record	**Applicant's Record**	**Respondent's Record**	**Children's Lawyer Record**
- Endorsements (only in 1st volume) - Pleadings - Financial statements Part II - All other documents	- Endorsements (only in 1st volume) - Pleadings - Financial statements Part II - Applicant's other documents	- Pleadings - Financial statements Part II - Respondent's other documents	- Documents

CHILD PROTECTION CONTINUING RECORDS			
SINGLE RECORD	**SEPARATE RECORDS**		
Continuing Record	**Applicant's Record**	**Respondent's Record**	**Children's Lawyer Record**
- red cover	- red cover	- blue cover	- red cover
Part I - Table of contents - Endorsements (only in 1st volume) - Pleadings Part II - All other documents	Part I - Table of contents - Endorsements (only in 1st volume) - Pleadings Part II - Applicant's other documents	Part I - Table of contents - Pleadings Part II - Respondent's other documents	Part I - Table of contents - Documents

STATUS REVIEW CONTINUING RECORDS			
SINGLE RECORD	**SEPARATE RECORDS**		
Continuing Record	**Applicant's Record**	**Respondent's Record**	**Children's Lawyer Record**
- red cover	- red cover	- blue cover	- red cover
- Table of contents	- Table of contents	- Table of contents	- Table of contents

STATUS REVIEW CONTINUING RECORDS			
SINGLE RECORD	**SEPARATE RECORDS**		
Continuing Record	**Applicant's Record**	**Respondent's Record**	**Children's Lawyer Record**
- Documents	- Documents	- Documents	- Documents

SUPPORT ENFORCEMENT CONTINUING RECORDS			
SINGLE RECORD	**SEPARATE RECORDS**		
Support Enforcement Record	**Director's Enforcement Record**	**Payor's Enforcement Record**	
- green cover	- green cover	- green cover	
- Table of contents - Endorsements (only in 1st volume) - Documents (incl. affidavits of service)	- Table of contents - Endorsements (only in 1st volume) - Documents (incl. affidavits of service)	- Table of contents - Documents (incl. affidavits of service)	

NEW RECORD: MOTION TO CHANGE			
SINGLE RECORD	**SEPARATE RECORDS**		
Continuing Record	**Applicant's Record**	**Respondent's Record**	**Children's Lawyer Record**
- red cover	- red cover	- blue cover	- red cover
Part I - Table of contents - Endorsements (only in 1st volume) - Pleadings - Financial statements Part II - All other documents	Part I - Table of contents - Endorsements (only in 1st volume) - Pleadings - Financial statements Part II - Applicant's other documents	Part I - Table of contents - Pleadings - Financial statements Part II - Respondent's other documents	Part I - Table of contents - Documents

Appendix B — Sample Cover

APPENDIX B – SAMPLE COVER

ONTARIO

Court File Number / *Numéro de dossier du greffe*

____
(Name of court / *Nom du tribunal)*

at / *situé(e) au* ____________________________
Court office address / *Adresse du greffe*

Part and Volume / *Partie et volume* : ____________

Applicant(s) / *Requérant(e)(s)*

Full legal name & address for service — street & number, municipality, postal code, telephone & fax numbers and e-mail address (if any). *Nom et prénom officiels et adresse aux fins de signification — numéro et rue, municipalité, code postal, numéros de téléphone et de télécopieur et adresse électronique (le cas échéant).*	Lawyer's name & address — street & number, municipality, postal code, telephone & fax numbers and e-mail address (if any). *Nom et adresse de l'avocat(e) — numéro et rue, municipalité, code postal, numéros de téléphone et de télécopieur et adresse électronique (le cas échéant).*

Respondent(s) / *Intimé(e)(s)*

Full legal name & address for service — street & number, municipality, postal code, telephone & fax numbers and e-mail address (if any). *Nom et prénom officiels et adresse aux fins de signification — numéro et rue, municipalité, code postal, numéros de téléphone et de télécopieur et adresse électronique (le cas échéant).*	Lawyer's name & address — street & number, municipality, postal code, telephone & fax numbers and e-mail address (if any). *Nom et adresse de l'avocat(e) — numéro et rue, municipalité, code postal, numéros de téléphone et de télécopieur et adresse électronique (le cas échéant).*

(Title of record in bold, font size 20 or equivalent / *Intitulé du dossier en caractères gras; police de taille 20 ou l'équivalent)*

Read these notes if this is an **Applicant's Record** *or a* **Respondent's Record.** / Veuillez prendre connaissance des remarques suivantes s'il s'agit d'un **Dossier du(de la) requérant(e)** ou d'un **Dossier de l'intimé(e).**

> **Note to the Respondent:** If you are served with an **Applicant's Record**, you must serve and file a separate Respondent's Record.
> ***À l'intimé(e) :*** *Si vous recevez signification d'un* ***Dossier du(de la) requérant(e)****, vous devez signifier et déposer un* ***Dossier de l'intimé(e)*** *distinct.*
>
> **Note to the Applicant:** If you are a served with a **Respondent's Record** after you have prepared the Continuing Record, the Continuing Record will be renamed **Applicant's Record.**
> ***Au(à la) requérant(e) :*** *Si vous recevez signification d'un* ***Dossier de l'intimé(e)*** *après avoir préparé le dossier continu, le dossier continu sera par la suite intitulé* ***Dossier du(de la) requérant(e).***

Appendix C — Sample Table of Contents

APPENDIX C – SAMPLE TABLE OF CONTENTS

ONTARIO

Court File Number

(Name of court)

Cumulative Table of Contents (Continuing Record)

at

Court office address

Applicant(s)

Full legal name & address for service — street & number, municipality, postal code, telephone & fax numbers and e-mail address (if any).	*Lawyer's name & address — street & number, municipality, postal code, telephone & fax numbers and e-mail address (if any).*

Respondent(s)

Full legal name & address for service — street & number, municipality, postal code, telephone & fax numbers and e-mail address (if any).	*Lawyer's name & address — street & number, municipality, postal code, telephone & fax numbers and e-mail address (if any).*

Document *(For an affidavit or transcript of evidence, include the name of the person who gave the affidavit or the evidence.)*	**Filed by** *(A = applicant or R = respondent)*	**Date of Document** *(d, m, y)*	**Date of Filing** *(d, m, y)*	**Part/Section/Tab**
Application	A	11/10/00	20/10/00	Part I, P – 1
Summary of Court Cases	A	11/10/00	20/10/00	Part I, P – 2
Financial Statement	A	11/10/00	20/10/00	Part I, F – 1
Answer	R	6/12/00	6/12/00	Part I, P – 3
Financial Statement	R	6/12/00	6/12/00	Part I, F – 2
Notice of Contempt Motion	R	5/6/02	5/6/02	Part II – 1
Affidavit (name of person)	R	5/6/02	5/6/02	Part II – 2
Affidavit in Response (name of person)	A	4/7/02	4/7/02	Part II – 3

☐ *Continued on next sheet*

(Français au verso)

NOTICE TO THE PROFESSION AMENDMENTS TO FAMILY LAW RULES (O. REG. 114/99) EFFECTIVE MAY 1, 2006

Amendments to the *Family Law Rules* (O. Reg. 114/99) will take effect on May 1, 2006. The amendments appear as O. Reg. 76/06 and will be published in the March 25, 2006 edition of the Ontario Gazette. The amendments can also be found at *www.e-laws.gov.on.ca*. Court forms can be found at *www.ontariocourtforms.on.ca*.

Highlights of the amendments include:

Child Protection Continuing Record

- The format and requirements for the continuing record in child protection cases have changed. These requirements appear in the following document: *Formal Requirements of the Child Protection Continuing Record under the Family Law Rules* (November 1, 2005), published by the Family Rules Committee and available on the website *www.ontariocourtforms.on.ca*.
- The formal requirements of the continuing record in cases other than child protection cases have not changed. These requirements appear in the following document: *Formal Requirements of the Continuing Record under the Family Law Rules* (November 1, 2005), published by the Family Rules Committee and available on the website *www.ontariocourtforms.on.ca*. The Family Rules Committee continues to consider how to improve the formal requirements of the continuing record in non-child protection cases.

Forms

- As of May 1, 2006, all forms under the Family Law Rules will be available from the new website *www.ontariocourtforms.on.ca* and will no longer be published on the "E-laws" website. Court users should refer to this new website to obtain current versions of the forms (version date September 1, 2005).
- The content of the following forms has been updated to ensure the consistency of the forms with current Ontario legislation and to make other technical changes: 6B, 8, 8A, 8B, 8D, 10, 13, 13.1, 13A, 13B, 15, 17A, 17C, 17E, 23C, 25D, 27C, 28, 28A, 28B, 30, 32B, 32D, 34D, 36A.

Rules

- Other amendments to the rules relate to technical drafting issues, the revocation of outdated transitional provisions, and the updating of the rules to ensure consistency with current Ontario legislation.

NOTICE TO THE PROFESSION AMENDMENTS TO FAMILY LAW RULES (O. REG. 114/99) EFFECTIVE NOVEMBER 30, 2006

Amendments to the *Family Law Rules* will take effect on November 30, 2006. The amendments appear as O. Reg. 519/06. The amendments can be found at *www.e-laws.gov.on.ca*. Court forms can be found at *www.ontariocourtforms.on.ca*.

The amendments implement the *Child and Family Services Statute Law Amendment Act, 2006*. The amendments create new court forms and amend existing forms to allow for the new types of orders that can be made as part of a child protection proceeding. Some forms amendments are consequential to the *Adoption Information Disclosure Act, 2005*.

The regulation also amends Rule 9, Continuing Record, for the continuing record in cases other than child protection cases. These amendments to the countinuing record come into effect on January 1, 2007. The new requirements appear in: *Formal Requirements of the Continuing Record under the Family Law Rules* (July 1, 2006) published by the Family Rules Committee and available at *www.ontariocourtforms.on.ca*.

FAMILY LAW RULES (SUPERIOR COURT OF JUSTICE AND ONTARIO COURT OF JUSTICE)

Made under the *Courts of Justice Act*

O. Reg. 114/99[Corrected Gazette 8/5/99 Vol. 132:19.]

as am. O. Reg. 441/99; 544/99; 250/00; 202/01; 337/02; 56/03; 91/03; 92/03; 89/04; 76/06; 519/06; 120/07; 439/07; 561/07; 151/08, ss. 1, 2(1)–(3), (4) (Fr.), (5)–(9), 3–10; 317/09; 386/09; 6/10; 51/10; 52/10.

1

---

[1]NOTICE TO THE PROFESSION FAMILY LAW RULES

The *Family Law Rules*, O. Reg. 114/99, is a new set of rules for family law cases in Superior Court of Justice, Family Court and Ontario Court of Justice locations. As a result of a delay in Family Court expansion, please note the revised implementation schedule for the new rules.

The Family Law rules will come into effect on September 15, 1999, as originally scheduled, in the following locations:

(a) all sites of the Ontario Court of Justice that are not affected by Family Court expansion and

(b) the Superior Court of Justice, Family Court site in London.

In the sites listed below, the *Family Law Rules* will come into effect on November 15, 1999. Until then, the rules of procedure that are currently in effect will continue to govern.

(a) all sites designated as expansion sites for the Superior Court of Justice, Family Court, namely:

(i) St. Catharines

(ii) York Region (Newmarket)

(iii) Durham Region (Whitby/Oshawa)

(iv) Peterborough

(v) Cobourg

(vi) Lindsay

(vii) Muskoka County

(viii) Ottawa — Carleton

(ix) L'Orignal

(x) Cornwall

(xi) Brockville

(xii) Perth

and

RULE 1 — GENERAL

SHORT TITLE

Citation

1. (1) These rules may be cited as the *Family Law Rules*.

Cases and Courts to Which Rules Apply

(2) These rules apply to all family law cases in the Family Court of the Superior Court of Justice, in the Superior Court of Justice and in the Ontario Court of Justice,

(a) under,

(i) the *Change of Name Act*,

(ii) Parts III, VI and VII of the *Child and Family Services Act*,

(iii) the *Children's Law Reform Act*, except sections 59 and 60,

(iv) the *Divorce Act* (Canada)

(v) the *Family Law Act*, except Part V,

(vi) the *Family Responsibility and Support Arrears Enforcement Act, 1996*,

(vii) sections 6 and 9 of the *Marriage Act*, and

(viii) the *Interjurisdictional Support Orders Act, 2002*;

(b) for the interpretation, enforcement or variation of a marriage contract, cohabitation agreement, separation agreement or paternity agreement;

(c) for a constructive or resulting trust or a monetary award as compensation for unjust enrichment between persons who have cohabited; and

(d) for annulment of a marriage or a declaration of validity or invalidity of a marriage.

(2.1) [Revoked O. Reg. 89/04, s. 1(2).]

Case Management in Family Court of Superior Court of Justice

(3) Despite subrule (2), rule 39 (case management in the Family Court of the Superior Court of Justice) applies only to cases in the Family Court of the Superior Court of Justice, which has jurisdiction in the following municipalities:

Regional Municipality of Durham
County of Frontenac
County of Haliburton
City of Hamilton
County of Lanark
United Counties of Leeds and Grenville
County of Lennox and Addington
County of Middlesex

(b) the existing Family Court sites of Hamilton — Wentworth, Simcoe County, Kingston, and Napanee

Territorial District of Muskoka
The part of The Regional Municipality of Niagara that was the County of Lincoln as it existed on December 31, 1969
County of Northumberland
City of Ottawa
County of Peterborough
United Counties of Prescott and Russell
County of Simcoe
United Counties of Stormont, Dundas and Glengarry
City of Kawartha Lakes
Regional Municipality of York

Case Management in Ontario Court of Justice

(4) Despite subrule (2), rule 40 (case management in the Ontario Court of Justice) applies only to cases in the Ontario Court of Justice.

Case Management in the Superior Court of Justice

(4.1) Despite subrule (2), rule 41 (case management in the Superior Court of Justice, other than the Family Court of the Superior Court of Justice) applies only to cases in the Superior Court of Justice that are not in the Family Court of the Superior Court of Justice.

Family Law Case Combined with Other Matter

(5) If a case in the court combines a family law case to which these rules apply with another matter to which these rules would not otherwise apply, the parties may agree or the court on motion may order that these rules apply to the combined case or part of it.

Conditions and Directions

(6) When making an order, the court may impose conditions and give directions as appropriate.

Matters not Covered in Rules

(7) If these rules do not cover a matter adequately, the court may give directions, and the practice shall be decided by analogy to these rules, by reference to the *Courts of Justice Act* and the Act governing the case and, if the court considers it appropriate, by reference to the Rules of Civil Procedure.

Failure to Follow Rules or Obey Order

(8) The court may deal with a failure to follow these rules, or a failure to obey an order in the case or a related case, by making any order that it considers necessary for a just determination of the matter, on any conditions that the court considers appropriate, including,

(a) an order for costs;

(b) an order dismissing a claim made by a party who has wilfully failed to follow the rules or obey the order.

Reference to Forms

(9) In these rules, when a form is referred to by number, the reference is to the form with that number that is described in the Table of Forms at the end of these rules and is available on the Internet through *www.ontariocourtforms.on.ca*.

Use of Forms

(9.1) The forms authorized by these rules and set out in the Table of Forms shall be used where applicable and may be adjusted as needed to fit the situation.

Format of Written Documents

(10) Every written document in a case,

(a) shall be legibly typed or printed;

(b) shall be on white paper, or on white or nearly white paper with recycled paper content; and

(c) may appear on one or both sides of the page.

Practice Directions

(11) In subrules (12), (12.1) and (12.2),

"practice direction" means a direction, notice, memorandum or guide for the purpose of governing, subject to these rules, the conduct of cases in any area.

Requirements for Practice Direction

(12) A practice direction shall be approved in advance by the Chief Justice or Chief Judge of the court, filed with the secretary of the Family Rules Committee and posted on the Ontario Courts website, and notice of the practice direction shall be published in the *Ontario Reports*.

Effective Date of Practice Direction

(12.1) A practice direction does not come into effect before it is filed and posted and notice of it is published as described in subrule (12).

Old Practice Directions

(12.2) Practice directions that were issued before these rules take effect no longer apply.

Transitional Provision

(13) If a case was started in the Superior Court of Justice, other than in the Family Court of the Superior Court of Justice, before July 1, 2004, the following applies:

1. The case or a step in the case shall be carried on under these rules on or after July 1, 2004.

2. If the case was not governed by the Family Case Management Rules for the Superior Court of Justice in Toronto or by the Essex Family Case Management Rules before July 1, 2004 and a step in the case is taken on or after that date, the timetable set out in subrule 41(5) and subrules 41(6), (7) and (8) apply as if the case started on the date on which the step was taken.

3. If the case was governed by the Family Case Management Rules for the Superior Court of Justice in Toronto before July 1, 2004, the timetable established for the case when it was started applies to the case on or after July 1, 2004.

4. If the case was governed by the Essex Family Case Management Rules before July 1, 2004 and a family consent timetable was made by the court before that date, the family consent timetable continues to apply to the case on or after July 1, 2004.

5. If the case was governed by the Essex Family Case Management Rules before July 1, 2004 but no family consent timetable was made by the court before that date,

i. the case management order expires on July 1, 2004, and

ii. if a step in the case is taken on or after July 1, 2004, the timetable set out in subrule 41(5) and subrules 41(6), (7) and (8) apply to the case as if the case started on the date on which the step was taken.

(14) [Repealed O. Reg. 76/06, s. 1(2).]

O. Reg. 441/99, s. 1; 544/99, s. 1; 202/01, s. 1; 56/03, s. 1; 89/04, s. 1; 76/06, s. 1; 439/07, s. 1; 561/07, s. 1

RULE 2 — INTERPRETATION

Definitions

2. (1) In these rules,

"address" means a person's street or municipal address, mailing address, telephone number, fax number and electronic mail address;

"appellant" means a person who starts an appeal;

"applicant" means a person who starts an application;

"application" means, as the context requires, the document that starts a case or the procedure by which new cases are brought to the court for a final order or provisional order;

"bond" includes a recognizance, and expressions that refer to the posting of a bond include the act of entering into a recognizance;

"case" means an application or any other method allowed in law for bringing a matter to the court for a final order or provisional order, and includes all motions, enforcements and appeals;

"change", when used to refer to an order or agreement, means to vary, suspend or discharge, or a variation, suspension or discharge (depending on whether the word is used as a verb or as a noun);

"child" means a child as defined in the Act governing the case or, if not defined in that Act, a person under the age of 18 years, and in a case under the *Divorce Act* (Canada) includes a "child of the marriage" within the meaning of that Act;

"child protection case" means a case under Part III of the *Child and Family Services Act*;

"clerk" means a person who has the authority of a clerk or a registrar of the court;

"contempt motion" means a motion for a contempt order;

"contempt order" means an order finding a person in contempt of court;

"continuing record" means the record made under Rule 9 containing, in accordance with these rules, written documents in a case that are filed with the court;

"corporation" *French version only.*

"court" means the court in which a case is being heard;

"default hearing" means a hearing under section 41 of the *Family Responsibility and Support Arrears Enforcement Act, 1996* in which a payor is required to come to court to explain why payment has not been made as required by a support order;

"Director of the Family Responsibility Office" means the Director of the Family Responsibility Office under the *Family Responsibility and Support Arrears Enforcement Act, 1996*, and "Director" has the same meaning, unless the context requires otherwise;

"document" means information, sound or images recorded by any method;

"enforcement" means the use of one or more remedies mentioned in rule 26 (enforcement of orders) to enforce an order;

"file" means to file with proof of service in the court office in the municipality,

(a) where the case or enforcement is started, or

(b) to which the case or enforcement is transferred;

"final order" means an order, other than a temporary order, that decides a claim in an application, including,

(a) an order made on motion that changes a final order,

(b) a judgment, and

(c) an order that decides a party's rights, in an issue between the parties or between a party and a non-party;

"government agency" means the Crown, a Crown agency, a municipal government or agency, a children's aid society or any other public body;

"income source" has the same meaning as in the *Family Responsibility and Support Arrears Enforcement Act, 1996*;

"lawyer" means a person authorized under the *Law Society Act* to practise law in Ontario;

"legal aid rate" means the rate payable by the Ontario Legal Aid Plan on an account submitted by a lawyer for copying in the lawyer's office;

"mail", when used as a noun, means ordinary or regular mail, and when used as a verb means to send by ordinary or regular mail;

"municipality" means a county, district, district municipality, regional municipality, the City of Toronto or a municipal corporation formed from the amalgamation of all the municipalities of a county, district, district municipality or regional municipality, and includes,

(a) an Indian reserve within the territorial area of a municipality, and

(b) the part of The Regional Municipality of Niagara that was the County of Lincoln as it existed on December 31, 1969;

"on motion" means on motion of a party or a person having an interest in the case;

"payment order" means a temporary or final order, but not a provisional order, requiring a person to pay money to another person, including,

(a) an order to pay an amount under Part I or II of the *Family Law Act* or the corresponding provisions of a predecessor Act,

(b) a support order,

(c) a support deduction order,

(d) an order under section 60 or subsection 154(2) of the *Child and Family Services Act*, or under the corresponding provision of a predecessor Act,

(e) a payment order made under rules 26 to 32 (enforcement measures) or under section 41 of the *Family Responsibility and Support Arrears Enforcement Act, 1996*,

(f) a fine for contempt of court,

(g) an order of forfeiture of a bond or recognizance,

(h) an order requiring a party to pay the fees and expenses of,

(i) an assessor, mediator or other expert named by the court, or

(ii) a person conducting a blood test to help determine a child's parentage, and

(i) the costs and disbursements in a case;

"payor" means a person required to pay money under an order or agreement, and includes the estate trustee of a payor who died;

"periodic payment" means an amount payable at regular intervals and includes an amount payable in instalments;

"property claim" means a claim,

(a) under Part I of the *Family Law Act*,

(b) for a constructive or resulting trust, or

(c) for a monetary award as compensation for unjust enrichment;

"provisional order" means an order that is not effective until confirmed by a court;

"recipient" means a person entitled to receive money or costs under a payment order or agreement, including,

(a) a guardian or person with custody of a child who is entitled to money for the child's benefit under an order,

(b) in the case of a support order made under the *Family Law Act*, an agency referred to in subsection 33(3) of that Act,

(c) in the case of a support order made under the *Divorce Act* (Canada), an agency referred to in subsection 20.1(1) of that Act,

(d) a children's aid society entitled to money under an order made under section 60 or subsection 154(2) of the *Child and Family Services Act*, or the corresponding provision in a predecessor Act,

(e) an assessor, mediator or other expert entitled to fees and expenses from the party named in the order, and

(f) the estate trustee of a person who was entitled to money under an order at the time of his or her death;

"Registrar General" means the Registrar General under the *Vital Statistics Act*;

"respondent" means a person against whom a claim is made in an application, answer or appeal;

"special party" means a party who is a child or who is or appears to be mentally incapable for the purposes of the *Substitute Decisions Act, 1992* in respect of an issue in the case and who, as a result, requires legal representation, but does not include a child in a custody, access, child protection, adoption or child support case;

"support deduction order" means a support deduction order as defined in section 1 of the *Family Responsibility and Support Arrears Enforcement Act, 1996*;

"support order" means an order described in subsection 34(1) of the *Family Law Act* or a support order as defined in subsection 2(1) of the *Divorce Act* (Canada) or in section 1 of the *Family Responsibility and Support Arrears Enforcement Act, 1996*;

"temporary order" means an order that says it is effective only for a limited time, and includes an interim order;

"transcript" includes an electronic recording;

"trial" includes a hearing;

"uncontested trial" means a trial at which only the party making the claim provides evidence and submissions.

Primary Objective

(2) The primary objective of these rules is to enable the court to deal with cases justly.

Dealing with Cases Justly

(3) Dealing with a case justly includes,

(a) ensuring that the procedure is fair to all parties;

(b) saving expense and time;

(c) dealing with the case in ways that are appropriate to its importance and complexity; and

(d) giving appropriate court resources to the case while taking account of the need to give resources to other cases.

Duty to Promote Primary Objective

(4) The court is required to apply these rules to promote the primary objective, and parties and their lawyers are required to help the court to promote the primary objective.

Duty to Manage Cases

(5) The court shall promote the primary objective by active management of cases, which includes,

(a) at an early stage, identifying the issues, and separating and disposing of those that do not need full investigation and trial;

(b) encouraging and facilitating use of alternatives to the court process;

(c) helping the parties to settle all or part of the case;

(d) setting timetables or otherwise controlling the progress of the case;

(e) considering whether the likely benefits of taking a step justify the cost;

(f) dealing with as many aspects of the case as possible on the same occasion; and

(g) if appropriate, dealing with the case without parties and their lawyers needing to come to court, on the basis of written documents or by holding a telephone or video conference.

O. Reg. 544/99, s. 2; 76/06, s. 2; 439/07, s. 2

RULE 3 — TIME

Counting Days

3. (1) In these rules or an order, the number of days between two events is counted as follows:

1. The first day is the day after the first event.
2. The last day is the day of the second event.

Counting Days — Short Periods

(2) If a rule or order provides a period of less than seven days for something to be done, Saturdays, Sundays and other days when all court offices are closed do not count as part of the period.

Day when Court Offices Closed

(3) If the last day of a period of time under these rules or an order falls on a day when court offices are closed, the period ends on the next day they are open.

Counting Days — Examples

(4) The following are examples of how time is counted under these rules:

1. Notice of a motion must be served not later than four days before the motion date (see subrule 14(11)). Saturday and Sunday are not counted, because the notice period is less than seven days (see subrule (2)). Service on the day set out in the left column below is in time for the motion to be heard on the day set out in the right column below.

Service on	Motion may be heard on the following
Monday	Friday
Tuesday	Monday
Wednesday	Tuesday
Thursday	Wednesday
Friday	Thursday
Saturday	Friday
Sunday	Friday

2. A respondent who is served with an application in Canada has 30 days to serve an answer (see subrule 10(1)). A respondent who is served with an application on October 1 is in time if the answer is served on or before October 31. A respondent served on November 1 is in time if the answer is served on or before December 1.

3. If the last day for doing something under these rules or an order is New Year's Day, January 1, which is a day when court offices are closed, the time expires on January 2. If January 2 is a Saturday, Sunday or other day when court offices are closed, the time expires on January 3. If January 3 is a day when court offices are closed, the time expires on January 4.

Order to Lengthen or Shorten Time

(5) The court may make an order to lengthen or shorten any time set out in these rules or an order, except that it may lengthen a time set out in subrule 33(1) (timetable for child protection cases) only if the best interests of the child require it.

Written Consent to Change Time

(6) The parties may, by consent in writing, change any time set out in these rules, except that they may not change a time set out in,

(a) clause 14(11)(c) (confirmation of motion);

(b) subrules 17(14) and (14.1) (confirmation of conference, late briefs);

(c) subrule 33(1) (timetable for child protection cases);

(d) rule 39 (case management in Family Court of Superior Court of Justice);

(e) rule 40 (case management in Ontario Court of Justice); or

(f) rule 41 (case management in the Superior Court of Justice (other than the Family Court of the Superior Court of Justice)).

Late Documents Refused by Court Office

(7) The staff at a court office shall refuse to accept a document that a person asks to file after,

(a) the time specified in these rules; or

(b) the later time specified in a consent under subrule (6), a statute that applies to the case, or a court order.

O. Reg. 544/99, s. 3; 202/01, s. 2; 76/06, s. 3

RULE 4 — REPRESENTATION

Representation for a Party

4. (1) A party may,

(a) appear without a lawyer or other representative;

(b) be represented by a lawyer; or

(c) be represented by a person who is not a lawyer, but only if the court gives permission in advance.

Private Representation of Special Party

(2) The court may authorize a person to represent a special party if the person is,

(a) appropriate for the task; and

(b) willing to act as representative.

Public Law Officer to Represent Special Party

(3) If there is no appropriate person willing to act as a special party's representative, the court may authorize the Children's Lawyer or the Public Guardian and Trustee to act as representative, but only with that official's consent.

Service of Authorization to Represent

(4) An order under subrule (2) or (3) shall be served immediately, by the person who asked for the order or by any other person named by the court,

(a) on the representative; and

(b) on every party in the case.

Representation of Party who Dies

(5) If a party dies after the start of a case, the court may make the estate trustee a party instead, on motion without notice.

Authorizing Representative for Party who Dies

(6) If the party has no estate trustee, the court may authorize an appropriate person to act as representative, with that person's consent, given in advance.

Lawyer for Child

(7) In a case that involves a child who is not a party, the court may authorize a lawyer to represent the child, and then the child has the rights of a party, unless the court orders otherwise.

Child's Rights Subject to Statute

(8) Subrule (7) is subject to section 38 (legal representation of child, protection hearing) and subsection 114(6) (legal representation of child, secure treatment hearing) of the *Child and Family Services Act.*

Choice of Lawyer

(9) A party appearing without a lawyer may choose a lawyer by,

(a) serving on every other party and filing a notice of change in representation (Form 4) containing the lawyer's consent to act; or

(b) having a lawyer come to court on the party's behalf.

Change in Representation

(10) Except as subrule (10.1) provides, a party represented by a lawyer may, by serving on every other party and filing a notice of change in representation (Form 4),

(a) change lawyers; or

(b) appear without a lawyer.

Exception, Child Protection Case Scheduled for Trial

(10.1) In a child protection case that has been scheduled for trial or placed on a trial list, a party may act under clause (10)(b) only with the court's permission, obtained in advance by motion made with notice.

Notice of Change in Representation

(11) A notice of change in representation shall,

(a) contain the party's address for service, if the party wants to appear without a lawyer; or

(b) show the name and address of the new lawyer, if the party wants to change lawyers.

Lawyer's Removal from the Case

(12) A lawyer may make a motion for an order to be removed from the case, with notice to the client and to,

(a) the Children's Lawyer, if the client is a child;

(b) the Public Guardian and Trustee, if the client is or appears to be mentally incapable in respect of an issue in the case.

Notice of Motion to Remove Lawyer

(13) Notice of a motion to remove a lawyer shall also be served on the other parties to the case, but the evidence in support of the motion shall not be served on them, shall not be put into the continuing record and shall not be kept in the court file after the motion is heard.

Affidavit in Support of Motion to Remove Lawyer

(14) The affidavit in support of the motion shall indicate what stage the case is at, the next event in the case and any scheduled dates.

Contents and Service of Order Removing Lawyer

(15) The order removing the lawyer from the case shall,

(a) set out the client's last known address for service; and

(b) be served on all other parties, served on the client by mail, fax or electronic mail at the client's last known address and filed immediately.

O. Reg. 91/03, s. 1

RULE 5 — WHERE A CASE STARTS AND IS TO BE HEARD

Where Case Starts

5. (1) Subject to sections 21.8 and 21.11 of the *Courts of Justice Act* (territorial jurisdiction — Family Court), a case shall be started,

(a) in the municipality where a party resides;

(b) if the case deals with custody of or access to a child, in the municipality where the child ordinarily resides, except for cases described in,

(i) section 22 (jurisdiction of an Ontario court) of the *Children's Law Reform Act*, and

(ii) subsection 48(2) (place for child protection hearing) and subsection 150(1) (place for adoption proceeding) of the *Child and Family Services Act*; or

(c) in a municipality chosen by all parties, but only with the court's permission given in advance in that municipality.

Starting Case — Danger to Child or Party

(2) Subject to sections 21.8 and 21.11 of the *Courts of Justice Act*, if there is immediate danger that a child may be removed from Ontario or immediate danger to a child's or party's health or safety, a party may start a case in any municipality and a motion may be heard in that municipality, but the case shall be transferred to a municipality referred to in subrule (1) immediately after the motion is heard, unless the court orders otherwise.

Clerk to Refuse Documents if Case in Wrong Place

(3) The clerk shall refuse to accept an application for filing unless,

(a) the case is started in the municipality where a party resides;

(b) the case deals with custody of or access to a child and is started in the municipality where the child ordinarily resides;

(c) the case is started in a municipality chosen by all parties and the order permitting the case to be started there is filed with the application; or

(d) the lawyer or party asking to file the application says in writing that the case is one that is permitted by clause (1)(b) or subrule (2) to be started in that municipality.

Place for Steps Other than Enforcement

(4) All steps in the case, other than enforcement, shall take place in the municipality where the case is started or transferred.

Place for Enforcement — Payment Orders

(5) All steps in enforcement of a payment order, including a motion to suspend a support deduction order, shall take place,

(a) in the municipality where the recipient resides;

(b) if the recipient does not reside in Ontario, in the municipality where the order is filed with the court for enforcement;

(c) if the person enforcing the order consents, in the municipality where the payor resides; or

(d) in a motion under section 26 (income source dispute) of the *Family Responsibility and Support Arrears Enforcement Act, 1996*, in the municipality where the income source resides.

Place for Enforcement — Other Orders

(6) All steps in the enforcement of an order other than a payment order shall take place,

(a) if the order involves custody of or access to a child,

(i) in the municipality where the child ordinarily resides, or

(ii) if the child does not ordinarily reside in Ontario, in the municipality to which the child has the closest connection;

(b) if the order involves property, in the municipality where the person enforcing the order resides or the municipality where the property is located; or

(c) in a municipality chosen by all parties, but only with the court's permission given in advance in that municipality.

Alternative Place for Enforcement — Order Enforced by Contempt Motion

(7) An order, other than a payment order, that is being enforced by a contempt motion may also be enforced in the municipality in which the order was made.

Transfer to Another Municipality

(8) If it is substantially more convenient to deal with a case or any step in the case in another municipality, the court may, on motion, order that the case or step be transferred there.

Change of Place for Child Protection Case

(9) Notice of a motion under subsection 48(3) of the *Child and Family Services Act* to transfer a case to a place within the jurisdiction of another children's aid society shall be served on the parties and the other children's aid society, with the evidence in support of the motion.

RULE 6 — SERVICE OF DOCUMENTS

Methods of Service

6. (1) Service of a document under these rules may be carried out by regular service or by special service in accordance with this rule, unless an Act, rule or order provides otherwise.

Age Restriction

(1.1) No person shall serve a document under these rules unless he or she is at least 18 years of age.

Regular Service

(2) Regular service of a document on a person is carried out by,

(a) mailing a copy to the person's lawyer or, if none, to the person;

(b) sending a copy by courier to the person's lawyer or, if none, to the person;

(c) depositing a copy at a document exchange to which the person's lawyer belongs;

(d) faxing a copy to the person's lawyer or, if none, to the person; or

(e) carrying out special service.

Special Service

(3) Special service of a document on a person is carried out by,

(a) leaving a copy,

(i) with the person to be served,

(ii) if the person is or appears to be mentally incapable in respect of an issue in the case, with the person and with the guardian of the person's property or, if none, with the Public Guardian and Trustee,

(iii) if the person is a child, with the child and with the child's lawyer, if any,

(iv) if the person is a corporation, with an officer, director or agent of the corporation, or with a person at any place of business of the corporation who appears to be managing the place, or

(v) if the person is a children's aid society, with an officer, director or employee of the society;

(b) leaving a copy with the person's lawyer of record in the case, or with a lawyer who accepts service in writing on a copy of the document;

(c) mailing a copy to the person, together with an acknowledgment of service in the form of a prepaid return postcard (Form 6), all in an envelope that is addressed to the person and has the sender's return address (but service under this clause is not valid unless the return postcard, signed by the person, is filed in the continuing record); or

(d) leaving a copy at the person's place of residence, in an envelope addressed to the person, with anyone who appears to be an adult person resident at the same address and, on the same day or on the next, mailing another copy to the person at that address.

Special Service — Documents that Could Lead to Imprisonment

(4) Special service of the following documents shall be carried out only by a method set out in subclause (3)(a), unless the court orders otherwise:

1. A notice of contempt motion.

2. A summons to witness.

3. A notice of motion or notice of default hearing in which the person to be served faces a possibility of imprisonment.

Special Service — Restriction on Who May Serve

(4.1) Subject to subrule (4.2), special service of the following documents shall be carried out by a person other than the party required to serve the document:

1. An application (Form 8, 8A, 8B, 8B.1, 8B.2, 8C, 8D, 8D.1, 34L or 34N).

2. A motion to change (Form 15) and change information form (Form 15A) or affidavit permitted under subrule 15(22), with required attachments.

3. A document listed in subrule (4).

Exceptions

(4.2) Subrule (4.1) does not apply if,

(a) the party required to serve the document or the person being served is a person referred to in clause 8(6)(c) (officials, agencies, etc.); or

(b) the court orders otherwise.

Regular Service at Address on Latest Document

(5) Regular service may be carried out at the address for service shown on the latest document filed by the person to be served.

Notice of Address Change

(6) A party whose address for service changes shall immediately serve notice of the change on the other parties and file it.

Service Outside Business Hours

(7) If a document is served by any method after 4 p.m. on a day when court offices are open or at any time on a day when they are not open, service is effective on the next day when they are open.

Hours of Fax Service

(8) Service of a document by fax may be carried out only before 4 p.m. on a day when court offices are open, unless the parties consent or the court orders otherwise.

Effective Date, Service by Mail

(9) Service of a document by mail is effective on the fifth day after it was mailed.

Effective Date, Service by Courier

(10) Service of a document by courier is effective on the day after the courier picks it up.

Effective Date, Service by Document Exchange

(11) Service by deposit at a document exchange is effective only if the copy deposited and an additional copy of the document are date-stamped by the document exchange in the presence of the person depositing the copy, and then service is effective on the day after the date on the stamp.

Information to be Included with Document Served by Fax

(12) A document that is served by fax shall show, on its first page,

(a) the sender's name, address, telephone number and fax number;

(b) the name of the person or lawyer to be served;

(c) the date and time of the fax;

(d) the total number of pages faxed; and

(e) the name and telephone number of a person to contact in case of transmission difficulties.

Maximum Length of Document that may be Faxed

(13) Service of a document or documents relating to a single step in a case may be carried out by fax only if the total number of pages (including any cover page or back sheet) is not more than 16, unless the parties consent in advance or the court orders otherwise.

Documents that may not be Faxed

(14) A trial record, appeal record, factum or book of authorities may not be served by fax at any time unless the person to be served consents in advance.

Substituted Service

(15) The court may, on motion without notice, order that a document be served by substituted service, using a method chosen by the court, if the party making the motion,

(a) provides detailed evidence showing,

(i) what steps have been taken to locate the person to be served, and

(ii) if the person has been located, what steps have been taken to serve the document on that person; and

(b) shows that the method of service could reasonably be expected to bring the document to the person's attention.

Service not Required

(16) The court may, on motion without notice, order that service is not required if,

(a) reasonable efforts to locate the person to be served have not been or would not be successful; and

(b) there is no method of substituted service that could reasonably be expected to bring the document to the person's attention.

Service by Advertisement

(17) If the court orders service by advertisement, Form 6A shall be used.

Approving Irregular Service

(18) When a document has been served by a method not allowed by these rules or by an order, the court may make an order approving the service if the document,

(a) came to the attention of the person to be served; or

(b) would have come to the person's attention if the person had not been evading service.

Proof of Service

(19) Service of a document may be proved by,

(a) an acceptance or admission of service, written by the person to be served or the person's lawyer;

(b) an affidavit of service (Form 6B);

(c) the return postcard mentioned in clause (3)(c); or

(d) the date stamp on a copy of the document served by deposit at a document exchange.

O. Reg. 6/10, s. 1

RULE 7 — PARTIES

Who are Parties — Case

7. (1) A person who makes a claim in a case or against whom a claim is made in a case is a party to the case.

Who are Parties — Motion

(2) For purposes of a motion only, a person who is affected by a motion is also a party, but this does not apply to a child affected by a motion relating to custody, access, child protection, adoption or child support.

Persons who must be Named as Parties

(3) A person starting a case shall name,

(a) as an applicant, every person who makes a claim;

(b) as a respondent,

(i) every person against whom a claim is made, and

(ii) every other person who should be a party to enable the court to decide all the issues in the case.

Parties in Cases Involving Children

(4) In any of the following cases, every parent or other person who has care and control of the child involved, except a foster parent under the *Child and Family Services Act*, shall be named as a party, unless the court orders otherwise:

1. A case about custody of or access to a child.

2. A child protection case.

3. A secure treatment case (Part VI of the *Child and Family Services Act*).

Party Added by Court Order

(5) The court may order that any person who should be a party shall be added as a party, and may give directions for service on that person.

Permanent Case Name and Court File Number

(6) The court file number given to a case and the description of the parties as applicants and respondents in the case shall remain the same on a motion to change an order, a status review application, an enforcement or an appeal, no matter who starts it, with the following exceptions:

1. In an enforcement of a payment order, the parties may be described instead as payors, recipients and garnishees.

2. In an appeal, the parties shall also be described as appellants and respondents.

3. When a case is transferred to another municipality, it may be given a new court file number.

4. An application under section 153.1 of the *Child and Family Services Act* to change or terminate an openness order shall be given a new court file number.

5. A motion to change an order made under section 57.1 of the *Child and Family Services Act* shall be given a new court file number.

O. Reg. 519/06, s. 1

RULE 8 — STARTING A CASE

Filing an Application

8. (1) To start a case, a person shall file an application (Form 8, 8A, 8B, 8B.1, 8B.2, 8C, 8D, 8D.1, 34L or 34N).

Change to Final Order or Agreement

(2) Subject to subrule 25(19) (changing order — fraud, mistake, lack of notice), a party who wants to ask the court to change a final order or an agreement for support filed under section 35 of the *Family Law Act* may do so only by a motion under rule 15 (if permitted to do so by that rule).

Exception

(2.1) Despite subrule (2), if a party who wants to ask the court to change a final order or agreement to which rule 15 applies also wants to make one or more related claims to which rule 15 does not apply, the party may file an application under subrule (1) to deal with the request for a change together with the related claim or claims and, in that case, subrules 15(11) to (13) apply with necessary modifications to the request.

Claims in Application

(3) An application may contain,

(a) a claim against more than one person; and

(b) more than one claim against the same person.

Claim for Custody or Access

(3.1) An application containing a claim for custody of or access to a child shall be accompanied by the applicable documents referred to in Rule 35.1.

Court Date Set when Application Filed

(4) When an application is filed, the clerk shall,

(a) set a court date, except as provided by subrule 39(7) (case management, standard track) and subrule 41(4) (case management, clerk's role); and

(b) seal the application with the court seal.

Service of Application

(5) The application shall be served immediately on every other party, and special service shall be used unless the party is listed in subrule (6).

Service on Officials, Agencies, etc.

(6) The application may be served by regular service,

(a) on a foster parent, at the foster parent's residence;

(b) on a representative of a band or native community, by serving the chief or other person who appears to be in charge of its management;

(c) on any of the following persons, at their place of business:

1. A Director appointed under section 5 of the *Child and Family Services Act*.

2. A local director appointed under section 16 of the *Child and Family Services Act*.

3. An administrator in charge of a secure treatment program under Part VI of the *Child and Family Services Act*.

4. A children's aid society.

5. The Minister of Community and Social Services.

6. An agency referred to in subsection 33(3) of the *Family Law Act* or subsection 20.1(1) of the *Divorce Act* (Canada).

7. The Director of the Family Responsibility Office.

8. The Children's Lawyer.

9. The Public Guardian and Trustee.

10. The Registrar General.

Serving Protection Application on Child

(7) In a child protection case in which the child is entitled to notice, the application shall be served on the child by special service.

Serving Secure Treatment Application on Child

(8) An application for secure treatment (Part VI of the *Child and Family Services Act*) shall be served on the child by special service.

Serving Application on Child's Lawyer

(9) If an order has been made for legal representation of a child under section 38 or subsection 114(6) of the *Child and Family Services Act* or under subrule 4(7), the applicant, or another party directed by the court, shall serve all documents in the continuing record and any status review application on the child's lawyer by regular service.

Serving Protection Application Before Start of Case

(10) If a child is brought to a place of safety (section 40, 42 or 43 of the *Child and Family Services Act*) or a homemaker remains or is placed on premises (subsection 78(2) of that Act), an application may be served without being sealed by the clerk, if it is filed on or before the court date.

Application not Served on or Before Court Date

(11) If an application is not served on a respondent on or before the court date, at the applicant's request the clerk shall set a new court date for that respondent and the applicant shall make the necessary change to the application and serve it immediately on that respondent.

O. Reg. 337/02, s. 1; 89/04, s. 2; 519/06, s. 2; 151/08, s. 1; 6/10, s. 2

RULE 8.1 — MANDATORY INFORMATION PROGRAM IN THE SUPERIOR COURT OF JUSTICE IN TORONTO [HEADING ADDED O. REG. 89/04, S. 3.]

Application of Rule

8.1 (1) This rule applies to,

(a) divorce cases started in the Superior Court of Justice in Toronto after July 1, 1998 in which any claim, other than a divorce, costs and the incorporation of the terms of an agreement or prior court order, is made; and

(b) cases governed by Parts I, II and III of the *Family Law Act* and Part III of the *Children's Law Reform Act* and started in the Superior Court of Justice in Toronto after July 1, 1998 in which any claim, other than costs, the incorporation of the terms of an agreement or prior court order and change of the terms of a final order, is made.

Exception

(2) Subrules (4) to (7) do not apply to,

(a) a person or agency referred to in subsection 33(3) of the *Family Law Act*;

(b) the Director of the Family Responsibility Office.

Content of Program

(3) The program referred to in this rule shall provide parties to cases referred to in subrule (1) with information about separation and the legal process, and may include information on topics such as,

(a) the options available for resolving differences, including alternatives to going to court;

(b) the impact the separation of parents has on children; and

(c) resources available to deal with problems arising from separation.

Attendance Compulsory

(4) Each party to a case shall attend the program no later than 45 days after the case is started.

Appointments to Attend

(5) The applicant shall arrange his or her own appointment to attend the program, obtain an appointment for the respondent from the person who conducts the program, and serve notice of the respondent's appointment with the application.

Certificate

(6) The person who conducts the program shall provide for each party who attends a certificate of attendance, which shall be filed as soon as possible, and in any event not later than 2 p.m. on the second day before the day of the case conference, if one is scheduled.

No Other Steps

(7) A party shall not take any step in the case before his or her certificate of attendance is filed, except that a respondent may serve and file an answer and a party may make an appointment for a case conference.

Exception

(8) The court may, on motion, order that any or all of subrules (4) to (7) do not apply to the party because of urgency or hardship or for some other reason in the interest of justice.

(9) [Repealed O. Reg. 561/07, s. 2.]

O. Reg. 89/04, s. 3; 561/07, s. 2

RULE 9 — CONTINUING RECORD

Continuing Record Created

9. (1) A person starting a case shall,

(a) prepare a single continuing record of the case, to be the court's permanent record of the case; and

(b) serve it on all other parties and file it, along with the affidavits of service or other documents proving that the continuing record was served.

(2) [Repealed O. Reg. 519/06, s. 3(1).]

Support Enforcement Continuing Record

(3) If a support order is filed with the Director of the Family Responsibility Office, the person bringing the case before the court shall prepare the continuing record, and the continuing record shall be called the support enforcement continuing record.

Child Protection Continuing Record

(4) In an application for a child protection order or an application for a status review of a child protection order, the continuing record shall be called the child protection continuing record.

(5) [Repealed O. Reg. 76/06, s. 4(3).]

Formal Requirements of Continuing Record

(6) In preparing and maintaining a continuing record and support enforcement continuing record under this rule, the parties shall meet the requirements set out in the document entitled "Formal Requirements of the Continuing Record under the *Family Law Rules*", dated July 1, 2006, published by the Family Rules Committee and available on the Internet through *www.ontariocourtforms.on.ca*.

Formal Requirements of Child Protection Continuing Record

(6.1) In preparing and maintaining a child protection continuing record under this rule, the parties shall meet the requirements set out in the document entitled "Formal Requirements of the Child Protection Continuing Record under the *Family Law Rules*", dated November 1, 2005, published by the Family Rules Committee and available on the Internet through *www.ontariocourtforms.on.ca*.

Separation of Single Record

(7) Instead of the single continuing record mentioned in subrule (1), the continuing record may be separated into separate records for the applicant and the respondent, in accordance with the following:

1. In a case other than a child protection case, the court may order separate records on its own initiative or at the request of either party on motion or at a case conference, settlement conference or trial management conference.

2. [Repealed O. Reg. 519/06, s. 3(3).]

3. If the court orders separate records and there is more than one applicant and respondent, the court may order separate records for each applicant and respondent.

4. If the record consists of separate records, the separate records are called the applicant's record and the respondent's record.

Combining Separated Records

(8) If the continuing record has been separated, the court may order the records to be combined into a single record on its own initiative or at the request of either party at a case conference, settlement conference or trial management conference.

Combining Separated Records on Consent

(9) If the continuing record has been separated, the parties may, if they agree, combine the separate records into a single continuing record, in which case the parties shall arrange together for the combining of the records.

By Whom Record is Separated or Combined

(10) If the court orders that the continuing record,

(a) be separated or combined on its own initiative, the court shall give directions as to which party shall separate or combine the record, as the case requires;

(b) be separated or combined at the request of a party at a case conference, settlement conference or trial management conference, the party that makes the request shall separate or combine the record, as the case requires, unless the court orders otherwise.

Maintaining Continuing Record

(11) The parties are responsible, under the clerk's supervision, for adding to a continuing record that has not been separated all documents filed in the case and, in the case of separated records, each party is responsible, under the clerk's supervision, for adding the documents the party files to the party's own record.

Duties of Party Serving Documents

(12) A party serving documents shall,

(a) if the continuing record has not been separated,

(i) serve and file any documents that are not already in the continuing record, and

(ii) serve with the documents an updated cumulative table of contents listing the documents being filed; and

(b) if the continuing record has been separated,

(i) serve and file any documents that are not already in the party's separate record, and

(ii) serve with the documents an updated cumulative table of contents listing the documents being filed in the party's separate record.

No Service or Filing of Documents Already in Record

(13) A party shall not serve or file any document that is already in the record, despite any requirement in these rules that the document be served and filed.

(14) [Repealed O. Reg. 519/06, s. 3(4).]

Documents Referred to by Tab in Record

(15) A party who is relying on a document in the record shall refer to it by its tab in the record, except in a support enforcement continuing record.

Documents Not to be Removed from Record

(16) No document shall be removed from the continuing record except by order.

Written Reasons for Order

(17) If the court gives written reasons for making an order,

(a) they may be endorsed by hand on an endorsement sheet, or the endorsement may be a short note on the endorsement sheet saying that written reasons are being given separately;

(b) the clerk shall add a copy of the reasons to the endorsements section of the record; and

(c) the clerk shall send a copy to the parties by mail, fax or electronic mail.

(18) [Repealed O. Reg. 519/06, s. 3(5).]

Appeal

(19) If a final order is appealed, only the notice of appeal and any order of the appeal court (and no other appeal document) shall be added to the record.

Transfer of Record if Case Transferred

(20) If the court transfers a case to another municipality the clerk shall, on request, transfer the record to the clerk at the court office in the other municipality, and the record shall be used there as if the case had started in the other municipality.

Confirmation of Support Order

(21) When a provisional support order or a provisional change to a support order is sent to a court in Ontario for confirmation,

(a) if the provisional order or change was made in Ontario, the clerk shall send the continuing record to the court office where the confirmation is to take place and the respondent shall update it as this rule requires; and

(b) if the provisional order or change was not made in Ontario, the clerk shall prepare the continuing record and the respondent shall update it as this rule requires.

Cases Started Before January 1, 2007

(22) Despite this rule, if a case was started before January 1, 2007, the version of this rule that applied to the case on December 31, 2006 as its application may have been modified by the court continues, subject to subrule (23), to apply to the case unless the court orders otherwise.

Exception, Cases Started Before January 1, 2007

(23) If a motion to change a final order is made on or after January 1, 2007 in respect of a case started before that date, this rule shall apply to the motion and to all documents filed afterwards.

(24) [Repealed O. Reg. 519/06, s. 3(6).]

O. Reg. 544/99, s. 4; 89/04, s. 4; 76/06, s. 4; 519/06, s. 3

RULE 10 — ANSWERING A CASE

Serving and Filing Answer

10. (1) A person against whom an application is made shall serve an answer (Form 10, 33B, 33B.1 or 33B.2) on every other party and file it within 30 days after being served with the application.

Time for Answer — Application Served Outside Canada or U.S.A.

(2) If an application is served outside Canada or the United States of America, the time for serving and filing an answer is 60 days.

Exception — Placement for Adoption

(2.1) In an application to dispense with a parent's consent before adoption placement, (Form 8D.1), the time for serving the answer is,

(a) 20 days, if the application is served in Canada or the United States of America;

(b) 40 days, if the application is served outside Canada or the United States of America.

Answer May Include Claim

(3) A respondent may include in the answer,

(a) a claim against the applicant;

(b) a claim against any other person, who then also becomes a respondent in the case.

Answer by Added Respondent

(4) Subrules (1) to (3) apply to a respondent added under subrule (3), except that the time for serving and filing an answer is 14 days after service on the added respondent, or 30 days if the added respondent is served outside Canada or the United States of America.

Claim for Custody or Access

(4.1) An answer that includes a claim for custody of or access to a child shall be accompanied by the applicable documents referred to in Rule 35.1.

No Answer or Answer Struck Out

(5) If a respondent does not serve and file an answer as this rule requires, or if the answer is struck out by an order,

(a) the respondent is not entitled to any further notice of steps in the case (except as subrule 25(13) (service of order) provides);

(b) the respondent is not entitled to participate in the case in any way;

(c) the court may deal with the case in the respondent's absence; and

(d) the clerk may set a date for an uncontested trial.

Reply

(6) A party may, within 10 days after being served with an answer, serve and file a reply (Form 10A) in response to a claim made in the answer.

O. Reg. 337/02, s. 2; 91/03, s. 2; 519/06, s. 4; 6/10, s. 3

RULE 11 — AMENDING AN APPLICATION, ANSWER OR REPLY

Amending Application without Court's Permission

11. (1) An applicant may amend the application without the court's permission as follows:

1. If no answer has been filed, by serving and filing an amended application in the manner set out in rule 8 (starting a case).

2. If an answer has been filed, by serving and filing an amended application in the manner set out in rule 8 and also filing the consent of all parties to the amendment.

Amending Answer without Court's Permission

(2) A respondent may amend the answer without the court's permission as follows:

1. If the application has been amended, by serving and filing an amended answer within 14 days after being served with the amended application.

2. If the application has not been amended, by serving and filing an amended answer and also filing the consent of all parties to the amendment.

Child Protection, Amendments Without Court's Permission

(2.1) In a child protection case, if a significant change relating to the child happens after the original document is filed,

(a) the applicant may serve and file an amended application, an amended plan of care or both; and

(b) the respondent may serve and file an amended answer and plan of care.

Amending Application or Answer with Court's Permission

(3) On motion, the court shall give permission to a party to amend an application, answer or reply, unless the amendment would disadvantage another party in a way for which costs or an adjournment could not compensate.

Claim for Custody or Access

(3.1) If an application or answer is amended to include a claim for custody of or access to a child that was not in the original application or answer, the amended application or amended answer shall be accompanied by the applicable documents referred to in Rule 35.1.

How Amendment is Shown

(4) An amendment shall be clearly shown by underlining all changes, and the rule or order permitting the amendment and the date of the amendment shall be noted in the margin of each amended page.

O. Reg. 91/03, s. 3; 6/10, s. 4

RULE 12 — WITHDRAWING, COMBINING OR SPLITTING CASES

Withdrawing Application, Answer or Reply

12. (1) A party who does not want to continue with all or part of a case may withdraw all or part of the application, answer or reply by serving a notice of withdrawal (Form 12) on every other party and filing it.

Withdrawal — Special Party's Application, Answer or Reply

(2) A special party's application, answer or reply may be withdrawn (whether in whole or in part) only with the court's permission, and the notice of motion for permission shall be served on every other party and on,

(a) the Children's Lawyer, if the special party is a child;

(b) the Public Guardian and Trustee, if the special party is not a child.

Costs Payable on Withdrawal

(3) A party who withdraws all or part of an application, answer or reply shall pay the costs of every other party in relation to the withdrawn application, answer, reply or part, up to the date of the withdrawal, unless the court orders or the parties agree otherwise.

Costs on Withdrawal by Government Agency

(4) Despite subrule (3), if the party is a government agency, costs are in the court's discretion.

Combining and Splitting Cases

(5) If it would be more convenient to hear two or more cases, claims or issues together or to split a case into two or more separate cases, claims or issues, the court may, on motion, order accordingly.

Splitting Divorce from Other Issues

(6) The court may, on motion, make an order splitting a divorce from the other issues in a case if,

(a) neither spouse will be disadvantaged by the order; and

(b) reasonable arrangements have been made for the support of any children of the marriage.

RULE 13 — FINANCIAL STATEMENTS

Financial Statement with Application, Answer or Motion

13. (1) If an application, answer or motion contains a claim for support, a property claim, or a claim for exclusive possession of the matrimonial home and its contents,

(a) the party making the claim shall serve and file a financial statement (Form 13 or 13.1) with the document that contains the claim; and

(b) the party against whom the claim is made shall serve and file a financial statement within the time for serving and filing an answer, reply or affidavit or other document responding to the motion, whether the party is serving an answer, reply or affidavit or other document responding to the motion or not.

Form 13 for Support Claim Without Property Claim

(1.1) If the application, answer or motion contains a claim for support but does not contain a property claim or a claim for exclusive possession of the matrimonial home and its contents, the financial statement used by the parties under these rules shall be in Form 13.

Form 13.1 for Property Claim With or Without Support Claim

(1.2) If the application, answer or motion contains a property claim or a claim for exclusive possession of the matrimonial home and its contents, the financial statement used by the parties under these rules shall be in Form 13.1, whether a claim for support is also included or not.

Exception, Certain Support Claims

(1.3) If the only claim for support contained in the application, answer or motion is a claim for child support in the amount specified in the table of the applicable child support guidelines, the party making the claim is not required to file a financial statement, unless the application, answer or motion also contains a property claim or a claim for exclusive possession of the matrimonial home and its contents.

(1.4) [Repealed O. Reg. 76/06, s. 5(1).]

Claim for Payment Order under CFSA

(2) If an application, answer or notice of motion contains a claim for a payment order under section 60 of the *Child and Family Services Act*, clause (1)(a) does not apply to the children's aid society but clause (1)(b) applies to the party against whom the claim is made.

Financial Statements in Custody and Access Cases

(3) If an application, answer or motion contains a claim for custody of or access to a child and this rule does not otherwise require the parties to serve and file financial statements, the court may order each party to serve and file a financial statement in Form 13 within the time decided by the court.

Financial Statement with Motion to Change Temporary Support Order

(4) Subject to subrule (1.3), the following requirements apply if a motion contains a request for a change in a temporary support order:

1. The party making the motion shall serve and file a financial statement (Form 13 or 13.1) with the notice of motion.

2. The party responding to the motion shall serve and file a financial statement as soon as possible after being served with the notice of motion, but in any event no later than two days before the motion date. Any affidavit in response to the motion shall be served and filed at the same time as the financial statement.

Exception — By Consent

(4.1) Parties to a consent motion to change a temporary support order do not need to serve and file financial statements if they file a consent agreeing not to serve and file them.

Financial Statement with Motion to Change Final Support Order or Support Agreement

(4.2) Subject to subrule (1.3), the following rules apply if a motion is made under rule 15 requesting a change to a final support order or a support agreement:

1. The party making the motion shall serve and file a financial statement (Form 13 or 13.1) with the motion to change (Form 15).

2. The party responding to the motion shall serve and file a financial statement within the time for serving and filing the response to motion to change (Form 15B) or returning the consent motion to change (Form 15C) to the party making the motion, as set out in subrule 15(10). Any response to motion to change (Form 15B) shall be served and filed at the same time as the financial statement.

3. Parties who bring the motion by filing a consent motion to change (Form 15C) shall each file a financial statement with the form, unless they indicate in the form that they agree not to do so.

4. Parties who bring the motion by filing a consent motion to change child support (Form 15D) do not need to serve or file financial statements.

Financial Statement Required by Response

(4.3) Subrule (4) or (4.2), as the case may be, applies with necessary modifications if a party makes a motion to change an order or agreement for which the party is not required by this rule to file a financial statement, and the party responding to the motion requests a change to a support order or support agreement.

No Financial Statement from Assignee

(5) The assignee of a support order is not required to serve and file a financial statement under subrule (4) or (4.2).

Financial Statement with Motion to Refrain

(5.1) A payor who makes a motion to require the Director of the Family Responsibility Office to refrain from suspending the payor's driver's licence shall, in accordance with subsection 35(7) of the *Family Responsibility and Support Arrears Enforcement Act, 1996*, serve and file with the notice of motion,

(a) a financial statement (Form 13 or 13.1) or a financial statement incorporated as Form 4 in Ontario Regulation 167/97 (*General*) made under that Act; and

(b) the proof of income specified in section 15 of the regulation referred to in clause (a).

Full Disclosure in Financial Statement

(6) A party who serves and files a financial statement shall,

(a) make full and frank disclosure of the party's financial situation;

(b) attach any documents to prove the party's income that the financial statement requires;

(c) follow the instructions set out in the form; and

(d) fully complete all portions of the statement.

Requirements for Filing

(7) The clerk shall not accept a party's financial statement for filing unless the following are attached to the form:

1. Proof of the party's current income.

2. One of the following, as proof of the party's income for the three previous years:

   i. For each of the three previous taxation years,

      A. the party's notice of assessment and, if any, notice of reassessment, or

      B. if a notice of assessment and a notice of reassessment are unavailable for a taxation year, a copy of the Income and Deductions printout provided by the Canada Revenue Agency for the party for the taxation year.

   ii. If the party swears or affirms a statement in the form that he or she is not required to and has chosen not to file an income tax return because of the *Indian Act* (Canada), some other proof of income for the three previous years.

Exception

(7.0.1) Subrule (7) does not apply to a financial statement filed under subrule (5.1).

Income Tax Returns

(7.1) Except in the case of a filing under subrule (5.1), income tax returns submitted in accordance with these rules are not required to be filed in the continuing record unless the court orders otherwise.

No Financial Statement by Consent — Spousal Support in Divorce

(8) Parties to a claim for spousal support under the *Divorce Act* (Canada) do not need to serve and file financial statements if they file a consent,

(a) agreeing not to serve and file financial statements; or

(b) agreeing to a specified amount of support, or to no support.

(9) [Repealed O. Reg. 151/08, s. 2(8).]

Documents not to be Filed without Financial Statement

(10) The clerk shall not accept a document for filing without a financial statement if these rules require the document to be filed with a financial statement.

Additional Financial Information

(11) If a party believes that another party's financial statement does not contain enough information for a full understanding of the other party's financial circumstances,

(a) the party shall ask the other party to give the necessary additional information; and

(b) if the other party does not give it within seven days, the court may, on motion, order the other party to give the information or to serve and file a new financial statement.

Updating Financial Statement

(12) Before any case conference, motion, settlement conference or trial, each party shall update the information in any financial statement that is more than 30 days old by serving and filing,

(a) a new financial statement; or

(b) an affidavit saying that the information in the last statement has not changed and is still true.

Minor Changes

(12.1) If there have been minor changes but no major changes to the information in a party's past statement, the party may serve and file, instead of a new financial statement, an affidavit with details of the changes.

Time for Updating

(12.2) The material described in subrules (12) and (12.1) shall be served and filed as follows:

1. For a case conference or settlement conference requested by a party, the requesting party shall serve and file at least seven days before the conference date and the other party shall serve and file at least four days before that date.

2. For a case conference or settlement conference that is not requested by a party, the applicant shall serve and file at least seven days before the conference date and the respondent shall serve and file at least four days before that date.

3. For a motion, the party making the motion shall serve and file at least seven days before the motion date and the other party shall serve and file at least four days before that date.

4. For a trial, the applicant shall serve and file at least seven days before the trial date and the respondent shall serve and file at least four days before that date.

Questioning on Financial Statement

(13) A party may be questioned under rule 20 on a financial statement provided under this rule, but only after a request for information has been made under clause (11)(a).

Net Family Property Statement

(14) Each party to a property claim under Part I of the *Family Law Act* shall serve and file a net family property statement (Form 13B) or, if the party has already served a net family property statement, an affidavit saying that the information in that statement has not changed and is still true,

(a) not less than seven days before a settlement conference; and

(b) not more than 30 days and not less than seven days before a trial.

Correcting and Updating Statement or Answer

(15) As soon as a party discovers that information in the party's financial statement or net family property statement or in a response the party gave under this rule is incorrect or incomplete, or that there has been a material change in the information provided, the party shall immediately serve on every other party to the claim and file the correct information or a new statement containing the correct information, together with any documents substantiating it.

Order to File Statement

(16) If a party has not served and filed a financial statement or net family property statement or information as required by this rule or an Act, the court may, on motion without notice, order the party to serve and file the document or information and, if it makes that order, shall also order the party to pay costs.

Failure to Obey Order to File Statement or Give Information

(17) If a party does not obey an order to serve and file a financial statement or net family property statement or to give information as this rule requires, the court may,

(a) dismiss the party's case;

(b) strike out any document filed by the party;

(c) make a contempt order against the party;

(d) order that any information that should have appeared on the statement may not be used by the party at the motion or trial;

(e) make any other appropriate order.

O. Reg. 544/99, s. 5; 202/01, s. 3; 92/03, s. 1; 89/04, s. 5; 76/06, s. 5; 151/08, s. 2(1)–(3), (5)–(9); 6/10, s. 5; 52/10, s. 1

RULE 14 — MOTIONS FOR TEMPORARY ORDERS [HEADING AMENDED O. REG. 89/04, S. 6(1).]

When to Make Motion

14. (1) A person who wants any of the following may make a motion:

1. A temporary order for a claim made in an application.

2. Directions on how to carry on the case.

3. A change in a temporary order.

Who May Make Motion

(2) A motion may be made by a party to the case or by a person with an interest in the case.

Parties to Motion

(3) A person who is affected by a motion is also a party, for purposes of the motion only, but this does not apply to a child affected by a motion relating to custody, access, child protection, adoption or child support.

No Motion Before Case Conference on Substantive Issues Completed

(4) No notice of motion or supporting evidence may be served and no motion may be heard before a case conference dealing with the substantive issues in the case has been completed.

(4.1) [Revoked O. Reg. 89/04, s. 6(3).]

Urgency, Hardship Etc.

(4.2) Subrule (4) does not apply if the court is of the opinion that there is a situation of urgency or hardship or that a case conference is not required for some other reason in the interest of justice.

(5) [Revoked O. Reg. 89/04, s. 6(5).]

Other Motions

(6) Subrule (4) does not apply to a motion,

(a) to change a temporary order under subrule 25(19) (fraud, mistake, lack of notice);

(b) for a contempt order under rule 31 or an order striking out a document under subrule (22);

(c) for summary judgment under rule 16;

(d) to require the Director of the Family Responsibility Office to refrain from suspending a licence;

(e) to limit or suspend a support deduction order;

(e.1) in a child protection case;

(e.2) made without notice, made on consent, that is unopposed or that is limited to procedural, uncomplicated or unopposed matters (Form 14B);

(e.3) made in an appeal;

(f) for an oral hearing under subrule 37(8) or 37.1(8); or

(g) to set aside the registration of an interjurisdictional support order made outside Canada.

Motion Involving Complicated Matters

(7) The judge who hears a motion involving complicated matters may,

(a) order that the motion or any part of it be heard as a trial; and

(b) give any directions that are necessary.

Motion by Telephone or Video Conference

(8) A party who wants a motion to be heard by telephone or video conference shall,

(a) obtain an appointment from the clerk for the hearing of the motion;

(b) make the necessary arrangements;

(c) serve a notice of the appointment and arrangements on all other parties, and file it; and

(d) participate in the motion as the notice specifies.

Documents for a Motion

(9) A motion, whether made with or without notice,

(a) requires a notice of motion (Form 14) and an affidavit (Form 14A); and

(b) may be supported by additional evidence.

Procedural, Uncomplicated or Unopposed Matters — Motion Form

(10) If a motion is limited to procedural, uncomplicated or unopposed matters, the party making the motion may use a motion form (Form 14B) instead of a notice of motion and affidavit.

Motion with Notice

(11) A party making a motion with notice shall,

(a) serve the documents mentioned in subrule (9) or (10) on all other parties, not later than four days before the motion date;

(b) file the documents as soon as possible after service, but not later than two days before the motion date; and

(c) file a confirmation (Form 14C) not later than 2 p.m. two days before the motion date.

No Late Documents

(11.1) No documents for use on the motion may be served or filed after 2 p.m. two days before the motion date.

Motion Without Notice

(12) A motion may be made without notice if,

(a) the nature or circumstances of the motion make notice unnecessary or not reasonably possible;

(b) there is an immediate danger of a child's removal from Ontario, and the delay involved in serving a notice of motion would probably have serious consequences;

(c) there is an immediate danger to the health or safety of a child or of the party making the motion, and the delay involved in serving a notice of motion would probably have serious consequences; or

(d) service of a notice of motion would probably have serious consequences.

Filing for Motion Without Notice

(13) The documents for use on a motion without notice shall be filed on or before the motion date, unless the court orders otherwise.

Order Made on Motion Without Notice

(14) An order made on motion without notice (Form 14D) shall require the matter to come back to the court and, if possible, to the same judge, within 14 days or on a date chosen by the court.

Service of Order Made Without Notice

(15) An order made on motion without notice shall be served immediately on all parties affected, together with all documents used on the motion, unless the court orders otherwise.

Withdrawing a Motion

(16) A party making a motion may withdraw it in the same way as an application or answer is withdrawn under rule 12.

Evidence on a Motion

(17) Evidence on a motion may be given by any one or more of the following methods:

1. An affidavit or other admissible evidence in writing.

2. A transcript of the questions and answers on a questioning under rule 20.

3. With the court's permission, oral evidence.

Affidavit Based on Personal Knowledge

(18) An affidavit for use on a motion shall, as much as possible, contain only information within the personal knowledge of the person signing the affidavit.

Affidavit Based on Other Information

(19) The affidavit may also contain information that the person learned from someone else, but only if,

(a) the source of the information is identified by name and the affidavit states that the person signing it believes the information is true; and

(b) in addition, if the motion is a contempt motion under rule 31, the information is not likely to be disputed.

Restrictions on Evidence

(20) The following restrictions apply to evidence for use on a motion, unless the court orders otherwise:

1. The party making the motion shall serve all the evidence in support of the motion with the notice of motion.

2. The party responding to the motion shall then serve all the evidence in response.

3. The party making the motion may then serve evidence replying to any new matters raised by the evidence served by the party responding to the motion.

4. No other evidence may be used.

No Motions Without Court's Permission

(21) If a party tries to delay the case or add to its costs or in any other way to abuse the court's process by making numerous motions without merit, the court may order the party not to make any other motions in the case without the court's permission.

Motion to Strike Out Document

(22) The court may, on motion, strike out all or part of any document that may delay or make it difficult to have a fair trial or that is inflammatory, a waste of time, a nuisance or an abuse of the court process.

Failure to Obey Order Made on Motion

(23) A party who does not obey an order that was made on motion is not entitled to any further order from the court unless the court orders that this subrule does not apply, and the court may on motion, in addition to any other remedy allowed under these rules,

(a) dismiss the party's case or strike out the party's answer or any other document filed by the party;

(b) postpone the trial or any other step in the case;

(c) make any other order that is appropriate, including an order for costs.

O. Reg. 544/99, s. 6; 202/01, s. 4; 56/03, s. 2; 91/03, s. 4; 89/04, s. 6; 151/08, s. 3

RULE 15 — MOTIONS TO CHANGE A FINAL ORDER OR AGREEMENT [HEADING AMENDED O. REG. 89/04, S. 7(1).]

15. (0.1) [Repealed O. Reg. 151/08, s. 4.]

(0.2) [Repealed O. Reg. 151/08, s. 4.]

Definition

(1) In this rule,

"assignee" means an agency or person to whom a support order or agreement that is the subject of a motion under this rule is assigned under the *Family Law Act* or the *Divorce Act* (Canada).

Application

(2) Subject to subrule (3), this rule only applies to a motion to change,

(a) a final order; or

(b) an agreement for support filed under section 35 of the *Family Law Act.*

(2.1) [Repealed O. Reg. 151/08, s. 4.]

Exception

(3) This rule does not apply to a motion or application to change an order made under the *Child and Family Services Act*, other than a final order made under section 57.1 of that Act.

Place of Motion

(4) Rule 5 (where a case starts) applies to a motion to change a final order or agreement as if the motion were a new case.

Motion to Change

(5) Subject to subrules (17) and (18), a party who wants to ask the court to change a final order or agreement shall serve and file,

(a) a motion to change (Form 15); and

(b) a change information form (Form 15A), with all required attachments.

Claim for Custody or Access

(5.1) If the motion includes a claim for custody of or access to a child, the documents referred to in subrule (5) shall be accompanied by the applicable documents referred to in Rule 35.1.

Service to Include Blank Forms

(6) The party making the motion shall serve on the other party a blank response to motion to change (Form 15B) and a blank consent motion to change (Form 15C) together with the documents referred to in subrule (5).

Special Service

(7) The documents referred to in subrules (5), (5.1) and (6) shall be served by special service (subrule 6(3)), and not by regular service.

Exception

(8) Despite subrule (7), service on the persons mentioned in subrule 8(6) (officials, agencies, etc.) may be made by regular service.

Response or Consent to Motion

(9) The following rules apply to a party who is served with a motion to change a final order or agreement:

1. If the party does not agree to the change or if the party wants to ask the court to make an additional or a different change to the final order or agreement, the party shall serve and file a response to motion to change (Form 15B), with all required attachments, within the time set out in clause (10)(a) or (b), as the case may be.

2. If the party agrees to the change or if the parties agree to a different change, the party shall complete the applicable portions of the consent motion to change (Form 15C) and shall, within the time set out in clause (10)(a) or (b), as the case may be,

i. return a signed copy of the consent motion to change to the party making the motion, and

ii. provide a copy of the signed consent motion to change to the assignee, if any.

Same

(10) The documents referred to in paragraphs 1 and 2 of subrule (9) shall be served and filed or returned and provided,

(a) no later than 30 days after the party responding to the motion receives the motion to change and the supporting documents, if that party resides in Canada or the United States of America; or

(b) no later than 60 days after the party responding to the motion receives the motion to change and the supporting documents, in any other case.

Service on Assignee Required

(11) In a motion to change a final order or agreement that has been assigned to an assignee, a party shall, in serving documents under subrule (5) or paragraph 1 of subrule (9), serve the documents on the assignee as if the assignee were also a party.

Assignee May Become Party

(12) On serving and filing a notice claiming a financial interest in the motion, an assignee becomes a respondent to the extent of the financial interest.

Sanctions if Assignee Not Served

(13) If an assignee is not served as required by subrule (11), the following rules apply:

1. The court may at any time, on motion by the assignee with notice to the other parties, set aside the changed order to the extent that it affects the assignee's financial interest.

2. The party who asked for the change has the burden of proving that the changed order should not be set aside.

3. If the changed order is set aside, the assignee is entitled to full recovery of its costs of the motion to set aside, unless the court orders otherwise.

No Response or Consent, or Response Struck Out

(14) If a party does not serve and file a response to motion to change (Form 15B) or return a consent motion to change (Form 15C) to the party making the motion as required under subrule (9), or if the party's response is struck out by an order,

(a) the party is not entitled to any further notice of steps in the case, except as subrule 25(13) (service of order) provides;

(b) the party is not entitled to participate in the case in any way; and

(c) the court may deal with the case in the party's absence.

Same, Request for Order

(15) If subrule (14) applies, the party making the motion to change may file a motion form (Form 14B) asking that the court make the order requested in the materials filed by the party, unless an assignee has filed a notice of financial interest in the motion and opposes the change.

Consent to Motion

(16) If a party returns to the party making the motion a consent motion to change (Form 15C) in accordance with subparagraph 2 i of subrule (9), the party making the motion shall complete and file the consent motion to change and, unless any assignee refuses to consent to the change being requested, the party making the motion shall file with the consent motion to change,

(a) a motion form (Form 14B) asking that the court make the order described in the consent motion to change;

(b) five copies of a draft order;

(c) a stamped envelope addressed to each party and to the assignee, if any; and

(d) if the order that is agreed on relates in whole or in part to a support obligation,

(i) a support deduction order information form prescribed under the *Family Responsibility and Support Arrears Enforcement Act, 1996*, and

(ii) a draft support deduction order.

Motion to Change on Consent

(17) Subject to subrule (18), if the parties to a final order or agreement want to ask the court to change the final order or agreement and the parties and any assignee agree to the change, the parties shall file,

(a) a change information form (Form 15A), with all required attachments;

(b) a consent motion to change (Form 15C);

(c) a motion form (Form 14B) asking that the court make the order described in the consent motion to change;

(d) five copies of a draft order;

(e) a stamped envelope addressed to each party and to the assignee, if any; and

(f) if the order that is agreed on relates in whole or in part to a support obligation,

(i) a support deduction order information form prescribed under the *Family Responsibility and Support Arrears Enforcement Act, 1996*, and

(ii) a draft support deduction order.

Motion to Change on Consent — Child Support Only

(18) If the parties to a final order or agreement want to ask the court to change the final order or agreement in relation only to a child support obligation, and the parties and any assignee agree to the change, the parties shall file,

(a) a consent motion to change child support (Form 15D), with all required attachments;

(b) five copies of a draft order;

(c) a stamped envelope addressed to each party and to the assignee, if any;

(d) a support deduction order information form prescribed under the *Family Responsibility and Support Arrears Enforcement Act, 1996*; and

(e) a draft support deduction order.

Consent After Response Filed

(19) If, at any time after a party has served and filed a response under paragraph 1 of subrule (9) and before the motion to change is heard, the parties and any assignee agree to an order that changes the final order or agreement that is the subject of the motion, the parties may proceed on consent by filing,

(a) a consent motion to change (Form 15C);

(b) a motion form (Form 14B) asking that the court make the order described in the consent motion to change;

(c) five copies of a draft order;

(d) a stamped envelope addressed to each party and to the assignee, if any; and

(e) if the order that is agreed on relates in whole or in part to a support obligation,

(i) a support deduction order information form prescribed under the *Family Responsibility and Support Arrears Enforcement Act, 1996*, and

(ii) a draft support deduction order.

Order, Agreement to be Attached

(20) A copy of any existing order or agreement that deals with custody, access or support shall be attached to every change information form (Form 15A) or consent motion to change child support (Form 15D).

Change not in Accordance with Child Support Guidelines

(21) Unless a motion to change a child support order or agreement is proceeding on the consent of the parties and any assignee, if a party asks that an order be made under this rule that is not in accordance with the tables in the applicable child support guidelines, the support recipient and the support payor shall each serve and file the evidence required by the following sections of the applicable child support guidelines, or the evidence that is otherwise necessary to satisfy the court that it should make the order asked for:

1. Section 4 (income over $150,000).

2. Section 5 (step-parent).

3. Section 7 (special expenses).

4. Section 8 (split custody).

5. Section 9 (shared custody).

6. Section 10 (undue hardship).

7. Section 21 (income and financial information).

Affidavit May Be Filed

(22) A party or parties who want to ask the court to change a final order or agreement may, instead of using a change information form (Form 15A), use an affidavit containing evidence necessary to satisfy the court that it should make the order asked for and, in that case, these rules apply to the affidavit as if it were a change information form.

Same

(23) A party who responds to a motion to change a final order or agreement by serving and filing a response to motion to change (Form 15B) may use an affidavit to provide evidence supporting his or her position instead of relying on the relevant portions of the form to provide the evidence or in addition to those portions of the form and, in that case, the affidavit is deemed to be part of the form.

Requirements for Affidavit

(24) Subrules 14(18) and (19) apply with necessary modifications to an affidavit provided in accordance with subrule (22) or (23).

Powers of Court — Motion on Consent or Unopposed

(25) If a motion to change a final order or agreement proceeds on the consent of the parties and any assignee or is unopposed, the clerk shall present the filed materials to a judge and the judge may,

(a) make the order asked for;

(b) require one or both parties to file further material; or

(c) require one or both parties to come to court.

Powers of Court — Directions

(26) If the court is of the opinion that a motion, whether proceeding on consent or not, cannot be properly dealt with because of the material filed, because of the matters in dispute or for any other reason, the court may give directions, including directions for a trial.

Powers of Court — Rule 14

(27) Subrules 14(21), (22) and (23) apply with necessary modifications to a motion to change a final order or agreement.

Motion Under Rule 14

(28) A motion under rule 14 may be made on a motion to change a final order or agreement.

Access to Listed Documents

(29) Subrule 19(2) (access to listed documents) applies with necessary modifications to a document mentioned in a form or affidavit used under this rule.

O. Reg. 544/99, s. 7; 89/04, s. 7; 519/06, s. 5; 151/08, s. 4; 6/10, s. 6

RULE 16 — SUMMARY JUDGMENT

When Available

16. (1) After the respondent has served an answer or after the time for serving an answer has expired, a party may make a motion for summary judgment for a final order without a trial on all or part of any claim made or any defence presented in the case.

Available in Any Case Except Divorce

(2) A motion for summary judgment under subrule (1) may be made in any case (including a child protection case) that does not include a divorce claim.

Divorce Claim

(3) In a case that includes a divorce claim, the procedure provided in rule 36 (divorce) for an uncontested divorce may be used, or the divorce claim may be split from the rest of the case under subrule 12(6).

Evidence Required

(4) The party making the motion shall serve an affidavit or other evidence that sets out specific facts showing that there is no genuine issue requiring a trial.

Evidence of Responding Party

(4.1) In response to the affidavit or other evidence served by the party making the motion, the party responding to the motion may not rest on mere allegations or denials but shall set out, in an affidavit or other evidence, specific facts showing that there is a genuine issue for trial.

Evidence not from Personal Knowledge

(5) If a party's evidence is not from a person who has personal knowledge of the facts in dispute, the court may draw conclusions unfavourable to the party.

No Issue for Trial

(6) If there is no genuine issue requiring a trial of a claim or defence, the court shall make a final order accordingly.

Only Issue Amount of Entitlement

(7) If the only genuine issue is the amount to which a party is entitled, the court shall order a trial to decide the amount.

Only Issue Question of Law

(8) If the only genuine issue is a question of law, the court shall decide the issue and make a final order accordingly.

Order Giving Directions

(9) If the court does not make a final order, or makes an order for a trial of an issue, the court may also,

(a) specify what facts are not in dispute, state the issues and give directions about how and when the case will go to trial (in which case the order governs how the trial proceeds, unless the trial judge orders otherwise to prevent injustice);

(b) give directions; and

(c) impose conditions (for example, require a party to pay money into court as security, or limit a party's pretrial disclosure).

Costs of Unsuccessful Motion

(10) If the party who made the motion has no success on the motion, the court shall decide the amount of the other party's costs of the motion on a full recovery basis and order the party who made the motion to pay them immediately, unless the motion was justified, although unsuccessful.

Costs — Bad Faith

(11) If a party has acted in bad faith, the court shall decide the costs of the motion on a full recovery basis and shall order the party to pay them immediately.

Motion for Summary Decision on Legal Issue

(12) The court may, on motion,

(a) decide a question of law before trial, if the decision may dispose of all or part of the case, substantially shorten the trial or save substantial costs;

(b) strike out an application, answer or reply because it sets out no reasonable claim or defence in law; or

(c) dismiss or suspend a case because,

(i) the court has no jurisdiction over it,

(ii) a party has no legal capacity to carry on the case,

(iii) there is another case going on between the same parties about the same matter, or

(iv) the case is a waste of time, a nuisance or an abuse of the court process.

Evidence on Motion for Summary Decision of Legal Issue

(13) On a motion under subrule (12), evidence is admissible only if the parties consent or the court gives permission.

O. Reg. 91/03, s. 5

RULE 17 — CONFERENCES

Conferences in Defended Cases

17. (1) In each case in which an answer is filed,

(a) a judge shall conduct at least one case conference, except as subrule (1.1) provides; and

(b) a judge may conduct a settlement conference, a trial management conference or both.

Exception, Case Conference Optional in Child Protection Case

(1.1) In a child protection case, a case conference may be conducted if,

(a) a party requests it; or

(b) the court considers it appropriate.

Undefended Cases

(2) If no answer is filed,

(a) the clerk shall, on request, schedule a case conference or set a date for an uncontested trial or, in an uncontested divorce case, prepare the documents for a judge; and

(b) settlement conference or trial management conference shall be conducted only if the court orders it.

Motions to Change Final Order or Agreement

(3) Subrule (1) applies, with necessary changes, to a motion to change a final order or agreement under rule 15, unless the motion is proceeding on the consent of the parties and any assignee or is unopposed.

Purposes of Case Conference

(4) The purposes of a case conference include,

(a) exploring the chances of settling the case;

(b) identifying the issues that are in dispute and those that are not in dispute;

(c) exploring ways to resolve the issues that are in dispute;

(d) ensuring disclosure of the relevant evidence;

(d.1) identifying any issues relating to any expert evidence or reports on which the parties intend to rely at trial;

(e) noting admissions that may simplify the case;

(f) setting the date for the next step in the case;

(g) setting a specific timetable for the steps to be taken in the case before it comes to trial;

(h) organizing a settlement conference, or holding one if appropriate; and

(i) giving directions with respect to any intended motion, including the preparation of a specific timetable for the exchange of material for the motion and ordering the filing of summaries of argument, if appropriate.

(4.1) A party who asks for a case conference shall serve and file a case conference notice (Form 17).

Purposes of Settlement Conference

(5) The purposes of a settlement conference include,

(a) exploring the chances of settling the case;

(b) settling or narrowing the issues in dispute;

(c) ensuring disclosure of the relevant evidence;

(c.1) settling or narrowing any issues relating to any expert evidence or reports on which the parties intend to rely at trial;

(d) noting admissions that may simplify the case;

(e) if possible, obtaining a view of how the court might decide the case;

(f) considering any other matter that may help in a quick and just conclusion of the case;

(g) if the case is not settled, identifying the witnesses and other evidence to be presented at trial, estimating the time needed for trial and scheduling the case for trial; and

(h) organizing a trial management conference, or holding one if appropriate.

Purposes of Trial Management Conference

(6) The purposes of a trial management conference include,

(a) exploring the chances of settling the case;

(b) arranging to receive evidence by a written report, an agreed statement of facts, an affidavit or another method, if appropriate;

(c) deciding how the trial will proceed;

(c.1) exploring the use of expert evidence or reports at trial, including the timing requirements for service and filing of experts' reports;

(d) ensuring that the parties know what witnesses will testify and what other evidence will be presented at trial;

(e) estimating the time needed for trial; and

(f) setting the trial date, if this has not already been done.

Combined Conference

(7) On the direction of the judge, part or all of a case conference, settlement conference and trial management conference may be combined.

Orders at Conference

(8) At a case conference, settlement conference or trial management conference the judge may, if it is appropriate to do so,

(a) make an order for document disclosure (rule 19), questioning (rule 20) or filing of summaries of argument on a motion, set the times for events in the case or give directions for the next step or steps in the case;

(a.1) order that the evidence of a witness at trial be given by affidavit;

(a.0.1) make an order respecting the use of expert witness evidence at trial or the service and filing of experts' reports;

(b) if notice has been served, make a temporary or final order;

(c) make an unopposed order or an order on consent; and

(d) on consent, refer any issue for alternative dispute resolution.

Conferences with a Non-Judge

(9) A case conference or settlement conference may be conducted by a person who has been named by the appropriate senior judge, unless a party requests a conference with a judge.

Settlement Conference with Judge Before Case Set for Trial

(10) A case shall not be scheduled for trial unless,

(a) a judge has conducted a settlement conference; or

(b) a judge has ordered that the case be scheduled for trial.

(11) [Repealed O. Reg. 151/08, s. 5(2).]

Enforcement — Conferences Optional

(12) In an enforcement, a case conference, settlement conference or trial management conference may be held at a party's request or on a judge's direction.

Parties to Serve Briefs

(13) For each conference, each party shall serve and file a case conference brief (Form 17A or Form 17B), settlement conference brief (Form 17C or Form 17D) or trial management conference brief (Form 17E), as appropriate.

Case Conference Brief in Child Protection Case

(13.0.1) In a child protection case, a case conference brief shall be served and filed only if a case conference is being held under subrule (1.1).

Time for Service of Briefs

(13.1) The party requesting the conference (or, if the conference is not requested by a party, the applicant) shall serve and file a brief not later than seven days before the date scheduled for the conference and the other party shall do so not later than four days before that date.

Parties to Confirm Attendance

(14) Not later than 2 p.m. two days before the date scheduled for the conference, each party shall file a confirmation (Form 14C).

No Late Briefs

(14.1) No brief or other document for use at the conference may be served or filed after 2 p.m. two days before the date scheduled for the conference.

Parties and Lawyers to Come to Conference

(15) The following shall come to each conference:

1. The parties, unless the court orders otherwise.

2. For each represented party, the lawyer with full knowledge of and authority in the case.

Participation by Telephone or Video Conference

(16) With permission obtained in advance from the judge who is to conduct a conference, a party or lawyer may participate in the conference by telephone or video conference.

Setting Up Telephone or Video Conference

(17) A party or lawyer who has permission to participate by telephone or video conference shall,

(a) make the necessary arrangements;

(b) serve a notice of the arrangements on all other parties and file it; and

(c) participate in the conference as the notice specifies.

Costs of Adjourned Conference

(18) If a conference is adjourned because a party is not prepared, has not served the required brief, has not made the required disclosure or has otherwise not followed these rules, the judge shall,

(a) order the party to pay the costs of the conference immediately;

(b) decide the amount of the costs; and

(c) give any directions that are needed.

Conference Agreement

(19) No agreement reached at a conference is effective until it is signed by the parties, witnessed and, in a case involving a special party, approved by the court.

Agreement Filed in Continuing Record

(20) The agreement shall be filed as part of the continuing record, unless the court orders otherwise.

Continuing Record, Trial Management Conference Briefs

(21) Trial management conference briefs form part of the continuing record.

Continuing Record, Case Conference Briefs

(22) Case conference briefs do not form part of the continuing record unless the court orders otherwise and shall be returned at the end of the conference to the parties who filed them or be destroyed by court staff immediately after the conference.

Deletions from Case Conference Brief Included in Record

(22.1) If the court orders that a case conference brief form part of the continuing record, that portion of the brief that deals with settlement of the case shall be deleted.

Continuing Record, Settlement Conference Briefs

(22.2) Settlement conference briefs do not form part of the continuing record and shall be returned at the end of the conference to the parties who filed them or be destroyed by the court staff immediately after the conference.

Confidentiality of Settlement Conference

(23) No brief or evidence prepared for a settlement conference and no statement made at a settlement conference shall be disclosed to any other judge, except in,

(a) an agreement reached at a settlement conference; or

(b) an order.

Settlement Conference Judge Cannot Hear Issue

(24) A judge who conducts a settlement conference about an issue shall not hear the issue, except as subrule (25) provides.

Exception, Child Protection Case

(25) In a child protection case, if a finding that the child is in need of protection is made without a trial and a trial is needed to determine which order should be made under section 57 of the *Child and Family Services Act*, any judge who has not conducted a settlement conference on that issue may conduct the trial.

O. Reg. 544/99, s. 8; 202/01, s. 5; 91/03, s. 6; 89/04, s. 8; 151/08, s. 5; 6/10, s. 7

RULE 18 — OFFERS TO SETTLE

Definition

18. (1) In this rule,

"offer" means an offer to settle one or more claims in a case, motion, appeal or enforcement, and includes a counter-offer.

Application

(2) This rule applies to an offer made at any time, even before the case is started.

Making an Offer

(3) A party may serve an offer on any other party.

Offer to be Signed by Party and Lawyer

(4) An offer shall be signed personally by the party making it and also by the party's lawyer, if any.

Withdrawing an Offer

(5) A party who made an offer may withdraw it by serving a notice of withdrawal, at any time before the offer is accepted.

Time-Limited Offer

(6) An offer that is not accepted within the time set out in the offer is considered to have been withdrawn.

Offer Expires When Court Begins to Give Decision

(7) An offer may not be accepted after the court begins to give a decision that disposes of a claim dealt with in the offer.

Confidentiality of Offer

(8) The terms of an offer,

(a) shall not be mentioned in any document filed in the continuing record; and

(b) shall not be mentioned to the judge hearing the claim dealt with in the offer, until the judge has dealt with all the issues in dispute except costs.

Accepting an Offer

(9) The only valid way of accepting an offer is by serving an acceptance on the party who made the offer, at any time before,

(a) the offer is withdrawn; or

(b) the court begins to give a decision that disposes of a claim dealt with in the offer.

Offer Remains Open Despite Rejection or Counter-Offer

(10) A party may accept an offer in accordance with subrule (9) even if the party has previously rejected the offer or made a counter-offer.

Costs not Dealt with in Offer

(11) If an accepted offer does not deal with costs, either party is entitled to ask the court for costs.

Court Approval, Offer Involving Special Party

(12) A special party may make, withdraw and accept an offer, but another party's acceptance of a special party's offer and a special party's acceptance of another party's offer are not binding on the special party until the court approves.

Failure to Carry Out Terms of Accepted Offer

(13) If a party to an accepted offer does not carry out the terms of the offer, the other party may,

(a) make a motion to turn the parts of the offer within the court's jurisdiction into an order; or

(b) continue the case as if the offer had never been accepted.

Costs Consequences of Failure to Accept Offer

(14) A party who makes an offer is, unless the court orders otherwise, entitled to costs to the date the offer was served and full recovery of costs from that date, if the following conditions are met:

1. If the offer relates to a motion, it is made at least one day before the motion date.

2. If the offer relates to a trial or the hearing of a step other than a motion, it is made at least seven days before the trial or hearing date.

3. The offer does not expire and is not withdrawn before the hearing starts.

4. The offer is not accepted.

5. The party who made the offer obtains an order that is as favourable as or more favourable than the offer.

Costs Consequences — Burden of Proof

(15) The burden of proving that the order is as favourable as or more favourable than the offer to settle is on the party who claims the benefit of subrule (14).

Costs — Discretion of Court

(16) When the court exercises its discretion over costs, it may take into account any written offer to settle, the date it was made and its terms, even if subrule (14) does not apply.

RULE 19 — DOCUMENT DISCLOSURE

Affidavit Listing Documents

19. (1) Every party shall, within 10 days after another party's request, give the other party an affidavit listing every document that is,

(a) relevant to any issue in the case; and

(b) in the party's control, or available to the party on request.

Access to Listed Documents

(2) The other party is entitled, on request,

(a) to examine any document listed in the affidavit, unless it is protected by a legal privilege; and

(b) to receive, at the party's own expense at the legal aid rate, a copy of any document that the party is entitled to examine under clause (a).

Access to Documents Mentioned in Court Papers

(3) Subrule (2) also applies, with necessary changes, to a document mentioned in a party's application, answer, reply, notice of motion, affidavit, financial statement or net family property statement.

Documents Protected by Legal Privilege

(4) If a party claims that a document is protected by a legal privilege, the court may, on motion, examine it and decide the issue.

Use of Privileged Documents

(5) A party who claims that a document is protected by a legal privilege may use it at trial only,

(a) if the other party has been allowed to examine the document and been supplied with a copy, free of charge, at least 30 days before the settlement conference; or

(b) on the conditions the trial judge considers appropriate, including an adjournment if necessary.

Documents of Subsidiary or Affiliated Corporation

(6) The court may, on motion, order a party to give another party an affidavit listing the documents that are,

(a) relevant to any issue in the case; and

(b) in the control of, or available on request to a corporation that is controlled, directly or indirectly, by the party or by another corporation that the party controls directly or indirectly.

Access to Listed Documents

(7) Subrule (2) also applies, with necessary changes, to any document listed in an affidavit ordered under subrule (6).

Documents Omitted from Affidavit or Found Later

(8) A party who, after serving an affidavit required under subrule (1) or (6), finds a document that should have been listed in it, or finds that the list is not correct or not complete, shall immediately serve on the other party a new affidavit listing the correct information.

Access to Additional Documents

(9) The other party is entitled, on request,

(a) to examine any document listed in an affidavit served under subrule (8), unless it is protected by a legal privilege; and

(b) to receive, free of charge, a copy of any document that the party is entitled to examine under clause (a).

Failure to Follow Rule or Obey Order

(10) If a party does not follow this rule or obey an order made under this rule, the court may, on motion, do one or more of the following:

1. Order the party to give another party an affidavit, let the other party examine a document or supply the other party with a copy free of charge.

2. Order that a document favourable to the party's case may not be used except with the court's permission.

3. Order that the party is not entitled to obtain disclosure under these rules until the party follows the rule or obeys the order.

4. Dismiss the party's case or strike out the party's answer.

5. Order the party to pay the other party's costs for the steps taken under this rule, and decide the amount of the costs.

6. Make a contempt order against the party.

7. Make any other order that is appropriate.

Document in Non-Party's Control

(11) If a document is in a non-party's control, or is available only to the non-party, and is not protected by a legal privilege, and it would be unfair to a party to go on with the case without the document, the court may, on motion with notice served on every party and served on the non-party by special service,

(a) order the non-party to let the party examine the document and to supply the party with a copy at the legal aid rate; and

(b) order that a copy be prepared and used for all purposes of the case instead of the original.

RULE 20 — QUESTIONING A WITNESS AND DISCLOSURE

Questioning — Procedure

20. (1) Questioning under this rule shall take place orally under oath or affirmation.

Cross-Examination

(2) The right to question a person includes the right to cross-examine.

Child Protection Case — Available as of Right

(3) In a child protection case, a party is entitled to obtain information from another party about any issue in the case,

(a) by questioning the other party, in which case the party shall serve the other party with a summons to witness (Form 23) by a method of special service set out in clause 6(3)(a); or

(b) by affidavit or by another method, in which case the party shall serve the other party with a request for information (Form 20).

Other Cases — Consent or Order

(4) In a case other than a child protection case, a party is entitled to obtain information from another party about any issue in the case,

(a) with the other party's consent; or

(b) by an order under subrule (5).

Order for Questioning or Disclosure

(5) The court may, on motion, order that a person (whether a party or not) be questioned by a party or disclose information by affidavit or by another method about any issue in the case, if the following conditions are met:

1. It would be unfair to the party who wants the questioning or disclosure to carry on with the case without it.

2. The information is not easily available by any other method.

3. The questioning or disclosure will not cause unacceptable delay or undue expense.

Questioning Special Party

(6) If a person to be questioned is a special party, the court may, on motion, order that someone else be questioned in addition to or in place of the person.

Questioning About Affidavit or Net Family Property Statement

(7) The court may make an order under subrule (5) that a person be questioned or disclose details about information in an affidavit or net family property statement.

Questioning or Disclosure — Preconditions

(8) A party who wants to question a person or obtain information by affidavit or by another method may do so only if the party,

(a) has served and filed any answer, financial statement or net family property statement that these rules require; and

(b) promises in writing not to serve or file any further material for the next step in the case, except in reply to the answers or information obtained.

Notice and Summons to Non-Party

(9) The court may make an order under this rule affecting a non-party only if the non-party has been served with the notice of motion, a summons to witness (Form 23) and the witness fee required by subrule 23(4), all by special service (subrule 6(3)).

Penalty for Failure to Obey Summons

(10) Subrule 23(7) (failure to obey summons to witness) applies, with necessary changes, if a person summoned under subrule (9) fails to obey the summons.

Place of Questioning

(11) The questioning shall take place in the municipality in which the person to be questioned lives, unless that person and the party who wants to do the questioning agree to hold it in another municipality.

Other Arrangements for Questioning

(12) If the person to be questioned and the party who wants to do the questioning do not agree on one or more of the following matters, the court shall, on motion, make an order to decide the matter:

1. The date and time for the questioning.

2. The person responsible for recording the questioning.

3. The method for recording the questioning.

4. Payment of the expenses of the person to be questioned, if a non-party.

Notice to Parties

(13) The parties shall, not later than three days before the questioning, be served with notice of the name of the person to be questioned and the address, date and time of the questioning.

Questioning Person Outside Ontario

(14) If a person to be questioned lives outside Ontario and will not come to Ontario for questioning, the court may decide,

(a) the date, time and place for the questioning;

(b) how much notice the person should be given;

(c) the person before whom the questioning will be held;

(d) the amount of the witness fee to be paid to the person to be questioned;

(e) the method for recording the questioning;

(f) where necessary, that the clerk shall issue,

(i) an authorization to a commissioner (Form 20A) who is to supervise the questioning outside Ontario, and

(ii) a letter of request (Form 20B) to the appropriate court or authorities outside Ontario, asking for their assistance in getting the person to be questioned to come before the commissioner; and

(g) any other related matter.

Commissioner's Duties

(15) A commissioner authorized under subrule (14) shall,

(a) supervise the questioning according to the terms of the court's authorization, these rules and Ontario's law of evidence, unless the law of the place where the questioning is to be held requires some other manner of questioning;

(b) make and keep a copy of the record of the questioning and, if possible, of the exhibits, if any;

(c) deliver the original record, any exhibits and the authorization to the clerk who issued it; and

(d) notify the party who asked for the questioning that the record has been delivered to the clerk.

Order to Bring Documents or Things

(16) An order for questioning and a summons to witness may also require the person to bring any document or thing that is,

(a) relevant to any issue in the case; and

(b) in the person's control or available to the person on request.

Other Rules Apply

(17) Subrules 19(2), (4) and (5) (right to examine document and obtain copy, documents protected by legal privilege, use of privileged documents) apply, with necessary changes, to the documents mentioned in the order.

Scope of Questions

(18) A person to be questioned may be asked about,

(a) the names of persons who might reasonably be expected to know about the claims in the case and, with the court's permission, their addresses;

(b) the names of the witnesses whom a party intends to call at trial and, with the court's permission, their addresses;

(c) the names, addresses, findings, conclusions and opinions of expert witnesses whom a party intends to call or on whose reports the party intends to rely at trial;

(d) if it is relevant to the case, the existence and details of any insurance policy under which the insurance company may be required to pay all or part of an order for the payment of money in the case or to pay back to a party money that the party has paid under an order; and

(e) any other matter in dispute in the case.

Refusal to Answer Question

(19) If a person being questioned refuses to answer a question,

(a) the court may, on motion,

(i) decide whether the question is proper,

(ii) give directions for the person's return to the questioning, and

(iii) make a contempt order against the person; and

(b) if the person is a party or is questioned on behalf or in place of a party, the party shall not use the information that was refused as evidence in the case, unless the court gives permission under subrule (20).

Court's Permission

(20) The court shall give permission unless the use of the information would cause harm to another party or an unacceptable delay in the trial, and may impose any appropriate conditions on the permission, including an adjournment if necessary.

Duty to Correct or Update Answers

(21) A person who has been questioned or who has provided information in writing by affidavit or by another method and who finds that an answer or information given was incorrect or incomplete, or is no longer correct or complete, shall immediately provide the correct and complete information in writing to all parties.

Lawyer Answering

(22) If there is no objection, questions may be answered by the lawyer for a person being questioned, and the answer shall be taken as the person's own answer unless the person corrects or changes it before the questioning ends.

Method for Recording Questioning

(23) All the questions and answers at a questioning shall be recorded electronically or manually.

Obligation to Keep Information Confidential

(24) When a party obtains evidence under this rule, rule 13 (financial statements) or rule 19 (document disclosure), the party and the party's lawyer may use the evidence and any information obtained from it only for the purposes of the case in which the evidence was obtained, subject to the exceptions in subrule (25).

Use of Information Permitted

(25) Evidence and any information obtained from it may be used for other purposes,

(a) if the person who gave the evidence consents;

(b) if the evidence is filed with the court, given at a hearing or referred to at a hearing;

(c) to impeach the testimony of a witness in another case; or

(d) in a later case between the same parties or their successors, if the case in which the evidence was obtained was withdrawn or dismissed.

Court May Lift Obligation of Confidentiality

(26) The court may, on motion, give a party permission to disclose evidence or information obtained from it if the interests of justice outweigh any harm that would result to the party who provided the evidence.

RULE 21 — REPORT OF CHILDREN'S LAWYER

REPORT OF CHILDREN'S LAWYER

21. When the Children's Lawyer investigates and reports on custody of or access to a child under section 112 of the *Courts of Justice Act*,

(a) the Children's Lawyer shall first serve notice on the parties and file it;

(b) the parties shall, from the time they are served with the notice, serve the Children's Lawyer with every document in the case that involves the child's custody, access, support, health or education, as if the Children's Lawyer were a party in the case;

(c) the Children's Lawyer has the same rights as a party to document disclosure (rule 19) and questioning witnesses (rule 20) about any matter involving the child's custody, access, support, health or education;

(d) within 90 days after serving the notice under clause (a), the Children's Lawyer shall serve a report on the parties and file it;

(e) within 30 days after being served with the report, a party may serve and file a statement disputing anything in it; and

(f) the trial shall not be held and the court shall not make a final order in the case until the 30 days referred to in clause (e) expire or the parties file a statement giving up their right to that time.

RULE 22 — ADMISSION OF FACTS

Meaning of Admission that Document Genuine

22. (1) An admission that a document is genuine is an admission,

(a) if the document is said to be an original, that it was written, signed or sealed as it appears to have been;

(b) if it is said to be a copy, that it is a complete and accurate copy; and

(c) if it is said to be a copy of a document that is ordinarily sent from one person to another (for example, a letter, fax or electronic message), that it was sent as it appears to have been sent and was received by the person to whom it is addressed.

Request to Admit

(2) At any time, by serving a request to admit (Form 22) on another party, a party may ask the other party to admit, for purposes of the case only, that a fact is true or that a document is genuine.

Copy of Document to be Attached

(3) A copy of any document mentioned in the request to admit shall be attached to it, unless the other party already has a copy or it is impractical to attach a copy.

Response Required within 20 Days

(4) The party on whom the request to admit is served is considered to have admitted, for purposes of the case only, that the fact is true or that the document is genuine, unless the party serves a response (Form 22A) within 20 days,

(a) denying that a particular fact mentioned in the request is true or that a particular document mentioned in the request is genuine; or

(b) refusing to admit that a particular fact mentioned in the request is true or that a particular document mentioned in the request is genuine, and giving the reasons for each refusal.

Withdrawing Admission

(5) An admission that a fact is true or that a document is genuine (whether contained in a document served in the case or resulting from subrule (4)), may be withdrawn only with the other party's consent or with the court's permission.

RULE 23 — EVIDENCE AND TRIAL

Trial Record

23. (1) At least 30 days before the start of the trial, the applicant shall serve and file a trial record containing a table of contents and the following documents:

1. The application, answer and reply, if any.

2. Any agreed statement of facts.

3. If relevant to an issue at trial, financial statements and net family property statements by all parties, completed not more than 30 days before the record is served.

3.1 If the trial involves a claim for custody of or access to a child, the applicable documents referred to in Rule 35.1.

4. Any assessment report ordered by the court or obtained by consent of the parties.

5. Any temporary order relating to a matter still in dispute.

6. Any order relating to the trial.

7. The relevant parts of any transcript on which the party intends to rely at trial.

8. [Repealed O. Reg. 6/10, s. 8(2).]

Respondent May Add to Trial Record

(2) Not later than seven days before the start of the trial, a respondent may serve, file and add to the trial record any document referred to in subrule (1) that is not already in the trial record.

Summons to Witness

(3) A party who wants a witness to give evidence in court or to be questioned and to bring documents or other things shall serve on the witness a summons to witness (Form 23), together with the witness fee set out in subrule (4).

Witness Fee

(4) A person summoned as a witness shall be paid, for each day that the person is needed in court or to be questioned,

(a) $50 for coming to court or to be questioned;

(b) travel money in the amount of,

(i) $5, if the person lives in the city or town where the person gives evidence,

(ii) 30 cents per kilometre each way, if the person lives elsewhere but within 300 kilometres of the court or place of questioning,

(iii) the cheapest available air fare plus $10 a day for airport parking and 30 cents per kilometre each way from the person's home to the airport and from the airport to the court or place of questioning, if the person lives 300 or more kilometres from the court or place of questioning; and

(c) $100 per night for meals and overnight stay, if the person does not live in the city or town where the trial is held and needs to stay overnight.

Meaning of "City or Town"

(4.1) For the purposes for subrule (4), a municipality shall be considered a city or town if it was a city or town on December 31, 2002.

Continuing Effect of Summons

(5) A summons to witness remains in effect until it is no longer necessary to have the witness present.

Summons for Original Document

(6) If a document can be proved by a certified copy, a party who wants a witness to bring the original shall not serve a summons on the witness for that purpose without the court's permission.

Failure to Obey Summons

(7) The court may issue a warrant for arrest (Form 32B) to bring a witness before the court if,

(a) the witness has been served as subrule (3) requires, but has not obeyed the summons; and

(b) it is necessary to have the witness present in court or at a questioning.

Interprovincial Summons to Witness

(8) A summons to a witness outside Ontario under the *Interprovincial Summonses Act* shall be in Form 23A.

Setting Aside Summons to Witness

(9) The court may, on motion, order that a summons to witness be set aside.

Attendance of a Prisoner

(10) If it is necessary to have a prisoner come to court or to be questioned, the court may order (Form 23B) the prisoner's custodian to deliver the prisoner on payment of the fee set out in the regulations under the *Administration of Justice Act.*

Calling Opposing Party as Witness

(11) A party may call the opposing party as a witness and may cross-examine the opposing party.

Attendance of Opposing Party

(11.1) A party who wishes to call an opposing party as a witness may have the opposing party attend,

(a) by serving a summons under subrule (3) on the opposing party; or

(b) by serving on the opposing party's lawyer, at least 10 days before the start of the trial, a notice of intention to call the opposing party as a witness.

Opposing Party Disobeying Summons

(12) When an opposing party has been served with a summons under subrule (3), the court may make a final order in favour of the party calling the witness, adjourn the case or make any other appropriate order, including a contempt order, if the opposing party,

(a) does not come to or remain in court as required by the summons; or

(b) refuses to be sworn or to affirm, to answer any proper question or to bring any document or thing named in the summons.

Reading Opposing Party's Answers into Evidence

(13) An answer or information given under rule 20 (questioning) by an opposing party may be read into evidence at trial if it is otherwise proper evidence, even if the opposing party has already testified at trial.

Reading Other Person's Answers into Evidence

(14) Subrule (13) also applies, with necessary changes, to an answer or information given by a person questioned on behalf of or in place of an opposing party, unless the trial judge orders otherwise.

Using Answers — Special Circumstances

(15) Subrule (13) is subject to the following:

1. If the answer or information is being read into evidence to show that a witness's testimony at trial is not to be believed, answers or information given by the witness earlier must be put to the witness as sections 20 and 21 of the *Evidence Act* require.

2. At the request of an opposing party, the trial judge may direct the party reading the answer or information into evidence to read in, as well, any other answer or information that qualifies or explains what the party has read into evidence.

3. A special party's answer or information may be read into evidence only with the trial judge's permission.

Rebutting Answers

(16) A party who has read answers or information into evidence at trial may introduce other evidence to rebut the answers or information.

Using Answers of Witness not Available for Trial

(17) The trial judge may give a party permission to read into evidence all or part of the answers or information given under rule 20 (questioning) by a person who is unable or unwilling to testify at the trial, but before doing so the judge shall consider,

(a) the importance of the evidence;

(b) the general principle that trial evidence should be given orally in court;

(c) the extent to which the person was cross-examined; and

(d) any other relevant factor.

Taking Evidence Before Trial

(18) The court may order that a witness whose evidence is necessary at trial may give evidence before trial at a place and before a person named in the order, and then may accept the transcript as evidence.

Taking Evidence Before Trial Outside Ontario

(19) If a witness whose evidence is necessary at trial lives outside Ontario, subrules 20(14) and (15) (questioning person outside Ontario, commissioner's duties) apply, with necessary changes.

Evidence by Affidavit or Electronic Recording

(20) The court may allow a witness to give evidence at trial by affidavit or electronic recording if,

(a) the parties consent;

(b) the witness is ill or unavailable to come to court for some other good reason;

(c) the evidence concerns minor or uncontroversial issues; or

(d) it is in the interests of justice to do so.

Direction, Evidence by Affidavit

(20.1) A direction made at a conference that the evidence of a witness be given by affidavit shall be followed at trial unless the trial judge orders otherwise.

Conditions for Use of Affidavit or Electronic Recording

(21) Evidence at trial by affidavit or electronic recording may be used only if,

(a) the use is in accordance with an order under subrule (20);

(b) the evidence is served at least 30 days before the start of the trial; and

(c) the evidence would have been admissible if given by the witness in court.

Affidavit Evidence at Uncontested Trial

(22) At an uncontested trial, evidence by affidavit in Form 14A or Form 23C and, if applicable, Form 35.1 may be used without an order under subrule (20), unless the court directs that oral evidence must be given.

Expert Witness Reports

(23) A party who wants to call an expert witness at trial shall serve on all other parties a report signed by the expert and containing the information listed in subrule (25),

(a) at least 90 days before the start of the trial; or

(b) in the case of a child protection case, at least 30 days before the start of the trial.

(c) [Repealed O. Reg. 6/10, s. 8(4).]

Same, Response

(24) A party who wants to call an expert witness at trial to respond to the expert witness of another party shall serve on all other parties a report signed by the expert and containing the information listed in subrule (25),

(a) at least 60 days before the start of the trial; or

(b) in the case of a child protection case, at least 14 days before the start of the trial.

Same, Contents

(25) A report provided for the purposes of subrule (1) or (2) shall contain the following information:

1. The expert's name, address and area of expertise.

2. The expert's qualifications and employment and educational experiences in his or her area of expertise.

3. The substance of the expert's proposed evidence.

Supplementary Report

(26) Any supplementary expert witness report shall be signed by the expert and served on all other parties,

(a) at least 30 days before the start of the trial; or

(b) in the case of a child protection case, at least 14 days before the start of the trial.

Failure to Serve Expert Witness Report

(27) A party who has not followed a requirement under subrule (23), (24) or (26) to serve and file an expert witness report, may not call the expert witness unless the trial judge allows otherwise.

O. Reg. 544/99, s. 9; 202/01, s. 6; 92/03, s. 2; 6/10, s. 8

RULE 24 — COSTS

Successful Party Presumed Entitled to Costs

24. (1) There is a presumption that a successful party is entitled to the costs of a motion, enforcement, case or appeal.

No Presumption in Child Protection Case or if Party is Government Agency

(2) The presumption does not apply in a child protection case or to a party that is a government agency.

Court's Discretion — Costs for or Against Government Agency

(3) The court has discretion to award costs to or against a party that is a government agency, whether it is successful or unsuccessful.

Successful Party Who has Behaved Unreasonably

(4) Despite subrule (1), a successful party who has behaved unreasonably during a case may be deprived of all or part of the party's own costs or ordered to pay all or part of the unsuccessful party's costs.

Decision on Reasonableness

(5) In deciding whether a party has behaved reasonably or unreasonably, the court shall examine,

(a) the party's behaviour in relation to the issues from the time they arose, including whether the party made an offer to settle;

(b) the reasonableness of any offer the party made; and

(c) any offer the party withdrew or failed to accept.

Divided Success

(6) If success in a step in a case is divided, the court may apportion costs as appropriate.

Absent or Unprepared Party

(7) If a party does not appear at a step in the case, or appears but is not properly prepared to deal with the issues at that step, the court shall award costs against the party unless the court orders otherwise in the interests of justice.

Bad Faith

(8) If a party has acted in bad faith, the court shall decide costs on a full recovery basis and shall order the party to pay them immediately.

Costs Caused by Fault of Lawyer or Agent

(9) If a party's lawyer or agent has run up costs without reasonable cause or has wasted costs, the court may, on motion or on its own initiative, after giving the lawyer or agent an opportunity to be heard,

(a) order that the lawyer or agent shall not charge the client fees or disbursements for work specified in the order, and order the lawyer or agent to repay money that the client has already paid toward costs;

(b) order the lawyer or agent to repay the client any costs that the client has been ordered to pay another party;

(c) order the lawyer or agent personally to pay the costs of any party; and

(d) order that a copy of an order under this subrule be given to the client.

Costs to be Decided at Each Step

(10) Promptly after each step in the case, the judge or other person who dealt with that step shall decide in a summary manner who, if anyone, is entitled to costs, and set the amount of costs.

Factors in Costs

(11) A person setting the amount of costs shall consider,

(a) the importance, complexity or difficulty of the issues;

(b) the reasonableness or unreasonableness of each party's behaviour in the case;

(c) the lawyer's rates;

(d) the time properly spent on the case, including conversations between the lawyer and the party or witnesses, drafting documents and correspondence, attempts to settle, preparation, hearing, argument, and preparation and signature of the order;

(e) expenses properly paid or payable; and

(f) any other relevant matter.

Payment of Expenses

(12) The court may make an order that a party pay an amount of money to another party to cover part or all of the expenses of carrying on the case, including a lawyer's fees.

Order for Security for Costs

(13) A judge may, on motion, make an order for security for costs that is just, based on one or more of the following factors:

1. A party ordinarily resides outside Ontario.

2. A party has an order against the other party for costs that remains unpaid, in the same case or another case.

3. A party is a corporation and there is good reason to believe it does not have enough assets in Ontario to pay costs.

4. There is good reason to believe that the case is a waste of time or a nuisance and that the party does not have enough assets in Ontario to pay costs.

5. A statute entitles the party to security for costs.

Amount and Form of Security

(14) The judge shall determine the amount of the security, its form and the method of giving it.

Effect of Order for Security

(15) Until the security has been given, a party against whom there is an order for security for costs may not take any step in the case, except to appeal from the order, unless a judge orders otherwise.

Failure to Give Security

(16) If the party does not give the security as ordered, a judge may, on motion, dismiss the party's case or strike out the party's answer or any other document filed by the party, and then subrule (15) no longer applies.

Security may be Changed

(17) The amount of the security, its form and the method of giving it may be changed by order at any time.

O. Reg. 544/99, s. 10

RULE 25 — ORDERS

Consent Order

25. (1) If the parties agree, the court may make an order under these rules or an Act without having the parties or their lawyers come to court.

Successful Party Prepares Draft Order

(2) The party in whose favour an order is made shall prepare a draft of the order (Form 25, 25A, 25B, 25C or 25D), unless the court orders otherwise.

Other Party may Prepare Draft Order

(3) If the party in whose favour an order is made does not have a lawyer or does not prepare a draft order within 10 days after the order is made, any other party may prepare the draft order, unless the court orders otherwise.

Approval of Draft Order

(4) A party who prepares an order shall serve a draft, for approval of its form and content, on every other party who was in court or was represented when the order was made (including a child who has a lawyer).

Settling Contents of Disputed Order

(5) Unless the court orders otherwise, a party who disagrees with the form or content of a draft order shall serve, on every party who was served under subrule (4) and on the party who served the draft order,

(a) a notice disputing approval (Form 25E);

(b) a copy of the order, redrafted as proposed; and

(c) notice of a time and date at which the clerk will settle the order by telephone conference.

Time and Date

(6) The time and date shall be set by the clerk and shall be within five days after service of the notice disputing approval.

Disputed Order — Settlement by Judge

(7) If unable to settle the order at the telephone conference, the clerk shall, as soon as possible, refer the order to the judge who made it, to be settled at a further telephone conference, unless the judge orders the parties to come to court for settlement of the order.

No Approval Required if no Response from Other Party

(8) If no approval or notice disputing approval (Form 25E) is served within 10 days after the draft order is served for approval, it may be signed without approval.

No Approval Required for Certain Orders

(9) If an order dismisses a motion, case or appeal, without costs, or is prepared by the clerk under subrule (11), it may be signed without approval.

No Approval Required in Emergencies

(10) If the delay involved in getting an order approved would have serious consequences, the judge who made it may sign it without approval.

When Clerk Prepares Order

(11) The clerk shall prepare the order for signature,

(a) within 10 days after it is made, if no party has a lawyer;

(b) as soon as it is made,

(i) if it is a support deduction order or alternative payment order under the *Family Responsibility and Support Arrears Enforcement Act, 1996* or an order under the *Interjurisdictional Support Orders Act, 2002*,

(i.1) if it is a restraining order under section 35 of the *Children's Law Reform Act* or section 46 of the *Family Law Act*,

(i.2) if it is an order terminating a restraining order referred to in subclause (i.1), or

(ii) if the judge directs the clerk to do so.

Restraining Orders

(11.1) A restraining order referred to in subclause 11(b)(i.1) shall be in Form 25F or 25G.

(11.2) An order terminating a restraining order referred to in subclause 11(b)(i.1) shall be in Form 25H.

Who Signs Order

(12) An order may be signed by the judge who made it or by the clerk.

Service of Order

(13) Unless the court orders otherwise, the person who prepared an order shall serve it, by regular service (subrule 6(2)) or by mail, fax or electronic mail to the person's last known address,

(a) on every other party, including a respondent to whom subrule 10(5) (no notice to respondent) applies;

(b) if a child involved in the case has a lawyer, on the lawyer; and

(c) on any other person named by the court.

Support Deduction Order Not Served

(14) A support deduction order under the *Family Responsibility and Support Arrears Enforcement Act, 1996* does not have to be served.

Service of Crown Wardship Order

(15) An order for Crown wardship under Part III of the *Child and Family Services Act* shall be served on the following persons, in addition to the ones mentioned in subrule (13):

1. The child, if that Act requires notice to the child.

2. Any foster parent or other person who is entitled to notice under subsection 39(3) of that Act.

3. A Director appointed under that Act.

Service of Secure Treatment Order

(16) An order for secure treatment under Part VI of the *Child and Family Services Act* shall be served on the administrator of the secure treatment program, in addition to the persons mentioned in subrule (13).

Service of Adoption Order

(17) An adoption order shall be served on the following persons, in addition to the ones mentioned in subrule (13):

1. The adopted child, if the child gave consent under subsection 137(6) of the *Child and Family Services Act.*

2. The persons mentioned in subsection 162(3) of that Act.

Effective Date

(18) An order is effective from the date on which it is made, unless it states otherwise.

Changing Order — Fraud, Mistake, Lack of Notice

(19) The court may, on motion, change an order that,

(a) was obtained by fraud;

(b) contains a mistake;

(c) needs to be changed to deal with a matter that was before the court but that it did not decide;

(d) was made without notice; or

(e) was made with notice, if an affected party was not present when the order was made because the notice was inadequate or the party was unable, for a reason satisfactory to the court, to be present.

Same

(20) Rule 14 applies with necessary modifications to a motion to change a final order under subrule (19) and, for the purpose, clause 14(6)(a) shall be read as if the reference to a temporary order were a reference to a final order.

O. Reg. 56/03, s. 3; 76/06, s. 6; 151/08, s. 6; 386/09, s. 1

RULE 26 — ENFORCEMENT OF ORDERS

Where to Enforce an Order

26. (1) The place for enforcement of an order is governed by subrules 5(5) and (6) (place for starting enforcement).

How to Enforce an Order

(2) An order that has not been obeyed may, in addition to any other method of enforcement provided by law, be enforced as provided by subrules (3) and (4).

Payment Orders

(3) A payment order may be enforced by,

(a) a request for a financial statement (subrule 27(1));

(b) a request for disclosure from an income source (subrule 27(7));

(c) a financial examination (subrule 27(11));

(d) seizure and sale (rule 28);

(e) garnishment (rule 29);

(f) a default hearing (rule 30), if the order is a support order;

(g) the appointment of a receiver under section 101 of the *Courts of Justice Act*; and

(h) registration under section 42 of the *Family Responsibility and Support Arrears Enforcement Act, 1996*.

Other Orders

(4) An order other than a payment order may be enforced by,

(a) a writ of temporary seizure of property (subrule 28(10));

(b) a contempt order (rule 31); and

(c) the appointment of a receiver under section 101 of the *Courts of Justice Act*.

Statement of Money Owed

(5) A statement of money owed shall be in Form 26, with a copy of the order that is in default attached.

Special Forms for Statement of Money Owed

(6) Despite subrule (5),

(a) if the *Family Responsibility and Support Arrears Enforcement Act, 1996* applies, a statement of arrears in the form used by the Director may be used instead of Form 26;

(b) if the *Interjurisdictional Support Orders Act, 2002* applies, a document receivable under section 49 of that Act may be used instead of Form 26.

Recipient's or Director's Entitlement to Costs

(7) Unless the court orders otherwise, the recipient or the Director is entitled to the costs,

(a) of carrying out a financial examination; and

(b) of issuing, serving, filing and enforcing a writ of seizure and sale, a writ of temporary seizure and a notice of garnishment and of changing them by statutory declaration.

Enforcement of Administrative Costs

(8) For the purpose of subrule (7), the recipient or the Director may collect under a writ of seizure and sale, a notice of garnishment or a statutory declaration changing either of them,

(a) the amounts set out in the regulations under the *Administration of Justice Act* and awarded under rule 24 (costs) for filing and renewing with the sheriff a writ of seizure and sale or a writ of temporary seizure;

(b) payments made to a sheriff, clerk, official examiner, court reporter or other public officer in accordance with the regulations under the *Administration of Justice Act* and awarded under rule 24 (costs), on filing with the sheriff or clerk a copy of a receipt for each payment or an affidavit setting out the payments made; and

(c) the actual expense for carrying out a financial examination, or any other costs to which the recipient or the Director is entitled under subrule (7), on filing with the sheriff or clerk an affidavit (Form 26A) setting out the items of expense in detail.

Affidavit for Filing Domestic Contract or Paternity Agreement

(9) An affidavit for filing a domestic contract or paternity agreement under subsection 35(1) of the *Family Law Act* shall be in Form 26B.

Director's Status

(10) If the Director enforces an order under the *Family Responsibility and Support Arrears Enforcement Act, 1996*, anything in these rules relating to enforcement by the person in whose favour the order was made applies to the Director.

Filing and Refiling with the Director

(11) A person who files or refiles a support order in the Director's office shall immediately send notice of the filing, by mail, fax or electronic mail to the clerk at any court office where the recipient is enforcing the order.

Transferring Enforcement from Recipient to Director

(12) A recipient who files a support order in the Director's office shall, on the Director's request, assign to the Director any enforcement that the recipient has started, and then the Director may continue with the enforcement as if the Director had started it.

Transferring Enforcement from Director to Recipient

(13) If the parties withdraw a support order from the Director's office, the Director shall, on the recipient's request, given to the Director at the same time as the notice of withdrawal, assign to the recipient any enforcement that the Director has started, and then the recipient may continue with the enforcement as if the recipient had started it.

Notice of Transfer of Enforcement

(14) A person who continues an enforcement under subrule (12) or (13) shall immediately send a notice of transfer of enforcement (Form 26C), by mail, fax or electronic mail to,

(a) all parties to the enforcement;

(b) the clerk at every court office where the enforcement is being carried on; and

(c) every sheriff who is involved with the enforcement at the time of transfer.

Place of Registration of Support Order Under the **Divorce Act** *(Canada)*

(15) If a person wants to enforce an order for support made outside Ontario under the *Divorce Act* (Canada), the order shall be registered in a court, as defined in subsection 20(1) of that Act, as follows:

1. If the recipient resides in Ontario, in the municipality where the recipient resides.

2. If the recipient does not reside in Ontario, in the municipality where the payor resides.

3. If neither the recipient nor the payor resides in Ontario, in the municipality where any property owned by the payor is located or, if the payor doesn't have any property, in any municipality.

Place of Registration of Custody or Access Order Under the **Divorce Act** *(Canada)*

(16) If a person wants to enforce an order involving custody of or access to a child that is made outside Ontario under the *Divorce Act* (Canada), the order shall be registered in a court, as defined in subsection 20(1) of that Act, in accordance with clause 5(6)(a) of these rules.

Registration Requirements

(17) The person requesting the registration shall send to the court a certified copy of the order and a written request that the order be registered under paragraph 20(3)(a) of the *Divorce Act* (Canada).

O. Reg. 544/99, s. 11; 56/03, s. 4; 89/04, s. 9

RULE 27 — REQUIRING FINANCIAL INFORMATION

Request for Financial Statement

27. (1) If a payment order is in default, a recipient may serve a request for a financial statement (Form 27) on the payor.

Effect of Request for Financial Statement

(2) Within 15 days after being served with the request, the payor shall send a completed financial statement (Form 13) to the recipient by mail, fax or electronic mail.

Frequency of Requests for Financial Statements

(3) A recipient may request a financial statement only once in a six-month period, unless the court gives the recipient permission to do so more often.

Application of Rule 13

(4) If a party is required under this rule to give a financial statement, the following subrules apply with necessary changes:

13(6) (full disclosure)

13(7) or (7.1) (income tax documents)

13(11) (additional information)

13(12) (updating financial statement)

13(15) (correcting and updating)

13(16) (order to file statement)

13(17) (failure to file).

Order for Financial Statement

(5) The court may, on motion, order a payor to serve and file a financial statement.

Failure to Obey Order

(6) If the payor does not serve and file a financial statement within 10 days after being served with the order, the court may, on motion with special service (subrule 6(3)), order that the payor be imprisoned continuously or intermittently for not more than 40 days.

Request for Statement of Income from Income Source

(7) If a payment order is in default, the recipient may serve a request for a statement of income (Form 27A) on an income source of the payor, requiring the income source to prepare and send to the recipient, by mail, fax or electronic mail a statement of income (Form 27B).

Frequency of Requests for Statement of Income

(8) A recipient may request a statement of income from an income source only once in a six-month period, unless the court gives the recipient permission to do so more often.

Order for Statement of Income

(9) The court may, on the recipient's motion, order an income source to serve and file a statement of income.

Income Source's Failure to Obey Order

(10) If the income source does not serve and file a statement of income within 10 days after being served with the order, the court may, on the recipient's motion, order the income source to post a bond (Form 32).

Appointment for Financial Examination

(11) If a payment order is in default, the recipient may serve on the payor, by special service (subrule 6(3)), an appointment for a financial examination (Form 27C), requiring the payor to,

(a) come to a financial examination;

(b) bring to the examination any document or thing named in the appointment that is in the payor's control or available to the payor on request, relevant to the enforcement of the order, and not protected by a legal privilege; and

(c) serve a financial statement (Form 13) on the recipient, not later than seven days before the date of the examination.

Financial Examination of Person Other than Payor

(12) If a payment order is in default and a person other than the payor may know about the matters listed in subrule (17), the recipient may require that person to come to a financial examination by serving a summons to witness (Form 23) and the witness fee (subrule 23(4)) on the person by special service (subrule 6(3)).

Place Where Financial Examination Held

(13) A financial examination shall be held,

(a) in a place where the parties and the person to be examined agree;

(b) where the person to be examined lives in Ontario, in the municipality where the person lives; or

(c) in a place chosen by the court.

Other Rules Apply

(14) Subrules 19(4), (5) and (8) (documents protected by legal privilege, use of privileged documents, documents omitted from affidavit) and 23(7) (failure to obey summons) apply to a financial examination, with necessary changes.

Notice of Time and Place of Examination

(15) A payor who is served with an appointment or a person who is served with a summons for a financial examination shall have at least 10 days' notice of the time and place of the examination.

Before Whom Examination is Held, Method of Recording

(16) A financial examination shall be held under oath or affirmation, before a person chosen by agreement of the payor and recipient or in accordance with subrule 20(12) (other arrangements for questioning), and shall be recorded by a method chosen in the same way.

Scope of Examination

(17) On a financial examination, the payor or other person may be questioned about,

(a) the reason for the payor's default;

(b) the payor's income and property;

(c) the debts owed to and by the payor;

(d) the disposal of any property by the payor either before or after the making of the order that is in default;

(e) the payor's past, present and future ability to pay under the order;

(f) whether the payor intends to obey the order, and any reason for not doing so; and

(g) any other matter relevant to the enforcement of the order.

Resistance to Examination

(18) Subrule (19) applies if a payor who is served with an appointment or a person who is served with a summons for a financial examination,

(a) does not come to the examination as required by the appointment or summons;

(b) does not serve on the recipient a financial statement as required by the appointment;

(c) comes to the examination, but does not bring a document or thing named in the appointment or summons; or

(d) comes to the examination, but refuses to take an oath or affirm or to answer a question.

Order for Another Examination

(19) The court may, on motion, make an order and give directions for another financial examination of the payor or other person and may in addition require the payor or person to post a bond (Form 32).

Imprisonment

(20) If a payor or other person, without sufficient excuse, fails to obey an order or direction made under subrule (19), the court may, on motion with special service (subrule 6(3)), order that the payor or person be imprisoned continuously or intermittently for not more than 40 days.

Imprisonment Power is Additional

(21) The court may exercise its power under subrule (20) in addition to or instead of its power of forfeiture under rule 32 (bonds, recognizances and warrants).

Frequency of Examinations

(22) A recipient may conduct only one financial examination of a payor and one financial examination of any other person in a six-month period, or more often with the court's permission.

O. Reg. 544/99, s. 12; 89/04, s. 10

RULE 28 — SEIZURE AND SALE

Issue of Writ of Seizure and Sale

28. (1) The clerk shall issue a writ of seizure and sale (Form 28) if a recipient files,

(a) a request for a writ of seizure and sale (Form 28A); and

(b) a statement of money owed (subrules 26(5) and (6)).

Statutory Declaration to Change Amount Owed

(2) The statutory declaration to sheriff mentioned in section 44 of the *Family Responsibility and Support Arrears Enforcement Act, 1996* shall be in Form 28B.

Statutory Declaration if Order Changed

(3) If a court changes a payment order that is being enforced by a writ of seizure and sale, a statutory declaration to sheriff (Form 28B) may be filed with the sheriff and once filed, it has the same effect as a declaration mentioned in subrule (2).

Duration of Writ

(4) A writ of seizure and sale continues in effect until,

(a) the recipient withdraws it under subrule (7); or

(b) the court orders otherwise under subrule (8).

Writ Issued Under Former Rules

(5) A writ directing the sheriff to seize and sell a payor's property that was issued by the court under the rules that applied before these rules take effect has the same legal effect as a writ of seizure and sale issued under these rules, and does not expire except as subrule (4) provides.

Notifying Sheriff of Payment Received

(6) If a writ of seizure and sale has been filed with a sheriff,

(a) the recipient shall, on the sheriff's request, provide a statutory declaration setting out details of all payments received by or on behalf of the recipient; and

(b) the sheriff shall update the writ accordingly.

Withdrawing Writ

(7) The person who obtained a writ to enforce an order shall immediately withdraw it from every sheriff's office where it has been filed if,

(a) the person no longer wants to enforce the order by a writ;

(b) in the case of a payment order, the payor's obligation to make periodic payments under the order has ended and all other amounts owing under it have been paid; or

(c) in the case of any other order, the person against whom the writ was issued has obeyed the order.

Order Changing, Withdrawing or Suspending Writ

(8) The court may, on motion, make an order changing the terms of a writ, withdrawing it or temporarily suspending it, even if the writ was issued by another court in Ontario.

Service of Order

(9) The person making the motion, or another person named by the court, shall serve a copy of the order on,

(a) every sheriff in whose office the writ has been filed; and

(b) if the writ was issued by the court in another place, or by another court, on the clerk of the court in the other place or the clerk of the other court.

Writ of Temporary Seizure of Property

(10) The court may, on motion with special service (subrule 6(3)), give permission to issue a writ of temporary seizure (Form 28C) directing the sheriff to take possession of and hold all or part of the land and other property of a person against whom an order has been made and to hold any income from the property until the writ is withdrawn or the court orders otherwise.

Electronic Writs

(11) If a recipient is entitled to the issue of a writ of seizure and sale by the Superior Court of Justice, the recipient is entitled to the electronic issue and filing of the writ in accordance with the *Rules of Civil Procedure*.

O. Reg. 544/99, s. 13; 89/04, s. 11

RULE 29 — GARNISHMENT

Issue of Notice or Notices of Garnishment

29. (1) The clerk shall issue as many notices of garnishment (Form 29A or 29B) as a recipient requests if the recipient files,

(a) a request for garnishment (Form 29) or an extra-provincial garnishment process referred to in section 50 of the *Family Responsibility and Support Arrears Enforcement Act, 1996*; and

(b) a statement of money owed (subrules 26(5) and (6)).

One Recipient and One Garnishee per Notice

(2) Each notice of garnishment shall name only one recipient and one garnishee.

Service on Payor and Garnishee

(3) The notice of garnishment shall be served on the payor and on the garnishee but the payor shall, in addition, be served with the documents filed under subrule (1).

Effect of Notice of Garnishment

(4) A notice of garnishment attaches,

(a) every debt that is payable by the garnishee to the payor at the time the notice is served; and

(b) every debt that is payable by the garnishee to the payor,

(i) after the notice is served, or

(ii) on the fulfilment of a condition after the notice is served.

Duration

(5) The notice of garnishment continues in effect from the time of service on the garnishee until it is withdrawn or stopped under this rule or until the court orders otherwise under this rule.

Financial Institution

(6) If the garnishee is a financial institution, the notice of garnishment and all further notices required to be served under this rule shall be served at the branch of the institution where the debt to the payor is payable, unless subrule (6.1) applies.

Federally Regulated Financial Institution — Garnishment Re Support

(6.1) If the garnishee is a financial institution to which the *Bank Act* (Canada), the *Cooperative Credit Associations Act* (Canada) or the *Trust and Loan Companies Act* (Canada) applies and the garnishment enforces a support order, the notice of garnishment and all further notices required to be served under this rule,

(a) shall be served at the designated office of the institution established for this purpose; and

(b) shall be accompanied by a statement to garnishee financial institution re support (Form 29J).

New Accounts

(6.2) Subrules (4) and (5) do not apply to money in an account opened after a notice of garnishment is served as described in subrule (6) or (6.1).

Joint Debts Garnishable

(7) Subrules (4) and (5) also apply to debts owed to the payor and another person jointly.

Procedure When Joint Debt Garnished

(8) If a garnishee has been served with a notice of garnishment and the garnishee owes a debt to which subrules (4) and (5) apply to the payor and another person jointly,

(a) the garnishee shall pay, in accordance with subrule (11), half of the debt, or the larger or smaller amount that the court orders;

(b) the garnishee shall immediately send the other person a notice to co-owner of debt (Form 29C) by mail, fax or electronic mail, to the person's address in the garnishee's records; and

(c) the garnishee shall immediately serve the notice to co-owner of debt on the recipient or the Director, depending on who is enforcing the order, and on the sheriff or clerk if the sheriff or clerk is to receive the money under subrule (11) or (12).

Joint Debt — Money to be Held

(9) Despite subrule (12), if served with notice under clause (8)(c), the sheriff, clerk or Director shall hold the money received for 30 days, and may pay it out when the 30 days expire, unless the other person serves and files a dispute within the 30 days.

Payment of Arrears Does not End Garnishment

(10) A notice of garnishment continues to attach future periodic payments even though the total amount owed when it was served is fully paid up.

Persons to Whom Garnishee Makes Payments

(11) A garnishee who has been served with a notice of garnishment shall make the required payments to,

(a) the Director, if the notice of garnishment relates to an order being enforced by the Director;

(b) the clerk, if the notice of garnishment does not relate to an order being enforced by the Director.

Clerk or Director to Pay Out Money

(12) On receiving money under a notice of garnishment, the Director or clerk shall, even if a dispute has been filed, but subject to subrules (9) and (13), immediately pay,

(a) to the recipient, any part of the money that comes within the priority created by subsection 4(1) of the *Creditors' Relief Act;* and

(b) to the sheriff, any part of the money that exceeds that priority.

Order that Subrule (12) Does not Apply

(13) The court may, at a garnishment hearing or on a motion to change the garnishment under this rule, order that subrule (12) does not apply.

Change in Garnishment, Indexed Support

(14) If a notice of garnishment enforces a support order that indexes periodic payments for inflation, the recipient may serve on the garnishee and on the payor a statutory declaration of indexed support (Form 29D) setting out the new amount to be paid under the order, and file the declaration with the court.

Effect of Statutory Declaration of Indexed Support

(15) A statutory declaration of indexed support requires the garnishee to pay the new amount set out in the declaration from the time it is served on the garnishee.

Garnishment Dispute

(16) Within 10 days after being served with a notice of garnishment or a statutory declaration of indexed support, a payor, garnishee or co-owner of a debt may serve on the other parties and file a dispute (Form 29E, 29F or 29G).

Notice of Garnishment Hearing

(17) The clerk shall, on request, issue a notice of garnishment hearing (Form 29H),

(a) within 10 days after a dispute is served and filed; or

(b) if the recipient says that the garnishee has not paid any money or has not paid enough money.

Service of Notice

(18) The clerk shall serve and file the notice not later than 10 days before the hearing.

Garnishment Hearing

(19) At a garnishment hearing, the court may make one or more of the following temporary or final orders:

1. An order dismissing the dispute.

2. An order that changes how much is being garnished on account of a periodic payment order. The court may make an order under this paragraph even if it does not have the authority to change the payment order itself.

2.1 An order that changes how much is being garnished on account of a periodic payment order and that, at the same time, changes the payment order itself. The court may make an order under this paragraph only if,

i. the payment order is one that the court has the authority to change, and

ii. the parties to the payment order agree to the change, or one of those parties has served and filed notice of a motion to have the change made.

3. An order changing how much is being garnished on account of a non-periodic payment order.

4. An order suspending the garnishment or any term of it, while the hearing is adjourned or until the court orders otherwise.

5. An order setting aside the notice of garnishment or any statutory declaration of indexed support.

6. An order that garnished money held or received by the clerk, Director or sheriff be held in court.

7. An order that garnished money that has been paid out in error to the recipient be paid into and held in court, returned to the garnishee or sent to the payor or to the co-owner of the debt.

8. An order that garnished money held in court be returned to the garnishee or be sent to the payor, the co-owner of the debt, the sheriff, the clerk or the Director.

9. An order deciding how much remains owing under a payment order that is being enforced by garnishment against the payor or garnishee.

10. If the garnishee has not paid what was required by the notice of garnishment or statutory declaration of indexed support, an order that the garnishee pay all or part of what was required.

11. An order deciding who is entitled to the costs of the garnishment hearing and setting the amount of the costs.

Changing Garnishment at Other Times

(20) The court may also use the powers listed in subrule (19), on motion or on its own initiative, even if the notice of garnishment was issued by another court,

(a) on a motion under section 7 of the *Wages Act;*

(b) if the court replaces a temporary payment order with a final payment order;

(c) if the court indexes or changes a payment order; or

(d) if the court allows an appeal.

Changing Garnishment When Ability to Pay Changes

(21) If there has been a material change in the payor's circumstances affecting the payor's ability to pay, the court may, on motion, use the powers listed in subrule (19).

Garnishee's Payment Pays Debt

(22) Payment of a debt by a garnishee under a notice of garnishment or statutory declaration of indexed support pays off the debt between the garnishee and the payor to the extent of the payment.

Notice by Garnishee — Payor not Working or Receiving Money

(23) Within 10 days after a payor stops working for or is no longer receiving any money from a garnishee, the garnishee shall send a notice as subrule (27) requires,

(a) saying that the payor is no longer working for or is no longer receiving any money from the garnishee;

(b) giving the date on which the payor stopped working for or receiving money from the garnishee and the date of the last payment to the payor from the garnishee; and

(c) giving the name and address of any other income source of the payor, if known.

Notice by Garnishee — Payor Working or Receiving Money Again

(24) Within 10 days after the payor returns to work for or starts to receive money again from the garnishee, the garnishee shall send another notice as subrule (27) requires, saying that the payor has returned to work for or started to receive money again from the garnishee.

Notice by Payor — Working or Receiving Money Again

(25) Within 10 days after returning to work for or starting to receive money again from the garnishee, the payor shall send a notice as subrule (27) requires, saying that the payor has returned to work for or started to receive money again from the garnishee.

Notice by Payor — New Income Source

(26) Within 10 days after starting to work for or receive money from a new income source, the payor shall send a notice as subrule (27) requires, saying that the payor has started to work for or to receive money from the new income source.

Notice Sent to Clerk and Recipient or Director

(27) A notice referred to in subrule (23), (24), (25) or (26) shall be sent to the clerk, and to the recipient or the Director (depending on who is enforcing the order), by mail, fax or electronic mail.

Notice by Clerk

(28) When the clerk receives a notice under subrule (26), the clerk shall immediately notify the recipient or the Director (depending on who is enforcing the order) by mail, fax or electronic mail.

New Notice of Garnishment

(29) If no written objection is received within 10 days of the clerk notifying the recipient or the Director that a notice under subrule (26) was received, the clerk shall,

(a) issue a new notice of garnishment directed to the new garnishee, requiring the same deductions as were required to be made, under the previous notice of garnishment or statutory declaration of indexed support, on the day that the notice under subrule (26) was received; and

(b) send a copy of the new notice of garnishment to the payor and the new garnishee, by mail, fax or electronic mail.

Effect of New Notice of Garnishment

(30) Issuing a new notice of garnishment under clause (29)(a) does not cancel any previous notice of garnishment or statutory declaration of indexed support.

Notice to Stop Garnishment

(31) The recipient shall immediately send a notice to stop garnishment (Form 29I), by mail, fax or electronic mail to the garnishee and payor and file it with the clerk if,

(a) the recipient no longer wants to enforce the order by garnishment; or

(b) the requirement to make periodic payments under the order has ended and all other amounts owing under the order have been paid.

Old Orders

(32) This rule applies, with necessary changes, to,

(a) an attachment order made under section 30 of the *Family Law Reform Act* (chapter 152 of the Revised Statutes of Ontario, 1980); and

(b) a garnishment order issued by the court under the rules that were in effect before January 1, 1985.

O. Reg. 544/99, s. 14; 56/03, s. 5; 76/06, s. 7

RULE 30 — DEFAULT HEARING

Issuing Notice of Default Hearing

30. (1) The clerk shall issue a notice of default hearing (Form 30),

(a) if the support order is being enforced by the recipient, when the recipient files a request for a default hearing (Form 30A) and a statement of money owed (subrule 26(5));

(b) if it is being enforced by the Director, when the Director files a statement of money owed.

Serving Notice of Default Hearing

(2) The notice of default hearing shall be served on the payor by special service (subrule 6(3)) and filed.

Payor's Dispute

(3) Within 10 days after being served with the notice, the payor shall serve on the recipient and file,

(a) a financial statement (Form 13); and

(b) a default dispute (Form 30B).

Updating Statement of Money Owed

(4) The recipient shall serve and file a new statement of money owed (subrule 26(5)) not more than seven days before the default hearing.

When Director to Update Statement

(5) Despite subrule 26(10), subrule (4) applies to the Director only if,

(a) the amount the Director is asking the court to enforce is greater than the amount shown in the notice of default hearing; or

(b) the court directs it.

Statement of Money Owed Presumed Correct

(6) The payor is presumed to admit that the recipient's statement of money owed is correct, unless the payor has filed a default dispute stating that the statement of money owed is not correct and giving detailed reasons.

Arrears Enforceable to Date of Hearing

(7) At the default hearing, the court may decide and enforce the amount owing as of the date of the hearing.

Conditional Imprisonment

(8) The court may make an order under clause 41(10)(h) or (i) of the *Family Responsibility and Support Arrears Enforcement Act, 1996*, suspending the payor's imprisonment on appropriate conditions.

Issuing Warrant of Committal

(9) If the recipient, on a motion with special service (subrule 6(3)) on the payor, states by affidavit (or by oral evidence, with the court's permission) that the payor has not obeyed a condition that was imposed under subrule (8), the court may issue a warrant of committal against the payor, subject to subsection 41(15) (power to change order) of the *Family Responsibility and Support Arrears Enforcement Act, 1996.*

O. Reg. 76/06, s. 8

RULE 31 — CONTEMPT OF COURT

When Contempt Motion Available

31. (1) An order, other than a payment order, may be enforced by a contempt motion made in the case in which the order was made, even if another penalty is available.

Notice of Contempt Motion

(2) The notice of contempt motion (Form 31) shall be served together with a supporting affidavit, by special service as provided in clause 6(3)(a), unless the court orders otherwise.

Affidavit for Contempt Motion

(3) The supporting affidavit may contain statements of information that the person signing the affidavit learned from someone else, but only if the requirements of subrule 14(19) are satisfied.

Warrant to Bring to Court

(4) To bring before the court a person against whom a contempt motion is made, the court may issue a warrant for the person's arrest if,

(a) the person's attendance is necessary in the interest of justice; and

(b) the person is not likely to attend voluntarily.

Contempt Orders

(5) If the court finds a person in contempt of the court, it may order that the person,

(a) be imprisoned for any period and on any conditions that are just;

(b) pay a fine in any amount that is appropriate;

(c) pay an amount to a party as a penalty;

(d) do anything else that the court decides is appropriate;

(e) not do what the court forbids;

(f) pay costs in an amount decided by the court; and

(g) obey any other order.

Writ of Temporary Seizure

(6) The court may also give permission to issue a writ of temporary seizure (Form 28C) against the person's property.

Limited Imprisonment or Fine

(7) In a contempt order under one of the following provisions, the period of imprisonment and the amount of a fine may not be greater than the relevant Act allows:

1. Section 38 of the *Children's Law Reform Act.*

2. Section 49 of the *Family Law Act.*

3. Section 53 of the *Family Responsibility and Support Arrears Enforcement Act, 1996.*

Conditional Imprisonment or Fine

(8) A contempt order for imprisonment or for the payment of a fine may be suspended on appropriate conditions.

Issuing Warrant of Committal

(9) If a party, on a motion with special service (subrule 6(3)) on the person in contempt, states by an affidavit in Form 32C (or by oral evidence, with the court's permission) that the person has not obeyed a condition imposed under subrule (8), the court may issue a warrant of committal against the person.

Payment of Fine

(10) A contempt order for the payment of a fine shall require the person in contempt to pay the fine,

(a) in a single payment, immediately or before a date that the court chooses; or

(b) in instalments, over a period of time that the court considers appropriate.

Corporation in Contempt

(11) If a corporation is found in contempt, the court may also make an order under subrule (5), (6) or (7) against any officer or director of the corporation.

Change in Contempt Order

(12) The court may, on motion, change an order under this rule, give directions and make any other order that is just.

RULE 32 — BONDS, RECOGNIZANCES AND WARRANTS

Warrant to Bring a Person to Court

32. (1) If a person does not come to court after being served with notice of a case, enforcement or motion that may result in an order requiring the person to post a bond,

(a) the court may issue a warrant for the person's arrest, to bring the person before the court, and adjourn the case to await the person's arrival; or

(b) the court may,

(i) hear and decide the case in the person's absence and, if appropriate, make an order requiring the person to post a bond, and

(ii) if the person has been served with the order and does not post the bond by the date set out in the order, issue a warrant for the person's arrest, on motion without notice, to bring the person before the court.

Form of Bond and Other Requirements

(2) A bond shall be in Form 32, does not need a seal, and shall,

(a) have at least one surety, unless the court orders otherwise;

(b) list the conditions that the court considers appropriate;

(c) set out an amount of money to be forfeited if the conditions are not obeyed;

(d) shall require the person posting the bond to deposit the money with the clerk immediately, unless the court orders otherwise; and

(e) name the person to whom any forfeited money is to be paid out.

Person Before Whom Recognizance to be Entered into

(3) A recognizance shall be entered into before a judge, a justice of the peace or the clerk.

Change of Conditions in a Bond

(4) The court may, on motion, change any condition in a bond if there has been a material change in a party's circumstances since the date of the order for posting the bond or the date of an order under this subrule, whichever is more recent.

Change in Bond under Children's Law Reform Act

(5) In the case of a bond under the *Children's Law Reform Act*, subrule (4) also applies to a material change in circumstances that affects or is likely to affect the best interests of the child.

Removal or Replacement of Surety

(6) The court may, on motion, order that a surety be removed or be replaced by another person as surety, in which case as soon as the order is made, the surety who is removed or replaced is free from any obligation under the bond.

Motion to Enforce Bond

(7) A person requesting the court's permission to enforce a bond under subsection 143(1) (enforcement of recognizance or bond) of the *Courts of Justice Act* shall serve a notice of forfeiture motion (Form 32A), with a copy of the bond attached, on the person said to have broken the bond and on each surety.

Forfeiture if no Deposit Made

(8) If an order of forfeiture of a bond is made and no deposit was required, or a deposit was required but was not made, the order shall require the payor or surety to pay the required amount to the person to whom the bond is payable,

(a) in a single payment, immediately or before a date that the court chooses; or

(b) in instalments, over a period of time that the court considers appropriate.

Change in Payment Schedule

(9) If time is allowed for payment under subrule (8), the court may, on a later motion by the payor or a surety, allow further time for payment.

Order for Forfeiture of Deposit

(10) If an order of forfeiture of a bond is made and a deposit was required and was made, the order shall direct the clerk to pay the required amount immediately to the person to whom the bond is made payable.

Cancelling Bond

(11) The court may, on motion, make an order under subrule (4), or an order cancelling the bond and directing a refund of all or part of the deposit, if,

(a) a payor or surety made a deposit under the bond;

(b) the conditions of the bond have not been broken; and

(c) the conditions have expired or, although they have not expired or do not have an expiry date, the payor or surety has good reasons for getting the conditions of the bond changed.

Form of Warrant for Arrest

(12) A warrant for arrest issued against any of the following shall be in Form 32B:

1. A payor who does not file a financial statement ordered under subsection 40(4) of the *Family Responsibility and Support Arrears Enforcement Act, 1996* or under these rules.

2. A payor who does not come to a default hearing under section 41 of the *Family Responsibility and Support Arrears Enforcement Act, 1996.*

3. An absconding respondent under subsection 43(1) or 59(2) of the *Family Law Act.*

4. An absconding payor under subsection 49(1) of the *Family Responsibility and Support Arrears Enforcement Act, 1996.*

5. A witness who does not come to court or remain in attendance as required by a summons to witness.

6. A person who does not come to court in a case that may result in an order requiring the person to post a bond under these rules.

7. A person who does not obey an order requiring the person to post a bond under these rules.

8. A person against whom a contempt motion is made.

9. Any other person liable to arrest under an order.

10. Any other person liable to arrest for committing an offence.

Bail on Arrest

(13) Section 150 (interim release by justice of the peace) of the *Provincial Offences Act* applies, with necessary changes, to an arrest made under a warrant mentioned in paragraph 1, 2, 3 or 4 of subrule (12).

Affidavit for Warrant of Committal

(14) An affidavit in support of a motion for a warrant of committal shall be in Form 32C.

Form of Warrant of Committal

(15) A warrant of committal issued to enforce an order of imprisonment shall be in Form 32D.

RULE 33 — CHILD PROTECTION

Timetable

33. (1) Every child protection case, including a status review application, is governed by the following timetable:

Step in the case	Maximum time for completion, from start of case
First hearing, if child has been apprehended	5 days
Service and filing of answers and plans of care	30 days
Temporary care and custody hearing	35 days
Settlement conference	80 days
Hearing	120 days

Case Management Judge

(2) Wherever possible, at the start of the case a judge shall be assigned to manage it and monitor its progress.

Court may Lengthen Times Only in Best Interests of Child

(3) The court may lengthen a time shown in the timetable only if the best interests of the child require it.

Parties may not Lengthen Times

(4) The parties may not lengthen a time shown in the timetable by consent under subrule 3(6).

Plan of Care or Supervision to be Served

(5) A party who wants the court to consider a plan of care or supervision shall serve it on the other parties and file it not later than seven days before a conference, even if that is sooner than the timetable would require.

Temporary Care and Custody Hearing — Affidavit Evidence

(6) The evidence at a temporary care and custody hearing shall be given by affidavit, unless the court orders otherwise.

Status Review

(6.1) A status review application under clause 64(2)(a) or (b) of the *Child and Family Services Act* shall be served at least 30 days before the date the order for society supervision or society wardship expires.

Forms for Child Protection Cases

(7) In a child protection case,

(a) an information for a warrant to apprehend a child shall be in Form 33;

(b) a warrant to apprehend a child shall be in Form 33A;

(c) an applicant's plan of care for a child shall be,

(i) if the applicant is a children's aid society, in Form 33B, and

(ii) if the applicant is not a children's aid society, in Form 33B.1;

(c.1) a respondent's answer and plan of care for a child shall be,

(i) if the respondent is not a children's aid society, in From 33B.1,

(ii) if the respondent is a children's aid society, in Form 10 and Form 33B;

(d) an agreed statement of facts in a child protection case shall be in Form 33C; and

(e) an agreed statement of facts in a status review application shall be in Form 33D.

Forms for Secure Treatment Cases

(8) In an application under Part VI (secure treatment) of the *Child and Family Services Act*, a consent signed by the child shall be in Form 33E and a consent signed by any other person shall be in Form 33F.

O. Reg. 91/03, s. 7; 76/06, s. 9

RULE 34 — ADOPTION

CFSA Definitions Apply

34. (1) The definitions in the *Child and Family Services Act* apply to this rule and, in particular,

"Director" means a Director within the meaning of the Act.

Meaning of "Act"

(2) In this rule,

"Act" means the *Child and Family Services Act.*

Use of Initials in Documents

(2.1) An applicant or respondent may be referred to by only the first letter of his or her surname in any document in the case, except that,

(a) the applicant's full names shall appear in the adoption order; and

(b) the child's full names shall appear in the adoption order, unless the court orders that the child's first name and the first letter of his or her surname be used.

Certified Copy of Order from Outside Ontario

(3) When this rule requires a copy of an order to be filed and the order in question was made outside Ontario, it shall be a copy that is certified by an official of the court or other authority that made it.

Material to be Filed with Adoption Applications

(4) The following shall be filed with every application for an adoption:

1. A certified copy of the statement of live birth of the child, or an equivalent that satisfies the court.

2. If required, the child's consent to adoption (Form 34) or a notice of motion and supporting affidavit for an order under subsection 137(9) of the Act dispensing with the child's consent.

3. If the child is not a Crown ward, an affidavit of parentage (Form 34A) or any other evidence about parentage that the court requires from the child's parent, or a person named by the court.

4. If the applicant has a spouse who has not joined in the application, a consent to the child's adoption by the spouse (Form 34B).

5. If required by the Act or by an order, a Director's or local director's statement on adoption (Form 34C) under subsection 149(1) or (6) of the Act.

6. An affidavit signed by the applicant (Form 34D) that includes details about the applicant's education, employment, health, background and ability to support and care for the child, a history of the relationship between the parent and the child and any other evidence relating to the best inter ests of the child, and states whether the child is an Indian or a native person.

Report of Child's Adjustment

(5) A report under subsection 149(5) or (6) of the Act of the child's adjustment in the applicant's home shall also be filed with the application if the child is under 16 years of age, or is 16 years of age or older but has not withdrawn from parental control and has not married.

Additional Material — Crown Ward

(6) If the child is a Crown ward, the following shall also be filed with the application:

1. A Director's consent to adoption (Form 34E).

2. A copy of any order under subsection 58(1) of the Act ending access to the child.

3. A copy of the order of Crown wardship.

4. Proof of service of the orders referred to in paragraphs 2 and 3, or a copy of any order dispensing with service.

5. An affidavit, signed by a person delegated by the local director of the children's aid society that has placed the child for adoption, stating that there is no appeal in progress from an order referred to in paragraph 2 or 3, or that the appeal period has expired without an appeal being filed, or that an appeal was filed but has been withdrawn or finally dismissed.

6. If the child is an Indian or native person, proof of 30 days written notice to the child's band or native community of the intention to place the child for adoption.

Additional Material — Child not Crown Ward

(7) If the child is not a Crown ward and is placed for adoption by a licensee or children's aid society, the following shall also be filed with the application:

1. A copy of any custody or access order that is in force and is known to the person placing the child, or to an applicant.

2. [Revoked O. Reg. 337/02, s. 3(4).]

3. A consent to adoption (Form 34F) under section 137 of the Act from every parent, other than the applicant, of whom the person placing the child or an applicant is aware. An order under section 138 of the Act dispensing with a parent's consent may be filed instead of the consent.

4. An affidavit (Form 34G) signed by the licensee or by an authorized employee of the children's aid society (depending on who is placing the child).

5. If the child is placed by a licensee, a copy of the licensee's licence to make the placement at the time of placing the child for adoption.

6. If the child is an Indian or native person, proof of 30 days written notice to the child's band or native community of the intention to place the child for adoption.

Additional Material — Relative or Step-parent

(8) If the applicant is the child's relative or the spouse of the child's parent, an affidavit from each applicant (Form 34H) shall also be filed with the application.

Application By Step-Parent or Relative

(9) An application by a relative of the child or the spouse of the child's parent,

(a) shall not be commenced until the 21-day period referred to in subsection 137(8) of the Act has expired; and

(b) shall be accompanied by the applicant's affidavit confirming that he or she did not receive a withdrawal of consent during the 21-day period.

Step-Parent Adoption, Parent's Consent

(10) An application by the spouse of the child's parent shall be accompanied by the parent's consent (Form 34I).

Independent Legal Advice, Child's Consent

(11) The consent of a child to be adopted (Form 34) shall be witnessed by a representative of the Children's Lawyer, who shall complete the affidavit of execution and independent legal advice contained in the form.

Independent Legal Advice, Consent of Parent Under 18

(11.1) The consent of a person under the age of 18 years who is a parent of the child to be adopted (Form 34F) shall be witnessed by a representative of the Children's Lawyer, who shall complete an affidavit of execution and independent legal advice (Form 34J).

Independent Legal Advice, Adult Parent's Consent

(12) The consent of an adult parent of the child to be adopted shall be witnessed by an independent lawyer, who shall complete the affidavit of execution and independent legal advice.

Copy of Consent for Person Signing

(13) A person who signs a consent to an adoption shall be given a copy of the consent and of the affidavit of execution and independent legal advice.

Withdrawal of Consent by Parent

(13.1) A parent who has given consent to an adoption under subsection 137(2) of the Act may withdraw the consent under subsection 137(8) of the Act in accordance with the following:

1. If the child is placed for adoption by a children's aid society, the parent who wishes to withdraw the consent shall ensure that the children's aid society receives the written withdrawal within 21 days after the consent was given.

2. If the child is placed for adoption by a licensee, the parent who wishes to withdraw the consent shall ensure that the licensee receives the written withdrawal within 21 days after the consent was given.

3. If a relative of the child or a spouse of a parent proposes to apply to adopt the child, the parent who wishes to withdraw the consent shall ensure that the relative or spouse receives the written withdrawal within 21 days after the consent was given.

Withdrawal of Consent by Child Aged Seven or Older

(13.2) A child who has given consent to an adoption under subsection 137(6) of the Act may withdraw the consent under subsection 137(8) of the Act in accordance with the following:

1. The withdrawal shall be signed within 21 days after the consent was given, and witnessed by the person who witnesses the consent under subrule (11) or by another representative of the Children's Lawyer.

2. The person who witnesses the withdrawal shall give the original withdrawal document to the child and promptly serve a copy on the children's aid society, licensee, relative or spouse, as the case may be, by regular service.

Motion to Withdraw Consent

(14) Despite subrule 5(4) (place for steps other than enforcement), a motion to withdraw a consent to an adoption under subsection 139(1) of the Act shall be made in,

(a) the municipality where the person who gave the consent lives; or

(b) in any other place that the court decides.

Clerk to Check Adoption Application

(15) Before the application is presented to a judge, the clerk shall,

(a) review the application and other documents filed to see whether they are in order; and

(b) prepare a certificate (Form 34K).

Dispensing With Consent Before Placement

(16) In an application to dispense with a parent's consent before placement for adoption,

(a) the applicant may be the licensee, a parent, the children's aid society or the person who wants to adopt;

(b) the respondent is the person who has not given consent;

(c) if an order that service is not required is sought, the request shall be made in the application and not by motion;

(d) if the application is being served, the applicant shall serve and file with it an affidavit (Form 14A) setting out the facts of the case;

(e) if the application is not being served, the applicant shall file with it an affidavit (Form 14A) setting out the facts of the case, and the clerk shall send the case to a judge for a decision on the basis of affidavit evidence.

Forms for Openness Applications

(17) In a case about an openness order under Part VII of the Act,

(a) an application for an openness order shall be in Form 34L;

(b) a consent to an openness order shall be in Form 34M;

(c) an application to change or terminate an openness order shall be in Form 34N; and

(d) an answer to an application to change or terminate an openness order shall be in Form 33B.2.

(18) [Spent December 31, 2004.]

O. Reg. 337/02, s. 3; 519/06, s. 6

RULE 35 — CHANGE OF NAME

Time for Application

35. (1) An application under subsection 7(3) (application to court for change of name) of the *Change of Name Act* shall be made within 30 days after the applicant is notified that the Registrar General has refused to make the requested change of name.

Service on the Registrar General

(2) The applicant shall serve the application and any supporting material on the Registrar General by delivering or mailing a copy of the documents to the Deputy Registrar General.

Registrar General's Reasons for Refusal

(3) Within 15 days after being served under subrule (2), the Registrar General may file reasons for refusing to make the requested change of name.

RULE 35.1 — CUSTODY AND ACCESS [HEADING ADDED O. REG. 6/10, S. 9.]

Definition

35.1 (1) In this rule,

"parent" means,

(a) a biological parent of a child,

(b) an adoptive parent of a child,

(c) an individual declared under Part II of the *Children's Law Reform Act* to be a parent of a child, and

(d) an individual presumed under section 8 of the *Children's Law Reform Act* to be the father of a child.

Affidavit in Support of Custody or Access Claim

(2) If an application, answer or motion to change a final order contains a claim for custody of or access to a child, the party making the claim shall serve and file an affidavit in support of claim for custody or access (Form 35.1), together with any other documents required by this rule, with the document that contains the claim.

Police Records Check

(3) Every person who makes a claim for custody of a child and who is not a parent of the child shall attach to the affidavit in support of claim for custody or access,

(a) a police records check obtained not more than 60 days before the person starts the claim; or

(b) if the person requested the police records check for the purposes of the claim but has not received it by the time he or she starts the claim, proof of the request.

Same

(4) If clause (3)(b) applies, the person shall serve and file the police records check no later than 10 days after receiving it.

Request for Report from Children's Aid Society

(5) Every person required to submit a request under subsection 21.2(2) of the *Children's Law Reform Act* for a report from a children's aid society shall provide to the court a copy of the request together with the affidavit in support of claim for custody or access.

Documents Shall be Refused

(6) If these rules require a document to be accompanied by the applicable documents referred to in this rule, the clerk shall not accept the document for filing without,

(a) an affidavit in support of claim for custody or access; and

(b) the documents referred to in subrules (3) and (5), if applicable.

Corrections and Updates

(7) As soon as a person discovers that information in his or her affidavit in support of claim for custody or access is incorrect or incomplete, or that there has been a change in the information provided in the affidavit, he or she shall immediately serve and file,

(a) a new affidavit in support of claim for custody or access (Form 35.1) containing the correct or updated information; or

(b) if the correction or change is minor, an affidavit in Form 14A describing the correction or change and indicating any effect it has on the person's plan for the care and upbringing of the child.

Associated Cases

(8) If the clerk provides to a person making a claim for custody of a child information in writing under subsection 21.3(1) of the *Children's Law Reform Act* respecting any current or previous family proceedings involving the child or any person who is a party to the claim and who is not a parent of the child, the person shall serve a copy of the written information on every other party.

Same

(9) If the written information provided by the clerk contains information indicating that the person making the claim was or is involved in family proceedings in which he or she was or is not involved, the person making the claim may serve with the copy of the written information an affidavit identifying those proceedings.

O. Reg. 6/10, s. 9

RULE 36 — DIVORCE

Application for Divorce

36. (1) Either spouse may start a divorce case by,

(a) filing an application naming the other spouse as a respondent; or

(b) filing a joint application with no respondent.

Joint Application

(2) In a joint application, the divorce and any other order sought shall be made only with the consent of both spouses.

Allegation of Adultery

(3) In an application for divorce claiming that the other spouse committed adultery with another person, that person does not need to be named, but if named, shall be served with the application and has all the rights of a respondent in the case.

Marriage Certificate and Central Divorce Registry Certificate

(4) The court shall not grant a divorce until the following have been filed:

1. A marriage certificate or marriage registration certificate, unless the application states that it is impractical to obtain a certificate and explains why.

2. A report on earlier divorce cases started by either spouse, issued under the *Central Registry of Divorce Proceedings Regulations* (Canada).

Divorce Based on Affidavit Evidence

(5) If the respondent files no answer, or files one and later withdraws it, the applicant shall file an affidavit (Form 36) that,

(a) confirms that all the information in the application is correct, except as stated in the affidavit;

(b) if no marriage certificate or marriage registration certificate has been filed, provides sufficient information to prove the marriage;

(c) contains proof of any previous divorce or the death of a party's previous spouse, unless the marriage took place in Canada;

(d) contains the information about arrangements for support of any children of the marriage required by paragraph 11(1)(b) of the *Divorce Act* (Canada), and attaches as exhibits the income and financial information required by section 21 of the child support guidelines; and

(e) contains any other information necessary for the court to grant the divorce.

Draft Divorce Order

(6) The applicant shall file with the affidavit,

(a) three copies of a draft divorce order (Form 25A);

(b) a stamped envelope addressed to each party; and

(c) if the divorce order is to contain a support order,

(i) an extra copy of the draft divorce order for the clerk to file with the Director of the Family Responsibility Office, and

(ii) two copies of a draft support deduction order.

Clerk to Present Papers to Judge

(7) When the documents mentioned in subrules (4) to (6) have been filed, the clerk shall prepare a certificate (Form 36A) and present the documents to a judge, who may,

(a) grant the divorce as set out in the draft order;

(b) have the clerk return the documents to the applicant to make any needed corrections; or

(c) grant the divorce but make changes to the draft order, or refuse to grant the divorce, after giving the applicant a chance to file an additional affidavit or come to court to explain why the order should be made without change.

Divorce Certificate

(8) When a divorce takes effect, the clerk shall, on either party's request,

(a) check the continuing record to verify that,

(i) no appeal has been taken from the divorce order, or any appeal from it has been disposed of, and

(ii) no order has been made extending the time for an appeal, or any extended time has expired without an appeal; and

(b) if satisfied of those matters, issue a divorce certificate (Form 36B) and mail it to the parties, unless the court orders otherwise.

(9) [Revoked O. Reg. 89/04, s. 12.]

O. Reg. 89/04, s. 12

RULE 37 — INTERJURISDICTIONAL SUPPORT ORDERS ACT, 2002 [HEADING AMENDED O. REG. 56/03, S. 6.]

Application

37. (1) This rule applies to cases under the Act.

Definitions

(2) In this rule,

"Act" means the *Interjurisdictional Support Orders Act, 2002*;

"appropriate authority" has the same meaning as in the Act;

"designated authority" has the same meaning as in the Act;

"general regulation" means Ontario Regulation 55/03;

"send", when used in reference to a person, means to,

(a) mail to the person's lawyer or, if none, to the person,

(b) send by courier to the person's lawyer or, if none, to the person,

(c) deposit at a document exchange to which the person's lawyer belongs, or

(d) fax to the person's lawyer or, if none, to the person.

Notice of Hearing

(3) When the court receives a support application or a support variation application the clerk shall, under section 10 or 33 of the Act,

(a) serve on the respondent, by special service,

(i) the notice of hearing mentioned in clause 10(b) or 33(b) of the Act (Form 37),

(ii) a copy of the documents sent by the designated authority, and

(iii) blank response forms; and

(b) send to the designated authority a copy of the notice of hearing and an information sheet (Form 37A).

Information And Documents To Be Provided By Respondent

(4) The respondent shall file, within 30 days after service of the notice of hearing,

(a) an answer in Form N under the general regulation,

(i) identifying any issues the respondent intends to raise with respect to the support application, and

(ii) containing the financial information referred to in subsection 21(1) of Ontario Regulation 391/97 (*Child Support Guidelines*), if the support application includes a claim for child support;

(b) an affidavit (Form 14A) setting out the evidence on which the respondent relies; and

(c) a financial statement in Form K under the general regulation.

Respondent's Financial Statement

(5) The respondent is required to file a financial statement whether he or she intends to dispute the claim or not.

Applicant's Financial Statement

(6) The fact that the applicant has provided financial information in a form different than that required by these rules does not affect the case.

Written Hearing

(7) Unless the court orders otherwise under subrule (9), the application shall be dealt with on the basis of written documents without the parties or their lawyers needing to come to court.

Request For Oral Hearing

(8) The respondent may request an oral hearing by filing a motion (Form 14B) within 30 days after being served with the notice of hearing.

Order For Oral Hearing

(9) The court may order an oral hearing, on the respondent's motion or on its own initiative, if it is satisfied that an oral hearing is necessary to deal with the case justly.

Direction to Request Further Information or Documents

(10) A direction to request further information or documents under clause 11(2)(a) or 34(2)(a) of the Act shall be in Form 37B, and a statement of the court's reasons for requesting further evidence shall be attached to the direction.

Direction to Be Sent to Respondent

(11) When a direction is sent to the designated authority under clause 11(2)(a) of the Act, the clerk shall also send a copy to the respondent.

Adjournment

(12) When the court adjourns the hearing under clause 11(2)(b) or 34(2)(b) of the Act, it shall specify the date on which the hearing is to continue.

Copies of Further Information or Documents

(13) When the court receives the further information or documents, the clerk shall promptly prepare a notice of continuation of hearing (Form 37C) and send it, with copies of the information or documents, to the respondent and to the designated authority.

Respondent's Affidavit

(14) If the respondent wishes to respond to the further information or documents, he or she shall file an affidavit (Form 14A) containing the response with the court, within 30 days after receiving the notice of continuation of hearing.

Preparation of Order

(15) The clerk shall prepare the order for signature as soon as it is made, in accordance with subrule 25(11).

Sending Copies of Order to Respondent and Designated Authority

(16) The court shall send,

(a) a copy of the order to the respondent, addressed to the respondent's last known address if sent by mail; and

(b) a certified copy of the order to the designated authority.

Sending Copy of Order to Appropriate Authority

(17) The designated authority shall send the certified copy of the order to the appropriate authority.

Notice of Registration, Order Made Outside Canada

(18) For the purpose of subsection 20(1) of the Act, the clerk of the Ontario court shall give notice of the registration of an order made outside Canada by providing a notice in Form 37D, as described in subrule (19), to any party to the order who is believed to ordinarily reside in Ontario.

Sending or Special Service

(19) If the party to whom notice is to be provided applied for the order in Ontario, the clerk shall send the notice to the party, but in any other case, the clerk shall serve the notice on the party by special service.

Motion to Set Aside Registration

(20) For the purpose of subsection 20(3) of the Act, a party shall give notice of a motion to set aside the registration of an order made outside Canada by,

(a) filing in the Ontario court a notice of motion (Form 14) setting out the grounds for the motion;

(b) sending the notice of motion and supporting documents to the claimant at the address shown in the order; and

(c) serving the notice of motion and supporting documents on the designated authority by regular service at least 10 days before the motion hearing date.

Designated Authority Need Not Appear On Motion

(21) The designated authority is not required to appear on the motion to set aside registration.

Notice of Decision or Order

(22) When the court makes a decision or order under section 20 of the Act, the clerk shall send copies of the order, with the court's reasons, if any,

(a) to each party, addressed to the party's last known address if sent by mail; and

(b) to the designated authority.

Party in Reciprocating Jurisdiction

(23) If a party ordinarily resides in a reciprocating jurisdiction and the order was originally sent to Ontario for registration by the appropriate authority there, the clerk may send it to that appropriate authority rather than sending it to the party as set out in clause (22)(a).

Provisional Orders

(24) When the court makes a provisional order under section 7 or 30 of the Act, the clerk shall send the following to the designated authority, to be sent to the reciprocating jurisdiction:

1. One copy of,

   i. the application (Form A under the general regulation),

   ii. the applicant's financial statement (Form K under the general regulation), and

   iii. a statement giving any information about the respondent's identification, whereabouts, income, assets and liabilities.

2. Three certified copies of,

   i. the applicant's evidence and, if reasonably possible, the exhibits, and

   ii. the provisional order.

Further Evidence

(25) When the court that made a provisional order receives a request for further evidence from the confirming court under subsection 7(4) or 30(4) of the Act, the clerk shall send to the applicant a notice for taking further evidence (Form 37E) and a copy of the documents sent by the confirming court.

O. Reg. 56/03, s. 6

RULE 37.1 — PROVISIONAL ORDERS AND CONFIRMATION OF PROVISIONAL ORDERS — DIVORCE ACT, FAMILY LAW ACT [HEADING ADDED O. REG. 56/03, S. 6.]

Application

37.1 (1) This rule applies to orders made under sections 18 and 19 of the *Divorce Act* (Canada) and under section 44 of the *Family Law Act.*

Definitions

(2) In this rule,

"confirming court" means,

(a) in the case of an order under section 19 of the *Divorce Act* (Canada), the court in Ontario or another province or territory of Canada that has jurisdiction to confirm a provisional variation of the order, or

(b) for the purpose of section 44 of the *Family Law Act,*

(i) the Ontario Court of Justice sitting in the municipality where the respondent resides, or

(ii) the Family Court of the Superior Court of Justice, if the respondent resides in an area where that court has jurisdiction;

"originating court" means,

(a) in the case of an order under section 18 of the *Divorce Act* (Canada), the court in Ontario or another province or territory of Canada that has jurisdiction under section 5 of that Act to deal with an application for a provisional variation of the order, or

(b) for the purpose of section 44 of the *Family Law Act*,

(i) the Ontario Court of Justice sitting in the municipality where the provisional order is made, or

(ii) the Family Court of the Superior Court of Justice when it makes the provisional order;

"send", when used in reference to a person, means to,

(a) mail to the person's lawyer or, if none, to the person,

(b) send by courier to the person's lawyer or, if none, to the person,

(c) deposit at a document exchange to which the person's lawyer belongs, or

(d) fax to the person's lawyer or, if none, to the person.

Documents To Be Sent To Confirming Court

(3) When the court makes a provisional order under section 18 of the *Divorce Act* (Canada) or section 44 of the *Family Law Act*, the clerk shall send the following to the confirming court (if it is in Ontario) or to the Attorney General to be sent to the confirming court (if it is outside Ontario):

1. One copy of,

i. the application (Form 8),

ii. the applicant's financial statement (Form 13),

iii. a statement giving any information about the respondent's identification, whereabouts, income, assets and liabilities, and

iv. if the confirming court is in another municipality in Ontario, proof that the application was served on the respondent.

2. Three certified copies of,

i. the applicant's evidence and, if reasonably possible, the exhibits, and

ii. the provisional order.

No Financial Statement From Foreign Applicant

(4) When a confirming court in Ontario receives a provisional order made outside Ontario, the applicant does not have to file a financial statement.

Notice of Confirmation Hearing

(5) A clerk of a confirming court in Ontario who receives a provisional order shall,

(a) serve on the respondent, by special service (subrule 6(3)),

(i) a notice of hearing (Form 37),

(ii) a copy of the documents sent by the originating court, and

(iii) blank response forms; and

(b) send a notice of hearing and an information sheet (Form 37A) to,

(i) the applicant,

(ii) the clerk of the originating court, and

(iii) the Attorney General, if the provisional order was made outside Ontario.

Respondent's Financial Statement

(6) A respondent at a confirmation hearing under section 19 of the *Divorce Act* (Canada) shall serve and file a financial statement (Form 13) within 30 days after service of the notice of confirmation hearing.

Written Hearing

(7) Unless the court orders otherwise under subrule (9), the application shall be dealt with on the basis of written documents without the parties or their lawyers needing to come to court.

Request For Oral Hearing

(8) The respondent may request an oral hearing by filing a motion (Form 14B) within 30 days after being served with the notice of hearing.

Order For Oral Hearing

(9) The court may order an oral hearing, on the applicant's motion or on its own initiative, if it is satisfied that an oral hearing is necessary to deal with the case justly.

Court Receives Request For Further Evidence

(10) When an originating court in Ontario receives a request for further evidence from the confirming court, the clerk shall send to the applicant a notice for taking further evidence (Form 37E) and a copy of the documents sent by the confirming court.

Court Sends Request For Further Evidence

(11) When a confirming court in Ontario requests further evidence from the originating court,

(a) the confirming court shall adjourn the confirmation hearing to a new date; and

(b) the clerk shall send to the originating court two certified copies of the evidence taken in the confirming court.

Continuing The Confirmation Hearing

(12) When a confirming court in Ontario receives further evidence from the originating court, the clerk shall promptly prepare a notice of continuation of hearing (Form 37C) and send it, with copies of the evidence, to the respondent and, if the provisional order was made outside Ontario, to the Attorney General.

Respondent's Affidavit

(13) If the respondent wishes to respond to the further evidence, he or she shall file an affidavit containing the response with the court, within 30 days after receiving the notice of continuation of hearing.

O. Reg. 56/03, s. 6

RULE 38 — APPEALS

Rules that Apply in Appeals to Divisional Court and Court of Appeal

38. (1) Rules 61, 62 and 63 of the *Rules of Civil Procedure* apply with necessary modifications, including those modifications set out in subrules (2) and (3),

(a) if an appeal lies to the Divisional Court or the Court of Appeal;

(b) if leave to appeal to the Divisional Court or the Court of Appeal is required,

in a family law case as described in subrule 1(2).

Modifications in Child Protection Appeals

(2) If the appeal is brought in a case under the *Child and Family Services Act*, the following time periods apply instead of the time periods mentioned in the referenced provisions of the *Rules of Civil Procedure*:

1. The time period referred to in clause 61.09(1)(a) shall be 14 days after filing the notice of appeal if there is no transcript.

2. The time period referred to in clause 61.09(1)(b) shall be 30 days after receiving notice that the evidence has been transcribed.

3. The time period referred to in clause 61.12(2) shall be 30 days after service of the appeal book and compendium, exhibit book, transcript of evidence, if any, and appellant's factum.

4. The time period referred to in clause 61.13(2)(a) shall be 30 days after the registrar receives notice that the evidence has been transcribed.

5. The time period referred to in clause 61.13(2)(b) shall be six months after filing the notice of appeal.

6. The time period referred to in subrule 62.02(2) for serving the notice of motion for leave to appeal shall be 30 days.

Appeal of Temporary Order in* Child and Family Services Act *Case

(3) In an appeal of a temporary order made in a case under the *Child and Family Services Act* and brought to the Divisional Court under clause 19(1)(b) of the *Courts of Justice Act*, the motion for leave to appeal shall be combined with the notice of appeal and heard together with the appeal.

Appeals to the Superior Court of Justice

(4) Subrules (5) to (45) apply to an appeal from an order of the Ontario Court of Justice to the Superior Court of Justice under,

(a) section 48 of the *Family Law Act*;

(b) section 73 of the *Children's Law Reform Act*;

(c) sections 69 and 156 of the *Child and Family Services Act*;

(d) section 40 of the *Interjurisdictional Support Orders Act, 2002*;

(e) section 40 of the *Courts of Justice Act*; and

(f) any other statute to which these rules apply, unless the statute provides for another procedure.

How to Start Appeal

(5) To start an appeal from a final order of the Ontario Court of Justice to the Superior Court of Justice under any of the provisions listed in subrule (4), a party shall,

(a) within 30 days after the date of the order or decision being appealed from, serve a notice of appeal (Form 38) by regular service on,

(i) every other party affected by the appeal or entitled to appeal,

(ii) the clerk of the court in the place where the order was made, and

(iii) if the appeal is under section 69 of the *Child and Family Services Act*, every other person entitled to notice under subsection 39(3) of that Act who appeared at the hearing; and

(b) within 10 days after serving the notice of appeal, file it.

Starting Appeal of Temporary Order

(6) Subrule (5) applies to the starting of an appeal from a temporary order of the Ontario Court of Justice to the Superior Court of Justice except that the notice of appeal shall be served within seven days after the date of the temporary order.

Same,* Child and Family Services Act *Case

(7) To start an appeal from a temporary order of the Ontario Court of Justice to the Superior Court of Justice in a case under the *Child and Family Services Act*, subrule (5) applies and the notice of appeal shall be served within 30 days after the date of the temporary order.

Name of Case Unchanged

(8) The name of a case in an appeal shall be the same as the name of the case in the order appealed from and shall identify the parties as appellant and respondent.

Appeal by Respondent

(9) If the respondent in an appeal also wants to appeal the same order, this rule applies, with necessary modifications, to the respondent's appeal, and the two appeals shall be heard together.

Grounds Stated in Notice of Appeal

(10) The notice of appeal shall state the order that the appellant wants the appeal court to make and the legal grounds for the appeal.

Other Grounds

(11) At the hearing of the appeal, no grounds other than the ones stated in the notice of appeal may be argued unless the court gives permission.

Transcript of Evidence

(12) If the appeal requires a transcript of evidence, the appellant shall, within 30 days after filing the notice of appeal, file proof that the transcript has been ordered.

Consultation With Respondent

(13) The appellant shall determine if the appeal requires a transcript of evidence in consultation with the respondent.

Agreement on Evidence to be Transcribed

(14) If the appellant and respondent agree about what evidence needs to be transcribed, the appellant shall order the agreed evidence transcribed.

No Agreement

(15) If the appellant and respondent cannot agree, the appellant shall order a transcript of all of the oral evidence from the hearing of the decision under appeal unless the court orders otherwise.

Court Reporter's Duty

(16) When the court reporter has completed the transcript, he or she shall promptly notify the appellant, the respondent and the court office in the court where the appeal will be heard.

Contents of Appellant's Appeal Record

(17) The appellant's appeal record shall contain a copy of the following documents, in the following order:

1. A table of contents describing each document, including each exhibit, by its nature and date and, for an exhibit, by exhibit number or letter.

2. The notice of appeal.

3. The order being appealed, as signed, and any reasons given by the court appealed from, as well as a further printed copy of the reasons if they are handwritten.

4. A transcript of the oral evidence.

5. Any other material that was before the court appealed from and that is necessary for the appeal.

Contents of Appellant's Factum

(18) The appellant's factum shall be not more than 30 pages long, shall be signed by the appellant's lawyer or, if none, by the appellant and shall consist of the following parts, containing paragraphs numbered consecutively from the beginning to the end of the factum:

1. Part 1: Identification. A statement identifying the appellant and respondent and the court appealed from, and stating the result in that court.

2. Part 2: Overview. A brief overview of the case and the issues on the appeal.

3. Part 3: Facts. A brief summary of the facts relevant to the appeal, with reference to the evidence by page and line as necessary.

4. Part 4: Issues. A brief statement of each issue, followed by a brief argument referring to the law relating to that issue.

5. Part 5: Order. A precise statement of the order the appeal court is asked to make, including any order for costs.

6. Part 6: Time estimate. An estimate of how much time will be needed for the appellant's oral argument, not including reply to the respondent's argument.

7. Part 7: List of authorities. A list of all statutes, regulations, rules, cases and other authorities referred to in the factum.

8. Part 8: Legislation. A copy of all relevant provisions of statutes, regulations and rules.

Respondent's Factum and Appeal Record

(19) The respondent shall, within the timeline set out in subrule (21) or (22), serve on every other party to the appeal and file,

(a) a respondent's factum (subrule (20)); and

(b) if applicable, a respondent's appeal record containing a copy of any material that was before the court appealed from which are necessary for the appeal but are not included in the appellant's appeal record.

Contents of Respondent's Factum

(20) The respondent's factum shall be not more than 30 pages long, shall be signed by the respondent's lawyer or, if none, by the respondent and shall consist of the following parts, containing paragraphs numbered consecutively from the beginning to the end of the factum:

1. Part 1: Overview. A brief overview of the case and the issues on the appeal.

2. Part 2: Facts. A brief statement of the facts in the appellant's factum that the respondent accepts as correct and the facts that the respondent says are incorrect, and a brief summary of any additional facts relied on by the respondent, with reference to the evidence by page and line as necessary.

3. Part 3: Issues. A statement of the respondent's position on each issue raised by the appellant, followed by a brief argument referring to the law relating to that issue.

4. Part 4: Additional issues. A brief statement of each additional issue raised by the respondent, followed by a brief argument referring to the law relating to that issue.

5. Part 5: Order. A precise statement of the order the appeal court is asked to make, including any order for costs.

6. Part 6: Time estimate. An estimate of how much time will be needed for the respondent's oral argument.

7. Part 7: List of authorities. A list of all statutes, regulations, rules, cases and other authorities referred to in the factum.

8. Part 8: Legislation. A copy of all relevant provisions of statutes, regulations and rules not included in the appellant's factum.

Timelines for Serving and Filing of Records and Factums Other Than in **Child and Family Services Act** *Cases*

(21) Except for appeals in cases under the *Child and Family Services Act*, the following timelines for serving appeal records and factums apply:

1. If a transcript is required, the appellant's appeal record and factum shall be served on the respondent and any other person entitled to be heard in the appeal and filed within 60 days from the date of receiving notice that evidence has been transcribed.

2. If no transcript is required, the appellant's appeal record and factum shall be served on the respondent and any other person entitled to be heard in the appeal and filed within 30 days of filing of the notice of appeal.

3. The respondent's appeal record and factum shall be served on the appellant and any other person entitled to be heard on the appeal and filed within 60 days from the serving of the appellant's appeal record and factum.

Timelines for Serving and Filing of Records and Factums in **Child and Family Services Act** *Cases*

(22) For appeals of cases under the *Child and Family Services Act*, the following timelines for serving appeal records and factums apply:

1. If a transcript is required, the appellant's appeal record and factum shall be served on the respondent and any other person entitled to be heard in the appeal and filed within 30 days from the date of receiving notice that evidence has been transcribed.

2. If no transcript is required, the appellant's appeal record and factum shall be served on the respondent and any other person entitled to be heard in the appeal and filed within 14 days of filing of the notice of appeal.

3. The respondent's appeal record and factum shall be served on the appellant and any other person entitled to be heard on the appeal and filed within 30 days from the serving of the appellant's appeal record and factum.

Scheduling of Hearing

(23) When the appellant's appeal record and factum have been filed and the respondent's factum and appeal record, if any, have been filed, or the time for their filing has expired, the clerk shall schedule the appeal for hearing.

Prompt Hearing of CFSA Appeals

(24) An appeal under the *Child and Family Services Act* shall be heard within 60 days after the appellant's factum and appeal record are filed.

Motions in Appeals

(25) If a person needs to bring a motion in an appeal, rule 14 applies with necessary modifications to the motion.

Security for Costs of Appeal

(26) On a motion by the respondent for security for costs, the court may make an order for security for costs that is just, if it is satisfied that,

(a) there is good reason to believe that the appeal is a waste of time, a nuisance, or an abuse of the court process and that the appellant has insufficient assets in Ontario to pay the costs of the appeal;

(b) an order for security for costs could be made against the appellant under subrule 24(13); or

(c) for other good reason, security for costs should be ordered.

Dismissal for Failure to Obey Order

(27) If an appellant does not obey an order under subrule (26), the court may on motion dismiss the appeal.

Motion for Summary Judgment in Appeal

(28) After the notice of appeal is filed, the respondent or any other person who is entitled to be heard on the appeal may make a motion for summary judgment or for summary decision on a legal issue without a hearing of the appeal, and rule 16 applies to the motion with necessary modifications.

Motion to Receive Further Evidence

(29) Any person entitled to be heard in the appeal may bring a motion to admit further evidence under clause 134(4)(b) of the *Courts of Justice Act*.

Motion for Dismissal for Delay

(30) If the appellant has not,

(a) filed proof that a transcript of evidence was ordered under subrule (12);

(b) served and filed the appeal record and factum within the timelines set out in subrule (21) or (22) or such longer time as may have been ordered by the court,

the respondent may file a procedural motion (Form 14B) to have the appeal dismissed for delay.

Withdrawal of Appeal

(31) The appellant may withdraw an appeal by serving a notice of withdrawal (Form 12) on every other party and filing it.

Deemed Withdrawal

(32) If a person serves a notice of appeal and does not file it within 10 days as required by clause (5)(b), the appeal shall be deemed to be withdrawn unless the court orders otherwise.

Automatic Stays Pending Appeal, Support Orders

(33) The service of a notice of appeal from a temporary or final order does not stay a support order or an order that enforces a support order.

Other Payment Orders

(34) The service of a notice of appeal from a temporary or final order stays, until the disposition of the appeal, any other payment order made under the temporary or final order.

Stay by Order of Court

(35) A temporary or final order may be stayed on any conditions that the court considers appropriate,

(a) by an order of the court that made the order;

(b) by an order of the Superior Court of Justice.

Expiry of Stay Granted by Court That Made Order

(36) A stay granted under clause (35)(a) expires if no notice of appeal is served and the time for service has expired.

Powers of Superior Court of Justice

(37) A stay granted under subrule (35) may be set aside or changed by the Superior Court of Justice.

Effect of Stay Generally

(38) If an order is stayed, no steps may be taken under the order or for its enforcement, except,

(a) by order of the Superior Court of Justice; or

(b) as provided in subrules (39) and (40).

Settling of Order

(39) A stay does not prevent the settling or signing of the order.

Writ of Execution

(40) A stay does not prevent the issue of a writ of seizure and sale or the filing of the writ in a sheriff's office or land registry office, but no instruction or direction to enforce the writ shall be given to a sheriff while the stay remains in effect.

Certificate of Stay

(41) If an order is stayed, the clerk of the court that granted the stay shall, if requested by a party to the appeal, issue a certificate of stay in Form 63A under the *Rules of Civil Procedure* with necessary modifications.

Stay of Support Order

(42) A party who obtains a stay of a support order shall obtain a certificate of stay under subrule (41) and file it immediately in the office of the Director of the Family Responsibility Office if the stay relates to a support order being enforced by the Director.

Certificate Filed With Sheriff's Office

(43) If a certificate of stay is filed with the sheriff's office, the sheriff shall not begin or continue enforcement of the order until satisfied that the stay is no longer in effect.

Request for Certificate

(44) A request for a certificate of stay under subrule (41) shall state whether the stay is under subrule (34) or by order under subrule (35) and, if under subrule (35), shall set out the particulars of the order.

Setting Aside Writ of Execution

(45) The court may set aside the issue or filing of a writ of seizure and sale if the party making the motion or the appellant gives security satisfactory to the court.

O. Reg. 89/04, s. 13; 76/06, s. 10

RULE 39 — CASE MANAGEMENT IN FAMILY COURT OF SUPERIOR COURT OF JUSTICE

Case Management in Certain Areas Only

39. (1) This rule applies only to cases in the Family Court of the Superior Court of Justice, which has jurisdiction in the municipalities listed in subrule 1(3).

Excluded Cases

(2) This rule does not apply to,

(a) enforcements;

(b) cases under rule 37 or 37.1; or

(c) cases under the *Child and Family Services Act*.

(d) [Repealed O. Reg. 439/07, s. 3(1).]

Parties May not Lengthen Times

(3) A time set out in this rule may be lengthened only by order of the case management judge and not by the parties' consent under subrule 3(6).

Fast Track

(4) Applications to which this rule applies, except the ones mentioned in subrule (7), and motions to change a final order or agreement are fast track cases (subrules (5) and (6)).

Fast Track — First Court Date

(5) In a fast track case the clerk shall, on or before the first court date,

(a) confirm that all necessary documents have been served and filed;

(b) refer the parties to sources of information about the court process, alternatives to court (including mediation), the effects of separation and divorce on children and community resources that may help the parties and their children;

(c) if an answer has been filed in response to an application, or if a response to motion to change (Form 15B) or a notice of financial interest has been filed in a motion to change a final order or agreement under rule 15, confirm that the case is ready for a hearing, case conference or settlement conference and schedule it accordingly;

(d) if no answer has been filed in response to an application, send the case to a judge for a decision on the basis of affidavit evidence or, on request of the applicant, schedule a case conference; and

(e) if no response to motion to change (Form 15B), consent motion to change (Form 15C) or notice of financial interest is filed in response to a motion to change a final order or agreement under rule 15, send the case to a judge for a decision on the basis of the evidence filed in the motion.

Fast Track — Case Management Judge Assigned at Start

(6) In a fast track case, a case management judge shall be assigned by the first time the case comes before a judge.

Standard Track

(7) Applications in which the applicant makes a claim for a divorce or a property claim are standard track cases (subrule (8)).

Features of Standard Track

(8) In a standard track case,

(a) the clerk shall not set a court date when the application is filed;

(b) a case management judge shall be assigned when a case conference or a motion is scheduled, whichever comes first; and

(c) the clerk shall schedule a case conference on any party's request.

Functions of Case Management Judge

(9) The case management judge assigned to a case,

(a) shall generally supervise its progress;

(b) shall conduct the case conference and the settlement conference;

(c) may schedule a case conference or settlement conference at any time, on the judge's own initiative; and

(d) shall hear motions in the case, when available to hear motions;

(e) [Repealed O. Reg. 76/06, s. 11(2).]

Substitute Case Management Judge

(10) If the case management judge is, for any reason, unavailable to continue as the case management judge, another case management judge may be assigned for part or all of the case.

Notice of Approaching Dismissal After 365 Days

(11) The clerk shall serve a notice of approaching dismissal (Form 39) for a case on the parties by mail, fax or electronic mail if the case has not been settled, withdrawn or scheduled or adjourned for trial before the 365th day after the date the case was started, and that time has not been lengthened by an order under subrule (3).

Exception

(11.1) Despite subrule (11), if a case conference or settlement conference is arranged before the 365th day after the date the case was started for a date on or later than the 365th day, the clerk shall not serve a notice of approaching dismissal except as set out in subrule (11.2).

Notice Sent if Conference Does Not Take Place

(11.2) If a case conference or settlement conference is arranged for a date on or later than the 365th day after the date the case was started, but the hearing does not take place on that date and is not adjourned by a judge, the clerk shall serve the notice of approaching dismissal on the parties by mail, fax or electronic mail.

Dismissal of Case

(12) A case for which a notice of approaching dismissal has been served shall be dismissed without further notice, unless one of the parties, within 60 days after the notice is served,

(a) obtains an order under subrule (3) to lengthen that time;

(b) files an agreement signed by all parties and their lawyers, if any, for a final order disposing of all issues in the case, and a notice of motion for an order carrying out the agreement;

(c) serves on all parties and files a notice of withdrawal (Form 12) that discontinues all outstanding claims in the case;

(d) schedules or adjourns the case for trial; or

(e) arranges a case conference or settlement conference for the first available date.

Same

(12.1) If a case conference or settlement conference is arranged for a date as described in clause (12)(e), but the hearing does not take place on that date and is not adjourned by a judge, the case shall be dismissed without further notice.

Dismissal After Notice

(12.2) The clerk shall dismiss a case under subrule (12) or (12.1) by preparing and signing an order dismissing the case, with no costs payable by any party.

Service of Dismissal Order by Clerk

(13) The clerk shall serve the order on each party by mail, fax or electronic mail.

Service of Dismissal Order by Lawyer on Client

(14) A lawyer who is served with a dismissal order on behalf of a client shall serve it on the client by mail, fax or electronic mail and file proof of service of the order.

Judge may Set Clerk's Order Aside

(14.1) The case management judge or another judge may, on motion, set aside an order of the clerk under subrule (12).

Transition

(15) Despite this rule, if the clerk served a notice of approaching dismissal before September 1, 2007, the version of this rule that applied to the case on August 31, 2007, as its application may have been modified by the court, continues to apply to the case unless the court orders otherwise.

O. Reg. 202/01, s. 7; 56/03, s. 7; 89/04, s. 14; 76/06, s. 11; 439/07, s. 3; 151/08, s. 7

RULE 40 — CASE MANAGEMENT IN ONTARIO COURT OF JUSTICE

Case Management in Certain Areas Only

40. (1) This rule applies only to cases in the Ontario Court of Justice.

Excluded Cases

(2) This rule does not apply to,

(a) enforcements;

(b) cases under rule 37 or 37.1; or

(c) cases under the *Child and Family Services Act*.

(d) [Repealed O. Reg. 439/07, s. 4(1).]

Parties may not Lengthen Times

(3) A time set out in this rule may be lengthened only by order and not by the parties' consent under subrule 3(6).

First Court Date

(4) The clerk shall, on or before the first court date,

(a) confirm that all necessary documents have been served and filed;

(b) refer the parties to sources of information about the court process, alternatives to court (including mediation), the effects of separation and divorce on children and community resources that may help the parties and their children;

(c) if an answer has been filed in response to an application, or if a response to motion to change (Form 15B) or a notice of financial interest has been filed in a motion to change a final order or agreement under rule 15, confirm that the case is ready for a hearing, case conference or settlement conference and schedule it accordingly;

(d) if no answer has been filed in response to an application, send the case to a judge for a decision on the basis of affidavit evidence or, on request of the applicant, schedule a case conference; and

(e) if no response to motion to change (Form 15B), consent motion to change (Form 15C) or notice of financial interest is filed in response to a motion to change a final order or agreement under rule 15, send the case to a judge for a decision on the basis of the evidence filed in the motion.

Notice of Approaching Dismissal After 365 Days

(5) The clerk shall serve a notice of approaching dismissal (Form 39) for a case on the parties by mail, fax or electronic mail if the case has not been settled, withdrawn or scheduled or adjourned for trial before the 365th day after the date the case was started, and that time has not been lengthened by an order under subrule (3).

Exception

(5.1) Despite subrule (5), if a case conference or settlement conference is arranged before the 365th day after the date the case was started for a date on or later than the 365th day, the clerk shall not serve a notice of approaching dismissal except as set out in subrule (5.2).

Notice Sent if Conference Does Not Take Place

(5.2) If a case conference or settlement conference is arranged for a date on or later than the 365th day after the date the case was started, but the hearing does not take place on that date and is not adjourned by a judge, the clerk shall serve the notice of approaching dismissal on the parties by mail, fax or electronic mail.

Dismissal of Case

(6) A case for which a notice of approaching dismissal has been served shall be dismissed without further notice, unless one of the parties, within 60 days after the notice is served,

(a) obtains an order under subrule (3) to lengthen that time;

(b) files an agreement signed by all parties and their lawyers, if any, for a final order disposing of all issues in the case, and a notice of motion for an order carrying out the agreement;

(c) serves on all parties and files a notice of withdrawal (Form 12) that discontinues all outstanding claims in the case;

(d) schedules or adjourns the case for trial; or

(e) arranges a case conference or settlement conference for the first available date.

Same

(6.1) If a case conference or settlement conference is arranged for a date as described in clause (6)(e), but the hearing does not take place on that date and is not adjourned by a judge, the case shall be dismissed without further notice.

Dismissal After Notice

(6.2) The clerk shall dismiss a case under subrule (6) or (6.1) by preparing and signing an order dismissing the case, with no costs payable by any party.

Service of Dismissal Order by Clerk

(7) The clerk shall serve the order on each party by mail, fax or electronic mail.

Service of Dismissal Order by Lawyer on Client

(8) A lawyer who is served with a dismissal order on behalf of a client shall serve it on the client by mail, fax or electronic mail and file proof of service of the order.

Judge May Set Clerk's Order Aside

(9) A judge may, on motion, set aside an order of the clerk under subrule (6).

Transition

(10) Despite this rule, if the clerk served a notice of approaching dismissal before September 1, 2007, the version of this rule that applied to the case on August 31, 2007, as its application may have been modified by the court, continues to apply to the case unless the court orders otherwise.

O. Reg. 202/01, s. 8; 56/03, s. 8; 89/04, s. 15; 76/06, s. 12; 439/07, s. 4; 151/08, s. 8

RULE 41 — CASE MANAGEMENT IN THE SUPERIOR COURT OF JUSTICE (OTHER THAN THE FAMILY COURT OF THE SUPERIOR COURT OF JUSTICE) [HEADING AMENDED O. REG. 89/04, S. 16.]

Case Management

41. (1) This rule applies only to cases in the Superior Court of Justice, other than cases in the Family Court of the Superior Court of Justice, started on or after July 1, 2004.

Excluded Cases

(2) This rule does not apply to,

(a) enforcements; or

(b) cases under rule 37 or 37.1.

Parties May Not Lengthen Times

(3) A time set out in this rule may be lengthened only by order of the court and not by the parties' consent under subrule 3(6).

Clerk's Role

(4) The clerk shall not set a court date when the application is filed, and the case shall come before the court when a case conference or a motion is scheduled, whichever comes first, and the clerk shall schedule a case conference on any party's request.

Notice of Approaching Dismissal After 365 Days

(5) The clerk shall serve a notice of approaching dismissal (Form 39) for a case on the parties by mail, fax or electronic mail if the case has not been settled, withdrawn or scheduled or adjourned for trial before the 365th day after the date the case was started, and that time has not been lengthened by an order under subrule (3).

Exception

(5.1) Despite subrule (5), if a case conference or settlement conference is arranged before the 365th day after the date the case was started for a date on or later than the 365th day, the clerk shall not serve a notice of approaching dismissal except as set out in subrule (5.2).

Notice Sent if Conference Does Not Take Place

(5.2) If a case conference or settlement conference is arranged for a date on or later than the 365th day after the date the case was started, but the hearing does not take place on that date and is not adjourned by a judge, the clerk shall serve the notice of approaching dismissal on the parties by mail, fax or electronic mail.

Dismissal of Case

(6) A case for which a notice of approaching dismissal has been served shall be dismissed without further notice, unless one of the parties, within 60 days after the notice is served,

(a) obtains an order under subrule (3) to lengthen that time;

(b) files an agreement signed by all parties and their lawyers, if any, for a final order disposing of all issues in the case, and a notice of motion for an order carrying out the agreement;

(c) serves on all parties and files a notice of withdrawal (Form 12) that discontinues all outstanding claims in the case;

(d) schedules or adjourns the case for trial; or

(e) arranges a case conference or settlement conference for the first available date.

Same

(6.1) If a case conference or settlement conference is arranged for a date as described in clause (6)(e), but the hearing does not take place on that date and is not adjourned by a judge, the case shall be dismissed without further notice.

Dismissal After Notice

(6.2) The clerk shall dismiss a case under subrule (6) or (6.1) by preparing and signing an order dismissing the case, with no costs payable by any party.

Service of Dismissal Order

(7) The clerk shall serve the order on each party by mail, fax or electronic mail.

Service of Dismissal Order by Lawyer on Client

(8) A lawyer who is served with a dismissal order on behalf of a client shall serve it on the client by mail, fax or electronic mail and file proof of service of the order.

Judge may Set Clerk's Order Aside

(9) A judge may, on motion, set aside an order of the clerk under subrule (6).

Transition

(10) Despite this rule, if the clerk served a notice of approaching dismissal before September 1, 2007, the version of this rule that applied to the case on August 31, 2007, as its application may have been modified by the court, continues to apply to the case unless the court orders otherwise.

O. Reg. 441/99, s. 2; 89/04, s. 16; 76/06, s. 13; 439/07, s. 5

RULE 42 — APPOINTMENT OF FAMILY CASE MANAGER IN THE FAMILY COURT OF THE SUPERIOR COURT OF JUSTICE IN OTTAWA

Scope

42. (1) This rule applies to cases in the Family Court of the Superior Court of Justice in the City of Ottawa if the cases relate to matters under the following Acts:

1. The *Child and Family Services Act*, subject to subrule (6).

2. The *Children 's Law Reform Act*.

3. The *Divorce Act* (Canada).

4. The *Family Law Act.*

5. The *Family Responsibility and Support Arrears Enforcement Act, 1996.*

Purpose

(2) The purpose of this rule is to promote the active management, in accordance with subrule 2(5), of cases to which this rule applies by conferring specified family law jurisdiction on a Family Case Manager.

Definition

(3) In this rule,

"Family Case Manager" means a person appointed under section 86.1 of the *Courts of Justice Act* by the Lieutenant Governor in Council as a case management master who is assigned to manage cases for the purposes of this rule.

Family Case Manager, Powers and Duties

(4) In a case to which this rule applies,

(a) the Family Case Manager may only exercise the powers and carry out the duties and functions that are specified in this rule; and

(b) the exercise of those powers and the performance of those duties and functions are subject to the restrictions specified in subrules (5) and (6).

No Jurisdiction

(5) The Family Case Manager has no jurisdiction in respect of,

(a) a power, duty or function that is conferred exclusively on a judge of a superior court by law or expressly on a judge by an Act;

(b) a case involving a special party;

(c) the determination of a right or interest of a party in real property; or

(d) the making of an order or hearing of a motion for an order,

(i) to change, set aside, stay or confirm an order of a judge,

(ii) to find a person in contempt of court,

(iii) to restrain the liberty of a person, including an order for imprisonment, a warrant for arrest or a warrant of committal,

(iv) to dismiss all or part of a party's case for a wilful failure by the party to follow these rules or obey an order in the case or a related case, if the *Family Responsibility and Support Arrears Enforcement Act, 1996* applies to the party's case,

(v) to split a divorce from other issues in a case under subrule 12(6),

(vi) to request the Children's Lawyer to act in accordance with subsection 89(3.1) or 112(2) of the *Courts of Justice Act*, or

(vii) to grant summary judgment.

***Limited Jurisdiction,* Child and Family Services Act**

(6) With respect to cases under the *Child and Family Services Act,*

(a) the Family Case Manager has jurisdiction only with respect to Part III of that Act (child protection case); and

(b) the jurisdiction of the Family Case Manager with respect to cases under Part III of that Act is not as broad as it is with respect to cases under the other Acts to which this rule applies but is subject to such further limitations as are specified in this rule.

Motions Under Rule 14

(7) The Family Case Manager may hear a motion that may be made under rule 14 and, on such a motion, may exercise only the following powers:

1. With respect to cases under an Act to which this rule applies other than the *Child and Family Services Act,* any power described in rule 14 other than a power described in subrule 14(21).

2. With respect to cases under Part III of the *Child and Family Services Act,* any power described in rule 14 other than a power described in subrule 14(21), (22) or (23).

Orders on Motion Under Rule 14

(8) If a motion under rule 14 is made in a case under an Act to which this rule applies other than the *Child and Family Services Act,* the Family Case Manager may make only the following orders:

1. An order under rules 3, 4, 5, 6, 7, 9, 10, 11, 12, 13, 18, 19 and 20.

2. An order for costs under rule 24 relating to a step in the case that the Family Case Manager dealt with.

3. An order under rule 25 relating to an order made by the Family Case Manager.

4. An order to change a temporary order made by the Family Case Manager.

5. An order under section 10 (Leave for blood tests and DNA tests) of the *Children's Law Reform Act.*

6. A temporary order for or relating to custody of or access to a child under section 21, 23, 25, 28, 29, 30, 32, 34, 39 or 40 of the *Children's Law Reform Act.*

7. A temporary order for custody of or access to a child under section 16 of the *Divorce Act* (Canada).

8. An order appointing a mediator under section 31 of the *Children's Law Reform Act* or section 3 (Mediation) of the *Family Law Act.*

9. A temporary order for or relating to support under section 33, clause 34(1)(a), (e), (f), (g) or (h), subsection 34(5) or section 37, 42 or 47 of the *Family Law Act.*

10. A temporary order for support under section 15.1 (Child support order) or 15.2 (Spousal support order) of the *Divorce Act* (Canada).

11. A temporary order under section 40 of the *Family Law Act.*

12. A temporary order dealing with property other than real property.

13. A support deduction order under section 10 (Support deduction orders to be made) of the *Family Responsibility and Support Arrears Enforcement Act, 1996.*

14. An order limiting or suspending a support deduction order.

15. An order under section 8 (Director to cease enforcement, termination of support obligation) of the *Family Responsibility and Support Arrears Enforcement Act, 1996* that terminates a support obligation or orders repayment from a person who received support.

16. An order that is necessary and incidental to the power to make a temporary order that is within the jurisdiction of the Family Case Manager.

Same, Child and Family Services Act

(9) If a motion under rule 14 is made in a case under the *Child and Family Services Act*, the Family Case Manager may make only the following orders:

1. An order under subrule 3(5) (order to lengthen or shorten time), if the motion is made on consent.

2. An order under rule 5 (where a case starts and is to be heard), if the motion is unopposed or made on consent.

3. An order under rule 6 (service of documents).

4. An order under subrule 7(5) (adding a party), if the motion is unopposed or made on consent.

5. An order under section 39 (parties and notice) or under subsection 48(3) (transfer of a proceeding) of the *Child and Family Services Act*, if the motion is unopposed or made on consent.

6. A finding that there is no person who should be presumed to be, or recognized in law as, the father of a child under section 8 of the *Children's Law Reform Act*.

7. An order granting an adjournment, if the motion is made on consent.

Temporary Order to be Continued

(10) An order for adjournment made under paragraph 7 of subrule (9) in a child protection case shall provide for the continuation of any temporary order made under subsection 51(2) (custody during adjournment) of the *Child and Family Services Act* that applies in respect of the case being adjourned.

(11) [Repealed O. Reg. 151/08, s. 9.]

Conferences

(12) Subject to subrule (13), the Family Case Manager may conduct a case conference, settlement conference or trial management conference instead of a judge under rule 17.

Same, Child and Family Services Act

(13) In a case under Part III of the *Child and Family Services Act*, the Family Case Manager shall not conduct a settlement conference without the consent of the parties and of the child's representative.

Application of Rule 17

(14) At a case conference, settlement conference or trial management conference conducted by the Family Case Manager, rule 17 applies subject to the following changes:

1. In a case to which this rule applies other than the *Child and Family Services Act*, the Family Case Manager may make any order described in rule 17 and, with respect to the temporary and final orders referred to in clause 17(8)(b),

i. the only temporary or final orders that the Family Case Manager may make are those described in subrule (8) of this rule, and

ii. the Family Case Manager shall not make a final order unless the parties consent to the order.

2. In a case under Part III of the *Child and Family Services Act*, the Family Case Manager,

i. may make any order described in rule 17 other than an order under subrule 17(18), and

ii. the only temporary or final orders that the Family Case Manager may make under clause 17(8)(b) are those described in subrule (9) of this rule.

3. A party to the conference may not request that the conference be conducted by a judge under subrule 17(9).

4. Despite clause 17(10)(a), a case may be scheduled for trial if the Family Case Manager conducted a settlement conference.

Enforcement Powers

(15) The Family Case Manager may exercise,

(a) any power that a court may exercise under rule 27 (requiring financial information) other than a power to order a person imprisoned under subrule 27(6), (20) or (21); and

(b) the powers relating to garnishment orders set out in subrules 29(5) and (19).

Sending Case to Judge

(16) Despite anything to the contrary in this rule, the Family Case Manager may at any time order that a matter assigned to him or her be adjourned and sent to a judge.

Appeal from Temporary Order

(17) Subrules 38(5) to (45) apply with necessary modifications to an appeal from a temporary order of the Family Case Manager.

Appeal from Final Order

(18) Subrules 38(1), (2) and (3) apply with necessary modifications to an appeal from a final order of the Family Case Manager.

Revocation

(19) This rule is revoked on June 30, 2012.

O. Reg. 441/99, s. 2; 120/07, s. 1; 151/08, s. 9; 51/10, s. 1

43. This Regulation comes into force on September 15, 1999.

TABLE OF FORMS

Form Number	**Form Title**	**Date of Form**
4	Notice of change in representation	September 1, 2005
6	Acknowledgment of service	September 1, 2005
6A	Advertisement	September 1, 2005
6B	Affidavit of service	November 15, 2009
8	Application (general)	June 15, 2007
8A	Application (divorce)	June 15, 2007
8B	Application (child protection and status review)	October 1, 2006
8B.1	Application (status review for Crown ward and former Crown ward)	October 1, 2006
8B.2	Application (general) (*Child and Family Services Act* cases other than child protection and status review)	October 1, 2006
8C	Application (secure treatment)	November 15, 2009
8D	Application (adoption)	September 1, 2005
8D.1	Application (dispense with parent's consent to adoption before placement)	September 1, 2005
8E	[Repealed O. Reg. 519/06, s. 7(1).]	
10	Answer	September 1, 2005
10A	Reply	September 1, 2005
12	Notice of withdrawal	September 1, 2005
13	Financial statement (support claims)	February 1, 2010
13.1	Financial statement (property and support claims)	February 1, 2010
13A	[Repealed O. Reg. 6/10, s. 10(2).]	
13B	Net family property statement	May 15, 2009
14	Notice of motion	June 15, 2007
14A	Affidavit (general)	September 1, 2005
14B	Motion form	September 1, 2005
14C	Confirmation	September 1, 2005
14D	Order on motion without notice	September 1, 2005
15	Motion to change	April 1, 2008
15A	Change information form	April 1, 2008
15B	Response to motion to change	April 1, 2008
15C	Consent motion to change	April 1, 2008
15D	Consent motion to change child support	April 1, 2008

TABLE OF FORMS

Form Number	Form Title	Date of Form
17	Conference notice	September 1, 2005
17A	Case conference brief — General	November 15, 2009
17B	Case conference brief for protection application or status review	November 15, 2009
17C	Settlement conference brief — General	November 15, 2009
17D	Settlement conference brief for protection application or status review	November 15, 2009
17E	Trial management conference brief	November 15, 2009
20	Request for information	September 1, 2005
20A	Authorization to commissioner	September 1, 2005
20B	Letter of request	September 1, 2005
22	Request to admit	September 1, 2005
22A	Response to request to admit	September 1, 2005
23	Summons to witness	September 1, 2005
23A	Summons to witness outside Ontario	September 1, 2005
23B	Order for prisoner's attendance	September 1, 2005
23C	Affidavit for uncontested trial	September 1, 2009
25	Order (general)	September 1, 2005
25A	Divorce order	September 1, 2005
25B	Secure treatment order	September 1, 2005
25C	Adoption order	September 1, 2005
25D	Order (uncontested trial)	September 1, 2005
25E	Notice disputing approval of order	September 1, 2005
25F	Restraining order	September 1, 2009
25G	Restraining order on motion without notice	September 1, 2009
25H	Order terminating restraining order	September 1, 2009
26	Statement of money owed	September 1, 2005
26A	Affidavit of enforcement expenses	September 1, 2005
26B	Affidavit for filing domestic contract or paternity agreement with court	September 1, 2005
26C	Notice of transfer of enforcement	September 1, 2005
27	Request for financial statement	September 1, 2005
27A	Request for statement of income	September 1, 2005
27B	Statement of income from income source	September 1, 2005
27C	Appointment for financial examination	September 1, 2005
28	Writ of seizure and sale	September 1, 2005
28A	Request for writ of seizure and sale	September 1, 2005
28B	Statutory declaration to sheriff	June 15, 2007
28C	Writ of temporary seizure	September 1, 2005
29	Request for garnishment	September 1, 2005
29A	Notice of garnishment (lump-sum debt)	September 1, 2005

TABLE OF FORMS

Form Number	Form Title	Date of Form
29B	Notice of garnishment (periodic debt)	September 1, 2005
29C	Notice to co-owner of debt	September 1, 2005
29D	Statutory declaration of indexed support	September 1, 2005
29E	Dispute (payor)	September 1, 2005
29F	Dispute (garnishee)	September 1, 2005
29G	Dispute (co-owner of debt)	September 1, 2005
29H	Notice of garnishment hearing	September 1, 2005
29I	Notice to stop garnishment	September 1, 2005
29J	Statement to garnishee financial institution re support	September 1, 2005
30	Notice of default hearing	September 1, 2005
30A	Request for default hearing	September 1, 2005
30B	Default dispute	September 1, 2005
31	Notice of contempt motion	September 1, 2005
32	Bond (recognizance)	September 1, 2005
32A	Notice of forfeiture motion	September 1, 2005
32B	Warrant for arrest	September 1, 2005
32C	Affidavit for warrant of committal	September 1, 2005
32D	Warrant of committal	September 1, 2005
33	Information for warrant to apprehend child	September 1, 2005
33A	Warrant to apprehend child	September 1, 2005
33B	Plan of care for child(ren) (Children's Aid Society)	October 1, 2006
33B.1	Answer and plan of care (parties other than Children's Aid Society)	October 1, 2006
33B.2	Answer (*Child and Family Services Act* cases other than child protection and status review)	October 1, 2006
33C	Statement of agreed facts (child protection)	September 1, 2005
33D	Statement of agreed facts (status review)	September 1, 2005
33E	Child's consent to secure treatment	September 1, 2005
33F	Consent to secure treatment (person other than child)	September 1, 2005
34	Child's consent to adoption	April 1, 2009
34A	Affidavit of parentage	September 1, 2005
34B	Non-parent's consent to adoption by spouse	June 15, 2007
34C	Director's or local director's statement on adoption	September 1, 2005
34D	Affidavit of adoption applicant(s), sworn/affirmed	April 1, 2009
34E	Director's consent to adoption	September 1, 2005
34F	Parent's or custodian's consent to adoption	April 1, 2009
34G	Affidavit of adoption licensee or society employee	September 1, 2005

TABLE OF FORMS

Form Number	Form Title	Date of Form
34H	Affidavit of adopting relative or stepparent	April 1, 2009
34I	Parent's consent to adoption by spouse	April 1, 2009
34J	Affidavit of execution and independent legal advice (Children's Lawyer)	April 1, 2009
34K	Certificate of clerk (adoption)	October 1, 2006
34L	Application for openness order	October 1, 2006
34M	Consent to openness order	October 1, 2006
34N	Application to change or terminate openness order	October 1, 2006
35.1	Affidavit in support of claim for custody or access	November 15, 2009
36	Affidavit for divorce	September 1, 2005
36A	Certificate of clerk (divorce)	September 1, 2005
36B	Certificate of divorce	September 1, 2005
37	Notice of hearing	September 1, 2005
37A	Information sheet	September 1, 2005
37B	Direction to request further information	September 1, 2005
37C	Notice of continuation of hearing	September 1, 2005
37D	Notice of registration of order	September 1, 2005
37E	Notice for taking further evidence	September 1, 2005
38	Notice of appeal	September 1, 2005
39	Notice of approaching dismissal	June 15, 2007

O. Reg. 76/06, s. 14; 519/06, s. 7; 439/07, s. 6; 151/08, s. 10; 317/09, s. 1; 386/09, s. 2; 6/10, s. 10; 52/10, s. 2

FORMS UNDER THE FAMILY LAW RULES

Form number	Title	Rule creating form
4	Notice of change in representation	4(10)
6	Acknowledgment of service	6(3)
6A	Advertisement	6(17)
6B	Affidavit of service	6(19)
8	Application (general)	8(1)
8A	Application (divorce)	8(1)
8B	Application (child protection and status review)	8(1)
8B.1	Application (status review for Crown ward and former Crown ward)	8(1)
8B.2	Application (general) (*Child and Family Services Act* cases other than child protection and status review)	8(1)
8C	Application (secure treatment)	8(1)
8D	Application (adoption)	8(1)
8D.1	Application (dispense with parent's consent to adoption before placement)	8(1)
8E	Summary of court cases	8(1)
10	Answer	10(1)
10A	Reply	10(6)
12	Notice of withdrawal	12(1)
13	Financial statement (support claims)	13(1)
13.1	Financial statement (property and support claims)	13(1)
13A	Direction to Canada Revenue Agency	13(7)
13B	Net family property statement	13(14)
14	Notice of motion	14(9)
14A	Affidavit (general)	14(9)
14B	Motion form	14(10)
14C	Confirmation	14(11)
14D	Order on motion without notice	14(14)
15	Change information form (motion to change child support)	15(10)
15A	Consent (motion to change child support)	15(10)
15B	Response to motion change [Proposed]	13(4.2)
15C	Consent motion to change [Proposed]	13(4.2)
15D	Consent motion to change child support [Proposed]	13(4.2)
17	Conference notice	17(13)
17A	Case conference brief — General	17(13)
17B	Case conference brief for protection application or status review	17(13)
17C	Settlement conference brief — General	17(13)

FORMS

Form number	Title	Rule creating form
17D	Settlement conference brief for protection application or status review	17(13)
17E	Trial management conference brief	17(13)
20	Request for information	20(3)
20A	Authorization to commissioner	20(14)
20B	Letter of request	20(14)
22	Request to admit	22(2)
22A	Response to request to admit	22(4)
23	Summons to witness	23(3)
23A	Summons to witness outside Ontario	23(8)
23B	Order for prisoner's attendance	23(10)
23C	Affidavit for uncontested trial	23(22)
25	Order (general)	25(2)
25A	Divorce order	25(2)
25B	Secure treatment order	25(2)
25C	Adoption order	25(2)
25D	Order (uncontested trial)	25(2)
25E	Notice disputing approval of order	25(5)
26	Statement of money owed	26(5)
26A	Affidavit of enforcement expenses	26(8)
26B	Affidavit for filing domestic contract or paternity agreement with court	26(9)
26C	Notice of transfer of enforcement	26(14)
27	Request for financial statement	27(1)
27A	Request for statement of income	27(7)
27B	Statement of income from income source	27(7)
27C	Appointment for financial examination	27(11)
28	Writ of seizure and sale	28(1)
28A	Request for writ of seizure and sale	28(1)
28B	Statutory declaration to sheriff	28(2)
28C	Writ of temporary seizure	28(10)
29	Request for garnishment	29(1)
29A	Notice of garnishment (lump-sum debt)	29(1)
29B	Notice of garnishment (periodic debt)	29(1)
29C	Notice to co-owner of debt	29(8)
29D	Statutory declaration of indexed support	29(14)
29E	Dispute (payor)	29(16)
29F	Dispute (garnishee)	29(16)
29G	Dispute (co-owner of debt)	29(16)
29H	Notice of garnishment hearing	29(17)
29I	Notice to stop garnishment	29(31)
29J	Statement to garnishee financial institution re support	29
30	Notice of default hearing	30(1)
30A	Request for default hearing	30(1)
30B	Default dispute	30(3)
31	Notice of contempt motion	31(2)
32	Bond (recognizance)	32(2)

FORMS UNDER THE FAMILY LAW RULES

Form number	Title	Rule creating form
32A	Notice of forfeiture motion	32(7)
32B	Warrant for arrest	32(12)
32C	Affidavit for warrant of committal	32(14)
32D	Warrant of committal	32(15)
33	Information for warrant to apprehend child	33(7)
33A	Warrant to apprehend child	33(7)
33B	Plan of care for child(ren) (Children's Aid Society)	33(7)
33B.1	Answer and plan of care (Parties other than Children's Aid Society)	33(7)
33B.2	Answer (*Child and Family Services Act* cases other than child protection and status review)	34(17)
33C	Statement of agreed facts (child protection)	33(7)
33D	Statement of agreed facts (status review)	33(7)
33E	Child's consent to secure treatment	33(8)
33F	Consent to secure treatment (person other than child)	33(8)
34	Child's consent to adoption	34(4)
34A	Affidavit of parentage	34(4)
34B	Non-parent's consent to adoption by spouse	34(4)
34C	Director's or local director's statement on adoption	34(4)
34D	Affidavit of adoption applicant(s)	34(4)
34E	Director's consent to adoption	34(6)
34F	Parent's or custodian's consent to adoption	34(7)
34G	Affidavit of adoption licensee or society employee	34(7)
34H	Affidavit of adopting relative or stepparent	34(8)
34I	Parent's consent to adoption by spouse	34(9)
34J	Affidavit of execution and independent legal advice (Children's Lawyer)	34(10)
34K	Certificate of clerk (adoption)	34(15)
34L	Application for openness order	34(17)
34M	Consent to openness order	34(17)
34N	Application to change or terminate openness order	34(17)
36	Affidavit for divorce	36(5)
36A	Certificate of clerk (divorce)	36(7)
36B	Certificate of divorce	36(8)
37	Notice of hearing	37(3)
37A	Information sheet	37(3)
37B	Direction to request further information	37(10)
37C	Notice of continuation of hearing	37(13)
37D	Notice of registration of order	37(18)
37E	Notice for taking further evidence	37(25)
38	Notice of appeal	38(2)
39	Notice of approaching dismissal	39(11)

FORM 4 — NOTICE OF CHANGE IN REPRESENTATION

[Repealed O. Reg. 76/06, s. 15.]

[Editor's Note: Forms 4 to 39 of the Family Law Rules have been repealed by O. Reg. 76/06, effective May 1, 2006. Pursuant to Family Law Rule 1(9), when a form is referred to by number, the reference is to the form with that number that is described in the Table of Forms at the end of these rules and which is available at www.ontariocourtforms.on.ca. For your convenience, the government form as published on this website is reproduced below.]

Court File Number ....

.... *(Name of Court)*

at... *Court office address*

Applicant(s)

Full legal name & address for service — street & number, municipality, postal code, telephone & fax numbers and e-mail address (if any).	*Lawyer's name & address — street & number, municipality, postal code, telephone & fax numbers and e-mail address (if any).*

Respondent(s)

Full legal name & address for service — street & number, municipality, postal code, telephone & fax numbers and e-mail address (if any).	*Lawyer's name & address — street & number, municipality, postal code, telephone & fax numbers and e-mail address (if any).*

Children's Lawyer

Name & address of Children's Lawyer's agent for service (street & number, municipality, postal code, telephone & fax numbers and e-mail address (if any)) and name of person represented.

TO ALL PARTIES AND THEIR LAWYERS

FROM *(name)*... *(Name, address, telephone & fax numbers and e-mail address)*

- ❏ I have chosen to be represented by a lawyer. See details in this box. →
- ❏ I have chosen a new lawyer. See details in this box. →
- ❏ I have decided to appear in court without a lawyer. Documents can be served on me at the address set out in this box. →
- ❏ I have the court's permission to be represented by a person who is not a lawyer. See details in this box. →

❑ I have the court's permission to appear in person at a child protection trial. Documents can be served on me at the address set out in this box. →

.... *(Date of signature)*

.... *(Signature)*

Notes:

1. *You must serve this notice on the lawyers for all of the other parties. If another party does not have a lawyer, you must serve it on the party. If you have been represented by a lawyer or other person who, because of this notice, is no longer going to represent you, you must also serve this notice on that lawyer or the other person who used to represent you.*

2. *You can serve by any method set out in rule 6 of the Family Law Rules, including mail, courier, and fax.*

3. *When you have served this notice, you must file it with the clerk of the court together with proof of service (form 6B). If you appeared without a lawyer and now you have chosen to be represented by a lawyer, you must attach that lawyer's consent to this notice.*

4. *If the case has been scheduled for trial, you must receive the court's permission to remove your lawyer and represent yourself.*

September 1, 2005

FORM 6 — ACKNOWLEDGEMENT OF SERVICE

[Repealed O. Reg. 76/06, s. 15.]

[Editor's Note: Forms 4 to 39 of the Family Law Rules have been repealed by O. Reg. 76/06, effective May 1, 2006. Pursuant to Family Law Rule 1(9), when a form is referred to by number, the reference is to the form with that number that is described in the Table of Forms at the end of these rules and which is available at www.ontariocourtforms.on.ca. For your convenience, the government form as published on this website is reproduced below.]

Court File Number ....

.... *(Name of court)*

at .... *Court office address*

You are asked to fill out and sign this card and to mail it immediately. If you do not return this card, the document(s) listed below may be personally served on you and you may be ordered to pay the costs of service.

My name is: (full legal name) ....

I may be served at: (address where court documents may be mailed to you) ....

I acknowledge receiving a copy of the following document(s):

❑ *Application dated* ....
❑ *Blank form of application*

❑ *Financial statement dated* ....

❑ *Blank form of financial statement*

❑ *Answer dated* ....
❑ *Blank form of answer*

❑ *Affidavit of (name)* .... *dated* ....

❑ *Notice of motion dated* ....

❑ *Statement of money owed dated* ....

❑ *(Other. Give title and date of document.)*

❑ ....

❑ ....

❑ ....

❑ ....

.... *Signature*

.... *Date of signature*

NOTICE: The address that you give above will be used in future to serve documents by mail until you inform the other parties and the court office of a new address for service.

September 1, 2005

FORM 6A — ADVERTISEMENT

[Repealed O. Reg. 76/06, s. 15.]

[Editor's Note: Forms 4 to 39 of the Family Law Rules have been repealed by O. Reg. 76/06, effective May 1, 2006. Pursuant to Family Law Rule 1(9), when a form is referred to by number, the reference is to the form with that number that is described in the Table of Forms at the end of these rules and which is available at www.ontariocourtforms.on.ca. For your convenience, the government form as published on this website is reproduced below.]

[*Name of court*]

NOTICE TO: (full legal name) ....

A CASE HAS BEEN STARTED AGAINST YOU IN COURT at (address: street & number, municipality, postal code) ....

The next court date is *(date)* .... at .... a.m./p/m. or as soon as possible after that time.

The court may make an order in this case that may affect your rights. You can get more information about this case from the court office at *(Write "the address above" or, if the court office is at a different address, give the street & number, municipality and postal code of the court office.)*

....

You may also get information about this case from *(name, address and telephone number of person publishing this advertisement)*

....

IF YOU DO NOT COME TO COURT, AN ORDER MAY BE MADE WITHOUT YOU AND BE ENFORCED AGAINST YOU.

September 1, 2005

FORM 6B — AFFIDAVIT OF SERVICE SWORN/AFFIRMED

[Repealed O. Reg. 76/06, s. 15.]

[Editor's Note: Forms 4 to 39 of the Family Law Rules have been repealed by O. Reg. 76/06, effective May 1, 2006. Pursuant to Family Law Rule 1(9), when a form is referred to by number, the reference is to the form with that number that is described in the Table of Forms at the end of these rules and which is available at www.ontariocourtforms.on.ca. For your convenience, the government form as published on this website is reproduced below.]

ONTARIO

Court File Number ....

.... *(Name of court)*

at .... *Court office address*

Applicant(s)

Full legal name & address for service — street & number, municipality, postal code, telephone & fax numbers and e-mail address (if any).	Lawyer's name & address — street & number, municipality, postal code, telephone & fax numbers and e-mail address (if any).

Respondent(s)

Full legal name & address for service — street & number, municipality, postal code, telephone & fax numbers and e-mail address (if any).	Lawyer's name & address — street & number, municipality, postal code, telephone & fax numbers and e-mail address (if any).

My name is (full legal name) ....

I live in (municipality & province) .... *and I swear/affirm that the following is true*:

1. On *(date)* ...., I served *(name of person to be served)* .... with the following document(s) in this case:

	Name of document	Author (if applicable)	Date when document signed, issued, sworn, etc.
	....	....	....
List the documents served	....	....	....
	....	....	....
	....	....	....

NOTE: You can leave out any part of this form that is not applicable.

2. I served the documents mentioned in paragraph 1 by:

Check one box only and go to indicated paragraph.

❑ special service. *(Go to paragraph 3 below if you used special service.)*

❑ mail. *(Go to paragraph 4 if you used mailed service.)*

❑ courier. *(Go to paragraph 5 if you used courier.)*

❑ deposit at a document exchange. *(Go to paragraph 6 if you used a document exchange.)*

❑ fax. *(Go to paragraph 7 if you used fax.)*

❑ substituted service or advertisement. *(Go to paragraph 8 if you used substituted service or advertisement.)*

3. I carried out special service of the document(s) on the person named in paragraph 1 at *(place or address)* .... by:

Check one box only. Strike out paragraphs 4 to 8 and go to paragraph 9.

❑ leaving a copy with the person.

❑ leaving a copy with *(name)* ....

❑ who is a lawyer who accepted service in writing on a copy of the document.

❑ who is the person's lawyer of record.

❑ who is the *(office or position)* .... of the corporation named in paragraph 1.

❑ mailing a copy to the person together with a prepaid return postcard in Form 6 in an envelope bearingthe sender's return address. This postcard, in which receipt of the document(s) is acknowledged, was returned and is attached to this affidavit.

❑ leaving a copy in a sealed envelope addressed to the person at the person's place of residence with *(name)* .... who provided me with identification to show that he/she was an adult person residing at the same address and by mailing another copy of the same document(s) on the same or following day to the person named in paragraph 1 at that place of residence.

❑ other *(Specify. See rule 6 for details.)*

....

....

4. I mailed the document(s) to be served by addressing the covering envelope to the person named in paragraph 1 at:

(Set out address.) .... which is the address

Check appropriate paragraph and strike out paragraphs 3, 5, 6, 7, 8, and 9.

❑ of the person's place of business.

❑ of a lawyer who accepted service on the person's behalf.

❑ of the person's lawyer of record.

❑ of the person's home.

❑ on the document most recently filed in court by the person.

❑ other *(Specify.)* ....

5. The document(s) to be served was/were placed in an envelope that was picked up at .... a.m./p.m. on *(date)* .... by *(name of courier service)* .... a private courier service, a copy of whose receipt is attached to this affidavit. The envelope was addressed to the person named in paragraph 1 at: *(Set out address.)* .... which is the address

Check appropriate paragraph and strike out paragraphs 3, 4, 6, 7, 8, and 9.

❑ of the person's place of business.

❑ of a lawyer who accepted service on the person's behalf.

❑ of the person's lawyer of record.

❑ of the person's home.

❑ on the document most recently filed in court by the person.

❑ other *(Specify.)* ....

6. The document(s) was/were deposited at a document exchange. The exchange's date stamp on the attached copy shows the date of deposit. *(Strike out paragraphs 3, 4, 5, 7, 8 and 9.)*

7. The document(s) to be served was/were faxed. The fax confirmation is attached to this affidavit. *(Strike out paragraphs 3, 4, 5, 6, 8 and 9.)*

8. An order of this court made on *(date)* .... allowed

❑ substituted service.

❑ service by advertisement. *(Attach advertisement.)*

The order was carried out as follows: *(Give details. Then go to paragraph 9 if you had to travel to serve substitutionally or by advertisement.)* ....

9. My relationship to, or affiliation with, any party in this case is as follows: ....

10. I am at least 18 years of age.

11. To serve the document(s), I had to travel .... kilometres. My fee for service of the document(s) is $ .... including travel.

Sworn/Affirmed before me at .... *municipality* in .... *province, state, or country* on .... *date* .... *Commissioner for taking affidavits (Type or print name below if signature is illegible.)*	.... *Signature* *(This form is to be signed in front of a lawyer, justice of the peace, notary public or commissioner for taking affidavits.)*

November 15, 2009

FORM 8 — APPLICATION (GENERAL)

[Editor's Note: Forms 4 to 39 of the Family Law Rules have been repealed by O. Reg. 76/06, effective May 1, 2006. Pursuant to Family Law Rule 1(9), when a form is referred to by number, the reference is to the form with that number that is described in the Table of Forms at the end of these rules and which is available at www.ontariocourtforms.on.ca. For your convenience, the government form as published on this website is reproduced below.]

Court File Number ....

SEAL

.... *(Name of court)*

at .... *Court office address*

Applicant(s)

Full legal name & address for service — street & number, municipality, postal code, telephone & fax numbers and e-mail address (if any).	*Lawyer's name & address — street & number, municipality, postal code, telephone & fax numbers and e-mail address (if any).*

Respondent(s)

Full legal name & address for service — street & number, municipality, postal code, telephone & fax numbers and e-mail address (if any).	*Lawyer's name & address — street & number, municipality, postal code, telephone & fax numbers and e-mail address (if any).*

Respondent(s)

TO THE RESPONDENT(S):

A COURT CASE HAS BEEN STARTED AGAINST YOU IN THIS COURT. THE DETAILS ARE SET OUT ON THE ATTACHED PAGES.

❑ *THE FIRST COURT DATE IS (date)* .... *AT* .... ❑ *a.m.* ❑ *p.m.* or as soon as possible after that time, at: *(address)*

....

....

NOTE: If this is a divorce case, no date will be set unless an Answer is filed. If you have also been served with a notice of motion, there may be an earlier court date and you or your lawyer should come to court for the motion.

❑ *THIS CASE IS ON THE FAST TRACK OF THE CASE MANAGEMENT SYSTEM.* A case management judge will be assigned by the time this case first comes before a judge.

❑ *THIS CASE IS ON THE STANDARD TRACK OF THE CASE MANAGEMENT SYSTEM. No court date has been set for this case* but, if you have been served with a notice of motion, it has a court date and you or your lawyer should come to court for the motion. A case management judge will not be assigned until one of the parties asks the clerk of the court to schedule a case conference or until a motion is scheduled, whichever comes first.

IF, AFTER 365 DAYS, THE CASE HAS NOT BEEN SCHEDULED FOR TRIAL, the clerk of the court will send out a warning that the case will be dismissed in 60 days unless the parties file proof that the case has been settled or one of the parties asks for a case conference or a settlement conference.

IF YOU WANT TO OPPOSE ANY CLAIM IN THIS CASE, you or your lawyer must prepare an Answer (Form 10 — a blank copy should be attached), serve a copy on the applicant(s) and file a copy in the court office with an Affidavit of Service (Form 6B). *YOU HAVE ONLY 30 DAYS AFTER THIS APPLICATION IS SERVED ON YOU (60 DAYS IF THIS APPLICATION IS SERVED ON YOU OUTSIDE CANADA OR THE UNITED STATES) TO SERVE AND FILE AN ANSWER. IF YOU DO NOT, THE CASE WILL GO AHEAD WITHOUT YOU AND THE COURT MAY MAKE AN ORDER AND ENFORCE IT AGAINST YOU.*

Check the box of the paragraph that applies to your case

❑ This case includes a claim for support. It does not include a claim for property or exclusive possession of the matrimonial home and its contents. You *MUST* fill out a Financial Statement (Form 13 — a blank copy attached), serve a copy on the applicant(s) and file a copy in the court office with an Affidavit of Service even if you do not answer this case.

❑ This case includes a claim for property or exclusive possession of the matrimonial home and its contents. You *MUST* fill out a Financial Statement (Form 13.1 — a blank copy attached), serve a copy on the applicant(s) and file a copy in the court office with an Affidavit of Service even if you do not answer this case.

IF YOU WANT TO MAKE A CLAIM OF YOUR OWN, you or your lawyer must fill out the claim portion in the Answer, serve a copy on the applicant(s) and file a copy in the court office with an Affidavit of Service.

- If you want to make a claim for support but do not want to make a claim for property or exclusive possession of the matrimonial home and its contents, you *MUST* fill out a Financial Statement (Form 13), serve a copy on the applicant(s) and file a copy in the court office.

- However, if your only claim for support is for child support in the table amount specified under the Child Support Guidelines, you do not need to fill out, serve or file a Financial Statement

- If you want to make a claim for property or exclusive possession of the matrimonial home and its contents, whether or not it includes a claim for support, you *MUST* fill out a Financial Statement (Form 13.1, not Form 13), serve a copy on the applicant(s), and file a copy in the court office.

YOU SHOULD GET LEGAL ADVICE ABOUT THIS CASE RIGHT AWAY. If you cannot afford a lawyer, you may be able to get help from your local Legal Aid Ontario office. *(See your telephone directory under LEGAL AID.)*

....

Date of issue *Clerk of the court*

FAMILY HISTORY

APPLICANT: . . . . Age: .... Birthdate: *(d, m, y)* ....

Resident in *(municipality & province)* ....

since *(date)* ....

Surname at birth: .... Surname just before marriage: ....

Divorced before? . . . . ❑ No ❑ Yes *(Place and date of previous divorce)*

....

RESPONDENT: . . . . Age: .... Birthdate: *(d, m, y)* ....

Resident in *(municipality & province)* ....

since *(date)* ....

Surname at birth: .... Surname just before marriage: ....

Divorced before? . . . . ❑ No ❑ Yes *(Place and date of previous divorce)*

....

RELATIONSHIP DATES:

❑ Married on *(date)* ....

❑ Started living together on *(date)* ....

❑ Separated on *(date)* ....

❑ Never lived together

❑ Still living together

THE CHILD(REN)

List all children involved in this case, even if no claim is made for these children.

Full legal name	Age	Birthdate (d, m, y)	Resident in (municipality & province)	Now Living With (name of person and relationship to child)

Full legal name	Age	Birthdate (d, m, y)	Resident in (municipality & province)	Now Living With (name of person and relationship to child)

PREVIOUS CASES OR AGREEMENTS

Have the parties or the children been in a court case before?

❑ No . . . . ❑ Yes

Have the parties made a written agreement dealing with any matter involved in this case?

❑ No . . . . ❑ Yes *(Give date of agreement. Indicate which of its terms are in dispute. Attach an additional page if you need more space.)*

CLAIM BY APPLICANT

I ASK THE COURT FOR THE FOLLOWING:

(Claims below include claims for temporary orders.)

Claims under the Divorce Act **(Check boxes in this column only if you are asking for a divorce and your case is in the Superior Court of Justice or Family Court of the Superior Court of Justice.)**	**Claims under the Family Law Act or Children's Law Reform Act**	**Claims relating to property** **(Check boxes in this column only if your case is in the Superior Court of Justice or Family Court of the Superior Court of Justice.)**
00 ❑ a divorce	10 ❑ support for me	20 ❑ equalization of net family properties
01 ❑ support for me	11 ❑ support for child(ren) — table amount	
02 ❑ support for child(ren) — table amount		21 ❑ exclusive possession of matrimonial home
	12 ❑ support for child(ren) — other than table amount	
03 ❑ support for child(ren) — other than table amount		22 ❑ exclusive possession of contents of matrimonial home
	13 ❑ custody of child(ren)	
04 ❑ custody of child(ren)	14 ❑ access to child(ren)	

Claims under the Divorce Act (Check boxes in this column only if you are asking for a divorce and your case is in the Superior Court of Justice or Family Court of the Superior Court of Justice.)	Claims under the Family Law Act or Children's Law Reform Act	Claims relating to property (Check boxes in this column only if your case is in the Superior Court of Justice or Family Court of the Superior Court of Justice.)
05 ❑ access to child(ren)	15 ❑ restraining/non-harassment order	23 ❑ freezing assets
		24 ❑ sale of family property
	16 ❑ indexing spousal support	
	17 ❑ declaration of parentage	
	18 ❑ guardianship over child's property	
Other claims	50 ❑ Other *(Specify.)*	
30 ❑ costs		
31 ❑ annulment of marriage		
32 ❑ prejudgment interest		

Give details of the order that you want the court to make. *(Include any amounts of support (if known) and the names of the children for whom support, custody or access is claimed.)*

IMPORTANT FACTS SUPPORTING MY CLAIM FOR DIVORCE

❑ *Separation*: The spouses have lived separate and apart since *(date)* .... and

❑ have not lived together again since that date in an unsuccessful attempt to reconcile.

❑ have lived together again during the following period(s) in an unsuccessful attempt to reconcile. *(Give dates.)*

❑ *Adultery*: The respondent has committed adultery. *(Give details. It is not necessary to name any other person involved but, if you do name the other person, then you must serve this application on the other person.)*

❑ *Cruelty*: The respondent has treated the applicant with physical or mental cruelty of such a kind as to make continued cohabitation intolerable. *(Give details.)*

IMPORTANT FACTS SUPPORTING MY OTHER CLAIM(S)

(Set out below the facts that form the legal basis for your other claim(s). Attach an additional page if you need more space.)

Put a line through any blank space left on this page. If additional space is needed, extra pages may be attached.

....	....
Date of signature	*Signature of applicant*

LAWYER'S CERTIFICATE

For divorce cases only

My name is: .... and I am the applicant's lawyer in this divorce case. I certify that I have complied with the requirements of section 9 of the *Divorce Act*.

....	....
Date	*Signature of Lawyer*

June 15, 2007

FORM 8A — APPLICATION (DIVORCE)

[Editor's Note: Forms 4 to 39 of the Family Law Rules have been repealed by O. Reg. 76/06, effective May 1, 2006. Pursuant to Family Law Rule 1(9), when a form is referred to by number, the reference is to the form with that number that is described in the Table of Forms at the end of these rules and which is available at www.ontariocourtforms.on.ca. For your convenience, the government form as published on this website is reproduced below.]

Court File Number ....

SEAL

.... *(Name of court)*

at .... *Court office address*

Applicant(s)

Full legal name & address for service — street & number, municipality, postal code, telephone & fax numbers and e-mail address (if any).	*Lawyer's name & address — street & number, municipality, postal code, telephone & fax numbers and e-mail address (if any).*

Respondent(s)

Full legal name & address for service — street & number, municipality, postal code, telephone & fax numbers and e-mail address (if any).	*Lawyer's name & address — street & number, municipality, postal code, telephone & fax numbers and e-mail address (if any).*

❑ *IN THIS CASE, THE APPLICANT IS CLAIMING DIVORCE ONLY.*

TO THE RESPONDENT(S): A COURT CASE FOR DIVORCE HAS BEEN STARTED AGAINST YOU IN THIS COURT. THE DETAILS ARE SET OUT ON THE ATTACHED PAGES.

THIS CASE IS ON THE STANDARD TRACK OF THE CASE MANAGEMENT SYSTEM. No court date has been set for this case but, if you have been served with a notice of motion, it has a court date and you or your lawyer should come to court for the motion. A case management judge will not be assigned until one of the parties asks the clerk of the court to schedule a case conference or until a motion is scheduled, whichever comes first.

IF, AFTER 365 DAYS, THE CASE HAS NOT BEEN SCHEDULED FOR TRIAL, the clerk of the court will send out a warning that the case will be dismissed within 60 days unless the parties file proof that the case has been settled or one of the parties asks for a case or a settlement conference.

IF YOU WANT TO OPPOSE ANY CLAIM IN THIS CASE, you or your lawyer must prepare an Answer (Form 10 — a blank copy should be attached), serve a copy on the applicant and file a copy in the court office with an Affidavit of Service (Form 6B). *YOU HAVE ONLY 30 DAYS AFTER THIS APPLICATION IS SERVED ON YOU (60 DAYS IF THIS APPLICATION IS SERVED ON YOU OUTSIDE CANADA OR THE UNITED STATES) TO SERVE AND FILE AN ANSWER. IF YOU DO NOT, THE CASE WILL GO AHEAD WITHOUT YOU AND THE COURT MAY MAKE AN ORDER AND ENFORCE IT AGAINST YOU.*

IF YOU WANT TO MAKE A CLAIM OF YOUR OWN, you or your lawyer must fill out the claim portion in the Answer, serve a copy on the applicant(s) and file a copy in the court office with an Affidavit of Service.

- If you want to make a claim for support but do not want to make a claim for property or exclusive possession of the matrimonial home and its contents, you *MUST* fill out a Financial Statement (Form 13), serve a copy on the applicant(s) and file a copy in the court office.
- However, if your only claim for support is for child support in the table amount specified under the Child Support Guidelines, you do not need to fill out, serve or file a Financial Statement.
- If you want to make a claim for property or exclusive possession of the matrimonial home and its contents, whether or not it includes a claim for support, you *MUST* fill out a Financial Statement (Form 13.1, not Form 13), serve a copy on the applicant(s), and file a copy in the court office.

YOU SHOULD GET LEGAL ADVICE ABOUT THIS CASE RIGHT AWAY. If you cannot afford a lawyer, you may be able to get help from your local Legal Aid Ontario office. *(See your telephone directory under LEGAL AID.)*

❑ *THIS CASE IS A JOINT APPLICATION FOR DIVORCE. THE DETAILS ARE SET OUT ON THE ATTACHED PAGES.* The application and affidavits in support of the application will be presented to a judge when the materials have been checked for completeness.

If you are requesting anything other than a simple divorce, such as support or property or exclusive possession of the matrimonial home and its contents, then refer to page 1 for instructions regarding the Financial Statement you should file.

....	....
Date of issue	*Clerk of the court*

FAMILY HISTORY

APPLICANT: . . . . Age: .... Birthdate: *(d, m, y)* ....

Resident in *(municipality & province)* ....

since *(date)* ....

Surname at birth: .... Surname just before marriage: ....

Divorced before? . . . . ❑ No ❑ Yes *(Place and date of previous divorce)* ....

RESPONDENT/JOINT APPLICANT:

Age: .... Birthdate: *(d, m, y)* ....

Resident in *(municipality & province)* ....

since *(date)* ....

Surname at birth: .... Surname just before marriage: ....

Divorced before? . . . . ❑ No ❑ Yes *(Place and date of previous divorce)* ....

RELATIONSHIP DATES:

❑ Married on *(date)* ....

❑ Started living together on *(date)* ....

❑ Separated on *(date)* ....

❑ Never lived together

THE CHILD(REN)

List all children involved in this case, even if no claim is made for these children.

Full legal name	**Age**	**Birthdate (d, m, y)**	**Resident in (municipality & province)**	**Now Living With (name of person and relationship to child)**

PREVIOUS CASES OR AGREEMENTS

Have the parties or the children been in a court case before?

❑ No . . . . ❑ Yes

Have the parties made a written agreement dealing with any matter involved in this case?

❑ No . . . . ❑ Yes *(Give date of agreement. Indicate which of its terms are in dispute. Attach an additional page if you need more space.)*

CLAIMS

USE THIS FRAME ONLY IF THIS CASE IS A JOINT APPLICATION FOR DIVORCE

WE JOINTLY ASK THE COURT FOR THE FOLLOWING:

Claims under the Divorce Act	*Claims under the Family Law Act or Children's Law Reform Act*	*Claims relating to property*
00 ❑ a divorce	10 ❑ spousal support	20 ❑ equalization of net family properties
01 ❑ spousal support	11 ❑ support for child(ren) — table amount	
02 ❑ support for child(ren) — table amount		21 ❑ exclusive possession of matrimonial home
	12 ❑ support for child(ren) — other than table amount	
03 ❑ support for child(ren) — other than table amount		22 ❑ exclusive possession of contents of matrimonial home
	13 ❑ custody of child(ren)	
04 ❑ custody of child(ren)	14 ❑ access to child(ren)	
05 ❑ access to child(ren)	15 ❑ restraining/non-harassment order	23 ❑ freezing assets
		24 ❑ sale of family property
	16 ❑ indexing spousal support	
	17 ❑ declaration of parentage	
	18 ❑ guardianship over child's property	
		Other claims
		30 ❑ costs
		31 ❑ annulment of marriage
		32 ❑ prejudgment interest
		50 ❑ Other *(Specify)*

USE THIS FRAME ONLY IF THE APPLICANT'S ONLY CLAIM IN THIS CASE IS FOR DIVORCE.

I ASK THE COURT FOR:
(Check if applicable.)

00 ❑ a divorce　　30 ❑ costs

IMPORTANT FACTS SUPPORTING THE CLAIM FOR DIVORCE

❑ *Separation*: The spouses have lived separate and apart since *(date)* .... and

❑ have not lived together again since that date in an unsuccessful attempt to reconcile.

❑ have lived together again during the following periods(s) in an unsuccessful attempt to reconcile: *(Give dates.)*

❑ *Adultery: (Name of spouse)* .... has committed adultery.

(Give details. It is not necessary to name any other person involved but if you do name the other person, then you must serve this application on the other person.)

❑ *Cruelty: (Name of spouse)* .... has treated *(name of spouse)* .... with physical or mental cruelty of such a kind as to make continued cohabitation intolerable. *(Give details.)*

USE THIS FRAME ONLY IF THIS CASE IS A JOINT APPLICATION FOR DIVORCE.
The details of the other order(s) that we jointly ask the court to make are as follows: *(Include any amounts of support and the names of the children for whom support, custody or access is to be ordered.)* *IMPORTANT FACTS SUPPORTING OUR CLAIM(S)* *(Set out the facts that form the legal basis for your claim(s). Attach an additional page if you need more space.)*

Put a line through any blank space left on this page.

Complete this section if your only claim is for a divorce. Your lawyer, if you are represented, must complete the Lawyer's Certificate below.

....	....
Date of signature	*Signature of applicant*

Complete this section if you are making a joint application for divorce. Your lawyer, if you are represented, must complete the Lawyer's Certificate below.

....	....
Date of signature	*Signature of joint applicant*
....	....
Date of signature	*Signature of joint applicant*

LAWYER'S CERTIFICATE

My name is: .... and I am the lawyer for *(name)* .... in this divorce case. I certify that I have complied with the requirements of section 9 of the *Divorce Act*.

....	....
Date	*Signature of Lawyer*

My name is: .... and I am the lawyer for *(name)* .... in this divorce case. I certify that I have complied with the requirements of section 9 of the *Divorce Act.*

....	....
Date	*Signature of Lawyer*

June 15, 2007

FORM 8B — APPLICATION (CHILD PROTECTION AND STATUS REVIEW)

[Editor's Note: Forms 4 to 39 of the Family Law Rules have been repealed by O. Reg. 76/06, effective May 1, 2006. Pursuant to Family Law Rule 1(9), when a form is referred to by number, the reference is to the form with that number that is described in the Table of Forms at the end of these rules and which is available at www.ontariocourtforms.on.ca. For your convenience, the government form as published on this website is reproduced below.]

Court File Number ....

SEAL

.... *(Name of court)*

at .... *Court office address*

Applicant(s) (In most cases, the applicant will be a children's aid society.)

Full legal name & address for service — street & number, municipality, postal code, telephone & fax numbers and e-mail address (if any).	*Lawyer's name & address — street & number, municipality, postal code, telephone & fax numbers and e-mail address (if any).*

Respondent(s) (In most cases, a respondent will be a "parent" within the meaning of section 37 of the *Child and Family Services Act.*)

Full legal name & address for service — street & number, municipality, postal code, telephone & fax numbers and e-mail address (if any).	*Lawyer's name & address — street & number, municipality, postal code, telephone & fax numbers and e-mail address (if any).*

Children's Lawyer

Name & address of Children's Lawyer's agent for service (street & number, municipality, postal code, telephone & fax numbers and e-mail address (if any)) and name of person represented.

TO THE RESPONDENT(S):

A COURT CASE HAS BEEN STARTED AGAINST YOU IN THIS COURT. THE DETAILS ARE SET OUT ON THE ATTACHED PAGES.

THE FIRST COURT DATE IS (date) .... *AT* .... ❑ *a.m.* ❑ *p.m.* or as soon as possible after that time, at: *(address)*

....

....

If you have also been served with a notice of motion, there may be an earlier court date and you or your lawyer should come to court for the motion.

IF YOU WANT TO OPPOSE ANY CLAIM IN THIS CASE, you or your lawyer must prepare an Answer and Plan of Care (Form 33B.1 — a blank copy should be attached), serve a copy on the children's aid society and all other parties and file a copy in the court office with an Affidavit of Service (Form 6B).

YOU HAVE ONLY 30 DAYS AFTER THIS APPLICATION IS SERVED ON YOU (60 DAYS IF THIS APPLICATION IS SERVED ON YOU OUTSIDE CANADA OR THE UNITED STATES) TO SERVE AND FILE AN ANSWER. IF YOU DO NOT, THE CASE WILL GO AHEAD WITHOUT YOU AND THE COURT MAY MAKE AN ORDER AND ENFORCE IT AGAINST YOU.

Check this box if this paragraph applies

> ❑ The children's aid society is also making a claim for child support. You *MUST* fill out a Financial Statement (Form 13 — a blank copy attached), serve a copy on the society and file a copy in the court office with an Affidavit of Service even if you do not answer this case.

WARNING: This case is subject to case management, which means that the case runs on a timetable. That timetable says that the following steps have to be finished by the following number of days from the start of this case:

Service and filing of answers and plans of care — 30 days

Temporary care & custody hearing — 35 days

Settlement conference — 80 days

Hearing — 120 days

You should consider getting legal advice about this case right away. If you cannot afford a lawyer, you may be able to get help from your local legal aid office. *(See your telephone directory under LEGAL AID).*

....

Date of issue *Clerk of the court*

THE CHILD(REN): (List all children involved in this case.)

Child's Full Legal Name	**Birthdate**	**Age**	**Sex**	**Full Legal Name of Mother**	**Full Legal Name of Father**	**Child's Religion**	**Child's Native Status**

CLAIM BY APPLICANT

NOTE: If this case is an application for a status review, strike out paragraph 1 and go immediately to paragraph 2.

1. The applicant children's aid society asks the court to make a finding under Part III of the *Child and Family Services Act* that the child(ren) named in this application is/are in need of protection because:

(Check the applicable box(es). In each checked paragraph, delete those portions of the text that are not relevant.)

❑ the child(ren) has/have suffered physical harm, inflicted by the person having charge of the child(ren) or caused by that person's

❑ failure to care for, provide for, supervise or protect the child(ren) adequately [subclause 37(2)(a)(i)].

❑ pattern of neglect in caring for, providing for, supervising or protecting the child(ren) [subclause 37(2)(a)(ii)].

❑ there is a risk that the child(ren) is/are likely to suffer physical harm inflicted by the person having charge of the child(ren) or caused by that person's

❑ failure to care for, provide for, supervise or protect the child(ren) adequately [subclause 37(2)(b)(i)].

❑ pattern of neglect in caring for, providing for, supervising or protecting the child(ren) [subclause 37(2)(b)(ii)].

❑ the child(ren) has/have been sexually molested or sexually exploited, by the person having charge of the child(ren) or by another person where the person having charge knows or should know of the possibility of sexual molestation or sexual exploitation and fails to protect the child(ren) [clause 37(2)(c)].

❑ there is a risk that the child(ren) is/are likely to be sexually molested or sexually exploited, by the person having charge of the child(ren) or by another person where the person having charge knows of should know of the possibility of sexual molestation or sexual exploitation and fails to protect the child(ren) [clause 37(2)(d)].

❑ the child(ren) require(s) medical treatment to cure, prevent or alleviate physical harm or suffering and the child(ren)'s parent or the person having charge of the child(ren) does not provide, or refuses or is unavailable or unable to consent to, the treatment [clause 37(2)(e)].

❑ the child(ren) has/have suffered emotional harm, demonstrated by serious anxiety, depression, withdrawal, self-destructive or aggressive behaviour, or delayed development and there are reasonable grounds to believe that the emotional harm suffered by the child(ren) results from the actions, failure to act or pattern of neglect on the part of the child(ren)'s parent or the person having charge of the child(ren) [clause 37(2)(f)].

❑ the child(ren) has/have suffered emotional harm, demonstrated by serious anxiety, depression, withdrawal, self-destructive or aggressive behaviour, or delayed development and the child(ren)'s parent or the person having charge of the child(ren) does not provide, or refuses or is unavailable or unable to consent to, services or treatment to remedy or alleviate the harm [clause 37(2)(f.1)].

❑ there is a risk that the child(ren) is/are likely to suffer emotional harm, demonstrated by serious anxiety, depression, withdrawal, self-destructive or aggressive behaviour, or delayed development resulting from the actions, failure to act or pattern of neglect on the part of the child(ren)'s parent or the person having charge of the child(ren) [clause 37(2)(g)].

❑ there is a risk that the child(ren) is/are likely to suffer emotional harm, demonstrated by serious anxiety, depression, withdrawal, self-destructive or aggressive behaviour, or delayed development and that the child(ren)'s parent or the person having charge of the child(ren) does not provide, or refuses or is unavailable or unable to consent to services or treatment to prevent the harm [clause 37(2)(g.1)].

❑ the child(ren) suffer(s) from a mental, emotional or developmental condition that, if not remedied, could seriously impair the child(ren)'s development and the child(ren)'s parent or the person having charge of the child(ren) does not provide, or refuses or is unavailable or unable to consent to, treatment to remedy or alleviate the condition [clause 37(2)(h)].

❑ the child(ren) has/have been abandoned [clause 37(2)(i)].

❑ the child(ren)'s parent has died or is unavailable to exercise his or her custodial rights over the child(ren) and has not made adequate provision for the child(ren)'s care and custody [clause 37(2)(i)].

❑ the child(ren) is/are in a residential placement and the child(ren)'s parent refuses or is unable or unwilling to resume the care and custody of the child(ren) [clause 37(2)(i)].

❑ the child(ren) is/are less than twelve years old and has/have killed or seriously injured another person or caused serious damage to another person's property; services or treatment are necessary to prevent a recurrence; and the child(ren)'s parent or the person having charge of the child(ren) does not provide, or refuses or is unavailable or unable to consent to, those services or treatment [clause 37(2)(j)].

❑ the child(ren) is/are less than twelve years old and has/have, on more than one occasion, injured another person or caused loss or damage to another person's property, with the encouragement of the person having charge of the child(ren) or because of that person's failure or inability to supervise the child(ren) adequately [clause 37(2)(k)].

❑ the child(ren)'s parent is unable to care for the child(ren) and the child(ren) is/are brought before the court with the parent's consent and, where the child(ren) is/are twelve years of age or older, with the child(ren)'s consent, to be dealt with under Part III of the *Child and Family Services Act* [clause 37(2)(l)].

2. *(name)* .... asks for an order,

❑ that the child(ren) be placed with *(name of custodian)* .... subject to the supervision of *(full legal name of supervising society)*

....

for a period of .... months, on the terms and conditions set out in the Appendix on page 7 of this Application form.

❑ that the child(ren) be made (a) ward(s) of *(full legal name of society)*

....

for a period of .... months

❑ that the child(ren) be made (a) ward(s) of *(full legal name of society)*

....

for a period of .... months and then returned to *(name of custodian)*

....

subject to the supervision of *(full legal name of supervising society)*

....

for a period of .... months, on the terms and conditions set out in the Appendix on page 7 of this Application form.

❑ that the child(ren) be made (a) ward(s) of the Crown and placed in the care of *(full legal name of caretaker society)* ....

❑ that *(name of homemaker)* .... be authorized to remain on the premises at *(address of premises where homemaker is placed)*

....

until *(date)* .... or until the person who is entitled to custody of the child(ren) returns to care for the child(ren), whichever is sooner.

❑ relating to access, the details of which are as follows: ....

....

....

❑ that *(name of person)* .... be restrained under s. 80 of the *Child and Family Services Act* from having any contact with *(name of child(ren) and/or any other caregiver)*

....

....

....

❑ relating to payment of support while the child(ren) is/are in care or subject to an order of supervision, the details of which are as follows:

....

....

....

....

....

....

....

....

❑ for court costs.

❑ other *(Specify.)* ....

Deemed orders under the *Children's Law Reform Act*:

❑ that the child(ren) be placed in the custody of *(name of custodian — cannot be a foster parent of the child)*

....

(This order shall be deemed to be an order under s. 28 of the Children's Law Reform Act.)

❑ relating to access, the details of which are as follows:

....

....

....

....

....

....

....

....

(This order shall be deemed to be an order under s. 28 of the Children's Law Reform Act.)

❑ that *(name of person)* .... be restrained under s. 57.1(3) of the *Child and Family Services Act* from having contact with *(name of child(ren) and/or any other caregiver)*

....

....

....

(This order shall be deemed to be an order under s. 35 of the Children's Law Reform Act.)

3. To the applicant's best knowledge, the child(ren)

❑ has/have never before been in the care of a society under an out-of-court agreement.

❑ has/have been in the care of a society under an out-of-court agreement. The details are as follows: *(Set out the number of times each child was in society care, when the care began and how long it lasted.)*

....

....

....

....

4. To the applicant's best knowledge, the parties or the child(ren) . . . ❑ have ❑ have not been in a court case before relating to the supervision, wardship (guardianship) or custody of or access to the child(ren). *(Provide details of any existing custody order, including whether made by a superior court or under the Divorce Act.)*

....

....

5. The parties . . . . . . ❑ have ❑ have not made a written agreement dealing with any matter involved in this case. *(If you checked the first box, give date of agreement and indicate which of its terms are in dispute. Attach an additional page if you need more space.)*

....

....

....

....

....

6. The following is a brief statement of the facts upon which the applicant is relying in this application.

(Set out the facts in numbered paragraphs. If you need more space, you may attach a page, but you must date and sign each additional page.)

....

....

....

....

....

....

....

....

....

Put a line through any blank space left on this page.

....	....
Date of signature	*Signature*
....	....
If applicant is a children's aid society, give office or position of person signing.	*Print or type name*

APPENDIX

The terms and conditions proposed for the child(ren)'s supervision are as follows: *(Set out terms and conditions in numbered paragraphs. Omit this page if no supervision is sought.)*

....

....

....

....

....

....

....

....

....

....

....

....

....

....

....

....

....

....

....

....

....

....

....

....

....

....

....

....

....

....

....

....

....

....

October 1, 2006

FORM 8B.1 — APPLICATION (STATUS REVIEW FOR CROWN WARD AND FORMER CROWN WARD)

[Editor's Note: Pursuant to Family Law Rule 1(9), when a form is referred to by number, the reference is to the form with that number that is described in the Table of Forms at the end of these rules and which is available at www.ontariocourtforms.on.ca. For your convenience, the government form as published on this website is reproduced below.]

Court File Number ....

SEAL

.... *(Name of court)*

at .... *Court office address*

Applicant(s) (In most cases, the applicant will be a children's aid society.)

Full legal name & address for service — street & number, municipality, postal code, telephone & fax numbers and e-mail address (if any).	*Lawyer's name & address — street & number, municipality, postal code, telephone & fax numbers and e-mail address (if any).*

Respondent(s) (In most cases, a respondent will be a "parent" within the meaning of section 37 of the *Child and Family Services Act*.)

Full legal name & address for service — street & number, municipality, postal code, telephone & fax numbers and e-mail address (if any).	*Lawyer's name & address — street & number, municipality, postal code, telephone & fax numbers and e-mail address (if any).*

Children's Lawyer

Name & address of Children's Lawyer's agent for service (street & number, municipality, postal code, telephone & fax numbers and e-mail address (if any)) and name of person represented.

TO THE RESPONDENT(S):

A COURT CASE HAS BEEN STARTED AGAINST YOU IN THIS COURT. THE DETAILS ARE SET OUT ON THE ATTACHED PAGES.

THE FIRST COURT DATE IS (date) .... *AT* .... ❑ a.m. ❑ p.m. or as soon as possible after that time, at: *(address)*

....

....

If you have also been served with a notice of motion, there may be an earlier court date, and you or your lawyer should come to court for the motion.

IF YOU WANT TO OPPOSE ANY CLAIM IN THIS CASE, you or your lawyer must prepare an Answer and Plan of Care (Form 33B.1 — a blank copy should be attached), serve a copy on the children's aid society and all other parties and file a copy in the court office with an Affidavit of Service (Form 6B).

YOU HAVE ONLY 30 DAYS AFTER THIS APPLICATION IS SERVED ON YOU (60 DAYS IF THIS APPLICATION IS SERVED ON YOU OUTSIDE CANADA OR THE UNITED STATES) TO SERVE AND FILE AN ANSWER. IF YOU DO NOT, THE CASE WILL GO AHEAD WITHOUT YOU AND THE COURT MAY MAKE AN ORDER AND ENFORCE IT AGAINST YOU.

Check this box if this paragraph applies

> ❑ The children's aid society is also making a claim for child support. You *MUST* fill out a Financial Statement (Form 13 — a blank copy attached), serve a copy on the society and file a copy in the court office with an Affidavit of Service even if you do not answer this case.

WARNING: This case is subject to case management, which means that the case runs on a timetable. That timetable says that the following steps have to be finished by the following number of days from the start of this case:

Service and filing of answers and plans of care — 30 days

Temporary care & custody hearing — 35 days

Settlement conference — 80 days

Hearing — 120 days

You should consider getting legal advice about this case right away. If you cannot afford a lawyer, you may be able to get help from your local legal aid office. *(See your telephone directory under LEGAL AID).*

....

Date of issue Clerk of the court

THE CHILD

Child's Full Legal Name	Birthdate	Age	Sex	Full Legal Name of Mother	Full Legal Name of Father	Child's Religion	Child's Native Status

CLAIM BY (name and relationship to child, if applicable) ....

1. (name) .... asks for an order,

❏ that the child be placed in the custody of *(name of custodian)* .... under s. 65.2 of the *Child and Family Services Act.*

❏ that the child be placed with *(name of custodian)* .... subject to the supervision of *(full legal name of supervising society)* .... for a period of .... months, on the terms and conditions set out in the Appendix on page 5 of this Application form.

❏ that the child be made a ward of the Crown and placed in the care of *(full legal name of caretaker society)* ....

❏ relating to access, the details of which are as follows: ....

❏ that *(name of person)* .... be restrained under s. 80 of the *Child and Family Services Act* from having any contact with *(name of child and/or any caregiver)* .... *(Provide details of restraining order being sought.)* ....

❏ relating to payment of support while the child is in care or subject to an order of supervision, the details of which are as follows: ....

❏ terminating the order dated *(date of order)* .... for *(type of order)* ....

❏ for court costs.

❏ other *(Specify.)* ....

2. The details of the child's history in the care of a society are as follows:

(Set out number of times the child was in the care of a society, when the care began, how long it lasted and the date(s) of the order(s) for Crown wardship and access.)

....

....

....

....

....

....

....

....

....

....

....

....

3. The following is a brief statement of the facts relied upon in this application.

(Set out the facts in numbered paragraphs. If you need more space, you may attach a page, but you must date and sign each additional page.)

....

....

....

....

....

....

....

....

....

....

....

....

....

Put a line through any blank space left on this page.

....	....
Date of signature	*Signature*
....	....
If applicant is a children's aid society, give office or position of person signing.	*Print or type name.*

APPENDIX

The terms and conditions proposed for the child's supervision are as follows: *(Set out terms and conditions in numbered paragraphs. Omit this page if no supervision is sought.)*

....

....

....

....

....

....

....

....

....

....

....

....

....

....

....

....

....

....

....

....

....

....

....

....

....

....

....

....

....

....

....

....

....

....

October 1, 2006

FORM 8B.2 — APPLICATION (GENERAL) (CHILD AND FAMILY SERVICES ACT CASES OTHER THAN CHILD PROTECTION AND STATUS REVIEW)

[Editor's Note: Pursuant to Family Law Rule 1(9), when a form is referred to by number, the reference is to the form with that number that is described in the Table of Forms at the end of these rules and which is available at www.ontariocourtforms.on.ca. For your convenience, the government form as published on this website is reproduced below.]

Court File Number ....

SEAL

.... *(Name of Court)*

at .... *Court office address*

Applicant(s) (In most cases, the applicant will be a children's aid society.)

Full legal name & address for service — street & number, municipality, postal code, telephone & fax numbers and e-mail address (if any).	*Lawyer's name & address — street & number, municipality, postal code, telephone & fax numbers and e-mail address (if any).*

Respondent(s) (In most cases, a respondent will be a "parent" within the meaning of section 37 of the *Child and Family Services Act*.)

Full legal name & address for service — street & number, municipality, postal code, telephone & fax numbers and e-mail address (if any).	*Lawyer's name & address — street & number, municipality, postal code, telephone & fax numbers and e-mail address (if any).*

Children's Lawyer

Name & address of Children's Lawyer's agent for service (street & number, municipality, postal code, telephone & fax numbers and e-mail address (if any)) and name of person represented.

TO THE RESPONDENT(S):

A COURT CASE HAS BEEN STARTED AGAINST YOU IN THIS COURT. THE DETAILS ARE SET OUT ON THE ATTACHED PAGES.

THE FIRST COURT DATE IS (date) .... *AT* .... ❑ a.m. ❑ p.m. or as soon as possible after that time, at: *(address)*

....

....

If you have also been served with a notice of motion, there may be an earlier court date and you or your lawyer should come to court for the motion.

IF YOU WANT TO OPPOSE ANY CLAIM IN THIS CASE, you or your lawyer must prepare an Answer (*Child and Family Services Act* Cases other than Child Protection and Status Review) (Form 33B.2 — a blank copy should be attached), serve a copy on the children's aid society and all other parties and file a copy in the court office with an Affidavit of Service (Form 6B).

YOU HAVE ONLY 30 DAYS AFTER THIS APPLICATION IS SERVED ON YOU (60 DAYS IF THIS APPLICATION IS SERVED ON YOU OUTSIDE CANADA OR THE UNITED STATES) TO SERVE AND FILE AN ANSWER. IF YOU DO NOT, THE CASE WILL GO AHEAD WITHOUT YOU AND THE COURT MAY MAKE AN ORDER AND ENFORCE IT AGAINST YOU.

Check this box if this paragraph applies

❑ The children's aid society is also making a claim for child support. You *MUST* fill out a Financial Statement (Form 13 — a blank copy attached), serve a copy on the society and file a copy in the court office with an Affidavit of Service even if you do not answer this case.

WARNING: This case is subject to case management, which means that the case runs on a timetable. That timetable says that the following steps have to be finished by the following number of days from the start of this case:

Service and filing of answers and plans of care — 30 days

Settlement conference — 80 days

Hearing — 120 days

You should consider getting legal advice about this case right away. If you cannot afford a lawyer, you may be able to get help from your local legal aid office. *(See your telephone directory under LEGAL AID).*

....

Date of issue *Clerk of the court*

THE CHILD(REN): (List all children involved in this case.)

Child's Full Legal Name	Birthdate	Age	Sex	Full Legal Name of Mother	Full Legal Name of Father	Child's Religion	Child's Native Status

CLAIM BY (name and relationship to child, if applicable) ....

1. (name) .... asks for an order: *(Specify the order being sought and the grounds upon which the application is being brought)*

❑ relating to access, the details of which are as follows: ....

❑ that *(name of person)* .... be restrained under s. 80 of the *Child and Family Services Act* from having any contact with *(name of child(ren) and/or any caregiver)* .... *(Provide details of restraining order being sought.)* ....

❑ relating to payment of support while the child(ren) is/are in care or subject to an order of supervision, the details of which are as follows: ....

❑ other *(Specify.)* ....

❑ for court costs of this application.

2. The existing orders relating to the child(ren) are as follows:

....

....

....

....

....

....

....

....

....

....

....

....

....

3. The following is a brief statement of the facts relied upon in this application.

(Set out the facts in numbered paragraphs. If you need more space, you may attach a page, but you must date and sign each additional page.)

....

....

....

....

....

....

....

....

....

....

....

....

....

Put a line through any blank space left on this page.

.... *Date of signature*	.... *Signature*
.... *If applicant is a children's aid society, give office or position of person signing.*	.... *Print or type name*

October 1, 2006

FORM 8C — APPLICATION FOR ❑ SECURE TREATMENT ❑ EXTENSION OF SECURE TREATMENT

[Repealed O. Reg. 76/06, s. 15.]

[Editor's Note: Forms 4 to 39 of the Family Law Rules have been repealed by O. Reg. 76/06, effective May 1, 2006. Pursuant to Family Law Rule 1(9), when a form is referred to by number, the reference is to the form with that number that is described in the Table of Forms at the end of these rules and which is available at www.ontariocourtforms.on.ca. For your convenience, the government form as published on this website is reproduced below.]

ONTARIO

Court File Number ....

SEAL

.... *(Name of court)*

at .... *Court office address*

Applicant(s)

Full legal name & address for service — street & number, municipality, postal code, telephone & fax numbers and e-mail address (if any).	*Lawyer's name & address — street & number, municipality, postal code, telephone & fax numbers and e-mail address (if any).*

Applicant(s)

Respondent(s)

Full legal name & address for service — street & number, municipality, postal code, telephone & fax numbers and e-mail address (if any).	*Lawyer's name & address — street & number, municipality, postal code, telephone & fax numbers and e-mail address (if any).*

Child

Full legal name of child:	*Lawyer's name & address — street & number, municipality, postal code, telephone & fax numbers and e-mail address (if any).*
Birth date (d, m, y):	
Sex:	

TO THE RESPONDENT(S) AND CHILD:

A COURT CASE HAS BEEN STARTED IN THIS COURT. THE DETAILS ARE SET OUT ON THE ATTACHED PAGES.

THE FIRST COURT DATE IS (date) .... *AT* .... ❑ a.m. ❑ p.m. or as soon as possible after that time, at *(address)* ....

Check applicable box.

1.

❑ I/We am/are the child's parent(s). *(Attach the consent of the parent(s) in Form 33F. If the child is 16 or 17 years old, the child's consent — Form 33E — must also be attached. In an application to extend treatment, the consent of the program administrator in Form 33F must also be attached. If the "child" is 18 or more years old, the "child's" consent to extend treatment in Form 33F must also be attached.)*

❑ I am an authorized officer of the applicant children's aid society that has custody of the child under an order made under Part III of the *Child and Family Services Act. (Attach the officer's consent in Form 33F. If the child is 16 or 17 years old, the child's consent — Form 33E — must also be attached. In an application to extend treatment, the administrator's consent in Form 33F must also be attached.)*

❑ I am a person (other than an administrator of the secure treatment program) who is caring for the child. *(To be used only where the child is less than 16 years of age. A consent of the child's parent — Form 33F — must be attached. In an application to extend treatment, the administrator's consent in Form 33F must also be attached.)*

❑ I am the child in this case and I am 16 or 17 years old. *(The child's consent — Form 33E — must be attached. In an application to extend treatment, the administrator's consent in Form 33F must also be attached.)*

❑ I am the person who has been committed to the secure treatment program in this case and I am 18 or more years old. *(To be used only in an application to extend treatment. Attach the consent of the program administrator on Form 33F.)*

❑ I am a physician qualified under the law of Ontario to practise medicine. *(To be used in an application for secure treatment only where the child is 16 years of age or more. A physician can apply to extend treatment, but only if the "child" is 18 or more years of age and only if separate consents in Form 33F, both from the administrator of the program and from the "child" are attached.)*

❑ I am the person in charge of the secure treatment program. *(To be used only in an application to extend secure treatment. Attach two consents in Form 33F — one from the administrator and the second from the child's parent or, if the child is in the care of a children's aid society, the society's consent. If the "child" is now 18 or more years old, the second consent in Form 33F must come from the "child".)*

2. I/We ask for an order under Part VI of the *Child and Family Services Act*

❑ committing the child . . . . ❑ extending the child's commitment

to the secure treatment program at: *(Name and address of secure treatment program.)*

....

....

3. I/We make this application because: *(NOTE: All three paragraphs — [a] and [b] and [c] — must be true in all cases.)*

❑ (a) the child has a mental disorder;

❑ (b) the secure treatment program would be effective to prevent the child from causing or attempting to cause serious bodily harm to himself/herself or to another person;

❑ (c) no less restrictive method of providing treatment appropriate for the child's mental disorder is appropriate in the circumstances;

Use this frame only in an application for secure treatment.
In addition to paragraphs (a), (b) and (c) above, all three paragraphs below — (d) and (e) and (f) — must ALSO be true.

❑ d) the child has, as a result of the mental disorder, within 45 days immediately before,

Check only one of these three boxes

❑ the date of this application for commitment to secure treatment,

❑ the child's detention or custody under the federal *Youth Criminal Justice Act* or Ontario's *Provincial Offences Act*,

❑ the child's admission as an involuntary patient to a psychiatric facility under the *Mental Health Act*,

caused or attempted to cause serious bodily harm to himself/herself or to another person;

❑ e) the child has:

{ ❑ within the 12 months immediately before this application for secure treatment on an occasion different from the one mentioned in clause (b) above caused or attempted to cause or by words or conduct, made a substantial threat to cause serious bodily harm to himself/herself or to another person, OR

{ ❑ caused or attempted to cause a person's death when causing or attempting to cause serious bodily harm to himself/herself or to another person; and

❑ f) treatment appropriate for the child's mental disorder is available at the program named in paragraph 2 above.

Use this frame only in an application to extend secure treatment.
In addition to paragraphs (a), (b) and (c) above, both paragraphs below — (d) and (e) — must ALSO be true.

❑ d)	the child is receiving, ❑ the treatment proposed when this court originally ordered secure commitment; ❑ other appropriate treatment; and
❑ e)	there is an appropriate plan for the child's care on release from the secure treatment program.

4. The following is a brief statement of the facts upon which this application is based. *(Set out the facts in numbered paragraphs with reference to the items in paragraph 3. If you need more space, you may attach a page, but you must date and sign each additional page.)*

....

....

....

....

Put a line through any blank space left on this page.

.... *Signature*	.... *Date of Signature*
.... *Signature*	.... *Date of Signature*

November 15, 2009

FORM 8D — APPLICATION (ADOPTION)

[Repealed O. Reg. 76/06, s. 15.]

[Editor's Note: Forms 4 to 39 of the Family Law Rules have been repealed by O. Reg. 76/06, effective May 1, 2006. Pursuant to Family Law Rule 1(9), when a form is referred to by number, the reference is to the form with that number that is described in the Table of Forms at the end of these rules and which is available at www.ontariocourtforms.on.ca. For your convenience, the government form as published on this website is reproduced below.]

Court File Number ....

By ❑ spouses jointly

❑ individual(s)

[SEAL]

.... *(Name of court)*

at .... *Court office address*

Applicant(s) (*The first letter of the applicant's surname may be used*)

Full legal name & address for service — street & number, municipality, postal code, telephone & fax numbers and e-mail address (if any).	Lawyer's name & address — street & number, municipality, postal code, telephone & fax numbers and e-mail address (if any).

Respondent(s) (*If there is a respondent, the first letter of respondent's surname may be used*)

Full legal name & address for service — street & number, municipality, postal code, telephone & fax numbers and e-mail address (if any).	Lawyer's name & address — street & number, municipality, postal code, telephone & fax numbers and e-mail address (if any).

THE APPLICANT(S) ASK FOR AN ORDER FOR THE ADOPTION OF:

(Give full legal name, date of birth, sex and birth registration number of person to be adopted. If this person is a Crown word or was placed for adoption by a licensee or children's aid society, you may use an initial for the surname.)

Full legal name ....

Date of birth..................................

Sex......... *Birth registration number* ....

The applicant(s) also ask for an order that the person's name after adoption be:

(full legal name of person after adoption) ....

Strike out the box below if it does not apply in this case.

> *NOTE TO THE RESPONDENTS:* You are also being served with a notice of motion to dispense with your consent to the adoption. The details of the motion can be found on the notice of motion and the attached affidavit(s).
>
> *IF YOU WANT TO OPPOSE THIS ADOPTION*, you or your lawyer must serve and file an answer (Form 10). *IF YOU DO NOT DO SO, THE COURT MAY DISPENSE WITH YOUR CONSENT WITHOUT YOU AND YOU WILL GET NO FURTHER NOTICE.*
>
> *YOU SHOULD GET LEGAL ADVICE ABOUT THIS CASE RIGHT AWAY.* If you cannot afford a lawyer, you may be able to get help from your local Legal Aid office. *(See your telephone directory under LEGAL AID).*

....	....
Date of signature	*Signature of applicant*
....	....
Date of signature	*Signature of co-applicant*
....	....
Date of issue by clerk of the court	*Signature of clerk of the court*

September 1, 2005

FORM 8D.1 — APPLICATION (DISPENSE WITH PARENT'S CONSENT TO ADOPTION BEFORE PLACEMENT)

[Repealed O. Reg. 76/06, s. 15.]

[Editor's Note: Forms 4 to 39 of the Family Law Rules have been repealed by O. Reg. 76/06, effective May 1, 2006. Pursuant to Family Law Rule 1(9), when a form is referred to by number, the reference is to the form with that number that is described in the Table of Forms at the end of these rules and which is available at www.ontariocourtforms.on.ca. For your convenience, the government form as published on this website is reproduced below.]

Court File Number ....

[SEAL]

.... *(Name of court)*

at .... *Court office address*

Applicant(s) (*The first letter of the applicant's surname may be used*)

Full legal name & address for service — street & number, municipality, postal code, telephone & fax numbers and e-mail address (if any).	*Lawyer's name & address — street & number, municipality, postal code, telephone & fax numbers and e-mail address (if any).*

Respondent(s) *(If there is a respondent, the first letter of respondent's surname may be used)*

Full legal name & address for service — street & number, municipality, postal code, telephone & fax numbers and e-mail address (if any).	*Lawyer's name & address — street & number, municipality, postal code, telephone & fax numbers and e-mail address (if any).*

THE APPLICANT(S) ASK FOR AN ORDER DISPENSING WITH THE CONSENT OF THE RESPONDENT(S) TO THE ADOPTION OF THE CHILD:

(Give full legal name, date of birth, sex and birth registration number (if known) of person to be adopted. If this person is to be placed for adoption by a licensee or children's aid society, you may use an initial for the surname.)

Full legal name ....

Date of birth..................................

Sex......... *Birth registration number* ....

❑ The applicant(s) also ask for an order that service of the applicant on the respondent(s) is not required.

NOTE TO THE RESPONDENT(S): a court case has been started against you in this court. The details are set out in the attached affidavit.

THE FIRST COURT DATE IS (date)........................ at .... a.m./p.m. or as soon as possible after that time, at: (address)

THIS CASE IS ON THE FAST TRACK OF THE CASE MANAGEMENT SYSTEM. A case management judge will be assigned by the time this case first comes before a judge.

IF YOU WANT TO OPPOSE THIS APPLICATION, you or your lawyer must prepare an *Answer* (Form 10 — a blank copy should be attached), serve a copy on the applicant(s) and file a copy in the court office with an *Affidavit of Service* (Form 6B). YOU HAVE ONLY 20 DAYS AFTER THIS APPLICATION IS SERVED ON YOU (40 DAYS IF THIS APPLICATION IS SERVED ON YOU OUTSIDE CANADA OR THE UNITED STATES) TO SERVE AND FILE AN ANSWER. IF YOU DO NOT DO SO, THE COURT MAY DISPENSE WITH YOUR CONSENT WITHOUT YOU.

If you want to make a claim of your own, you or your lawyer must fill out the claim portion in the *Answer*, serve a copy on the applicant(s) and file a copy in the court office with an *Affidavit of Service*. YOU SHOULD GET LEGAL ADVICE ABOUT THIS CASE RIGHT AWAY. If you cannot afford a lawyer, you may be able to get help from your local Legal Aid office. *(See your telephone directory under LEGAL AID).*

....	....
Date of signature	*Signature of applicant*
....	....
Date of signature	*Signature of co-applicant*
....	....
Date of issue by clerk of the court	*Signature of clerk of the court*

September 1, 2005

FORM 10 — ANSWER

[Repealed O. Reg. 76/06, s. 15.]

[Editor's Note: Forms 4 to 39 of the Family Law Rules have been repealed by O. Reg. 76/06, effective May 1, 2006. Pursuant to Family Law Rule 1(9), when a form is referred to by number, the reference is to the form with that number that is described in the Table of Forms at the end of these rules and which is available at www.ontariocourtforms.on.ca. For your convenience, the government form as published on this website is reproduced below.]

Court File Number ....

.... *(Name of court)*

at.. *Court office address*

Applicant(s)

Full legal name & address for service — street & number, municipality, postal code, telephone & fax numbers and e-mail address (if any).	*Lawyer's name & address — street & number, municipality, postal code, telephone & fax numbers and e-mail address (if any).*

Respondent(s)

Full legal name & address for service — street & number, municipality, postal code, telephone & fax numbers and e-mail address (if any).	*Lawyer's name & address — street & number, municipality, postal code, telephone & fax numbers and e-mail address (if any).*

Name & address of Children's Lawyer's agent for service (street & number, municipality, postal code, telephone & fax numbers and e-mail address (if any)) and name of person represented.

INSTRUCTIONS: FINANCIAL STATEMENT

COMPLETE A FINANCIAL STATEMENT (Form 13) IF:

- you are making or responding to a claim for spousal support; or
- you are responding to a claim for child support; or
- you are making a claim for child support in an amount different from the table amount specified under the Child Support Guidelines.

You must complete all parts of the form UNLESS you are ONLY responding to a claim for child support in the table amount specified under the Child Support Guidelines AND you agree with the claim. In that case, only complete Parts 1, 2 and 3.

COMPLETE A FINANCIAL STATEMENT (Form 13.1) IF:

- you are making or responding to a claim for property or exclusive possession of the matrimonial home and its contents; or
- you are making or responding to a claim for property or exclusive possession of the matrimonial home and its contents together with other claims for relief.

TO THE APPLICANT(S):

If you are making a claim against someone who is not an applicant, insert the person's name and address here.

AND TO: *(full legal name)*... an added respondent, of *(address of added party)*...

My name is *(full legal name)* ....

1. I agree with the following claim(s) made by the applicant: *(Refer to the numbers alongside the boxes on page 3 of the application form.)*

2. I do not agree with the following claim(s) made by the applicant: *(Again, refer to the numbers alongside the boxes on page 3 of the application form.)*

3. ❑ I am asking that the applicant's claim (except for the parts with which I agree) be dismissed with costs.

4. ❑ I am making a claim of my own.

   (Attach a "Claim by Respondent" page and include it as page 3. Otherwise, do not attach it.)

5. ❑ THE FAMILY HISTORY, as set out in the application

   ❑ is correct.

   ❑ is not correct.

   (If it is not correct, attach your own FAMILY HISTORY page and underline those parts that are different from the applicant's version.)

6. The important facts that form the legal basis for my position in paragraph 2 are as follows:

(In numbered paragraphs, set out the facts for your position. Attach an additional sheet and number it if you need more space.)

Put a line through any blank space left an this page.

.... *Date of signature*

.... *Respondent's signature*

CLAIM BY RESPONDENT

Fill out a separate claim page for each person against whom you are making your claim(s).

7. THIS CLAIM IS MADE AGAINST

❑ THE APPLICANT

❑ AN ADDED PARTY, whose name is: *(full legal name)*

(If your claim is against an added party, make sure that this person's name appears an page 1 of this form.)

8. I ASK THE COURT FOR THE FOLLOWING:

(Claim below include claims for temporary orders.)

Claims under the *Divorce Act*

(Check boxes in this column only if you are asking for a divorce and your case is in the Superior Court of Justice or Family Court of the Superior Court of Justice.)

00 ❑ a divorce

01 ❑ support for me

02 ❑ support for child(ren)-table amount

03 ❑ support for child(ren)-other than table amount

04 ❑ custody of child(ren)

05 ❑ access to child(ren)

Claims under the *Family Law Act* or *Children's Law Reform Act*

10 ❑ support for me

11 ❑ support for child(ren)-table amount

12 ❑ support for child(ren)-other than table amount

13 ❑ custody of child(ren)

14 ❑ access to child(ren)

15 ❑ restraining/non-harassment order

16 ❑ indexing spousal support

17 ❑ declaration of parentage

18 ❑ guardianship over child's property

Claims relating to property

(Check boxes in this column only if your case is in the Superior Court of Justice or Family Court of the Superior Court of Justice.)

20 ❑ equalization of net family properties

21 ❑ exclusive possession of matrimonial home

22 ❑ exclusive possession of contents of matrimonial home

23 ❑ freezing assets

24 ❑ sale of family property

Other claims

30 ❑ costs

31 ❑ annulment of marriage

32 ❑ prejudgment interest

Claims relating to child protection

40 ❑ access

41 ❑ lesser protection order

42 ❑ return of child(ren) to my care

43 ❑ place child(ren) into care of *(name)*..................................

44 ❑ children's aid society wardship for .... months

45 ❑ society supervision of my child(ren)

50 ❑ Other *(Specify.)*

Give details of the order that you want the court to make. *(Include any amounts of support (if known) and the name(s) of the child(ren) for whom support, custody or access is claimed.)*

IMPORTANT FACTS SUPPORTING MY CLAIM(S)

(In numbered paragraphs, set out the facts that form the legal basis for your claim(s). Attach an additional page and number it if you need more space.)

Put a line through any blank space left an this page.

.... *Date of signature*

.... *Respondent's signature*

LAWYER'S CERTIFICATE

For divorce cases only

My name is: ....

and I am the respondent's lawyer in this divorce case. I certify that I have complied with the requirements of section 9 of the *Divorce Act*.

______________________	______________________
Date	*Signature of Lawyer*

September 1, 2005

FORM 10A — REPLY BY ❑ APPLICANT ❑ ADDED RESPONDENT

[Repealed O. Reg. 76/06, s. 15.]

[Editor's Note: Forms 4 to 39 of the Family Law Rules have been repealed by O. Reg. 76/06, effective May 1, 2006. Pursuant to Family Law Rule 1(9), when a form is referred to by number, the reference is to the form with that number that is described in the Table of Forms at the end of these rules and which is available at www.ontariocourtforms.on.ca. For your convenience, the government form as published on this website is reproduced below.]

Court File Number ....

.... *(Name of court)*

at.. *Court office address*

Applicant(s)

Full legal name & address for service — street & number, municipality, postal code, telephone & fax numbers and e-mail address (if any).	*Lawyer's name & address — street & number, municipality, postal code, telephone & fax numbers and e-mail address (if any).*

Respondent(s)

Full legal name & address for service — street & number, municipality, postal code, telephone & fax numbers and e-mail address (if any).	*Lawyer's name & address — street & number, municipality, postal code, telephone & fax numbers and e-mail address (if any).*

Children's Lawyer

Name & address of Children's Lawyer's agent for service (street & number, municipality, postal code, telephone & fax numbers and e-mail address (if any)) and name of person represented.

INSTRUCTIONS: FINANCIAL STATEMENT

COMPLETE A FINANCIAL STATEMENT (Form 13) IF:

- you are responding to a claim for spousal support; or
- you are responding to a claim for child support.

You must complete all parts of the form UNLESS you are ONLY responding to a claim for child support in the table amount specified under the Child Support Guidelines AND you agree with the claim. In that case, only complete Parts 1, 2 and 3.

COMPLETE A FINANCIAL STATEMENT (Form 13.1) IF:

- you are responding to a claim for property or exclusive possession of the matrimonial home and its contents; or
- you are responding to a claim for property or exclusive possession of the matrimonial home and its contents together with other claims for relief.

TO ALL PARTIES:

1. My name is *(full legal name)* ....

2. I agree with the following claim(s) made by the respondent in his/her answer: *(Refer to the numbers alongside the boxes on page 3 of the answer form.)*

3. I do not agree with the following claim(s) made by the respondent: *(Again, refer to the numbers alongside the boxes on page 3 of the answer form.)*

4. ❑ I am asking that the respondent's claim (except for the parts with which I agree) be dismissed with costs.

5. The important facts supporting my position in paragraph 3 are as follows:

(In numbered paragraphs, set out the reasons for your position. Attach an additional sheet and number it if you need more space.)

Put a line through any space left an this page.

.... *Date of signature*

.... *Signature*

September 1, 2005

FORM 12 — NOTICE OF WITHDRAWAL

[Repealed O. Reg. 76/06, s. 15.]

[Editor's Note: Forms 4 to 39 of the Family Law Rules have been repealed by O. Reg. 76/06, effective May 1, 2006. Pursuant to Family Law Rule 1(9), when a form is referred to by number, the reference is to the form with that number that is described in the Table of Forms at the end of these rules and which is available at www.ontariocourtforms.on.ca. For your convenience, the government form as published on this website is reproduced below.]

Court File Number ....

.... *(Name of court)*

at .... *Court office address*

Applicant(s)

Full legal name & address for service — street & number, municipality, postal code, telephone & fax and e-mail address (if any)	*Lawyer's name & address — street & number, municipality, postal code, telephone & fax numbers and e-mail address (if any)*

Respondent(s)

Full legal name & address for service — street & number, municipality, postal code, telephone & fax numbers and e-mail address (if any)	*Lawyer's name & address — street & number, municipality, postal code, telephone & fax numbers and e-mail address (if any)*

TO ALL PARTIES:

My name is *(full legal name)* ....

I withdraw this

❑ application dated *(date)* ....

❑ answer dated *(date)* ....

❑ notice of default hearing dated *(date)* ....

❑ notice of motion dated *(date)* ....

❑ *(Other; specify.)*

against *(names of parties against who there is to be a withdrawal)* ....

❑ completely.

❑ regarding *(state limited nature of withdrawal.)*
....
....

.... *Signature of party making withdrawal or of party's lawyer*

.... *Date of signature*

NOTE TO OTHER PARTIES: If a case, an enforcement, a motion, etc., has been wholly or partly withdrawn against you by this notice, you are entitled to your costs from the party making the withdrawal unless the court orders otherwise or unless the parties agree otherwise.

September 1, 2005

FORM 13 — FINANCIAL STATEMENT (SUPPORT CLAIMS) SWORN/AFFIRMED

[Repealed O. Reg. 76/06, s. 15.]

[Editor's Note: Forms 4 to 39 of the Family Law Rules have been repealed by O. Reg. 76/06, effective May 1, 2006. Pursuant to Family Law Rule 1(9), when a form is referred to by number, the reference is to the form with that number that is described in the Table of Forms at the end of these rules and which is available at www.ontariocourtforms.on.ca. For your convenience, the government form as published on this website is reproduced below.]

ONTARIO

Court File Number ....

.... *(Name of court)*

at .... *Court office address*

Applicant(s)

Full legal name & address for service — street & number, municipality, postal code, telephone & fax numbers and e-mail address (if any).	***Lawyer's name & address — street & number, municipality, postal code, telephone & fax numbers and e-mail address (if any).***

Respondent(s)

Full legal name & address for service — street & number, municipality, postal code, telephone & fax numbers and e-mail address (if any).	***Lawyer's name & address — street & number, municipality, postal code, telephone & fax numbers and e-mail address (if any).***

INSTRUCTIONS

You must complete this form if you are making or responding to a claim for child or spousal support or a claim to change support, unless your only claim for support is a claim for child support in the table amount under the *Child Support Guidelines*.

You may also be required to complete and attach additional schedules based on the claims that have been made in your case or your financial circumstances:

- If you have income that is not shown in Part I of the financial statement (for example, partnership income, dividends, rental income, capital gains or RRSP income), you must also complete *Schedule A*.

- If you have made or responded to a claim for child support that involves undue hardship or a claim for spousal support, you must also complete *Schedule B*.

- If you or the other party has sought a contribution towards special or extraordinary expenses for the child(ren), you must also complete *Schedule C.*

NOTES: You must fully and truthfully complete this financial statement, including any applicable schedules. Failure to do so may result in serious consequences.

If you are making or responding to a claim for property, an equalization payment or the matrimonial home, you must complete Form 13.1: Financial Statement (Property and Support Claims) instead of this form.

1. My name is (full legal name) ....

I live in (municipality & province) ....

and I swear/affirm that the following is true:

PART 1: — INCOME

2. I am currently

❑ employed by *(name and address of employer)* ....

❑ self-employed, carrying on business under the name of *(name and address of business)* ....

❑ unemployed since *(date when last employed)* ....

3. I attach proof of my year-to-date income from all sources, including my most recent *(attach all that are applicable)*:

❑ pay cheque stub ❑ social assistance stub ❑ pension stub ❑ workers' compensation stub

❑ employment insurance stub and last Record of Employment

❑ statement of income and expenses/ professional activities (for self-employed individuals)

❑ other (e.g. a letter from your employer confirming all income received to date this year)

4. Last year, my gross income from all sources was $ .... *(do not subtract any taxes that have been deducted from this income).*

5. ❑ I am attaching all of the following required documents to this financial statement as proof of my income over the past three years, if they have not already been provided:

- a copy of my personal income tax returns for each of the past three taxation years, including any materials that were filed with the returns. *(Income tax returns must be served but should NOT be filed in the continuing record, unless they are filed with a motion to refrain a driver's license suspension.)*

- a copy of my notices of assessment and any notices of reassessment for each of the past three taxation years;

- where my notices of assessment and reassessment are unavailable for any of the past three taxation years, an Income and Deductions printout from the Canada Revenue Agency for each of those years, whether or not I filed an income tax return.

  Note: An Income and Deductions printout is available from Canada Revenue Agency. Please call customer service at 1-800-959-8281.

OR

❑ I am an Indian within the meaning of the *Indian Act* (Canada) and I have chosen not to file income tax returns for the past three years. I am attaching the following proof of income for the last three years *(list documents you have provided)*:

....

....

(In this table you must show all of the income that you are currently receiving.)

	Income Source	**Amount Received/Month**
1.	Employment income (before deductions)	$
2.	Commissions, tips and bonuses	$
3.	Self-employment income (Monthly amount before expenses: $ ....)	$
4.	Employment Insurance benefits	$
5.	Workers' compensation benefits	$
6.	Social assistance income (including ODSP payments)	$
7.	Interest and investment income	$
8.	Pension income (including CPP and OAS)	$
9.	Spousal support received from a former spouse/partner	$
10.	Child Tax Benefits or Tax Rebates (e.g. GST)	$
11.	Other sources of income (e.g. RRSP withdrawals, capital gains) *(*attach Schedule A and divide annual amount by 12)*	$
12.	*Total monthly income from all sources*:	$
13.	*Total monthly income X 12 = Total annual income*:	$

14. Other Benefits

Provide details of any non-cash benefits that your employer provides to you or are paid for by your business such as medical insurance coverage, the use of a company car, or room and board.

Item	**Details**	**Yearly Market Value**
		$
		$
		$
		$

PART 2: — EXPENSES

Expense	**Monthly Amount**
Automatic Deductions	
CPP contributions	$
El premiums	$
Income taxes	$
Employee pension contributions	$
Union dues	$
SUBTOTAL	$
Housing	
Rent or mortgage	$
Property taxes	$
Property insurance	$
Condominium fees	$
Repairs and maintenance	$
SUBTOTAL	$
Utilities	
Water	$
Heat	$
Electricity	$
Telephone	$
Cell phone	$
Cable	$
Internet	$
SUBTOTAL	$
Household Expenses	
Groceries	$
Household supplies	$
Meals outside the home	$
Pet care	$
Laundry and Dry Cleaning	$
SUBTOTAL	$
Daycare expense	$
Babysitting costs	$
SUBTOTAL	$
Transportation	
Public transit, taxis	$
Gas and oil	$
Car insurance and license	$
Repairs and maintenance	$
Parking	$

Expense	Monthly Amount
Car Loan or Lease Payments	$
SUBTOTAL	$
Health	
Health insurance premiums	$
Dental expenses	$
Medicine and drugs	$
Eye care	$
SUBTOTAL	$
Personal	
Clothing	$
Hair care and beauty	$
Alcohol and tobacco	$
Education (*specify*)	$
Entertainment/recreation (including children)	$
Gifts	$
SUBTOTAL	$
Other expenses	
Life Insurance premiums	$
RRSP/RESP withdrawals	$
Vacations	$
School fees and supplies	$
Clothing for children	$
Children's activities	$
Summer camp expenses	$
Debt payments	$
Support paid for other children	$
Other expenses not shown above (*specify*)	$
SUBTOTAL	$
Total Amount of Monthly Expenses	$
Total Amount of Yearly Expenses	$

PART 3: — ASSETS

Type	Details		Value or Amount
State Address of Each Property and Nature of Ownership			
Real Estate	1		$
	2		$
	3		$
Year and Make			

Type	**Details**		**Value or Amount**
Cars, Boats, Vehicles	1		$
	2		$
	3		$
		Address Where Located	
Other Possessions of Value (e.g. computers, jewellery, collections)	1		$
	2		$
	3		$
		Type — Issuer — Due Date — Number of Shares	
Investments (e.g. bonds, shares, term deposits and mutual funds)	1		$
	2		$
	3		$
		Name and Address of Institution *Account Number*	
Bank Accounts	1		$
	2		$
	3		$
		Type and Issuer *Account Number*	
Savings Plans R.R.S.P.s Pension Plans R.E.S.P.s	1		$
	2		$
	3		$
		Type — Beneficiary — Face Amount	Cash Surrender Value
Life Insurance	1		$
	2		$
	3		$
		Name and Address of Business	
	1		$

Type		Details	Value or Amount
Interest in Business (**attach separate year-end statement for each business)*	2		$
	3		$
		Name and Address of Debtors	
	1		$
Money Owed to You *(for example, any court judgments in your favour, estate money and income tax refunds)*	2		$
	3		$
		Description	
Other Assets	1		$
	2		$
	3		$

Total Value of All Property	$

PART 4: — DEBTS

Type of Debt	Creditor (name and address)	Full Amount Now Owing	Monthly Payments	Are Payments Being Made?
Mortgages, Lines of Credits or other Loans from a Bank, Trust or Finance Company		$	$	❑ Yes ❑ No
		$	$	❑ Yes ❑ No
		$	$	❑ Yes ❑ No
		$	$	❑ Yes ❑ No

Type of Debt	Creditor (name and address)	Full Amount Now Owing	Monthly Payments	Are Payments Being Made?
Outstanding Credit Card Balances		$	$	❑ Yes ❑ No
		$	$	❑ Yes ❑ No
Unpaid Support Amounts		$	$	❑ Yes ❑ No
		$	$	❑ Yes ❑ No
		$	$	❑ Yes ❑ No
Other Debts		$	$	❑ Yes ❑ No
		$	$	❑ Yes ❑ No
		$	$	❑ Yes ❑ No

Total Amount of Debts Outstanding	$

PART 5: — SUMMARY OF ASSETS AND LIABILITIES

Total Assets	$
Subtract Total Debts	$
Net Worth	$

NOTE: This financial statement must be updated no more than 30 days before any court event by either completing and filing:

- *a new financial statement with updated information, or*
- *an affidavit in Form 14A setting out the details of any minor changes or confirming that the information contained in this statement remains correct.*

Sworn/Affirmed before me at ....
municipality

in ....
province, state or country

on ....

Date *Commissioner for taking affidavits*
(Type or print name below if signature is illegible.)

....
Signature
(This form is to be signed in front of a lawyer, justice of the peace, notary public or commissioner for taking affidavits.)

SCHEDULE A — ADDITIONAL SOURCES OF INCOME

Line	Income Source	Annual Amount
1.	Net partnership income	$
2.	Net rental income (Gross annual rental income of $ ....)	$
3.	Total amount of dividends received from taxable Canadian corporations	$
4.	Total capital gains ($ ....) less capital losses ($ ....)	$
5.	Registered retirement savings plan withdrawals	$
6.	Any other income *(specify source)*	$

Subtotal:	$

SCHEDULE B — OTHER INCOME EARNERS IN THE HOME

Complete this part only if you are making or responding to a claim for undue hardship or spousal support. Check and complete all sections that apply to your circumstances.

1. ❏ I live alone.

2. ❏ I am living with *(full legal name of person you are married to or cohabiting with)* ....

3. ❏ I/we live with the following other adult(s): ....

4. ❏ I/we have *(give number)* .... child(ren) who live(s) in the home.

5. My spouse/partner ❏ works at *(place of work or business)* ....

❏ does not work outside the home.

6. My spouse/partner ❏ earns *(give amount)* $ .... per ....

❏ does not earn any income.

7. ❏ My spouse/partner or other adult residing in the home contributes about $ .... Per .... towards the household expenses.

SCHEDULE C — SPECIAL OR EXTRAORDINARY EXPENSES FOR THE CHILD(REN)

Child's Name	Expense	Amount/yr.	Available Tax Credits or Deductions*
1.		$	$
2.		$	$
3.		$	$
4.		$	$
5.		$	$
6.		$	$

Child's Name	Expense	Amount/yr.	Available Tax Credits or Deductions*
7.		*$*	*$*
8.		*$*	*$*
9.		*$*	*$*
10.		*$*	*$*

Total Net Annual Amount	*$*
Total Net Monthly Amount	*$*

Notes:

* *Some of these expenses can be claimed in a parent's income tax return in relation to a tax credit or deduction (for example childcare costs). These credits or deductions must be shown in the above chart.*

❑ I attach proof of the above expenses.

❑ I earn $ .... per year which should be used to determine my share of the above expenses.

NOTE:

Pursuant to the Child Support Guidelines, a court can order that the parents of a child share the costs of the following expenses for the child:

- Necessary childcare expenses;
- Medical insurance premiums and certain health-related expenses for the child that cost more than $100 annually;
- Extraordinary expenses for the child's education;
- Post-secondary school expenses; and,
- Extraordinary expenses for extracurricular activities.

February 1, 2010

FORM 13.1 — FINANCIAL STATEMENT (PROPERTY AND SUPPORT CLAIMS) SWORN/AFFIRMED

[Repealed O. Reg. 76/06, s. 15.]

[Editor's Note: Forms 4 to 39 of the Family Law Rules have been repealed by O. Reg. 76/06, effective May , 2006. Pursuant to Family Law Rule 1(9), when a form is referred to by number, the reference is to the form ith that number that is described in the Table of Forms

at the end of these rules and which is available at ww.ontariocourtforms.on.ca. For your convenience, the government form as published on this website is reproduced below.]

ONTARIO

Court File Number ....

.... *(Name of court)*

at .... *Court office address*

Applicant(s)

Full legal name & address for service — street & number, municipality, postal code, telephone & fax numbers and e-mail address (if any).	**Lawyer's name & address — street & number, municipality, postal code, telephone & fax numbers and e-mail address (if any).**

Respondent(s)

Full legal name & address for service — street & number, municipality, postal code, telephone & fax numbers and e-mail address (if any).	**Lawyer's name & address — street & number, municipality, postal code, telephone & fax numbers and e-mail address (if any).**

INSTRUCTIONS

1. USE THIS FORM IF:

- you are making or responding to a claim for property or exclusive possession of the matrimonial home and its contents; or

- you are making or responding to a claim for property or exclusive possession of the matrimonial home and its contents together with other claims for relief.

2. USE FORM 13 INSTEAD OF THIS FORM IF:

- you are making or responding to a claim for support but NOT making or responding to a claim for property or exclusive possession of the matrimonial home and its contents.

3. If you have income that is not shown in Part I of the financial statement (for example, partnership income, dividends, rental income, capital gains or RRSP income), you must also complete *Schedule A*.

4. If you or the other party has sought a contribution towards special or extraordinary expenses for the child(ren), you must also complete *Schedule B*.

NOTE: You must fully and truthfully complete this financial statement, including any applicable schedules. Failure to do so may result in serious consequences.

1. My name is (full legal name) ....

I live in (municipality & province) ....

and I swear/affirm that the following is true:

PART 1: — INCOME

2. I am currently

❑ employed by *(name and address of employer)* ....

❑ self-employed, carrying on business under the name of (name and address of business) ....

❑ unemployed since *(date when last employed)* ....

3. I attach proof of my year-to-date income from all sources, including my most recent *(attach all that are applicable)*:

❑ pay cheque stub ❑ social assistance stub ❑ pension stub ❑ workers' compensation stub

❑ employment insurance stub and last Record of Employment

❑ statement of income and expenses/ professional activities (for self-employed individuals)

❑ other (e.g. a letter from your employer confirming all income received to date this year)

4. Last year, my gross income from all sources was $ .... *(do not subtract any taxes that have been deducted from this income).*

5. I am attaching all of the following required documents to this financial statement as proof of my income over the past three years, if they have not already been provided:

- a copy of my personal income tax returns for each of the past three taxation years, including any materials that were filed with the returns. *(Income tax returns must be served but should NOT be filed in the continuing record, unless they are filed with a motion to refrain a driver's license suspension.)*

- a copy of my notices of assessment and any notices of reassessment for each of the past three taxation years;

- where my notices of assessment and reassessment are unavailable for any of the past three taxation years, an Income and Deductions printout from the Canada Revenue Agency for each of those years, whether or not I filed an income tax return.

  Note: An Income and Deductions printout is available from Canada Revenue Agency. Please call customer service at 1-800-959-8281.

OR

❑ I am an Indian within the meaning of the *Indian Act* (Canada) and I have chosen not to file income tax returns for the past three years. I am attaching the following proof of income for the last three years *(list documents you have provided)*:

....

....

(In this table you must show all of the income that you are currently receiving.)

	Income Source	Amount Received/Month
1.	Employment income (before deductions)	$
2.	Commissions, tips and bonuses	$
3.	Self-employment income (Monthly amount before expenses: $ ....)	$
4.	Employment Insurance benefits	$
5.	Workers' compensation benefits	$
6.	Social assistance income (including ODSP payments)	$
7.	Interest and investment income	$
8.	Pension income (including CPP and OAS)	$
9.	Spousal support received from a former spouse/partner	$
10.	Child Tax Benefits or Tax Rebates (e.g. GST)	$
11.	Other sources of income (e.g. RRSP withdrawals, capital gains) *(*attach Schedule A and divide annual amount by 12)*	$
12.	*Total monthly income from all sources*:	$
13.	*Total monthly income X 12 = Total annual income*:	$

14. Other Benefits

Provide details of any non-cash benefits that your employer provides to you or are paid for by your business such as medical insurance coverage, the use of a company car, or room and board.

Item	Details	Yearly Market Value
		$
		$
		$
		$

PART 2: — EXPENSES

Expense	Monthly Amount
Automatic Deductions	
CPP contributions	$
El premiums	$
Income taxes	$
Employee pension contributions	$
Union dues	$
SUBTOTAL	$
Housing	
Rent or mortgage	$
Property taxes	$
Property insurance	$

Expense	**Monthly Amount**
Condominium fees	$
Repairs and maintenance	$
SUBTOTAL	$
Utilities	
Water	$
Heat	$
Electricity	$
Telephone	$
Cell phone	$
Cable	$
Internet	$
SUBTOTAL	$
Household Expenses	
Groceries	$
Household supplies	$
Meals outside the home	$
Pet care	$
Laundry and Dry Cleaning	$
SUBTOTAL	$
Childcare Costs	
Daycare expense	$
Babysitting costs	$
SUBTOTAL	$
Transportation	
Public transit, taxis	$
Gas and oil	$
Car insurance and license	$
Repairs and maintenance	$
Parking	$
Car Loan or Lease Payments	$
SUBTOTAL	$
Health	
Health insurance premiums	$
Dental expenses	$
Medicine and drugs	$
Eye care	$
SUBTOTAL	$
Personal	
Clothing	$
Hair care and beauty	$
Alcohol and tobacco	$

Expense	Monthly Amount
Education (*specify*)	$
Entertainment/recreation (including children)	$
Gifts	$
SUBTOTAL	$
Other expenses	
Life Insurance premiums	$
RRSP/RESP withdrawals	$
Vacations	$
School fees and supplies	$
Clothing for children	$
Children's activities	$
Summer camp expenses	$
Debt payments	$
Support paid for other children	$
Other expenses not shown above (*specify*)	$
SUBTOTAL	$
Total Amount of Monthly Expenses	$
Total Amount of Yearly Expenses	$

PART 3: — OTHER INCOME EARNERS IN THE HOME

Complete this part only if you are making or responding to a claim for undue hardship or spousal support. Check and complete all sections that apply to your circumstances.

1. ❑ I live alone.

2. ❑ I am living with *(full legal name of person you are married to or cohabiting with)* ....

3. ❑ I/we live with the following other adult(s): ....

4. ❑ I/we have *(give number)* .... child(ren) who live(s) in the home.

5. My spouse/partner ❑ works at *(place of work or business)* ....

❑ does not work outside the home.

6. My spouse/partner ❑ earns *(give amount)* $ .... per ....

❑ does not earn any income.

7. My spouse/partner or other adult residing in the home contributes about $ .... per .... towards the household expenses.

PART 4: — ASSETS IN AND OUT OF ONTARIO

If any sections of Parts 4 to 9 do not apply, do not leave blank, print "NONE" in the section.

The date of marriage is: *(give date)* ....

The valuation date is: *(give date)* ....

The date of commencement of cohabitation is (if different from date of marriage): *(give date)* ....

PART 4(A): — LAND

Include any interest in land owned on the dates in each of the columns below, including leasehold interests and mortgages. Show estimated market value of your interest, but do not deduct encumbrances or costs of disposition; these encumbrances and costs should be shown under Part 5, "Debts and Other Liabilities".

Nature & Type of Ownership (Give your percentage interest where relevant.)	**Address of Property**	**Estimated Market Value of YOUR Interest**		
		on date of marriage	**on valuation date**	**today**
		$	$	$
	15. TOTAL VALUE OF LAND		$	$

PART 4(B): — GENERAL HOUSEHOLD ITEMS AND VEHICLES

Show estimated market value, not the cost of replacement for these items owned on the dates in each of the columns below. Do not deduct encumbrances or costs of disposition; these encumbrances and costs should be shown under Part 5, "Debts and Other Liabilities".

Item	**Description**	**Indicate if NOT in your possession**	**Estimated Market Value of YOUR Interest**		
			on date of marriage	**on valuation date**	**today**
Household goods & furniture			$	$	$
Cars, boats, vehicles			$	$	$
Jewellery, art, electronics, tools, sports & hobby equipment			$	$	$
Other special items			$	$	$

Item	Description	Indicate if NOT in your possession	Estimated Market Value of YOUR Interest		
			on date of marriage	on valuation date	today
16. TOTAL VALUE OF GENERAL HOUSEHOLD ITEMS AND VEHICLES				$	$

PART 4(C): — BANK ACCOUNTS, SAVINGS, SECURITIES AND PENSIONS

Show the items owned on the dates in each of the columns below by category, for example, cash, accounts in financial institutions, pensions, registered retirement or other savings plans, deposit receipts, any other savings, bonds, warrants, options, notes and other securities. Give your best estimate of the market value of the securities if the items were to be sold on the open market.

Category	INSTITUTION (including location)/ DESCRIPTION (including issuer and date)	Account number	Amount/Estimated Market Value		
			on date of marriage	on valuation date	today
			$	$	$
17. TOTAL VALUE OF ACCOUNTS, SAVINGS, SECURITIES AND PENSIONS				$	$

PART 4(D): — LIFE AND DISABILITY INSURANCE

List all policies in existence on the dates in each of the columns below.

Company, Type & Policy No.	Owner	Beneficiary	Face Amount	Cash Surrender Value		
				on date of marriage	on valuation date	today
				$	$	$
18. TOTAL CASH SURRENDER VALUE OF INSURANCE POLICIES					$	$

PART 4(E): — BUSINESS INTERESTS

Show any interest in an unincorporated business owned on the dates in each of the columns below. An interest in an incorporated business may be shown here or under "BANK ACCOUNTS, SAVINGS, SECURITIES, AND PENSIONS" in Part 4(c). Give your best estimate of the market value of your interest.

Name of Firm or Company	Interest	Estimated Market Value of YOUR Interest		
		on date of marriage	on valuation date	today
		$	$	$
19. TOTAL VALUE OF BUSINESS INTERESTS			$	$

PART 4(F): — MONEY OWED TO YOU

Give details of all money that other persons owe to you on the dates in each of the columns below, whether because of business or from personal dealings. Include any court judgments in your favour, any estate money and any income tax refunds owed to you.

Details	Amount Owed to You		
	on date of marriage	on valuation date	today
	$	$	$
20. TOTAL OF MONEY OWED TO YOU		$	$

PART 4(G): — OTHER PROPERTY

Show other property or assets owned on the dates in each of the columns below. Include property of any kind not listed above. Give your best estimate of market value.

Category	Details	Estimated Market Value of YOUR interest		
		on date of marriage	on valuation date	today
		$	$	$
21. TOTAL VALUE OF OTHER PROPERTY			$	$
22. VALUE OF ALL PROPERTY OWNED ON THE VALUATION DATE (Add items [15] to [21].)			$	$

PART 5: — DEBTS AND OTHER LIABILITIES

Show your debts and other liabilities on the dates in each of the columns below. List them by category such as mortgages, charges, liens, notes, credit cards, and accounts payable. Don't forget to include:

- *any money owed to the Canada Revenue Agency*;

- *contingent liabilities such as guarantees or warranties given by you (but indicate that they are contingent); and*

- *any unpaid legal or professional bills as a result of this case.*

Category	Details	Amount Owing		
		on date of marriage	on valuation date	today
		$	$	$
23. TOTAL OF DEBTS AND OTHER LIABILITIES			$	$

PART 6: — PROPERTY, DEBTS AND OTHER LIABILITIES ON DATE OF MARRIAGE

Show by category the value of your property, debts and other liabilities, calculated as of the date of your marriage. (In this part, do not include the value of a matrimonial home or debts or other liabilities directly related to its purchase or significant improvement, if you and your spouse ordinarily occupied this property as your family residence at the time of separation.)

Category and details	Value on date of marriage	
	Assets	Liabilities
Land	$	$
General household items & vehicles	$	$
Bank accounts, savings, securities & pensions	$	$
Life & disability insurance	$	$
Business interests	$	$
Money owed to you	$	$
Other property *(Specify.)*	$	$
Debts and other liabilities *(Specify.)*	$	$
TOTALS	$	$
24. NET VALUE OF PROPERTY OWNED ON DATE OF MARRIAGE *(From the total of the "Assets" column, subtract the total of the "Liabilities" column.)*	$	$

Category and details	Value on date of marriage	
	Assets	Liabilities
25. VALUE OF ALL DEDUCTIONS (Add items [23] and [24].)	$	$

PART 7: — EXCLUDED PROPERTY

Show by category the value of property owned on the valuation date that is excluded from the definition of "net family property" (such as gifts or inheritances received after marriage).

Category	Details	Value on valuation date
		$
	26. TOTAL VALUE OF EXCLUDED PROPERTY	$

PART 8: — DISPOSED-OF PROPERTY

Show by category the value of all property that you disposed of during the two years immediately preceding the making of this statement, or during the marriage, whichever period is shorter.

Category	Details	Value
		$
	27. TOTAL VALUE OF DISPOSED-OF PROPERTY	$

PART 9: — CALCULATION OF NET FAMILY PROPERTY

	Deductions	BALANCE
Value of all property owned on valuation date (from item [22] above)		$
Subtract value of all deductions (from item [25] above)	$	$
Subtract total value of excluded property (from item [26] above)	$	$
28. NET FAMILY PROPERTY		$

NOTE: This financial statement must be updated no more than 30 days before any court event by either completing and filing:

- *a new financial statement with updated information, or*
- *an affidavit in Form 14A setting out the details of any minor changes or confirming that the information contained in this statement remains correct.*

Sworn/Affirmed before me .... at *municipality* in .... *province, state or country* on .... *Date* *Commissioner for taking affidavits* *(Type or print name below if signature is illegible.)*	.... *Signature* *(This form is to be signed in front of a lawyer, justice of the peace, notary public or commissioner for taking affidavits.)*

SCHEDULE A: — ADDITIONAL SOURCES OF INCOME

Line	Income Source	Annual Amount
1.	Net partnership income	$
2.	Net rental income (Gross annual rental income of $ ....)	$
3.	Total amount of dividends received from taxable Canadian corporations	$
4.	Total capital gains ($ ....) less capital losses ($ ....)	$
5.	Registered retirement savings plan withdrawals	$
6.	Any other income *(specify source)*	$

Subtotal:	$

SCHEDULE B: — SPECIAL OR EXTRAORDINARY EXPENSES FOR THE CHILD(REN)

Child's Name	Expense	Amount/yr.	Available Tax Credits or Deductions*
1.		$	$
2.		$	$
3.		$	$
4.		$	$
5.		$	$
6.		$	$
7.		$	$
8.		$	$
9.		$	$
10.		$	$

Child's Name	Expense	Amount/yr.	Available Tax Credits or Deductions*

Total Net Annual Amount	$
Total Net Monthly Amount	$

Notes:

* *Some of these expenses can be claimed in a parent's income tax return in relation to a tax credit or deduction (for example childcare costs). These credits or deductions must be shown in the above chart.*

❑ I attach proof of the above expenses.

❑ I earn $ .... per year which should be used to determine my share of the above expenses.

NOTE: Pursuant to the Child Support Guidelines, a court can order that the parents of a child share the costs of the following expenses for the child:

- Necessary childcare expenses;
- Medical insurance premiums and certain health-related expenses for the child that cost more than $100 annually;
- Extraordinary expenses for the child's education;
- Post-secondary school expenses; and,
- Extraordinary expenses for extracurricular activities.

February 1, 2010

FORM 13A — [REPEALED O. REG. 6/10, S. 10(2).]

[Repealed O. Reg. 6/10, s. 10(2).]

FORM 13B — NET FAMILY PROPERTY STATEMENT

[Repealed O. Reg. 76/06, s. 15.]

[Editor's Note: Forms 4 to 39 of the Family Law Rules have been repealed by O. Reg. 76/06, effective May 1, 2006. Pursuant to Family Law Rule 1(9), when a form is referred to by

number, the reference is to the form with that number that is described in the Table of Forms at the end of these rules and which is available at www.ontariocourtforms.on.ca. For your convenience, the government form as published on this website is reproduced below.]

ONTARIO

Court File Number

....

(Name of court)

at ....

Court office address

Applicant(s)

Full legal name & address for service — street & number, municipality, postal code, telephone & fax numbers and e-mail address (if any)..	*Lawyer's name & address — street & number, municipality, postal code, telephone & fax numbers and e-mail address (if any)..*

Respondent(s)

Full legal name & address for service — street & number, municipality, postal code, telephone & fax numbers and e-mail address (if any)..	*Lawyer's name & address — street & number, municipality, postal code, telephone & fax numbers and e-mail address (if any)..*

My name is *(full legal name)* ....

The valuation date for the following material is *(date)* ....

(Complete the tables by filling in the columns for both parties, showing your assets, debts, etc., and those of your spouse.)

TABLE 1: Value of assets owned on valuation date (List in the order of the categories in the financial statement.)		
ITEM	**APPLICANT**	**RESPONDENT**
1.	$	$

TABLE 1: Value of assets owned on valuation date (List in the order of the categories in the financial statement.)		
ITEM	**APPLICANT**	**RESPONDENT**
TOTAL 1	$	$

TABLE 2: Value of debts and liabilities on valuation date (List in the order of the categories in the financial statement.)		
ITEM	**APPLICANT**	**RESPONDENT**
1.	$	$
TOTAL 2	$	$

TABLE 3: Net value on date of marriage of property (other than a matrimonial home) after deducting debts or other liabilities on date of marriage (other than those relating directly to the purchase or significant improvement of a matrimonial home) (List in the order of the categories in the financial statement.)		
3(a) PROPERTY ITEM	*APPLICANT*	*RESPONDENT*
	$	$
TOTAL OF PROPERTY ITEMS	*$*	*$*
3(b) DEBT ITEM		
TOTAL OF DEBT ITEMS	*$*	*$*
NET TOTAL 3 [3(a) minus 3(b)]	*$*	*$*

TABLE 4: Value or property excluded under subsection 4(2) of the Family Law Act (List in the order of the categories in the financial statement.)		
ITEM	**APPLICANT**	**RESPONDENT**
	$	$
TOTAL 4	$	$

TOTAL 2 (from page 2)	$	$
TOTAL 3 (from page 2)	$	$
TOTAL 4 (from page 3)	$	$
TOTAL 5 ([Total 2] + [Total 3] +[Total 4])	$	$

TOTAL 1 (from page 1)	$	$
TOTAL 5 (from above)	$	$
TOTAL 6: NET FAMILY PROPERTY ([Total 1] minus [Total 5])	$	$

.... *Date of signature* .... *Signature*

May 15, 2009

FORM 14 — NOTICE OF MOTION

[Repealed O. Reg. 76/06, s. 15.]

[Editor's Note: Forms 4 to 39 of the Family Law Rules have been repealed by O. Reg. 76/06, effective May 1, 2006. Pursuant to Family Law Rule 1(9), when a form is referred to by number, the reference is to the form with that number that is described in the Table of Forms at the end of these rules and which is available at www.ontariocourtforms.on.ca. For your convenience, the government form as published on this website is reproduced below.]

Court File Number ....

.... *(Name of court)*

at .... *Court office address*

Applicant(s)

Full legal name & address for service — street & number, municipality, postal code, telephone & fax numbers and e-mail address (if any).	*Lawyer's name & address — street & number, municipality, postal code, telephone & fax numbers and e-mail address (if any).*

Respondent(s)

Full legal name & address for service — street & number, municipality, postal code, telephone & fax numbers and e-mail address (if any).	*Lawyer's name & address — street & number, municipality, postal code, telephone & fax numbers and e-mail address (if any).*

The person making this motion or the person's lawyer must contact the clerk of the court by telephone or otherwise to choose a time and date when the court could hear this motion.

TO THE PARTIES:

THE COURT WILL HEAR A MOTION on (date) .... *at* .... *a.m./p.m., or as soon as possible after that time, at (place of hearing)*

This motion will be made by *(name of person making the motion)* .... who will be asking the court for an order for the item(s) listed on page 2 of this notice.

❑ A copy of the affidavit(s) in support of this motion is/are served with this notice.

❑ A notice of a case conference is served with this notice to change an order.

If this material is missing, you should talk to the court office immediately.

The person making this motion is also relying on the following documents in the continuing record: *(List documents.)*

If you want to oppose this motion or to give your own views, you should talk to your own lawyer and prepare your own affidavit, serve it on all other parties not later than 4 days before the date above and file it at the court office not later than 2 days before that date. Only written and affidavit evidence will be allowed at a motion unless the court gives permission for oral testimony. You may bring your lawyer to the motion.

IF YOU DO NOT COME TO THE MOTION, THE COURT MAY MAKE AN ORDER WITHOUT YOU AND ENFORCE IT AGAINST YOU.

....
Date of signature

....
Signature of person making this motion or of person's lawyer

Typed or printed name of person or of person's lawyer, address for service, telephone & fax numbers and e-mail address (if any)

NOTE TO PERSON MAKING THIS MOTION: You MUST file a confirmation (Form 14C) not later than 2:00 p.m. 2 days before the date set out above.

If this is a motion to change past and future support payments under an order that has been assigned to a government agency, you must also serve this notice on that agency. If you do not, the agency can ask the court to set aside any order that you may get in this motion and can ask for costs against you.

State the order or orders requested on this motion.

June 15, 2007

FORM 14A — AFFIDAVIT (GENERAL)

[Repealed O. Reg. 76/06, s. 15.]

[Editor's Note: Forms 4 to 39 of the Family Law Rules have been repealed by O. Reg. 76/06, effective May 1, 2006. Pursuant to Family Law Rule 1(9), when a form is referred to by number, the reference is to the form with that number that is described in the Table of Forms at the end of these rules and which is available at www.ontariocourtforms.on.ca. For your convenience, the government form as published on this website is reproduced below.]

Court File Number ....

.... *(Name of court)*

at .... *Court office address*

Applicant(s)

Full legal name & address for service — street & number, municipality, postal code, telephone & fax and e-mail address (if any)	*Lawyer's name & address — street & number, municipality, postal code, telephone & fax numbers and e-mail address (if any)*

Respondent(s)

Full legal name & address for service — street & number, municipality, postal code, telephone & fax numbers and e-mail address (if any)	*Lawyer's name & address — street & number, municipality, postal code, telephone & fax numbers and e-mail address (if any)*

My name is (full legal name)

I live in (municipality & province) and I swear/affirm that the following is true:

Set out the statements of fact in consecutively numbered paragraphs. Where possible, each numbered paragraph should consist of one complete sentence and be limited to a particular statement of fact. If you learned a fact from someone else, you must give that person's name and state that you believe that fact to be true.

1.

Put a line through any blank space left on this page.

Sworn/Affirmed before me at .... *municipality* in .... *province, state or country* on .... *date*	
Commissioner for taking affidavits (Type or print name below if signature is illegible.)	*Signature* *(This form is to be signed in front of a lawyer, justice of the peace, notary public or commissioner for taking affidavits.)*

September 1, 2005

FORM 14B — MOTION FORM

[Repealed O. Reg. 76/06, s. 15.]

[Editor's Note: Forms 4 to 39 of the Family Law Rules have been repealed by O. Reg. 76/06, effective May 1, 2006. Pursuant to Family Law Rule 1(9), when a form is referred to by number, the reference is to the form with that number that is described in the Table of Forms at the end of these rules and which is available at www.ontariocourtforms.on.ca. For your convenience, the government form as published on this website is reproduced below.]

Court File Number ....

.... *(Name of court)*

at .... *Court office address*

Names of parties:

Applicant: ....

Hearing date: ....

Respondent: ....

Name of case management judge: ....

This form is filed by:

❑ applicant
❑ respondent
❑ other *(Specify.)*
....

This motion is made:

❑ with the consent of all persons affected
❑ with notice to all persons affected — opposition expected

❑ with notice to all persons affected — unopposed
❑ without notice

NOTE TO PERSON MAKING THIS MOTION: If this is a motion to change past and future support payments under an order that has been assigned to a government agency, you must also serve this Notice on that agency. If you do not, the agency can ask the court to set aside any order that you may get in this motion and can ask for court costs against you.

Order that you want the court to make: (If you need more space, add an extra sheet but do not make any changes to this form.)

Laws and rules on which you are relying: (Give name of statute and section numbers; name of regulation and section numbers; and rule numbers.)

....

....

I want the court to deal with this motion:

- ❑ by relying only on written material.
- ❑ by conference telephone call *(An appointment for such a call must be arranged in advance; see rule 14 of the Family Law Rules).)*
- ❑ in a hearing at which affected persons may attend personally.

At this motion, I am relying on the following material:

- ❑ Tabs/pages .... of the continuing record
- ❑ Pages .... of the transcript of the evidence of *(name of person)* ...., dated .... *(Relevant parts of transcript must be highlighted.)*

This party's lawyer (Give lawyer's name, firm, telephone & fax number and e-mail address. If no lawyer, give party's name, and address for service, telephone & fax number and e-mail address.)	**Other party's lawyer (Give lawyer's name, firm, telephone & fax number and e-mail address. If no lawyer, give party's name, and address for service, telephone & fax number and e-mail address.)**

.... *Signature*

.... *Date of signature*

September 1, 2005

FORM 14C — CONFIRMATION

[Repealed O. Reg. 76/06, s. 15.]

[Editor's Note: Forms 4 to 39 of the Family Law Rules have been repealed by O. Reg. 76/06, effective May 1, 2006. Pursuant to Family Law Rule 1(9), when a form is referred to by number, the reference is to the form with that number that is described in the Table of Forms at the end of these rules and which is available at www.ontariocourtforms.on.ca. For your convenience, the government form as published on this website is reproduced below.]

Court File Number

(Name of court)

Form 14C: Confirmation

at ____

Court office address

Applicant(s)

Full legal name & address for service — street & number, municipality, postal code, telephone & fax numbers and e-mail address (if any).	*Lawyer's name & address — street & number, municipality, postal code, telephone & fax numbers and e-mail address (if any).*

Respondent(s)

Full legal name & address for service — street & number, municipality, postal code, telephone & fax numbers and e-mail address (if any).	*Lawyer's name & address — street & number, municipality, postal code, telephone & fax numbers and e-mail address (if any).*
Name & address of Children's Lawyer's agent (street & number, municipality, postal code, telephone & fax numbers and e-mail address (if any)) and name of person represented.	

1. My name is *(full legal name)* ....
and I am ❑ the lawyer for *(name)* ....
❑ *(Other. Specify.)* ....

2. I have ❑ not been able to contact the opposing lawyer or party in this case to confirm the matters set out in paragraphs 3 to 7 below because: *(Give reason for inability to contact other side).*
❑ contacted the opposing lawyer or party and have confirmed the matters set out in paragraphs 3 to 7 below.

3. The scheduled date and time for this
❑ motion ❑ case conference ❑ settlement conference ❑ trial management conference
is *(date)* .... at .... am/pm.
(complete only if motion is being confirmed)
❑ A case conference was held on the issues in this motion before Justice ....
❑ A case conference has not been held on the issues in this motion.

4. This matter is going ahead
❑ on all the issues.
❑ on only the following issues: *(Specify.)* ....
❑ for a consent order regarding: *(Specify.)* ....
❑ for an adjournment on consent to *(date)* .... because *(Give reason.)* ....
❑ for a contested adjournment to *(date)* .... asked for by *(name of person asking for adjournment)* .... because *(Give reason.)* ....

5. The judge should read pages/tabs .... of the continuing record.

6. Total time estimate: applicant: .... minutes; respondent .... minutes; for a total of .... minutes.

7. The case management judge for this case is Justice ....

....	....
Date of signature	*Lawyer's or party's signature*

September 1, 2005

FORM 14D — ORDER ON MOTION WITHOUT NOTICE

[Repealed O. Reg. 76/06, s. 15.]

[Editor's Note: Forms 4 to 39 of the Family Law Rules have been repealed by O. Reg. 76/06, effective May 1, 2006. Pursuant to Family Law Rule 1(9), when a form is referred to by number, the reference is to the form with that number that is described in the Table of Forms at the end of these rules and which is available at www.ontariocourtforms.on.ca. For your convenience, the government form as published on this website is reproduced below.]

Court File Number ....

[SEAL]

.... *(Name of court)*

at .... *Court office address*

Applicant(s)

Full legal name & address for service — street & number, municipality, postal code, telephone & fax numbers and e-mail address (if any)	Lawyer's name & address — street & number, municipality, postal code, telephone & fax numbers and e-mail address (if any)

Respondent(s)

Full legal name & address for service — street & number, municipality, postal code, telephone & fax numbers and e-mail address (if any)	Lawyer's name & address — street & number, municipality, postal code, telephone & fax numbers and e-mail address (if any)

.... *Judge (print or type name)*

.... *Date of order*

The court heard a motion made by *(name of person or persons who made the motion)* .... without notice to *(name)* ....

The following persons were in court *(names of parties and lawyers in court at time of the motion)* ....

For this motion, the court read *(list the documents filed on the motion)* ....

The court also received and heard submissions on behalf of *(name or names)* ....

THIS COURT ORDERS THAT:

Put a line through any blank space left on this page.

.... *Date of signature*

.... *Signature of judge or clerk of the court*

NOTICE TO (name)

This order has been made without notice to you. If you want the court to change this order, you must act as quickly as possible after the order comes to your attention, by serving an affidavit and a notice of motion on the other parties and by filing them together with proof of service at the court office.

September 1, 2005

FORM 15 — MOTION TO CHANGE

[Repealed O. Reg. 76/06, s. 15.]

[Editor's Note: Forms 4 to 39 of the Family Law Rules have been repealed by O. Reg. 76/06, effective May 1, 2006. Pursuant to Family Law Rule 1(9), when a form is referred to by number, the reference is to the form with that number that is described in the Table of Forms at the end of these rules and which is available at www.ontariocourtforms.on.ca. For your convenience, the government form as published on this website is reproduced below.]

ONTARIO

Court File Number

....

(Name of court)

at ....

Court office address

❑ *the order of Justice ...., dated ....*

❑ *the agreement for support between the parties, dated ...., filed with the court on ....*

Applicant(s)

Full legal name & address for service — street & number, municipality, postal code, telephone & fax numbers and e-mail address (if any).	*Lawyer's name & address — street & number, municipality, postal code, telephone & fax numbers and e-mail address (if any).*

Respondent(s)

Full legal name & address for service — street & number, municipality, postal code, telephone & fax numbers and e-mail address (if any).	*Lawyer's name & address — street & number, municipality, postal code, telephone & fax numbers and e-mail address (if any).*

Assignee (if applicable)

Full legal name & address for service — street & number, municipality, postal code, telephone & fax numbers and e-mail address (if any).	*Lawyer's name & address — street & number, municipality, postal code, telephone & fax numbers and e-mail address (if any).*

NOTE: If you are seeking to change a support term in an agreement that has not already been filed with the court pursuant to s. 35 of the Family Law Act, you must file the agreement and Form 26B (Affidavit for Filing Domestic Contract or Paternity Agreement with Court) before bringing this motion to change.

If the order or agreement for support has been assigned to a person or agency, the assignee must be served with this form and the Change Information Form (Form 15A). The assignee's consent to change an order or agreement for support may be necessary. It is the responsibility of the person seeking the change to the order or agreement to determine if the order or agreement has been assigned. You can do this by submitting a Confirmation of Assignment form. The Confirmation of Assignment form is available through the Ministry of the Attorney General website or at the court office.

TO: (name(s) of party(ies)) ....

(Name of party bringing motion) .... has brought a motion to change

❑ the order of Justice ...., dated ....

❑ the agreement between you and *(name of party bringing this motion)* ...., dated ....

❑ *THE FIRST COURT DATE IS* ...., at .... ❑ a.m. ❑ p.m. or as soon as possible after that time, at *(address of court)* ....

❑ *NO COURT DATE HAS BEEN SET FOR THIS CASE.* A case management judge will not be assigned until one of the parties asks the clerk of the court to schedule a case conference and serves a Conference Notice (Form 17).

IF, AFTER 365 DAYS, THE CASE HAS NOT BEEN SCHEDULED FOR TRIAL, the clerk of the court will send out a warning that the case will be dismissed in 60 days unless the parties file proof that the case has been settled or one of the parties asks for a case or a settlement conference.

(To be completed by the party bringing this motion — check the box of any paragraph that applies to your case:)

❑ This case does not include any claim to change support, and a financial statement is therefore not attached.

❑ The case only includes a claim to change child support in accordance with the table amount specified under the Child Support Guidelines and a financial statement is therefore not attached.

❑ This case includes a claim to change support other than child support in the amount specified in the table of the applicable child support guidelines, and a financial statement is attached. You MUST fill out a Financial Statement (Form 13 or 13.1), serve a copy on the person(s) bringing the motion to change and file a copy in the court office with an Affidavit of Service (Form 6B) even if you do not respond to this case.

IF YOU CONSENT TO THE CHANGES BEING SOUGHT IN THIS MOTION, you or your lawyer must complete the Consent Motion to Change (Form 15C — a blank copy should be attached) and return a copy to the person(s) bringing the motion and any assignee, if applicable, within 30 days of being served (60 days if the motion to change is served on you outside Canada or the United States). The person(s) bringing the motion may then file the consent with the court and may obtain a court order based on the consent. If a first court date has been scheduled, you do not need to attend court on that date unless specifically directed by the court to do so.

IF YOU WANT TO OPPOSE ANY CHANGE BEING SOUGHT IN THIS MOTION OR WANT TO REQUEST A CHANGE OF YOUR OWN, you or your lawyer must complete the Response to Motion to Change (Form 15B — a blank copy should be attached), serve a copy on the person(s) bringing the motion and file a copy in the court office with an Affidavit of Service (Form 6B). *YOU HAVE ONLY 30 DAYS AFTER THIS MOTION TO CHANGE IS SERVED ON YOU (60 DAYS IF THE MOTION TO CHANGE IS SERVED ON YOU OUTSIDE CANADA OR THE UNITED STATES) TO SERVE AND FILE A RESPONSE TO A MOTION TO CHANGE. IF YOU DO NOT, THE CASE WILL GO AHEAD WITHOUT YOU AND THE COURT MAY MAKE AN ORDER AND ENFORCE IT AGAINST YOU.*

NOTE: If you want to make your own claim to change support, you MUST also fill out a Financial Statement (Form 13 or 13.1), serve a copy on the person(s) bringing the motion and file a copy in the court office with an Affidavit of Service (Form 6B) UNLESS your only claim for support is for child support in the table amount specified under the Child Support Guidelines.

YOU SHOULD GET LEGAL ADVICE ABOUT THIS CASE RIGHT AWAY. If you cannot afford a lawyer, you may be able to get help from your local Legal Aid Ontario Office. (See your telephone directory under LEGAL AID.)

....

Date of issue by the clerk of the court *Clerk of the court*

CLAIM BY (name(s) of person(s) bringing motion) ....

I ASK THE COURT TO CHANGE THE EXISTING COURT ORDER OR SUPPORT AGREEMENT BY MAKING AN ORDER AS FOLLOWS: (complete only those items that affect the terms of the order or agreement that you are seeking to change.)

❑ *1.* An order that *(name(s) of party(ies) or person(s))* .... have custody of the following child(ren): *(name(s) and birthdate(s) of child(ren))* ....

❑ *2.* An order that *(name(s) of party(ies) or person(s))* .... have access to the following child(ren): *(name(s) and birthdate(s) of child(ren))* .... as follows: *(give details of access)* ....

❑ *3.* An order that *(name(s) of party(ies) and/or person(s))* .... and .... have joint custody of the following child(ren): *(name(s) and birthdate(s) of child(ren))* ....

❑ *4.* An order for the following residential/access arrangements for the child(ren): *(name(s) and birthdate(s) of child(ren)* ....

❑ *5.* Order(s) dealing with child support as follows:

❑ The order/agreement for child support, dated ...., be terminated for the following child(ren): *(insert name(s) and birthdate(s) of child(ren))* ...., effective *(date)* ....

❑ Based on the payor's annual income of $ ...., *(name of party)* .... pay *(name of party)* .... $ .... per month for the following child(ren): *(name(s) and birthdate(s) of child(ren))* .... with payments to start on *(date)* ....

❑ This amount is the table amount listed in the Child Support Guidelines.

❑ This amount is more than the table amount listed in the Child Support Guidelines.

❑ This amount is less than the table amount listed in the Child Support Guidelines.

❑ Starting on *(date)* ...., *(name of party)* .... pay to *(name of party)* .... $ .... for the following special or extraordinary expenses:

Child's Name	**Type of Expense**	**Total Amount of Expense**	**Payor's Share**	**Terms of Payment (frequency of payment, date due, etc.)**
		$	$	
		$	$	
		$	$	
		$	$	
		$	$	

❑ Other: *(give details)* ....

6. ❑ Orders dealing with the outstanding child support owed as follows:

❑ The child support owed to *(name of recipient)* .... be fixed at $ .... as of *(date)* ....

❑ *(Name of payor)* .... pay to *(name of recipient)* .... $ .... per month, with payments to begin on *(date)* .... until the full amount owing is paid.

❑ The child support owed to *(name of agency or other person)* .... be fixed at $ .... as of *(date)* ....

❑ *(Name of payor)* .... pay to *(name of agency or other person)* .... $ .... per month, with payments to begin on *(date)* .... until the full amount owing is paid.

7. ❑ An order that the spousal support be changed as follows:

❑ The order/agreement for spousal support, dated .... be terminated effective *(date)* ....

❑ *(Name of party)* .... pay spousal support to *(name of party)* .... in the amount of $ .... per month, effective on *(date)* ....

❑ Other *(give details of the order you want the court to make)* ....

8. ❑ An order that the outstanding spousal support owed be paid as follows:

❑ The spousal support owed to *(name of recipient)* .... be fixed at $ .... as of *(date)* ....

❑ *(Name of payor)* .... pay to *(name of recipient)* .... $ .... per month, with payments to begin on *(date)* .... until the full amount owing is paid.

❑ The spousal support owed to *(name of agency or other person)* .... be fixed at $ .... as of *(date)* ....

❑ *(Name of payor)* .... pay to *(name of agency or other person)* .... $ .... per month, with payments to begin on *(date)* .... until the full amount owing is paid.

9. ❑ I ask that the term(s) of the order of Justice *(name of judge)* ...., dated ...., for *(give details)* .... be changed as follows: *(give details of the order you want the court to make)* ....

10. ❑ I ask the court for the following order: ....

The information and facts supporting my motion to change are set out in the Change Information Form (Form 15A) attached.

....	....
Date of signature	*Signature of person bringing the motion or person's lawyer*

April 1, 2008

FORM 15A — CHANGE INFORMATION FORM

[Repealed O. Reg. 76/06, s. 15.]

[Editor's Note: Forms 4 to 39 of the Family Law Rules have been repealed by O. Reg. 76/06, effective May 1, 2006. Pursuant to Family Law Rule 1(9), when a form is referred to by number, the reference is to the form with that number that is described in the Table of Forms at the end of these rules and which is available at www.ontariocourtforms.on.ca. For your convenience, the government form as published on this website is reproduced below.]

ONTARIO

Court File Number

....

(Name of court)

at ....

Court office address

Applicant(s)

Full legal name & address for service — street & number, municipality, postal code, telephone & fax numbers and e-mail address (if any).	*Lawyer's name & address — street & number, municipality, postal code, telephone & fax numbers and e-mail address (if any).*

Respondent(s)

Full legal name & address for service — street & number, municipality, postal code, telephone & fax numbers and e-mail address (if any).	*Lawyer's name & address — street & number, municipality, postal code, telephone & fax numbers and e-mail address (if any).*

Assignee (if applicable)

Full legal name & address for service — street & number, municipality, postal code, telephone & fax numbers and e-mail address (if any).	*Lawyer's name & address — street & number, municipality, postal code, telephone & fax numbers and e-mail address (if any).*

PART 1 — GENERAL INFORMATION

(This part should be filled out to the best ability of the party asking for a change in an order or support agreement.)

My name is (full legal name) ....

I live in (municipality & province) ....

and I swear/affirm that the following is true:

1. I am the ❑ applicant ❑ respondent

2. The applicant, *(applicant's full legal name)* .... was born on *(date of birth)* .... lives in *(municipality & province)* .... and, at the present time, is

❑ married

❑ separated

❑ living in a spousal relationship

❑ other *(specify)* ....

The applicant is the ❑ support recipient ❑ support payor

3. The respondent, *(respondent's full legal name)* .... was born on *(date of birth)* .... lives in *(municipality & province)* and, at the present time, is

❑ married

❑ separated

❑ living in a spousal relationship

❑ other *(specify)* ....

The respondent is the ❑ support recipient ❑ support payor

4. This order/agreement

❑ has never been assigned

❑ has been assigned to

❑ the Ontario Ministry of Community and Social Services

❑ Ontario Works in *(name of location)* ....

❑ the municipality of *(name)* ....

❑ other *(specify)* ....

The details of the assignment are: *(Give date of assignment, indicate whether it is still in effect, add any other relevant information known to you and attach a copy of the Confirmation of Assignment Form.)*

....

....

....

....

5. The applicant and the respondent:

❑ started living together on *(date)* ....

❑ were married on *(date)* ....

❑ never lived together

❑ separated on *(date)* ....

❑ were divorced on *(date)* ....

6. The following chart gives basic information about the child(ren) in this case:

(List all child(ren) involved in this case, even those for whom no support is being claimed.)

Child's full legal name	**Age**	**Birthdate (d, m, y)**	**Lives in (municipality & province)**	**Now living with (name of person and relationship to child)**	**Support claimed for child? (YES or NO)**

Child's full legal name	Age	Birthdate (d, m, y)	Lives in (municipality & province)	Now living with (name of person and relationship to child)	Support claimed for child? (YES or NO)

7. I attach a copy of the existing ❑ court order ❑ agreement

that contains the term(s) to be changed.

8. The existing custody and access arrangements for the child(ren) are as follows:

Child's name	Custody/Access Arrangement

9. The details of the existing order/agreement with respect to support are as follows:

Date of order or agreement	Present child support payment	Other terms of child support	Present support payment (if any) for spouse
	$ .... *per*		$ .... *per* ....

10. The payment status of the existing order/agreement as of today is as follows:

❑ all payments have been made

❑ arrears are owing as follows:

Child support owed to recipient	Child support owed to other(s) (such as Ministry of Community and Social Services)	Spousal support owed to recipient	Spousal support owed to other(s) (such as Ministry of Community and Social Services)
$	$	$	$ ....

CUSTODY/ACCESS

(Complete only if you are asking for a change in an order for custody or access.)

11. I ask that *(name(s) of party(ies) and/or person(s))* .... have custody of the following child(ren): *(name(s) and birthdate(s) of child(ren))* ....

12. I ask that *(name of party)* .... have access to the following child(ren): *(name(s) and birthdate(s) of child(ren))* .... as follows: *(give details of access)* ....

OR

13. I ask that *(name(s) of party(ies) and/or person(s))* .... and .... have joint custody of the following child(ren): *(name(s) and birthdate(s) of child(ren))* ....

14. I ask for the following residential/access arrangements for the child(ren): .... *(name(s) and birthdate(s) of child(ren))* ....

15. The order I am asking the court to make is in the best interests of the child(ren) for the following reasons: *(give details)*

....

....

CHILD SUPPORT

(Complete this section only if you are asking for a change in child support.)

16. I am asking to change the child support in the order/agreement because:

❑ The order/agreement was made before the applicable Child Support Guidelines came into effect.

❑ The following change in circumstances has taken place: *(Give details of change in circumstances.)*

....

....

❑ The parties agree to the termination of the support order/agreement, dated ...., for the following child(ren): *(name(s) and birthdate(s) of child(ren))* ...., as of *(date)* ....

❑ Other: *(give details)*

17. I ask that the child support be changed as follows:

❑ The order/agreement for child support dated .... be terminated for the following child(ren): *(insert name(s) and birthdate(s) of child(ren))* .... effective *(date)* ....

❑ Based on the payor's income of $ .... per year, *(name of party)* .... pay child support to *(name of party)* .... in the amount of $ .... per month for the following child(ren) *(name(s) and birthdate(s) of child(ren))* .... with payments to start on *(date)* ....

❑ This amount is the table amount listed in the Child Support Guidelines.

❑ This amount is more than the table amount listed in the Child Support Guidelines.

❑ This amount is less than the table amount listed in the Child Support Guidelines. *(If this box is checked, you must complete paragraph 18.)*

❑ Starting on *(date)* ...., *(name of party)* .... pay to *(name of party)* .... $ .... for the following special or extraordinary expenses:

Child's Name	Type of Expense	Total Amount of Expense	Payor's Share	Terms of Payment (frequency of payment, date due, etc.)
		$	$	
		$	$	
		$	$	
		$	$	
		$	$	
		$	$	

❑ Other: *(give details)* ....

18.

❑ I am asking that child support be changed to an amount that is less than the table amount listed in the Child Support Guidelines. The reason(s) for my request is/are that:

❑ The parties agree to a different amount.

❑ I have attached a separate sheet to this form that explains why this is an appropriate amount of child support.

❑ The recipient is getting social assistance payments from a public agency whose consent to this arrangement is needed. I am attaching the agency's consent to this form.

❑ As can be seen from paragraphs 6 and 8 above, the parties have shared custody of the child(ren) *(the payor has a child at least 40% of the time).*

❑ I have attached a separate sheet to this form that compares the table amounts from the Child Support Guidelines for each of the parties, shows the increased cost of the shared custody arrangement, the financial circumstances of each party and of each child for whom support is claimed.

❑ The parties are agreeing to this arrangement and I have attached a separate sheet to this form that explains why this is an appropriate amount of child support.

❑ As can be seen from paragraphs 6 and 8 above, custody of the children is split between the parties. I have attached a separate sheet to this form that calculates the difference between the amount that each party would otherwise pay to the other under the Child Support Guidelines.

❑ A child is 18 or more years old and I attach to this form a separate sheet that calculates the amount of support for this child.

❑ A child contributes to his/her own support and I attach to this form a separate sheet showing the amount of the child's own income and/or assets.

❑ The payor's annual income is over $150,000 and I have attached to this form a separate sheet that calculates the amount of support that I want to be put in an order.

❑ Under the order/agreement, *(name(s) of child(ren))* .... is/are the subject of special provisions that I have detailed on a separate sheet that I have attached to this form.

❑ The payor stands in the place of a parent to *(name(s) of child(ren))* .... and I attach to this form a separate sheet that gives the details of another parent's duty to pay support for this/these child(ren), as well as the details of the calculation of the amount of support requested.

❑ The amount listed in the Child Support Guidelines would cause undue hardship to me or to the child(ren) for whom support is claimed. I attach to this form a separate sheet that compares the standards of living of the parties and calculates the amount of support that should be paid.

19. I ask that the outstanding child support owed be paid as follows:

❑ The child support owed to *(name of recipient)* .... be fixed at $ .... as of *(date)* ....

❑ *(Name of payor)* .... pay to *(name of recipient)* .... $ .... per month, with payments to begin on *(date)* .... until the full amount owing is paid.

❑ The child support owed to *(name of agency or other person)* .... be fixed at $ .... as of *(date)* ....

❑ *(Name of payor)* .... pay to *(name of agency or other person)* .... $ .... per month, with payments to begin on *(date)* .... until the full amount owing is paid.

SPOUSAL SUPPORT

(Complete only if you are asking for a change in spousal support.)

20. I am asking to change the spousal support in the order/agreement because:

❑ The following change in circumstances has taken place: *(give details of change in circumstances.)*

....

....

....

❑ Spousal support should no longer be paid as of *(date)* .... for the following reasons: *(give details)* ....

❑ The parties consent to the termination of the spousal support order/agreement, dated ...., as of *(date)* ....

❑ Other *(give details)*: ....

21. I ask that the spousal support be changed as follows:

❑ The order/agreement for spousal support, dated ...., be terminated effective *(date)* ....

❑ *(Name of party)* .... pay spousal support to *(name of party)* .... in the amount of $ .... per month, effective on *(date)* ....

❑ Other *(give details of the order you want the court to make)* ....

22. I ask that the outstanding spousal support owed be paid as follows:

❑ The spousal support owed to *(name of recipient)* .... be fixed at $ .... as of *(date)* ....

❑ *(Name of payor)* .... pay to *(name of recipient)* .... $ .... per month, with payments to begin on *(date)* .... until the full amount owing is paid.

❑ The spousal support owed to *(name of agency or other person)* .... be fixed at $ .... as of *(date)* ....

❑ *(Name of payor)* .... pay to *(name of agency or other person)* .... $ .... per month, with payments to begin on *(date)* until the full amount owing is paid.

OTHER

(Complete if applicable.)

23. I ask that the term(s) of the order of Justice *(name of judge)* ...., dated ...., for *(give details)* .... be changed as follows: *(give details of the order you want the court to make)* ....

24. I ask that the court make this order for the following reasons: ....

Sworn/Affirmed before me at .... *municipality*	.... *Signature*
in .... *province, state or country*	*(This form is to be signed in front of a lawyer, justice of the peace, notary public or commissioner for taking affidavits.)*
on .... *date* .... *Commissioner for taking affidavits* *(Type or print name below if signature is illegible.)*	

PART 2 — INFORMATION FROM SUPPORT PAYOR

DO NOT COMPLETE THIS PART IF THE PARTIES ARE ONLY CONSENTING TO TERMINATE A SUPPORT OBLIGATION OR IF THE MOTION TO CHANGE DOES NOT INCLUDE A CLAIM TO CHANGE CHILD SUPPORT.

My name is (full legal name) ....

I live in (municipality & province) .... *and I swear/affirm that the following is true:*

25. I am the support payor in this case.

26. I attach the following financial information about myself:

(a) a copy of every personal income tax return that I filed with Canada Revenue Agency for the 3 most recent taxation years;

(b) a copy of every notice of assessment or re-assessment from Canada Revenue Agency of those returns; and

(c)

❑ *(applies only if you are an employee)* proof of this year's earnings from my employer as required by clause 21(1)(c) of the Child Support Guidelines.

❑ *(applies only if you are self-employed, or you are a partner in a partnership or you control a corporation or are a beneficiary under a trust)* the documents listed in clauses 21(1)(d), (e), (f) or (g) of the Child Support Guidelines.

27. My total income

❑ will be $ .... for this year;

❑ was $ .... for last year; and

❑ was $ .... for the year before that.

28. On the basis of my annual income, the table amount from the Child Support Guidelines for *(number of child(ren))* .... child(ren) is $ .... per month.

29. My financial statement ❑ is attached. ❑ is not attached.

Sworn/Affirmed before me at	.... *municipality*	.... *Signature* *(This form is to be signed in front of a lawyer, justice of the peace, notary public or commissioner for taking affidavits.)*
in	*province, state or country*	
on .... *date*	.... *Commissioner for taking affidavits* *(Type or print name below if signature is illegible.)*	

PART 3 — INFORMATION FROM SUPPORT RECIPIENT

DO NOT COMPLETE THIS PART IF THE PARTIES ARE ONLY CONSENTING TO TERMINATE A SUPPORT OBLIGATION OR IF THE MOTION TO CHANGE DOES NOT INCLUDE A CLAIM TO CHANGE CHILD SUPPORT.

My name is (full legal name) ....

I live in (municipality & province) .... *and I swear/affirm that the following is true:*

30. I am the support recipient in this case.

Fill in paragraphs 31 and 32 only if:

- *the change for which you are asking is for an amount that is different from the Child Support Guidelines;*
- *the change for which you are asking relates to a child*
  - *over the age of 18 years,*
  - *for whom the payor stands in the place of a parent, or*
  - *with respect to whom the payor has access or physical custody not less than 40% of the time over the course of the year;*
- *each party has custody of one or more children;*
- *the payor's annual income as determined under the guidelines is more than $150,000;*
- *either party claims that an order according to the guidelines would result in undue hardship; or*
- *there is a claim for special or extraordinary expenses.*

31. I attach the following financial information about myself:

(a) a copy of every personal income tax return that I filed with Canada Revenue Agency for the 3 most recent taxation years;

(b) a copy of every notice of assessment or re-assessment from Canada Revenue Agency of those returns; and

(c)

❏ *(applies only if you are an employee)* proof of this year's earnings from my employer as required by clause 21(1)(c) of the Child Support Guidelines.

❏ *(applies only if you are self-employed, or you are a partner in a partnership or you control a corporation or are a beneficiary under a trust)* the documents listed in clauses 21(1)(d), (e), (f) or (g) of the Child Support Guidelines.

32. My total income

❏ will be $ .... for this year;

❏ was $ .... for last year; and

❏ was $ .... for the year before that.

33. My financial statement ❏ is attached. ❏ is not attached.

Sworn/Affirmed before me at .... *municipality* in .... *province, state or country*	.... *Signature* *(This form is to be signed in front of a lawyer, justice of the peace, notary public or commissioner for taking affidavits.)*

on ....

date *Commissioner for taking affidavits*
(Type or print name below if signature is illegible.)

April 1, 2008

FORM 15B — RESPONSE TO MOTION TO CHANGE

ONTARIO

Court File Number

....

(Name of court)

at ....

Court office address

Applicant(s)

Full legal name & address for service — street & number, municipality, postal code, telephone & fax numbers and e-mail address (if any).	*Lawyer's name & address — street & number, municipality, postal code, telephone & fax numbers and e-mail address (if any).*

Respondent(s)

Full legal name & address for service — street & number, municipality, postal code, telephone & fax numbers and e-mail address (if any).	*Lawyer's name & address — street & number, municipality, postal code, telephone & fax numbers and e-mail address (if any).*

Assignee (if applicable)

Full legal name & address for service — street & number, municipality, postal code, telephone & fax numbers and e-mail address (if any).	*Lawyer's name & address — street & number, municipality, postal code, telephone & fax numbers and e-mail address (if any).*

PART 1 — GENERAL INFORMATION

My name is (full legal name) ....

I live in (municipality and province) .... *and I swear/affirm that the following is true*:

1. I am the ❑ applicant ❑ respondent

2. I am the ❑ support payor ❑ support recipient

3. This order/agreement ❑ has never been assigned

❑ has been assigned to

❑ the Ontario Ministry of Community and Social Services

❑ Ontario Works in *(name of location)* ....

❑ the municipality of *(name)* ....

❑ other *(specify)* ....

The details of the assignment are: *(give date of assignment, indicate whether it is still in effect and add any other relevant information known to you.)*

....

....

4. ❑ I agree with the information set out in paragraphs 1 through 10 of the Change Information Form (Form 15A), dated ....

❑ I agree with the information set out in paragraphs 1 through 10 of the Change Information Form (Form 15A), dated .... EXCEPT as follows: *(give details of the information with which you do not agree and attach any documents that support your position.)*

....

....

....

5. ❑ I agree with the claims made by *(name of person bringing motion to change)* .... in paragraphs .... of the Motion to Change (Form 15), dated ....

❑ I disagree with the claims made by *(name of person bringing motion to change)* in paragraphs .... of the Motion to Change (Form 15), dated ....

6. ❑ I am asking that the motion to change (except for the parts with which I agree) be dismissed with costs.

CLAIM BY RESPONDING PARTY

(Complete only if you are asking the court to change the existing order or support agreement.)

7. ❑ I am asking the court to make a change of my own, the details of which are set out below.

CUSTODY/ACCESS

(Complete only if you are asking for a change in a custody or access order.)

8. I ask that *(name of party)* .... have custody of the following child(ren): *(name(s) and birthdate(s) of child(ren))* ....

9. I ask that *(name of party)* .... have access to the following child(ren): *(name(s) and birthdate(s) of child(ren))* .... as follows: *(give details of access)* ....

OR

10. I ask that *(name(s) of party(ies) and/or person(s))* .... and .... have joint custody of the following child(ren): *(name(s) and birthdate(s) of child(ren))* ....

11. I ask for the following residential/access arrangements for the child(ren): *(include name(s) and birthdate(s) of child(ren))*

....

....

....

12. The order I am asking the court to make is in the best interests of the child(ren) for the following reasons: *(give details)*

....

....

....

CHILD SUPPORT

(Complete this section only if you are asking for a change in child support.)

13. I am asking to change the child support in the order/agreement because:

❑ the order/agreement was made before the applicable Child Support Guidelines came into effect.

❑ the following change in circumstances has taken place: *(give details of change in circumstances.)*

....

....

....

....

❑ the parties agree to the termination of the support order/agreement, dated ...., for the following child(ren): *(name(s) and birthdate(s) of child(ren))* .... as of *(date)* ....

❑ Other: *(give details)* ....

14. I ask that the child support be changed as follows:

❑ The order/agreement for child support, dated ...., be terminated for the following child(ren): *(name(s) and birthdate(s) of child(ren))* .... effective *(date)* ....

❑ Based on the payor's annual income of $ ...., *(name of party)* .... pay child support to *(name of party)* .... in the amount of $ .... per month for the following child(ren): *(name(s) and birthdate(s) of child(ren))* .... with payments to start on *(date)* ....

❑ This amount is the table amount listed in the Child Support Guidelines.

❑ This amount is more than the table amount listed in the Child Support Guidelines.

❑ This amount is less than the table amount listed in the Child Support Guidelines. *(If this box is checked, you must complete paragraph 15.)*

❑ Starting on *(date)* ...., *(name of party)* .... pay to *(name of party)* .... $ .... for the following special or extraordinary expenses:

Child's Name	Type of Expense	Total Amount of Expense	Payor's Share	Terms of payment (frequency of payment, date due, etc.)
		$	$	
		$	$	
		$	$	
		$	$	
		$	$	

❑ Other: *(give details)* ....

15. I am asking that child support be changed to an amount that is less than the table amount listed in the Child Support Guidelines The reason(s) for my request is/are that:

❑ The parties agree to a different amount.

❑ I have attached a separate sheet to this form that explains why this is an appropriate amount of child support.

❑ The recipient is getting social assistance payments from a public agency whose consent to this arrangement is needed. I am attaching the agency's consent to this form.

❑ The parties have shared custody to the child(ren) *(the payor has a child at least 40% of the time).*

❑ I have attached a separate sheet to this form that compares the table amounts from the Child Support Guidelines for each of the parties, shows the increased cost of the shared custody arrangement, the financial circumstances of each party and of each child for whom support is claimed.

❑ The parties are agreeing to this arrangement and I have attached a separate sheet to this form that explains why this is an appropriate amount of child support.

❑ Custody of the children is split between the parties. I have attached a separate sheet to this form that calculates the difference between the amount that each party would otherwise pay to the other under the Child Support Guidelines.

❑ A child is 18 or more years old and I attach to this form a separate sheet that calculates the amount of support for this child.

❑ A child contributes to his/her own support and I attach to this form a separate sheet showing the amount of the child's own income and/or assets.

❑ The payor's annual income is over $150,000 and I have attached to this form a separate sheet that calculates the amount of support that I want to be put in an order.

❑ Under the order/agreement, *(name(s) of child(ren))* .... is/are the subject of special provisions that I have detailed on a separate sheet that I have attached to this form.

❑ The payor stands in the place of a parent to *(name(s) of child(ren)* .... and I attach to this form a separate sheet that gives the details of another parent's duty to pay support for this/these child(ren), as well as the details of the calculation of the amount of support requested.

❑ The amount listed in the Child Support Guidelines would cause undue hardship to me or to the child(ren) for whom support is claimed. I attach to this form a separate sheet that compares the standards of living of the parties and calculates the amount of support that should be paid.

16. I ask that the outstanding child support owed be paid as follows:

❑ The child support owed to *(name of recipient)* .... be fixed at $ .... as of *(date)* .... and *(name of payor)* .... pay to *(name of recipient)* .... $ .... per month, with payments to begin on *(date)* .... until the full amount owing is paid.

❑ The child support owed to *(name of agency or other person)* .... be fixed at $ .... as of *(date)* .... and *(name of payor)* .... pay to *(name of agency or other person)* .... $ .... per month, with payments to begin on *(date)* .... until the full amount owing is paid.

SPOUSAL SUPPORT

(Complete only if you are asking for a change in spousal support.)

17. I am asking to change the spousal support in the order/agreement because:

❑ The following change in circumstances has taken place: *(give details of change in circumstances.)*

....

....

....

....

❑ Spousal support should no longer be paid as of *(date)* .... for the following reasons: *(give details)*

....

....

....

❑ The parties consent to the termination of the spousal support order/agreement, dated ...., as of *(date)* ....

❑ Other *(specify)* ....

18. I ask that the spousal support be changed as follows:

❑ The order/agreement for spousal support, dated ...., be terminated effective *(date)* ....

❑ *(Name of party)* .... pay spousal support to *(name of party)* .... in the amount of $ .... per month, effective on *(date)* ....

❑ Other: *(give details of the order you want the court to make)* ....

19. I ask that the outstanding spousal support owed be paid as follows:

❑ The spousal support owed to *(name of recipient)* .... be fixed at $ .... as of *(date)* ....

❑ *(Name of payor)* .... pay to *(name of recipient)* .... $ .... per month, with payments to begin on *(date)* .... until the full amount owing is paid.

❑ The spousal support owed to *(name of agency or other person)* be fixed at $ .... as of *(date)* ....

❑ *(Name of payor)* .... pay to *(name of agency or other person)* .... $ .... per month, with payments to begin on *(date)* .... until the full amount owing is paid.

OTHER

(Complete if applicable)

20. I ask that the term of the order of Justice *(name of judge)* ...., dated ...., for *(give details)* .... be changed as follows: *(give details of the order you want the court to make)* ....

21. I ask that the court make the order set out in paragraph 20 for the following reasons:

....

....

....

....

....

....

....

22. I ask the court to make the following additional order:

....

....

....

....

....

....

....

23. I ask the court to make the order set out in paragraph 22 for the following reasons:

....

....

....

....

....

....

....

Sworn/Affirmed before me at .... *municipality* in .... *province, state or country* on .... *date* *Commissioner for taking affidavits* *(Type or print name below if signature is illegible.)*	.... *Signature* *(This form is to be signed in front of a lawyer, justice of the peace, notary public or commissioner for taking affidavits.)*

PART 2 — INFORMATION FROM SUPPORT PAYOR

DO NOT COMPLETE THIS PART IF THE PARTIES ARE ONLY CONSENTING TO TERMINATE A SUPPORT OBLIGATION OR IF THE MOTION TO CHANGE DOES NOT INCLUDE A CLAIM TO CHANGE CHILD SUPPORT.

My name is (full legal name) ....

I live in (municipality and province) .... *and I swear/affirm that the following is true*:

24. I am the support payor in this case.

25. I attach the following financial information about myself:

(a) a copy of every personal income tax return that I filed with Canada Revenue Agency for the 3 most recent taxation years;

(b) a copy of every notice of assessment or re-assessment from Canada Revenue Agency of those returns; and

(c) ❑ *(applies only if you are an employee)* proof of this year's earnings from my employer as required by clause 21(1)(c) of the Child Support Guidelines.

❑ *(applies only if you are self-employed, or you are a partner in a partnership or you control a corporation or are a beneficiary under a trust)* the documents listed in clauses 21(1)(d), (e), (f) or (g) of the Child Support Guidelines.

26. My total income

❑ will be $ .... for this year;

❑ was $ .... for last year; and

❑ was $ .... for the year before that.

27. On the basis of my annual income, the table amount from the Child Support Guidelines for *(number of children)* .... child(ren) is $ .... per month.

28. My financial statement ❑ is attached. ❑ is not attached.

Sworn/Affirmed before me at .... *municipality* in .... *province, state or country* on .... *date* *Commissioner for taking affidavits* *(Type or print name below if signature is illegible.)*	.... *Signature* *(This form is to be signed in front of a lawyer, justice of the peace, notary public or commissioner for taking affidavits.)*

PART 3 — INFORMATION FROM SUPPORT RECIPIENT

DO NOT COMPLETE THIS PART IF THE PARTIES ARE ONLY CONSENTING TO TERMINATE A SUPPORT OBLIGATION OR IF THE MOTION TO CHANGE DOES NOT INCLUDE A CLAIM TO CHANGE CHILD SUPPORT.

My name is (full legal name)

I live in (municipality and province) .... *and I swear/affirm that the following is true:*

29. I am the support recipient in this case.

Fill in paragraphs 30 and 31 only if:

- *the change for which you are asking is for an amount that is different from the Child Support Guidelines;*
- *the change for which you are asking relates to a child*
    - *over the age of 18 years,*
    - *for whom the payor stands in the place of a parent, or*

- *with respect to whom the payor has access or physical custody not less than 40% of the time over the course of the year*;

- *each party has custody of one or more children*;
- *the payor's annual income as determined under the guidelines is more than $150,000*;
- *either party claims that an order according to the guidelines would result in undue hardship; or*
- *there is a claim for special or extraordinary expenses.*

30. I attach the following financial information about myself:

(a) a copy of every personal income tax return that I filed with Canada Revenue Agency for the 3 most recent taxation years;

(b) a copy of every notice of assessment or re-assessment from Canada Revenue Agency of those returns; and

(c) ❑ *(applies only if you are an employee)* proof of this year's earnings from my employer as required by clause 21(1)(c) of the Child Support Guidelines.

❑ *(applies only if you are self-employed, or you are a partner in a partnership or you control a corporation or are a beneficiary under a trust)* the documents listed in clauses 21(1)(d), (e), (f) or (g) of the Child Support Guidelines.

31. My total income

❑ will be $ .... for this year;

❑ was $ .... for last year; and

❑ was $ .... for the year before that.

32. My financial statement ❑ is attached. ❑ is not attached.

Sworn/Affirmed before me at .... *municipality* in .... *province, state or country* on .... *date* *Commissioner for taking affidavits* *(Type or print name below if signature is illegible.)*	.... *Signature* *(This form is to be signed in front of a lawyer, justice of the peace, notary public or commissioner for taking affidavits.)*

April 1, 2008

FORM 15C — CONSENT MOTION TO CHANGE

ONTARIO

Court File Number

....

(Name of court)

at ....

Court office address

Applicant(s)

Full legal name & address for service — street & number, municipality, postal code, telephone & fax numbers and e-mail address (if any).	*Lawyer's name & address — street & number, municipality, postal code, telephone & fax numbers and e-mail address (if any).*

Respondent(s)

Full legal name & address for service — street & number, municipality, postal code, telephone & fax numbers and e-mail address (if any).	*Lawyer's name & address — street & number, municipality, postal code, telephone & fax numbers and e-mail address (if any).*

Assignee (if applicable)

Full legal name & address for service — street & number, municipality, postal code, telephone & fax numbers and e-mail address (if any).	*Lawyer's name & address — street & number, municipality, postal code, telephone & fax numbers and e-mail address (if any).*

EACH OF YOU SHOULD CONSIDER GETTING A LAWYER'S ADVICE BEFORE SIGNING THIS CONSENT.

IF YOU ARE SEEKING TO CHANGE A SUPPORT ORDER OR AGREEMENT THAT HAS BEEN ASSIGNED TO A PERSON OR AGENCY, YOU MUST SERVE ALL DOCUMENTS ON THE ASSIGNEE AND OBTAIN THE ASSIGNEE'S CONSENT TO ANY CHANGE THAT MAY AFFECT THE ASSIGNEE'S FINANCIAL INTEREST. FAILURE TO OBTAIN THE ASSIGNEE'S CONSENT MAY RESULT IN A COURT SETTING ASIDE AN ORDER AND ORDERING COSTS AGAINST THE PARTY WHO DID NOT PROVIDE NOTICE. IT IS THE RESPONSIBILITY OF THE PERSON SEEKING THE CHANGE TO DETERMINE IF THE ORDER HAS BEEN ASSIGNED. YOU CAN DO THIS BY SUBMITTING A CONFIRMATION OF ASSIGNMENT FORM. THE CONFIRMATION OF ASSIGNMENT FORM IS AVAILABLE THROUGH THE MINISTRY OF THE ATTORNEY GENERAL WEBSITE OR AT THE COURT OFFICE.

1. We know that each of us has the right to get advice from his or her own lawyer about this case and understand that signing this consent may result in a final court order that will be enforced.

2. ❑ We have filed/are filing Financial Statements (Form 13 or 13.1) with the court.

❑ We have agreed not to file any Financial Statements with the court.

3. ❑ We have attached the existing final order or support agreement and ask the court to make an order that changes that order or agreement as set out below.

CUSTODY/ACCESS

(Complete only if the parties are asking for a change in a custody or access order.)

4. ❑ We agree that *(name(s) of person(s) or party(ies))* .... shall have custody of the following child(ren):

Child's full legal name	**Birthdate (d, m, y)**	**Age**	**Sex**

❑ We agree that *(name(s) of person(s) or party(ies))* .... shall have access to: *(name(s) and birthdate(s) of child(ren))* .... as follows: *(give details of access order)* ....

OR

5. ❑ We agree that *(names of parties or persons)* .... and .... shall have joint custody of the following child(ren):

Child's full legal name	**Birthdate (d, m, y)**	**Age**	**Sex**

❑ We agree that the residential/access arrangements for the child(ren) *(name(s) and birthdate(s) of child(ren))* .... shall be as follows: ....

CHILD SUPPORT

(Complete only if the parties are asking for a change in child support.)

6. We agree to an order for child support that is:

❑ equal to or more than what is in the Child Support Guidelines.

❑ none (no child support).

❑ less than what is in the Child Support Guidelines for the following reasons: ....

7. The party receiving support ❑ is ❑ is not receiving social assistance.

8. We agree that child support shall be as follows:

❑ Based on the payor's annual income of $ ...., *(name of party)* .... shall pay to *(name of party)* .... $ .... per month for the following child(ren) *(name(s) and birthdate(s) of child(ren))* .... with payments to begin on *(date)* ....

❑ Starting on *(date)* ...., *(name of party)* .... shall pay *(name of party)* .... $ .... for the following special or extraordinary expenses:

Child's Name	Type of Expense	Total Amount of Expense	Payor's Share	Terms of Payment (frequency of payment, date due, etc.)
		$	$	
		$	$	
		$	$	
		$	$	
		$	$	

❑ *(Complete only if the parties are agreeing to special or extraordinary expenses.)* The recipient's total annual income is $ ....

❑ The order or agreement for child support, with respect to the child(ren) *(name(s) and birthdate(s) of child(ren))* ...., dated ...., shall be terminated as of *(date)* ....

Complete if applicable:

9. We also agree that the outstanding child support owed be paid off as follows:

❑ The child support owed to *(name of recipient)* .... shall be fixed at $ .... as of *(date)* .... and *(name of payor)* .... shall pay *(name of recipient)* .... $ .... per month, with payments to begin on *(date)* .... until the full amount owing has been paid.

❑ The child support owed to *(name of agency or other person)* .... shall be fixed at $ .... as of *(date)* .... and *(name of payor)* .... shall pay *(name of agency or other person)* .... $ .... per month, with payments to begin on *(date)* .... until the full amount owing has been paid.

SPOUSAL SUPPORT

(Complete only if the parties are seeking a change in spousal support.)

10. We agree that the spousal support payments should be as follows:

❑ *(Name of party)* .... shall pay to *(name of party)* .... the amount of $ .... per month, with payments to begin on *(date)* ....

❑ The order or agreement for spousal support, dated ...., shall be terminated as of *(date)* ....

11. We agree that the outstanding spousal support owed be paid off as follows:

❑ The spousal support owed to *(name of recipient)* .... shall be fixed at $ .... as of *(date)* .... and *(name of payor)* .... shall pay *(name of recipient)* .... $ .... per month, with payments to begin on *(date)* .... until the full amount owing has been paid.

❑ The spousal support owed to *(name of agency or other person)* .... shall be fixed at $ .... as of *(date)* .... and *(name of payor)* .... shall pay *(name of recipient)* .... $ .... per month, with payments to begin on *(date)* .... until the full amount owing has been paid.

NOTE: If money is owed to an agency or other person (an assignee), a representative of that agency or the other person must consent to the change in the order.

OTHER

(Complete if applicable.)

12. We agree that paragraph(s) *(specify which paragraphs of the order are to be changed)* .... of the order of Justice *(name of judge)* ...., dated ...., shall be changed as follows: *(give details of the order you want the court to make)* ....

The parties do not need to sign this consent at the same time. Each party must sign in the presence of his or her witness who shall sign immediately after that party.

NOTE: The witness cannot be one of the parties. If the witness does not know the party, the witness should see identification that proves that the person signing the consent is the same person who is a party to the consent.

.... *Applicant's signature*	.... *Respondent's signature*
.... *Date of applicant's signature*	.... *Date of respondent's signature*
.... *Signature of witness*	.... *Signature of witness*
.... *Type or print name of witness to applicant's signature*	.... *Type or print name of witness to respondent's signature*
.... *Address of witness*	.... *Address of witness*
.... *Telephone number of witness*	.... *Telephone number of witness*

ASSIGNEE'S CONSENT

....	....
Signature of person authorized to sign on behalf of assignee	*Date of signature*

....

Print name and title of person signing the consent

....	....
Witness's signature	*Name of witness (type or print legibly)*

April 1, 2008

FORM 15D — CONSENT MOTION TO CHANGE CHILD SUPPORT

ONTARIO

Court File Number

....

(Name of court)

at ....

Court office address

Applicant(s)

Full legal name & address for service — street & number, municipality, postal code, telephone & fax numbers and e-mail address (if any).	*Lawyer's name & address — street & number, municipality, postal code, telephone & fax numbers and e-mail address (if any).*

Respondent(s)

Full legal name & address for service — street & number, municipality, postal code, telephone & fax numbers and e-mail address (if any).	*Lawyer's name & address — street & number, municipality, postal code, telephone & fax numbers and e-mail address (if any).*

Assignee (if applicable)

Full legal name & address for service — street & number, municipality, postal code, telephone & fax numbers and e-mail address (if any).	*Lawyer's name & address — street & number, municipality, postal code, telephone & fax numbers and e-mail address (if any).*

Instructions to the Parties:

IF YOU ARE SEEKING TO CHANGE A CHILD SUPPORT TERM IN AN AGREEMENT THAT HAS NOT ALREADY BEEN FILED WITH THE COURT PURSUANT TO SECTION 35 OF THE FAMILY LAW ACT, YOU MUST FILE THE AGREEMENT AND FORM 26B (Affidavit for Filing Domestic Contract or Paternity Agreement with Court) BEFORE BRINGING THIS MOTION TO CHANGE.

EACH OF YOU SHOULD CONSIDER GETTING A LAWYER'S ADVICE BEFORE SIGNING THIS CONSENT.

IF YOU ARE SEEKING TO CHANGE A CHILD SUPPORT ORDER OR AGREEMENT THAT HAS BEEN ASSIGNED TO A PERSON OR AGENCY, YOU MUST OBTAIN THE ASSIGNEE'S CONSENT TO ANY CHANGE THAT MAY AFFECT THE ASSIGNEE'S FINANCIAL INTEREST. FAILURE TO OBTAIN THE ASSIGNEE'S CONSENT MAY RESULT IN A COURT SETTING ASIDE AN ORDER AND ORDERING COSTS AGAINST THE PARTY WHO DID NOT PROVIDE NOTICE. IT IS THE RESPONSIBILITY OF THE PERSON SEEKING THE CHANGE TO DETERMINE IF THE ORDER HAS BEEN ASSIGNED. YOU CAN DO THIS BY SUBMITTING A CONFIRMATION OF ASSIGNMENT FORM. THE CONFIRMATION OF ASSIGNMENT FORM IS AVAILABLE THROUGH THE MINISTRY OF THE ATTORNEY GENERAL WEBSITE OR AT THE COURT OFFICE.

TO THE COURT:

This motion to change child support is filed by the parties with the consent of the applicant and respondent and, if applicable, the assignee.

We ask the court to make the order requested in this motion by relying on this form only.

1. We know that each of us has the right to get advice from his or her own lawyer about this case and understand that signing this consent may result in a final court order that will be enforced.

2. We have attached the existing agreement or order for child support and ask the court to make an order that changes that order or agreement as set out below.

Check the following box(es) that apply:

3. The total annual income of the person paying support is $ ....

The payor ❑ is ❑ is not self-employed.

4. Proof of income for the payor was provided to the recipient by: *(check at least one)*

❑ Most recent income tax return

❑ Most recent notice of income tax assessment

❑ Current pay stub

❑ Business records

❑ Other *(provide details)* ....

5. *(Name of party)* .... shall pay to *(name of party)* .... $ .... per month for the following child(ren) *(name(s) and birthdate(s) of child(ren))*

.... with payments to begin on *(date)* ....

6. ❑ This amount is the table amount listed in the Child Support Guidelines.

❑ This amount is more than the table amount listed in the Child Support Guidelines.

❑ This amount is less than the table amount listed in the Child Support Guidelines for the following reasons: *(give details)* ....

7. Starting on *(date)* ...., *(name of party)* .... shall pay *(name of party)* .... $ .... for the following special or extraordinary expenses:

Child's Name	**Type of Expense**	**Total Amount of Expense**	**Payor's Share**	**Terms of Payment (frequency of payment, date due, etc.)**
		$	$	
		$	$	
		$	$	
		$	$	
		$	$	

(Complete paragraphs 8 and 9 only if the parties are agreeing to special or extraordinary expenses.)

8. ❑ The recipient's total annual income is $ ....

9. ❑ Proof of income for the recipient was provided to the payor by: *(check at least one)*

❑ Most recent income tax return

❑ Most recent notice of income tax assessment

❑ Current pay stub

❑ Business records

❑ Other *(provide details)* ....

10. ❑ The order or agreement for child support, with respect to the child(ren) *(name(s) and birthdate(s) of child(ren))* ...., dated ...., should be terminated as of *(date)* ....

Complete applicable paragraphs if there is outstanding child support owing

11. ❑ The child support owed to *(name of recipient)* .... shall be fixed at $ .... as of *(date)* ....

12. ❑ *(Name of payor)* .... shall pay *(name of recipient)* .... $ .... per month, with payments to begin on *(date)* .... until the full amount owing is paid.

13. ❑ The child support owed to *(name of agency or other person)* .... shall be fixed at $ .... as of *(date)* ....

14. ❑ *(Name of payor)* .... shall pay to *(name of agency or other person)* .... $ .... per month, with payments to begin on *(date)* .... until the full amount owing is paid.

NOTE: If money is owed to an agency or other person (an assignee), a representative of that agency or the other person must consent to the change in the order.

The parties do not need to sign this consent at the same time. Each party must sign in the presence of his or her witness who shall sign immediately after that party.

NOTE: The witness cannot be one of the parties. If the witness does not know the party, the witness should see identification that proves that the person signing the consent is the same person who is a party to the consent.

....	....
Applicant's signature	*Respondent's signature*
....	....
Date of applicant's signature	*Date of respondent's signature*
....	....
Signature of witness	*Signature of witness*
....	....
Type or print name of witness to applicant's signature	*Type or print name of witness to respondent's signature*
....	....
Address of witness	*Address of witness*
....	....
Telephone number of witness	*Telephone number of witness*

ASSIGNEE'S CONSENT

....	....
Signature of person authorized to sign on behalf of assignee	*Date of signature*

....

Print name and title of person signing the consent

....	....
Witness's signature	*Name of witness (type or print legibly)*

April 1, 2008

FORM 17 — CONFERENCE NOTICE

[Repealed O. Reg. 76/06, s. 15.]

[Editor's Note: Forms 4 to 39 of the Family Law Rules have been repealed by O. Reg. 76/06, effective May 1, 2006. Pursuant to Family Law Rule 1(9), when a form is referred to by number, the reference is to the form with that number that is described in the Table of Forms

at the end of these rules and which is available at www.ontariocourtforms.on.ca. For your convenience, the government form as published on this website is reproduced below.]

Court File Number

____

(Name of court)

____

Form 17: Conference Notice

at ______________________________________

Court office address

Applicant(s)

Full legal name & address for service — street & number, municipality, postal code, telephone & fax numbers and e-mail address (if any).	*Lawyer's name & address — street & number, municipality, postal code, telephone & fax numbers and e-mail address (if any).*

Respondent(s)

Full legal name & address for service — street & number, municipality, postal code, telephone & fax numbers and e-mail address (if any).	*Lawyer's name & address — street & number, municipality, postal code, telephone & fax numbers and e-mail address (if any).*
Name & address of Children's Lawyer's agent (street & number, municipality, postal code, telephone & fax numbers and e-mail address (if any)) and name of person represented.	

TO: (name of party or parties or lawyer(s))

A ❏ *CASE CONFERENCE* ❏ *SETTLEMENT CONFERENCE* ❏ *TRIAL MANAGEMENT CONFERENCE*

WILL BE HELD at *(place of conference)* ....

at .... *a.m./p.m. on (date)* ....

The conference has been arranged at the request of

❏ the applicant ❏ the respondent

❏ the case management judge ❏ *(Other; specify.)* ....

to deal with the following issues:

You must participate at that time and date by

❏ coming to court at the address set out above.

❏ video-conference or telephone at *(location of video terminal or telephone)* ....

as agreed under arrangements already made by *(name of person)* .... for video/telephone conferencing

IF YOU DO NOT PARTICIPATE AS SET OUT ABOVE, THE CASE MAY GO ON WITHOUT YOU OR THE COURT MAY DISMISS THE CASE.

....

Date of signature *Signature of clerk of the court*

NOTE: The party requesting the conference (or, if the conference is not requested by a party, the applicant) must serve and file a case conference brief (Form 17A or 17B), settlement conference brief (Form 17C or 17D) or trial management conference brief (Form 17E) not later than seven days before the date scheduled for the conference. The other party must serve and file a brief not later than four days before the conference date. Each party must also file a confirmation (Form 14C) not later than 2 p.m. two days before the conference.

September 1, 2005

FORM 17A — CASE CONFERENCE BRIEF — GENERAL

[Repealed O. Reg. 76/06, s. 15.]

[Editor's Note: Forms 4 to 39 of the Family Law Rules have been repealed by O. Reg. 76/06, effective May 1, 2006. Pursuant to Family Law Rule 1(9), when a form is referred to by number, the reference is to the form with that number that is described in the Table of Forms at the end of these rules and which is available at www.ontariocourtforms.on.ca. For your convenience, the government form as published on this website is reproduced below.]

ONTARIO

Court File Number ....

.... *(Name of court)*

at .... *Court office address*

Name of party filing this brief	**Date of case conference**

Applicant(s)

Full legal name & address for service — street & number, municipality, postal code, telephone & fax numbers and e-mail address (if any).	*Lawyer's name & address — street & number, municipality, postal code, telephone & fax numbers and e-mail address (if any).*

Respondent(s)

Full legal name & address for service — street & number, municipality, postal code, telephone & fax numbers and e-mail address (if any).	*Lawyer's name & address — street & number, municipality, postal code, telephone & fax numbers and e-mail address (if any).*

Name & address of Children's Lawyer's agent (street & number, municipality, postal code, telephone & fax numbers and e-mail address (if any)) and name of person represented.

PART 1: — FAMILY FACTS

1. APPLICANT: . . . . Age: .... Birthdate: *(d, m, y)* ....

2. RESPONDENT: . . . . Age: .... Birthdate: *(d, m, y)* ....

3. RELATIONSHIP DATES:

❑ Married on *(date)* ....

❑ Separated on *(date)* ....

❑ Started living together on *(date)* ....

❑ Never lived together

❑ Other *(Explain.)* ....

4. The basic information about the child(ren) is as follows:

Child's full legal name	**Age**	**Birthdate (d, m, y)**	**Grade/Year and school**	**Now living with**

PART 2: — ISSUES

5. What are the issues in this case that *HAVE* been settled:

❑ child custody
❑ access
❑ restraining order
❑ spousal support
❑ child support
❑ ownership of property
❑ possession of home
❑ equalization of net family property

❑ other *(Specify.)* ....

6. What are the issues in this case that have *NOT* yet been settled:

❑ child custody
❑ access
❑ restraining order
❑ spousal support
❑ child support
❑ ownership of property
❑ possession of home
❑ equalization of net family property *(Attach Net Family Property Statement, Form 13B)*

❑ other *(Specify.)* ....

7. If child or spousal support is an issue, give the income of the parties:

Applicant: . . . . $ .... per year for the year 20..........

Respondent: . . . . $ .... per year for the year 20..........

8. Have you explored any ways to settle the issues that are still in dispute in this case?

❑ No. . . . . ❑ Yes. *(Give details.)* ....

9. Have any of the issues that have been settled been turned into a court order or a written agreement?

❑ No.
❑ Yes. ❑ an order dated ....
❑ a written agreement that is attached.

10. Have the parents attended a family law or parenting education session?

❑ No. (Should they attend one? ....)

❑ Yes. *(Give details.)* ....

PART 3: — ISSUES FOR THIS CASE CONFERENCE

11. What are the issues for this case conference? What are the important facts for this case conference?

....

....

....

....

....

....

....

12. What is your proposal to resolve these issues? ....

13. Do you want the court to make a temporary or final order at the case conference about any of these issues?

❑ No. . . . . ❑ Yes. *(Give details.)* ....

PART 4: — FINANCIAL INFORMATION

NOTE: If a claim for support has been made in this case, you must serve and file a new financial statement (Form 13 or 13.1), if it is different from the one filed in the continuing record or if the one in the continuing record is more than 30 days old. If there are minor changes but no major changes in your financial statement, you can serve and file an affidavit with details of the changes instead of a new financial statement. If you have not yet filed a financial statement in the continuing record, you must do it now. The page/tab number of the financial statement in the continuing record is ....

14. If a claim is being made for child support and a claim is made for special expenses under the child support guidelines, give details of those expenses or attach additional information.

....

....

....

....

....

....

....

....

....

....

15. If a claim is made for child support and you claim that the Child Support Guidelines table amount should not be ordered, briefly outline the reasons here or attach an additional page.

....

....

....

....

....

....

....

....

....

....

PART 5: — PROCEDURAL ISSUES

16. If custody or access issues are not yet settled:

(a) Is a custody or access assessment needed?

❑ No. ❑ Yes. *(Give names of possible assessors.)*
....

(b) Does a child or a parent under 18 years of age need legal representation from the Office of the Children's Lawyer?

❑ No. . . . . ❑ Yes. *(Give details and reasons.)*
....

17. Does any party need an order for the disclosure of documents, the questioning of witnesses, a property valuation or any other matter in this case?

❑ No. . . . . ❑ Yes. *(Give details.)* ....

18. Are any other procedural orders needed?

❑ No. . . . . ❑ Yes. *(Give details.)* ....

19. Have all the persons who should be parties in this case been added as parties?

❑ Yes. . . . . ❑ No. *(Who needs to be added?)*

....

20. Are there issues that may require expert evidence or a report?

❑ No. . . . . . . ❑ Yes. *(If yes, provide details such as: the type of expert evidence; whether the parties will be retaining a joint expert; who the expert will be; who will be paying the expert; how long it will take to obtain a report, etc.)*

....

....

....

21. Are there any other issues that should be reviewed at the case conference?

❑ No. . . . . ❑ Yes. *(Give details.)* ....

....	....
Date of party's signature	*Signature of party*
....	....
Date of lawyer's signature	*Signature of party's lawyer*

November 15, 2009

FORM 17B — CASE CONFERENCE BRIEF FOR ❑ PROTECTION APPLICATION ❑ STATUS REVIEW

[Repealed O. Reg. 76/06, s. 15.]

[Editor's Note: Forms 4 to 39 of the Family Law Rules have been repealed by O. Reg. 76/06, effective May 1, 2006. Pursuant to Family Law Rule 1(9), when a form is referred to by number, the reference is to the form with that number that is described in the Table of Forms at the end of these rules and which is available at www.ontariocourtforms.on.ca. For your convenience, the government form as published on this website is reproduced below.]

ONTARIO

Court File Number ....

.... *(Name of court)*

at .... *Court office address*

Name of party filing this brief	**Date of case conference**

Applicant(s)

Full legal name & address for service — street & number, municipality, postal code, telephone & fax numbers and e-mail address (if any).	*Lawyer's name & address — street & number, municipality, postal code, telephone & fax numbers and e-mail address (if any).*

Respondent(s)

Full legal name & address for service — street & number, municipality, postal code, telephone & fax numbers and e-mail address (if any).	*Lawyer's name & address&street & number, municipality, postal code, telephone & fax numbers and e-mail address (if any).*

Respondent(s)

Full legal name & address for service — street & number, municipality, postal code, telephone & fax numbers and e-mail address (if any).	*Lawyer's name & address — street & number, municipality, postal code, telephone & fax numbers and e-mail address (if any).*

Respondent(s)

Full legal name & address for service — street & number, municipality, postal code, telephone & fax numbers and e-mail address (if any).	*Lawyer's name & address — street & number, municipality, postal code, telephone & fax numbers and e-mail address (if any).*

Name & address of Children's Lawyer's agent (street & number, municipality, postal code, telephone & fax numbers and e-mail address (if any)) and name of person represented.

PART 1: — BASIC INFORMATION ABOUT THE CHILD(REN)

1. The basic information about the child(ren) is as follows:

Child's full legal name	**Age**	**Birthdate (d, m, y)**	**Full legal name of every parent of child and relationship to child (See subsection 37(1) of the *Child and Family Services Act*.)**	**Date of apprehension of child**

2. Where is the child living at the time of this conference?

....

3. What is the total length of time that any child less than six years old has been in care? *(Attach more detail if necessary.)*

Name of child .... Total length of time ....

4. What is the total length of time any child six years old or more has been in care? *(Attach more details if necessary.)*

Name of child .... Total length of time ....

5. What religious faith, if any, is the child being raised in? *(Give the name of the child and the child's religion.)*

....

....

6. Is any child an Indian or native person?

❑ No. ❑ Yes. *(Give the name, address, band number and telephone number of the band to which the child belongs.)*

....

....

....

....

7. If the child was brought to a place of safety before the hearing, name the person from whose care and the place from which the child was removed.

....

....

8. Has everyone who is entitled to notice in this case been served?

❑ Yes. ❑ No. *(Do you want an order for substituted service on any person or an order that service is not required? Give details.)*

....

....

....

....

....

....

PART 2: — OUTSTANDING ISSUES

(Complete only Part 2A — Protection Application or Part 2B — Status Review, not both)

Part 2A — Protection Application

9. The parties have reached an agreement or the court has made an order on the following issues:

❑ findings of fact set out in Part 1 above

❑ temporary care and custody . . . . ❑ access

❑ finding that child is in need of protection

❑ placing the child(ren) with *(name of person)* .... for .... months under supervision.

❑ society wardship for .... months. . . . . ❑ Crown wardship with access

❑ *(Other. Specify.)* .... ❑ Crown wardship without access

The details of this agreement or order are: ....

10. What are the issues in this case that have *NOT* yet been resolved?

❑ findings of fact set out in Part 1 above

❑ temporary care and custody . . . . ❑ access

❑ finding that child is in need of protection

❑ placing the child(ren) with *(name of person)* .... for .... months under supervision.

❑ society wardship for .... months. . . . . ❑ Crown wardship with access

❑ *(Other. Specify.)* .... ❑ Crown wardship without access

Part 2B — Status Review

11. The parties have reached an agreement or the court has made an order on the following issues:

❑ temporary care and custody . . . . ❑ access

❑ placing the child(ren) with *(name of person)* .... for .... months under supervision.

❑ society wardship for .... months. . . . . ❑ Crown wardship with access

❑ *(Other. Specify.)* .... ❑ Crown wardship without access

The details of this agreement or order are: ....

12. What are the issues in this case that have *NOT* yet been resolved?

❑ temporary care and custody . . . . ❑ access

❑ placing the child(ren) with *(name of person)* .... for .... months under supervision.

❑ society wardship for .... months. . . . . ❑ Crown wardship with access

❑ *(Other. Specify.)* .... ❑ Crown wardship without access

PART 3: — ISSUES FOR THIS CASE CONFERENCE

13. Have you explored any ways to settle the issues that are still in dispute in this case?

❑ No. . . . . ❑ Yes. *(Give details.)* ....

14. What are the issues for this case conference? What are the important facts for this case conference?

....

....

....

....

....

15. What is your proposal to resolve these issues? ....

16. Are any of the issues in this case urgent?

❑ No. . . . . ❑ Yes. *(Identify the issues and give details of why the issues are urgent.)*

....

....

....

....

PART 4: — PROCEDURAL ISSUES

17. Does any party or the Children's Lawyer want an assessment?

❑ No. . . . . . ❑ Yes. *(Give names of possible assessors and the type of assessment recommended.)*

....

....

....

....

....

18. Do the other parties agree with the proposal for an assessment?

❑ No. . . . . ❑ Yes. *(Give names of possible assessors, the type of assessment, who will be assessed, and how long it will take.)*

....

....

....

....

....

19. Have you served a plan of care on the other parties?

❑ No. . . . . ❑ Yes. *(A copy of the plan of care must be filed in the continuing record.)* The plan can be found at tab/page .... of the continuing record.

20. Does a child or a parent under 18 years of age need legal representation from the Office of the Children's Lawyer?

❑ No. . . . . ❑ Yes. *(Give details and reasons.)*
....

21. Do you want an order for the disclosure of documents, the questioning of witnesses or any other matter in this case?

❑ No. . . . . ❑ Yes. *(Give details.)* ....

22. Are there issues that may require expert evidence or a report?

❑ No. . . . . . . ❑ Yes. *(If yes, provide details such as: the type of expert evidence; whether the parties will be retaining a joint expert; who the expert will be; who will be paying the expert; how long it will take to obtain a report, etc.)*

....

....

....

....

....

23. Are there any other issues that should be reviewed at the case conference?

❑ No. . . . . ❑ Yes. *(Give details.)* ....

....	....
Date of party's signature	*Signature of party*
....	....
Date of lawyer's signature	*Signature of party's lawyer*

November 15, 2009

FORM 17C — SETTLEMENT CONFERENCE BRIEF — GENERAL

[Repealed O. Reg. 76/06, s. 15.]

[Editor's Note: Forms 4 to 39 of the Family Law Rules have been repealed by O. Reg. 76/06, effective May 1, 2006. Pursuant to Family Law Rule 1(9), when a form is referred to by number, the reference is to the form with that number that is described in the Table of Forms at the end of these rules and which is available at www.ontariocourtforms.on.ca. For your convenience, the government form as published on this website is reproduced below.]

ONTARIO

Court File Number ....

.... *(Name of court)*

at .... *Court office address*

Name of party filing this brief	**Date of settlement conference**

Applicant(s)

Full legal name & address for service — street & number, municipality, postal code, telephone & fax numbers and e-mail address (if any).	*Lawyer's name & address — street & number, municipality, postal code, telephone & fax numbers and e-mail address (if any).*

Respondent(s)

Full legal name & address for service — street & number, municipality, postal code, telephone & fax numbers and e-mail address (if any).	*Lawyer's name & address — street & number, municipality, postal code, telephone & fax numbers and e-mail address (if any).*

Name & address of Children's Lawyer's agent (street & number, municipality, postal code, telephone & fax numbers and e-mail address (if any)) and name of person represented.

PART 1: — FAMILY FACTS

1. *APPLICANT*: . . . . Age: .... Birthdate: *(d, m, y)* ....

2. *RESPONDENT*: . . . . Age: .... Birthdate: *(d, m, y)* ....

3. *RELATIONSHIP DATES*:

❑ Married on *(date)* ....

❑ Separated on *(date)* ....

❑ Started living together on *(date)* ....

❑ Never lived together

❑ Other *(Explain.)* ....

4. The basic information about the child(ren) is as follows:

Child's full legal name	**Age**	**Birthdate (d, m, y)**	**Grade/Year and school**	**Now living with**

PART 2: — ISSUES

If you want to refer to anything else that is not in the continuing record and that does not need to be in the continuing record, you must attach it to this brief. In particular, attach any valuations or experts' reports that are not in the record.

If you want to refer to a report or document that has already been filed in the continuing record, just give the page number(s) or tab number of that document in the continuing record.

If you are updating a document that is already in the continuing record, you must file the updated document in the continuing record and then refer to it by the page number(s) or tab numbers of that update in the continuing record.

5. What are the issues in this case that *HAVE* been settled:

❑ child custody
❑ access
❑ restraining order
❑ spousal support
❑ child support
❑ ownership of property
❑ possession of home
❑ equalization of net family property

❑ other *(Specify.)* ....

6. What are the issues in this case that have *NOT* yet been settled:

❑ child custody
❑ access
❑ restraining order
❑ spousal support
❑ child support
❑ ownership of property
❑ possession of home
❑ equalization of net family property *(Attach Net Family Property Statement, Form 13B)*

❑ other *(Specify.)* ....

7. If child or spousal support is an issue, give the income of the parties:

Applicant: . . . . $ .... per year for the year 20..........

Respondent: . . . . $ .... per year for the year 20..........

8. What are the issues for this settlement conference? What are the important facts for this settlement conference?

....

....

....

....

....

9. Do you want the court to make a temporary or final order about any of these issues at the settlement conference?

❑ No . . . . ❑ Yes. *(Give details.)* ....

10. Have any of these issues that have been settled been turned into a court order or a written agreement?

❑ No.
❑ Yes ❑ an order dated ....
❑ a written agreement that is attached.

11. Are any of the issues in this case urgent?

❑ No. . . . . ❑ Yes. *(Identify the issues and give details of why the issues are urgent.)*

....

....

....

....

....

....

PART 3: — PROCEDURAL MATTERS

12. If there is a custody or access assessment in this case, is it finished?

❑ Yes. *(If it is not already filed in the continuing record, file it now. Give the tab/page number(s) of the assessment: ....)*

❑ No. *(Explain why the assessment is not ready.)*

....

....

....

....

13. Are there issues that may require expert evidence or a report?

❑ No. . . . . . . ❑ Yes. *(If yes, provide details such as: the type of expert evidence; whether the parties will be retaining a joint expert; who the expert will be; who will be paying the expert; how long it will take to obtain a report, etc.)*

....

....

....

....

....

....

14. Have all of the reports you intend to rely on been provided to all of the parties and the Children's Lawyer (if involved)?

❏ No. . . . . ❏ Yes.

If not, when will they be provided? ....

15. If the Children's Lawyer is involved in this case, has the Children's Lawyer told the parties what its position is on the issues involving the children?

❏ Yes. *(What is the Children's Lawyer's position? Explain below.)*

❏ No. *(Explain below.)*

....

....

....

....

....

....

....

16. Have the parties finished the disclosing of documents and the questioning of witnesses?

❏ Yes. . . . . ❏ No. *(State what has not been done.)*
....

17. Are there any further procedural orders needed in this case?

❏ No. . . . . ❏ Yes. *(Explain.)* ....

18. I estimate that the trial time needed for my part of this trial is .... days; the other side's part of this trial is .... days.

PART 4: — OFFER TO SETTLE

19. The following is my offer to settle the outstanding issues in this case:

❏ offer to settle all issues . . . . ❏ offer to settle some of the issues

NOTE: If you have already made an offer and it is still open for acceptance, attach a copy to this brief. If you have not made an offer to settle, you must make one here. If you do not have enough information about all the issues, make a partial offer on those issues for which you do have enough information.
The other side can accept your offer. And if the other side does accept it, the accepted offer becomes a binding contract and can be turned into a court order that can be enforced against you. The other side can make a counter-offer.

In your offer for child support, give detailed calculations for any claim for special expenses or for undue hardship. If your offer deals with spousal support, it will be helpful to your case if you attach detailed calculations showing the effect of income tax on any proposed support order.

....

....

....

....

....

....

....

....

....

....

....

....

....

....

....

....

....

....

....

....

....

Put a line through any space left on this page. If additional space is needed, extra pages may be attached.

....	....
Date of party's signature	*Signature of party*
....	....
Date of lawyer's signature	*Signature of party's lawyer*

November 15, 2009

FORM 17D — SETTLEMENT CONFERENCE BRIEF FOR ❑ PROTECTION APPLICATION ❑ STATUS REVIEW

[Repealed O. Reg. 76/06, s. 15.]

[Editor's Note: Forms 4 to 39 of the Family Law Rules have been repealed by O. Reg. 76/06, effective May 1, 2006. Pursuant to Family Law Rule 1(9), when a form is referred to by number, the reference is to the form with that number that is described in the Table of Forms at the end of these rules and which is available at www.ontariocourtforms.on.ca. For your convenience, the government form as published on this website is reproduced below.]

ONTARIO

Court File Number ....

.... *(Name of court)*

at .... *Court office address*

Name of Party Filing this Brief	**Date of settlement conference**

Applicant(s)

Full legal name & address for service — street & number, municipality, postal code, telephone & fax numbers and e-mail address (if any).	*Lawyer's name & address — street & number, municipality, postal code, telephone & fax numbers and e-mail address (if any).*

Respondent(s)

Full legal name & address for service — street & number, municipality, postal code, telephone & fax numbers and e-mail address (if any).	*Lawyer's name & address — street & number, municipality, postal code, telephone & fax numbers and e-mail address (if any).*

Respondent(s)

Full legal name & address for service — street & number, municipality, postal code, telephone & fax numbers and e-mail address (if any).	*Lawyer's name & address — street & number, municipality, postal code, telephone & fax numbers and e-mail address (if any).*

Respondent(s)

Full legal name & address for service — street & number, municipality, postal code, telephone & fax numbers and e-mail address (if any).	*Lawyer's name & address — street & number, municipality, postal code, telephone & fax numbers and e-mail address (if any).*

Respondent(s)

Children's Lawyer

Name & address of Children's Lawyer's agent (street & number, municipality, postal code, telephone & fax numbers and e-mail address (if any)) and name of person represented.

PART 1: — BASIC INFORMATION ABOUT THE CHILD(REN)

1. The basic information about the child(ren) is as follows:

Child's full legal name	**Age**	**Birthdate (d, m, y)**	**Full legal name of every parent of child and relationship to child (See subsection 37(1) of the Child and Family Services Act.)**	**Date of apprehension of child**

2. Where is the child living at the time of this conference?

....

3. What is the total length of time that any child less than six years old has been in care? *(Attach more detail if necessary).*

Name of child .... Total length of time ....

4. What is the total length of time any child six years old or more has been in care? *(Attach more details if necessary.)*

Name of child .... Total length of time ....

5. Is any child an Indian or native person?

❑ No. . . . ❑ Yes. *(Give the name, address, band number and telephone number of the band to which the child belongs.)*

....

....

....

6. What religious faith, if any, is the child being raised in? *(Give the name of the child and the child's religion.)*

....

7. If the child was brought to a place of safety before the hearing, name the person from whose care and the place from which the child was removed.

....

8. Has everyone who is entitled to notice in this case been served?

❑ Yes. . . . ❑ No. *(Do you want an order for substituted service on any person or an order that service is not required? Give details.)*

....

....

....

....

....

....

....

PART 2: — OUTSTANDING ISSUES

NOTE: If you want to refer to a report or document that has already been filed in the continuing record, just give the page number(s) or tab number of that document in the continuing record. If you are updating a document that is already in the continuing record, you must file the updated document in the continuing record and then refer to it by the page number(s) or tab numbers of that update in the continuing record. If you want to refer to anything else that is not in the continuing record and that does not need to be in the continuing record, you must attach it to this brief.

(Complete only Part 2A — Protection Application or Part 2B — Status Review, not both)

Part 2A — Protection Application

9. The parties have reached an agreement or the court has made an order on the following issues:

- ❑ findings of fact set out in Part 1 above
- ❑ temporary care and custody
- ❑ finding that child is in need of protection
- ❑ placing the child(ren) with *(name of person)* .... for .... months under supervision.
- ❑ society wardship for .... months.
- ❑ *(Other. Specify.)* ....
- ❑ payment order
- ❑ access
- ❑ Crown wardship with access
- ❑ Crown wardship without access

The details of this agreement or order are: ....

10. What are the issues in this case that have NOT yet been resolved and what needs to happen to resolve them?

....

....

11. Are any of the issues in this case urgent?

❑ No. ❑ Yes. *(Identify the issues and give details of why the issues are urgent.)*

....

....

Part 2B — Status Review

12. The parties have reached an agreement or the court has made an order on the following issues:

❑ temporary care and custody ❑ payment order

❑ placing the child(ren) with *(name of person)* .... for .... months under supervision.

❑ society wardship for .... months. ❑ access

❑ *(Other. Specify.)* .... ❑ Crown wardship with access

.... ❑ Crown wardship without access

The details of this agreement or order are: ....

13. What are the issues in this case that have NOT yet been resolved and what needs to happen to resolve them?

....

....

14. Are any of the issues in this case urgent?

❑ No. . . . . ❑ Yes. *(Identify the issues and give details of why the issues are urgent.)*

....

....

....

PART 3: — PROCEDURAL ISSUES

15. If there is an assessment in this case, is it finished?

❑ Yes. *(If it is not already filed in the continuing record, file it now. Give the tab/page number(s) of the assessment: ....)*

❑ No. *(Explain why the assessment is not ready.)* ....

16. Are there any other assessments necessary or not yet completed?

❑ No. . . . . . ❑ Yes. *(Give details of the type of assessment, who will be assessed and any issues relating to the timing or completion of the assessment.)*

....

....

....

17. If the Children's Lawyer is involved in this case, has the Children's Lawyer told the parties what its position is on the issues involving the child(ren)?

❑ Yes. *(What is the Children's Lawyer's position? Explain below.)* . . . . . ❑ No. *(Explain below.)*

....

....

....

18. Have you served and filed a plan of care?

❑ No. . . . . ❑ Yes. *(A copy of the plan of care must be filed in the continuing record.)* The plan can be found at tab/page .... of the continuing record.

19. Have the parties finished the disclosing of documents and the questioning of witnesses?

❑ Yes. . . . . ❑ No. *(State what has not been done.)* ....

20. Are there issues that require expert evidence or a report?

❑ No. . . . . . . ❑ Yes. *(If yes, provide details such as: the type of expert evidence; whether the parties will be retaining a joint expert; who the expert will be; who will be paying the expert; how long it will take to obtain a report, etc.)*

....

....

....

21. Have all of the reports you intend to rely on been provided to all of the parties and the Children's Lawyer (if involved)?

❑ No. . . . . ❑ Yes.

If no, when will they be provided? ....

22. Are there any further procedural orders needed in this case?

❑ No. . . . . ❑ Yes. *(Explain.)* ....

23. Has an order been made for affidavit evidence at trial? *(Give details.)* ....

PART 4: — OFFER TO SETTLE

24. The following is my offer to settle the outstanding issues in this case:

If you have already made an offer and it is still open for acceptance, attach a copy of this brief. The other side can accept your offer. And if the other side does accept it, the accepted offer becomes a binding contract and can be turned into a court order that can be enforced against you. The other side can make a counter-offer.

....

....

....

....

....

....

....

....

....

....

....

....

....

....

....

....

....

....

....

....

....

....

....

....

....

....

....

....

....

Put a line through any space left on this page. If additional space is needed, extra pages may be attached.

....	....
Date of party's signature	*Signature of party*
....	....
Date of lawyer's signature	*Signature of party's lawyer*

November 15, 2009

FORM 17E — TRIAL MANAGEMENT CONFERENCE BRIEF

[Repealed O. Reg. 76/06, s. 15.]

[Editor's Note: Forms 4 to 39 of the Family Law Rules have been repealed by O. Reg. 76/06, effective May 1, 2006. Pursuant to Family Law Rule 1(9), when a form is referred to by number, the reference is to the form with that number that is described in the Table of Forms at the end of these rules and which is available at www.ontariocourtforms.on.ca. For your convenience, the government form as published on this website is reproduced below.]

ONTARIO

Court File Number ....

.... *(Name of court)*

at .... *Court office address*

Name of Party Filing this Brief	**Date of trial management conference**

Applicant(s)

Full legal name & address for service — street & number, municipality, postal code, telephone & fax numbers and e-mail address (if any).	*Lawyer's name & address — street & number, municipality, postal code, telephone & fax numbers and e-mail address (if any).*

Respondent(s)

Full legal name & address for service — street & number, municipality, postal code, telephone & fax numbers and e-mail address (if any).	*Lawyer's name & address — street & number, municipality, postal code, telephone & fax numbers and e-mail address (if any).*

Name & address of Children's Lawyer's agent (street & number, municipality, postal code, telephone & fax numbers and e-mail address (if any)) and name of person represented.

PART 1: — THE ISSUES

1. What are the issues in this case that *HAVE* been settled or about which an order has been made:

Child protection cases

❏ access ❏ finding in need of protection

❏ placing the child(ren) with *(name of person)* .... for .... months under supervision.

❑ society wardship for .... months. ❑ Crown wardship.
❑ other *(Specify.)* ....

All other cases

❑ child custody ❑ spousal support ❑ possession of home
❑ access ❑ child support ❑ equalization of net family property
❑ restraining order ❑ ownership of property
❑ other *(Specify.)* ....

Attach a copy of any agreement that the judge should read to prepare for the trial management conference.

2. What are the issues in this case that have *NOT* yet been settled:

Child protection cases

❑ access ❑ finding in need of protection
❑ placing the child(ren) with *(name of person)* .... for .... months under supervision.
❑ society wardship for .... months. ❑ Crown wardship.
❑ other *(Specify.)* ....

All other cases

❑ child custody ❑ spousal support ❑ possession of home
❑ access ❑ child support ❑ equalization of net family property *(Attach net family property statement, Form 13B.)*
❑ restraining order ❑ ownership of property
❑ other *(Specify.)* ....

3. Where is the child living at the time of this conference? ....

4. Are any of the issues in this case urgent?

❑ No. . . . . ❑ Yes. *(Identify the issues and give details of why the issues are urgent.)*

....

....

....

PART 2: — ISSUES FOR TRIAL

5. Attach an outline of your opening statement for the trial, including:

(a) what you consider to be the undisputed facts;

(b) the theory of your case on the disputed issues;

(c) a brief summary of the evidence you plan to present at trial; and

(d) the orders you are asking the trial judge to make.

6. These are the witnesses whom I plan to have testify for me, the topics about which they will testify and my current estimate of the length of time for the testimony of each witness, including cross-examination:

Name of witness	**Topic about which witness will testify**	**Current time estimate for witness**

7. I estimate that the trial time needed for my part of this trial is .... days; the other side's part of this trial is .... days.

PART 3: — PROCEDURAL MATTERS

8. Have the parties signed a statement of agreed facts?

❑ Yes. *(Attach a copy.)* . . . . ❑ No. *(Explain why not.)* ....

9. Have the parties finished the disclosing of documents and the questioning of witnesses?

❑ Yes. . . . . ❑ No. *(Indicate what has not been done.)* ....

10. Are there any expert reports that you intend to rely on at trial?

❑ No. . . . ❑ Yes. *(Give details about the reports such as who prepared them and the issues addressed.)*

....

....

....

....

11. Have all of the reports you intend to rely on been provided to all of the parties and the Children's Lawyer (if involved)?

❑ No. . . . . ❑ Yes.

If no, when will they be provided? ....

12. Attach a list of the relevant orders in this case.

13. Are there any orders or directions for trial that have not been carried out?

❑ No. . . . . ❑ Yes. *(Explain.)* ....

14. Have the parties produced a joint document brief?

❑ Yes. *(Attach a copy.)* . . . . ❑ No. *(Explain why not.)* ....

15. Has an order been made for affidavit evidence at trial?

❑ Yes. . . . . ❑ No. *(Explain.)* ....

13. Are there any preliminary or procedural matters that need to be dealt with before or at the start of the trial?

❑ No. . . . . ❑ Yes. *(Explain.)*

....

....

....

....

....

....

....

....

....

....

....

....

....

....

14. Have you served a request to admit?

❑ Yes. . . . . ❑ No. *(Explain.)*

....

....

....

....

....

....

....

....

....

....

....

....

....

....

.... *Date of party's signature*	.... *Signature of party*
.... *Date of lawyer's signature*	.... *Signature of party's lawyer*

November 15, 2009

FORM 20 — REQUEST FOR INFORMATION

[Repealed O. Reg. 76/06, s. 15.]

[Editor's Note: Forms 4 to 39 of the Family Law Rules have been repealed by O. Reg. 76/06, effective May 1, 2006. Pursuant to Family Law Rule 1(9), when a form is referred to by number, the reference is to the form with that number that is described in the Table of Forms at the end of these rules and which is available at www.ontariocourtforms.on.ca. For your convenience, the government form as published on this website is reproduced below.]

Court File Number ....

.... *(Name of court)*

at .... *Court office address*

Applicant(s)

Full legal name & address for service — street & number, municipality, postal code, telephone & fax and e-mail address (if any).	*Lawyer's name & address — street & number, municipality, postal code, telephone & fax numbers and e-mail address (if any).*

Respondent(s)

Full legal name & address for service — street & number, municipality, postal code, telephone & fax numbers and e-mail address (if any).	*Lawyer's name & address — street & number, municipality, postal code, telephone & fax numbers and e-mail address (if any).*

TO: (name of party) ....

This is a request for information in writing under subrule 20(2) of the *Family Law Rules.*

I request that the information be provided within .... days by

❑ an affidavit from *(name of person(s))*....................................
❑ a letter from *(name of person(s))*....................................
(Other. Specify.)

....

The information that I am requesting is as follows: (Be as specific as possible. If you want more than one piece of information, number the requested pieces of information.)

....

....

IF YOU DO NOT PROVIDE THE INFORMATION AS REQUESTED,

(1) A SUMMONS MAY BE SERVED ON YOU, REQUIRING YOU TO BE QUESTIONED ABOUT IT; or

(2) A MOTION MAY BE MADE TO THE COURT FOR AN ORDER REQUIRING YOU TO PROVIDE THE INFORMATION AND YOU MAY BE ORDERED TO PAY THE COSTS OF THE MOTION.

.... *Signature*

.... *Date of signature*

September 1, 2005

FORM 20A — AUTHORIZATION TO COMMISSIONER

[Repealed O. Reg. 76/06, s. 15.]

[Editor's Note: Forms 4 to 39 of the Family Law Rules have been repealed by O. Reg. 76/06, effective May 1, 2006. Pursuant to Family Law Rule 1(9), when a form is referred to by number, the reference is to the form with that number that is described in the Table of Forms at the end of these rules and which is available at www.ontariocourtforms.on.ca. For your convenience, the government form as published on this website is reproduced below.]

Court File Number ....

[SEAL]

.... *(Name of court)*

at .... *Court office address*

Applicant(s)

Full legal name & address for service — street and number, municipality, postal code, telephone & fax numbers and e-mail address (if any).	*Lawyer's name & address — street and number, municipality, postal code, telephone & fax numbers and e-mail address (if any).*

Respondent(s)

Full legal name & address for service — street and number, municipality, postal code, telephone & fax numbers and e-mail address (if any).	*Lawyer's name & address — street and number, municipality, postal code, telephone & fax numbers and e-mail address (if any).*

TO (full legal name and address of commissioner) ....

THE COURT HAS NAMED YOU A COMMISSIONER to take evidence in this case. A copy of the order naming you is attached.

THE COURT GIVES YOU FULL POWER to take the necessary steps to take the evidence mentioned in the attached order.

If the parties consent, you also have the power to take the evidence of any other witnesses who may be found in *(name of province, territory, state or country)* ....

In carrying out your duties under this commission, you must follow,

(a) the terms of the attached order; and

(b) the instructions set out below.

As soon as

❑ an audio recording

❑ a video recording

❑ a transcript

of the evidence is finished, you must deliver it to the clerk of the court along with this commission.

.... *Signature*

.... *Date of signature*

NOTE: Attach the court's order naming the commissioner

INSTRUCTIONS TO COMMISSIONER

1. You are to question the witness(es) according to subrules 20(14), (15) and 23(19) of the *Family Law Rules* to the extent that it is possible to do so. Subrules 20(14), (15) and 23(19) state as follows:

Questioning Person Outside Ontario

20. (14) If a person to be questioned lives outside Ontario and will not come to Ontario for questioning, the court may decide,

(a) the date, the time and place for the questioning;

(b) how much notice the person should be given;

(c) the person before whom the questioning will be held;

(d) the amount of the witness fee to be paid to the person to be questioned;

(e) the method for recording the questioning;

(f) where necessary, that the clerk shall issue,

(i) an authorization to a commissioner (Form 20A) who is to supervise the questioning outside Ontario, and

(ii) a letter of request (Form 20B) to the appropriate court or authorities outside Ontario, asking for their assistance in getting the person to be questioned to come before the commissioner; and

(g) any other related matter.

Commissioner's Duties

(15) A commissioner authorized under subrule (14) shall,

(a) supervise the questioning according to the terms of the court's authorization, these rules and Ontario's law of evidence, unless the law of the place where the questioning is to be held requires some other manner of questioning;

(b) make and keep a copy of the record of the questioning and, where possible, of the exhibits, if any;

(c) deliver the original record, any exhibits and the authorization to the clerk who issued it; and

(d) notify the party who asked for the questioning that the record has been delivered to the clerk.

Taking Evidence Before Trial Outside Ontario

23. (19) If a witness whose evidence is necessary at trial lives outside Ontario, subrules 20(14) and (15) (questioning person outside Ontario, commissioner's duties) apply with necessary changes.

2. The law of Ontario applies to the taking of evidence, unless the law of the province, territory, state or country where you supervise the questioning requires you to follow some other manner of questioning.

3. Before you begin your duties under this commission, you yourself must take the following oath or affirmation:

I, *(commissioner's name)* ....

❑ swear
❑ affirm

that I will,

(a) according to the best of my skill and knowledge, truly and faithfully and without bias to any of the parties to this case, take the evidence of every witness questioned under this commission, and

(b) cause the evidence to be

❑ recorded
❑ recorded and transcribed

and sent to the court.

(*In an oath, add the words:* "So help me God.")

Sworn/Affirmed before me at .... *municipality* in .... *province, state or country* on .... *date*	
Commissioner for taking affidavits (Type or print name below if signature is illegible.)	*Signature* *(This form is to be signed in front of a lawyer, justice of the peace, notary public or commissioner for taking affidavits.)*

You may take this oath or affirmation before any person listed in section 45 of Ontario's *Evidence Act* who is authorized to take affidavits or to administer oaths or affirmations outside Ontario. Section 45 of the *Evidence Act* states:

Oaths, etc., administered outside Ontario

45. (1) An oath, affidavit, affirmation or statutory declaration administered, sworn, affirmed or made outside Ontario before,

(a) a judge;

(b) a magistrate;

(c) an officer of a court of justice;

(d) a commissioner for taking affidavits or other competent authority of the like nature;

(e) a notary public;

(f) the head of a city, town, village, township or other municipality;

(g) an officer of any of Her Majesty's diplomatic or consular services, including an ambassador, envoy, minister, chargé d'affaires, counsellor, secretary, attaché, consul-general, consul, vice-consul, pro-consul, consular agent, acting consul-general, acting consul, acting vice-consul and acting consular agent;

(h) an officer of the Canadian diplomatic, consular or representative services, including, in addition to the diplomatic and consular officers mentioned in clause (g), a high commissioner, permanent delegate, acting high commissioner, acting permanent delegate, counsellor and secretary; or

(i) a Canadian Government trade commissioner or assistant trade commissioner,

exercising his or her functions or having jurisdiction or authority as such in the place in which it is administered, sworn, affirmed or made, is as valid and effectual to all intents and purposes as if it had been duly administered, sworn, affirmed or made in Ontario before a commissioner for taking affidavits in Ontario.

Idem

(2) An oath, affidavit, affirmation or statutory declaration administered, sworn, affirmed or made outside Ontario before a notary public for Ontario or before a commissioner for taking affidavits in Ontario is as valid and effectual to all intents and purposes as if it had been duly administered, sworn, affirmed or made in Ontario before a commissioner for taking affidavits in Ontario.

Admissibility

(3) A document that purports to be signed by a person mentioned in subsection (1) or (2) in testimony of an oath, affidavit, affirmation or statutory declaration having been administered, sworn, affirmed or made before him or her, and on which the person's office is shown below his or her signature, and

(a) in the case of a notary public, that purports to have impressed thereon or attached thereto his or her official seal;

(b) in the case of a person mentioned in clause (1)(f), that purports to have impressed thereon or attached thereto the seal of the municipality;

(c) in the case of a person mentioned in clause (1)(g), (h) or (l), that purports to have impressed thereon or attached thereto his or her seal or the seal or stamp of his or her office or of the office to which he or she is attached,

is admissible in evidence without proof of his or her signature or of his or her office or official character or of the seal or stamp and without proof that he or she was exercising his or her functions or had jurisdiction or authority in the place in which the oath, affidavit, affirmation or statutory declaration was administered, sworn, affirmed or made.

4. The party who wants the witness to be questioned must:

(a) give at least .... days notice of the date for the questioning; and,

(b) where the attached order says so, pay the witness appearance money.

5. You must arrange:

(a) to have the evidence recorded in a manner set out in the attached order; and

(b) where the order says so, to have it transcribed.

You must administer the following oath or affirmation to the person who records the evidence in shorthand and, where necessary, to the person who transcribes and written, audio or video recording of the evidence:

You

❏ swear
❏ affirm

that you will truly and accurately
❏ record
❏ transcribe
❏ record and transcribe

all questions put to all witnesses and their answers in keeping with the directions of the commissioner. (*In an oath, add the words:* "So help you God.")

6. To each witness whose evidence you take, you must administer the following oath or affirmation:

You

❏ swear

❏ affirm

that the evidence that you are about to give about the matters in dispute between the parties in this case shall be the truth, the whole truth and nothing but the truth. (*In an oath, add the words:* "So help you God.")

7. Where any witness does not understand the language in which he or she is being questioned or is deaf or mute, his or her evidence must be given through an interpreter. You must first administer the following oath or affirmation to the interpreter:

You

❏ swear
❏ affirm

that you understand the .... language and the language in which the examination is to be conducted and that you will truly interpret the
❏ oath
❏ affirmation

to all witnesses, all questions put to the witness and the answers of the witness, to the best of your skill and understanding. (*In an oath, add the words:* "So help you God.")

8. You must:

(a) fill out the certificate on the next page;

(b) make a copy of

(i) the audio or video record of the evidence,

(ii) any transcript of the evidence, and

(iii) where possible, any exhibits;

(c) keep the copies in your care until the court finishes this case;

(d) mail or deliver the originals, together with this commission and your certificate, to the clerk of the court; and

(e) immediately notify the party who asked for this questioning that the material has been sent to the clerk of the court.

COMMISSIONER'S CERTIFICATE

My name is *(full legal name)* .... and I certify that:

❑ I administered the proper to *(name)* ....

❑ oath
❑ affirmation

who was the person who
❑ recorded the evidence by shorthand.
❑ transcribed the evidence.

❑ I administered the proper to *(name of witness(es))*

❑ oath
❑ affirmation

whose evidence was taken and recorded.

❑ I administered the proper to *(name of interpreter)*

❑ oath
❑ affirmation

who was the interpreter through whom the evidence was given.

❑ The evidence of the witness(es) was properly taken and accurately

❑ recorded
❑ recorded and transcribed.

.... *Commissioner's signature*

.... *Date of signature*

September 1, 2005

FORM 20B — LETTER OF REQUEST

[Repealed O. Reg. 76/06, s. 15.]

[Editor's Note: Forms 4 to 39 of the Family Law Rules have been repealed by O. Reg. 76/06, effective May 1, 2006. Pursuant to Family Law Rule 1(9), when a form is referred to by

number, the reference is to the form with that number that is described in the Table of Forms at the end of these rules and which is available at www.ontariocourtforms.on.ca. For your convenience, the government form as published on this website is reproduced below.]

Court File Number ....

[SEAL]

.... *(Name of court)*

at .... *Court office address*

Applicant(s)

Full legal name & address for service — street and number, municipality, postal code, telephone & fax numbers and e-mail address (if any).	*Lawyer's name & address — street and number, municipality, postal code, telephone & fax numbers and e-mail address (if any).*

Respondent(s)

Full legal name & address for service — street and number, municipality, postal code, telephone & fax numbers and e-mail address (if any).	*Lawyer's name & address — street and number, municipality, postal code, telephone & fax numbers and e-mail address (if any).*

TO THE JUDICIAL AUTHORITIES OF (name of province, state or country): ....

A CASE HAS BEEN STARTED IN THIS COURT INVOLVING THE PERSONS NAMED ABOVE. EVIDENCE BEFORE THIS COURT SHOWS THAT A WITNESS LIVING IN YOUR JURISDICTION SHOULD BE QUESTIONED THERE. THIS COURT HAS ISSUED A COMMISSION TO (name and address of commissioner): ....

TO QUESTION (name and address of witness): ....

YOU ARE REQUESTED to have (name of witness) ....

(a) appear before the commissioner by the method normally used in your jurisdiction;

(b) answer questions under oath or affirmation; and

(c) bring to the examination the documents or things listed on the back of this request.

YOU ARE ALSO REQUESTED TO allow the commissioner to have the witness questioned according to Ontario's law of evidence, to Ontario's rules of court and to the commission issued by this court.

AND WHEN YOU REQUEST IT, the courts in Ontario are ready and willing to do the same for you in a similar case.

THIS LETTER OF REQUEST is signed and sealed by a court order made on *(date of order)* ....

.... *Clerk of the court*

.... *Date of signature*

(Give the date of every document that the witness should bring and give enough of a description of each document or thing that the witness must bring to identify it.)

....

....

Put a line through any blank space left on this page. If you need more space, add a sheet and number the page.

September 1, 2005

FORM 22 — REQUEST TO ADMIT

[Repealed O. Reg. 76/06, s. 15.]

[Editor's Note: Forms 4 to 39 of the Family Law Rules have been repealed by O. Reg. 76/06, effective May 1, 2006. Pursuant to Family Law Rule 1(9), when a form is referred to by number, the reference is to the form with that number that is described in the Table of Forms at the end of these rules and which is available at www.ontariocourtforms.on.ca. For your convenience, the government form as published on this website is reproduced below.]

Court File Number ....

.... *(Name of court)*

at .... *Court office address*

Applicant(s)

Full legal name & address for service — street & number, municipality, postal code, telephone & fax and e-mail address (if any).	*Lawyer's name & address — street & number, municipality, postal code, telephone & fax numbers and e-mail address (if any). .*

Respondent(s)

Full legal name & address for service — street & number, municipality, postal code, telephone & fax numbers and e-mail address (if any).	*Lawyer's name & address — street & number, municipality, postal code, telephone & fax numbers and e-mail address (if any).*

TO: *(name of party)*

YOU MUST RESPOND TO THIS REQUEST WITHIN 20 DAYS AFTER BEING SERVED WITH IT.

You make your response by serving a Response to Request to Admit in Form 22A, a blank copy of which should be attached to this request. If the blank form is missing, contact your own lawyer or the court office as soon as possible.

IF YOU DO NOT RESPOND WITHIN THE TIME GIVEN, THIS CASE WILL GO TO COURT ON THE BASIS THAT YOU ARE ADMITTING, for the purposes of this case only, THAT THE FACTS SET OUT BELOW ARE TRUE AND THAT THE DOCUMENTS DESCRIBED BELOW ARE GENUINE.

You are requested to admit, only for the purposes of this case, that the following facts are true: *(If you need more space to list additional facts, attach an extra sheet.)*

1. ....

2. ....

3. ....

4. ....

5. ....

You are requested to admit, only for the purposes of this case, that the following documents are genuine. *(Being "genuine" also means:*

- *that a document that claims to be an original was written, signed or sealed as it appears to have been;*
- *that a document claiming to be a copy is a true copy of the original; and*
- *where the document claims to be a copy of a letter, fax, electronic-mail message or other document ordinarily sent from one person to another, that it was sent as it appears to have been sent and received by the person to whom it was addressed.*

Describe each document and identify it by date, type of document, author, name of person to whom it was sent, etc. Indicate whether the document is an original or a copy. If you need more space to list additional documents, attach a sheet.)

1. ....

2. ....

3. ....

4. ....

5. ....

A copy of each document named above is attached to this Request, except for: *(Give the number of any document that you are NOT attaching and state your reason for not doing so. Generally, you must attach copies of all the documents mentioned unless the other party already has a copy or it is impractical to attach a copy.)*

.... *Signature*

.... *Date of signature*

September 1, 2005

FORM 22A — RESPONSE TO REQUEST TO ADMIT

[Repealed O. Reg. 76/06, s. 15.]

[Editor's Note: Forms 4 to 39 of the Family Law Rules have been repealed by O. Reg. 76/06, effective May 1, 2006. Pursuant to Family Law Rule 1(9), when a form is referred to by number, the reference is to the form with that number that is described in the Table of Forms at the end of these rules and which is available at www.ontariocourtforms.on.ca. For your convenience, the government form as published on this website is reproduced below.]

Court File Number ....

.... *(Name of court)*

at .... *Court office address*

Applicant(s)

Full legal name & address for service — street & number, municipality, postal code, telephone & fax and e-mail address (if any).	*Lawyer's name & address — street & number, municipality, postal code, telephone & fax numbers and e-mail address (if any).*

Respondent(s)

Full legal name & address for service — street & number, municipality, postal code, telephone & fax numbers and e-mail address (if any).	*Lawyer's name & address — street & number, municipality, postal code, telephone & fax numbers and e-mail address (if any).*

TO: (name of party)

This is my response to your Request to Admit of (date) .... *that was served on me on (date)* ....

(Refer to the facts and documents according to the numbering set out in the Request to Admit.)

1. I admit that the following facts are true: *(fact numbers)* ....

2. I admit that the following documents are genuine: *(document numbers)* ....

3. I deny that the following facts are true: *(fact numbers)* ....

4. I deny that the following documents are genuine: *(document numbers)* ....

5. I refuse to admit the following facts for the following reasons: *(If you need more space, attach a sheet.)*

Fact number	**My reasons**

6. I refuse to admit that the following documents are genuine for the following reasons: *(If you need more space, attach a sheet.)*

Document number	**My reasons**

.... *Signature*

.... *Date of signature*

September 1, 2005

FORM 23 — SUMMONS TO WITNESS

[Repealed O. Reg. 76/06, s. 15.]

[Editor's Note: Forms 4 to 39 of the Family Law Rules have been repealed by O. Reg. 76/06, effective May 1, 2006. Pursuant to Family Law Rule 1(9), when a form is referred to by number, the reference is to the form with that number that is described in the Table of Forms at the end of these rules and which is available at www.ontariocourtforms.on.ca. For your convenience, the government form as published on this website is reproduced below.]

Court File Number ....

.... *(Name of court)*

at .... *Court office address*

Applicant(s)

Full legal name & address for service — street & number, municipality, postal code, telephone & fax and e-mail address (if any).	*Lawyer's name & address — street & number, municipality, postal code, telephone & fax numbers and e-mail address (if any).*

Respondent(s)

Full legal name & address for service — street & number, municipality, postal code, telephone & fax numbers and e-mail address (if any).	*Lawyer's name & address — street & number, municipality, postal code, telephone & fax numbers and e-mail address (if any).*

TO: (full legal name of witness) .... *of (address: street & number, municipality, postal code)* ....

YOU MUST:

(1) come to (address: street & number, municipality) .... *on (date)* ...., *at* .... *a.m./p.m.;*

(2) give evidence in the case or examination before (court or other person) ....

(3) bring with you the documents and things listed on the back of this summons; and

(4) remain there until this case or examination is finished or until the person conducting it says otherwise.

With this summons, you should get a fee that is calculated for .... day(s) of attendance as follows:

Appearance allowance of $ .... daily	$
Travel allowance of $ .... each way	$
Overnight hotel and meal allowance	$
TOTAL	$

If the case or examination takes up more of your time, you will be entitled to an additional fee.

Date of issue	*IF YOU DO NOT COME AND REMAIN AS REQUIRED BY THIS SUMMONS, A WARRANT MAY BE ISSUED FOR YOUR ARREST.*

(Give the date of every document that the witness must bring and give enough of a description to identify each document or thing that the witness must bring.)

Draw a line through any blank space left on this page. If you need more space, you can add pages and number them.

Name, address, telephone & fax numbers and e-mail address of person or lawyer who prepared this summons.	

September 1, 2005

FORM 23A — SUMMONS TO WITNESS OUTSIDE ONTARIO

[Repealed O. Reg. 76/06, s. 15.]

[Editor's Note: Forms 4 to 39 of the Family Law Rules have been repealed by O. Reg. 76/06, effective May 1, 2006. Pursuant to Family Law Rule 1(9), when a form is referred to by number, the reference is to the form with that number that is described in the Table of Forms at the end of these rules and which is available at www.ontariocourtforms.on.ca. For your convenience, the government form as published on this website is reproduced below.]

Court File Number ....

[SEAL]

.... *(Name of court)*

at .... *Court office address*

Applicant(s)

Full legal name & address for service — street and number, municipality, postal code, telephone & fax and e-mail address (if any).	*Lawyer's name & address — street and number, municipality, postal code, telephone & fax numbers and e-mail address (if any).*

Respondent(s)

Full legal name & address for service — street and number, municipality, postal code, telephone & fax and e-mail address (if any).	*Lawyer's name & address — street and number, municipality, postal code, telephone & fax numbers and e-mail address (if any).*

TO: *(full legal name of witness)* .... of *(address: street & number, municipality, postal code)* ....

YOU MUST:

(1) come to *(address: street & number, municipality)* .... on *(date)* ...., at .... a.m./p.m.;

(2) give evidence in the case or examination before (court or other person) ....

(3) bring with you the documents and things listed on the back of this Summons; and

(4) remain there until this case or examination is finished or until the person conducting it says otherwise.

With this *Summons,* you should get a fee that is calculated for .... day(s) of attendance as follows:

Appearance allowance of $20 for each day that you are away from home ($60 minimum)		$	
Travel allowance	$		
Overnight hotel for minimum of 3 days ($60 minimum)			$
Meal allowance for minimum of 3 days ($60 minimum)			$
TOTAL		$	

If the case or examination takes up more of your time, you will be entitled to an additional fee.

IF YOU DO NOT COME AND REMAIN AS REQUIRED BY THIS SUMMONS, A WARRANT MAY BE ISSUED FOR YOUR ARREST.

.... *Date of issue*

.... *Signature of the clerk of the court*

(Give the date of every document that the witness must bring and give enough of a description to identify each document or thing that the witness must bring.)

Draw a line through any blank space left on this page. If you need more space, you can add pages and number them.

This summons was issued at the request of and inquiies may be directed to: *(Name, address, telephone number & fax numbers and e-mail address of person or lawyer who requested this summons.)*	

JUDGE'S CERTIFICATE

I, *(name)* ...., a judge of the *(name of court)* .... CERTIFY THAT I have heard and examined *(name of party or parties who have asked for this Summons or of his, her or their lawyer)* .... who seek(s) to compel the attendance of *(name of witness(es))* .... to produce documents or other articles or to testify, or both, in an Ontario case in the *(name of court in which witness is to appear)* .... involving *(names of parties in the case and court file number)* ....

I FURTHER CERTIFY THAT I am persuaded that the appearance of *(name of witness(es))* .... as a witness/witnesses in the case is necessary for the due adjudication of the case, and, in relation to the nature and importance of cause or proceeding, is reasonable and essential to the due administration of justice in Ontario.

The *Interprovincial Summonses Act* makes the following provision for the immunity of *(name of witness(es))* ....

A person who is required to attend before a court in Ontario by a summons adopted by a court outside Ontario shall be deemed, while within Ontario for the purposes for which the summons was issued, not to have submitted to the jurisdiction of the courts of Ontario other than as a witness in the proceedings in which the person is summoned and shall be absolutely immune from seizure of goods, service of process, execution of judgment, garnishment, imprisonment or molestation of any kind relating to a legal or judicial right, cause, action, proceeding or process within the jurisdiction of the Legislature of Ontario except only those proceedings grounded on events occurring during or after the required attendance of the person in Ontario.

.... *(Signature of judge)*

.... *(Date of signature)*

[SEAL OF THE COURT]

September 1, 2005

FORM 23B — ORDER FOR PRISONER'S ATTENDANCE

[Repealed O. Reg. 76/06, s. 15.]

[Editor's Note: Forms 4 to 39 of the Family Law Rules have been repealed by O. Reg. 76/06, effective May 1, 2006. Pursuant to Family Law Rule 1(9), when a form is referred to by number, the reference is to the form with that number that is described in the Table of Forms at the end of these rules and which is available at www.ontariocourtforms.on.ca. For your convenience, the government form as published on this website is reproduced below.]

Court File Number ....

[SEAL]

.... *(Name of court)*

at .... *Court office address*

Applicant(s)

Full legal name & address for service — street & number, municipality, postal code, telephone & fax numbers and e-mail address (if any).	*Lawyer's name & address — street & number, municipality, postal code, telephone & fax numbers and e-mail address (if any).*

Respondent(s)

Full legal name & address for service — street & number, municipality, postal code, telephone & fax numbers and e-mail address (if any).	*Lawyer's name & address — street & number, municipality, postal code, telephone & fax numbers and e-mail address (if any).*

.... *Judge (print or type name)*

.... *Date of order*

TO THE OFFICERS OF (name of correctional institution)

AND TO ALL PEACE OFFICERS IN ONTARIO:

THIS COURT has found that a prisoner at the institution or facility named above, *(prisoner's full legal name)* is

- ❑ a party in this case;
- ❑ a witness whose presence is necessary to decide an issue in this case.

THIS COURT ORDERS THAT:

1. You produce the prisoner before

   ❑ this court
   ❑ *(Specify other officer before whom attendance is required)*

on *(date)* ...., at .... a.m./p.m. at *(address)* .... to enable the prisoner to come to court or to an examination in this case.

2. The prisoner be returned and re-admitted immediately afterwards to the correctional institution or other facility from which he/she was brought.

.... *Date of signature*

.... *Signature of judge or clerk of the court*

September 1, 2005

FORM 23C — AFFIDAVIT FOR UNCONTESTED TRIAL, DATED

[Repealed O. Reg. 76/06, s. 15.]

[Editor's Note: Forms 4 to 39 of the Family Law Rules have been repealed by O. Reg. 76/06, effective May 1, 2006. Pursuant to Family Law Rule 1(9), when a form is referred to by number, the reference is to the form with that number that is described in the Table of Forms at the end of these rules and which is available at www.ontariocourtforms.on.ca. For your convenience, the government form as published on this website is reproduced below.]

ONTARIO

Court File Number

....

(Name of court)

at ....

Court office address

Applicant(s)

Full legal name & address for service — street & number, municipality, postal code, telephone & fax numbers and e-mail address (if any).	*Lawyer's name & address — street & number, municipality, postal code, telephone & fax numbers and e-mail address (if any).*

Respondent(s)

Full legal name & address for service — street & number, municipality, postal code, telephone & fax numbers and e-mail address (if any).		*Lawyer's name & address — street & number, municipality, postal code, telephone & fax numbers and e-mail address (if any).*

My name is (full legal name) ....

I live in (municipality & province) ....

and I swear/affirm that the following is true:

1. I am the applicant in this case.

2. There is/are *(number)* .... child(ren) from our relationship, namely:

Full Legal Name	**Age**	**Birthdate (d, m, y)**	**Resident in (municipality & province)**	**Now living with (name of person and relationship to child)**

3. I am asking for the following order:

❑ custody of the child(ren) named above

❑ access to the child(ren) named above

❑ support for *(name of recipient(s))* ....

❑ a restraining order against the respondent *(name)* .... *(date of birth)* ....

❑ other *(specify)* ....

4. The respondent and I were:

❑ married on *(date)* ....

❑ separated on *(date)* ....

❑ started living together on *(date)* ....

❑ never lived together.

CUSTODY AND ACCESS

Fill out this section if you are claiming custody of one or more of the children.

5. An order giving me custody of the child(ren) is in the best interests of the child(ren) because: *(Give reasons.)*

....

....

....

....

....

....

6. An order giving the respondent access to the children

❑ is . . . . ❑ is not

in the best interests of the child(ren) because: *(Give reasons.)*

....

....

....

....

....

....

7. If an order for access is made, it should be:

❑ reasonable access on reasonable notice;

❑ reasonable access on reasonable notice including but not limited to the terms below:

❑ on the following terms:

❑ every other weekend from .... p.m. on Friday until .... p.m. on Sunday or Monday, if Monday is a statutory holiday, starting on *(date)* ....

❑ alternate spring breaks, starting in *(year)* ....

❑ .... weeks during the summer vacation, to be decided by the parties before April 1 of each year.

❑ one half of the winter break, starting on *(date)* .... and ending on *(date)* .... to be shared as follows:

....

....

....

❑ List any other special days such as religious festivals, Christmas Day, birthdays, Mother's Day, Father's Day, etc., and indicate with which person the children will be on each day. *(Specify dates and times.)*

....

....

....

❑ other *(Specify.)* ....

CHILD SUPPORT

Fill out this section if you are claiming child support.

8. I am claiming support for *(number)* .... child(ren).

9. To the best of my knowledge, the source(s) of the respondent's income is/are *(Check one or more boxes as circumstances require.)*

❑ employment income at *(employer's name and address)* ....

❑ commissions, tips, overtime, bonuses, etc.

❑ self-employment as *(name or nature of respondent's business)* ....

❑ other *(Specify.)* ....

10. I believe that the respondent's current annual income from all income sources is $ .... for the following reasons: *(Give your reasons for believing the dollar amount set out.)*

....

....

....

....

....

....

....

....

SPOUSAL SUPPORT

Fill out this section if you are claiming support for yourself.

11. I need spousal support for the following reasons: *(Give details of your financial needs.)*

....

....

....

....

....

....

....

....

....

....

....

....

....

RESTRAINING ORDER

Fill out this section if you are claiming a restraining order against the respondent.

12. I need an order to restrain the respondent *(full legal name of person restrained)* .... *(date of birth of person restrained)* .... from

❑ a) contacting or communicating directly or indirectly with the following people *(full legal name and date(s) of birth of person[s] protected by this order)*

Name	**Birthdate (d,m,y)**

❑ except through *(name of person or agency)* .... to arrange access to the child(ren).

❑ except to permit access to the child(ren) *(names and birthdates)* .... on *(dates/days and times)* ....

❑ except through or in the presence of counsel.

❑ except through or in the presence of counsel or a clinical investigator from the Office of the Children's Lawyer, if the Children's Lawyer is appointed to represent the child(ren).

❑ b) coming within .... ❑ metres . . . . ❑ yards ❑ feet of *(locations and addresses)*

....

....

at any time or for any purpose

❑ except under the following conditions: *(provide details of conditions, including time(s), purpose(s) of exception(s) and address(es) as applicable)*

....

....

....

❑ c) *(any additional terms)* ....

I need a restraining order for the following reasons:

....

....

....

....

....

LACK OF SERVICE

Fill out this section if the respondent is not going to be served or has not been served.

NOTE: The Family Law Rules require all documents to be served on the opposing party. The court will make an order even without service, but only in very unusual circumstances such as: *1.* *An emergency situation where there is not enough time to serve documents or where serving them would put you or your child in danger or would have other serious consequences.* *2.* *Where the court is satisfied that every effort has been made to find the other party and that it is impossible to serve him or her by any means.*

13. My application/motion is not being served on the respondent for the following reasons:

....

....

....

....

....

....

....

OTHER ISSUES

....

....

....

....

....

....

....

....

....

....

....

....

....

....

Put a line through any blank space left on this page.

Sworn/Affirmed before me at .... *municipality*		
in .... *province, state or country*		.... *Signature*
on .... *Date*	.... *Commissioner for taking affidavits (Type or print name below if signature is illegible.)*	*(This form is to be signed in front of a lawyer, justice of the peace, notary public or commissioner for taking affidavits.)*

September 1, 2009

FORM 25 — ORDER (GENERAL) ❑ TEMPORARY ❑ FINAL

[Repealed O. Reg. 76/06, s. 15.]

[Editor's Note: Forms 4 to 39 of the Family Law Rules have been repealed by O. Reg. 76/06, effective May 1, 2006. Pursuant to Family Law Rule 1(9), when a form is referred to by number, the reference is to the form with that number that is described in the Table of Forms at the end of these rules and which is available at www.ontariocourtforms.on.ca. For your convenience, the government form as published on this website is reproduced below.]

❑ Temporary

❑ Final

Court File Number ....

[SEAL]

.... *(Name of court)*

at .... Court office address

Applicant(s)

Full legal name & address for service — street & number, municipality, postal code, telephone & fax numbers and e-mail address (if any)	*Lawyer's name & address — street & number, municipality, postal code, telephone & fax numbers and e-mail address (if any)*

Respondent(s)

Full legal name & address for service — street & number, municipality, postal code, telephone & fax numbers and e-mail address (if any)	*Lawyer's name & address — street & number, municipality, postal code, telephone & fax numbers and e-mail address (if any)*

.... *Judge (print or type name)*

.... *Date of order*

The court heard an application/motion made by *(name of person or persons)*

....

The following persons were in court *(names of parties and lawyers in court)*

....

The court received evidence and heard submissions on behalf of *(name or names)*

....

THIS COURT ORDERS THAT:

....

Put a line through any blank space left on this page. If additional space is needed, extra pages may be attached.

.... *Date of signature*

.... *Signature of judge or clerk of the court*

September 1, 2005

FORM 25A — DIVORCE ORDER

[Repealed O. Reg. 76/06, s. 15.]

[Editor's Note: Forms 4 to 39 of the Family Law Rules have been repealed by O. Reg. 76/06, effective May 1, 2006. Pursuant to Family Law Rule 1(9), when a form is referred to by number, the reference is to the form with that number that is described in the Table of Forms at the end of these rules and which is available at www.ontariocourtforms.on.ca. For your convenience, the government form as published on this website is reproduced below.]

Court File Number ....

[SEAL]

.... *(Name of court)*

at .... *Court office address*

Applicant(s)

Full legal name & address for service — street & number, municipality, postal code, telephone & fax numbers and e-mail address (if any)	*Lawyer's name & address — street & number, municipality, postal code, telephone & fax numbers and e-mail address (if any)*

Respondent(s)

Full legal name & address for service — street & number, municipality, postal code, telephone & fax numbers and e-mail address (if any)	*Lawyer's name & address — street & number, municipality, postal code, telephone & fax numbers and e-mail address (if any)*

.... *Judge (print or type name)*

.... *Date of order*

The court considered an application of *(name)* .... on *(date)*

The following persons were in court *(Give names of parties and lawyers in court. This paragraph may be struck out if the divorce is uncontested.)*

The court received evidence and considered submissions on behalf of *(name or names)* ....

THIS COURT ORDERS THAT:

1. *(full legal names of spouses)*

   who were married at *(place)* ....

   on *(date)* ....

   be divorced and that the divorce take effect 31 days after the date of this order.

If the court decides that the divorce should take effect earlier, replace "31" with the smaller number.

(Add further paragraphs where the court orders other relief.) ....

Put a line through any blank space left on this page. If additional space is needed, extra pages may be attached.

.... *Date of signature*

.... *Signature of judge or clerk of the court*

NOTE: Neither spouse is free to remarry until this order takes effect, at which time you can get a Certificate of Divorce from the court office.

September 1, 2005

FORM 25B — SECURE TREATMENT ORDER

[Repealed O. Reg. 76/06, s. 15.]

[Editor's Note: Forms 4 to 39 of the Family Law Rules have been repealed by O. Reg. 76/06, effective May 1, 2006. Pursuant to Family Law Rule 1(9), when a form is referred to by number, the reference is to the form with that number that is described in the Table of Forms at the end of these rules and which is available at www.ontariocourtforms.on.ca. For your convenience, the government form as published on this website is reproduced below.]

Court File Number ....

.... *(Name of court)*

at .... *Court office address*

Applicant(s)

Full legal name & address for service — street & number, municipality, postal code, telephone & fax numbers and e-mail address (if any)	*Lawyer's name & address — street & number, municipality, postal code, telephone & fax numbers and e-mail address (if any)*

Respondent(s)

Full legal name & address for service — street & number, municipality, postal code, telephone & fax numbers and e-mail address (if any)	*Lawyer's name & address — street & number, municipality, postal code, telephone & fax numbers and e-mail address (if any)*

.... *Judge (print or type name)*

.... *Date of order*

The court heard an application of *(name of person or persons)* ....

The following persons were in court *(names of parties and lawyers in court)* ....

The court received evidence and heard submissions on behalf of *(name or names)* ....

THIS COURT ORDERS THAT:

❑ *(child's full legal name)* .... be committed to the secure treatment programme at *(name and address of program)* .... for a period of .... days, beginning on *(date)* ....

❑ the commitment of *(child's full legal name)* .... to the secure treatment program at *(name and address of program)* .... be extended for a period of .... days, beginning on *(date)* ....

❑ this application for an order
  ❑ of commitment

  ❑ extending the commitment

of *(child's full legal name)* .... to the secure treatment programme at *(name and address of program)* .... be dismissed.

❏ *(Other. Specify.)*
....
....

Put a line through any blank space left on this page. If additional space is needed, extra pages may be attached.

.... *Date of signature*

.... *Signature of judge or clerk of the court*

NOTE TO ADMINISTRATOR OF SECURE TREATMENT PROGRAM: Subsection 118(3) of the Child and Family Services Act states:

> *In the calculation of a child's period of commitment, time spent in the secure treatment program before an order has been made under section 117 (commitment) or pending an application under section 120 (extension) shall be counted.*

NOTE FURTHER that section 125 of the Child and Family Services Act authorizes a peace officer to take a child to a place where there is a secure treatment program if an order for the child's commitment to the secure treatment program has been made under section 117.

September 1, 2005

FORM 25C — ADOPTION ORDER

[Repealed O. Reg. 76/06, s. 15.]

[Editor's Note: Forms 4 to 39 of the Family Law Rules have been repealed by O. Reg. 76/06, effective May 1, 2006. Pursuant to Family Law Rule 1(9), when a form is referred to by number, the reference is to the form with that number that is described in the Table of Forms at the end of these rules and which is available at www.ontariocourtforms.on.ca. For your convenience, the government form as published on this website is reproduced below.]

Court File Number ....

[SEAL]

.... *(Name of court)*

at .... *Court office address*

Applicant(s)

Full legal name & address for service — street & number, municipality, postal code, telephone & fax numbers and e-mail address (if any)	*Lawyer's name & address — street & number, municipality, postal code, telephone & fax numbers and e-mail address (if any)*

.... *Judge (print or type name)*

.... *Date of order*

The court heard an application of *(name of person or persons)*

....

The following persons were in court *(names of parties and lawyers in court)*

....

The court received evidence and heard submissions on behalf of *(name or names)*

....

The person to be adopted is:

Name before adoption (Give full legal name of person to be adopted, unless the court orders otherwise.)	**Date of Birth**	**Place of birth** (municipality, province and country)	**Sex**	**Birth registration number**

THIS COURT ORDERS THAT:

1. The person is adopted as the child of *(name of applicant or applicants)*

   ....

2. The name of the person shall now be *(person's full legal name)*

   ....

.... *Date of signature*

.... *Signature of judge or clerk of the court*

FOR ADMINISTRATIVE PURPOSES ONLY:

- ❑ crown ward adoption
- ❑ licensed private adoption
- ❑ CAS non-ward adoption
- ❑ relative adoption
- ❑ stepparent adoption
- ❑ international adoption
- ❑ section 146(1)(b) adoption

September 1, 2005

FORM 25D — ORDER (UNCONTESTED TRIAL) ❑ TEMPORARY ❑ FINAL

[Repealed O. Reg. 76/06, s. 15.]

[Editor's Note: Forms 4 to 39 of the Family Law Rules have been repealed by O. Reg. 76/06, effective May 1, 2006. Pursuant to Family Law Rule 1(9), when a form is referred to by number, the reference is to the form with that number that is described in the Table of Forms at the end of these rules and which is available at www.ontariocourtforms.on.ca. For your convenience, the government form as published on this website is reproduced below.]

Court File Number

(Name of court)

Form 25D: Order (Uncontested Trial)
❑ Temporary
❑ Final

SEAL

at

Court office address

Judge (print or type name)

Date of order

Applicant(s)

Full legal name & address for service — street & number, municipality, postal code, telephone & fax numbers and e-mail address (if any).	*Lawyer's name & address — street & number, municipality, postal code, telephone & fax numbers and e-mail address (if any).*

Respondent(s)

Full legal name & address for service — street & number, municipality, postal code, telephone & fax numbers and e-mail address (if any)	*Lawyer's name & address — street & number, municipality, postal code, telephone & fax numbers and e-mail address (if any).*

Name & address of Children's Lawyer's agent (street & number, municipality, postal code, telephone & fax numbers and e-mail address (if any)) and name of person represented.

The court considered an application/motion made by *(name of person or persons)*
The following persons were in court *(names of parties and lawyers in court)*
The court received evidence and submissions on behalf of *(name or names)*

This order affects the following children:

Child's full legal name	*Date of birth (d, m, y)*	*Sex*

PARENTAGE

❑ *1.* *THIS COURT FINDS that:*

❑ each child mentioned above is a child of the marriage within the meaning of the *Divorce Act* (Canada).

❑ the applicant and respondent are parents of each child mentioned above within the meaning of the *Family Law Act* and the *Children's Law Reform Act*.

❑ other *(Specify.)*

CUSTODY

❑ *2.* *THIS COURT ORDERS that (name(s))* .... *shall have*

❑ temporary ❑ final

❑ sole ❑ joint

custody of each child mentioned above.

ACCESS

❑ *3.* *THIS COURT ORDERS that (name(s))* .... *shall have*

❑ temporary ❑ final

access to each child mentioned above. The terms of access are:

❑ reasonable access on reasonable notice;

❑ reasonable access on reasonable notice including but not limited to the terms below;

❑ as follows:

❑ every other weekend from .... p.m. on Friday until .... p.m. on Sunday or Monday, if Monday is a statutory holiday, starting on *(date)* ....

❑ alternate spring breaks, starting in *(year)* ....

❑ .... weeks during the summer vacation, to be decided by the parties before April 1 of each year.

❑ one-half of the winter break, starting on *(date)* .... and ending on *(date)* .... to be shared as follows:

❑ List any other special days such as religious festivals, Christmas Day, birthdays, Mother's Day, Father's Day, etc., and indicate with which person the children will be on each day. *(Specify dates and times.)*

❑ other *(Specify.)*

CHILD SUPPORT

❑ *4.* *THIS COURT FINDS that (name of payor)* .... has an income of $ .... *and IT ORDERS that (name of payor)* .... pay to *(name of recipient)* .... the sum of $ .... per month for the support of the child(ren) named above, starting on *(date)* ....

Fill in this frame only if there is a claim for add-ons for the child(ren).

THIS COURT FINDS that (name of recipient) .... has an income of $ .... *and IT ORDERS that (name of payor)* .... pay to *(name of recipient)* .... the sum of $ .... per month for the special or extraordinary expenses (add-ons) of the child(ren) named above, starting on *(date)* ....

The details of this amount are as follows:

Name of child	*Nature of special or extraordinary expense*	*Amount*

SPOUSAL SUPPORT

❑ *5.* *THIS COURT ORDERS that (name of payor)* .... pay to *(name of recipient)* .... ❑ temporary ❑ final spousal support in the amount of $ .... per .... starting on *(date)* ....

❑ *6.* *THIS COURT ORDERS that* the support under paragraph 5 of this order be indexed and changed annually according to the indexing factor in subsection 34(6) of the *Family Law Act*.

SUPPORT MONEY OWED

❑ *7.* *THIS COURT FINDS that* the amount of support owed is $ .... as of *(date)* ....

AND THIS COURT ORDERS that (name of payor) .... pay off this amount

❑ by *(date)* ....

❑ at the rate of $ .... per .... starting on *(date)* ....

SUPPORT — ENFORCEMENT

❑ *8.* *THIS COURT ORDERS that* unless the support order is withdrawn from the office of the Director of the Family Responsibility Office, it shall be enforced by the Director and amounts owing under the order shall be paid to the Director, who shall pay them to the person to whom they are owed.

❑ *9.* *THIS COURT ORDERS that* the clerk issue a support deduction order under section 11 of the *Family Responsibility and Support Arrears Enforcement Act* for the periodic support.

PROPERTY

❑ *10.* *THIS COURT ORDERS that*

DISCLOSURE

❑ *11.* *THIS COURT ORDERS that (name)* .... serve and file the following before the next court date:

❑ a current financial statement.

❑ other *(Specify.)*

OTHER MATTERS

❑ *12.* *THIS COURT ORDERS that*

COSTS

❑ *13.* *THIS COURT ORDERS that* costs be paid by *(name)* .... to *(name)* .... fixed at $ ....

ADJOURNMENT

❑ *14.* *THIS COURT ORDERS that* the matter(s) of .... be adjourned to *(date)* .... at *(time)* .... for: *(purpose)*

Interest

❑ *15.* *THIS COURT ORDERS that* interest be payable on amounts owing under this order at the rate of ....% per year.

Put a line through any space left on this page. If additional space is needed, extra pages may be attached.

....

Date of signature *Signature of judge or clerk of the court*

September 1, 2005

FORM 25E — NOTICE DISPUTING APPROVAL OF ORDER

[Repealed O. Reg. 76/06, s. 15.]

[Editor's Note: Forms 4 to 39 of the Family Law Rules have been repealed by O. Reg. 76/06, effective May 1, 2006. Pursuant to Family Law Rule 1(9), when a form is referred to by number, the reference is to the form with that number that is described in the Table of Forms at the end of these rules and which is available at www.ontariocourtforms.on.ca. For your convenience, the government form as published on this website is reproduced below.]

Court File Number ....

.... *(Name of court)*

at .... *Court office address*

Applicant(s)

Full legal name & address for service — street & number, municipality, postal code, telephone & fax and e-mail address (if any). .	Lawyer's name & address — street & number, municipality, postal code, telephone & fax numbers and e-mail address (if any).

Respondent(s)

Full legal name & address for service — street & number, municipality, postal code, telephone & fax numbers and e-mail address (if any).	Lawyer's name & address — street & number, municipality, postal code, telephone & fax numbers and e-mail address (if any).

TO: (name of parties)

....

I disagree with the proposed wording of the order in this case for the following reasons: *(Give your reasons.)*

....

....

I am asking for a reworded order. A copy of my version of the order is attached.

THE CLERK OF THE COURT WILL SETTLE THE WORDING OF THE ORDER on *(date)* .... at .... a.m./p.m., or as soon as possible after that time at *(place for settling order)* ....

IF YOU DO NOT COME, THE CLERK OF THE COURT MAY SIGN THE ORDER WITH WORDING THAT MAY BE DIFFERENT FROM THE VERSION FIRST PROPOSED.

.... *Signature*

.... *Date of signature*

September 1, 2005

FORM 25F — RESTRAINING ORDER

SEAL

ONTARIO

Court File Number

....

(Name of court)

at ....

Court office address

❑ *Temporary* ❑ *Final*

Applicant(s)

....	*Full legal name & address for service — street & number, municipality, postal code, telephone & fax numbers and e-mail address (if any).*	*Lawyer's name & address — street & number, municipality, postal code, telephone & fax numbers and e-mail address (if any).*
Judge (print or type name)		

Respondent(s)

....	*Full legal name & address for service — street & number, municipality, postal code, telephone & fax numbers and e-mail address (if any).*	*Lawyer's name & address — street & number, municipality, postal code, telephone & fax numbers and e-mail address (if any).*
Date of order		

THIS COURT ORDERS THAT:

1. ...., born ...., shall not

(Court staff to insert here relevant clauses as ordered by judge in Endorsement.)

2. This restraining order is effective ....

3. This restraining order shall remain in effect until ....

❑ A separate order with additional terms relating to this family case was also made on this date.

In support of this order, this court heard a .... made by the .... for a restraining order under ....

The .... was made with notice to ....

The following persons were in court *(list names of parties and lawyers in court)*:

....

....

....

....

....

....

The court read the following materials filed in support of a request for this order:

....

....

....

....

....

....

The court heard submissions in support of a request for this order from:

....

....

....

....

....

....

....	....
Date of signature	*Signature of judge or clerk of the court*

Note: This order will be registered against the person being restrained on the Canadian Police Information Centre (CPIC) Database. Disobeying this order is a criminal offence punishable by fine or imprisonment. Any police or peace officer with jurisdiction over the place where the order was disobeyed may arrest the person being restrained without a warrant in accordance with section 495 of the Criminal Code of Canada.

September 1, 2009

FORM 25G — RESTRAINING ORDER ON MOTION WITHOUT NOTICE

SEAL

ONTARIO

Court File Number

....
(Name of court)

at ....
Court office address

	Applicant(s)	
....	*Full legal name & address for service — street & number, municipality, postal code, telephone & fax numbers and e-mail address (if any).*	*Lawyer's name & address — street & number, municipality, postal code, telephone & fax numbers and e-mail address (if any).*
Judge (print or type name)		
	Respondent(s)	
....	*Full legal name & address for service — street & number, municipality, postal code, telephone & fax numbers and e-mail address (if any).*	*Lawyer's name & address — street & number, municipality, postal code, telephone & fax numbers and e-mail address (if any).*
Date of order		

THIS COURT ORDERS THAT:

1. ...., born ...., shall not

(Court staff to insert here relevant clauses as ordered by judge in Endorsement.)

2. This restraining order is effective ....

3. This restraining order shall remain in effect until ....

4. This matter is adjourned to *(date and time)* .... to review this restraining order.

5. A copy of this order together with the notice of motion, dated ...., and affidavit of ...., sworn/affirmed on ...., shall be served immediately on *(insert full legal name of person restrained by this order)* .... by *(specify type of service)* ....

❑ A separate order with additional terms relating to this family case was also made on this date.

In support of this order, this court heard a motion made by the .... for a restraining order under ....

The motion was made without notice to ....

The following persons were in court *(list names of parties and lawyers in court)*

....

....

....

....

....

The court read the following materials filed in support of a request for this order

....

....

....

....

....

The court heard submissions in support of a request for this order from

....

....

....

....

....

....

....

Date of signature *Signature of judge or clerk of the court*

NOTICE TO (name) ....

If you want to oppose this motion or to give your own views, you must serve an Affidavit (general) (Form 14A). If you think the court should make a different order, you must serve an Affidavit (general) (Form 14A) and a Notice of Motion (Form 14). In either case, you must serve these materials on the other party and file the materials together with proof of service at the court office on or before 2 p.m. on *(insert date)* .... If you do not have a lawyer, you should ask the court office about serving the documents for you.

Note: This order will be registered against the person being restrained on the Canadian Police Information Centre (CPIC) Database. Disobeying this order is a criminal offence punishable by fine or imprisonment. Any police or peace officer with jurisdiction over the place where the order was disobeyed may arrest the person being restrained without a warrant in accordance with section 495 of the Criminal Code of Canada.

September 1, 2009

FORM 25H — ORDER TERMINATING RESTRAINING ORDER, DATED

SEAL

ONTARIO

Court File Number

....

(Name of court)

at ....

Court office address

....

	Applicant(s)	
....	*Full legal name & address for service — street & number, municipality, postal code, telephone & fax numbers and e-mail address (if any).*	*Lawyer's name & address — street & number, municipality, postal code, telephone & fax numbers and e-mail address (if any).*
Judge (print or type name)		

	Respondent(s)	
....	*Full legal name & address for service — street & number, municipality, postal code, telephone & fax numbers and e-mail address (if any).*	*Lawyer's name & address — street & number, municipality, postal code, telephone & fax numbers and e-mail address (if any).*
Date of order		

THIS COURT ORDERS THAT:

1. The restraining order made by Justice ...., on ...., shall be terminated, effective ....

In support of this order, the following persons were in court *(names of parties and lawyers in court)* ....

The court read the following materials filed in support of a request for this order ....

The court heard submissions in support of a request for this order from ....

....

Date of signature *Signature of judge or clerk of the court*

Note: This order will be sent to police services to advise them to remove the terminated restraining order from the Canadian Police Information Centre (CPIC) Database.

September 1, 2009

FORM 26 — STATEMENT OF MONEY OWED

[Repealed O. Reg. 76/06, s. 15.]

[Editor's Note: Forms 4 to 39 of the Family Law Rules have been repealed by O. Reg. 76/06, effective May 1, 2006. Pursuant to Family Law Rule 1(9), when a form is referred to by number, the reference is to the form with that number that is described in the Table of Forms at the end of these rules and which is available at www.ontariocourtforms.on.ca. For your convenience, the government form as published on this website is reproduced below.]

Court File Number ....

.... *(Name of court)*

at .... *Court office address*

dated ....

Recipient(s)

Full legal name & address for service — street & number, municipality, postal code, telephone & fax and e-mail address (if any).	*Lawyer's name & address — street & number, municipality, postal code, telephone & fax numbers and e-mail address (if any).*

Payor

Full legal name & address for service — street & number, municipality, postal code, telephone & fax numbers and e-mail address (if any).	*Lawyer's name & address — street & number, municipality, postal code, telephone & fax numbers and e-mail address (if any).*

My name is (full legal name)

I live in (municipality & province) and I swear/affirm that the following is true:

1. I am

   ❑ a person entitled to money under an order, a domestic contract or a paternity agreement that is enforceable in this court.

   ❑ a child's custodian or guardian entitled to money for the child's benefit under an order, domestic contract or paternity agreement that is enforceable in this court.

   ❑ an assignee of a person or of a child's custodian or guardian entitled to money under an order, domestic contract or paternity agreement that is enforceable in this court.

   ❑ an agent of the Director of the Family Responsibility Office.

❑ *(Other. Specify.)*

2. I attach a copy of the

❑ *court order*
❑ paternity agreement

❑ domestic contrac
❑ bond/recognizance

and it has not been changed by a court order or agreement of the parties, except *(Write "NIL" if there has been no change.)*

3. The total of the periodic payments that remain unpaid today is $.......... The detailed calculation of this total is attached to this statement. *(See reverse side for instructions.)*

4. The amount of interest on the unpaid periodic payments between the date of each default and today is $.......... The detailed interest calculations are attached to this statement. *(See reverse side for instructions.)*

Put a line through any blank space left on this page.

INSTRUCTIONS FOR COMPLETING FORM 26 (STATEMENT OF MONEY OWED)

Paragraph 3:

Write "NIL",

(a) if the periodic portion of your order, domestic contract or paternity agreement is fully paid up today; or

(b) if your order, domestic contract or paternity agreement does not require the payor to make periodic payments.

If you are claiming unpaid amounts of periodic payments under a support order, a fine or forfeiture to be paid by instalments, a domestic contract or a paternity agreement, you *MUST* attach one or more separate sheets as an appendix to this *Statement*. There you must set out a history or a diary of the payor's payments and defaults. The diagram to the right shows one way to set out this history or diary. The final total in this diary of payments and defaults must be the same as the dollar amount in paragraph 3.

DATE	**AMOUNT DUE (Add to TOTAL)**	**AMOUNT PAID (Subtract from TOTAL)**	**TOTAL amount owing**
4 Sept. 1998	$250.00		$250.00
10 Sept. 1998		$250.00	$ 0.00
18 Sept. 1998	$250.00		$250.00
24 Sept. 1998		$150.00	$100.00
2 Oct. 1998	$250.00		$350.00
12 Oct. 1998		$125.00	$225.00
16 Oct. 1998	$250.00		$475.00
30 Oct. 1998	$250.00		$725.00
30 Oct. 1998	$250.00		$975.00

Paragraph 4:

Write "NIL",

(a) if you don't want to claim any interest on unpaid periodic payments; or

(b) if your order, domestic contract or paternity agreement actually forbids you to claim interest. (if your order, domestic contract or paternity agreement says nothing about interest, you can still claim it if you want.)

Even though the payor is fully paid up today on periodic payments and even though the dollar amount that you are claiming in paragraph 3 is "NIL", there may be interest owing from the times when the payor was behind in payments. You may therefore wish to make a claim for that unpaid interest here. If you are not barred from claiming interest and wish to do so, you *MUST* attach one or more work sheets as an appendix to this *Statement*. On those work sheets,

(c) you must set out your method of computing interest. Unless the court order, domestic contract or paternity agreement specifically allows you to compound interest, you must use simple interest.

(d) you must indicate the appropriate rate of interest. This rate can sometimes be set out in your order, domestic contract or paternity agreement, but if it is not, then you must rely on the rate allowed by section 127 of the *Courts of Justice Act*. You can also get this information from the court office.

(e) for each overdue or partially overdue payment, calculate in dollars and cents the amount of interest allowed by subsection 129(2) of the *Courts of Justice Act*, from the date when it was due until today or until the date of full payment of that overdue amount, whichever date is earlier.

Paragraph 5:

Write "NIL",

(a) if the lump sum (whether by way of order, forfeiture, fine or support in a domestic contract or paternity agreement) is fully paid up today; or

(b) if there is no requirement on the payor to pay any lump sum.

If there have been partial payments on the lump sum, you *MUST* attach one or more separate sheets as an appendix to this Statement. There, you must set out a history or a diary of the payor's partial payments, similar to the diagram on the right. The final total in this history must be the same as the dollar amount that you are claiming in paragraph 5.

DATE	AMOUNT DUE (Add to TOTAL)	AMOUNT PAID (Subtract from TOTAL)	TOTAL amount owing
1 Dec. 1998	$24,000.00		$24,000.00
29 Dec. 1998		$4,700.00	$19,300.00
12 Feb. 1999		$1,800.00	$17,500.00
6 May 1999		$1,226.40	$16,273.60

Paragraph 6:

Write "NIL",

(a) if you don't want to claim any interest on the lump-sum amount.

(b) if your order, domestic contract or paternity agreement forbids you to claim interest.

Even though the lump sum has been paid up and even though the dollar amount that you are claiming in paragraph 5 is "NIL", the interest earned on it during a time when payment was overdue may still be owing and you may wish to claim it here. If you are not barred from claiming interest and wish to do so, you *MUST* attach one or more work sheets as an appendix to this *Statement.* On those work sheets,

(c) you must set out your method of computing interest. You must use simple interest unless the court order, domestic contract or paternity agreement specifically allows you to compound interest.

(d) you must indicate the appropriate rate of interest. This rate may sometimes be set out in your order, domestic contract or paternity agreement, but if it is not, then you must rely on the rate allowed by section 127 of the *Courts of Justice Act.* You can also get this information from the court office.

(e) for each partial payment, calculate in dollars and cents the amount of interest from the date of the order, domestic contract or paternity agreement until the date of the partial payment. Interest on any balance still outstanding today will be calculated from the date of the order, contract or agreement until today.

5. The amount of the lump-sum

❑ support

❑ equalization payment

❑ costs

❑ fine for contempt of court

❑ *(Other. Specify.)*

....

....

that remains unpaid today is $ .... The detailed calculation is attached to this statement. *(See reverse side for instructions.)*

6. The total amount of unpaid interest on the lump sum up to today is $ .... The detailed calculation is attached to this statement. *(See reverse side of page 1 for instructions.)*

7. The amount of court costs remaining unpaid today is $ .... The detailed calculation is attached to this statement. *(See reverse side of this sheet of for instructions.)*

8. The amount of unpaid interest on court costs up to today is $ .... The detailed calculation is attached to this statement. *(See reverse side of this sheet for instructions.)*

Creditor's Relief Provisions

9. Of the money in paragraphs 5 and 6, I attribute $ .... of the total to lump-sum support. *(See reverse side of this sheet for instructions.)*

10. Of the money in paragraphs 3 and 4, I attribute $ .... of the total to periodic support. *(See reverse side of this sheet for instructions.)*

INSTRUCTIONS FOR COMPLETING FORM 26 (STATEMENT OF MONEY OWED) (CONTINUED)

Paragraph 7:

Write "NIL",

(a) if the court costs are fully paid up today; or

(b) if the court did not award costs to you.

If there have been partial payments on the court costs, you MUST attach one or more separate sheets as an appendix to this *Statement.* There, you must set out the history or diary of the payor's partial payments, as illustrated by the diagram alongside the note to paragraph 5. The final total in this diary must be the same as the dollar amount that you are claiming in paragraph 7.

Paragraph 8:

Write "NIL",

(a) if you don't want to claim any interest on court costs; or

(b) if your order forbids you to claim any interest on costs.

Even though the court costs may be paid up today and the dollar amount that you are claiming in paragraph 8 is "NIL", the interest earned on those costs during the time when payment on them was overdue may still be owing and you may wish to claim that interest here. If you are claiming interest on court costs, you MUST attach one or more work sheets as an appendix to this *Statement.* On those work sheets,

(c) you must set out your method of computing interest. You must use simple accrual unless the court has specifically allowed you to compound your interest.

(d) you must indicate the appropriate rate of interest prevailing on the date when the order was made or the rate allowed by the court when it made the order. You can get this information from the court office.

(e) for each partial payment, you must calculate in dollars and cents the amount of interest from the date of the order until the date of the partial payment. Interest on any balance still outstanding today will run from the date of the order until today.

Paragraph 9:

Write "NIL" if your lump-sum claim has nothing to do with support or maintenance. Otherwise, figure out what portion of your lump-sum claim deals with support or maintenance. You are entitled to include the interest earned on that amount.

This figure will be needed by the clerk of the court and by others, such as the sheriff, because they are required by law to give your claim for lump-sum support priority over the claims of other people with orders against the payor under the *Creditors' Relief Act*. Section 4 of that Act states:

Priority for support orders

4. (1) A support or maintenance order has priority over other judgment debts regardless of when an enforcement process is issued or served,

(a) if the order is for periodic payments, in the amount of the arrears owing under the order at the time of seizure or attachment; and

(b) if the order is for a lump sum payment, in the amount of the lump sum.

Support orders rank equally

(2) Support or maintenance orders rank equally with one another.

Enforcement process

(3) Process for the enforcement of a support or maintenance order shall be identified on its face as being for support or maintenance.

Crown bound

(4) Subsection (1) binds the Crown in right of Ontario.

Paragraph 10:

Write "NIL" if your claim has nothing to do with periodic support or maintenance. Otherwise, figure out what portion of your claim deals with periodic support or maintenance. You are entitled to include the interest earned on that amount.

This figure together with the one in paragraph 9 will be needed by the clerk of the court and by others, such as the sheriff, to determine the priority that your support arrears should have over the claims of other people with orders against the payor. See subsection 4(1) of the *Creditors' Relief Act*.

11. The total of the sums in paragraphs 9 and 10 is $ ....

12. I have carried out the computations in this statement and the attached sheets correctly to the best of my ability.

Final Total

13. The total amount enforceable in this court that I am claiming against the payor is as follows:

(a)	unpaid amounts of periodic payments (paragraph 3)	$ ....
(b)	interest on unpaid amounts of periodic payments (paragraph 4)	$ ....
(c)	unpaid lump-sum debt (paragraph 5)	$ ....
(d)	interest on unpaid lump-sum debt (paragraph 6)	$ ....
(e)	unpaid court costs (paragraph 7)	$ ....
(f)	interest on unpaid court costs (paragraph 8)	$ ....
	TOTAL	$ ....

Put a line through any blank space left on this page.

Sworn/Affirmed before me at .... *munic-ipality* in .... *province, state or country* on .... *date*	
Commissioner for taking affidavits (Type or print name below if signa-ture is illegible.)	*Signature* *(This form is to be signed in front of a lawyer, justice of the peace, notary public or commissioner for taking affi-davits.)*

NOTE: To this statement, you must attach a photocopy of the order, domestic contract, paternity agreement, bond or recognizance that you will be enforcing through the court. In the case of a bond or recognizance, you must also attach a photocopy of the order of forfeiture. If court costs were determined separately, you should include a photocopy of the order or certificate of costs.

Pages of computer print-out are acceptable provided that they generally conform to the examples or diagrams provided in the instructions above.

Appendix

.... *(A, B, C, etc.)*

(page ....) *(page number)*

DATE	**AMOUNT DUE (Add to TOTAL)**	**AMOUNT PAID (subtract from TOTAL)**	**TOTAL (Amount still owing)**

DATE	AMOUNT DUE (Add to TOTAL)	AMOUNT PAID (subtract from TOTAL)	TOTAL (Amount still owing)

CALCULATION OF INTEREST

1. The calculations below relate to interest earned on *(State nature of order, judgment or contract)*

2. The calculations below use:

- ❑ simple interest;
- ❑ compound interest, compounded *(State frequency of compounding)*
- ❑ *(Other. Specify.)*

  ....
  ....

3. The rate of interest permitted by law is ....% per (frequency) ....

4. The calculation of the interest is detailed as follows:

....

....

September 1, 2005

FORM 26A — AFFIDAVIT OF ENFORCEMENT EXPENSES

[Repealed O. Reg. 76/06, s. 15.]

[Editor's Note: Forms 4 to 39 of the Family Law Rules have been repealed by O. Reg. 76/06, effective May 1, 2006. Pursuant to Family Law Rule 1(9), when a form is referred to by number, the reference is to the form with that number that is described in the Table of Forms at the end of these rules and which is available at www.ontariocourtforms.on.ca. For your convenience, the government form as published on this website is reproduced below.]

Court File Number ....

.... *(Name of court)*

at .... *Court office address*

dated ....

Recipient(s)

Full legal name & address for service — street & number, municipality, postal code, telephone & fax and e-mail address (if any).	*Lawyer's name & address — street & number, municipality, postal code, telephone & fax numbers and e-mail address (if any).*

Payor

Full legal name & address for service — street & number, municipality, postal code, telephone & fax numbers and e-mail address (if any).	*Lawyer's name & address — street & number, municipality, postal code, telephone & fax numbers and e-mail address (if any).*

My name is (full legal name)

....

I live in (municipality & province) and I swear/affirm that the following is true:

1. I am

❑ a person entitled to money under an order, a domestic contract or a paternity agreement that is enforceable in this court.

❑ child's custodian or guardian entitled to money for the child's benefit under an order, domestic contract or paternity agreement that is enforceable in this court.

❑ an assignee of a person or of a child's custodian or guardian entitled to money under an order, domestic contract or paternity agreement that is enforceable in this court.

❑ an agent of the Director of the Family Responsibility Office.

❑

(Other. Specify.)
....
....

Attach copy of order, contract or agreement.

2. To enforce the order, domestic contract or paternity agreement, I took the following steps for which I am claiming costs under the rules of the court:

❑ A financial examination of the payor was carried out.
❑ A writ of seizure and sale was issued, filed and enforced.
❑ A notice of garnishment was issued, served, filed and enforced.
❑ A writ of seizure and sale was changed by way of a statutory declaration.
❑ A notice of garnishment was changed by way of a statutory declaration.
❑ *(Other. Specify.)*
....
....

Put a line through any blank space left on this page.

3. The details of my claim are as follows: *(For each item of expense, give the date when it was paid and the amount. Where receipts are available, please attach them and identify them in numbered sequence.)*

ITEM OF EXPENSE	DATE	AMOUNT	Receipt No.
			1
			2
			3
			4
			5
			6
			7
			8
			9
			10
			11
			12

ITEM OF EXPENSE	DATE	AMOUNT	Receipt No.
			13
			14
			15
			16
			17
			18
			19
			20
			21
			22
			23

Notes:

If you need more space, you may attach extra sheets and number them.

Sworn/Affirmed before me at .... *municipality* in .... *province, state or country* on .... *date*	
	Signature
Commissioner for taking affidavits (Type or print name below if signature is illegible.)	*(This form is to be signed in front of a lawyer, justice of the peace, notary public or commissioner for taking affidavits.)*

September 1, 2005

FORM 26B — AFFIDAVIT FOR FILING DOMESTIC CONTRACT OR PATERNITY AGREEMENT WITH COURT

[Repealed O. Reg. 76/06, s. 15.]

[Editor's Note: Forms 4 to 39 of the Family Law Rules have been repealed by O. Reg. 76/06, effective May 1, 2006. Pursuant to Family Law Rule 1(9), when a form is referred to by number, the reference is to the form with that number that is described in the Table of Forms at the end of these rules and which is available at www.ontariocourtforms.on.ca. For your convenience, the government form as published on this website is reproduced below.]

Court File Number ....

.... *(Name of court)*

at .... *Court office address*

Recipient(s)

Full legal name & address for service — street & number, municipality, postal code, telephone & fax and e-mail address (if any).	*Lawyer's name & address — street & number, municipality, postal code, telephone & fax numbers and e-mail address (if any).*

Payor

Full legal name & address for service — street & number, municipality, postal code, telephone & fax numbers and e-mail address (if any).	*Lawyer's name & address — street & number, municipality, postal code, telephone & fax numbers and e-mail address (if any).*

My name is (full legal name)

....

I live in (municipality & province)

....

and I swear/affirm that the following is true:

1. I attach a copy of a

❑ marriage contract

❑ separation agreement

❑ cohabitation agreement

❑ paternity agreement

for filing with the court so that its support provisions can be enforced or changed as if they were a court order.

2. The contract/agreement has not been set aside or disregarded by a court nor has it been changed by agreement of the parties.

Sworn/Affirmed before me at .... *municipality* in .... *province, state or country* on .... *date*	
Commissioner for taking affidavits (Type or print name below if signature is illegible.)	*Signature* *(This form is to be signed in front of a lawyer, justice of the peace, notary public or commissioner for taking affidavits.)*

September 1, 2005

FORM 26C — NOTICE OF TRANSFER OF ENFORCEMENT

[Repealed O. Reg. 76/06, s. 15.]

[Editor's Note: Forms 4 to 39 of the Family Law Rules have been repealed by O. Reg. 76/06, effective May 1, 2006. Pursuant to Family Law Rule 1(9), when a form is referred to by number, the reference is to the form with that number that is described in the Table of Forms at the end of these rules and which is available at www.ontariocourtforms.on.ca. For your convenience, the government form as published on this website is reproduced below.]

Court File Number ....

.... *(Name of court)*

at .... *Court office address*

Recipient(s)

Full legal name & address for service — street & number, municipality, postal code, telephone & fax and e-mail address (if any).	*Lawyer's name & address — street & number, municipality, postal code, telephone & fax numbers and e-mail address (if any).*

Payor

Full legal name & address for service — street & number, municipality, postal code, telephone & fax numbers and e-mail address (if any).	*Lawyer's name & address — street & number, municipality, postal code, telephone & fax numbers and e-mail address (if any).*

TO THE PARTIES IN THIS ENFORCEMENT,

TO THE CLERK OF THE COURT at (list court locations out of which enforcement was carried out)

....

....

AND TO THE SHERIFF FOR (list areas where sheriff has been involved with enforcement)

....

....

❑ I am the recipient named above. The attached

❑ order

❑ domestic contract

❑ paternity agreement

has been withdrawn from the enforcement program run by the Director of the Family Responsibility Office. At my request, the Director assigned to me the enforcement measure(s) listed on the back of this sheet that were started by the Director.

❑ My name is *(full legal name)* ....

I am an authorized agent of the Director of the Family Responsibility Office. The recipient(s) *(name of recipient(s))* .... filed the attached

❑ order

❑ domestic contract

❏ paternity agreement

in the Director's office to be enforced. At my request, the recipient(s) assigned to the Director the enforcement measure(s) listed on the back of this sheet that were started by the recipient(s).

.... *Signature*

.... *Date of signature*

ENFORCEMENT MEASURES BEING TRANSFERRED		
NAME OF ENFORCEMENT MEASURE	**WHERE STARTED**	**WHEN STARTED**

Notes:

If you need more space, you may attach extra sheets and number them.

September 1, 2005

FORM 27 — REQUEST FOR FINANCIAL STATEMENT

[Repealed O. Reg. 76/06, s. 15.]

[Editor's Note: Forms 4 to 39 of the Family Law Rules have been repealed by O. Reg. 76/06, effective May 1, 2006. Pursuant to Family Law Rule 1(9), when a form is referred to by number, the reference is to the form with that number that is described in the Table of Forms at the end of these rules and which is available at www.ontariocourtforms.on.ca. For your convenience, the government form as published on this website is reproduced below.]

Court File Number ....

.... *(Name of court)*

at .... *Court office address*

Recipient(s)

Full legal name & address for service — street & number, municipality, postal code, telephone & fax and e-mail address (if any).	*Lawyer's name & address — street & number, municipality, postal code, telephone & fax numbers and e-mail address (if any).*

Payor

Full legal name & address for service — street & number, municipality, postal code, telephone & fax and e-mail address (if any).	*Lawyer's name & address — street & number, municipality, postal code, telephone & fax numbers and e-mail address (if any).*

TO (name of party)

....

I claim that you have missed payments under an order, domestic contract or paternity agreement, a copy of which is attached to this notice.

YOU MUST PREPARE A FINANCIAL STATEMENT (Form 13) within 15 days of being served with this notice. A blank form of financial statement should accompany or be attached to this notice. If it is missing, you should contact your own lawyer or the court office immediately.

YOU MUST MAIL your completed financial statement within the next 15 days to: *(person & address)*

....

IF YOU DO NOT MAIL THE COMPLETED FINANCIAL STATEMENT AS REQUIRED BY THIS NOTICE, THE COURT MAY ORDER YOU TO DO SO AND YOU MAY THEN BE REQUIRED TO PAY THE COSTS. IF YOU DISOBEY THE ORDER, THE COURT MAY MAKE AN ORDER FOR YOUR IMPRISONMENT.

.... *Signature*

.... *Date of signature*

September 1, 2005

FORM 27A — REQUEST FOR STATEMENT OF INCOME

[Repealed O. Reg. 76/06, s. 15.]

[Editor's Note: Forms 4 to 39 of the Family Law Rules have been repealed by O. Reg. 76/06, effective May 1, 2006. Pursuant to Family Law Rule 1(9), when a form is referred to by number, the reference is to the form with that number that is described in the Table of Forms at the end of these rules and which is available at www.ontariocourtforms.on.ca. For your convenience, the government form as published on this website is reproduced below.]

Court File Number ....

.... *(Name of court)*

at .... *Court office address*

Recipient(s)

Full legal name & address for service — street & number, municipality, postal code, telephone & fax and e-mail address (if any).	*Lawyer's name & address — street & number, municipality, postal code, telephone & fax numbers and e-mail address (if any).*

Payor

Full legal name & address for service — street & number, municipality, postal code, telephone & fax and e-mail address (if any).	*Lawyer's name & address — street & number, municipality, postal code, telephone & fax numbers and e-mail address (if any).*

TO (name and address of income source)

....

I claim that the payor has missed payments under an order, domestic contract or paternity agreement.

YOU MUST PREPARE A STATEMENT OF INCOME in Form 27B concerning the payor named above. A blank form of statement of income should accompany or be attached to this notice. If it is missing, you should contact your own lawyer or the court office immediately.

YOU MUST MAIL the completed statement of income within 10 days of being served with this notice to: *(person & address)*

....

IF YOU DO NOT MAIL THE COMPLETED STATEMENT OF INCOME AS REQUIRED BY THIS NOTICE, THE COURT MAY ORDER YOU TO DO SO AND YOU MAY THEN BE REQUIRED TO PAY THE COURT COSTS.

.... *Signature*

.... *Date of Signature*

September 1, 2005

FORM 27B — STATEMENT OF INCOME FROM INCOME SOURCE

[Repealed O. Reg. 76/06, s. 15.]

[Editor's Note: Forms 4 to 39 of the Family Law Rules have been repealed by O. Reg. 76/06, effective May 1, 2006. Pursuant to Family Law Rule 1(9), when a form is referred to by number, the reference is to the form with that number that is described in the Table of Forms at the end of these rules and which is available at www.ontariocourtforms.on.ca. For your convenience, the government form as published on this website is reproduced below.]

Court File Number ....

.... *(Name of court)*

at .... *Court office address*

Recipient(s)

Full legal name & address for service — street & number, municipality, postal code, telephone & fax and e-mail address (if any).	*Lawyer's name & address — street & number, municipality, postal code, telephone & fax numbers and e-mail address (if any).*

Payor

Full legal name & address for service — street & number, municipality, postal code, telephone & fax numbers and e-mail address (if any).	*Lawyer's name & address — street & number, municipality, postal code, telephone & fax numbers and e-mail address (if any).*

1. My name is *(full legal name)*

   ....

2.

   ❑ I am
   - ❑ an income source of the payor.
   - ❑ an employee of an income source of the payor.
   - ❑ *(Other, specify)*

     ....
     ....

OR

❑ Neither I nor the organization for which I work is an income source of the payor for the following reasons:
- ❑ there is no money owed to the payor on any basis mentioned in paragraph 3 below.
- ❑ the payor has never worked for me or my organization.
- ❑ the payor has worked for me or my organization but stopped working on :*(date)*

  ....
- ❑ *(Other, specify.)*

  ....
  ....

(Strike out paragraph 3 if you are not an income source.)

3. I owe money to the payor on the following basis: *(check one or more boxes below)*

   ❑ wages or salary of $.......... per ....

   ❑ overtime that, over the past 6 months, has amounted to $..........

   ❑ commission, bonus, piece-work allowance or other performance-related payment that, over the past 6 months, has amounted to $..........

   ❑ benefits under an accident, disability or sickness plan that, over the past 6 months, has amounted to $..........

   ❑ a disability, retirement or other pension of $.......... per ....

   ❑ an annuity paying $.......... per ....

❑ vacation pay/severance pay of $ ....

❑ *(Other. specify.)*

....

....

.... *Signature*

.... *Date of signature*

September 1, 2005

FORM 27C — APPOINTMENT FOR FINANCIAL EXAMINATION

[Repealed O. Reg. 76/06, s. 15.]

[Editor's Note: Forms 4 to 39 of the Family Law Rules have been repealed by O. Reg. 76/06, effective May 1, 2006. Pursuant to Family Law Rule 1(9), when a form is referred to by number, the reference is to the form with that number that is described in the Table of Forms at the end of these rules and which is available at www.ontariocourtforms.on.ca. For your convenience, the government form as published on this website is reproduced below.]

Court File Number ....

.... *(Name of court)*

at .... *Court office address*

Recipient(s)

Full legal name & address for service — street & number, municipality, postal code, telephone & fax numbers and e-mail address (if any).	*Lawyer's name & address — street & number, municipality, postal code, telephone & fax numbers and e-mail address (if any).*

Payor

Full legal name & address for service — street & number, municipality, postal code, telephone & fax numbers and e-mail address (if any).	*Lawyer's name & address — street & number, municipality, postal code, telephone & fax numbers and e-mail address (if any).*

TO: *(full legal name of person to be examined)*

....

I claim that you have missed payments under an order, domestic contract or paternity agreement, a copy of which is attached. The purpose of this examination is to find out,

(a) your ability to pay the amount of the money owing; and

(b) your ability to continue obeying the order, domestic contract or paternity agreement.

YOU MUST PREPARE a financial statement in Form 13 and serve it on the recipient or on the recipient's lawyer at least 7 days before the date of the examination. A blank form of financial statement should accompany or be attached to this notice. If it is missing, you should talk to your own lawyer or the court office immediately.

YOU MUST THEN COME TO A FINANCIAL EXAMINATION to be held on *(date)* .... at .... a.m./p.m. at *(place of examination):*

....

You can bring your own lawyer.

YOU MUST BRING WITH YOU TO THE FINANCIAL EXAMINATION the documents or things in your possession or control that are listed on the back of this sheet.

IF YOU DO NOT COME TO THE FINANCIAL EXAMINATION, THE COURT MAY MAKE AN ORDER WITHOUT YOU AND ENFORCE IT AGAINST YOU.

.... *Signature*

.... *Date of signature*

(Set out the nature and the date of every document and give enough OC details to identify every document and thing that the payor is to bring to the examination. Write "NIL" if no document or thing is to be brought to the examination.)

- ❑ A copy of the income tax return that you filed with the Canada Revenue Agency (together with all material filed with the return) for the years .... and a copy of any notice of assessment or reassessment that you received from the Agency for those years.
- ❑ Proof of your income (including pay stubs) for the past .... month(s).
- ❑ A print-out from every bank, trust company, loan corporation, credit union or *caisse populaire* in which you have maintained an account for the past .... month(s) showing all the transactions carried out in account during that period of time.

  ....

  ....

Put a line through any blank space left on this page.

September 1, 2005

FORM 28 — WRIT OF SEIZURE AND SALE

[Repealed O. Reg. 76/06, s. 15.]

[Editor's Note: Forms 4 to 39 of the Family Law Rules have been repealed by O. Reg. 76/06, effective May 1, 2006. Pursuant to Family Law Rule 1(9), when a form is referred to by number, the reference is to the form with that number that is described in the Table of Forms at the end of these rules and which is available at www.ontariocourtforms.on.ca. For your convenience, the government form as published on this website is reproduced below.]

Court File Number

[SEAL] ....

(Name of court)

at ....

Form 28: Writ of Seizure and Sale

Court office address

Recipient(s)

Full legal name & address for service — street & number, municipality, postal code, telephone & fax numbers and e-mail address (if any).	*Lawyer's name & address — street & number, municipality, postal code, telephone & fax numbers and e-mail address (if any).*

Payor

Full legal name & address for service — street & number, municipality, postal code, telephone & fax numbers and e-mail address (if any).	*Lawyer's name & address — street & number, municipality, postal code, telephone & fax numbers and e-mail address (if any).*

TO THE SHERIFF FOR THE (name of area) ....

An order, domestic contract or paternity agreement that is enforceable in this court and that requires the payor to make payments to the recipient is in default.

YOU ARE THEREFORE DIRECTED TO SEIZE AND TO SELL the personal and real property within your area of *(Give full legal name of person or corporation, etc., against whom the writ shall be issued.)*

Surname of payor or name of corporation, etc.		
First given name (individual only)	*Second given name, if any (individual only)*	*Third given name, if any (individual only)*

and to realize from that sale the following sums:

Insert amount to be realized from paragraph 4(b) of the request for a writ of seizure and sale. Insert date that statement of money owed was sworn/affirmed.

(a) $.......... and interest on it at the rate of ....% per year, beginning on *(date)* ....and

(b) your fees and expenses in enforcing this writ.

(Check appropriate box)

Priority for support payments: insert amount from paragraph 3 of request for a writ of seizure and sale.

❑ The sum to be realized includes unpaid support of $ ....
YOU ARE THEREFORE REQUIRED, under subsection 4(1) of the *Creditors' Relief Act*, to give priority to this amount over other judgments and orders.

Assignment of costs to Legal Aid Ontario: insert amount from paragraph 4(c) of request for writ of seizure and sale.

❑ An *Assignment of Judgment of Costs* in the amount of $ .... has been made in favour of Legal Aid Ontario.
YOU ARE THEREFORE REQUIRED, under subsections 46(4) and 47(1) of the *Legal Aid Services Act, 1998*, to deduct this sum from the proceeds of the sale and to pay it to Legal Aid Ontario.

Fine, bond or recognizance

❑ This Writ enforces the sum of $ .... as

- ❑ a fine for contempt of this court
- ❑ a forfeited bond or a forfeited recognizance

and made payable to ❑ Her Majesty the Queen

❑ other *(Specify.)*

YOU ARE THEREFORE REQUIRED, under subsection 143(3) of the *Courts of Justice Act*, to proceed immediately to execute this Writ without a direction to enforce.

YOU ARE FURTHER DIRECTED TO PAY OUT THESE PROCEEDS ACCORDING TO LAW AND TO REPORT ON THE EXECUTION OF THIS WRIT IF REQUIRED BY THE PARTY OR BY THE PARTY'S LAWYER WHO FILED THIS WRIT.

.... *Date of signature*

.... *Signature of the clerk of the court*

Court File Number ....

Name of Payor: ....

Name of recipient(s): ....

FEES				*Full legal name of filing party*:
Fee	*Item*	*Officer*		*Filing party's address for service*:
			....	
			(Name of court)	
			at	*Name, address, telephone & fax numbers and e-mail address (if any) of filing party's lawyer:*
			Court office address	
			Writ of Seizure and Sale	
				Note: This writ has no automatic expiry date. It remains in effect: (a) until it is withdrawal by or on behalf of the party who filed it; or (b) until it is set aside or suspended by order of a court in Ontario.

September 1, 2005

FORM 28A — REQUEST FOR WRIT OF SEIZURE AND SALE

[Repealed O. Reg. 76/06, s. 15.]

[Editor's Note: Forms 4 to 39 of the Family Law Rules have been repealed by O. Reg. 76/06, effective May 1, 2006. Pursuant to Family Law Rule 1(9), when a form is referred to by number, the reference is to the form with that number that is described in the Table of Forms at the end of these rules and which is available at www.ontariocourtforms.on.ca. For your convenience, the government form as published on this website is reproduced below.]

Court File Number ....

.... *(Name of court)*

at .... *Court office address*

Recipient(s)

Full legal name & address for service — street & number, municipality, postal code, telephone & fax and e-mail address (if any).	*Lawyer's name & address — street & number, municipality, postal code, telephone & fax numbers and e-mail address (if any).*

Payor

Full legal name & address for service — street & number, municipality, postal code, telephone & fax numbers and e-mail address (if any).	*Lawyer's name & address — street & number, municipality, postal code, telephone & fax numbers and e-mail address (if any).*

TO THE CLERK OF THE COURT:

1. I am

❑ the person who signed the attached statement of money owed.
❑ the lawyer for the person who signed the attached statement of money owed.
❑ other *(Specify.)* ....

2. The attached statement of money owed contains a claim for $ .... *(Insert the sum from paragraph 13 of the statement of money owed.)*

....

....

3. This claim includes *unpaid support* of $ ...., an amount that has priority over all other judgment debts of the payor's creditors.

4. I request that a writ of seizure and sale be issued, directed to the sheriff of each of the following areas: *(list the areas)* ....

(a) to seize and sell the payor's real and personal property within that area;

(b) to realize from that seizure and sale

❑ the sum set out in paragraph 2 above;
❑ the sum of $ .... *(Set out a sum less than that in paragraph 2 above if you do not want to have all of it enforced by seizure and sale.)*; and

(c) to pay out the proceeds according to law, including payment of $ .... *(write "NIL" if no assignment was made)* to the Legal Aid Ontario in accordance with the attached *Assignment of Judgment of Costs* in favour of Legal Aid Ontario.

.... *Signature*

.... *Date of signature*

NOTE: You must file this request and a freshly prepared statement of money owed in Form 26 with the clerk of the court. If you completed paragraph 4(c) of this request with a dollar amount, a copy of the assignment of costs must be attached to this request and to each writ of seizure and sale that you file with a sheriff and a land registrar.

September 1, 2005

FORM 28B — STATUTORY DECLARATION TO SHERIFF

[Repealed O. Reg. 76/06, s. 15.]

[Editor's Note: Forms 4 to 39 of the Family Law Rules have been repealed by O. Reg. 76/06, effective May 1, 2006. Pursuant to Family Law Rule 1(9), when a form is referred to by number, the reference is to the form with that number that is described in the Table of Forms at the end of these rules and which is available at www.ontariocourtforms.on.ca. For your convenience, the government form as published on this website is reproduced below.]

Court File Number ....

.... *(Name of court)*

at .... *Court office address*

Recipient(s)

Full legal name & address for service — street & number, municipality, postal code, telephone & fax numbers and e-mail address (if any).	*Lawyer's name & address — street & number, municipality, postal code, telephone & fax numbers and e-mail address (if any).*

Payor

Full legal name & address for service — street & number, municipality, postal code, telephone & fax numbers and e-mail address (if any).	*Lawyer's name & address — street & number, municipality, postal code, telephone & fax numbers and e-mail address (if any).*

My name is (full legal name) ....

I live in (municipality & province) ....

and I declare that the following is true:

1. I am

❑ a recipient under a payment order.

❑ an assignee of a recipient under a payment order.

❑ an agent of the Director of the Family Responsibility Office.

❑ other *(Specify.)* ....

2. On *(date)* .... a writ of seizure and sale was issued in this case, a copy of which is attached.

3. Since then, the amount owed by the payor has changed and, as of today, the amount owed stands at $ .... with interest on it at the rate of .... % per year beginning on *(date when interest begins)* ....

4. Since then, the payor has:

❑ legally changed his/her name from .... to ....

❑ used the following alias(es): ....

❑ used the following spelling variation(s) of his or her name or alias(es): ....

5. The amount in paragraph 3 includes unpaid support of $ .... which, under subsection 4(1) of the *Creditors' Relief Act*, gets priority over other judgments and orders.

6. An additional *Assignment of Judgment of Costs* in the amount of *(write NIL if none)* $ .... has been made in favour of Legal Aid Ontario which, under subsections 46(4) and 47(1) of the *Legal Aid Services Act, 1998*, must be deducted from the proceeds of the sale and paid to Legal Aid Ontario.

7. The amount in paragraph 3 includes $ .... as a fine for contempt of this court, a forfeited bond or a forfeited recognizance arising out of a civil proceeding and made payable to, . . . ❑ Her Majesty the Queen ❑ other *(Specify.)* .... and, under subsection 143(3) of the *Courts of Justice Act*, the writ of seizure and sale can be executed immediately to collect that amount without a direction to enforce.

Declared before me at .... *municipality* in .... *province, state or country* on .... *date* .... *Commissioner for taking affidavits* *(Type or print name below if signature is illegible.)*	.... *Signature* *(This form is to be signed in front of a lawyer, justice of the peace, notary public or commissioner for taking affidavits.)*

June 15, 2007

FORM 28C — WRIT OF TEMPORARY SEIZURE

[Repealed O. Reg. 76/06, s. 15.]

[Editor's Note: Forms 4 to 39 of the Family Law Rules have been repealed by O. Reg. 76/06, effective May 1, 2006. Pursuant to Family Law Rule 1(9), when a form is referred to by number, the reference is to the form with that number that is described in the Table of Forms at the end of these rules and which is available at www.ontariocourtforms.on.ca. For your convenience, the government form as published on this website is reproduced below.]

Court File Number

[SEAL] ....

(Name of court)

at .... *Form 28C: Writ of Temporary Seizure*

Court office address

Applicant(s)/Recipient(s) (Strike out inapplicable term.)

Full legal name & address for service — street & number, municipality, postal code, telephone & fax numbers & e-mail address (if any).	*Lawyer's name & address — street & number, municipality, postal code, telephone & fax numbers & e-mail address (if any).*

Respondent/Payor (Strike out inapplicable term.)

Full legal name & address for service — street & number, municipality, postal code, telephone & fax numbers & e-mail address (if any).	*Lawyer's name & address — street & number, municipality, postal code, telephone & fax numbers & e-mail address (if any).*

TO THE SHERIFF FOR THE (name of area) ....

On a motion made by *(name of moving party)* ....

the court gave its permission on *(date)* .... to issue this writ.

YOU ARE THEREFORE DIRECTED TO SEIZE AND TO HOLD the following property within your area of (Give full legal name of person or corporation, etc. against whom the writ shall be issued.)

Surname of respondent/payor or name of corporation, etc.		
First given name (individual only)	*Second given name, if any (individual only)*	*Third given name, if any (individual only)*

Give description of property to be taken and held.

YOU ARE ALSO DIRECTED TO COLLECT AND TO HOLD any income from the property until the writ is withdrawn or until further order of the court.

.... *Date of signature*

.... *Signature of the clerk of the court*

September 1, 2005

FORM 29 — REQUEST FOR GARNISHMENT

[Repealed O. Reg. 76/06, s. 15.]

[Editor's Note: Forms 4 to 39 of the Family Law Rules have been repealed by O. Reg. 76/06, effective May 1, 2006. Pursuant to Family Law Rule 1(9), when a form is referred to by number, the reference is to the form with that number that is described in the Table of Forms at the end of these rules and which is available at www.ontariocourtforms.on.ca. For your convenience, the government form as published on this website is reproduced below.]

Court File Number ....

.... *(Name of court)*

at .... *Court office address*

Recipient(s)

Full legal name & address for service — street & number, municipality, postal code, telephone & fax and e-mail address (if any).	*Lawyer's name & address — street & number, municipality, postal code, telephone & fax numbers and e-mail address (if any).*

Payor

Full legal name & address for service — street & number, municipality, postal code, telephone & fax numbers and e-mail address (if any).	*Lawyer's name & address — street & number, municipality, postal code, telephone & fax numbers and e-mail address (if any).*

TO THE CLERK OF THE COURT:

1. I am

❑ the person who signed the attached statement of money owed.
❑ the lawyer for the person who signed the attached statement of money owed.

❑ an agent for the Director of the Family Responsibility Office.
❑ *(Other, specify.)*

....
....

2. I want to enforce by way of garnishment the sum of $.........., which is the money claimed in the attached statement of money owed. *(If you want to collect ongoing periodic payments as well as arrears, check the box below.)*

❑ I also want the garnishment to collect ongoing payments of $.......... per *(period)*

3. I request that a separate notice of garnishment be issued and sent to each person named in the Appendix to this form, who, I have reason to believe, owes or will owe money to the payor in the amounts described in that Appendix.

.... *Signature of person making request or of person's lawyer*

.... *Date of signature*

NOTE: You must attach one or more sheets as an Appendix in which you name the person or persons who owe or will owe money to the payor. You must also prepare and attach a fresh statement of money owed in Form 26 (one prepared within the past 30 days) to this request and file it with the clerk of the court.

If

(a) the payor's obligation to pay the order, domestic contract or paternity agreement that you are enforcing by this garnishment should expire or be discharged, and

(b) there is no more money owed by the payor under that order, domestic contract or paternity agreement,

or if you simply decide that you no longer want to enforce the order, domestic contract or paternity agreement by means of this garnishment, you must immediately fill out and serve a notice to stop garnishment in Form 29H on the payor and on each garnishee and file it, together with proof of service, with the clerk of the court at the above court office.

Appendix — (page..........)

Name of Garnishee: ....

Garnishee's address: ....

Amount that the garnishee owes or will owe to the payor:

❑ *periodic amounts*
  ❑ *of $..........*

  ❑ *whose dollar figure I do not know*

that are or will be paid on (State frequency of payments. Write "UNKNOWN" if you do not know.) ....

❑ *lump-sum amount*
  ❑ *of $..........*

  ❑ *whose dollar figure I do not know.*

Description of debt owed by the garnishee to the payor:

❑ *wages, commissions or other employment income.*

❑ *rental payments*

❑ *money held at a bank, credit union, etc.*

❑ *pension payments*

❑ *(Other. Specify.)*
....
....

September 1, 2005

FORM 29A — NOTICE OF GARNISHMENT (LUMP-SUM DEBT)

[Repealed O. Reg. 76/06, s. 15.]

[Editor's Note: Forms 4 to 39 of the Family Law Rules have been repealed by O. Reg. 76/06, effective May 1, 2006. Pursuant to Family Law Rule 1(9), when a form is referred to by number, the reference is to the form with that number that is described in the Table of Forms at the end of these rules and which is available at www.ontariocourtforms.on.ca. For your convenience, the government form as published on this website is reproduced below.]

Court File Number ....

[SEAL]

.... *(Name of court)*

at .... *Court office address*

Recipient	Payor
Full legal name & address for service — street & number, municipality, postal code, telephone & fax and e-mail address (if any).	*Full legal name & address for service — street & number, municipality, postal code, telephone & fax and e-mail address (if any).*
Lawyer's name & address — street & number, municipality, postal code, telephone & fax numbers and e-mail address (if any).	*Lawyer's name & address — street & number, municipality, postal code, telephone & fax numbers and e-mail address (if any).*

TO: (garnishee's full legal name and address)

....

ALL DEDUCTIONS MADE UNDER THIS NOTICE MUST TO BE PAID TO

❑ the clerk of the court

❑ the Director of the Family Responsibility Office

at *(address)*...

The payor *(name)* .... has missed payments under a court order, a domestic contract or a paternity agreement that is enforceable in this court or that is enforceable by a garnishment process from outside Ontario and recognized by this court.

The recipient claims that you owe or will owe the payor a debt in the form of one or more lump-sum amounts.. (A debt to the payor includes both a debt payable to the payor alone and a joint debt payable to the payor and one or more other persons.)

YOU MUST THEREFORE PAY TO the clerk of the court or the Director of the Family Responsibility Office (as indicated above)

(a) within 10 days after service of this Notice upon you, ALL MONEY THAT IS NOW PAYABLE BY YOU TO THE PAYOR; and

(b) within 10 days after any future amount becomes payable, ALL MONEY THAT BECOMES PAYABLE BY YOU TO THE PAYOR.

The total amount of your payments is not to exceed $.......... *(Insert the dollar amount by adding the sums in paragraphs 5, 6, 7 and 8 of the statement of money owed or such lesser amount as the recipient chooses to have enforced by way of garnishment.)*

If your debt is jointly owed to the payor and to one or more other persons, you must pay half of the amount now payable or that becomes payable or such fraction as the court may order.

This notice is legally binding on you until it is changed or terminated.

(Check box below if appropriate.)

❑ This notice of garnishment enforces the support provisions of a court order, domestic contract or paternity agreement. Under subsection 4(1) of the *Creditors' Relief Act, YOU MUST GIVE THIS NOTICE OF GARNISHMENT PRIORITY OVER ALL OTHER NOTICES OF GARNISHMENT*, no matter when these other competing notices of garnishment were served on you. For details of the extent of this priority, you should talk to your own lawyer.

Your payment in accordance with this notice is, to the extent of the payment, a valid discharge of your debt to the payor and, in the case of a joint debt to the payor and one or more other persons, a valid discharge of your debt to the payor and the other person(s).

If your debt is jointly owed to the payor and to one or more other persons, *YOU MUST IMMEDIATELY MAIL a notice to co-owner of the debt (Form 29C) to the following persons:*

(a) each other person to whom the joint debt is owed, at the address shown in your own records;

(b) the recipient or the Director of the Family Responsibility Office, depending on who is enforcing the order; and

(c) the clerk of the court.

A blank Form 29C should be attached to this notice. If it is missing, you should talk to your own lawyer or the court office.

If you have reason to believe that you should not to be making the payments required of you by this notice, you have the right to serve a dispute in Form 29F on the parties and file it at the court office within 10 days after service of this notice upon you. You may consult with your lawyer about this. A blank Form 29F (*Dispute from Garnishee*) should be attached to this notice. If it is missing, you should talk to your own lawyer or the court office. You can serve by any method set out in rule 6 of the *Family Law Rules,* including mail, courier and fax. If you serve Form 29F and file it at the court office, the court may hold a garnishment hearing to determine the rights of the parties. In the meantime, serving and filing a dispute does not stop the operation of this notice of garnishment.

If you are the payor's employer,

(a) Section 56.1 of Ontario's *Employment Standards Act* make it unlawful to dismiss or suspend an employee or to threaten to do so on the ground that a garnishment process has been issued in respect of the employee;

(b) section 7 of Ontario's *Wages Act* says that you cannot deduct more than:

(i) 50% of any wages (after statutory deductions) payable to your employee for the enforcement of support; and

(ii) 20% of any wages (after statutory deductions) payable to your employee for the enforcement of money not connected to support.

These percentages can be increased or decreased only by an order of the court. If a copy of such an order is attached to this notice or if it is ever served on you, you must use the percentage given in that court order; and

(c) the *Family Law Rules* state that you MUST give to the clerk of the court and to the person who asked for this garnishment, within 10 days after the end of the payor's employment with you, a written notice,

(i) indicating that the payor has ceased to be employed by you, and

(ii) setting out the date on which the employment ended and the date of the payor's last remuneration from you.

IF YOU DO NOT OBEY THIS NOTICE, THE COURT MAY ORDER YOU TO PAY THE FULL AMOUNT OWED AND THE COSTS INCURRED BY THE RECIPIENT.

IF YOU PAY ANYONE OTHER THAN AS DIRECTED ON THE FRONT OF THIS SHEET, THE COURT MAY ORDER YOU TO MAKE ANOTHER PAYMENT, BUT THIS TIME, TO THE PERSON NAMED IN THIS NOTICE.

.... *Signature of the clerk of the court*

.... *Date of signature*

NOTICE TO THE PAYOR: You have the right to serve and file a dispute in Form 29E at the court office within 10 days after service of this notice on you. You may want to talk to a lawyer about this. A blank Form 29E (Dispute from Payor) should have accompanied this notice when it was served on you. If it is missing, you should talk to your own lawyer or the court office immediately. You can serve by any method set out in rule 6 of the Family Law Rules, including mail, courier and fax. If you serve Form 29E and file it at the court office, the court may hold a garnishment hearing to decide the rights of the parties.

If the garnishee is your employer, the Family Law Rules say that you MUST, within 10 days after the end of your employment with the garnishee, give the clerk of the court and (depending on who is enforcing the garnishment) the recipient or the Director of the Family Responsibility Office, a written notice,

(a) indicating that your employment with the garnishee is ended; and

(b) setting out the date on which your employment ended and the date of your last pay from the garnishee.

Within 10 days after you start any new job or go back to your old one, you MUST give a further written notice giving the name and address of your new employer or saying that you have gone back to work with of your former employment.

September 1, 2005

FORM 29B — NOTICE OF GARNISHMENT (PERIODIC DEBT)

[Repealed O. Reg. 76/06, s. 15.]

[Editor's Note: Forms 4 to 39 of the Family Law Rules have been repealed by O. Reg. 76/06, effective May 1, 2006. Pursuant to Family Law Rule 1(9), when a form is referred to by number, the reference is to the form with that number that is described in the Table of Forms at the end of these rules and which is available at www.ontariocourtforms.on.ca. For your convenience, the government form as published on this website is reproduced below.]

Court File Number ....

[SEAL]

.... *(Name of court)*

at .... *Court office address*

Recipient	Payor
Full legal name & address for service — street & number, municipality, postal code, telephone & fax and e-mail address (if any).	*Full legal name & address for service — street & number, municipality, postal code, telephone & fax and e-mail address (if any).*
Lawyer's name & address — street & number, municipality, postal code, telephone & fax numbers and e-mail address (if any).	*Lawyer's name & address — street & number, municipality, postal code, telephone & fax numbers and e-mail address (if any).*

TO: *(garnishee's full legal name and address)*

....

ALL DEDUCTIONS MADE UNDER THIS NOTICE MUST TO BE PAID TO

❑ the clerk of the court

❑ the Director of the Family Responsibility Office

at *(address)* ....

The payor *(name)* .... has missed payments under a court order, domestic contract or paternity agreement that is enforceable in this court or that is enforceable by a garnishment process from outside Ontario and recognized by this court. The recipient claims that you owe or will owe the payor a debt in the form of wages, salary, pension payments, rent, annuity or other debt that you pay out periodically or by instalments. (A debt to the payor includes both a debt payable to the payor alone and a debt payable jointly to the payor and one or more other persons.)

Check the first circle if you want the garnishment to deduct fixed dollar amounts. If you want the garnishment to deduct by way of percentage, check the second circle below.

❍ *YOU MUST IMMEDIATELY THEREFORE DEDUCT FROM ALL SUCH PAYMENTS MADE BY YOU,*

Insert the dollar amount and frequency as stated in the periodic portion of the order, domestic contract or paternity agreement

❑ to satisfy the payor's ongoing duty to make periodic payments under the order, domestic contract or paternity agreement THE SUM OF $ .... on every *(state frequency)* .... or the equivalent sum according to your regular or established cycle of payment to the payor; and

"Accumulated debts" includes lump-sum orders, fines, forfeitures, accumulated arrears of periodic payments, court costs and interest

❑ to reduce the payor's accumulated debts of $ .... to the recipient under the order, domestic contract or paternity agreement, THE SUM OF $ .... on every (*state frequency*) .... or the equivalent sum according to your regular or established cycle of payment to the payor, OR

Check this circle only if you want the garnishment to deduct by way of percentage.

❍ *YOU MUST IMMEDIATELY THEREFORE DEDUCT FROM ALL SUCH PAYMENTS MADE BY YOU,*

Unless a court order says otherwise, you can deduct no more than 50% of the payor's wages to collect support and no more than 20% to collect

money unrelated to support. There is no percentage ceiling on the deductions from non-wages.

❑ ....% of all wages that are now payable by you to the payor, and

❑ ....% of any debt (other than wages) now payable by you to the payor periodically or by instalments

AND YOU MUST PAY THIS DEDUCTION to clerk or the Director (as indicated above) within 10 days after service of this notice upon you. If your debt is jointly owed to the payor and to one or more other persons, you must pay half of the amount now payable or that becomes payable or such fraction as the court may order.

THIS NOTICE LEGALLY BINDS YOU TO CONTINUE PAYING THESE DEDUCTIONS within 10 days after each payment becomes payable by you to the payor, until this notice is changed or terminated.

(Check box below if appropriate.)

❑ This notice of garnishment enforces the support provisions of a court order, domestic contract or paternity agreement. Under subsection 4(1) of the *Creditors' Relief Act, YOU MUST GIVE THIS NOTICE OF GARNISHMENT PRIORITY OVER ALL OTHER NOTICES OF GARNISHMENT,* no matter when these other competing notices of garnishment were served on you. For details of the extent of this priority, you should talk to your own lawyer.

Your payment in accordance with this *Notice* is, to the extent of the payment, a valid discharge of your debt to the payor and, in the case of a joint debt to the payor and one or more other persons, a valid discharge of your debt to the payor and the other person(s).

If your debt is jointly owed to the payor and to one or more other persons, *YOU MUST IMMEDIATELY MAIL a notice to co-owner of the debt (Form 29C) to the following persons:*

(a) each other person to whom the joint debt is owed, at the address shown in your own records;

(b) the recipient or the Director of the Family Responsibility Office, depending on who is enforcing the order; and

(c) the clerk of the court.

A blank Form 29C should be attached to this notice. If it is missing, you should talk to your own lawyer or the court office.

.If you have reason to believe that you should not to be making the payments required of you by this notice, you have the right to serve and file a dispute in Form 29F at the court office within 10 days after service of this notice upon you. You may consult with your lawyer about this. A blank Form 29F (*Dispute from Garnishee*) should be attached to this notice. If it is missing, you should talk to your own lawyer or the court office. You can serve by any method set out in rule 6 of the *Family Law Rules,* including mail, courier and fax. If you serve Form 29F and file it at the court office, the court may hold a garnishment hearing to determine the rights of the parties. In the meantime, serving and filing a dispute does not stop the operation of this notice of garnishment.

If you are the payor's employer,

(a) Section 56.1 of Ontario's *Employment Standards Act* make it unlawful to dismiss or suspend an employee or to threaten to do so on the ground that a garnishment process has been issued in respect of the employee;

(b) section 7 of Ontario's *Wages Act* says that you cannot deduct more than:

(i) 50% of any wages (after statutory deductions) payable to your employee for the enforcement of support; and

(ii) 20% of any wages (after statutory deductions) payable to your employee for the enforcement of money not connected to support.

These percentages can be increased or decreased only by an order of the court. If a copy of such an order is attached to this *Notice* or if it is ever served on you, you must use the percentage given in that court order; and

(c) the *Family Law Rules* state that you MUST give to the clerk of the court and to the person who asked for this garnishment, within 10 days after the end of the payor's employment with you, a written notice,

(i) indicating that the payor has ceased to be employed by you, and

(ii) setting out the date on which the employment ended and the date of the payor's last remuneration from you.

IF YOU DO NOT OBEY THIS NOTICE, THE COURT MAY ORDER YOU TO PAY THE FULL AMOUNT OWED AND THE COSTS INCURRED BY THE RECIPIENT.

IF YOU PAY ANYONE OTHER THAN AS DIRECTED ON THE FRONT OF THIS SHEET, THE COURT MAY ORDER YOU TO MAKE ANOTHER PAYMENT, BUT THIS TIME, TO THE PERSON NAMED IN THIS NOTICE.

.... *Signature of the clerk of the court*

.... *Date of signature*

NOTICE TO THE PAYOR: You have the right to serve and file a dispute in Form 29E at the court office within 10 days after service of this notice on you. You may want to talk to a lawyer about this. A blank Form 29E (Dispute from Payor) should have accompanied this notice when it was served on you. If it is missing, you should talk to your own lawyer or the court office immediately. You can serve by any method set out in rule 6 of the Family Law Rules, including mail, courier and fax. If you serve Form 29E and file it at the court office, the court may hold a garnishment hearing to decide the rights of the parties.

If the garnishee is your employer, the Family Law Rules say that you MUST, within 10 days after the end of your employment with the garnishee, give the clerk of the court and (depending on who is enforcing the garnishment) the recipient or the Director of the Family Responsibility Office, a written notice,

(a) indicating that your employment with the garnishee is ended; and

(b) setting out the date on which your employment ended and the date of your last pay from the garnishee.

Within 10 days after you start any new job or go back to your old one, you MUST give a further written notice giving the name and address of your new employer or saying that you have gone back to work with of your former employment.

September 1, 2005

FORM 29C — NOTICE TO CO-OWNER OF DEBT

[Repealed O. Reg. 76/06, s. 15.]

[Editor's Note: Forms 4 to 39 of the Family Law Rules have been repealed by O. Reg. 76/06, effective May 1, 2006. Pursuant to Family Law Rule 1(9), when a form is referred to by number, the reference is to the form with that number that is described in the Table of Forms at the end of these rules and which is available at www.ontariocourtforms.on.ca. For your convenience, the government form as published on this website is reproduced below.]

Court File Number ....

.... *(Name of court)*

at .... *Court office address*

Recipient(s)	**Payor**
Full legal name & address for service — street & number, municipality, postal code, telephone & fax and e-mail address (if any).	*Full legal name & address for service — street & number, municipality, postal code, telephone & fax and e-mail address (if any).*
Lawyer's name & address — street & number, municipality, postal code, telephone & fax numbers and e-mail address (if any).	*Lawyer's name & address — street & number, municipality, postal code, telephone & fax numbers and e-mail address (if any).*

TO: (co-owner's full legal name and address)

A court case between the recipient and the payor has resulted in a court order requiring the payor to pay money to the recipient. The recipient or a person enforcing this order on the recipient's behalf has served me or my business with a notice of garnishment, claiming to intercept a debt that I or my business is supposed to owe and to pay to the payor. Under the law, a debt to the payor includes both a debt payable to the payor alone and a debt payable jointly to the payor and one or more other persons. According to my records or the records of my business, you are such an "other person" who shares in the debt that I or my business owe to the payor.

❑ In accordance with this notice of garnishment, I have paid out one half

❑ In accordance with a court order, I have paid out $.......... of the debt that I or my business jointly owes to you and the payor. This money is being held for 30 days by:

❑ the clerk of the court

❑ the Director of the Family Responsibility Office

at *(address)* ....

IF YOU BELIEVE THAT I OR MY BUSINESS HAVE PAID OUT MONEY THAT LEGALLY BELONGS TO YOU, you have 30 days from the service of this notice to serve Form 29G (*Dispute from Co-owner of Debt*) and file it with the court. You can get a copy of this form from your own lawyer or from the court office. You must then serve a completed copy of this form to the following persons:

(a) me or my business at the address given below;

(b) the payor and the recipient; and

(c) the clerk of the court or the Director, depending on who is holding the money.

You can serve by any method set out in rule 6 of the *Family Law Rules,* including mail, courier and fax. Once you have served this form, you must then file it with the court with proof of service (Form 6B). The court may then hold a garnishment hearing to determine your rights.

IF YOU FAIL TO DO THIS WITHIN 30 DAYS, you may not later challenge the recipient's garnishment of the debt that I or my business jointly owes to you and the payor.

.... *Signature of person preparing this notice or of person's lawyer*

.... Date of signature

.... *Typed or printed name, address for service, telephone & fax numbers and e-mail address of person or of person's lawyer*

September 1, 2005

FORM 29D — STATUTORY DECLARATION OF INDEXED SUPPORT

[Repealed O. Reg. 76/06, s. 15.]

[Editor's Note: Forms 4 to 39 of the Family Law Rules have been repealed by O. Reg. 76/06, effective May 1, 2006. Pursuant to Family Law Rule 1(9), when a form is referred to by number, the reference is to the form with that number that is described in the Table of Forms at the end of these rules and which is available at www.ontariocourtforms.on.ca. For your convenience, the government form as published on this website is reproduced below.]

Court File Number ....

.... *(Name of court)*

at .... *Court office address*

Recipient(s)

Full legal name & address for service — street & number, municipality, postal code, telephone & fax and e-mail address (if any).	*Lawyer's name & address — street & number, municipality, postal code, telephone & fax numbers and e-mail address (if any).*

Payor

Full legal name & address for service — street & number, municipality, postal code, telephone & fax numbers and e-mail address (if any).	*Lawyer's name & address — street & number, municipality, postal code, telephone & fax numbers and e-mail address (if any).*

Garnishee

Full legal name & address for service — street & number, municipality, postal code, telephone & fax numbers and e-mail address (if any).	*Lawyer's name & address — street & number, municipality, postal code, telephone & fax numbers and e-mail address (if any).*

My name is (full legal name) ....

I live in (municipality & province) .... *and I declare that the following is true:*

1. I am

- ❑ a recipient under a support order or the support provisions of a domestic contract or paternity agreement.
- ❑ an assignee of a recipient under a support order or the support provisions of a domestic contract or paternity agreement.
- ❑ an agent of the Director of the Family Responsibility Office.
- ❑ *(Other. Specify.)*

  ....

  ....

2. On *(date)* ...., a notice of garnishment was issued to the garnishee to enforce a support order or the support provisions of a domestic contract or paternity agreement that indexed the periodic payments for inflation.

3. On *(date)* ...., the amount of support was automatically adjusted for inflation as set out in the order, contract or agreement.

4. As a result of this adjustment, the garnishee should now be making the following deductions: *(State new level of deductions)*

Put a line through any blank space left on this page.

Declared before before me at .... *municipality* in .... *province, state or country* on .... *date*

____
Commissioner for taking affidavits (Type or print name below if signature is illegible.)

____
Signature
(This form is to be signed in front of a lawyer, justice of the peace, notary public or commissioner for taking affidavits.)

NOTE: This declaration must be served on the garnishee and the payor together with blank forms of dispute and must then be filed with the clerk of the court. You can serve by any means allowed in rule 6 of the Family Law Rules, including mail, courier nad fax. The filing with the clerk of the court must be accompanied by proof of service (Form 6B).

NOTICE TO GARNISHEE: From the moment that you are served with this declaration, you must treat the notice of garnishment as if it now required you to make the deductions set out in paragraph 4 of this declaration. Failure to do so is the same as disobeying the Notice of Garnishment.

NOTICE TO PAYOR AND GARNISHEE: You have the right to serve and file a dispute in Form 29E (Dispute from Payor) or Form 29F (Dispute from Garnishee) at the court office within 10 days after service of this declaration on you if you have legal reasons for objecting to the changes to the notice of garnishment. You may want to talk to a lawyer about this. A blank form of dispute should have accompanied this declaration when it was served on you. If it is missing, you should talk to your own lawyer or the court office immediately. If this is what you want to do, you must serve your dispute on the other parties. You can serve by any means allowed in rule 6 of the Family Law Rules, including mail, courier nad fax. Once the dispute has been served, you must file it with the clerk of the court. The filing must be accompanied by proof of service (Form 6B). If you serve and file your dispute, the court may hold a garnishment hearing to decide the rights of the parties.

September 1, 2005

FORM 29E — DISPUTE (PAYOR)

[Repealed O. Reg. 76/06, s. 15.]

[Editor's Note: Forms 4 to 39 of the Family Law Rules have been repealed by O. Reg. 76/06, effective May 1, 2006. Pursuant to Family Law Rule 1(9), when a form is referred to by number, the reference is to the form with that number that is described in the Table of Forms at the end of these rules and which is available at www.ontariocourtforms.on.ca. For your convenience, the government form as published on this website is reproduced below.]

Court File Number ....

.... *(Name of court)*

at .... *Court office address*

Recipient(s)

Full legal name & address for service — street & number, municipality, postal code, telephone & fax and e-mail address (if any).	*Lawyer's name & address — street & number, municipality, postal code, telephone & fax numbers and e-mail address (if any).*

Payor

Full legal name & address for service — street & number, municipality, postal code, telephone & fax numbers and e-mail address (if any).	*Lawyer's name & address — street & number, municipality, postal code, telephone & fax numbers and e-mail address (if any).*

Garnishee

Full legal name & address for service — street & number, municipality, postal code, telephone & fax numbers and e-mail address (if any).	*Lawyer's name & address — street & number, municipality, postal code, telephone & fax numbers and e-mail address (if any).*

My name is (full legal name) ....

I live in (municipality & province) .... *and I swear/affirm that the following is true:*

1. I am the payor in this garnishment case.

2. I dispute

❑ the notice of garnishment issued on

❑ the statutory declaration of indexed support made on

(date) ...., for the following reason(s): *(State the reason or reasons for your dispute in numbered paragraphs.)*

Put a line through any blank space left on this page.

NOTE: Merely serving and filing this dispute will not stop the garnishment process. It can be stopped at the recipient's request if the receipient agrees with the reasons for your dispute. It can also be stopped by a court order at a garnishment hearing. If you want the court to hold a hearing, you must check the box in the frame below.

❑	NOTICE TO THE CLERK OF THE COURT AND TO ALL PARTIES: I am making a request for a garnishment hearing in which the court can rule on this dispute.

Sworn/Affirmed before me at .... *municipality* in .... *province, state or country* on .... *date*	
	Signature
Commissioner for taking affidavits (Type or print name below if signature is illegible.)	*(This form is to be signed in front of a lawyer, justice of the peace, notary public or commissioner for taking affidavits.)*

NOTICE TO RECIPIENT: Please examine this dispute. If you disagree with it and if the payor has not asked for a garnishment hearing, you yourself may ask to have a court hearing. You may want to talk to your own lawyer about this. You have 10 days from the date of being served with this document to decide whether to have a court hearing. If you want a hearing, you or your lawyer have 10 days within which to ask the clerk of the court, either in person or in writing, to mail out to you, to the payor, to the garnishee and to the co-owner of a joint debt (if any) a notice of garnishment hearing (Form 29H). At that hearing, the judge will give you and the other parties a chance to be heard and may make an order that can affect the rights of all parties.

September 1, 2005

FORM 29F — DISPUTE (GARNISHEE)

[Repealed O. Reg. 76/06, s. 15.]

[Editor's Note: Forms 4 to 39 of the Family Law Rules have been repealed by O. Reg. 76/06, effective May 1, 2006. Pursuant to Family Law Rule 1(9), when a form is referred to by number, the reference is to the form with that number that is described in the Table of Forms at the end of these rules and which is available at www.ontariocourtforms.on.ca. For your convenience, the government form as published on this website is reproduced below.]

Court File Number ....

.... *(Name of court)*

at .... *Court office address*

Recipient(s)

Full legal name & address for service — street & number, municipality, postal code, telephone & fax and e-mail address (if any).	*Lawyer's name & address — street & number, municipality, postal code, telephone & fax numbers and e-mail address (if any).*

Payor

Full legal name & address for service — street & number, municipality, postal code, telephone & fax numbers and e-mail address (if any).	*Lawyer's name & address — street & number, municipality, postal code, telephone & fax numbers and e-mail address (if any).*

Garnishee

Full legal name & address for service — street & number, municipality, postal code, telephone & fax numbers and e-mail address (if any).	*Lawyer's name & address — street & number, municipality, postal code, telephone & fax numbers and e-mail address (if any).*

1 I am the garnishee in this garnishment case.

2. I am not legally required to pay

❑ the amounts set out in the notice of garnishment issued on
❑ the changed amounts set out in the statutory declaration of indexed support made on

(date) ...., for the following reason(s):

❑ I do not owe and do not expect to owe any money to the payor because:
❑ the payor has never worked for me.

❑ the payor stopped working for me on *(date)* ....

❑ I owed the payor money and paid it in full by *(date)* ....

❑ I do not hold any money in trust for or to the credit of the payor.
❑ *(Other. Specify.)*
....
....

❑ I owe or will owe money to the payor, but it cannot be seized by garnishment because *(State reasons for legal exemption.)*
❑ *(Other grounds. Specify.)*
....
....

Put a line through any blank space left on this page.

NOTE: Merely serving and filing this dispute will not stop the garnishment process. It can be stopped at the recipient's request if the receipient agrees with the reasons for your dispute. It can also be stopped by a court order at a garnishment hearing. If you want the court to hold a hearing, you must check the box in the frame below.

❑	*NOTICE TO THE CLERK OF THE COURT AND TO ALL PARTIES: I am making a request for a garnishment hearing in which the court can rule on this dispute.*

.... *Signature of garnishee*

.... *Date of signature*

NOTICE TO RECIPIENT: Please examine this dispute. If you disagree with it and if the garnishee has not asked for a garnishment hearing, you yourself may ask to have a court hearing. You may want to talk to your own lawyer about this. You have 10 days from the date of being served with this document to decide whether to have a court hearing. If you want a hearing, you or your lawyer have 10 days within which to ask the clerk of the court, either in person or in writing, to mail out to you, to the payor, to the garnishee and to the co-owner of a joint debt (if any) a notice of garnishment hearing (Form 29H). At that hearing, the judge will give you and the other parties a chance to be heard and may make an order that can affect the rights of all parties.

September 1, 2005

FORM 29G — DISPUTE (CO-OWNER OF DEBT)

[Repealed O. Reg. 76/06, s. 15.]

[Editor's Note: Forms 4 to 39 of the Family Law Rules have been repealed by O. Reg. 76/06, effective May 1, 2006. Pursuant to Family Law Rule 1(9), when a form is referred to by number, the reference is to the form with that number that is described in the Table of Forms at the end of these rules and which is available at www.ontariocourtforms.on.ca. For your convenience, the government form as published on this website is reproduced below.]

Court File Number ....

.... *(Name of court)*

at .... *Court office address*

Recipient(s)

Full legal name & address for service — street & number, municipality, postal code, telephone & fax and e-mail address (if any).	*Lawyer's name & address — street & number, municipality, postal code, telephone & fax numbers and e-mail address (if any).*

Payor

Full legal name & address for service — street & number, municipality, postal code, telephone & fax numbers and e-mail address (if any).	*Lawyer's name & address — street & number, municipality, postal code, telephone & fax numbers and e-mail address (if any).*

Garnishee

Full legal name & address for service — street & number, municipality, postal code, telephone & fax numbers and e-mail address (if any).	*Lawyer's name & address — street & number, municipality, postal code, telephone & fax numbers and e-mail address (if any).*

1. I am a person who shares in the debt that the garnishee in this garnishment case is supposed to owe to the payor.

2. I make a claim on the money that the garnishee paid out and that is being temporarily held for the recipient's benefit as follows: *(In separately numbered paragraphs, indicate the amount that you are claiming to be yours and set out the legal basis for your claim.)*

Put a line through any blank space left on this page.

NOTE: Merely serving and filing this dispute will not stop the garnishment process. It can be stopped at the recipient's request if the receipient agrees with the reasons for your dispute. It can also be stopped by a court order at a garnishment hearing. If you want the court to hold a hearing, you must check the box in the frame below.

❑	NOTICE TO THE CLERK OF THE COURT AND TO ALL PARTIES: I am making a request for a garnishment hearing in which the court can rule on this dispute.

.... *Signature of co-owner of debt*

.... *Date of signature*

NOTICE TO RECIPIENT: Please examine this dispute. If you disagree with it and if the co-owner of the debt has not asked for a garnishment hearing, you yourself may ask to have a court hearing. You may want to talk to your own lawyer about this. You have 10 days from the date of being served with this document to decide whether to have a court hearing. If you want a hearing, you or your lawyer have 10 days within which to ask the clerk of the court, either in person or in writing, to mail out to you, to the payor, to the garnishee and to the co-owner of a joint debt (if any) a notice of garnishment hearing (Form 29H). At that hearing, the judge will give you and the other parties a chance to be heard and may make an order that can affect the rights of all parties.

September 1, 2005

FORM 29H — NOTICE OF GARNISHMENT HEARING

[Repealed O. Reg. 76/06, s. 15.]

[Editor's Note: Forms 4 to 39 of the Family Law Rules have been repealed by O. Reg. 76/06, effective May 1, 2006. Pursuant to Family Law Rule 1(9), when a form is referred to by number, the reference is to the form with that number that is described in the Table of Forms at the end of these rules and which is available at www.ontariocourtforms.on.ca. For your convenience, the government form as published on this website is reproduced below.]

Court File Number ....

[SEAL]

.... *(Name of court)*

at .... *Court office address*

Recipient(s)

Full legal name & address for service — street & number, municipality, postal code, telephone & fax and e-mail address (if any).	*Lawyer's name & address — street & number, municipality, postal code, telephone & fax numbers and e-mail address (if any).*

Payor

Full legal name & address for service — street & number, municipality, postal code, telephone & fax numbers and e-mail address (if any).	*Lawyer's name & address — street & number, municipality, postal code, telephone & fax numbers and e-mail address (if any).*

Garnishee

Full legal name & address for service — street & number, municipality, postal code, telephone & fax numbers and e-mail address (if any).	*Lawyer's name & address — street & number, municipality, postal code, telephone & fax numbers and e-mail address (if any).*

TO THE PARTIES:

THE COURT WILL HOLD A HEARING on *(date)* ...., at .... a.m./p.m. or as soon as possible after that time, at *(place of hearing)* .... because *(Check the appropriate box or boxes.)*

❑ a dispute has been filed by the
- ❑ payor
- ❑ garnishee
- ❑ co-owner of a debt

❑ it is claimed that the garnishee has not paid any money

❑ it is claimed that the garnishee has paid less than the required amount money

and the clerk of the court has received a request that a garnishment hearing be held.

IF YOU DO NOT COME TO COURT, AN ORDER MAY BE MADE WITHOUT YOU AND ENFORCED AGAINST YOU.

.... *Signature of the clerk of the court*

.... *Date of signature*

NOTE: Where a dispute has been served and filed, a photocopy of it should be attached to this notice. If it is missing, you should talk to the court office immediately.

September 1, 2005

FORM 29I — NOTICE TO STOP GARNISHMENT

[Repealed O. Reg. 76/06, s. 15.]

[Editor's Note: Forms 4 to 39 of the Family Law Rules have been repealed by O. Reg. 76/06, effective May 1, 2006. Pursuant to Family Law Rule 1(9), when a form is referred to by number, the reference is to the form with that number that is described in the Table of Forms at the end of these rules and which is available at www.ontariocourtforms.on.ca. For your convenience, the government form as published on this website is reproduced below.]

Court File Number ....

.... *(Name of court)*

at .... *Court office address*

Recipient(s)

Full legal name & address for service — street & number, municipality, postal code, telephone & fax and e-mail address (if any).	*Lawyer's name & address — street & number, municipality, postal code, telephone & fax numbers and e-mail address (if any).*

Payor

Full legal name & address for service — street & number, municipality, postal code, telephone & fax numbers and e-mail address (if any).	*Lawyer's name & address — street & number, municipality, postal code, telephone & fax numbers and e-mail address (if any).*

Garnishee

Full legal name & address for service — street & number, municipality, postal code, telephone & fax numbers and e-mail address (if any).	*Lawyer's name & address — street & number, municipality, postal code, telephone & fax numbers and e-mail address (if any).*

TO: (name of garnishee) .... *AND TO*

❑ *THE CLERK OF THE COURT*:

❑ *THE SHERIFF OF (area)* ....

My name is: *(full legal name)* ....

I am

❑ the person who asked for the garnishment in this case.

❑ the lawyer for the person who asked for the garnishment in this case.

❑ the person who continued this garnishment under a transfer of enforcement.

❑ the lawyer for the person who continued this garnishment under a transfer of enforcement.

❑ an agent for the Director of the Family Responsibility Office.
❑ *(Other. Specify.)*

....
....

The notice of garnishment issued on *(date)* ...., by the clerk of the court is withdrawn today.

YOU ARE THEREFORE DIRECTED TO STOP FURTHER PAYMENTS UNDER THE GARNISHMENT.

.... *Signature of person withdrawing garnishment*

.... *Date of signature*

September 1, 2005

FORM 29J — STATEMENT TO GARNISHEE FINANCIAL INSTITUTION RE SUPPORT

[Repealed O. Reg. 76/06, s. 15.]

[Editor's Note: Forms 4 to 39 of the Family Law Rules have been repealed by O. Reg. 76/06, effective May 1, 2006. Pursuant to Family Law Rule 1(9), when a form is referred to by number, the reference is to the form with that number that is described in the Table of Forms at the end of these rules and which is available at www.ontariocourtforms.on.ca. For your convenience, the government form as published on this website is reproduced below.]

Court File Number ....

____

(Name of court)

at ______________________________

Court office address

Recipient(s)

Full legal name & address for service — street & number, municipality, postal code, telephone & fax numbers and e-mail address (if any).	*Lawyer's name & address — street & number, municipality, postal code, telephone & fax numbers and e-mail address (if any).*

Payor

Full legal name & address for service — street & number, municipality, postal code, telephone & fax numbers and e-mail address (if any).	*Lawyer's name & address — street & number, municipality, postal code, telephone & fax numbers and e-mail address (if any).*

Payor

Garnishee

Full legal name & address for service — street & number, municipality, postal code, telephone & fax numbers and e-mail address (if any).	*Lawyer's name & address — street & number, municipality, postal code, telephone & fax numbers and e-mail address (if any).*

My name is *(full legal name)* . . . .

I live in *(municipality & province)* . . . .

The following statements are true to the best of my knowledge:

1. I am

❑ a recipient under a support order or the support provisions of a domestic contract or paternity agreement that is enforceable by this court.

❑ an assignee of a recipient under a support order or the support provisions of a domestic contract or paternity agreement.

❑ an agent of the Director of the Family Responsibility Office.

2. The payor's full name is

❑ . . . .
❑ unknown.

3. The payor commonly uses the name(s): . . . .

(Either paragraph 4 or 5 must be completed. If both known, complete both.)

4. The payor's date of birth is . . . .

5. The payor's social insurance number is . . . .

Date of signature	*Signature*

NOTE: Under rule 29(6.1) of the Family Law Rules, this form (29J) must be attached to Forms 29A, 29B, 29D, 29E, 29G, 29H or 29I when they are served on a bank or other financial institution at a central location. Under regulations made under the federal Bank Act, Cooperative Credit Associations Act and Trust and Loan Companies Act, a notice of garnishment for support payments against a bank or other federally regulated financial institution must be served on a central location established and published by each bank or financial institution.

September 1, 2005

FORM 30 — NOTICE OF DEFAULT HEARING

[Repealed O. Reg. 76/06, s. 15.]

[Editor's Note: Forms 4 to 39 of the Family Law Rules have been repealed by O. Reg. 76/06, effective May 1, 2006. Pursuant to Family Law Rule 1(9), when a form is referred to by number, the reference is to the form with that number that is described in the Table of Forms at the end of these rules and which is available at www.ontariocourtforms.on.ca. For your convenience, the government form as published on this website is reproduced below.]

Court File Number ....

[SEAL]

.... *(Name of court)*

at .... *Court office address*

Recipient(s)

Full legal name & address for service — street and number, municipality, postal code, telephone & fax numbers and e-mail address (if any).	*Lawyer's name & address — street and number, municipality, postal code, telephone & fax numbers and e-mail address (if any).*

Payor

Full legal name & address for service — street and number, municipality, postal code, telephone & fax numbers and e-mail address (if any).	*Lawyer's name & address — street and number, municipality, postal code, telephone & fax numbers and e-mail address (if any).*

TO (name of payor) ....

YOU MUST COME TO COURT on (date) ...., at .... a.m./p.m. or as soon after that time as the court can hear the matter, at *(place of hearing)* ....

It is claimed by the recipient or on the recipient's behalf that you have missed support payments under an order, domestic contract or paternity agreement. Details of the claim against you can be found in the attached copy of the statement of money owed. If it is missing, you should contact the court office immediately. The court has been asked to hold a default hearing under section 41 of the *Family Responsibility and Support Arrears Enforcement Act,* in which you will be required to explain not only the missed payments mentioned in the statement of money owed, but also any payments missed right up to the day when the court holds the hearing.

YOU MUST FILL OUT the attached blank forms of the financial statement (Form 13) and the default dispute (Form 30B), serve a copy of the completed forms on the recipient's lawyer, or on the recipient if the recipient has no lawyer, or on the Director of the Family Responsibility Office, and then file the completed forms, together with proof of service (Form 6B), at the court office, all within 10 days after service of this notice on you. You can use any method of service allowed under rule 6 of the Family Law Rules, including mail, courier or fax. If the blank forms are missing, you must talk to the court office immediately.

IF YOU DO NOT FILL OUT AND SERVE THE FINANCIAL STATEMENT OR IF YOU DO NOT COME TO COURT AS REQUIRED BY THIS NOTICE, A WARRANT MAY BE ISSUED FOR YOUR ARREST TO BRING YOU TO COURT.

You should bring with you to the default hearing any documents (such as cancelled cheques) that you need to prove that you made payments that are claimed to be missing. You may bring your own lawyer with you.

AT THE DEFAULT HEARING, THE COURT MAY MAKE AN ORDER AGAINST YOU, INCLUDING AN ORDER FOR YOUR IMPRISONMENT FOR UP TO 180 DAYS. YOU MAY ALSO BE ORDERED TO PAY COSTS.

IF YOU PAY THE AMOUNT OF THE MISSING PAYMENTS ON OR BEFORE THE DAY OF THE HEARING, YOU MAY STILL BE REQUIRED TO COME TO COURT AND TO PAY COSTS.

.... *Signature of clerk of the court*

.... *Date of signature*

September 1, 2005

FORM 30A — REQUEST FOR DEFAULT HEARING

[Repealed O. Reg. 76/06, s. 15.]

[Editor's Note: Forms 4 to 39 of the Family Law Rules have been repealed by O. Reg. 76/06, effective May 1, 2006. Pursuant to Family Law Rule 1(9), when a form is referred to by number, the reference is to the form with that number that is described in the Table of Forms at the end of these rules and which is available at www.ontariocourtforms.on.ca. For your convenience, the government form as published on this website is reproduced below.]

Court File Number ....

.... *(Name of court)*

at .... *Court office address*

Recipient(s)

Full legal name & address for service — street & number, municipality, postal code, telephone & fax and e-mail address (if any).	*Lawyer's name & address — street & number, municipality, postal code, telephone & fax numbers and e-mail address (if any).*

Payor

Full legal name & address for service — street & number, municipality, postal code, telephone & fax numbers and e-mail address (if any).	*Lawyer's name & address — street & number, municipality, postal code, telephone & fax numbers and e-mail address (if any).*

TO THE CLERK OF THE COURT:

1. I am

❑ the person who signed the attached statement of money owed.
❑ the lawyer for the person who signed the attached statement of money owed.

❏ *(Other. Specify.)*
....
....

2. The payor has missed support payments in the amount of $ ...., as detailed in the attached statement of money owed.

3. I request that a notice of default hearing be issued requiring the payor to come to court to explain the missed payments at a hearing under section 41 of the *Family Responsibility and Support Arrears Enforcement Act.*

.... *Signature*

.... *Date of signature*

NOTE: You must prepare and attach a fresh statement of money owed (one that has been prepared within the past 30 days) to this request when you file it with the clerk of the court. Then, in the week leading up to the default hearing, you must file an updated statement of money owed.

September 1, 2005

FORM 30B — DEFAULT DISPUTE

[Repealed O. Reg. 76/06, s. 15.]

[Editor's Note: Forms 4 to 39 of the Family Law Rules have been repealed by O. Reg. 76/06, effective May 1, 2006. Pursuant to Family Law Rule 1(9), when a form is referred to by number, the reference is to the form with that number that is described in the Table of Forms at the end of these rules and which is available at www.ontariocourtforms.on.ca. For your convenience, the government form as published on this website is reproduced below.]

Court File Number ....

.... *(Name of court)*

at .... *Court office address*

Recipient(s)

Full legal name & address for service — street & number, municipality, postal code, telephone & fax and e-mail address (if any).	*Lawyer's name & address — street & number, municipality, postal code, telephone & fax numbers and e-mail address (if any).*

Payor

Full legal name & address for service — street & number, municipality, postal code, telephone & fax numbers and e-mail address (if any).	*Lawyer's name & address — street & number, municipality, postal code, telephone & fax numbers and e-mail address (if any).*

My name is *(full legal name)* ....

I live in *(municipality & province)* .... and I swear/affirm that the following is true:

1. I am the person named as payor in this case.

(Check off and fill in appropriate paragraphs below. Paragraphs that do not apply to you may be struck out and initialled.)

❑ 2. I have not missed any support payments as claimed in the statement of money owed because: *(Set out your reasons for saying that there are no missed payments.)*

❑ 3. I do not owe the amount claimed in the statement of money owed. I owe instead the sum of $........... The reason for the difference in the amounts is:

(Set out your explanation, if any and if known, for the difference. If you have paid all the money that you claim to owe here, ignore and strike out paragraphs 4 and 5 below; if not, go to paragraph 5 on the other side to give your reasons for non-payment.)

Put a line through any blank space left on this page.

❑ 4. I owe the amount claimed in the statement of money owed. *(Go to paragraph 5 below to give your reasons for not paying.)*

❑ 5. My reasons for not paying the money that I owe are: *(State your reasons.)*

Put a line through any blank space left on this page.

Sworn/Affirmed before me at .... *municipality* in .... *province, state or country* on .... *date*	
Commissioner for taking affidavits (Type or print name below if signature is illegible.)	*Signature* *(This form is to be signed in front of a lawyer, justice of the peace, notary public or commissioner for taking affidavits.)*

September 1, 2005

FORM 31 — NOTICE OF CONTEMPT MOTION

[Repealed O. Reg. 76/06, s. 15.]

[Editor's Note: Forms 4 to 39 of the Family Law Rules have been repealed by O. Reg. 76/06, effective May 1, 2006. Pursuant to Family Law Rule 1(9), when a form is referred to by number, the reference is to the form with that number that is described in the Table of Forms at the end of these rules and which is available at www.ontariocourtforms.on.ca. For your convenience, the government form as published on this website is reproduced below.]

Court File Number ....

[SEAL]

.... *(Name of court)*

at .... Court office address

Applicant(s)/Recipient(s) (Strike out inapplicable term.)

Full legal name & address for service — street and number, municipality, postal code, telephone & fax numbers and e-mail address (if any).	*Lawyer's name & address — street and number, municipality, postal code, telephone & fax numbers and e-mail address (if any).*

Respondent/Payor (Strike out inapplicable term.)

Full legal name & address for service — street and number, municipality, postal code, telephone & fax numbers and e-mail address (if any).	*Lawyer's name & address — street and number, municipality, postal code, telephone & fax numbers and e-mail address (if any).*

TO: (name of person against whom contempt motion is made) ....

The person making this motion or the person's lawyer must contact the clerk of the court by telephone or otherwise to choose a time and date when the court could hear this motion

YOU MUST COME TO COURT AT: (place of hearing) ....

ON (date) ...., at .... a.m./p.m. and to remain until the court has dealt with the case.

A motion will be made by *(moving party's name)* .... for a finding that you are in contempt of the court because you: *(Briefly state details of contempt.)* ....

The evidence against you is set out in the affidavit(s) attached to this notice. If the document(s) is/are missing, you must talk to the court office immediately.

IF YOU ARE FOUND IN CONTEMPT OF THE COURT, THE COURT MAY MAKE AN ORDER TO IMPRISON YOU, TO PAY A FINE AND TEMPORARILY TO SEIZE YOUR PROPERTY. YOU MAY ALSO BE ORDERED TO PAY COSTS.

IF YOU DO NOT COME TO COURT, A WARRANT MAY BE ISSUED FOR YOUR ARREST TO BRING YOU TO COURT.

.... Signature of person making this motion or of person's lawyer

.... Date of signature

.. Typed or printed name, address for service, telephone and fax numbers and e-mail address of person or of person's lawyer

September 1, 2005

FORM 32 — BOND (RECOGNIZANCE)

[Repealed O. Reg. 76/06, s. 15.]

[Editor's Note: Forms 4 to 39 of the Family Law Rules have been repealed by O. Reg. 76/06, effective May 1, 2006. Pursuant to Family Law Rule 1(9), when a form is referred to by number, the reference is to the form with that number that is described in the Table of Forms at the end of these rules and which is available at www.ontariocourtforms.on.ca. For your convenience, the government form as published on this website is reproduced below.]

Court File Number ....

[SEAL]

.... *(Name of court)*

at .... *Court office address*

Applicant(s)/Recipient(s) (Strike out inapplicable term.)

Full legal name & address for service — street and number, municipality, postal code, telephone & fax numbers and e-mail address (if any).	*Lawyer's name & address — street and number, municipality, postal code, telephone & fax numbers and e-mail address (if any).*

Respondent/Payor (Strike out inapplicable term.)

Full legal name & address for service — street and number, municipality, postal code, telephone & fax numbers and e-mail address (if any).	*Lawyer's name & address — street and number, municipality, postal code, telephone & fax numbers and e-mail address (if any).*

TO THE COURT:

My name is *(full legal name)* ....

I live in *(municipality and province)* ....

I ACKNOWLEDGE THAT I OWE

❑ Her Majesty the Queen

❑ *(name of person who can legally collect the money from me)* ....

the amount of $ ....,

❑ that will be immediately deposited in full with the clerk of the court by me or by one or more of my sureties and that will be forfeited,

❑ that, by the court's permission, will not need to be deposited with the clerk of the court but that can be collected from me and from one or more of my sureties in the same way that an order for the payment of money may be enforced by this court,

if I do not comply with any one or more of the following conditions:

(List the conditions in numbered paragraphs. Indicate the duration of each condition with the words, "... until [expiry date]" or a similar phrase wherever the judge has imposed an expiry date.)

Put a line through any blank space left on this page or on the reverse page.

.... *Signature of person under bond (recognizance)*

NOTE: A recognizance must be signed in front of the clerk of the court or the judge. No seal is needed for a bond

(Complete the following unless the court did not require any surety. No seals are needed for a bond.)

By signing below, each surety agrees to become indebted in the same way as the person giving the bond or recognizance if that person does not comply with the terms on this form.

Full legal name and address of first surety		*Full legal name and address of second surety*
Signature of first surety		*Signature of second surety*
Full legal name and address of third surety		*Full legal name and address of fourth surety*
Signature of third surety		*Signature of fourth surety*

If this form is a recognizance, the following must be completed.

This recognizance was signed before me at *(municipality)* .... on *(date)* ....

.... *Signature of judge or clerk of the court*

NOTE TO THE BOND GIVER AND TO ANY SURETY: If there is a material change in circumstances, you may make a motion to the court to change any condition of this bond (recognizance).

September 1, 2005

FORM 32A — NOTICE OF FORFEITURE MOTION

[Repealed O. Reg. 76/06, s. 15.]

[Editor's Note: Forms 4 to 39 of the Family Law Rules have been repealed by O. Reg. 76/06, effective May 1, 2006. Pursuant to Family Law Rule 1(9), when a form is referred to by number, the reference is to the form with that number that is described in the Table of Forms at the end of these rules and which is available at www.ontariocourtforms.on.ca. For your convenience, the government form as published on this website is reproduced below.]

Court File Number ....

.... *(Name of court)*

at .... *Court office address*

Applicant(s)/Recipient(s) (Strike out inapplicable term.)

Full legal name & address for service — street & number, municipality, postal code, telephone & fax and e-mail address (if any).	*Lawyer's name & address — street & number, municipality, postal code, telephone & fax numbers and e-mail address (if any).*

Respondent/Payor (Strike out inapplicable term.)

Full legal name & address for service — street & number, municipality, postal code, telephone & fax numbers and e-mail address (if any).	*Lawyer's name & address — street & number, municipality, postal code, telephone & fax numbers and e-mail address (if any).*

TO: *(name of person who entered into recognizance or who posted bond)* ....

AND TO: *(name of surety or sureties)* ....

The person making this motion or the person's lawyer must contact the clerk of the court by telephone or otherwise to choose a time and date when the court could hear this motion

THE COURT WILL HEAR A MOTION ON *(date)* ...., at .... a.m./p.m., or as soon as possible after that time at: *(place of hearing)* ....

The motion is being made by *(moving party's name)* .... who will be asking the court to make an order of forfeiture in respect of

❏ a recognizance entered into

❏ a bond posted

by *(name of person who entered into recognizance or who posted bond)* ....

on *(date)* .... A copy of the bond/recognizance should be attached to this notice. Details of the grounds of the motion are set out in the affidavit(s) that accompany this notice. If the document(s) is/are missing, you should talk to the court office immediately.

IF YOU DO NOT COME TO COURT FOR THIS MOTION, AN ORDER OF FORFEITURE MAY BE MADE WITHOUT YOU AND MAY BE ENFORCED AGAINST YOU.

.... *Signature of person making this motion or of person's lawyer*

.... *Date of signature*

.... *Typed or printed name, address for service, telephone and fax numbers and e-mail address of person or of person's lawyer*

September 1, 2005

FORM 32B — WARRANT FOR ARREST

[Repealed O. Reg. 76/06, s. 15.]

[Editor's Note: Forms 4 to 39 of the Family Law Rules have been repealed by O. Reg. 76/06, effective May 1, 2006. Pursuant to Family Law Rule 1(9), when a form is referred to by number, the reference is to the form with that number that is described in the Table of Forms at the end of these rules and which is available at www.ontariocourtforms.on.ca. For your convenience, the government form as published on this website is reproduced below.]

Court File Number ....

[SEAL]

.... *(Name of court)*

at .... *Court office address*

TO ALL PEACE OFFICERS IN THE PROVINCE OF ONTARIO:

I COMMAND YOU TO ARREST *(name of person to be arrested)* .... on the grounds that this person is:

❑ a payor who has failed to file a financial statement at the request of the Director of the Family Responsibilty Office.
See subsection 40(4) of the Family Responsibility and Support Arrears Enforcement Act.

❑ a payor who has failed to file a financial statement, as required by a notice of default hearing.
See subsection 41(7) of the Family Responsibility and Support Arrears Enforcement Act.

❑ a payor who has failed to appear before the court to explain a default in a support order, domestic contract or paternity agreement that is enforceable in this court, as required by a notice of default hearing.
See subsection 41(7) of the Family Responsibility and Support Arrears Enforcement Act.

❑ a payor who is about to leave Ontario intending to evade his or her responsibilities under a support order, domestic contract or paternity agreement that is enforceable in this court.
See subsection 49(1) of the Family Responsibility and Support Arrears Enforcement Act.

❑ a respondent in an application for support who is about to leave Ontario, intending to evade his or her responsibilities under the *Family Law Act.*
See subsection 43(1) of the Family Law Act.

❑ a respondent in an application to incorporate a paternity agreement in an order of the court, who is about to leave Ontario, intending to evade his or her responsibilities under the agreement.
See subsection 59(2) of the Family Law Act.

❑ a witness whose presence is necessary to determine an issue in a proceeding, who has been served with a summons to witness and who has failed to attend or to remain in attendance as required by the summons to witness.
See subrules 20(9), 23(7) and 27(19) of the Family Law Rules.

❑ a person who has failed to appear at a proceeding that may result in an order requiring him or her to enter into a recognizance or to post a bond.
See subrule 32(1) of the Family Law Rules.

❑ a person who has failed to enter into a recognizance or to post a bond as required by an order of this court.
See rule 32(1) of the Family Law Rules.

❑ a person against whom a motion for contempt of the court is brought, whose attendance at the motion for contempt is necessary in the interests of justice and who appears not likely to appear voluntarily at the motion.
See subrule 31(4) of the Family Law Rules.

❑ *(Other. Specify the grounds and the statutory of regulatory authority to issue this warrant.)*

AND I FURTHER COMMAND YOU to bring this person immediately to court in the municipality in which he or she may be found to be dealt with according to law, and if the court is not then sitting, to bring this person to a justice of the peace as soon as possible to be dealt with according to law.

.... *Signature of judge*

.... *Date of issue*

.... *Print or type name of judge*

.... *Date on which this warrant expires*

(Insert all available information)

Full legal name of person to be arrested				*Birth date (d,m,y)*	*Sex*
Aliases or nicknames					
Residential address				*Telephone number*	
Employment address				*Telephone number*	
Height	*Weight*	*Hair colour*	*Hair style*	*Eye colour*	*Complexion*
Driver's licence			*Year, make & model of automobile*		
Licence plate & province			*Social insurance number*		
Clubs, associations or union affiliation					
Most recent date & occasion when residential address was verified by personal service					
Name & address of person to be contacted for further information				*Telephone number*	

.... *(Name of court)*

at ....

.... *Court office address*

WARRANT OF ARREST

I have informed this arrested person of his/her right to a lawyer.

.... *Date of arrest*

.... *Signature of arresting office*

.... *Printed name of arresting officer*

(In space below, set out address and telephone number where arresting officer may be contacted.)

....

....

September 1, 2005

FORM 32C — AFFIDAVIT FOR WARRANT OF COMMITTAL

[Repealed O. Reg. 76/06, s. 15.]

[Editor's Note: Forms 4 to 39 of the Family Law Rules have been repealed by O. Reg. 76/06, effective May 1, 2006. Pursuant to Family Law Rule 1(9), when a form is referred to by number, the reference is to the form with that number that is described in the Table of Forms at the end of these rules and which is available at www.ontariocourtforms.on.ca. For your convenience, the government form as published on this website is reproduced below.]

Court File Number ....

.... *(Name of court)*

at .... *Court office address*

Applicant(s)/Recipient(s) (Strike out inapplicable term.)

Full legal name & address for service — street & number, municipality, postal code, telephone & fax and e-mail address (if any).	*Lawyer's name & address — street & number, municipality, postal code, telephone & fax numbers and e-mail address (if any).*

Respondent/Payor (Strike out inapplicable term.)

Full legal name & address for service — street & number, municipality, postal code, telephone & fax numbers and e-mail address (if any).	*Lawyer's name & address — street & number, municipality, postal code, telephone & fax numbers and e-mail address (if any).*

My name is *(full legal name)* ....

I live in *(municipality & province)* .... and I swear/affirm that the following is true:

1. I am

   ❑ a recipient under a payment order.

   ❑ an assignee of a recipient under a payment order.

   ❑ an agent of the Director of the Family Responsibility Office.
   ❑ *(Other. Specify.)*
   ....
   ....

2. I am the person who

   ❑ asked the payor to file a financial statement.

   ❑ asked to payor to come to a financial examination.

❑ began a default hearing against the payor.

❑ made a contempt motion.

❑ *(Other; specify.)*
....
....

3. I make this motion to ask the court to issue a warrant of committal.

4. On *(date)* ...., the court made an order of imprisonment, a photocopy of which is attached to this affidavit, committing,

❑ the payor to prison for disobeying the court's order to file a financial statement,

❑ the payor to prison for disobeying the court's order or direction about a financial examination,

❑ the payor to prison for missing support payments,

❑ *(name)* .... to prison for contempt of court,

❑ *(Other; specify.)*
....
....

for a period of .... days, but the committal was suspended on certain conditions set out in the order of imprisonment.

5. The respondent/payor was

❑ in court or his/her lawyer or agent was in court when this order of conditional imprisonment was made.

❑ not in court nor was his/her lawyer or agent was in court when the order of conditional imprisonment was made, but the order was served on him/her on *(date)* ....

6. The conditions that were broken and the circumstances of the breach are as follows: *(Set out conditions of the suspended imprisonment that were broken and details of the breach.)*

❑ Payment of the sum of $.......... was due by *(date)* .... but no payment was made by that day.
❑ Payment of the sum of $.......... was due by *(date)* .... but only a partial payment of $.......... was made by that day.
❑ *(Other; specify.)*
....
....

Put a line through any blank space left on this page.

Sworn/Affirmed before me at .... *municipality* in .... *province, state or country* on .... *date*	
Commissioner for taking affidavits (Type or print name below if signature is illegible.)	*Signature* *(This form is to be signed in front of a lawyer, justice of the peace, notary public or commissioner for taking affidavits.)*

Note to Moving Party: You must attach a photocopy of the court's order of conditional imprisonment to this Affidavit

September 1, 2005

FORM 32D — WARRANT OF COMMITTAL

[Repealed O. Reg. 76/06, s. 15.]

[Editor's Note: Forms 4 to 39 of the Family Law Rules have been repealed by O. Reg. 76/06, effective May 1, 2006. Pursuant to Family Law Rule 1(9), when a form is referred to by number, the reference is to the form with that number that is described in the Table of Forms at the end of these rules and which is available at www.ontariocourtforms.on.ca. For your convenience, the government form as published on this website is reproduced below.]

Court File Number ....

[SEAL]

.... *(Name of court)*

at .... *Court office address*

TO ALL PEACE OFFICERS IN THE PROVINCE OF ONTARIO;

AND TO THE OFFICERS OF THE: *(name and address of correctional institution)* ....

THIS WARRANT IS FOR THE COMMITTAL OF *(full legal name of person to be imprisoned)* ....

THIS COURT FOUND THAT this person:

❑ disobeyed the court's order to file a financial statement;
❑ disobeyed the court's order or direction about a financial examination;

❑ without valid reason missed support payments as required by an order, domestic contract or paternity agreement resulting in an order being made under the *Family Responsibility and Support Arrears Enforcement Act, 1996*;

❑ was in contempt of court;

❑ other *(Specify.)* ....

AS PUNISHMENT, THE COURT COMMITTED THIS PERSON to prison for a term of .... days, to be served,

❑ continuously

❑ intermittently on *(pattern of intermittent sentence)* ....

and to be served
❑ consecutively with any other term of imprisonment now being served or about to be served.

❑ *(Set out alternative arrangement with respect to other terms of imprisonment.)* ....

Check one or both boxes as appropriate. Otherwise strike out and initial.

❑ AND THE COURT DIRECTED THAT this order of imprisonment be suspended on one or more conditions. The court later found that this person broke one or more of the conditions and, as a result, the court has ordered the removal of the suspension from the order of imprisonment;

❑ AND THE COURT ORDERED THAT this person be subject to immediate release from custody upon receipt by the officers of the correctional institution or other secure facility of the sum of
(specify amount) $........... .

I THEREFORE COMMAND YOU TO BRING THIS PERSON SAFELY TO THE CORRECTIONAL INSTITUTION OR SECURE FACILITY NAMED ABOVE AND TO DELIVER HIM/HER TO THE OFFICERS OF THAT INSTITUTION OR FACILITY, TOGETHER WITH THIS WARRANT.

AND I COMMAND YOU, THE OFFICERS OF THE CORRECTIONAL INSTITUTION OR SECURE FACILITY, TO ADMIT THIS PERSON INTO CUSTODY IN YOUR INSTITUTION OR FACILITY AND TO DETAIN HIM/HER THERE UNTIL THIS WARRANT EXPIRES.

This warrant expires,

(a) in a case under the *Family Responsibility and Support Arrears Enforcement Act, 1996*, when this person has completed the prescribed term of imprisonment; or

(b) in other cases, when this person has completed the prescribed term of imprisonment, subject to section 28 (remission of sentence) of the *Ministry of Correctional Services Act*; or

(c) when you, the officers of the correctional institution or secure facility, receive the sum named above; or

(d) upon further order of this court,

whichever event happens first.

.... *Signature of judge*

.... *Date of issue*

.... *Print or type name of judge*

NOTE: Completion of the prescribed term of imprisonment does not discharge arrears of support or maintenance. A description of the person to be imprisoned is set out on page 2 of this warrant.

(Insert all available information)

<table>
<tr><td colspan="4">Full legal name of person to be arrested</td><td colspan="2">Birth date (d,m,y)</td><td>Sex</td></tr>
<tr><td colspan="7">Aliases or nicknames</td></tr>
<tr><td colspan="4">Residential address</td><td colspan="3">Telephone number</td></tr>
<tr><td colspan="4">Employment address</td><td colspan="3">Telephone number</td></tr>
<tr><td>Height</td><td>Weight</td><td>Hair colour</td><td>Hair style</td><td>Eye colour</td><td colspan="2">Complexion</td></tr>
<tr><td colspan="3">Driver's licence</td><td colspan="4">Year, make and model of automobile</td></tr>
<tr><td colspan="3">Licence plate & province</td><td colspan="4">Social insurance number</td></tr>
<tr><td colspan="7">Clubs, associations or union affiliation</td></tr>
<tr><td colspan="4">Most recent date & occasion when residential address was verified by personal service</td><td colspan="3">Family Responsibility Office Case No. (if applicable)</td></tr>
</table>

Name & address of person to be contacted for further information	*Telephone number*

.... *(Name of court)*

.... *Court office address*

WARRANT OF COMMITTAL

September 1, 2005

FORM 33 — INFORMATION FOR WARRANT TO APPREHEND CHILD

[Repealed O. Reg. 76/06, s. 15.]

[Editor's Note: Forms 4 to 39 of the Family Law Rules have been repealed by O. Reg. 76/06, effective May 1, 2006. Pursuant to Family Law Rule 1(9), when a form is referred to by number, the reference is to the form with that number that is described in the Table of Forms at the end of these rules and which is available at www.ontariocourtforms.on.ca. For your convenience, the government form as published on this website is reproduced below.]

Court file number ....

.... *(Name of court)*

at .... *Court office address* ....

My name is *(full legal name)* ....

I live in *(municipality & province)* .... and I swear/affirm that the following is true:

1. I am

- ❑ a child protection worker employed by *(full legal name of children's aid society)*
- ❑ *(Give occupation or title.)*.................................. a peace officer in the province of Ontario, employed in *(name of office out of which you work)*

2. I have reasonable and probable grounds to believe and do believe that *(child's full legal name)* is a child in need of protection for the following reasons: *(Set out grounds for belief.)*

....

....

3. I have reasonable and probable grounds to believe and do believe that a course of action less restrictive than the child's removal to a place of safety is not available or will not adequately protect the child, for the following reasons: *(Set out grounds for belief.)*

....

....

(Strike out paragraph 4 if not applicable.)

4. I have reasonable and probable grounds to believe that the child may be found at *(Give full municipal address or a precise description of the premises where the child may be located.)* ....

Put a line through any blank space left on this page.

Sworn/Affirmed before me at .... *municipality* in .... *province, state or country* on .... *date*	
	Signature
Commissioner for taking affidavits (Type or print name below if signature is illegible.)	*(This form is to be signed in front of a lawyer, justice of the peace, notary public or commissioner for taking affidavits.)*

September 1, 2005

FORM 33A — WARRANT TO APPREHEND CHILD

[Repealed O. Reg. 76/06, s. 15.]

[Editor's Note: Forms 4 to 39 of the Family Law Rules have been repealed by O. Reg. 76/06, effective May 1, 2006. Pursuant to Family Law Rule 1(9), when a form is referred to by number, the reference is to the form with that number that is described in the Table of Forms at the end of these rules and which is available at www.ontariocourtforms.on.ca. For your convenience, the government form as published on this website is reproduced below.]

Court file number ....

.... *(Name of court)*

at .... *Court office address*

TO ALL CHILD PROTECTION WORKERS AND PEACE OFFICERS IN THE PROVINCE OF ONTARIO:

On the basis of an information sworn before me under Part III of the *Child and Family Services Act* respecting the child named or described at the bottom of this warrant, I am satisfied that there are reasonable and probable grounds to believe:

(a) that the child is in need of protection; and

(b) that a course of action less restrictive than the child's removal to a place of safety is not available or will not adequately protect the child.

(Check box below only if the child's whereabouts are known. Otherwise, strike out the paragraph below and initial the deletion.)

❑ I am further satisfied, on the basis of that information, that the child may now be found at *(Give full municipal address or a precise description of the premises where the child may be located.)*

....

....

I THEREFORE AUTHORIZE YOU TO BRING THIS CHILD to a "place of safety" within the meaning of the *Child and Family Services Act.*

This warrant expires at .... a.m./p.m. on *(date)* ....

.... *Signature of justice of the peace*

.... *Print or type name of justice of the peace*

.... *Date of signature*

.... *Municipality where this warrant was signed*

NOTE: Any changes, alterations or corrections to this form must be initialled by the justice of the peace. It is a criminal offence for any other person to change the wording of this warrant after it has been signed by the justice of the peace.

DESCRIPTION: *Insert all available information*

Full legal name of child to be apprehended				*Birth date (d,m,y)*		*Sex*
Aliases or nicknames						
Residential address				*Telephone number*		
Present whereabouts of child				*Telephone number*		
Height	*Weight*	*Hair colour*	*Hair style*	*Eye colour*	*Complexion*	
Other features						
Name & address of person to be contacted for further information				*Telephone number*		

.... *(Name of court)*

at ....

.... *Court office address*

Warrant to Apprehend Child

September 1, 2005

FORM 33B — PLAN OF CARE FOR CHILD(REN) (CHILDREN'S AID SOCIETY)

[Editor's Note: Forms 4 to 39 of the Family Law Rules have been repealed by O. Reg. 76/06, effective May 1, 2006. Pursuant to Family Law Rule 1(9), when a form is referred to by number, the reference is to the form with that number that is described in the Table of Forms at the end of these rules and which is available at www.ontariocourtforms.on.ca. For your convenience, the government form as published on this website is reproduced below.]

Court File Number ....

.... *(Name of court)*

at .... *Court office address*

Applicant(s) (In most cases, the applicant will be a children's aid society.)

Full legal name & address for service — street & number, municipality, postal code, telephone & fax numbers and e-mail address (if any).	*Lawyer's name & address — street & number, municipality, postal code, telephone & fax numbers and e-mail address (if any).*

Respondent(s) (In most cases, a respondent will be a "parent" within the meaning of section 37 of the Child and Family Services Act.)

Full legal name & address for service — street & number, municipality, postal code, telephone & fax numbers and e-mail address (if any).	*Lawyer's name & address — street & number, municipality, postal code, telephone & fax numbers and e-mail address (if any).*

Children's Lawyer

Name & address of Children's Lawyer's agent for service (street & number, municipality, postal code, telephone & fax numbers and e-mail address (if any)) and name of person represented.

Fill out only those paragraphs that apply and strike out others.

1. I am/We are *(full legal name)* .... and I am/we are *(state your position with children's aid society)* ....

2. The child(ren) in this case is/are:

Child's Full Legal Name	Birthdate	Sex

3. ❑ After the court makes a finding that the child(ren) is/are in need of protection under Part III of the *Child and Family Services Act*, I/we ask the court to make an order.

❑ The court previously found on *(date)* .... that the child(ren) was/were in need of protection under Part III of the *Child and Family Services Act*, and the court made an order on *(date)* .... I/We now ask the court to make a further order.

The details of the order that I/we now ask the court to make are as follows: *(Give details of the order you now want the court to make. If you want the order to include any supervision by the children's aid society, give details of any terms and conditions of supervision.)*

....

....

....

Put a line through any blank space left on this page.

4. The services that the family and child(ren) need and that will be provided are as follows: *(Give details of the service needed, who needs it and who will be providing it.)*

....

....

....

....

....

....

....

....

....

....

....

5. The children's aid society expects the respondent(s) to carry out certain conditions before it would feel that supervision or wardship of the child(ren) is no longer needed. Very serious consequences could result if those conditions are broken. These conditions are: *(Set out conditions and estimate the time needed to achieve them.)*

....

....

....

....

....

....

....

....

....

....

....

....

....

....

....

....

....

....

....

....

....

Put a line through any blank space left on this page.

6. The child(ren) cannot be adequately protected while in the care of the respondent(s) because: *(State reasons.)*

....

....

....

....

....

....

....

....

7. The following efforts have been made in the past to protect the child(ren) while in the care of the respondent(s): *(Describe the efforts made. If no efforts were made, give explanation.)*

....

....

....

....

....

....

....

....

8. The following efforts are planned to keep up the child(ren)'s contact with the respondent(s): *(Describe plans. Write "Nil" if there are no plans.)*

....

....

....

....

....

....

....

....

9. The following arrangements have been or are being made to recognize the importance of the child's culture and to preserve his/her heritage, traditions and cultural identity:

....

....

....

....

....

....

....

Put a line through any blank space left on this page.

PART 3

10. The children's aid society has removed the child(ren) from the care of the respondent(s) and intends to make this removal ❑ temporary.

❑ permanent. *(If the children's aid society is not seeking an order of Crown wardship, please provide details of the efforts by the children's aid society to provide a long-term, stable placement for the child.)*

....

....

....

....

....

....

....

....

11. (To be completed if the children's aid society is seeking an order of Crown wardship.)

Efforts will be made to assist the child to develop a positive, secure and enduring relationship within a family through one of the following methods:

❑ adoption ..... ❑ a custody order under s. 65.2(1) ❑ a plan for customary care

other *(Please provide available details.)*

....

....

....

....

....

12. This plan of care was served on and its details explained to the respondent(s) and others named below:

Print name of person to whom this plan was explained	Print name of person who explained plan	Date of explanation

Print name of person to whom this plan was explained	Print name of person who explained plan	Date of explanation

Put a line through any blank space left on this page.

.... *Date of signature*

.... *Signature*

.... *Date of signature*

.... *Signature*

October 1, 2006

FORM 33B.1 — ANSWER AND PLAN OF CARE (PARTIES OTHER THAN CHILDREN'S AID SOCIETY)

[Editor's Note: Forms 4 to 39 of the Family Law Rules have been repealed by O. Reg. 76/06, effective May 1, 2006. Pursuant to Family Law Rule 1(9), when a form is referred to by number, the reference is to the form with that number that is described in the Table of Forms at the end of these rules and which is available at www.ontariocourtforms.on.ca. For your convenience, the government form as published on this website is reproduced below.]

Court File Number ....

.... (Name of court)

at .... *Court office address*

Applicant(s)

Full legal name & address for service — street & number, municipality, postal code, telephone & fax numbers and e-mail address (if any).	*Lawyer's name & address — street & number, municipality, postal code, telephone & fax numbers and e-mail address (if any).*

Respondent(s)

Full legal name & address for service — street & number, municipality, postal code, telephone & fax numbers and e-mail address (if any).	*Lawyer's name & address — street & number, municipality, postal code, telephone & fax numbers and e-mail address (if any).*

Respondent(s)

Children's Lawyer

Name & address for service for Children's Lawyer's agent — street & number, municipality, postal code, telephone & fax numbers and e-mail address (if any)) and name of person represented.

TO THE APPLICANT(S):

(Note to the respondent(s): If you are making a claim against someone who is not an applicant, insert the person's name and address here.)

AND TO: (full legal name) ...., *an added respondent, of (address for service of added party)* ....

(Note to the respondent(s): You must complete, serve, file and update this form if any significant changes regarding the child(ren) occur after you sign this form.)

I am/We are *(full legal name(s))* .... and I am/we are *(state your relationship to the child(ren))* ....

PART 1

1. The child(ren) in this case is/are:

Child's Full Legal Name	Birthdate	Age	Sex	Full Legal Name of Mother	Full Legal Name of Father	Child's Religion	Child's Native Status

2. The following people have had the child(ren) in their care and custody during the past year:

Child's Name	Name of Other Caregiver(s)	Period of Time with Caregiver(s) (d,m,y to d,m,y)

Child's Name	**Name of Other Caregiver(s)**	**Period of Time with Caregiver(s) (d,m,y to d,m,y)**

PART 2

3. If this is a child protection application, complete this Part, then go to Part 4. *(If this is a status review, complete Part 3, then go to Part 4.)*

(Check applicable box(es).)

❏ I/We agree with the following facts in

❏ paragraph 6 of the application (Form 8B).

❏ paragraph 3 of the application (Form 8B.1).

(Refer to the numbered paragraph(s) under paragraph 6/paragraph 3 of the application.)

....

....

....

....

....

....

....

....

....

....

....

❏ I/We disagree with the following facts in

❏ paragraph 6 of the application (Form 8B).

❏ paragraph 3 of the application (Form 8B.1).

(Refer to the numbered paragraph(s) under paragraph 6/paragraph 3 of the application.)

....

....

....

....

....

....

....

....

....

....

....

NOTE: If you intend to dispute the children's aid society's position at the temporary care and custody hearing, an affidavit in Form 14A MUST also be served on the parties and filed at court.

(Attach an additional page and number it if you need more space.)

PART 3

4. If this is a status review, complete this Part, then go to Part 4. *(If this is a protection application, complete Part 2, then go to Part 4.)*

(Check applicable box(es).)

❑ I/We agree with the following facts in

❑ paragraph 6 of the application (Form 8B).

❑ paragraph 3 of the application (Form 8B.1).

(Refer to the numbered paragraph(s) under paragraph 6/paragraph 3 of the application.)

....

....

....

....

....

....

....

....

....

....

....

....

❑ I/We disagree with the following facts in

❑ paragraph 6 of the application (Form 8B).

❑ paragraph 3 of the application (Form 8B.1).

(Refer to the numbered paragraph(s) under paragraph 6/paragraph 3 of the application.)

....

....

....

....

....

....

....

....

....

....

....

....

(Attach an additional page and number it if you need more space.)

PART 4

5. What placement and terms of placement do you believe would be in the child(ren)'s best interests? *(You should include in your plan of care at least the following information. If your plan is not the same for a particular child, then complete a separate plan for that child.)*

(a) Where will you live?

(b) Who, if anyone, will live with you?

(c) Where will the child(ren) live?

(d) What school or daycare will the child(ren) attend?

(e) What days and hours will the child(ren) attend school or daycare?

(f) Are you enrolled in school or counselling?

(g) If you are enrolled in counselling, where do you attend counselling?

(h) What support services will you be using for the child(ren)?

(i) Do you have support from your family or community?

(j) If you have support from your family or community, who will help you and how will they help you?

(k) What will the child(ren)'s activities be?

(l) What will your source of income be?

(m) Do you go to work or school?

(n) If you go to work or school, what are the details, including the days and hours you work or go to school, and who will look after your child(ren) while you are there?

....

....

....

....

(o) State why you feel that this plan would be in the child(ren)'s best interests.

(Attach an additional page and number it if you need more space.)

....

....

....

....

....

....

....

....

....

....

....

....

....

....

....

....

....

....

6. These are the people who have information that would support my plan:

Name	Information

PART 5

Claims by Respondent(s)

(Fill out a separate claim page for each person against whom you are making a claim(s).)

7. THIS CLAIM IS MADE AGAINST

❑ *THE CHILDREN'S AID SOCIETY (OR OTHER APPLICANT)*

❑ *AN ADDED PARTY*, whose name is *(full legal name)* ....

(If you claim against an added party, make sure that the person's name appears on page 1 of this form.)

....

....

8. I/WE ASK THE COURT FOR THE FOLLOWING ORDER:

(Claims below include claims for temporary orders.)

Claims relating to child protection	
❑	access
❑	lesser protection order
❑	return of child(ren) to my/our care
❑	place child(ren) into the custody of *(name)* .... *(s. 57.1, deemed custody order under the Children's Law Reform Act)*
❑	place child(ren) into the custody of *(name)* .... *(s. 65.2(1)(b), custody order for former Crown ward)*
❑	society wardship for .... months
❑	place child(ren) into the care and custody of *(name)* .... subject to society supervision
❑	costs
❑	other *(Specify.)* ....

Give details of the order that you want the court to make. *(Include the name(s) of the child(ren) for whom custody or access is claimed.)*

....

....

....

....

IMPORTANT FACTS SUPPORTING MY/OUR CLAIM(S)

(In numbered paragraphs, set out the facts that form the legal basis for your claim(s). Attach an additional page and number it if you need more space.)

....

....

....

....

Put a line through any space left on this page.

....

Date of signature *Signature*

.... *Date of signature*

.... *Signature*

October 1, 2006

FORM 33B.2 — ANSWER (CHILD AND FAMILY SERVICES ACT CASES OTHER THAN CHILD PROTECTION AND STATUS REVIEW)

[Editor's Note: Pursuant to Family Law Rule 1(9), when a form is referred to by number, the reference is to the form with that number that is described in the Table of Forms at the end of these rules and which is available at www.ontariocourtforms.on.ca. For your convenience, the government form as published on this website is reproduced below.]

Court File Number ....

.... *(Name of court)*

at .... *Court office address*

Applicant(s)

Full legal name & address for service — street & number, municipality, postal code, telephone & fax numbers and e-mail address (if any).	*Lawyer's name & address — street & number, municipality, postal code, telephone & fax numbers and e-mail address (if any).*

Respondent(s)

Full legal name & address for service — street & number, municipality, postal code, telephone & fax numbers and e-mail address (if any).	*Lawyer's name & address — street & number, municipality, postal code, telephone & fax numbers and e-mail address (if any).*

Children's Lawyer

Name & address for service for Children's Lawyer's agent — street & number, municipality, postal code, telephone & fax numbers and e-mail address (if any) and name of person represented.

TO THE APPLICANT(S):

(Note to the respondent(s): If you are making a claim against someone who is not an applicant, insert the person's name and address here.)

AND TO: (full legal name) ...., *an added respondent, of (address for service of added party)* ....

(Note to the respondent(s): You must complete, serve, file and update this form if any significant changes regarding the child(ren) occur after you sign this form.)

I am/We are *(full legal name(s))* .... and I am/we are *(state your relationship to the child(ren))* ....

1. The child(ren) in this case is/are:

Child's Full Legal Name	Birthdate	Age	Sex	Full Legal Name of Mother	Full Legal Name of Father	Child's Religion	Child's Native Status

2. ❑ I/We agree with the following facts in paragraph 3 of the application (Form 8B.2). *(Refer to the numbered paragraph(s) under paragraph 3 of the application.)*

....

....

....

....

....

....

....

....

....

....

....

....

....

....

....

....

❑ I/We disagree with the following facts in paragraph 3 of the application (Form 8B.2). *(Refer to the numbered paragraph(s) under paragraph 3 of the application.)*

....

....

....

....

....

....

....

....

....

....

....

....

....

....

....

....

(Attach an additional page and number it if you need more space.)

3. Do you agree that the court should make the order requested?

❑ Yes . . . . ❑ No

Give reasons:

....

....

....

....

....

....

....

....

....

....

....

....

....

....

....

....

....

....

....

....

....

....

....

....

....

....

....

....

....

....

....

....

....

(Attach an additional page and number it if you need more space.)

IMPORTANT FACTS SUPPORTING MY/OUR POSITION

(In numbered paragraphs, set out the facts that form the legal basis for your position. Attach an additional page and number it if you need more space.)

....

....

....

....

....

....

....

....

....

....

....

....

....

....

....

....

....

....

....

....

....

....

....

....

....

....

....

....

Put a line through any blank space left on this page.

....	....
Date of signature	*Signature*
....	....
Date of signature	*Signature*

October 1, 2006

FORM 33C — STATEMENT OF AGREED FACTS (CHILD PROTECTION)

[Repealed O. Reg. 76/06, s. 15.]

[Editor's Note: Forms 4 to 39 of the Family Law Rules have been repealed by O. Reg. 76/06, effective May 1, 2006. Pursuant to Family Law Rule 1(9), when a form is referred to by number, the reference is to the form with that number that is described in the Table of Forms at the end of these rules and which is available at www.ontariocourtforms.on.ca. For your convenience, the government form as published on this website is reproduced below.]

Court File Number ....

.... *(Name of court)*

at .... *Court office address*

Applicant(s) [In most cases, the applicant will be a children's aid society.]

Full legal name & address for service — street & number, municipality, postal code, telephone & fax numbers and e-mail address (if any).	*Lawyer's name & address — street & number, municipality, postal code, telephone & fax numbers and e-mail address (if any).*

Respondent(s) [In most cases, a respondent will be a "parent" within the meaning of section 37 of the *Child and Family Services Act*.]

Full legal name & address for service — street & number, municipality, postal code, telephone & fax numbers and e-mail address (if any).	*Lawyer's name & address — street & number, municipality, postal code, telephone & fax numbers and e-mail address (if any).*

THE PEOPLE SIGNING THIS AGREEMENT ARE:

(Give full legal name. If you are a respondent, state your relationship to the child(ren). If you are an employee of the children's aid society, state your position within the society.)

Print or type full legal name	*Relationship to child OR position within children's aid society*
Signature	*Date of signature*
Print or type full legal name	*Relationship to child OR position within children's aid society*
Signature	*Date of signature*
Print or type full legal name	*Relationship to child OR position within children's aid society*
Signature	*Date of signature*
Print or type full legal name	*Relationship to child OR position within children's aid society*
Signature	*Date of signature*

WE AGREE:

(a) that the statements made on this form are true; and

(b) that this form may be filed with the court and may be read to the court as evidence, without affecting anyone's right to test that evidence by cross-examination or to bring in other evidence.

1. The information about the child(ren) in this case is as follows:

Full legal name of first child:	*Date of birth*	*Age*	*Sex*
Child's religion			
Child's Indian or native status			
Name of child's band or native community			
If child was apprehended, address and identity of place from which child was removed			

Full legal name of child's mother by birth or by adoption			
Full legal name of child's father by birth or by adoption			
Father's status as "parent" under statute			

Full legal name of second child:	*Date of birth*	*Age*	*Sex*
Child's religion			
Child's Indian or native status			
Name of child's band or native community			
If child was apprehended, address and identity of place from which child was removed			
Full legal name of child's mother by birth or by adoption			
Full legal name of child's father by birth or by adoption			
Father's status as "parent" under statute			

Full legal name of third child:	*Date of birth*	*Age*	*Sex*
Child's religion			
Child's Indian or native status			
Name of child's band or native community			
If child was apprehended, address and identity of place from which child was removed			
Full legal name of child's mother by birth or by adoption			
Full legal name of child's father by birth or by adoption			
Father's status as "parent" under statute			

Notes:

If there are more children, attach a sheet and number it.

2. The details of the children's aid society's previous involvement with one or more of these children in this case are as follows:

(Write "Nil" if no involvement. Indicate any involvement with children's aid society in another part of Ontario or a child protection agency outside Ontario. Please remember that this is a statement of AGREED FACTS. That means that you must not set out something as a fact if another party disagrees with it. If you cannot agree at all about anything, write: "No agreement reached.")

....

....

3. The child(ren) was/were apprehended because:

(If there was no apprehension, write "Nil". Again, there must be full agreement by all parties. Any point on which there is disagreement must be excluded. If there is no agreement at all on anything, write "No agreement reached.")

....

....

4. We agree that the court should make a finding that the child(ren) is/are in need of protection on the following reason(s):

(Use only the reasons listed on page 3 of the application [Form 8B]. Any reason on which there is disagreement must be excluded. If there is no agreement at all, write, "No agreement reached." In any event, the court can always make some other finding.)

....

....

4.1 The following important events relating to the child(ren)'s best interests have occurred since the date this application began:

5. We agree that the order that would best serve the best interests of the child(ren) is:

(Again, list only the terms and conditions on which there is full agreement by all parties. If there is no agreement at all, write, "No agreement reached." In any event, the court is always free to make some other order. If the order on which you all agree would remove the child(ren) from the care of the person who had the child(ren) before the case started, explain why less disruptive options would not be enough to protect the child(ren).)

....

....

Put a line through any blank space left on this page.

September 1, 2005

FORM 33D — STATEMENT OF AGREED FACTS (STATUS REVIEW)

[Repealed O. Reg. 76/06, s. 15.]

[Editor's Note: Forms 4 to 39 of the Family Law Rules have been repealed by O. Reg. 76/06, effective May 1, 2006. Pursuant to Family Law Rule 1(9), when a form is referred to by number, the reference is to the form with that number that is described in the Table of Forms at the end of these rules and which is available at www.ontariocourtforms.on.ca. For your convenience, the government form as published on this website is reproduced below.]

Court File Number ....

.... *(Name of court)*

at .... *Court office address*

Applicant(s) [In most cases, the applicant will be a children's aid society.]

Full legal name & address for service — street & number, municipality, postal code, telephone & fax numbers and e-mail address (if any).	*Lawyer's name & address — street & number, municipality, postal code, telephone & fax numbers and e-mail address (if any).*

Respondent(s) [In most cases, a respondent will be a "parent" within the meaning of section 37 of the Child and Family Services Act.]

Full legal name & address for service — street & number, municipality, postal code, telephone & fax e-mail e-mail address (if any).	*Lawyer's name & address — street & number, municipality, postal code, telephone & fax numbers and e-mail address (if any).*

THE PEOPLE SIGNING THIS AGREEMENT ARE:

(Give full legal name. If you are a respondent, state your relationship to the child(ren). If you are an employee of the children's aid society, state your position within the society.)

Print or type full legal name	*Relationship to child OR position within children's aid society*
Signature	*Date of signature*
Print or type full legal name	*Relationship to child OR position within children's aid society*
Signature	*Date of signature*
Print or type full legal name	*Relationship to child OR position within children's aid society*
Signature	*Date of signature*
Print or type full legal name	*Relationship to child OR position within children's aid society*
Signature	*Date of signature*

WE AGREE:

(a) that the statements made on this form are true; and

(b) that this form may be filed with the court and may be read to the court as evidence, without affecting anyone's right to test that evidence by cross-examination or to bring in other evidence.

1. The information about the child(ren) in this case is as follows:

Full legal name of first child:	*Date of birth*	*Age*	*Sex*
Child's religion			
Child's Indian or native status			
Name of child's band or native community			
If child was apprehended, address and identity of place from which child was removed			
Full legal name of child's mother by birth or by adoption			
Full legal name of child's father by birth or by adoption			
Father's status as "parent" under statute			

Full legal name of second child:	*Date of birth*	*Age*	*Sex*
Child's religion			
Child's Indian or native status			
Name of child's band or native community			
If child was apprehended, address and identity of place from which child was removed			
Full legal name of child's mother by birth or by adoption			
Full legal name of child's father by birth or by adoption			
Father's status as "parent" under statute			

Full legal name of third child:	*Date of birth*	*Age*	*Sex*
Child's religion			
Child's Indian or native status			
Name of child's band or native community			
If child was apprehended, address and identity of place from which child was removed			
Full legal name of child's mother by birth or by adoption			
Full legal name of child's father by birth or by adoption			
Father's status as "parent" under statute			

Notes:

If there are more children, attach a sheet and number it.

2. The most recent protection order dealing with the child(ren) in paragraph 1 was made on *(date)* .... and it said that: *(State substance of order.)*

....

....

3. Since the order under review was made the following person(s) has/have become a "parent" under Part III of the *Child and Family Services Act*:

Full legal name	**Relationship to child**

4. Since that order was made, the following important events have happened: *(Describe only the events on which you can ALL agree. Please remember that this is a statement of AGREED FACTS. That means that you must not set out something as a fact if at least one of the persons signing this statement disagrees with it. If you cannot agree at all about anything, write: "No agreement reached.")*

....

....

5. We agree that an order of the court is needed now and that it would best serve the best interests of the child(ren) because: *(If there is no agreement that an order needs to be made, write: "No agreement reached on need for an order." If you agree that an order needs to be made, give reasons for it and set out its terms and conditions. If any person disagrees with a*

reason, term or condition, then you must not include that reason, term or condition. If you cannot agree on any reasons, write: "No agreement reached on reasons for order." If you cannot agree on any terms or conditions of the order, write: "No agreement reached on terms and conditions of order.")

....

....

Put a line through any blank space left on this page.

September 1, 2005

FORM 33E — CHILD'S CONSENT TO SECURE TREATMENT

[Repealed O. Reg. 76/06, s. 15.]

[Editor's Note: Forms 4 to 39 of the Family Law Rules have been repealed by O. Reg. 76/06, effective May 1, 2006. Pursuant to Family Law Rule 1(9), when a form is referred to by number, the reference is to the form with that number that is described in the Table of Forms at the end of these rules and which is available at www.ontariocourtforms.on.ca. For your convenience, the government form as published on this website is reproduced below.]

Court File Number ....

.... *(Name of court)*

at .... *Court office address*

Applicant(s)

Full legal name & address for service — street & number, municipality, postal code, telephone & fax numbers and e-mail address (if any).	*Lawyer's name & address — street & number, municipality, postal code, telephone & fax numbers and e-mail address (if any).*

Child

Full legal name of child: *Birthdate:* *Sex:*	*Lawyer's name & address — street and number, municipality, postal code, telephone & fax numbers and e-mail address (if any).*

1. My name is *(child's full legal name)* ....

2. I know that the applicant(s) is/are asking the court to make an order

❑ to send me to and maybe have me locked up for my own protection at

❑ to keep me for a longer time and maybe keep me locked up for my own protection at

❑ to get me released from

(name and address of program) ....

3. I know that

- ❑ I have a right to be in court when this case is heard by the judge, but I agree not to come to court and to let the court make whatever order needs to be made without me.
- ❑ the court usually needs to hear witnesses before it can make an order in this case, but I agree that the court can make the order without having to hear witnesses in person and can reach its decision on evidence found in the reports and other documents that the applicant(s) can show to the judge.

4. I have talked with a lawyer

(a) who has explained these things to me, and

(b) who has explained what it means for me to sign this consent, and

(c) who is going to witness my signature of this form.

.... *Signature of child*

.... *Signature of lawyer*

.... *Date of signatures*

NOTE: This consent must be witnessed by an independent lawyer who is to provide an affidavit of independent legal advice on the reverse side of this sheet.

NOTE: A consent to dispense with oral evidence is not effective for more than 180 days after the court's order.

AFFIDAVIT OF EXECUTION AND INDEPENDENT LEGAL ADVICE

My name is (full legal name) .... *and I swear/affirm that the following is true:*

1. I am a member of the Bar of *(name of jurisdiction)* .... and am not acting for any other person in this secure treatment case.

2. I explained to *(child's full legal name)* .... about

- ❑ the nature and effect of
  - ❑ secure treatment;
  - ❑ an extension of secure treatment;
  - ❑ release from secure treatment;
- ❑ the consequences of not attending the hearing; and
- ❑ the consequences of a hearing where a court proceeds without hearing oral evidence;

in language appropriate to his/her age to the best of my knowledge and skills.

3. After my explanation, the child told me that he/she wanted to sign this consent.

4. I was present at and witnessed the signing of this consent by the child.

Sworn/Affirmed before me at .... *municipality* in .... *province, state or country* on .... *date*	
______________________________	______________________________ *Signature*

Commissioner for taking affidavits (Type or print name below if signature is illegible.)	*(This form is to be signed in front of a lawyer, justice of the peace, notary public or commissioner for taking affidavits.)*

September 1, 2005

FORM 33F — CONSENT TO SECURE TREATMENT (PERSON OTHER THAN CHILD)

[Repealed O. Reg. 76/06, s. 15.]

[Editor's Note: Forms 4 to 39 of the Family Law Rules have been repealed by O. Reg. 76/06, effective May 1, 2006. Pursuant to Family Law Rule 1(9), when a form is referred to by number, the reference is to the form with that number that is described in the Table of Forms at the end of these rules and which is available at www.ontariocourtforms.on.ca. For your convenience, the government form as published on this website is reproduced below.]

Court File Number ....

.... *(Name of court)*

at .... *Court office address*

Applicant(s)

Full legal name & address for service — street & number, municipality, postal code, telephone & fax and e-mail address (if any).	*Lawyer's name & address — street & number, municipality, postal code, telephone & fax numbers and e-mail address (if any).*

Child

Full legal name of child: *Birthdate:* *Sex:*	*Lawyer's name & address — street and number, municipality, postal code, telephone & fax numbers and e-mail address (if any).*

Name and address of secure treatment program in this case

....

....

My name is *(full legal name)* .... and I am

❑ the administrator of the secure treatment program. I consent to this application for

❑ the child's commitment to the program.

❑ an extension of the child's commitment to the program.

❑ an extension of the commitment to the program of the person admitted into it who has now attained the age of eighteen years.

❑ the child's parent. I consent to

❑ this application for the commitment of my child who is in the care of a person other than the administrator of the secure treatment program.

❑ my child's commitment to the secure treatment program for a period of 180 days in this application brought by *(full legal name of applicant children's aid society)*

❑ this application by the administrator of the secure treatment program for an extension of my child's admission to the program.

❑ an authorized representative of the Minister of Community and Social Services for Ontario. I consent to the admission of the child who is less than twelve years old to the secure treatment program

❑ temporarily while this case for an order of commitment or for an order extending it is adjourned.

❑ on the court's final order of commitment or extending commitment.

❑ an officer of *(full legal name of children's aid society)* .... I am authorized, on behalf of the society, to consent to this application of the administrator of the secure treatment program for an extension of the child's commitment to that program.

❑ the person who is the subject of this case. I am 18 years of age or more. I consent to this application to extend my commitment to the secure treatment program to which I am now admitted.

.... *Signature*

.... *Date of signature*

September 1, 2005

FORM 34 — CHILD'S CONSENT TO ADOPTION

[Editor's Note: Forms 4 to 39 of the Family Law Rules have been repealed by O. Reg. 76/06, effective May 1, 2006. Pursuant to Family Law Rule 1(9), when a form is referred to by number, the reference is to the form with that number that is described in the Table of Forms at the end of these rules and which is available at www.ontariocourtforms.on.ca. For your convenience, the government form as published on this website is reproduced below.]

ONTARIO

Court File Number

....

(Name of court)

at ....

Court office address

Applicant(s) (The first letter of the applicant's surname may be used)

Full legal name & address for service — street & number, municipality, postal code, telephone & fax numbers and e-mail address (if any)..	*Lawyer's name & address — street & number, municipality, postal code, telephone & fax numbers and e-mail address (if any)..*

Respondent(s) (If there is a respondent, the first letter of the respondent's surname may be used)

Full legal name & address for service — street & number, municipality, postal code, telephone & fax numbers and e-mail address (if any)..	*Lawyer's name & address — street & number, municipality, postal code, telephone & fax numbers and e-mail address (if any)..*

1. My name is *(child's full legal name)* ....

2. I was born on *(give date of birth)* ....

3. I know that the applicant(s) is/are asking the court to make an order to adopt me.

4. I agree to being adopted by the applicant(s).

5. I have been given a chance to get counselling.

6. I understand the nature and effect of this consent. I understand that I may withdraw this consent within 21 days by attending at the office of the lawyer who witnessed the consent located at *(give address)* .... or by attending at the office of another authorized representative of the Children's Lawyer and signing a written notice of withdrawal.

7. I understand that once I turn eighteen years old, I can apply for a copy of my original birth registration, if any, and a copy of my adoption order.

8. I understand that once I turn nineteen years old, my birth parent(s) can apply for information from my original birth registration, if any, any substituted birth registration and my adoption order. This information would include my full legal name after adoption.

9. I have spoken to a lawyer ❑ who has explained adoption to me,

❑ who has explained what it means for me to sign this consent,

❑ who has told me what to do if I want to change my mind about this consent,

❑ who has told me about my rights and the rights of other persons with respect to the disclosure of adoption information,

❑ who is going to witness my signing of this form.

To be completed only where the child is 12 years of age or older.

10. I agree that my name after adoption will be *(full legal name after adoption)*

....

....	....
Date of signatures	*Signature of child*
	....

Signature of Children's Lawyer

AFFIDAVIT OF EXECUTION AND INDEPENDENT LEGAL ADVICE

My name is (full legal name) ....

and I swear/affirm that the following is true:

1. I am a member of the Bar of *(name of jurisdiction)* .... and am an agent of the Office of the Children's Lawyer.

2. I am not acting for any other person in this adoption case.

3. I explained to *(child's full legal name)* .... about

- ❑ the nature and effect of adoption under the law of Ontario
- ❑ the nature and effect of this consent
- ❑ the circumstances under which this consent may be withdrawn
- ❑ his/her rights and the rights of other persons with respect to the disclosure of adoption information

in language appropriate to his/her age to the best of my knowledge and skills.

4. After my explanation, the child told me that he/she wanted to sign this consent.

5. I was present at and witnessed the signing of this consent by the child.

Sworn/Affirmed before me at	.... *municipality*	.... *Signature* *(This form is to be signed in front of a lawyer, justice of the peace, notary public or commissioner for taking affidavits.)*
in	*province, state or country*	
on .... *date*	.... *Commissioner for taking affidavits* *(Type or print name below if signature is illegible.)*	

April 1, 2009

FORM 34A — AFFIDAVIT OF PARENTAGE

[Repealed O. Reg. 76/06, s. 15.]

[Editor's Note: Forms 4 to 39 of the Family Law Rules have been repealed by O. Reg. 76/06, effective May 1, 2006. Pursuant to Family Law Rule 1(9), when a form is referred to by number, the reference is to the form with that number that is described in the Table of Forms at the end of these rules and which is available at www.ontariocourtforms.on.ca. For your convenience, the government form as published on this website is reproduced below.]

Court File Number ....

.... *(Name of court)*

at .... *Court office address*

Applicant(s) ***(If the applicant is unknown at the time this affidavit is sworn/affirmed or if the applicant's name is not to be disclosed to the person swearing/affirming this affidavit, leave this box blank)***

Full legal name & address for service — street & number, municipality, postal code, telephone & fax and e-mail address (if any).	*Lawyer's name & address — street & number, municipality, postal code, telephone & fax numbers and e-mail address (if any).*

Respondent(s) ***(If there is a respondent, the first letter of the respondent's surname may be used)***

Full legal name & address for service — street & number, municipality, postal code, telephone & fax numbers and e-mail address (if any).	*Lawyer's name & address — street & number, municipality, postal code, telephone & fax numbers and e-mail address (if any).*

My name is *(full legal name)* ....

I live in *(municipality & province)* .... and I swear/affirm that the following is true:

1. The child's full legal name is: *(Give full legal name, date of birth, sex and birth registration number if known of person to be adopted. If this person was placed for adoption by a licensee or children's aid society, you may use an initial for the surname.)*

.... *Full legal name* .... *Date of Birth* .... *Sex* .... *Birth registration number*

2. I am *(State your relationship to the child.)* ....

3. The child was born on *(date)* ...., in *(municipality, province, etc.)*

4. The child's birth was registered with the vital statistics register of *(province)* ...., under the following name(s):

....

Check applicable box(es).

5.

❑ The child's biological father is *(father's full legal name)* ....

❑ I do not know the identity of the child's biological father. The only information that I have about his identity is as follows *(Give what information you have about who the father might be.)*

....

6. *(Name of person familiar with legal meaning of "parent")* .... has reviewed with me those categories of persons who qualify as "parents" for the purposes of the *Child and Family Services Act* and whose consents have to be obtained before the child can be adopted.

Check off all boxes below that apply to your situation.

7. The review mentioned in paragraph 6 included an examination of the following checklist:

(a) Within the 300-day period before the child's birth,

❑ the mother's husband *(husband's full legal name)* .... died.

❑ the mother got a divorce from *(spouse's full legal name)* ....

❑ the mother's cohabitation with *(man's full legal name)* .... that lasted for a period of *(State duration of relationship.)* .... came to an end.

❑ the mother was not cohabiting with anyone in a relationship of some permanence.

(b) At the time of the child's birth, the child's mother was

❑ not married.

❑ married to *(husband's full legal name)* ....

❑ not cohabiting with any man.

❑ cohabiting with *(man's full legal name)* .... for a period of *(State duration of relationship.)* ....

(c) After the child's birth, the child's mother

❑ remained unmarried to this day, to the best of my knowledge and information.

❑ was married to a man who has never acknowledged that he is the father of the child.

❑ was married on *(date of marriage)* .... to *(husband's full legal name)* ...., who acknowledged that he is the father of the child.

(d) Under Ontario's *Vital Statistics Act* or under similar legislation in another province or territory in Canada,

❑ no man, to the best of my knowledge and information,

❑ *(man's full legal name)* ....

has certified the child's birth as the child's father.

(e) As of today's date,

❑ no man has, to the best of my knowledge and information, been recognized by a court in Canada

❑ *(man's full legal name)* .... has been recognized by *(name of court)* ....

to be the father of the child.

(f) In the 12 months before the child was placed for adoption,

❑ no person,

❑ *(person's full legal name)* ....

has demonstrated a settled intention to treat the child as a child of his or her own family.

(g) In the 12 months before the child was placed for adoption,

❑ no person has acknowledged to me or, to the best of my knowledge and information, to any other person or agency,

❑ *(person's full legal name)* .... acknowledged

❑ to me

❑ to *(name of other person or agency)* ....

parentage of the child and provided for the child's support.

(h) A statutory declaration

❑ has, to the best of my knowledge and information, never been filed by any person,

❑ was filed by *(person's full legal name)* ....

with the office of the Registrar General acknowledging parentage of the child.

(i) There is

❑ no written agreement or court order requiring any person,

❑ a written agreement made on *(date)* ...., at *(municipality, etc.)* ...., requiring *(person's full name)* ....

❑ an order of *(name of court)* ...., made on *(date)* ...., at *(municipality, etc.)* .... requiring *(person's full legal name)* ....

to provide for the child's support.

(j) There is

❑ no written agreement or court order giving any person,

❑ a written agreement made on *(date)* ...., at *(municipality, etc.)* ...., giving *(person's full legal name)* ....

❑ an order of *(name of court)* ...., made on *(date)* .... at *(municipality, etc.)* ...., giving *(person's full legal name)* ....

custody of or access to the child.

8. The review in paragraphs 6 and 7 indicates that, other than the child's mother,

❑ no other person,

❑ *(full legal name of person(s))* ....

meets/meet the definition of "parent" whose consent would therefore be required before the child could be adopted.

Sworn/Affirmed before me at .... *municipality* in .... *province, state or country* on .... *date*	
Commissioner for taking affidavits (Type or print name below if signature is illegible.)	*Signature* *(This form is to be signed in front of a lawyer, justice of the peace, notary public or commissioner for taking affidavits.)*

September 1, 2005

FORM 34B — NON-PARENT'S CONSENT TO ADOPTION BY SPOUSE

[Repealed O. Reg. 76/06, s. 15.]

[Editor's Note: Forms 4 to 39 of the Family Law Rules have been repealed by O. Reg. 76/06, effective May 1, 2006. Pursuant to Family Law Rule 1(9), when a form is referred to by number, the reference is to the form with that number that is described in the Table of Forms at the end of these rules and which is available at www.ontariocourtforms.on.ca. For your convenience, the government form as published on this website is reproduced below.]

Court File Number ....

.... *(Name of court)*

at .... *Court office address*

Applicant(s) (The first letter of the applicant's surname may be used)

Full legal name & address for service — street & number, municipality, postal code, telephone & fax numbers and e-mail address (if any).	*Lawyer's name & address — street & number, municipality, postal code, telephone & fax numbers and e-mail address (if any).*

Respondent(s) (If there is a respondent, the first letter of the respondent's surname may be used)

Full legal name & address for service — street & number, municipality, postal code, telephone & fax numbers and e-mail address (if any).	*Lawyer's name & address — street & number, municipality, postal code, telephone & fax numbers and e-mail address (if any).*

1. My name is *(full legal name)* .... and I live in *(municipality & province)* ....

2. The applicant is my "spouse" within the meaning of Part VII of the *Child and Family Services Act.*

3. I am not a "parent" of the child in this case within the meaning of Part VII of the *Child and Family Services Act.*

4. I consent to the adoption of: *(Give full legal name, date of birth, sex and birth registration number if known of person to be adopted. If this person is a Crown ward or was placed for adoption by a licensee or children's aid society, you may use an initial for the surname.)*

....	....	....	....
Full legal name	*Date of birth*	*Sex*	*Birth registration number*

by my spouse *(spouse's full legal name)* ....

....
Date of signatures

....
Signature of non-parent

....
Signature of independent lawyer

NOTE: This consent must be witnessed by an independent lawyer who is to provide an affidavit of execution and independent legal advice on the next sheet of this form.

AFFIDAVIT OF EXECUTION AND INDEPENDENT LEGAL ADVICE

My name is (full legal name) .... *and I swear/affirm that the following is true*:

1. I am a member of the Bar of *(name of jurisdiction)* .... and I am not acting for any other person in this adoption case.

2. I explained to *(non-parent's full legal name)* .... about

- ❑ the nature and effect of adoption under the law of Ontario;
- ❑ the nature and effect of this consent;
- ❑ the circumstances under which this consent may be withdrawn; and
- ❑ the right to counselling.

3. After my explanation, he/she told me that he/she wanted to sign this consent.

4. I was present at and witnessed the signing of this consent.

Sworn/Affirmed before me at ....
municipality

in ....
province, state or country

....
Signature

on .... *date*	.... *Commissioner for taking affidavits* *(Type or print name below if signature is illegible.)*	*(This form is to be signed in front of a lawyer, justice of the peace, notary public or commissioner for taking affidavits.)*

June 15, 2007

FORM 34C — DIRECTOR'S OR LOCAL DIRECTOR'S STATEMENT ON ADOPTION

[Repealed O. Reg. 76/06, s. 15.]

[Editor's Note: Forms 4 to 39 of the Family Law Rules have been repealed by O. Reg. 76/06, effective May 1, 2006. Pursuant to Family Law Rule 1(9), when a form is referred to by number, the reference is to the form with that number that is described in the Table of Forms at the end of these rules and which is available at www.ontariocourtforms.on.ca. For your convenience, the government form as published on this website is reproduced below.]

Court File Number ....

.... *(Name of court)*

at .... *Court office address*

Applicant(s) ***(The first letter of the applicant's surname may be used)***

Full legal name & address for service — street & number, municipality, postal code, telephone & fax and e-mail address (if any).	*Lawyer's name & address — street & number, municipality, postal code, telephone & fax numbers and e-mail address (if any).*

Child ....

(Child's full legal name. If this person is a Crown ward or was placed by a licensee or children's aid society, you may use an initial for the surname.)

.... *Date of birth* ...... *Sex* .... *Birth registration number*

A local director of a children's aid society may complete this form only where the child was placed for adoption by the society and the child has resided in the home of the applicant(s) for at least 6 months.

1. My name is *(full legal name)* ...., and I am

- ❑ appointed as a Director under the *Child and Family Services Act.*
- ❑ the local director of *(full legal name of children's aid society)* ....

2. The child in this adoption case

- ❑ is less than 16 years of age.
- ❑ is less than 18 years of age and has not withdrawn from parental control.

3. The child has resided in the home of the applicant(s) since *(date)* ....

4. Having regard to the child's best interests, I recommend:

- ❑ that the period of residence be dispensed with and that an order be made for the child's adoption by the applicant(s).
- ❑ that the court make an order of temporary custody of the child in favour of the applicant(s) for a period not exceeding one year on the terms set out on the other side of this form.
- ❑ because the child has resided in the home of the applicant(s) for at least 6 months, that an order be made for the child's adoption by the applicant(s).
- ❑ that an order for the child's adoption not be made for reasons set out on the other side of this form.

5. The report on the child's adjustment in the home of the applicant(s) is attached to this form.

6. There are

- ❑ no additional circumstances to which I want to draw the court's attention.
- ❑ additional circumstances set out on the back of this form to which I want to draw the court's attention.

.... *Date of Signature*

.... *Signature*

NOTE TO THE APPLICANT(S): If you disagree with any of the statements made in this document, you will have a chance to challenge it in court and to present your own evidence.

NOTE TO DIRECTOR OR LOCAL DIRECTOR: If, in the Director's or local director's opinion, it would not be in the child's best interest to make the order, this form and any attachments must be filed with the court and served on the applicant(s) at least 30 days before the adoption hearing.

(Set out any additional circumstances to which the court's attention should be drawn. If more space is needed, an additional page may be attached.)

....

....

(Set out proposed terms of the temporary custody order or the reasons for recommending against the making of an adoption order. If more space is needed, an additional page may be attached.)

....

....

September 1, 2005

FORM 34D — AFFIDAVIT OF ADOPTION APPLICANT(S), SWORN/AFFIRMED

[Editor's Note: Forms 4 to 39 of the Family Law Rules have been repealed by O. Reg. 76/06, effective May 1, 2006. Pursuant to Family Law Rule 1(9), when a form is referred to by number, the reference is to the form with that number that is described in the Table of Forms at the end of these rules and which is available at www.ontariocourtforms.on.ca. For your convenience, the government form as published on this website is reproduced below.]

ONTARIO

Court File Number

....

(Name of court)

at ....

Court office address

Applicant(s) (The first letter of the applicant's surname may be used)

Full legal name & address for service — street & number, municipality, postal code, telephone & fax numbers and e-mail address (if any).	*Lawyer's name & address — street & number, municipality, postal code, telephone & fax numbers and e-mail address (if any).*

Respondent(s) (If there is a respondent, the first letter of the respondent's surname may be used)

Full legal name & address for service — street & number, municipality, postal code, telephone & fax numbers and e-mail address (if any).	*Lawyer's name & address — street & number, municipality, postal code, telephone & fax numbers and e-mail address (if any).*

Child .... *(Child's full legal name. If this person is a Crown ward or was placed by a licensee or children's aid society, you may use an initial for the surname.)*

....

Date of birth *Sex* *Birth registration number*

My/Our name(s) is/are (full legal name(s)) ....

I/We live in (municipality & province) ....

and I/we swear/affirm that the following is true:

1. I am/We are the applicant(s) for the adoption of the child in this case and reside in Ontario.

2. My/Our birthdate(s) is/are: *(For two persons, indicate which birthdate belongs to whom.)*

....

....

3. The details of my/our background are as follows: *(Give details of your health, education, employment, ability to support and care for the child and any other relevant background material. If you need more space, you may add a page.)*

....

....

....

....

....

....

....

....

....

....

Put a line through any blank space left on this page.

4. The child is a resident of Ontario and is:

❑ my/our grandchild by blood, marriage or adoption.

❑ my/our grandnephew/grandniece by blood, marriage or adoption.

❑ my/our nephew/niece by blood, marriage or adoption.

❑ a child of my spouse.

❑ a member of my/our band or native community.

❑ not related to me/us.

5. The history of my/our relationship with the child is as follows: *(Give details of history of your relationship with the child. If you need more space, you may add a page.)*

....

....

....

....

....

....

....

....

....

....

....

....

....

....

....

....

....

....

....

....

....

....

....

....

....

....

....

....

....

....

....

Put a line through any blank space left on this page.

Check applicable box.

6.

❑ I am the sole applicant for this child's adoption and if an adoption order is made, I will be the child's only legal parent.

❑ I am the sole applicant for this child's adoption. If an adoption order is made, I will be joining with *(spouse's full legal name)* ...., who is my spouse within the meaning of Part VII of the *Child and Family Services Act*, and together, we will be the child's only legal parents.

❑ We are applying for this child's adoption jointly as spouses within the meaning of Part VII of the *Child and Family Services Act*. If an adoption order is made, we will be the child's only legal parents.

7. I/We understand and appreciate the special role of an adopting parent.

8. No payment or reward of any kind was made, given, received or agreed to be made, given or received by me/us or, to the best of my/our knowledge, by any other person in connection with,

(a) the adoption of this child;

(b) this child's placement for adoption;

(c) the giving of any consent to this child's adoption; or

(d) any negotiations or arrangements leading up to this child's adoption, except for what is permitted by the *Child and Family Services Act* and the regulations made under that Act.

9. I/We understand the importance of the child's culture and will make efforts to preserve his/her traditions, heritage and cultural identity.

10. I/We understand that once the child turns eighteen years old, he/she can apply for a copy of his/her original birth registration, if any, and a copy of his/her adoption order.

11. I/We understand that once the child turns nineteen years old, his/her birth parent(s) can apply for information from his/her original birth registration, if any, any substituted birth registration, and his/her adoption order. This information would include the child's full legal name after adoption.

12. I/We understand the provisions of the *Vital Statistics Act* and the *Child and Family Services Act* related to the disclosure of adoption information.

13. I/We want to bring to the court's attention the following additional facts about the child's best interests: *(Give any additional facts. If you need more space, you may add a page.)*

....

....

....

....

....

....

....

....

....

Put a line through any blank space left on this page.

Sworn/Affirmed before me at .... *municipality* in .... *province, state or country* on .... *date* .... *Commissioner for taking affidavits* *(Type or print name below if signature is illegible.)*	.... *Signature* *(This form is to be signed in front of a lawyer, justice of the peace, notary public or commissioner for taking affidavits.)*

April 1, 2009

FORM 34E — DIRECTOR'S CONSENT TO ADOPTION

[Repealed O. Reg. 76/06, s. 15.]

[Editor's Note: Forms 4 to 39 of the Family Law Rules have been repealed by O. Reg. 76/06, effective May 1, 2006. Pursuant to Family Law Rule 1(9), when a form is referred to by number, the reference is to the form with that number that is described in the Table of Forms at the end of these rules and which is available at www.ontariocourtforms.on.ca. For your convenience, the government form as published on this website is reproduced below.]

Court File Number ....

.... *(Name of court)*

at .... *Court office address*

Applicant(s) ***(The first letter of the applicant's surname may be used)***

Full legal name & address for service — street & number, municipality, postal code, telephone & fax and e-mail address (if any).	*Lawyer's name & address — street & number, municipality, postal code, telephone & fax numbers and e-mail address (if any).*

Child ....

(Child's full legal name. If this person is a Crown ward or was placed by a licensee or children's aid society, you may use an initial for the surname.)

.... *Date of birth* ...... *Sex* .... *Birth registration number*

1. My name is *(full legal name)* ...., and I am appointed as a Director under the *Child and Family Services Act.*

2. The child in this adoption case became a Crown ward on *(date)* .... and was placed into the care of *(full legal name of children's aid society)* ....

3. The are no outstanding access orders with respect to this child

4. I consent to this child's adoption by the applicant(s).

.... *Date of signature*

.... *Signature*

September 1, 2005

FORM 34F — PARENT'S OR CUSTODIAN'S CONSENT TO ADOPTION

[Editor's Note: Forms 4 to 39 of the Family Law Rules have been repealed by O. Reg. 76/06, effective May 1, 2006. Pursuant to Family Law Rule 1(9), when a form is referred to by number, the reference is to the form with that number that is described in the Table of Forms

at the end of these rules and which is available at www.ontariocourtforms.on.ca. For your convenience, the government form as published on this website is reproduced below.]

ONTARIO

Court File Number

....

(Name of court)

at ....

Court office address

1. My name is (full legal name) .... *I was born on (date of birth)* .... *and I live at (address)* ....

2. The child in this case is: *(Give child's full legal name, date of birth, sex and birth registration number, if available.)*

....	....	....	....
Full legal name	*Date of birth*	*Sex*	*Birth registration number*

3. I am a parent of the child within the meaning of Part VII of the Child and Family Services Act because I am (Check appropriate paragraph below.)

❑ the child's mother.

❑ the child's father.

❑ the person presumed to be the child's father under section 8 of the *Children's Law Reform Act.*

❑ an individual having lawful custody of the child.

❑ an individual who, during the 12 months before the child was placed for adoption, has demonstrated a settled intention to treat the child as a member of his/her family.

❑ an individual who, during the 12 months before the child was placed for adoption, has acknowledged parentage of the child and has provided for the child's support.

❑ an individual who is required to provide for the child or who has custody of or access to the child under a written agreement or a court order.

❑ an individual who has acknowledged parentage of the child under section 12 of the *Children's Law Reform Act.*

4. I consent to the adoption of this child.

5. I understand the nature and effect of this consent. I understand that I may withdraw this consent as follows:

- If the child is placed for adoption by a children's aid society, by ensuring that the children's aid society located at *(address)* .... receives my written notice of withdrawal within 21 days after my consent was given.

- If the child is placed for adoption by a licensee, by ensuring that the licensee located at *(address)* .... receives my written notice of withdrawal within 21 days after my consent was given.

- If a relative of the child or the spouse of a parent proposes to apply to adopt the child, by ensuring that the proposed applicant receives my written notice of withdrawal within 21 days after my consent was given.

6. I understand that, after the 21 days have passed, I am not allowed to withdraw this consent unless I first get the court's permission, and then only if my child has not yet been placed for adoption and if I can show that it is in the child's best interests that this consent be withdrawn.

7. I understand the nature of an adoption order and that, if an adoption order is made, I will no longer be a legal parent to the child.

8. I understand that once the child turns eighteen years old, he/she can apply for a copy of his/her original birth registration, if any, and a copy of his/her adoption order. I understand that my full legal name may be included on such copies.

9. I understand that once the child turns nineteen years old, his/her birth parent(s) may apply for information from his/her original birth registration, if any, any substituted birth registration, and his/her adoption order. This information would include the child's full legal name after adoption.

10. I understand my right to ask and to be told whether an adoption order has been made for the child.

11. I understand my rights and the rights of other persons with respect to the disclosure of adoption information.

12. No payment or reward of any kind was made, given, received or agreed to be made, given or received by me/us or, to the best of my/our knowledge, by any other person in connection with,

(a) the adoption of this child;

(b) this child's placement for adoption;

(c) the giving of any consent to this child's adoption; or

(d) any negotiations or arrangements leading up to this child's adoption,

except for what is permitted by the *Child and Family Services Act* and the regulations made under that Act.

13. I have had a chance to get counselling about this consent.

14. I have had independent legal advice about this consent.

....

Date of signatures *Signature of parent*

....

Signature of independent lawyer

NOTE: This consent must be witnessed by an independent lawyer who is to provide an affidavit of execution and independent legal advice below. If the person giving this consent is less than 18 years old, the consent must be accompanied by Form 34J (Affidavit of Execution and Independent Legal Advice (Children's Lawyer)), instead of the Affidavit of Execution and Independent Legal Advice that accompanies this form.

AFFIDAVIT OF EXECUTION AND INDEPENDENT LEGAL ADVICE

My name is (full legal name) ....

and I swear/affirm that the following is true:

1. I am a member of the Bar of *(name of jurisdiction)* .... and I am not acting for any other person in this adoption case.

2. I explained to *(parent's full legal name)* .... about

- ❑ the nature and effect of adoption under the law of Ontario;
- ❑ the nature and effect of this consent;
- ❑ the circumstances under which this consent may be withdrawn;
- ❑ his/her rights and the rights of other persons with respect to the disclosure of adoption information;
- ❑ the right to counselling.

3. After my explanation, he/she told me that he/she wanted to sign this consent.

4. I was present at and witnessed the signing of this consent.

Sworn/Affirmed before me at .... *municipality* in .... *province, state or country* on .... *date* .... *Commissioner for taking affidavits* *(Type or print name below if signature is illegible.)*	.... *Signature* *(This form is to be signed in front of a lawyer, justice of the peace, notary public or commissioner for taking affidavits.)*

April 1, 2009

FORM 34G — AFFIDAVIT OF ADOPTION LICENSEE OR SOCIETY EMPLOYEE

[Repealed O. Reg. 76/06, s. 15.]

[Editor's Note: Forms 4 to 39 of the Family Law Rules have been repealed by O. Reg. 76/06, effective May 1, 2006. Pursuant to Family Law Rule 1(9), when a form is referred to by number, the reference is to the form with that number that is described in the Table of Forms at the end of these rules and which is available at www.ontariocourtforms.on.ca. For your convenience, the government form as published on this website is reproduced below.]

Court File Number ....

.... *(Name of court)*

at .... *Court office address*

Applicant(s) ***(The first letter of the applicant's surname may be used)***

Full legal name & address for service — street & number, municipality, postal code, telephone & fax and e-mail address (if any).	*Lawyer's name & address — street & number, municipality, postal code, telephone & fax numbers and e-mail address (if any).*

Respondent(s) ***(If there is a respondent, the first letter of the respondent's surname may be used)***

Full legal name & address for service — street & number, municipality, postal code, telephone & fax numbers and e-mail address (if any)	*Lawyer's name & address — street & number, municipality, postal code, telephone & fax numbers and e-mail address (if any).*

My name is *(full legal name)* ....

I live in *(municipality & province)* .... and I swear/affirm that the following is true:

1. The name of the child being placed for adoption is: *(Give child's full legal name, date of birth, sex and birth registration number, if known of person to be adopted. If this person is a Crown ward or was placed for adoption by a licensee or children's aid society, you may use an initial for the surname.)*

.... *Full legal name* .... *Date of birth* ...... *Sex* .... *Birth registration number*

2. I am

❑ a person licensed under Part IX of the *Child and Family Services Act* to place the child for adoption.

❑ an employee of *(full legal name of children's aid society)* .... authorized to place the child for adoption.

❑ an employee of *(full legal name of adoption agency)* .... which is licensed under Part IX of the *Child and Family Services Act* to place the child for adoption.

3. I have made reasonable inquiries about the existence of any outstanding orders of custody of or access to the child. To the best of my knowledge,

❑ there is no outstanding order.

❑ the outstanding order(s) is/are as follows: *(For each order, give the name of the court, date of order, name of judge, court file number and full legal name(s) of the person(s) given custody or access under the order.)*

....

....

4. I have made reasonable inquiries about the existence of any person — other than the person(s) who already filed a consent — who is a "parent" of the child within the meaning of Part VII of the *Child and Family Services Act*. To the best of my knowledge,

❑ there is no other "parent".

❑ the other "parent(s)" is/are: *(For each person, state his or her full legal name, address and an explanation why a consent is not yet available.)*

....

....

5. I have made reasonable inquiries about the existence of any other application for the adoption of this child. To the best of my knowledge,

❑ there has been no other adoption application with respect to this child.

❑ the details of the other adoption application(s) are as follows: *(For each application, state the name and location of the court before which the application was brought, the date of the application, the full legal name(s) of the applicant(s) and the result of the application.)*

....

....

6. I have made reasonable inquiries whether the person(s) who filed the consent(s) in this application withdrew the consent(s) or whether a court had set aside the consent(s). To the best of my knowledge,

❑ no consent was withdrawn or set aside.

❑ the details of the withdrawal or of the setting aside are as follows: *(Specify details.)*

....

....

7. The child in this adoption case

❑ is 7 or more years old and I have therefore offered the child a chance to get counselling about the consent. This offer of counselling

❑ was accepted and the child received counselling.

❑ was turned down by the child.

I also ensured that the child received independent legal advice from *(lawyer's name)* ....

❑ is less than 7 years old and no counselling or independent legal advice was offered.

8. I offered the child's parent(s) a chance to get counselling about the consent and the offer

❑ was accepted by *(name of parent(s) who accepted offer)* .... and counselling was provided.

❑ was turned down by *(name of parent(s) who refused offer)* ....

9. The parent(s) received independent legal advice from *(name of lawyer(s))* ....

10. To the best of my knowledge, no person has given, received or agreed to give or receive any payment or reward of any kind in connection with

(a) the adoption of the child;

(b) the child's placement for adoption;

(c) the giving of any consent to the child's adoption; or

(d) any negotiations or arrangements leading up to the child's adoption,

except for what is permitted by the *Child and Family Services Act* and the regulations made under it.

Sworn/Affirmed before me at .... *municipality* in .... *province, state or country* on .... *date*	

Commissioner for taking affidavits (Type or print name below if signature is illegible.)	Signature (This form is to be signed in front of a lawyer, justice of the peace, notary public or commissioner for taking affidavits.)

September 1, 2005

FORM 34H — AFFIDAVIT OF ADOPTING RELATIVE OR STEPPARENT, SWORN/AFFIRMED

[Repealed O. Reg. 76/06, s. 15.]

[Editor's Note: Forms 4 to 39 of the Family Law Rules have been repealed by O. Reg. 76/06, effective May 1, 2006. Pursuant to Family Law Rule 1(9), when a form is referred to by number, the reference is to the form with that number that is described in the Table of Forms at the end of these rules and which is available at www.ontariocourtforms.on.ca. For your convenience, the government form as published on this website is reproduced below.]

ONTARIO

Court File Number

....

(Name of court)

at ....

Court office address

Applicant(s) (The first letter of the applicant's surname may be used)

Full legal name & address for service — street & number, municipality, postal code, telephone & fax numbers and e-mail address (if any).	*Lawyer's name & address — street & number, municipality, postal code, telephone & fax numbers and e-mail address (if any).*

Respondent(s) (If there is a respondent, the first letter of the respondent's surname may be used)

Full legal name & address for service — street & number, municipality, postal code, telephone & fax numbers and e-mail address (if any).	*Lawyer's name & address — street & number, municipality, postal code, telephone & fax numbers and e-mail address (if any).*

My name is (full legal name) ....

I live in (municipality & province) ....

and I swear/affirm that the following is true:

1. I was born on *(date of your own birth)* ....

2. The name of the child whom I want to adopt is *(Give full legal name, date of birth, sex and birth registration number if known)*

....	....	....	....
Full legal name	*Date of birth*	*Sex*	*Birth registration number*

3. I am the applicant in this adoption and am this child's

❑ stepparent.

❑ aunt/uncle by blood, marriage or adoption.

❑ grandparent by blood, marriage or adoption.

❑ great-aunt/great-uncle by blood, marriage or adoption.

4. I have made reasonable inquiries about the existence of any outstanding orders of custody of or access to the child. To the best of my knowledge,

❑ there is no outstanding order.

❑ the outstanding order(s) is/are as follows: *(For each order, give the name of the court, date of order, name of judge, court file number and full legal name(s) of the person(s) given custody or access under the order.)*

....

....

....

....

....

....

Put a line through any space left on this page.

5. I have made reasonable inquiries about the existence of any person — other than the person(s) who already filed a consent — who is a "parent" of the child within the meaning of Part VII of the *Child and Family Services Act*. To the best of my knowledge,

❑ there is no other "parent".

❑ the other "parent(s)" is/are: (For each parent, state his or her full legal name, address and an explanation why a consent is not yet available.)

....

....

6. I have made reasonable inquiries about the existence of any other application for the adoption of this child. To the best of my knowledge,

❑ there has been no other adoption application with respect to this child.

❑ the details of the other adoption application(s) are as follows: *(For each application, state the name and location of the court before which the application was brought, the date of the application, the full legal name(s) of the applicant(s) and the result of the application.)*

....

....

....

....

7. I have made reasonable inquiries whether the person(s) who filed the consent(s) in this application withdrew the consent(s) or whether a court had set aside the consent(s). To the best of my knowledge,

❑ no consent was withdrawn or set aside.

❑ the details of the withdrawal or of the setting aside are as follows: *(Specify details.)*

....

....

....

....

8. The child in this adoption case

❑ is 7 or more years old and I have therefore offered the child a chance to get counselling about the consent. This offer of counselling

❑ was accepted and the child received counselling.

❑ was turned down by the child.

I also ensured that the child received independent legal advice from *(lawyer's name)*

....

❑ is less than 7 years old and no counselling or independent legal advice was offered.

9. I offered the child's parent(s) a chance to get counselling about the consent and the offer

❑ was accepted by *(name of parent(s) who accepted offer)* .... and counselling was provided.

❑ was turned down by *(name of parent(s) who refused offer)*

....

Put a line through any space left on this page.

10. I also ensured that the parent(s) received independent legal advice from (name of lawyer(s))

....

11. To the best of my knowledge, no person has given, received or agreed to give or receive any payment or reward of any kind in connection with,

(a) the adoption of the child;

(b) the child's placement for adoption;

(c) the giving of any consent to the child's adoption; or

(d) any negotiations or arrangements leading up to the child's adoption,

except for what is permitted by the *Child and Family Services Act* and the regulations made under it.

12. I understand that once the child turns eighteen years old, he/she can apply for a copy of his/her original birth registration, if any, and a copy of his/her adoption order.

13. I understand that once the child turns nineteen years old, his/her birth parent(s) can apply for information from his/her original birth registration, if any, any substituted birth registration and his/her adoption order. This information would include the child's full legal name after adoption.

14. I understand the provisions of the *Vital Statistics Act* and the *Child and Family Services Act* related to the disclosure of adoption information.

Sworn/Affirmed before me at .... *municipality*

in .... *province, state or country*

on .... *date*

.... *Commissioner for taking affidavits* *(Type or print name below if signature is illegible.)*

.... *Signature* *(This form is to be signed in front of a lawyer, justice of the peace, notary public orcommissioner for taking affidavits.)*

April 1, 2009

FORM 34I — PARENT'S CONSENT TO ADOPTION BY SPOUSE

[Editor's Note: Forms 4 to 39 of the Family Law Rules have been repealed by O. Reg. 76/06, effective May 1, 2006. Pursuant to Family Law Rule 1(9), when a form is referred to by number, the reference is to the form with that number that is described in the Table of Forms at the end of these rules and which is available at www.ontariocourtforms.on.ca. For your convenience, the government form as published on this website is reproduced below.]

ONTARIO

Court File Number

....

(Name of court)

at ....

Court office address

Applicant(s) (The first letter of the applicant's surname may be used)

Full legal name & address for service — street & number, municipality, postal code, telephone & fax numbers and e-mail address (if any).	*Lawyer's name & address — street & number, municipality, postal code, telephone & fax numbers and e-mail address (if any).*

Respondent(s) (If there is a respondent, the first letter of the respondent's surname may be used)

Full legal name & address for service — street & number, municipality, postal code, telephone & fax numbers and e-mail address (if any).	*Lawyer's name & address — street & number, municipality, postal code, telephone & fax numbers and e-mail address (if any).*

Child .... *(Child's full legal name. If this person is a Crown ward or was placed by a licensee or children's aid society, you may use an initial for the surname.)*

....	....	....
Date of birth	*Sex*	*Birth registration number*

1. My name is (full legal name) .... *I was born on (date of birth)* .... *and I live at (address)* ....

2. The applicant is my "spouse" within the meaning of Part VII of the *Child and Family Services Act.*

3. I am a parent of the child within the meaning of Part VII of the *Child and Family Services Act* because I am *(Check appropriate paragraph below.)*

❑ the child's mother.

❑ the child's father.

❑ the person presumed to be the child's father under section 8 of the *Children's Law Reform Act.*

❑ an individual having lawful custody of the child.

❑ an individual who, during the 12 months before the child was placed for adoption, has demonstrated a settled intention to treat the child as a member of his/her family.

❑ an individual who, during the 12 months before the child was placed for adoption, has acknowledged parentage of the child and has provided for the child's support.

❑ an individual who is required to provide for the child or who has custody of or access to the child under a written agreement or a court order.

❑ an individual who has acknowledged parentage of the child under section 12 of the *Children's Law Reform Act.*

4. I consent to the adoption of the child by my spouse.

5. I understand the nature and effect of this consent. I understand that I may withdraw my consent by ensuring that the proposed applicant receives my written notice of withdrawal within 21 days after my consent was given.

6. I understand that, after the 21 days have passed, I am not allowed to withdraw this consent unless I first get the court's permission and if I can show that it is in the child's best interests that this consent be withdrawn.

7. I understand the nature of an adoption order. I understand that, if an adoption order were made, my spouse would be joining me in the role of a parent and, together, we would be the child's only legal parents. An adoption order would require me to share my parental rights and responsibilities with my spouse equally and permanently until a court ordered otherwise.

8. I understand my rights and the rights of other persons with respect to the disclosure of adoption information.

9. No payment or reward of any kind was made, given, received or agreed to be made, given or received by me/us or, to the best of my/our knowledge, by any other person in connection with,

(a) the adoption of this child;

(b) this child's placement for adoption;

(c) the giving of any consent to this child's adoption; or

(d) any negotiations or arrangements leading up to this child's adoption,

except for what is permitted by the *Child and Family Services Act* and the regulations made under that Act.

10. I had a chance to seek counselling with respect to this consent.

11. I have had independent legal advice with respect to this consent.

....	....
Date of signatures	*Signature of parent*
	....
	Signature of independent lawyer

NOTE: This consent must be witnessed by an independent lawyer who is to provide an affidavit of execution and independent legal advice below. If the person giving this consent is less than 18 years old, the consent must be accompanied by Form 34J (Affidavit of Execution and Independent Legal Advice (Children's Lawyer)), instead of the Affidavit of Execution and Independent Legal Advice that accompanies this form.

AFFIDAVIT OF EXECUTION AND INDEPENDENT LEGAL ADVICE

My name is (full legal name) ....

and I swear/affirm that the following is true:

1. I am a member of the Bar of *(name of jurisdiction)* .... and I am not acting for any other person in this adoption case.

2. I explained to *(parent's full legal name)* .... about

❑ the nature and effect of adoption under the law of Ontario;

❑ the nature and effect of this consent;

❑ the circumstances under which this consent may be withdrawn;
❑ his/her rights and the rights of other persons with respect to the disclosure of adoption information;
❑ the right to counselling.

3. After my explanation, he/she told me that he/she wanted to sign this consent.

4. I was present at and witnessed the signing of this consent.

Sworn/Affirmed before me at .... *municipality* in .... *province, state or country* on .... *date* .... *Commissioner for taking affidavits* *(Type or print name below if signature is illegible.)*	.... *Signature* *(This form is to be signed in front of a lawyer, justice of the peace, notary public or commissioner for taking affidavits.)*

April 1, 2009

FORM 34J — AFFIDAVIT OF EXECUTION AND INDEPENDENT LEGAL ADVICE (CHILDREN'S LAWYER), SWORN/AFFIRMED

[Repealed O. Reg. 76/06, s. 15.]

[Editor's Note: Forms 4 to 39 of the Family Law Rules have been repealed by O. Reg. 76/06, effective May 1, 2006. Pursuant to Family Law Rule 1(9), when a form is referred to by number, the reference is to the form with that number that is described in the Table of Forms at the end of these rules and which is available at www.ontariocourtforms.on.ca. For your convenience, the government form as published on this website is reproduced below.]

ONTARIO

Court File Number

....
(Name of court)

at ....
Court office address

My name is (full legal name) ....

and I swear/affirm that the following is true:

1. I am an authorized representative of the Office of the Children's Lawyer in the adoption of:

Full legal name of child	*Date of birth (d, m, y) and sex*

2. I explained to *(minor parent's full legal name)* .... about

❑ the nature and effect of adoption under the law of Ontario;

❑ the nature and effect of a consent to adoption;

❑ the right to counselling;

❑ his/her rights and the rights of other persons with respect to the disclosure of adoption information;

❑ the right upon request to be advised whether an adoption order has been made,

in language appropriate to his/her age to the best of my knowledge and skills.

3. I also explained that he/she could withdraw the consent within 21 days by a written notice. I gave him/her the address where the written notice would have to be served. I also explained that, after the 21 days had passed, he/she could withdraw the consent only with the court's permission but only if the child had not yet been placed with a person for adoption and if he/she could convince the court that it would be in the child's best interests to have the consent withdrawn.

4. After my explanation, he/she told me that he/she wanted to sign the consent to adoption and I believe that this reflects his/her true wishes.

5. I was present at and witnessed the signing of the consent.

Sworn/Affirmed before me at .... *municipality* in .... *province, state or country* on .... *date* .... *Commissioner for taking affidavits (Type or print name below if signature is illegible.)*	.... *Signature (This form is to be signed in front of a lawyer,justice of the peace, notary public orcommissioner for taking affidavits.)*

April 1, 2009

FORM 34K — CERTIFICATE OF CLERK (ADOPTION)

[Editor's Note: Forms 4 to 39 of the Family Law Rules have been repealed by O. Reg. 76/06, effective May 1, 2006. Pursuant to Family Law Rule 1(9), when a form is referred to by number, the reference is to the form with that number that is described in the Table of Forms at the end of these rules and which is available at www.ontariocourtforms.on.ca. For your convenience, the government form as published on this website is reproduced below.]

Court File Number ....

.... *(Name of court)*

at .... *Court office address*

Applicant(s) (The first letter of the applicant's surname may be used)

Full legal name & address for service — street & number, municipality, postal code, telephone & fax numbers and e-mail address (if any).	*Lawyer's name & address — street & number, municipality, postal code, telephone & fax numbers and e-mail address (if any).*

Respondent(s) (If there is a respondent, the first letter of the surname may be used)

Full legal name & address for service — street & number, municipality, postal code, telephone & fax numbers and e-mail address (if any).	*Lawyer's name & address — street & number, municipality, postal code, telephone & fax numbers and e-mail address (if any).*

If the appropriate box on the left cannot be checked, check the box on the right margin and describe the deficiency by the box.

The clerk of the court certifies as follows:

1. MATERIAL COMMON TO ALL ADOPTION CASES — *Deficiency*

(a) ❑ An application for adoption (Form 8D in *Family Law Rules*) has been filed. — 1(a) ❑

(b) ❑ A certified copy of the statement of live birth has been filed (Form 2 in regulation under *Vital Statistics Act*). — 1(b) ❑

❑ A certified copy of a change of birth registration has been filed (Form 2 in regulation under *Vital Statistics Act*).

❑ Equivalent proof of details of birth has been filed.

(c) ❑ The person to be adopted is 7 years of age or over and has filed a consent to adoption (Form 34 in *Family Law Rules*). — 1(c) ❑

❑ A court order dispensing with the consent of the person to be adopted has been filed.

(d) ❑ An affidavit of parentage has been filed (Form 34A in *Family Law Rules*). 1(d) ❑

❑ Other evidence of who is or is not a "parent" has been filed.

(e) ❑ A report on the child's adjustment in the applicant's home: 1(e) ❑

❑ is required by the Act (where a child had been "placed" for adoption through a licensee, a society or otherwise). That report has been filed.

❑ had been ordered by the court in the case of an adoption by a stepparent or relative. That report has been filed.

❑ has not been required in this case.

(f) ❑ The applicant has a "spouse" who is not a "parent" and who has not joined in the application. That spouse's consent (Form 34B in *Family Law Rules*) has been filed. 1(f) ❑

❑ A court order dispensing with the spouse's consent has been filed, together with,

(i) ❑ proof of service of this order.

(ii) ❑ a certified copy of an order dispensing with service.

(g) ❑ The Director's or local director's statement (with recommendations) on the adoption (Form 34C in *Family Law Rules*): 1(g) ❑

❑ is required by the Act (where a child had been "placed" for adoption through a licensee, a society or otherwise). That statement has been filed.

❑ had been ordered by the court in the case of an adoption by a stepparent or relative. That statement has been filed.

❑ has not been required in this case.

(h) ❑ The affidavit of each adoption applicant (Form 34D in *Family Law Rules*) has been filed. 1(h) ❑

(i) ❑ A draft adoption order (Form 25C in *Family Law Rules*) has been filed. 1(i) ❑

(j) ❑ This is a joint application by spouses and 1(j) ❑

(i) ❑ a certificate of the applicants' marriage had been filed.

(ii) ❑ other proof of the applicants' spousal status has been filed.

(k) ❑ Other joint application *(Specify.)* 1(k) ❑

....

(l) ❑ *(Other. Specify.)* 1(l) ❑

....

2. *ADDITIONAL MATERIAL FOR CROWN WARDSHIP ADOPTIONS*

(a) ❑ The Director's consent to adoption (Form 34E in *Family Law Rules*) has been filed. 2(a) ❑

(b) ❑ There is no outstanding access order to this Crown ward. 2(b) ❑

❑ A certified copy of an order terminating access to this Crown ward has been filed, together with,

(i) ❑ proof of service of this order.

(ii) ❑ a certified copy of an order dispensing with service.

(c) ❑ A certified copy of the Crown wardship order has been filed together with, 2(c) ❑

(i) ❑ proof of service of this order.

(ii) ❑ a certified copy of an order dispensing with service.

(d) ❑ A copy of any openness order has been filed (if applicable). 2(d) ❑

(e) ❑ An affidavit from the local director has been filed, stating that no appeal of the orders mentioned in clauses (b) and (c) above had been launched or that the appeal period had expired. 2(e) ❑

(f) ❑ The child is an Indian or native person and the society has filed the affidavit of service of its notice on the child's band or native community setting out the society's intention to place the child for adoption. 2(f) ❑

(g) ❑ *(Other. Specify.)* 2(g) ❑

....

3. *ADDITIONAL MATERIAL FOR NON-WARD ADOPTION THROUGH LICENSEE OR SOCIETY*

(a) ❑ The child has been placed by a children's aid society. 3(a) ❑

❑ The child has been placed by a licensee within the time frame allowed by the licence, a copy of which has been filed.

(b) ❑ An affidavit (Form 34G in *Family Law Rules*) of the licensee or of an authorized employee of the children's aid society has been filed. 3(b) ❑

(c) ❑ The person filing the affidavit knows of no custody or access order involving the child. 3(c) ❑

❑ Certified copy/copies of the custody or access order(s) involving the child has/have been filed together with,

(i) ❑ proof of service of this order.

(ii) ❑ a certified copy of an order dispensing with service.

(d) ❑ A consent (Form 34F in *Family Law Rules*) to adoption from the child's mother has been filed. 3(d) ❑

❑ The consent, which was signed by the mother when she was under 18 years of age, is accompanied by a certificate of the Children's Lawyer (Form 34J in *Family Law Rules*).

❑ The child's mother has, outside Ontario, signed a form of consent that is not an Ontario consent form and that is accompanied by:

(i) ❑ a certified translation of the document into English/French.

(ii) ❑ evidence that the foreign consent complies with the laws of the place where the mother made it.

❑ A certified copy of an order dispensing with the mother's consent has been filed, together with proof of service of the order.

(e) ❑ A consent (Form 34F in *Family Law Rules*) to adoption from the child's biological father has been filed. 3(e) ❑

❑ The consent, which was signed by the father when he was under 18 years of age, is accompanied by a certificate of the Children's Lawyer (Form 34J in *Family Law Rules*).

❑ The child's biological father has, outside Ontario, signed a form of consent that is not an Ontario consent form and that is accompanied by:

(i) ❑ a certified translation of the document into English/French.

(ii) ❑ evidence that the foreign consent complies with the laws of the place where the biological father made it.

❑ A certified copy of an order dispensing with the biological father's consent has been filed, together with proof of service of the order.

❑ The court has ruled that the biological father does not have the status of "parent" under Part VII of the *Child and Family Services Act*.

(f) ❑ A consent (Form 34F in *Family Law Rules*) to adoption from any other person who is a "parent" under Part VII of the *Child and Family Services Act* has been filed. 3(f) ❑

❑ The consent, which was signed by the other "parent" when he/she was under 18 years of age, is accompanied by a certificate of the Children's Lawyer (Form 34J in *Family Law Rules*).

❑ This other "parent" has, outside Ontario, signed a form of consent that is not an Ontario consent form and that is accompanied by:

(i) ❑ a certified translation of the document into English/French.

(ii) ❑ evidence that the foreign consent complies with the laws of the place where the other "parent" made it.

❑ A certified copy of an order dispensing with the other "parent's" consent has been filed, together with proof of service of the order.

(g) ❑ The child is an Indian or native person and an affidavit of service of the notice on the child's band or native community about the intention to place the child for adoption has been filed. 3(g) ❑

(h) ❑ *(Other. Specify.)* 3(h) ❑

....

4. *ADDITIONAL MATERIAL FOR ADOPTION BY RELATIVE OR STEP-PARENT OR WHERE CHILD HAS RESIDED WITH APPLICANT FOR AT LEAST TWO YEARS*

(a) ❑ There are no custody or access orders involving the child. 4(a) ❑

❑ Certified copy/copies of the custody or access order(s) involving the child has/have been filed together with,

(i) ❑ proof of service of this order.

(ii) ❑ a certified copy of an order dispensing with service.

(b) ❑ A consent (Form 34F in *Family Law Rules*) to adoption from the child's mother has been filed. 4(b) ❑

❑ The consent, which was signed by the mother when she was under 18 years of age, is accompanied by a certificate of the Children's Lawyer (Form 34J in *Family Law Rules*).

❑ The child's mother has, outside Ontario, signed a form of consent that is not an Ontario consent form and that is accompanied by:

(i) ❑ a certified translation of the document into English/French.

(ii) ❑ evidence that the foreign consent complies with the laws of the place where the mother made it.

❑ A certified copy of an order dispensing with the mother's consent has been filed, together with proof of service of the order.

(c) ❑ A consent (Form 34F in *Family Law Rules*) to adoption from the child's biological father has been filed. 4(c) ❑

❑ The consent, which was signed by the father when he was under 18 years of age, is accompanied by a certificate of the Children's Lawyer (Form 34J in *Family Law Rules*).

❑ The child's biological father has, outside Ontario, signed a form of consent that is not an Ontario consent form and that is accompanied by:

(i) a certified translation of the document into English/French.

(ii) ❑ evidence that the foreign consent complies with the laws of the place where the biological father made it.

❑ A certified copy of an order dispensing with the biological father's consent has been filed, together with proof of service of the order.

❑ The court has ruled that the biological father does not have the status of "parent" under Part VII of the *Child and Family Services Act*.

(d) ❑ A consent (Form 34F in *Family Law Rules*) to adoption from any other person who is a "parent" under Part VII of the *Child and Family Services Act* has been filed. 4(d) ❑

❑ The consent, which was signed by the other "parent" when he/she was under 18 years of age, is accompanied by a certificate of the Children's Lawyer (Form 34J in *Family Law Rules*).

❑ This other "parent" has, outside Ontario, signed a form of consent that is not an Ontario consent and that is accompanied by:

(i) ❑ a certified translation of the document into English/French.

(ii) ❑ evidence that the foreign consent complies with the laws of the place where the other "parent" made it.

❑ A certified copy of an order dispensing with the other "parent's" consent has been filed, together with proof of service of the order.

(e) ❑ The affidavit (Form 34H in *Family Law Rules*) of the stepparent or of each adoption applicant has been filed. 4(e) ❑

(f) ❑ This is a stepparent adoption and the spouse of the adopting stepparent has filed a consent (Form 34I in *Family Law Rules*). 4(f) ❑

(g) ❑ *(Other. Specify.)* 4(g) ❑

....

....	....
Date of Signature	*Signature of clerk of the court*

October 1, 2006

FORM 34L — APPLICATION FOR OPENNESS ORDER

[Editor's Note: Pursuant to Family Law Rule 1(9), when a form is referred to by number, the reference is to the form with that number that is described in the Table of Forms at the end of these rules and which is available at www.ontariocourtforms.on.ca. For your convenience, the government form as published on this website is reproduced below.]

Court File Number ....

SEAL

.... *(Name of court)*

at .... *Court office address*

Applicant (In all cases, the applicant will be a children's aid society.)

Full legal name & address for service — street & number, municipality, postal code, telephone & fax numbers and e-mail address (if any).	*Lawyer's name & address — street & number, municipality, postal code, telephone & fax numbers and e-mail address (if any).*

Respondent(s) (Persons entitled to notice.)

Full legal name & address for service — street & number, municipality, postal code, telephone & fax numbers and e-mail address (if any).	*Lawyer's name & address — street & number, municipality, postal code, telephone & fax numbers and e-mail address (if any).*

Children's Lawyer

Name & address of Children's Lawyer's agent for service (street & number, municipality, postal code, telephone & fax numbers and e-mail address (if any)) and name of person represented.

TO THE RESPONDENT(S):

A COURT APPLICATION HAS BEEN STARTED IN THIS COURT FOR AN OPENNESS ORDER. THE DETAILS ARE SET OUT ON THE ATTACHED PAGES.

THE FIRST COURT DATE IS (date) .... *AT* .... ❑ a.m. ❑ p.m. or as soon as possible after that time, at: *(address)* ....

You should consider getting legal advice about this case right away. If you cannot afford a lawyer, you may be able to get help from your local legal aid office. *(See your telephone directory under LEGAL AID.)*

....

Date of issue *Clerk of the court*

THE CHILD

Child's Full Legal Name	*Birthdate*	*Sex*	*Child's Native Status*

Crown Wardship Order:

Court File Number	*Court Office Address*	*Name of Judge*	*Date of Order*
Details of Order			

1. The applicant asks for an order that: *(Provide details of openness order.)*

....

....

....

....

....

....

2. The openness order will permit the continuation of a relationship with a person that is beneficial and meaningful to the child for the following reasons:

....

....

....

....

....

....

3. The openness order is in the best interests of the child for the following reasons:

....

....

....

....

....

Put a line through any blank space left on this page.

.... *Date of signature*	.... *Signature*
.... *If applicant is a children's aid society, give office or position of person signing.*	.... *Print or type name.*

October 1, 2006

FORM 34M — CONSENT TO OPENNESS ORDER

[Editor's Note: Pursuant to Family Law Rule 1(9), when a form is referred to by number, the reference is to the form with that number that is described in the Table of Forms at the end

of these rules and which is available at www.ontariocourtforms.on.ca. For your convenience, the government form as published on this website is reproduced below.]

Court File Number ....

.... *(Name of court)*

at .... *Court office address*

Applicant (In all cases, the applicant will be a children's aid society.)

Full legal name & address for service — street & number, municipality, postal code, telephone & fax numbers and e-mail address (if any).	*Lawyer's name & address — street & number, municipality, postal code, telephone & fax numbers and e-mail address (if any).*

Respondent(s) (Persons entitled to notice.)

Full legal name & address for service — street & number, municipality, postal code, telephone & fax numbers and e-mail address (if any).	*Lawyer's name & address — street & number, municipality, postal code, telephone & fax numbers and e-mail address (if any).*

Children's Lawyer

Name & address of Children's Lawyer's agent for service (street & number, municipality, postal code, telephone & fax numbers and e-mail address (if any)) and name of person represented.

THE CHILD

Child's Full Legal Name	*Birthdate*	*Sex*	*Child's Native Status*

Crown Wardship Order:

Court File Number	*Court Office Address*	*Name of Judge*	*Date of Order*
Details of Order			

The parties and the child, if the child is 12 years of age or older, agree to the following:

1. The openness order will permit the continuation of a relationship with a person that is beneficial and meaningful to the child for the following reasons:

....

....

....

....

....

....

2. The openness order is in the best interests of the child for the following reasons:

....

....

....

....

....

....

....

....

....

....

3. For the reasons set out above, we ask the court to make the following order: *(Provide details of openness order.)*

....

....

....

....

....

....

....

....

....

....

Applicant's name and position within the children's aid society: ....

.... *Date* .... *Applicant's signature* .... *Witness' signature*

Signature of person who will be permitted to communicate with or have a relationship with the child if order is made:

.... *Date* .... *Respondent's signature* .... *Witness' signature*

Signature of person with whom the children's aid society has placed or intends to place the child for adoption:

.... *Date* .... *Respondent's signature* .... *Witness' signature*

If applicable, children's aid society that will supervise or participate in the arrangement under the openness order:

.... *Date* .... *Respondent's signature* .... *Witness' signature*

CHILD'S CONSENT

If child is 12 years of age or older:

.... *Date* .... *Child's signature* .... *Witness' signature*

October 1, 2006

FORM 34N — APPLICATION TO CHANGE OR TERMINATE OPENNESS ORDER

[Editor's Note: Pursuant to Family Law Rule 1(9), when a form is referred to by number, the reference is to the form with that number that is described in the Table of Forms at the end of these rules and which is available at www.ontariocourtforms.on.ca. For your convenience, the government form as published on this website is reproduced below.]

Court File Number ....

SEAL

.... *(Name of court)*

at .... *Court office address*

Applicant(s)

Full legal name & address for service — street & number, municipality, postal code, telephone & fax numbers and e-mail address (if any).	*Lawyer's name & address — street & number, municipality, postal code, telephone & fax numbers and e-mail address (if any).*

Respondent(s)

Full legal name & address for service — street & number, municipality, postal code, telephone & fax numbers and e-mail address (if any).	*Lawyer's name & address — street & number, municipality, postal code, telephone & fax numbers and e-mail address (if any).*

Respondent(s)

Children's Lawyer

Name & address of Children's Lawyer's agent for service (street & number, municipality, postal code, telephone & fax numbers and e-mail address (if any)) and name of person represented.

TO THE RESPONDENT(S):

A COURT CASE HAS BEEN STARTED AGAINST YOU IN THIS COURT. THE DETAILS ARE SET OUT ON THE ATTACHED PAGES.

THE FIRST COURT DATE IS (date) .... *AT* .... ❑ a.m. ❑ p.m. or as soon as possible after that time, at: *(address)* ....

If you have also been served with a notice of motion, there may be an earlier court date, and you or your lawyer should come to court for the motion.

IF YOU WANT TO OPPOSE ANY CLAIM IN THIS CASE, you or your lawyer must prepare an Answer (*Child and Family Services Act* Cases other than Child Protection and Status Review) (Form 33B.2 — a blank copy should be attached), serve a copy on the children's aid society and all other parties and file a copy in the court office with an Affidavit of Service (Form 6B).

YOU HAVE ONLY 30 DAYS AFTER THIS APPLICATION IS SERVED ON YOU (60 DAYS IF THIS APPLICATION IS SERVED ON YOU OUTSIDE CANADA OR THE UNITED STATES) TO SERVE AND FILE AN ANSWER. IF YOU DO NOT, THE CASE WILL GO AHEAD WITHOUT YOU AND THE COURT MAY MAKE AN ORDER AND ENFORCE IT AGAINST YOU.

You should consider getting legal advice about this case right away. If you cannot afford a lawyer, you may be able to get help from your local legal aid office. *(See your telephone directory under LEGAL AID).*

....

Date of issue *Clerk of the court*

THE CHILD

Child's Full Legal name	Birthdate	Age	Sex	Date of Crown Wardship Order (if pre-adoption application under s. 145.2 of the Child and Family Services Act)	Date of Adoption Order (if post-adoption application under s. 153 of the Child and Family Services Act)

Details of Openness Order to be Changed or Terminated:

Name of Judge	Date of Order	Details of Openness Order

1. The applicant asks for an order: *(if applicable)*

❑ granting permission under s. 153.1(2) of the *Child and Family Services Act* to *(name of person seeking contact)* .... to bring an application to change the order of Justice *(name of judge)* ...., dated *(date of order)* .... for the following reasons:

....

....

....

....

....

....

....

....

....

2. The applicant asks for an order that:

❑ (a) the order, made by Justice *(name of judge)* .... on *(date of order)* .... be changed as follows:

....

....

....

....

....

....

....

....

....

OR

❑ (b) the order, made by Justice *(name of judge)* .... on *(date of order)* .... be terminated.

3. The following circumstances have changed:

....

....

....

....

....

....

....

....

....

....

....

....

....

....

....

....

....

....

4. (a) The proposed change to the openness order would continue a relationship that is beneficial and meaningful to the child for the following reasons:

....

....

....

....

....

....

....

....

....

....

....

....

....

....

....

....

OR

❑ (b) The proposed termination of the openness order would terminate a relationship that is no longer beneficial and meaningful to the child for the following reasons:

....

....

....

....

....

....

....

....

....

....

....

....

....

....

5. The proposed order is in the best interests of the child for the following reasons:

....

....

....

....

....

....

....

....

....

....

....

....

....

....

Put a line through any blank space left on this page.

.... *Date of signature*	.... *Signature*
.... *If applicant is a children's aid society, give office or position of person signing.*	.... *Print or type name*

October 1, 2006

FORM 35.1 — AFFIDAVIT IN SUPPORT OF CLAIM FOR CUSTODY OR ACCESS, DATED

ONTARIO

Court File Number ....

.... *(Name of court)*

at .... *Court office address*

Applicant(s)

Full legal name & address for service — street & number, municipality, postal code, telephone & fax numbers and e-mail address (if any).	*Lawyer's name & address — street & number, municipality, postal code, telephone & fax numbers and e-mail address (if any).*

Respondent(s)

Full legal name & address for service — street & number, municipality, postal code, telephone & fax numbers and e-mail address (if any).	*Lawyer's name & address — street & number, municipality, postal code, telephone & fax numbers and e-mail address (if any).*

AFFIDAVIT IN SUPPORT OF CLAIM FOR CUSTODY OR ACCESS

(If you need more space, attach extra pages.)

My name is (full legal name) ....

My date of birth is (d, m, y) ....

I live in: (name of city, town or municipality and province, state or country if outside of Ontario)

....

I swear/affirm that the following is true:

PART A: — TO BE COMPLETED BY ALL PERSONS SEEKING CUSTODY OR ACCESS

(Write "N/A" if any of the paragraphs do not apply to you or the child(ren).)

1. During my life, I have also used or been known by the following names:

....

....

2. The child(ren) in this case is/are:

Child's full legal name	**Birthdate (d, m, y)**	**Age**	**Full legal name(s) of parent(s)**	**Name(s) of all people the child lives with now (include address if the child does not live with you)**	**My relationship to the child (specify if parent, grandparent, family friend, etc.)**

3. I am also the parent of or have acted as a parent (for example, as a step-parent, legal guardian etc.) to the following child(ren): (include the full legal names and birthdates of any child(ren) not already listed in paragraph 2)

Child's Full Legal Name	**Birthdate (d, m, y)**	**My relationship to the child (specify if parent, step-parent, grandparent, etc.)**	**Name(s) of the person(s) with whom the child lives now (if the child is under 18 years old)**

4. I am or have been a party in the following court case(s) involving custody of or access to any child: (Including the child(ren) in this case or any other child(ren). Do not include cases involving a children's aid society in this section. Attach a copy of any custody or access court order(s) or endorsement(s) you have.)

Court location	**Names of parties in the case**	**Name(s) of child(ren)**	**Court orders made (include dates of orders)**

5. I have been a party or person responsible for the care of a child in the following child protection court case(s): (attach a copy of any relevant court order(s) or endorsement(s) you have)

Court location	**Names of people involved in the case**	**Name of children's aid society**	**Court orders made (include dates of orders)**

6. I have been found guilty of the following criminal offence(s) for which I have not received a pardon:

Charge	Approximate date of finding of guilt	Sentence received

7. I am now charged with the following criminal offence(s):

Charge	Date of next court appearance	Terms of release while waiting for trial (attach copy of bail or other release conditions, if any)

8. When the court is assessing a person's ability to act as a parent, s. 24(4) of the Children's Law Reform Act requires the court to consider whether the person has at any time committed violence or abuse against:

- his or her spouse;
- a parent of the child to whom the claim for custody or access relates;
- a member of the person's household; or
- any child.

I am aware of the following violence or abuse the court should consider under s. 24(4) of the Children's Law Reform Act: (describe incident(s) or episode(s) and provide information about the nature of the violence or abuse, who committed the violence and who the victim(s) was/were)

....

....

....

....

....

....

9. To the best of my knowledge, since birth, the child(ren) in this case has/have lived with the following caregiver(s): (including a parent, legal guardian, children's aid society etc.)

Child's Name	Name(s) of Caregiver(s) (if the child was in the care of a children's aid society, give the name of that children's aid society)	Period(s) of Time with Caregiver(s) (d,m,y to d,m,y)

Child's Name	Name(s) of Caregiver(s) (if the child was in the care of a children's aid society, give the name of that children's aid society)	Period(s) of Time with Caregiver(s) (d,m,y to d,m,y)

10. My plan for the care and upbringing of the child(ren) is as follows:

a) I plan to live at the following address: ....

b) The following people (other than the child(ren) involved in this case) will be living with me:

Full legal name and other names this person has used	Birthdate (d, m, y)	Relationship to you	Has a child of this person ever been in the care of a children's aid society? (if yes, give details)	Has this person been found guilty of a criminal offence (for which he/she has not received a pardon) or is he/she currently facing criminal charges? (if yes, give details)

c) *Decisions for the child(ren) (including education, medical care, religious upbringing, extra-curricular activities, etc.) will be made as follows*:

❑ *jointly by me and (name(s) of person(s))* ....

❑ *by me*

❑ *by (name(s) of person(s))* ....

(If necessary, provide additional details below.)

....

....

d) ❑ *I am a stay-at-home parent.*

❑ *I work*: . . . . ❑ *full time.* ❑ *part time.*

❑ *I attend school*: . . . . ❑ *full time.* ❑ *part time.*

at: (name of your place of work or school) ....

❑ *I anticipate that my plans for work and/or school may change as follows: (complete if you know or expect that you will be doing something different from what you are doing now))*

....

....

e) *The child(ren) will attend school, daycare or be cared for by others on a regular basis as follows*:

....

....

....

....

....

f) *My plan for the child(ren) to have regular contact with others, including the child(ren)'s parent(s) and family members, is as follows*:

....

....

....

....

....

g) Check the appropriate box:

❑ *The child(ren) does not/do not have any special medical, educational, mental health or developmental needs.*

❑ *The child or one or more of the children has/have the following special needs and will receive support and services for those needs as follows: (if a child does not have special needs, you do not have to include information about that child below)*

Name of child	**Special need(s)**	**Description of child's needs**	**Support or service child will be receiving (include the names of any doctors, counsellors, treatment centres, etc. that are or will be providing support or services to the child)**
	❑ medical ❑ educational ❑ mental health ❑ developmen-tal ❑ other		
	❑ medical ❑ educational ❑ mental health ❑ developmen-tal ❑ other		

Name of child	Special need(s)	Description of child's needs	Support or service child will be receiving (include the names of any doctors, counsellors, treatment centres, etc. that are or will be providing support or services to the child)
	❑ medical ❑ educational ❑ mental health ❑ developmen-tal ❑ other		
	❑ medical ❑ educational ❑ mental health ❑ developmen-tal ❑ other		

h) *I will have support from the following relatives, friends or community services in caring for the child(ren)*:

....

....

....

11. I acknowledge that the court needs up-to-date and accurate information about my plan in order to make a custody or access order in the best interests of the child(ren) (subrule 35.1(7)). If, at any time before a final order is made in this case,

a) there are any changes in my life or circumstances that affect the information provided in this affidavit; or

b) I discover that the information in this affidavit is incorrect or incomplete,

I will immediately serve and file either:

a) an updated affidavit in support of claim for custody or access (Form 35.1); or,

b) if the correction or change is minor, an affidavit in Form 14A describing the correction or change and indicating any effect it has on my plan for the care and upbringing of the child(ren).

.... *(Initial here to show you have read this paragraph and you understand it.)*

NOTE: If you are not the parent of the child for whom you are seeking an order of custody or access, you must complete Part B of this affidavit.

You are a parent of a child if:

a) you are the biological parent of the child;

b) you are the adoptive parent of the child;

c) a court has declared that you are the child's parent under the *Children's Law Reform Act*; or

d) you are presumed to be a father under section 8 of the *Children's Law Reform Act.*

If you are completing Part B, you do not have to swear/affirm the affidavit at this point. You will swear/affirm at the end of Part B.

Sworn/Affirmed before me at .... *municipality* in .... *province, state, or country* on .... *Date* .... *Commissioner for taking affidavits (Type or print name below if signature is illegible.)*	.... *Signature* *(This form is to be signed in front of a lawyer, justice of the peace, notary public or commissioner for taking affidavits.)*

PART B — TO BE COMPLETED ONLY BY A NON-PARENT SEEKING A CUSTODY ORDER

You are not a parent of a child unless:

a) you are the biological parent of the child;

b) you are the adoptive parent of the child;

c) a court has declared that you are the child's parent under the *Children's Law Reform Act*; or

d) you are presumed to be a father under section 8 of the *Children's Law Reform Act.*

NOTICE: If you are a non-parent claiming custody of a child, court staff will conduct a search of the databases maintained by the Ontario courts to identify previous or current family court cases in which you or the child(ren) may have been or may be involved and provide you with a list of those cases. This information will be shared with the court and you must provide a copy to any other party.

If the list contains information about someone other than you, you may swear or affirm an affidavit indicating that you are not the same person as the person named in the list.

In addition to the information in Part A, I swear/affirm that the following is true:

12. To the best of my knowledge, the child(ren) in this case has/have been involved in the following custody/ access or child protection court cases: (do NOT include cases in which the child was charged under the Youth Criminal Justice Act (Canada))

Child(ren)'s name(s)	Type of Case	Details of Case

13. You must file a police records check with the court. Choose the option below that applies to you:

❑ *I have attached to this affidavit a copy of my police records check, dated (date of report from local police force) .... Since the date that the attached police records check was completed, I have been found guilty of or charged with the following offence(s):*

....

....

....

❑ *On (date) ...., I sent a request to (name of local police force) .... for a police records check.*

I agree to serve and file the police records check with the court within 10 days after the day I receive it.

I understand that the court may not make an order for custody of the child(ren) until I have filed the police records check.

14. Since I turned 18 years old or became a parent, whichever was earlier, I have lived in the following places:

Approximate dates (month/year to month/year)	City, town or municipality where you lived (if outside of Ontario, give name of province, state or country)

15. I have provided a signed consent form to the court, which authorizes each of the children's aid societies listed below to send a report to me and to the court indicating:

- *whether the society has any records within the meaning of the Children's Law Reform Act regulations relating to me; and*
- *the date(s) on which any files were opened and/or closed (if applicable).*

i) Name of children's aid society: ....

ii) Name of children's aid society: ....

iii) Name of children's aid society: ....

iv) Name of children's aid society: ....

v) Name of children's aid society: ....

vi) Name of children's aid society: ....

16. I understand that if any report from a children's aid society indicates that the children's aid society has records related to me, then, unless the court orders otherwise, that report will be shared with:

a) the court;

b) any other parties in this case; and

c) the child(ren)'s lawyer, if there is one in this case.

If I wish to bring a motion asking the court not to release all or part of this report, I understand that I must file my motion with the court no later than *20 days* from the day that the last report is received by the court.

I also understand that any report indicating that a children's aid society has no records relating to me will not be shared with the court, any other party or the child(ren)'s lawyer.

.... *(Initial here to show that you have read this paragraph and you understand it.)*

Sworn/Affirmed before me at .... *municipality*		
in .... *province, state, or country*		.... *Signature*
on .... *Date*	.... *Commissioner for taking affidavits (Type or print name below if signature is illegible.)*	*(This form is to be signed in front of a lawyer, justice of the peace, notary public or commissioner for taking affidavits.)*

November 15, 2009

FORM 36 — AFFIDAVIT FOR DIVORCE

[Repealed O. Reg. 76/06, s. 15.]

[Editor's Note: Forms 4 to 39 of the Family Law Rules have been repealed by O. Reg. 76/06, effective May 1, 2006. Pursuant to Family Law Rule 1(9), when a form is referred to by number, the reference is to the form with that number that is described in the Table of Forms at the end of these rules and which is available at www.ontariocourtforms.on.ca. For your convenience, the government form as published on this website is reproduced below.]

Court File Number ....

.... *(Name of court)*

at .... *Court office address*

Applicant

Full legal name & address for service — street & number, municipality, postal code, telephone & fax and e-mail address (if any).	*Lawyer's name & address — street & number, municipality, postal code, telephone & fax numbers and e-mail address (if any).*

Respondent(s)

Full legal name & address for service — street & number, municipality, postal code, telephone & fax numbers and e-mail address (if any).	*Lawyer's name & address — street & number, municipality, postal code, telephone & fax numbers and e-mail address (if any).*

My name is (full legal name) ....

I live in (municipality & province) .... *and I swear/affirm that the following is true:*

1. I am the applicant in this divorce case.

2. There is no chance of a reconciliation between the respondent and me.

3. All the information in the application in this case is correct, except: *(State any corrections or changes to the information in the application. Write "NONE" if there are no corrections or changes.)*

4.

❑ The certificate or registration of my marriage to the respondent has been signed and sealed by the Registrar General of Ontario and

❑ has been filed with the application.

❑ is attached to this affidavit.

❑ The certificate of my marriage to the respondent was issued outside Ontario. It is called *(title of certificate)* .... It was issued at *(place of issue)* .... on *(date)* .... by *(name and title of person who issued certificate)* .... and the information in it about my marriage is correct.

❑ I have not been able to get a certificate or registration of my marriage. I was married to the respondent on *(date)* .... at *(place of marriage)* .... The marriage was performed by *(name and title)* .... who had the authority to perform marriages in that place.

5. The legal basis for the divorce is:

❑ that the respondent and I have been separated for at least one year. We separated on *(date)* ....

❑ *(Other. Specify.)*

....

....

6. I do not know about and I am not involved in any arrangement to make up or to hide evidence or to deceive the court in this divorce case.

Strike out the following paragraphs if they do not apply.

7. I do not want to make a claim for a division of property in this divorce case, even though I know that it may be legally impossible to make such a claim after the divorce.

8. I want the divorce order to include the following paragraph numbers of the attached consent, settlement, separation agreement or previous court order: *(List the numbers of the paragraphs that you want included in the divorce order.)*

....

9. There are (number) .... children of the marriage. They are:

Full legal name of child	Birthdate (d,m,y)

10. The custody and access arrangements for the child(ren) are as follows: *(Give summary.)*

....

....

11. These are the arrangements that have been made for the support of the child(ren) of the marriage:

(a) The income of the party paying child support is $.......... per year.

(b) The number of children for whom support is supposed to be paid is *(number)* ....

(c) The amount of support that should be paid according to the applicable table in the child support guidelines is $.......... per month.

(d) The amount of child support actually being paid is $.......... per month.

(NOTE: — Where the dollar amounts in clauses (c) and (d) are different, you must fill out the frame on the next page. If the amounts in clauses (c) and (d) are the same, skip the frame and go directly to paragraph 12.)

Fill out the information in this frame only if the amounts in paragraphs 11(c) and 11(d) are different. If they are the same, go to paragraph 12

(a) Child support is already covered by:

(i) ❑ a court order dated *(date)* .... that was made before the child support guidelines came into effect (before 1 May 1997). I attach a copy of the order

(ii) ❑ a domestic contract order dated *(date)* .... that was made before the child support guidelines came into effect (before 1 May 1997). I attach a copy of the contract

(iii) ❑ a court order or written agreement dated *(date)* .... made after the guidelines came into effect that has some direct or indirect benefits for the child(ren). I attach a copy.

(iv) ❑ a written consent between the parties dated *(date)* .... agreeing to the payment of an amount different from that set out in the guidelines.

(b) The child support clauses of this order or agreement require payment of $ .... per .... in child support.

(c) These child support clauses

❑ are not indexed for any automatic cost-of-living increases.

❑ are indexed according to *(Give indexing formula)*

....

(d) These child support clauses

❑ have not been changed since the day the order or agreement was made.

❑ have been changed on *(Give dates and details of changes)*

....

(e) *(If you ticked off box (i) above, you can go to paragraph 12. If you ticked off boxes (ii), (iii) or (iv) above, then fill out the information after box of the corresponding number below. For example, if you ticked off box (iii) above, you would fill out the information alongside box (iii) below.)*

(ii) ❑ The amount being paid under this agreement is a fair and reasonable arrangement for the support of the child(ren) because: *(Give reasons.)*

....

....

(iii) ❑ The order or agreement directly or indirectly benefits the child(ren) because: *(Give details of benefits.)*

....

....

(iv) ❑ The amount to which the parties have consented is reasonable for the support of the child(ren) because: *(Give reasons.)*

....

....

12. I am claiming costs in this case. The details of this claim are as follows: *(Give details.)*

....

....

13. The respondent's address last known to me is: *(Give address.)*

....

....

Put a line through any blank space left on this page.

Sworn/Affirmed before me at .... *municipality* in .... *province, state or country* on .... *date*

____

____
Signature

Commissioner for taking affidavits (Type or print name below if signature is illegible.)	*(This form is to be signed in front of a lawyer, justice of the peace, notary public or commissioner for taking affidavits.)*

September 1, 2005

FORM 36A — CERTIFICATE OF CLERK (DIVORCE)

[Repealed O. Reg. 76/06, s. 15.]

[Editor's Note: Forms 4 to 39 of the Family Law Rules have been repealed by O. Reg. 76/06, effective May 1, 2006. Pursuant to Family Law Rule 1(9), when a form is referred to by number, the reference is to the form with that number that is described in the Table of Forms at the end of these rules and which is available at www.ontariocourtforms.on.ca. For your convenience, the government form as published on this website is reproduced below.]

Court File Number ....

.... *(Name of court)*

at .... *Court office address*

Applicant's last name ....

Respondent's last name ....

If the appropriate box on the left cannot be checked, check the box on the right margin and describe the deficiency by that box.

The clerk of the court certifies as follows:

Check if applicable and complete the rest of the certificate as if the divorce had been claimed by the applicant.

❑ Divorce claimed only by the respondent.

				Deficiency	
1.	*PRELIMINARY*				
	(a)	❑	No answer filed	1(a)	❑
		❑	Answer was withdrawn — Continuing record tab/page number		
		❑	Order dated ...., under subrule 12(6), splitting divorce from rest of the case — continuing record tab/page number		
		❑	Answer struck out by order dated .... — Continuing record tab/page number		
		❑	Joint application — no respondent		
	(b)	❑	Clearance certificate from Central Divorce Registry	1(b)	❑
2.	*PROOF OF SERVICE*			2	❑
		❑	Affidavit of service		
		❑	Person's lawyer accepted service		
		❑	Joint application — no service necessary		
3.	*METHOD OF SERVICE*			3	❑
		❑	Left copy with person to be served		

Deficiency

- ❑ Left copy with person's lawyer
- ❑ Mailed copy to person and received acknowledgement signed by person
- ❑ Left copy at person's residence with adult resident and mailed another copy
- ❑ Signed acknowledgement of service filed
- ❑ other *(Specify.)* ....

Service took place in *(province or country)* ....

Service was carried out on *(date)* ....

4. *GROUNDS FOR DIVORCE* 4 ❑

- ❑ Separation since *(date)* ...., affidavit sworn more that one year after separation
- ❑ Adultery
- ❑ Cruelty

5. *ONTARIO RESIDENCE* 5 ❑

Application should indicate that at least one spouse must have been Ontario resident for at least a year.

- ❑ Applicant resident in Ontario since *(date)* ....
- ❑ Respondent resident in Ontario since *(date)* ....

6. *CLAIMS* 6 ❑

- ❑ Only claim for divorce
- ❑ Claim for child support *[details in part 9 below]*
- ❑ Claim for custody/access — details in application
- ❑ Claim for spousal support — details in application
- ❑ Claim for property — details in application
- ❑ Claim to include provisions of consent, agreement or previous court order — details in application
- ❑ Costs

7. *PROOF OF MARRIAGE* 7 ❑

Marriage took place

- ❑ in Canada
- ❑ outside Canada
  - ❑ Marriage certificate or registration of marriage filed — details agree with those in application — Continuing record tab/page number ....
  - ❑ No certificate — details of marriage set out in affidavit — Continuing record tab/page number ....
  - ❑ Previous divorce or death certificate filed — Continuing record tab/page number ....

8. *AFFIDAVITS* 8 ❑

- ❑ Applicant's affidavit — Continuing record tab/page number ....
- ❑ Respondent's affidavit — Continuing record tab/page number ....
- ❑ Affidavit of *(name)*.................................. — Continuing record tab/page number ....
- ❑ Affidavit complies with Form 36 and is properly completed — Continuing record tab/page number ....

9. *CHILDREN* 9 ❑

- ❑ No children of the marriage
- ❑ There are children of the marriage
- ❑ Child support guidelines information supplied — Continuing record tab/page number ....
  - ❑ Payor's income
  - ❑ table amount

Deficiency

- ❑ recipient's income *[REQUIRED for specil expenses (add-ons), split custody, shared custody, payor is stepparent, child over 18, payor's income more than $150,000, claim of undue hardship]*
- ❑ details of special expenses (add-ons)
- ❑ agreement/consent with explanation for claim less than table amount

10. *DRAFT ORDER* 10 ❑

The following material has been filed:

- ❑ 3 copies of draft order — no support claimed.
- ❑ 4 copies of draft order + 2 drafts of support deduction order — support claimed
- ❑ Stamped envelope for each party
- ❑ Address for service of order on respondent is same as
  - ❑ on application
  - ❑ on documents filed by respondent
  - ❑ in applicant's affidavit
- ❑ Draft order in same terms as application
- ❑ Draft order in same terms as consent, minutes of settlement, or agreement filed — Continuing record tab/page number ....
- ❑ Request for early effective date for divorce; agreements and undertakings filed not to appeal — Continuing record tab/page number ....

11. *NOTICE TO APPLICANT* 11 ❑

- ❑ Applicant notified of deficiencies but requests to submit papers to judge despite them.

.... *Date of signature*

.... *Signature of clerk of the court*

September 1, 2005

FORM 36B — CERTIFICATE OF DIVORCE

[Repealed O. Reg. 76/06, s. 15.]

[Editor's Note: Forms 4 to 39 of the Family Law Rules have been repealed by O. Reg. 76/06, effective May 1, 2006. Pursuant to Family Law Rule 1(9), when a form is referred to by number, the reference is to the form with that number that is described in the Table of Forms at the end of these rules and which is available at www.ontariocourtforms.on.ca. For your convenience, the government form as published on this website is reproduced below.]

Court File Number ....

[SEAL]

.... *(Name of court)*

at .... *Court office address*

Applicant

Full legal name & address for service — street and number, municipality, postal code, telephone & fax numbers and e-mail address (if any).	*Lawyer's name & address — street and number, municipality, postal code, telephone & fax numbers and e-mail address (if any).*

Respondent(s)

Full legal name & address for service — street and number, municipality, postal code, telephone & fax numbers and e-mail address (if any).	*Lawyer's name & address — street and number, municipality, postal code, telephone & fax numbers and e-mail address (if any).*

I CERTIFY THAT the marriage of *(full legal names of the spouses)* .... that was solemnized at *(place of marriage)* on *(date of marriage)* .... was dissolved by an order of this court made on *(date of divorce order)* ....

The divorce took effect on *(date when order took effect)* ....

.... *Signature of clerk of the court*

.... *Date of signature*

NOTE: This certificate can only be issued on or after the date on which the divorce takes effect.

September 1, 2005

FORM 37 — NOTICE OF HEARING

[Repealed O. Reg. 76/06, s. 15.]

[Editor's Note: Forms 4 to 39 of the Family Law Rules have been repealed by O. Reg. 76/06, effective May 1, 2006. Pursuant to Family Law Rule 1(9), when a form is referred to by number, the reference is to the form with that number that is described in the Table of Forms at the end of these rules and which is available at www.ontariocourtforms.on.ca. For your convenience, the government form as published on this website is reproduced below.]

Court File Number ....

[SEAL]

____

(Name of court)

at ______________________________

Court office address

Applicant(s)

Full legal name & address for service — street & number, municipality, postal code, telephone & fax numbers and e-mail address (if any).	*Lawyer's name & address — street & number, municipality, postal code, telephone & fax numbers and e-mail address (if any).*

Respondent(s)

Full legal name & address for service — street & number, municipality, postal code, telephone & fax numbers and e-mail address (if any).	*Lawyer's name & address — street & number, municipality, postal code, telephone & fax numbers and e-mail address (if any).*

NOTICE:

THE COURT WILL HOLD A WRITTEN HEARING on *(date)* . . . .

at .... a.m./p.m., or as soon as possible after that time at *(place of hearing)* . . . .

This court has received

❑ An application under the *Interjurisdictional Support Orders Act, 2002* for
❑ an order ❑ a change of an order
❑ A provisional ❑ an order ❑ change of an order
❑ in another part of Ontario ❑ outside Ontario

The details are set out in the attached materials.

IF YOU WANT TO OPPOSE ANY CLAIM IN THIS CASE, you or your lawyer must prepare an Answer (a blank copy of which is attached) and file a copy in the court office. YOU HAVE ONLY 30 DAYS AFTER THIS NOTICE IS SERVED ON YOU TO FILE AN ANSWER TO THIS CASE.

Whether or not you wish to oppose a claim in this case, YOU MUST FILE A FINANCIAL STATEMENT (a blank copy of which is attached) with the court office WITHIN 30 DAYS AFTER THIS NOTICE IS SERVED ON YOU.

If you want to ask for an oral hearing, you must prepare a motion (Form 14B — blank copy attached), and file a copy in the court office WITHIN 30 DAYS AFTER THIS NOTICE IS SERVED ON YOU.

The court will only consider the written materials in this case on the date noted above. UNLESS THE COURT ORDERS OTHERWISE, THERE IS NO NEED FOR YOU TO COME TO COURT OR TO HAVE A LAWYER THERE TO ARGUE YOUR CASE. If an order is made or the judge requires you to be present or provide further evidence, you will be notified.

IF YOU DO NOT FILE WRITTEN MATERIALS, THE COURT MAY MAKE AN ORDER WITHOUT YOUR WRITTEN ANSWER AND ENFORCE IT AGAINST YOU.

You should get legal advice about this case right away. If you cannot afford a lawyer, you may be able to get help from your local Legal Aid office. (See your telephone directory under LEGAL AID.)

Date of signature	Signature of registrar or clerk of the court

NOTE: *A copy of the application should be attached to this notice, along with a copy of the applicant's financial statement, a copy of any provisional order and a copy of the applicant's evidence. Also attached to this notice should be a blank Financial Statement that you must fill out and file. If a provisional order was made in another part of Ontario, you must serve and file your financial statement.*

If any of these documents is missing, you should talk to the court office at the address at the top of this form immediately.

September 1, 2005

FORM 37A — INFORMATION SHEET

[Repealed O. Reg. 76/06, s. 15.]

[Editor's Note: Forms 4 to 39 of the Family Law Rules have been repealed by O. Reg. 76/06, effective May 1, 2006. Pursuant to Family Law Rule 1(9), when a form is referred to by number, the reference is to the form with that number that is described in the Table of Forms at the end of these rules and which is available at www.ontariocourtforms.on.ca. For your convenience, the government form as published on this website is reproduced below.]

Court File Number ....

(Name of court)

at

Court office address

Applicant(s)

Full legal name & address for service — street & number, municipality, postal code, telephone & fax numbers and e-mail address (if any).	*Lawyer's name & address — street & number, municipality, postal code, telephone & fax numbers and e-mail address (if any).*

Respondent(s)

Full legal name & address for service — street & number, municipality, postal code, telephone & fax numbers and e-mail address (if any).	*Lawyer's name & address — street & number, municipality, postal code, telephone & fax numbers and e-mail address (if any).*

TO THE APPLICANT(S):

The respondent(s) was/were served with a notice of

❑ *Interjurisdictional Support Orders Act, 2002* hearing.
❑ confirmation hearing.

A copy of this notice is attached to this sheet. It is being sent to you FOR YOUR INFORMATION ONLY.

THERE IS NO NEED FOR YOU TO COME TO THIS HEARING OR TO HAVE A LAWYER THERE TO ARGUE YOUR CASE FOR YOU.

You will be told about what happens at the hearing by the office where you submitted your application. If you have any questions, you should talk to your own lawyer or the office where you submitted your application.

Date of signature	*Signature of registrar or clerk of the court*

September 1, 2005

FORM 37B — DIRECTION TO REQUEST FURTHER INFORMATION

[Repealed O. Reg. 76/06, s. 15.]

[Editor's Note: Forms 4 to 39 of the Family Law Rules have been repealed by O. Reg. 76/06, effective May 1, 2006. Pursuant to Family Law Rule 1(9), when a form is referred to by number, the reference is to the form with that number that is described in the Table of Forms at the end of these rules and which is available at www.ontariocourtforms.on.ca. For your convenience, the government form as published on this website is reproduced below.]

Court File Number ....

[SEAL]

(Name of court)

at ________________

Court office address

Applicant(s)

Full legal name & address for service — street & number, municipality, postal code, telephone & fax numbers and e-mail address (if any).	*Lawyer's name & address — street & number, municipality, postal code, telephone & fax numbers and e-mail address (if any).*

Applicant(s)

Respondent(s)

Full legal name & address for service — street & number, municipality, postal code, telephone & fax numbers and e-mail address (if any).	*Lawyer's name & address — street & number, municipality, postal code, telephone & fax numbers and e-mail address (if any).*

TO THE (check appropriate box(es))

- ❑ APPLICANT(S):
- ❑ THE ONTARIO INTERJURISDICTIONAL SUPPORT ORDERS UNIT:

This court considered the application for support or the application to change a support order

on *(date)* ....

THE COURT ADJOURNED THE HEARING OF THE CASE TO *(date)* ....

❑ You, the applicant, are directed to provide the information or documents required by the court.

❑ You, the Ontario Interjurisdictional Support Orders Unit, are directed to contact the applicant or appropriate authority in the reciprocating jurisdiction to request the information or documents required by the court.

This court requires the following information or documents: *(attach extra paper if necessary, or transcript noting information and documents required).*

....

....

The information or documents must be filed with this court at the address at the top of this form at least 30 days before the court date. At the hearing, a temporary order:

- ❑ was not made;
- ❑ was made — details will be sent; or
- ❑ was made — a certified copy of the temporary order is attached.

Date of signature	*Signature of registrar or clerk of the court*

NOTE: *A copy of the respondent's evidence and a copy of the court's reasons for seeking further evidence should be attached to this form. If either of these is missing, you should talk to the court office at the address at the top of this form immediately.*

September 1, 2005

FORM 37C — NOTICE OF CONTINUATION OF HEARING

[Repealed O. Reg. 76/06, s. 15.]

[Editor's Note: Forms 4 to 39 of the Family Law Rules have been repealed by O. Reg. 76/06, effective May 1, 2006. Pursuant to Family Law Rule 1(9), when a form is referred to by number, the reference is to the form with that number that is described in the Table of Forms at the end of these rules and which is available at www.ontariocourtforms.on.ca. For your convenience, the government form as published on this website is reproduced below.]

Court File Number ....

[SEAL]

____
(Name of court)

at ______________________________
Court office address

Applicant(s)

Full legal name & address for service — street & number, municipality, postal code, telephone & fax numbers and e-mail address (if any).	*Lawyer's name & address — street & number, municipality, postal code, telephone & fax numbers and e-mail address (if any).*

Respondent(s)

Full legal name & address for service — street & number, municipality, postal code, telephone & fax numbers and e-mail address (if any).	*Lawyer's name & address — street & number, municipality, postal code, telephone & fax numbers and e-mail address (if any).*

TO THE RESPONDENT(S):

THE COURT WILL CONTINUE A WRITTEN HEARING on *(date)* . . . .

at .... a.m./p.m., or as soon as possible after that time at *(place of hearing)* . . . .

This case was adjourned on *(adjournment date)* . . . .

so that the case could be sent to the originating jurisdiction for further evidence.

The originating jurisdiction has now sent to this court further evidence, a copy of which is attached. This court will therefore consider this case at the time and place shown above.

IF YOU WISH TO RESPOND TO THE FURTHER EVIDENCE, YOU OR YOUR LAWYER MUST FILE AN AFFIDAVIT IN RESPONSE (Form 14A — blank copy attached) WITHIN 30 DAYS AFTER YOU RECEIVE THIS NOTICE.

If you want to ask for an oral hearing, you must prepare a motion (Form 14B — blank copy attached), and file a copy in the court office WITHIN 30 DAYS AFTER THIS NOTICE IS SERVED ON YOU.

The court will only consider the written materials in this case on the date noted above. UNLESS THE COURT ORDERS OTHERWISE, THERE IS NO NEED FOR YOU TO COME TO COURT OR TO HAVE A LAWYER THERE TO ARGUE YOUR CASE. If an order is made or the judge requires you to be present or provide further evidence, you will be notified.

Date of signature	*Signature of registrar or clerk of the court*

NOTE: *A copy of the applicant's further evidence taken in the originating jurisdiction should be attached to this notice. If it is missing, you should talk to the court office at the address at the top of this form immediately.*

September 1, 2005

FORM 37D — NOTICE OF REGISTRATION OF ORDER

[Repealed O. Reg. 76/06, s. 15.]

[Editor's Note: Forms 4 to 39 of the Family Law Rules have been repealed by O. Reg. 76/06, effective May 1, 2006. Pursuant to Family Law Rule 1(9), when a form is referred to by number, the reference is to the form with that number that is described in the Table of Forms at the end of these rules and which is available at www.ontariocourtforms.on.ca. For your convenience, the government form as published on this website is reproduced below.]

Court File Number ....

[SEAL]

(Name of court)

at

Court office address

Applicant(s)

Full legal name & address for service — street & number, municipality, postal code, telephone & fax numbers and e-mail address (if any).	*Lawyer's name & address — street & number, municipality, postal code, telephone & fax numbers and e-mail address (if any).*

Respondent(s)

Full legal name & address for service — street & number, municipality, postal code, telephone & fax numbers and e-mail address (if any).	*Lawyer's name & address — street & number, municipality, postal code, telephone & fax numbers and e-mail address (if any).*

TO THE *(check appropriate box(es))*

❑ APPLICANT(S):
❑ RESPONDENT(S):

The *(name of court)* . . . .

at *(place where court presides)* . . . .

has asked the courts in Ontario to enforce

❑ an order for the payment of support for dependants.
❑ the support provisions of a written agreement between you and the other party.

This order/agreement has been registered with this Ontario court on *(date of registration)* .... under the *Interjurisdictional Support Orders Act, 2002*.

If you have reason to believe that:

(a) you did not have notice or a reasonable opportunity to be heard;

(b) the order/agreement is contrary to public policy in Ontario; or

(c) the court that made the order did not have jurisdiction to make it,

you may make a motion (Forms 14 and 14A) to have the registration set aside, but you must do so within 30 days after receiving this notice. You must mail notice of your own motion to the Ontario Interjurisdictional Support Orders Unit at: (address)

. . . .

You may use any method of service set out in rule 6 of the *Family Law Rules*, including mail, courier or fax.

If you choose not to challenge the registration, the order/agreement will be enforced against you as if it were an order of an Ontario court. You have the right at any time to apply for a change of this order/agreement if there has been a material change in circumstances since the making of the order/agreement.

Date of signature	*Signature of registrar or clerk of the court*

September 1, 2005

FORM 37E — NOTICE FOR TAKING FURTHER EVIDENCE

[Repealed O. Reg. 76/06, s. 15.]

[Editor's Note: Forms 4 to 39 of the Family Law Rules have been repealed by O. Reg. 76/06, effective May 1, 2006. Pursuant to Family Law Rule 1(9), when a form is referred to by number, the reference is to the form with that number that is described in the Table of Forms at the end of these rules and which is available at www.ontariocourtforms.on.ca. For your convenience, the government form as published on this website is reproduced below.]

Court File Number ....

[SEAL]

(Name of court)

at ______________________________

Court office address

Applicant(s)

Full legal name & address for service — street & number, municipality, postal code, telephone & fax numbers and e-mail address (if any).	*Lawyer's name & address — street & number, municipality, postal code, telephone & fax numbers and e-mail address (if any).*

Respondent(s)

Full legal name & address for service — street & number, municipality, postal code, telephone & fax numbers and e-mail address (if any).	*Lawyer's name & address — street & number, municipality, postal code, telephone & fax numbers and e-mail address (if any).*

TO THE APPLICANT(S):

The provisional

❑ order in this case

❑ change of the order made by the *(name of court)* . . . .

on (date) . . . .

has come before a judge of the *(name and address of court)* . . . .

That other court requires further evidence from you. The details are set out in the attached material.

If you want to continue your application for support or for a change in support, you or your lawyer must prepare an affidavit (Form 14A — blank copy attached) of your further evidence and file it in this court office.

The other court will continue the hearing on *(insert date, if known)* ....
Your affidavit evidence must be filed in this court 30 days before that date so it can be sent to the other court in time for the hearing.

IF YOU DO NOT FILE FURTHER AFFIDAVIT EVIDENCE, THE PROVISIONAL ORDER/CHANGE OF AN ORDER MAY NOT BE CONFIRMED BY THE OTHER COURT.

Date of signature	*Signature of registrar or clerk of the court*

NOTE: *A copy of the respondent's evidence and a copy of the other court's reasons for seeking further evidence should be attached to this notice. If either of these is missing, you should talk to the court office at the address at the top of this form immediately.*

September 1, 2005

FORM 38 — NOTICE OF APPEAL

[Repealed O. Reg. 76/06, s. 15.]

[Editor's Note: Forms 4 to 39 of the Family Law Rules have been repealed by O. Reg. 76/06, effective May 1, 2006. Pursuant to Family Law Rule 1(9), when a form is referred to by number, the reference is to the form with that number that is described in the Table of Forms at the end of these rules and which is available at www.ontariocourtforms.on.ca. For your convenience, the government form as published on this website is reproduced below.]

Court File Number

____

(Name of court)

____

Form 38:
Notice of Appeal

at _______________________________

Court office address

Applicant(s) *Check the appropriate box:* ❑ *Appellant* ❑ *Respondent in this appeal*

Full legal name & address for service — street & number, municipality, postal code, telephone & fax numbers and e-mail address (if any).	*Lawyer's name & address — street & number, municipality, postal code, telephone & fax numbers and e-mail address (if any).*

Respondent(s) *Check the appropriate box:* ❑ *Appellant* ❑ *Respondent in this appeal*

Full legal name & address for service — street & number, municipality, postal code, telephone & fax numbers and e-mail address (if any).	*Lawyer's name & address — street & number, municipality, postal code, telephone & fax numbers and e-mail address (if any).*
Name & address of Children's Lawyer's agent (street & number, municipality, postal code, telephone & fax numbers and e-mail address (if any)) and name of person represented.	

My name is (name of party making this appeal) ....

I APPEAL TO THE (name of court) ....

at (municipality) ....

from the following order or decision:

Date of order: ....

Name of court that made it: ....

Name of judge who made it: ....

Place where it was made: ....

It was: ❑ a final order. ❑ a temporary order.

I ask that this order be set aside and that an order be made as follows: (Set out briefly the order that you want the appeal court to make.)

The legal grounds for my appeal are: (Set out in numbered paragraphs the legal basis of your appeal.)

Draw a line through any space left on this page.

NOTE TO THE APPELLANT: You have 30 days to serve this notice on the other parties in the case and you must file it with the clerk of the appeal court with proof of service (Form 6B) within 10 days after that.

NOTE TO THE RESPONDENT: If you want to oppose this appeal, you or your lawyer must prepare a respondent's factum required by subrule 38(9) of the *Family Law Rules*, serve a copy on the appellant(s) and file a copy with the clerk of the appeal court with proof of service (Form 6B). You must serve and file a respondent's factum at least 3 days before the hearing of the appeal. If you do not, the appeal will go ahead without you and the court may make a new order and enforce it against you.

....	....
Date of signature	*Signature*

September 1, 2005

FORM 39 — NOTICE OF APPROACHING DISMISSAL

[Repealed O. Reg. 76/06, s. 15.]

[Editor's Note: Forms 4 to 39 of the Family Law Rules have been repealed by O. Reg. 76/06, effective May 1, 2006. Pursuant to Family Law Rule 1(9), when a form is referred to by number, the reference is to the form with that number that is described in the Table of Forms at the end of these rules and which is available at www.ontariocourtforms.on.ca. For your convenience, the government form as published on this website is reproduced below.]

Court File Number ....

.... *(Name of court)*

at .... Court office address

Applicant(s)

Full legal name & address for service — street & number, municipality, postal code, telephone & fax numbers and e-mail address (if any).	*Lawyer's name & address — street & number, municipality, postal code, telephone & fax numbers and e-mail address (if any).*

Respondent(s)

Full legal name & address for service — street & number, municipality, postal code, telephone & fax numbers and e-mail address (if any).	*Lawyer's name & address — street & number, municipality, postal code, telephone & fax numbers and e-mail address (if any).*

TO ALL PARTIES:

1. THE CLERK OF THE COURT WILL DISMISS THIS CASE WITHOUT FURTHER NOTICE unless, within 60 days after service of this notice, one of the parties:

(a) obtains an order under subrule 39(3), 40(3) or 41(3) to lengthen the time to do anything described below;

(b) files an agreement signed by all parties and their lawyers, if any, for a final order disposing of all issues in the case, and a notice of motion for an order carrying out the agreement;

(c) serves on all parties and files a notice of withdrawal (Form 12) that discontinues all outstanding claims in the case;

(d) schedules or adjourns the case for trial; or

(e) arranges a case conference or settlement conference for the first available date.

2. If a case conference or settlement conference is arranged for a date as described in clause 1(e) but the hearing does not take place on that date and is not adjourned by a judge, the case will be dismissed without further notice.

3. Any temporary orders, including temporary orders for support and interim restraining orders under section 46 of the *Family Law Act* or under section 35 of the *Children's Law Reform Act*, will expire upon the dismissal of the case.

Put a line through any blank space left on this page.

....	....
Date of signature	*Signature of clerk of the court*

June 15, 2007

CLASS PROCEEDINGS

TABLE OF CONTENTS

INTRODUCTION

I.

This section contains the various components of the class proceedings legislative package, *i.e.*, the two Acts — the *Class Proceedings Act, 1992*, S.O. 1992, c. 6 (which establishes the procedure for class actions) and the *Law Society Amendment Act (Class Proceedings Funding)*, 1992, S.O. 1992, c. 7 (which provides a funding mechanism for class actions) — and the regulations made under the latter Act (O. Reg. 771/92) which regulate applications to the Class Proceedings Committee for financial assistance from the Class Proceedings Fund. (The Class Proceedings Committee has issued two Practice Directions which are reproduced following the Rule 12 Highlights in the main volume.)

The text of U.S. Federal Rules of Civil Procedure, Rule 23 is also included.

In the Annual Survey of Recent Developments in Civil Procedure in this and earlier editions will be found an analysis of the case law decided under the Act.

The essay "Ontario's New Class Proceedings Legislation — An Analysis," which was written at the time the legislation came into effect, is again reproduced below without any attempt to update it in light of decided case law.

Further analysis can be found in two articles which have been published by the Authors since the legislation came into effect — G. Watson "Initial Interpretations of Ontario's Class Proceedings Act — the Anaheim and Breast Implant Cases" (1993), 18 C.P.C. (3d) 344 and M. McGowan, "Certification of Class Actions in Ontario: A Comparison to Rule 23 of the U.S. Federal Rules of Civil Procedure" (1993), 16 C.P.C. (3d) 172 and in the Annual Surveys in earlier editions of Watson & McGowan.

CLASS PROCEEDINGS ACT, 1992

S.O. 1992, c. 6

as am. S.O. 2006, c. 19, Sched. C, s. 1(1).

Summary of Contents

CLASS PROCEEDINGS

Summary of Contents

Section 1

Definitions

1. In this Act,

"common issues" means,

(a) common but not necessarily identical issues of fact, or

(b) common but not necessarily identical issues of law that arise from common but not necessarily identical facts;

"court" means the Superior Court of Justice but does not include the Small Claims Court;

"defendant" includes a respondent;

"plaintiff" includes an applicant.

2006, c. 19, Sched. C, s. 1(1)

Section 2

Plaintiff's class proceeding

2. (1) One or more members of a class of persons may commence a proceeding in the court on behalf of the members of the class.

Motion for certification

(2) A person who commences a proceeding under subsection (1) shall make a motion to a judge of the court for an order certifying the proceeding as a class proceeding and appointing the person representative plaintiff.

Idem

(3) A motion under subsection (2) shall be made,

(a) within ninety days after the later of,

(i) the date on which the last statement of defence, notice of intent to defend or notice of appearance is delivered, and

(ii) the date on which the time prescribed by the rules of court for delivery of the last statement of defence, notice of intent to defend or a notice of appearance expires without its being delivered; or

(b) subsequently, with leave of the court.

Section 3

Defendant's class proceeding

3. A defendant to two or more proceedings may, at any stage of one of the proceedings, make a motion to a judge of the court for an order certifying the proceedings as a class proceeding and appointing a representative plaintiff.

Section 4

Classing defendants

4. Any party to a proceeding against two or more defendants may, at any stage of the proceeding, make a motion to a judge of the court for an order certifying the proceeding as a class proceeding and appointing a representative defendant.

Section 5

Certification

5. (1) The court shall certify a class proceeding on a motion under section 2, 3 or 4 if,

(a) the pleadings or the notice of application discloses a cause of action;

(b) there is an identifiable class of two or more persons that would be represented by the representative plaintiff or defendant;

(c) the claims or defences of the class members raise common issues;

(d) a class proceeding would be the preferable procedure for the resolution of the common issues; and

(e) there is a representative plaintiff or defendant who,

(i) would fairly and adequately represent the interests of the class,

(ii) has produced a plan for the proceeding that sets out a workable method of advancing the proceeding on behalf of the class and of notifying class members of the proceeding, and

(iii) does not have, on the common issues for the class, an interest in conflict with the interests of other class members.

Idem, subclass protection

(2) Despite subsection (1), where a class includes a subclass whose members have claims or defences that raise common issues not shared by all the class members, so that, in the opinion of the court, the protection of the interests of the subclass members requires that they be separately represented, the court shall not certify the class proceeding unless there is a representative plaintiff or defendant who,

(a) would fairly and adequately represent the interests of the subclass;

(b) has produced a plan for the proceeding that sets out a workable method of advancing the proceeding on behalf of the subclass and of notifying subclass members of the proceeding; and

(c) does not have, on the common issues for the subclass, an interest in conflict with the interests of other subclass members.

Evidence as to size of class

(3) Each party to a motion for certification shall, in an affidavit filed for use on the motion, provide the party's best information on the number of members in the class.

Adjournments

(4) The court may adjourn the motion for certification to permit the parties to amend their materials or pleadings or to permit further evidence.

Certification not a ruling on merits

(5) An order certifying a class proceeding is not a determination of the merits of the proceeding.

Section 6

Certain matters not bar to certification

6. The court shall not refuse to certify a proceeding as a class proceeding solely on any of the following grounds:

1. The relief claimed includes a claim for damages that would require individual assessment after determination of the common issues.

2. The relief claimed relates to separate contracts involving different class members.

3. Different remedies are sought for different class members.

4. The number of class members or the identity of each class member is not known.

5. The class includes a subclass whose members have claims or defences that raise common issues not shared by all class members.

Section 7

Refusal to certify, proceeding may continue in altered form

7. Where the court refuses to certify a proceeding as a class proceeding, the court may permit the proceeding to continue as one or more proceedings between different parties and, for the purpose, the court may,

(a) order the addition, deletion or substitution of parties;

(b) order the amendment of the pleadings or notice of application; and

(c) make any further order that it considers appropriate.

Section 8

Contents of certification order

8. (1) An order certifying a proceeding as a class proceeding shall,

(a) describe the class;

(b) state the names of the representative parties;

(c) state the nature of the claims or defences asserted on behalf of the class;

(d) state the relief sought by or from the class;

(e) set out the common issues for the class; and

(f) specify the manner in which class members may opt out of the class proceeding and a date after which class members may not opt out.

Subclass protection

(2) Where a class includes a subclass whose members have claims or defences that raise common issues not shared by all the class members, so that, in the opinion of the court, the protection of the interests of the subclass members requires that they be separately represented, subsection (1) applies with necessary modifications in respect of the subclass.

Amendment of certification order

(3) The court, on the motion of a party or class member, may amend an order certifying a proceeding as a class proceeding.

Section 9

Opting out

9. Any member of a class involved in a class proceeding may opt out of the proceeding in the manner and within the time specified in the certification order.

Section 10

Where it appears conditions for certification not satisfied

10. (1) On the motion of a party or class member, where it appears to the court that the conditions mentioned in subsections 5(1) and (2) are not satisfied with respect to a class proceeding, the court may amend the certification order, may decertify the proceeding or may make any other order it considers appropriate.

Proceeding may continue in altered form

(2) Where the court makes a decertification order under subsection (1), the court may permit the proceeding to continue as one or more proceedings between different parties.

Powers of court

(3) For the purposes of subsections (1) and (2), the court has the powers set out in clauses 7(a) to (c).

Section 11

Stages of class proceedings

11. (1) Subject to section 12, in a class proceeding,

(a) common issues for a class shall be determined together;

(b) common issues for a subclass shall be determined together; and

(c) individual issues that require the participation of individual class members shall be determined individually in accordance with sections 24 and 25.

Separate judgments

(2) The court may give judgment in respect of the common issues and separate judgments in respect of any other issue.

Section 12

Court may determine conduct of proceeding

12. The court, on the motion of a party or class member, may make an order it considers appropriate respecting the conduct of a class proceeding to ensure its fair and expeditious determination and, for the purpose, may impose such terms on the parties as it considers appropriate.

Section 13

Court may stay any other proceeding

13. The court, on its own initiative or on the motion of a party or class member, may stay any proceeding related to the class proceeding before it, on such terms as it considers appropriate.

Section 14

Participation of class members

14. (1) In order to ensure the fair and adequate representation of the interests of the class or any subclass or for any other appropriate reason, the court may, at any time in a class proceeding, permit one or more class members to participate in the proceeding.

Idem

(2) Participation under subsection (1) shall be in whatever manner and on whatever terms, including terms as to costs, the court considers appropriate.

Section 15

Discovery of parties

15. (1) Parties to a class proceeding have the same rights of discovery under the rules of court against one another as they would have in any other proceeding.

Discovery of class members with leave

(2) After discovery of the representative party, a party may move for discovery under the rules of court against other class members.

Idem

(3) In deciding whether to grant leave to discover other class members, the court shall consider,

(a) the stage of the class proceeding and the issues to be determined at that stage;

(b) the presence of subclasses;

(c) whether the discovery is necessary in view of the claims or defences of the party seeking leave;

(d) the approximate monetary value of individual claims, if any;

(e) whether discovery would result in oppression or in undue annoyance, burden or expense for the class members sought to be discovered; and

(f) any other matter the court considers relevant.

Idem

(4) A class member is subject to the same sanctions under the rules of court as a party for failure to submit to discovery.

Section 16

Examination of class members before a motion or application

16. (1) A party shall not require a class member other than a representative party to be examined as a witness before the hearing of a motion or application, except with leave of the court.

Idem

(2) Subsection 15(3) applies with necessary modifications to a decision whether to grant leave under subsection (1).

Section 17

Notice of certification

17. (1) Notice of certification of a class proceeding shall be given by the representative party to the class members in accordance with this section.

Court may dispense with notice

(2) The court may dispense with notice if, having regard to the factors set out in subsection (3), the court considers it appropriate to do so.

Order respecting notice

(3) The court shall make an order setting out when and by what means notice shall be given under this section and in so doing shall have regard to,

(a) the cost of giving notice;

(b) the nature of the relief sought;

(c) the size of the individual claims of the class members;

(d) the number of class members;

(e) the places of residence of class members; and

(f) any other relevant matter.

Idem

(4) The Court may order that notice be given,

(a) personally or by mail;

(b) by posting, advertising, publishing or leafleting;

(c) by individual notice to a sample group within the class; or

(d) by any means or combination of means that the court considers appropriate.

Idem

(5) The court may order that notice be given to different class members by different means.

Contents of notice

(6) Notice under this section shall, unless the court orders otherwise,

(a) describe the proceeding, including the names and addresses of the representative parties and the relief sought;

(b) state the manner by which and time within which class members may opt out of the proceeding;

(c) describe the possible financial consequences of the proceeding to class members;

(d) summarize any agreements between representative parties and their solicitors respecting fees and disbursements;

(e) describe any counterclaim being asserted by or against the class, including the relief sought in the counterclaim;

(f) state that the judgment, whether favourable or not, will bind all class members who do not opt out of the proceeding;

(g) describe the right of any class member to participate in the proceeding;

(h) give an address to which class members may direct inquiries about the proceeding; and

(i) give any other information the court considers appropriate.

Solicitations of contributions

(7) With leave of the court, notice under this section may include a solicitation of contributions from class members to assist in paying solicitor's fees and disbursements.

Section 18

Notice where individual participation is required

18. (1) When the court determines common issues in favour of a class and considers that the participation of individual class members is required to determine individual issues, the representative party shall give notice to those members in accordance with this section.

Idem

(2) Subsections 17(3) to (5) apply with necessary modifications to notice given under this section.

Contents of notice

(3) Notice under this section shall,

(a) state that common issues have been determined in favour of the class;

(b) state that class members may be entitled to individual relief;

(c) describe the steps to be taken to establish an individual claim;

(d) state that failure on the part of a class member to take those steps will result in the member not being entitled to assert an individual claim except with leave of the court;

(e) give an address to which class members may direct inquiries about the proceeding; and

(f) give any other information that the court considers appropriate.

Section 19

Notice to protect interests of affected persons

19. (1) At any time in a class proceeding, the court may order any party to give such notice as it considers necessary to protect the interests of any class member or party or to ensure the fair conduct of the proceeding.

Idem

(2) Subsections 17(3) to (5) apply with necessary modifications to notice given under this section.

Section 20

Approval of notice by the court

20. A notice under section 17, 18 or 19 shall be approved by the court before it is given.

Section 21

Delivery of notice

21. The court may order a party to deliver, by whatever means are available to the party, the notice required to be given by another party under section 17, 18 or 19, where that is more practical.

Section 22

Costs of notice

22. (1) The court may make any order it considers appropriate as to the costs of any notice under section 17, 18 or 19, including an order apportioning costs among parties.

Idem

(2) In making an order under subsection (1), the court may have regard to the different interests of a subclass.

Section 23

Statistical evidence

23. (1) For the purposes of determining issues relating to the amount or distribution of a monetary award under this Act, the court may admit as evidence statistical information that would not otherwise be admissible as evidence, including information derived from sampling, if the information was compiled in accordance with principles that are generally accepted by experts in the field of statistics.

Idem

(2) A record of statistical information purporting to be prepared or published under the authority of the Parliament of Canada or the legislature of any province or territory of Canada may be admitted as evidence without proof of its authenticity.

Notice

(3) Statistical information shall not be admitted as evidence under this section unless the party seeking to introduce the information has,

(a) given reasonable notice of it to the party against whom it is to be used, together with a copy of the information;

(b) complied with subsections (4) and (5); and

(c) complied with any requirement to produce documents under subsection (7).

Contents of notice

(4) Notice under this section shall specify the source of any statistical information sought to be introduced that,

(a) was prepared or published under the authority of the Parliament of Canada or the legislature of any province or territory of Canada;

(b) was derived from market quotations, tabulations, lists, directories or other compilations generally used and relied on by members of the public; or

(c) was derived from reference material generally used and relied on by members of an occupational group.

Idem

(5) Except with respect to information referred to in subsection (4), notice under this section shall,

(a) specify the name and qualifications of each person who supervised the preparation of statistical information sought to be introduced; and

(b) describe any documents prepared or used in the course of preparing the statistical information sought to be introduced.

Cross-examination

(6) A party against whom statistical information is sought to be introduced under this section may require, for the purposes of cross-examination, the attendance of any person who supervised the preparation of the information.

Production of documents

(7) Except with respect to information referred to in subsection (4), a party against whom statistical information is sought to be introduced under this section may require the party seeking to introduce it to produce for inspection any document that was prepared or used in the course of preparing the information, unless the document discloses the identity of persons responding to a survey who have not consented in writing to the disclosure.

Section 24

Aggregate assessment of monetary relief

24. (1) The court may determine the aggregate or a part of a defendant's liability to class members and give judgment accordingly where,

(a) monetary relief is claimed on behalf of some or all class members;

(b) no questions of fact or law other than those relating to the assessment of monetary relief remain to be determined in order to establish the amount of the defendant's monetary liability; and

(c) the aggregate or a part of the defendant's liability to some or all class members can reasonably be determined without proof by individual class members.

Average or proportional application

(2) The court may order that all or a part of an award under subsection (1) be applied so that some or all individual class members share in the award on an average or proportional basis.

Idem

(3) In deciding whether to make an order under subsection (2), the court shall consider whether it would be impractical or inefficient to identify the class members entitled to share in the award or to determine the exact shares that should be allocated to individual class members.

Court to determine whether individual claims need to be made

(4) When the court orders that all or a part of an award under subsection (1) be divided among individual class members, the court shall determine whether individual claims need to be made to give effect to the order.

Procedures for determining claims

(5) Where the court determines under subsection (4) that individual claims need to be made, the court shall specify procedures for determining the claims.

Idem

(6) In specifying procedures under subsection (5), the court shall minimize the burden on class members and, for the purpose, the court may authorize,

(a) the use of standardized proof of claim forms;

(b) the receipt of affidavit or other documentary evidence; and

(c) the auditing of claims on a sampling or other basis

Time limits for making claims

(7) When specifying procedures under subsection (5), the court shall set a reasonable time within which individual class members may make claims under this section.

Idem

(8) A class member who fails to make a claim within the time set under subsection (7) may not later make a claim under this section except with leave of the court.

Extension of time

(9) The court may give leave under subsection (8) if it is satisfied that,

(a) there are apparent grounds for relief;

(b) the delay was not caused by any fault of the person seeking the relief; and

(c) the defendant would not suffer substantial prejudice if leave were given.

Court may amend subs. (1) judgment

(10) The court may amend a judgment given under subsection (1) to give effect to a claim made with leave under subsection (8) if the court considers it appropriate to do so.

Section 25

Individual issues

25. (1) When the court determines common issues in favour of a class and considers that the participation of individual class members is required to determine individual issues, other than those that may be determined under section 24, the court may,

(a) determine the issues in further hearings presided over by the judge who determined the common issues or by another judge of the court;

(b) appoint one or more persons to conduct a reference under the rules of court and report back to the court; and

(c) with the consent of the parties, direct that the issues be determined in any other manner.

Directions as to procedure

(2) The court shall give any necessary directions relating to the procedures to be followed in conducting hearings, inquiries and determinations under subsection (1), including directions for the purpose of achieving procedural conformity.

Idem

(3) In giving directions under subsection (2), the court shall choose the least expensive and most expeditious method of determining the issues that is consistent with justice to class members and the parties and, in so doing, the court may,

(a) dispense with any procedural step that it considers unnecessary; and

(b) authorize any special procedural steps, including steps relating to discovery, and any special rules, including rules relating to admission of evidence and means of proof, that it considers appropriate.

Time limits for making claims

(4) The court shall set a reasonable time within which individual class members may make claims under this section.

Idem

(5) A class member who fails to make a claim within the time set under subsection (4) may not later make a claim under this section except with leave of the court.

Extension of time

(6) Subsection 24(9) applies with necessary modifications to a decision whether to give leave under subsection (5).

Determination under cl. (1)(c) deemed court order

(7) A determination under clause (1)(c) is deemed to be an order of the court.

Section 26

Judgment distribution

26. (1) The court may direct any means of distribution of amounts awarded under section 24 or 25 that it considers appropriate.

Idem

(2) In giving directions under subsection (1), the court may order that,

(a) the defendant distribute directly to class members the amount of monetary relief to which each class member is entitled by any means authorized by the court, including abatement and credit;

(b) the defendant pay into court or some other appropriate depository the total amount of the defendant's liability to the class until further order of the court; and

(c) any person other than the defendant distribute directly to class members the amount of monetary relief to which each member is entitled by any means authorized by the court.

Idem

(3) In deciding whether to make an order under clause (2)(a), the court shall consider whether distribution by the defendant is the most practical way of distributing the award for any reason, including the fact that the amount of monetary relief to which each class member is entitled can be determined from the records of the defendant.

Idem

(4) The court may order that all or a part of an award under section 24 that has not been distributed within a time set by the court be applied in any manner that may reasonably be expected to benefit class members, even though the order does not provide for monetary relief to individual class members, if the court is satisfied that a reasonable number of class members who would not otherwise receive monetary relief would benefit from the order.

Idem

(5) The court may make an order under subsection (4) whether or not all class members can be identified or all of their shares can be exactly determined.

Idem

(6) The court may make an order under subsection (4) even if the order would benefit,

(a) persons who are not class members; or

(b) persons who may otherwise receive monetary relief as a result of the class proceeding.

Supervisory role of the court

(7) The court shall supervise the execution of judgments and the distribution of awards under section 24 or 25 and may stay the whole or any part of an execution or distribution for a reasonable period on such terms as it considers appropriate.

Payment of awards

(8) The court may order that an award made under section 24 or 25 be paid,

(a) in a lump sum, forthwith or within a time set by the court; or

(b) in instalments, on such terms as the court considers appropriate.

Costs of distribution

(9) The court may order that the costs of distribution of an award under section 24 or 25, including the costs of notice associated with the distribution and the fees payable to a person administering the distribution, be paid out of the proceeds of the judgment or may make such other order as it considers appropriate.

Return of unclaimed amounts

(10) Any part of an award for division among individual class members that remains unclaimed or otherwise undistributed after a time set by the court shall be returned to the party against whom the award was made, without further order of the court.

Section 27

Contents of judgment on common issues

27. (1) A judgment on common issues of a class or subclass shall,

(a) set out the common issues;

(b) name or describe the class or subclass members;

(c) state the nature of the claims or defences asserted on behalf of the class or subclass; and

(d) specify the relief granted.

Effect of judgment on common issues

(2) A judgment on common issues of a class or subclass does not bind,

(a) a person who has opted out of the class proceeding; or

(b) a party to the class proceeding in any subsequent proceeding between the party and a person mentioned in clause (a).

Idem

(3) A judgment on common issues of a class or subclass binds every class member who has not opted out of the class proceeding, but only to the extent that the judgment determines common issues that,

(a) are set out in the certification order;

(b) relate to claims or defences described in the certification order; and

(c) relate to relief sought by or from the class or subclass as stated in the certification order.

Section 28

Limitations

28. (1) Subject to subsection (2), any limitation period applicable to a cause of action asserted in a class proceeding is suspended in favour of a class member on the commencement of the class proceeding and resumes running against the class member when,

(a) the member opts out of the class proceeding;

(b) an amendment that has the effect of excluding the member from the class is made to the certification order;

(c) a decertification order is made under section 10;

(d) the class proceeding is dismissed without an adjudication on the merits;

(e) the class proceeding is abandoned or discontinued with the approval of the court; or

(f) the class proceeding is settled with the approval of the court, unless the settlement provides otherwise.

Idem

(2) Where there is a right of appeal in respect of an event described in clauses (1)(a) to (f), the limitation period resumes running as soon as the time for appeal has expired without an appeal being commenced or as soon as any appeal has been finally disposed of.

Section 29

Discontinuance and abandonment

29. (1) A proceeding commenced under this Act and a proceeding certified as a class proceeding under this Act may be discontinued or abandoned only with the approval of the court, on such terms as the court considers appropriate.

Settlement without court approval not binding

(2) A settlement of a class proceeding is not binding unless approved by the court.

Effect of settlement

(3) A settlement of a class proceeding that is approved by the court binds all class members.

Notice: dismissal, discontinuance, abandonment or settlement

(4) In dismissing a proceeding for delay or in approving a discontinuance, abandonment or settlement, the court shall consider whether notice should be given under section 19 and whether any notice should include,

(a) an account of the conduct of the proceeding;

(b) a statement of the result of the proceeding; and

(c) a description of any plan for distributing settlement funds.

Section 30

Appeals: refusals to certify and decertification orders

30. (1) A party may appeal to the Divisional Court from an order refusing to certify a proceeding as a class proceeding and from an order decertifying a proceeding.

Appeals: certification orders

(2) A party may appeal to the Divisional Court from an order certifying a proceeding as a class proceeding, with leave of the Superior Court of Justice as provided in the rules of court.

Appeals: judgments on common issues and aggregate awards

(3) A party may appeal to the Court of Appeal from a judgment on common issues and from an order under section 24, other than an order that determines individual claims made by class members.

Appeals by class members on behalf of the class

(4) If a representative party does not appeal or seek leave to appeal as permitted by subsection (1) or (2), or if a representative party abandons an appeal under subsection (1) or (2), any class member may make a motion to the court for leave to act as the representative party for the purposes of the relevant subsection.

Idem

(5) If a representative party does not appeal as permitted by subsection (3), or if a representative party abandons an appeal under subsection (3), any class member may make a motion to the Court of Appeal for leave to act as the representative party for the purposes of subsection (3).

Appeals: individual awards

(6) A class member may appeal to the Divisional Court from an order under section 24 or 25 determining an individual claim made by the member and awarding more than $3,000 to the member.

Idem

(7) A representative plaintiff may appeal to the Divisional Court from an order under section 24 determining an individual claim made by a class member and awarding more than $3,000 to the member.

Idem

(8) A defendant may appeal to the Divisional Court from an order under section 25 determining an individual claim made by a class member and awarding more than $3,000 to the member.

Idem

(9) With leave of the Superior Court of Justice as provided in the rules of court, a class member may appeal to the Divisional Court from an order under section 24 or 25,

(a) determining an individual claim made by the member and awarding $3,000 or less to the member; or

(b) dismissing an individual claim made by the member for monetary relief.

Idem

(10) With leave of the Superior Court of Justice as provided in the rules of court, a representative plaintiff may appeal to the Divisional Court from an order under section 24,

(a) determining an individual claim made by a class member and awarding $3,000 or less to the member; or

(b) dismissing an individual claim made by a class member for monetary relief.

Idem

(11) With leave of the Superior Court of Justice as provided in the rules of court, a defendant may appeal to the Divisional Court from an order under section 25,

(a) determining an individual claim made by a class member and awarding $3,000 or less to the member; or

(b) dismissing an individual claim made by a class member for monetary relief.

2006, c. 19, Sched. C, s. 1(1) (Table 1)

Section 31

Costs

31. (1) In exercising its discretion with respect to costs under subsection 131 (1) of the *Courts of Justice Act*, the court may consider whether the class proceeding was a test case, raised a novel point of law or involved a matter of public interest.

Liability of class members for costs

(2) Class members, other than the representative party, are not liable for costs except with respect to the determination of their own individual claims.

Small claims

(3) Where an individual claim under section 24 or 25 is within the monetary jurisdiction of the Small Claims Court where the class proceeding was commenced, costs related to the claim shall be assessed as if the claim had been determined by the Small Claims Court.

Section 32

Agreements respecting fees and disbursements

32. (1) An agreement respecting fees and disbursements between a solicitor and a representative party shall be in writing and shall,

(a) state the terms under which fees and disbursements shall be paid;

(b) give an estimate of the expected fee, whether contingent on success in the class proceeding or not; and

(c) state the method by which payment is to be made, whether by lump sum, salary or otherwise.

Court to approve agreements

(2) An agreement respecting fees and disbursements between a solicitor and a representative party is not enforceable unless approved by the court, on the motion of the solicitor.

Priority of amounts owed under approved agreement

(3) Amounts owing under an enforceable agreement are a first charge on any settlement funds or monetary award.

Determination of fees where agreement not approved

(4) If an agreement is not approved by the court, the court may,

(a) determine the amount owing to the solicitor in respect of fees and disbursements;

(b) direct a reference under the rules of court to determine the amount owing; or

(c) direct that the amount owing be determined in any other manner.

Section 33

Agreements for payment only in the event of success

33. (1) Despite the *Solicitors Act* and *An Act Respecting Champerty*, being chapter 327 of Revised Statutes of Ontario, 1897, a solicitor and a representative party may enter into a written agreement providing for payment of fees and disbursements only in the event of success in a class proceeding.

Interpretation, success in a proceeding

(2) For the purposes of subsection (1), success in a class proceeding includes,

(a) a judgment on common issues in favour of some or all class members; and

(b) a settlement that benefits one or more class members.

Definitions

(3) For the purposes of subsections (4) to (7),

"base fee" means the result of multiplying the total number of hours worked by an hourly rate;

"multiplier" means a multiple to be applied to a base fee.

Agreements to increase fees by a multiplier

(4) An agreement under subsection (1) may permit the solicitor to make a motion to the court to have his or her fees increased by a multiplier.

Motion to increase fee by a multiplier

(5) A motion under subsection (4) shall be heard by a judge who has,

(a) given judgment on common issues in favour of some or all class members; or

(b) approved a settlement that benefits any class member.

Idem

(6) Where the judge referred to in subsection (5) is unavailable for any reason, the regional senior judge shall assign another judge of the court for the purpose.

Idem

(7) On the motion of a solicitor who has entered into an agreement under subsection (4), the court,

(a) shall determine the amount of the solicitor's base fee;

(b) may apply a multiplier to the base fee that results in fair and reasonable compensation to the solicitor for the risk incurred in undertaking and continuing the proceeding under an agreement for payment only in the event of success; and

(c) shall determine the amount of disbursements to which the solicitor is entitled, including interest calculated on the disbursements incurred, as totalled at the end of each six-month period following the date of the agreement.

Idem

(8) In making a determination under clause (7)(a), the court shall allow only a reasonable fee.

Idem

(9) In making a determination under clause (7)(b), the court may consider the manner in which the solicitor conducted the proceeding.

Section 34

Motions

34. (1) The same judge shall hear all motions before the trial of the common issues.

Idem

(2) Where a judge who has heard motions under subsection (1) becomes unavailable for any reason, the regional senior judge shall assign another judge of the court for the purpose.

Idem

(3) Unless the parties agree otherwise, a judge who hears motions under subsection (1) or (2) shall not preside at the trial of the common issues.

Section 35

Rules of court

35. The rules of court apply to class proceedings.

Section 36

Crown bound

36. This Act binds the Crown.

Section 37

Application of Act

37. This Act does not apply to,

(a) a proceeding that may be brought in a representative capacity under another Act;

(b) a proceeding required by law to be brought in a representative capacity; and

(c) a proceeding commenced before this Act comes into force.

Section 38

Commencement

38. This Act comes into force on a day to be named by proclamation of the Lieutenant Governor.

Section 39

Short title

39. The short title of this Act is the *Class Proceedings Act, 1992.*

LAW SOCIETY AMENDMENT ACT (CLASS PROCEEDINGS FUND), 1992

S.O. 1992, c. 7

Section 1

1. Section 52 of the Law Society Act is amended by striking out "53 to 59" in the first and second lines and substituting "53 to 59.5" and by adding the following definitions:

"class proceeding" means a proceeding certified as a class proceeding on a motion made under section 2 or 3 of the *Class Proceedings Act, 1992*;

"Committee" means the Class Proceedings Committee referred to in section 59.2,

"defendant" includes a respondent;

"plaintiff" includes an applicant.

Section 2

2. Subsection 55(1) of the Act is amended by adding the following paragraph:

4. The provision of costs assistance to parties to class proceedings and to proceedings commenced under the *Class Proceedings Act, 1992*.

Regulations

3. The Act is amended by adding the following sections:

Class Proceedings Fund

59.1 (1) The board shall,

(a) establish an account of the Foundation to be known as the Class Proceedings Fund;

(b) within sixty days after this Act comes into force, endow the Class Proceedings Fund with $300,000 from the funds of the Foundation;

(c) within one year after the day on which the endowment referred to in clause (b) is made, endow the Class Proceedings Fund with a further $200,000 from the funds of the Foundation; and

(d) administer the Class Proceedings Fund in accordance with this Act and the. regulations.

Purposes of the Class Proceedings Fund

(2) The Class Proceedings Fund shall be used for the following purposes:

1. Financial support for plaintiffs to class proceedings and to proceedings commenced under the *Class Proceedings Act, 1992*, in respect of disbursements related to the proceeding.

2. Payments to defendants in respect of costs awards made in their favour against plaintiffs who have received financial support from the Fund.

Application of s. 56

(3) Funds in the Class Proceedings Fund are funds of the Foundation within the meaning of section 56, but payments out of the Class Proceedings Fund shall relate to the administration or purposes of the Fund.

Class Proceedings Committee

59.2 (1) The Class Proceedings Committee is established and shall be composed of,

(a) one member appointed by the Foundation;

(b) one member appointed by the Attorney General; and

(c) three members appointed jointly by the Foundation and the Attorney General.

Term of office

(2) Each member of the Class Proceedings Committee shall hold office for a period of three years and is eligible for re-appointment.

Quorum

(3) Three members of the Committee constitute a quorum.

Vacancies

(4) Where there are not more than two vacancies in the membership of the Committee, the remaining members constitute the Committee for all purposes.

Remuneration

(5) The members of the Committee shall serve without remuneration, but each member is entitled to compensation for expenses incurred in carrying out the functions of the Committee.

Applications by plaintiff

59.3 (1) A plaintiff to a class proceeding or to a proceeding commenced under section 2 of the *Class Proceedings Act, 1992* may apply to the Committee for financial support from the Class Proceedings Fund in respect of disbursements related to the proceeding.

Idem

(2) An application under subsection (1) shall not include a claim in respect of solicitor's fees.

Committee may authorize payment

(3) The Committee may direct the board to make payments from the Class Proceedings Fund to a plaintiff who makes a application under subsection (1), in the amount that the Committee considers appropriate.

Idem

(4) In making a decision under subsection (3), the Committee may have regard to,

(a) the merits of the plaintiff's case;

(b) whether the plaintiff has made reasonable efforts to raise funds from other

(c) whether the plaintiff has a clear and reasonable proposal for the use of any funds awarded;

(d) whether the plaintiff has appropriate financial controls to ensure that any funds awarded are spent for the purposes of the award; and

(e) any other matter that the Committee considers relevant.

Supplementary funding

(5) A plaintiff who has received funding under subsection (3) may apply to the Committee at any time up to the end of the class proceeding for supplementary funding and the Committee may direct the board to make further payments from the Class Proceedings Fund to the plaintiff if the Committee is of the opinion, having regard to all the circumstances, that it is appropriate to do so.

Board shall make payments

(6) The board shall make payments in accordance with any directions given by the Committee under this section.

Applications by defendants

59.4 (1) A defendant to a proceeding may apply to the board for payment from the Class Proceedings Fund in respect of a costs award made in the proceeding in the defendant's favour against a plaintiff who has received financial support from the Class Proceedings Fund in respect of the proceeding.

Board shall make payments

(2) The board shall make payments applied for in accordance with subsection (1) from the Class Proceedings Fund, subject to any limits or tariffs applicable to such payments prescribed by the regulations.

Plaintiff not liable

(3) A defendant who has the right to apply for payment from the Class Proceedings Fund in respect of a costs award against a plaintiff may not recover any part of the award from the plaintiff.

Regulations

59.5 (1) The Lieutenant Governor in Council may make regulations,

(a) respecting the administration of the Class Proceedings Fund;

(b) establishing procedures for making applications under sections 59.3 and 59.4;

(c) establishing criteria in addition to those set out in section 59.3 for decisions of the Committee under section 59.3;

(d) establishing limits and tariffs for payments under sections 59.3 and 59.4;

(e) prescribing conditions of awards under section 59.3;

(f) providing for the assessment of costs in respect of which a claim is made under section 59.4;

(g) providing for levies in favour of the Class Proceedings Fund against awards and settlement funds in proceedings in respect of which a party receives financial support from the Class Proceedings Fund.

Idem

(2) A regulation made under clause (1)(d) may provide for different limits and tariffs for different stages and types of proceedings.

Idem

(3) A regulation made under clause (1)(g) may provide for levies that exceed the amount of financial support received by the parties to a proceeding.

Idem

(4) A regulation made under clause (1)(g) may provide for levies based on a formula that takes the amount of an award or settlement fund into account.

Idem

(5) A levy under clause (1)(g) against a settlement fund or monetary award is a charge on the fund or award.

Section 4

Commencement

4. This Act comes into force on a day to be named by proclamation of the Lieutenant Governor. [in force January 1, 1993, Ontario Gazette: Vol. 125-52, December 26, 1992, p. 3284]

Section 5

Short title

5. The short title of this Act is the *Law Society Amendment Act (Class Proceedings Funding), 1992.*

CLASS PROCEEDINGS REGULATION

Made under the *Law Society Act*

O. Reg. 771/92

as am. O. Reg. 535/95.

Definitions

1. In this Regulation,

"defendant applicant" means an applicant for payment under section 59.4 of the Act;

"plaintiff applicant" means an applicant for financial support under section 59.3 of the Act;

"plaintiff recipient" means a recipient of an award of financial support under section 59.3 of the Act.

Application by plaintiffs under section 59.3 of the act

2. A plaintiff applicant shall make a separate application for financial assistance in respect of each of the following stages in a proceeding:

1. Steps taken up to the end of the hearing of a motion for an order certifying the proceeding as a class proceeding.

2. Appeals of orders relating to certification.

3. Steps other than those described in paragraphs 1 and 2 taken up to the end of discovery or cross-examination on affidavits.

4. Steps other than those described in paragraphs 1 to 3 concerning the determination of common issues.

5. Appeals from a judgment on common issues.

6. Steps other than those described in paragraphs 1 to 5.

3. (1) Every plaintiff applicant shall provide six copies of the following information and documents to the Committee:

1. If the applicant is an individual, his or her name, address, telephone number and fax number, if any.

2. If the applicant is a corporation, its name, head office address, telephone number and fax number and a copy of its articles of incorporation.

3. Each defendant's name.

4. A statement indicating which of the stages in the proceeding, as set out in paragraphs 1 to 6 of section 2, the application addresses.

5. A copy of the pleadings and any court order relating to the proceeding.

6. A description of the class and an estimate of the number of members in the class.

7. A legal opinion describing and assessing the merits of the applicant's case, and any other information and documents the applicant considers appropriate for this purpose.

8. If the applicant has not yet applied for certification of the proceeding as a class proceeding, a statement indicating when the applicant will do so.

9. If the proceeding has not yet been certified as a class proceeding, a legal opinion assessing the likelihood that it will be certified.

10. A statement of the financial support being requested, itemized according to the purposes for which it is being requested.

11. Such information and documents as the applicant considers appropriate to address each of the matters described in clauses 59.3(4)(b) to (d) of the Act.

12. An affidavit by the applicant stating that the information provided by him, her or it in connection with the application is true.

13. Authorization to the Committee and to the board to verify the information provided by the applicant in connection with the application.

14. The name and address of the applicant's lawyer.

15. A statement by the lawyer indicating that he or she will accept payments from the Class Proceedings Fund in connection with the application and will use them for the purposes for which the payments are made.

(2) Despite subsection (1), a plaintiff applicant who makes more than one application in respect of a proceeding is not required to resubmit information and documents provided on a previous application.

(3) A plaintiff applicant is entitled to make oral submissions to the Committee concerning the applicant's first application for financial support relating to a particular proceeding.

4. The Committee shall not award financial support in respect of a particular expert unless the Committee approves the use of the expert and the amount of the disbursements relating to the expert.

Criteria for decisions respecting plaintiff's applications

5. In making a decision under subsection 59.3(3) of the Act, the Committee may have regard to the following matters:

1. The extent to which the issues in the proceeding affect the public interest.

2. If the application for financial support is made before the proceeding is certified as a class proceeding, the likelihood that it will be certified.

3. The amount of money in the Fund that has been allocated to provide financial support in respect of other applications or that may be required to make payments to defendants under section 59.4 of the Act.

Conditions of financial support for plaintiffs

6. (1) A plaintiff applicant is not entitled to receive payment of an award under section 59.3 of the Act until he, she or it provides the board with,

(a) a statement of disbursements to which the award relates, certified by the lawyer who made the disbursements to be complete and accurate; or

(b) such other proof that the disbursements have been made as the board considers appropriate.

(2) The board may make a payment relating to a disbursement that the plaintiff recipient's lawyer has not yet paid if the board considers that, in the circumstances, the plaintiff recipient would otherwise suffer undue hardship.

7. (1) The plaintiff recipient shall use the money paid under section 59.3 of the Act only for the purpose for which financial support is authorized in the award.

(2) If the plaintiff recipient wishes to use any money awarded for a different purpose, he, she or it shall obtain the consent of the Committee before doing so.

(3) A plaintiff recipient who fails to comply with this section shall repay the amount of the payment.

8. (1) The conditions set out in this section apply with respect to every payment of financial support made under section 59.3 of the Act.

(2) A plaintiff recipient who fails to comply with a condition set out in this section shall, at the request of the board, repay the amount of the payment.

(3) The plaintiff recipient shall notify the defendant in the proceeding,

(a) that the recipient has received financial support from the Class Proceedings Fund in respect of the proceeding;

(b) that there is a charge in favour of the Fund on any award and settlement funds in the proceeding; and

(c) that the amount of the charge is determined under section 10.

(4) If the proceeding is certified as a class proceeding, the plaintiff recipient shall notify the other class members.

(a) that the recipient has received financial support from the Class Proceedings Fund in respect of the proceeding;

(b) that there will be a levy that reduces the amount of any award or settlement funds to which the class members may become entitled;

(c) that the amount of the levy is the sum of,

(i) the amount of any financial support paid under section 59.3 of the Act, excluding any amount repaid by a plaintiff, and

(ii) 10 per cent of the amount of the award or settlement funds, if any, to which one or more persons in the class is entitled.

(5) The plaintiff recipient shall give the notice required by subsection (4) on the first occasion that he, she or it is required to give any notice to other class members under the *Class Proceedings Act, 1992* that falls after he, she or it is first awarded financial support in the proceeding by the Committee.

(6) The plaintiff recipient shall give notice to the board of all motions in the proceeding relating to settlement.

(7) The plaintiff recipient shall provide the board with the following information and documents:

1. Details respecting any change in the information provided in the application for financial support.

2. On request, a copy of every document filed with the court in the proceeding.

3. On request, a copy of every order made by the court in the proceeding.

(8) The plaintiff recipient shall allow the board to review records relating to disbursements for which financial support is claimed or paid.

9. If the proceeding to which the award relates is discontinued or abandoned, the plaintiff recipient shall, at the request of the board, repay the amount of any payments from the Class Proceedings Fund.

Levies against awards and settlement funds

10. (1) This section applies in a proceeding in respect of which a party receives financial support from the Class Proceedings Fund.

(2) A levy is payable in favour of the Fund,

(a) when a monetary award is made in favour of one or more persons in a class that includes a plaintiff who received financial support under section 59.3 of the Act; or

(b) when the proceeding is settled and one or more persons in such a class is entitled to receive settlement funds.

(3) The amount of the levy is the sum of,

(a) the amount of any financial support paid under section 59.3 of the Act, excluding any amount repaid by a plaintiff; and

(b) 10 per cent of the amount of the award or settlement funds, if any, to which one or more persons in a class that includes a plaintiff who received financial support under section 59.3 of the Act is entitled.

(4) [Revoked O. Reg. 535/95, s. 1.]

O. Reg. 535/95, s. 1

Applications by defendants under section 59.4 of the act

11. Every defendant applicant shall provide the following information and documents to the board:

1. If the applicant is an individual, his or her name, address, telephone number and fax number, if any.

2. If the applicant is a corporation, its name, head office address, telephone number and fax number.

3. An affidavit by the applicant containing.

   i. a statement that costs have been awarded in favour of the applicant against the plaintiff, and indicating the stage of the proceeding at which the order was made,

   ii. a statement whether the court order fixed the amount of the costs to be paid by the plaintiff and, if so, setting out the amount,

   iii. a statement that the order awarding costs has not been appealed and that the certificate, if any, of the assessment officer has not been appealed, and

   iv. a statement that the time for appealing the order and the certificate, if any, has expired.

4. If the court order did not fix the amount of the costs to be paid by the plaintiff, either a certificate of assessment of costs or an agreed bill of costs.

5. The name and address of the person to whom payment from the Class Proceedings Fund is to be made.

6. The name and address of the applicant's lawyer.

Administration of the fund

12. Payments from the Class Proceedings Fund to a plaintiff recipient shall be made only to the recipient's lawyer.

13. The board shall compile the following information each year for inclusion in its annual report:

1. The number of applications under section 59.3 of the Act that were made, listed by those stages in the proceeding that are set out in paragraphs 1 to 6 of section 2.

2. The number of those applications, listed by stages in the proceeding,

   i. in which an award was made, and

   ii. in which no award was made.

3. The number of proceedings for which financial support was awarded under section 59.3 of the Act.

4. The total amount of money awarded to applicants under section 59.3 of the Act, listed by type of disbursement.

5. The total amount of money paid from the Class Proceedings Fund to applicants under section 59.3 of the Act.

6. The number of applicants who received financial support under section 59.3 of the Act before the proceeding was certified as a class proceeding and whose proceedings were certified.

7. The number of applicants who received financial support under section 59.3 of the Act,

i. who received judgment on common issues in their favour at trial, or

ii. whose proceedings settled.

8. The number of applications by defendants under section 59.4 of the Act.

9. The total amount of money paid from the Fund to defendants under section 59.4 of the Act.

10. A brief description of each proceeding for which a plaintiff was awarded financial support under section 59.3 of the Act and the amount awarded for each type of disbursement.

Commencement

14. This Regulation comes into force on the 1st day of January, 1993.

RULE 12 — CLASS PROCEEDINGS AND OTHER REPRESENTATIVE PROCEEDINGS

[am. O. Regs. 770/92; 465/93; 288/99; 504/00 (Fr.); 113/01; 575/07]

DEFINITIONS

12.01 In rules 12.02 to 12.06,

"Act" means the *Class Proceedings Act, 1992*;

"Foundation" means The Law Foundation of Ontario;

"Fund" means the Class Proceedings Fund of the Foundation.

O. Reg. 770/92, s. 5; 465/93, s. 2(2)

TITLE OF PROCEEDING

12.02 (1) In a proceeding commenced under subsection 2(1) of the Act, the title of the proceeding shall include, after the names of the parties, "Proceeding under the *Class Proceedings Act, 1992*".

(2) In a proceeding referred to in section 3 or 4 of the Act, the notice of motion for an order certifying the proceeding, the order certifying it and all subsequent documents shall include, after the names of the parties, "Proceeding under the *Class Proceedings Act, 1992*".

O. Reg. 770/92, s. 5

DISCOVERY OF CLASS MEMBERS

12.03 (1) For the purpose of subrule 31.11(1) (reading in examination), a class member who is examined for discovery under subsection 15(2) of the Act is examined in addition to the party.

(2) Rule 31.10 (discovery of non-parties) and clause 34.15(1)(b) (sanctions for default or misconduct) do not apply when a class member is examined for discovery under subsection 15(2) of the Act.

O. Reg. 770/92, s. 5

COSTS

Application of Rule

12.04 (1) This rule applies to class proceedings in which the plaintiff or applicant has received financial support from the Fund.

Notice to Foundation, Opportunity to Participate

(2) If the court is of the opinion that the defendant or respondent may be entitled to an award of costs, the court shall direct the plaintiff or applicant to give notice to the Foundation.

(3) When the court has made a direction under subsection (2),

(a) no order for costs or assessment of costs shall be made unless the Foundation has had an opportunity to present evidence and make submissions in respect of costs; and

(b) the Foundation is a party for the purpose of an appeal in relation to costs.

Failure to Accept Defendant's Offer

(4) Subrule 49.10(2) (costs consequences of offer) does not apply.

O. Reg. 770/92, s. 5; 113/01, s. 1

CONTENTS OF JUDGMENTS AND ORDERS

12.05 (1) A judgment in a class proceeding or an order approving a settlement, discontinuance or abandonment of a class proceeding under section 29 of the Act shall contain directions with respect to,

(a) the distribution of amounts awarded under section 24 or 25 of the Act, and the costs of distribution;

(b) the payment of amounts owing under an enforceable agreement made under section 32 of the Act between a lawyer and a representative party;

(c) the payment of the costs of the proceeding; and

(d) the payment of any levy in favour of the Fund under clause 59.5(1)(g) of the *Law Society Act*.

(2) An order certifying two or more proceedings as a class proceeding under section 3 of the Act or decertifying a class proceeding under section 10 of the Act shall contain directions with respect to pleadings and other procedural matters.

O. Reg. 770/92, s. 5; 575/07, s. 1, item 6

LEAVE TO APPEAL

Leave to be Obtained from Another Judge

12.06 (1) Leave to appeal to the Divisional Court under subsection 30(2), (9), (10) or (11) of the Act shall be obtained from a judge other than the judge who made the order.

Certification Order — Grounds

(2) Leave to appeal from an order under subsection 30(2) of the Act shall be granted only on the grounds provided in subrule 62.02(4).

Order Awarding $3,000 or less or Dismissing Claim — Grounds

(3) Leave to appeal from an order under subsection 30(9), (10) or (11) of the Act shall not be granted unless,

(a) there has been a miscarriage of justice; or

(b) the order may be used as a precedent in determining the rights of other class members or the defendant in the proceeding under section 24 or 25 of the Act and there is good reason to doubt the correctness of the order.

Procedure

(4) Subrules 62.02(2), (3), (5), (6), (7) and (8) (procedure on motion for leave to appeal) apply to the motion for leave to appeal.

O. Reg. 465/93, s. 2(3)

PROCEEDING AGAINST REPRESENTATIVE DEFENDANT

12.07 Where numerous persons have the same interest, one or more of them may defend a proceeding on behalf or for the benefit of all, or may be authorized by the court to do so.

O. Reg. 465/93, s. 2(3)

PROCEEDING BY UNINCORPORATED ASSOCIATION OR TRADE UNION

12.08 Where numerous persons are members of an unincorporated association or trade union and a proceeding under the *Class Proceedings Act, 1992* would be an unduly expensive or inconvenient means for determining their claims, one or more of them may be authorized by the court to bring a proceeding on behalf of or for the benefit of all.

O. Reg. 288/99, s. 9

Certification Order — Grounds

(2) Leave to appeal from an order under subsection 30(2) of the Act shall be granted only on the grounds provided in subrule 62.02(4).

Order Awarding $3,000 or Less or Dismissing Claim — Grounds

(3) Leave to appeal from an order under subsection 30(9), (10) or (11) of the Act shall not be granted unless,

(a) there has been a miscarriage of justice; or

(b) the order may be used as a precedent in determining the rights of other class members or the defendant in the proceeding under section 24 or 25 of the Act and there is good reason to doubt the correctness of the order.

Procedure

(4) Subrules 62.02(2), (3), (6), (6.1), (7) and (8) (procedure on motion for leave to appeal) apply to the motion for leave to appeal.

O. Reg. 465/93, s. 2 (1).

PROCEEDING AGAINST REPRESENTATIVE DEFENDANT

12.07 Where numerous persons have the same interest, one or more of them may defend a proceeding on behalf or for the benefit of all, or may be authorized by the court to do so.

O. Reg. 465/93, s. 2 (1).

PROCEEDING BY UNINCORPORATED ASSOCIATION OR TRADE UNION

12.08 Where numerous persons are members of an unincorporated association or trade union and a proceeding under the *Class Proceedings Act, 1992* would be an unduly expensive or inconvenient means for determining their claims, one or more of them may be authorized by the court to bring a proceeding on behalf of or for the benefit of all.

O. Reg. 258/98, s. 9.

U.S. FEDERAL RULES OF CIVIL PROCEDURE RULE 23. CLASS ACTIONS

(a) Prerequisites to a Class Action. One or more members of a class may sue or be sued as representative parties on behalf of all only if (1) the class is so numerous that joinder of all members is impracticable, (2) there are questions of law or fact common to the class, (3) the claims or defenses of the representative parties are typical of the claims or defenses of the class, and (4) the representative parties will fairly and adequately protect the interests of the class.

b) Class Actions Maintainable. An action may be maintained as a class action if the prerequisites of subdivision (a) are satisfied, and in addition:

(1) the prosecution of separate actions by or against individual members of the class would create a risk of

(A) inconsistent or varying adjudications with respect to individual members of the class which would establish incompatible standards of conduct for the party opposing the class, or

(B) adjudications with respect to individual members of the class which would as a practical matter be dispositive of the interests of the other members not parties to the adjudications or substantially impair or impede their ability to protect their interests; or

(2) the party opposing the class has acted or refused to act on grounds generally applicable to the class, thereby making appropriate final injunctive relief or corresponding declaratory relief with respect to the class as a whole; or

(3) the court finds that the questions of law or fact common to the members of the class predominate over any questions affecting only individual members, and that a class action is superior to other available methods for the fair and efficient adjudication of the controversy. The matters pertinent to the findings include: (A) the interest of members of the class in individually controlling the prosecution or defense of separate actions; (B) the extent and nature of any litigation concerning the controversy already commenced by or against members of the class; (C) the desirability or undesirability of concentrating the litigation of the claims in the particular forum; (D) the difficulties likely to be encountered in the management of a class action.

(c) Determination by Order Whether Class Action to be Maintained; Notice; Judgment; Actions Conducted Partially as Class Actions.

(1) As soon as practicable after the commencement of an action brought as a class action, the court shall determine by order whether it is to be so maintained. An order under this subdivision may be conditional, and may be altered or amended before the decision on the merits.

(2) In any class action maintained under subdivision (b)(3), the court shall direct to the member of the class the best notice practicable under the circumstances, including individual notice to all members who can be identified through reasonable effort. The notice shall advise each member that (A) the court will exclude the

member from the class if the member so requests by a specified date; (B) the judgment, whether favorable or not, include all members who do not request exclusion; and (C) any member who does not request exclusion may, if the member desires, enter an appearance through counsel.

(3) The judgment in an action maintained as a class action under subdivision (b)(1) (b)(2), whether or not favorable to the class, shall include and describe those whom the court finds to be members of the class. The judgment in an action maintained as a class action under subdivision (b)(3), whether or not favorable to the class, shall include and specify or describe those to whom the notice provided in subdivision (c)(2) was directed, and who have not requested exclusion, and whom the court finds to be members of the class.

(4) When appropriate (A) an action may be brought or maintained as a class action with respect to particular issues, or (B) a class may be divided into subclasses and each subclass treated as a class, and the provisions of this rule shall then be construed and applied accordingly.

(d) *Orders in Conduct of Actions.* In the conduct of actions to which this rule applies, the court may make appropriate orders: (1) determining the course of proceedings or prescribing measures to prevent undue repetition or complication in the presentation of evidence or argument; (2) requiring, for the protection of the members of the class or otherwise for the fair conduct of the action, that notice be given in such manner as the court may direct to some or all of the members of any step in the action, or of the proposed extent of the judgment, or of the opportunity of members to signify whether they consider the representation fair and adequate, to intervene and present claims or defenses, or otherwise to come into the action; (3) imposing conditions on the representative parties or on intervenors; (4) requiring that the pleadings be amended to eliminate therefrom allegations as to representation of absent persons, and that the action proceed accordingly; (5) dealing with similar procedural matters. The orders may be combined with an order under Rule 16, and may be altered or amended as may be desirable from time to time.

(e) Dismissal or Compromise. A class action shall not be dismissed or compromised without the approval of the court, and notice of the proposed dismissal or compromise shall be given to all members of the class in such manner as the court directs.

JUDICIAL REVIEW PROCEDURE ACT

R.S.O. 1990, c. J.1

as am. S.O. 2002, c. 17, Sched. F, s. 1; 2006, c. 19, Sched. C, s. 1(1).

Section 1

Definitions

1. In this Act,

"application for judicial review" means an application under subsection 2(1);

"court" means the Superior Court of Justice;

"licence" includes any permit, certificate, approval, registration or similar form of permission required by law;

"municipality" has the same meaning as in the *Municipal Affairs Act*;

"party" includes a municipality, association of employers, a trade union or council of trade unions which may be a party to any of the proceedings mentioned in subsection 2(1);

"statutory power" means a power or right conferred by or under a statute,

(a) to make any regulation, rule, by-law or order, or to give any other direction having force as subordinate legislation,

(b) to exercise a statutory power of decision,

(c) to require any person or party to do or to refrain from doing any act or thing that, but for such requirement, such person or party would not be required by law to do or to refrain from doing,

(d) to do any act or thing that would, but for such power or right, be a breach of the legal rights of any person or party;

"statutory power of decision" means a power or right conferred by or under a statute to make a decision deciding or prescribing,

(a) the legal rights, powers, privileges, immunities, duties or liabilities of any person or party, or

(b) the eligibility of any person or party to receive, or to the continuation of, a benefit or licence, whether the person or party is legally entitled thereto or not,

and includes the powers of an inferior court.

2002, c. 17, Sched. F, s. 1; 2006, c. 19, Sched. C, s. 1(1)

Cross Reference: Re "statutory power of decision," see also cases under the *Statutory Powers Procedure Act*, s. 1(1), below.

Case Law

Statutory Power of Decision — s. 1 — Cases Where Power or Right Held to Be Statutory Power of Decision

Hasan v. 260 Wellesley Residence Ltd. (1995), 24 O.R. (3d) 335, 126 D.L.R. (4th) 363, 83 O.A.C. 280 (Div. Ct.).

In signing a judgment in relation to an application brought under the *Landlord and Tenant Act*, the local registrar was engaged in the exercise of a statutory power of decision as defined in s. 1 of the Act. However, as s. 113(8) of the *Landlord and Tenant Act* provided an adequate alternate remedy to that of judicial review, an application for judicial review of the local registrar's decision was dismissed.

MacPump Developments Ltd. v. Sarnia (City) (1994), 20 O.R. (3d) 755, 24 M.P.L.R. (2d) 1, 120 D.L.R. (4th) 662, 75 O.A.C. 378; additional reasons (January 19, 1995), Doc. CA C16439 (C.A.).

Resolutions were passed by a city council pursuant to s. 100(1) of the *Municipal Act* establishing a judicial inquiry into the sale of land. The resolutions constituted an order or direction made in the exercise of the power granted by statute and had the force of subordinate legislation. The resolutions therefore constituted the exercise of a statutory power within the meaning of that phrase as defined in s. 1 of the Act.

Middlesex (County) v. Ontario (Minister of Municipal Affairs) (1993), 10 O.R. (3d) 1, 9 Admin. L.R. (2d) 206, 12 M.P.L.R. (2d) 208, 95 D.L.R. (4th) 676, 60 O.A.C. 185 (Div. Ct.).

Actions taken by the Minister of Municipal Affairs under the *Municipal Boundary Negotiations Act* in relation to the resolution of a boundary dispute were taken in the exercise of a statutory power, and therefore were reviewable by the court.

Hamilton-Wentworth (Regional Municipality) v. Ontario (Minister of Transportation) (1991), 2 O.R. (3d) 716, 49 Admin. L.R. 169, 45 C.L.R. 257, 78 D.L.R. (4th) 289, 46 O.A.C. 246 (Div. Ct.); leave to appeal to Ont. C.A. refused (August 12, 1991), Doc. A-48/91.

A decision by the Minister of Transportation not to provide any further funding for the construction of a highway project is not subject to judicial review. To rule otherwise would be trenching on the exclusive control of the legislature in relation to fiscal matters.

Ainsworth Electric Co. v. Exhibition Place (1987), 58 O.R. (2d) 432, 35 M.P.L.R. 56, 36 D.L.R. (4th) 299, 19 O.A.C. 216 (Div. Ct.).

A decision by a board of governors to hire a single in-house electrical contractor rather than continue with a system which had resulted in business for a number of contractors was a commercial decision. The courts have no authority, in the exercise of their prerogative jurisdiction, to review a commercial business decision.

Collins v. Pension Comm. (Ont.) (1986), 56 O.R. (2d) 274, 21 Admin. L.R. 186, 33 B.L.R. 265, 31 D.L.R. (4th) 86, C.E.B. & P.G.R. 8019, 16 O.A.C. 24 (Div. Ct.).

Where the Ontario Pension Commission had consented to the removal of surplus funds from a pension plan, the consent was subject to review as a statutory power of decision, because it determined the legal rights of both the employer and the pension plan members.

Metro. Bd. of Commrs. of Police v. Ont. Mun. Employees' Retirement Bd. (1985), 53 O.R. (2d) 83, 23 D.L.R. (4th) 414, 13 O.A.C. 19 (Div. Ct.).

Where a board purported to exercise a statutory authority in determining the applicant's pension plan contributions, the decision was subject to judicial review as it affected the rights of the applicant.

Prysiazniuk v. Hamilton-Wentworth (Reg. Mun.) (1985), 51 O.R. (2d) 339, 10 O.A.C. 208 (Div. Ct.).

Where the decision of a commissioner effectively deprives the applicant of his livelihood, and seriously threatens the well-being of the residents being cared for by the applicant, the decision is subject to judicial review.

Re Temple and Ont. Liquor Licence Bd. (1982), 41 O.R. (2d) 214, 145 D.L.R. (3d) 480 (Div. Ct.).

The Liquor Licence Board of Ontario, in deciding whether an applicant is entitled to a liquor licence (pursuant to s. 6 of the *Liquor Licence Act*), exercises a statutory power of decision.

Re Grant Bus Lines Ltd. and Ont. Pension Comm. (1980), 30 O.R. (2d) 180, 116 D.L.R. (3d) 336; affirmed (1981), 33 O.R. (2d) 652, 125 D.L.R. (3d) 325 (C.A.); leave to appeal to Supreme Court of Canada refused 41 N.R. 374.

Where the Ontario Pension Commission declares that an employer's contributions vest in the employees, it exercises a statutory power of decision and the employer is entitled to a hearing before the decision is made.

Re Aamco Automatic Transmissions Inc. and Simpson (1980), 29 O.R. (2d) 565, 113 D.L.R. (3d) 650 (Div. Ct.).

The Director of the Consumer Protection Division who proposes an order to cease and desist from unfair practices pursuant to s. 6(2) of the *Business Practices Act* exercises a statutory power of decision which is subject to judicial review.

Re Keeprite Workers Independent Union and Keeprite Products Ltd. (1980), 29 O.R. (2d) 513, 114 D.L.R. (3d) 162 (C.A.); leave to appeal to Supreme Court of Canada refused 35 N.R. 85.

An arbitrator appointed by a collective agreement subject to the *Labour Relations Act* who makes findings of facts and evidence exercises a "statutory power of decision".

Re Olympia & York Devs. Ltd. and Toronto (1980), 29 O.R. (2d) 353, 113 D.L.R. (3d) 695 (Div. Ct.).

A municipality, in refusing to permit development pursuant to a by-law passed under s. 35(a) of the *Planning Act*, exercises a statutory power of decision.

Re Chadwill Coal Co. and McCrae (1976), 14 O.R. (2d) 393, (sub nom. Chadwill Coal Co. v. Ont. Treasurer & Min. of Economics) 1 M.P.L.R. 25 (Div. Ct.).

Where hearing officers appointed pursuant to the *Ontario Planning and Development Act*, 1973 made a decision to make recommendations, the decision was held to be the exercise of a statutory power of decision within the definition of the Act.

Statutory Power of Decision — s. 1 — Cases Where Power or Right Held Not to Be Statutory Power of Decision

Masters v. Ontario (1994), 18 O.R. (3d) 551, 27 Admin. L.R. (2d) 152, 115 D.L.R. (4th) 319, 72 O.A.C. 1 (Div. Ct.).

The government retained outside counsel to investigate and report on allegations of sexual harassment made against the Agent General for Ontario in New York. The Agent subsequently resigned, but brought an application for judicial review claiming certain declaratory relief, and an order in the nature of *certiorari* quashing the report. A motion to strike out the requests for declaratory relief was granted, and upheld on appeal. The application was not brought in relation to the exercise of a statutory power of decision as required by s. 2(1)2 of the Act, and therefore declaratory relief was not available.

Aboutown Transportation Ltd. v. London (City) (1992), 9 O.R. (3d) 143, 10 M.P.L.R. (2d) 164 (Gen. Div.).

In awarding a contract for the provision of transit services to the physically disabled, a municipality was not exercising a statutory power of decision. The court should be wary about undertaking judicial review of commercial decision-making by municipal corporations, absent very extraordinary circumstances.

Ayerst, McKenna & Harrison Inc. v. Ontario (Attorney-General) (1992), 8 O.R. (3d) 90, 88 D.L.R. (4th) 763, 54 O.A.C. 230 (Div. Ct.).

Recommendations made by a committee to the Ministry of Health regarding the designation of a generic drug were not a statutory power of decision, as no legal rights of the applicant were prescribed by the committee's actions.

Apotex Inc. v. Ontario (Minister of Health) (1989), 71 O.R. (2d) 525, 44 Admin. L.R. 130, 65 D.L.R. (4th) 622, 36 O.A.C. 355 (Div. Ct.).

A decision by the Minister of Health to recommend the designation of a generic drug under the Ontario Drug Benefit Formulary, and a decision by the Lieutenant-Governor to make such a designation, are decisions which are subject to judicial review.

Haber v. Wellesley Hospital (1986), 56 O.R. (2d) 553, 31 D.L.R. (4th) 607, 16 O.A.C. 215; additional reasons 56 O.R. (2d) 553 at 569, 31 D.L.R. (4th) 607 at 624 (Div. Ct.); affirmed (1988), 62 O.R. (2d) 756, 46 D.L.R. (4th) 575, 24 O.A.C. 239 (C.A.); leave to appeal to S.C.C. refused 63 O.R. (2d) x, 46 D.L.R. (4th) vi, 88 N.R. 317, 30 O.A.C. 77n.

The recommendations of a Medical Advisory Committee are not subject to judicial review where the recommendations are not automatically acted upon, and the applicant is entitled to receive a fair hearing after the recommendations are made.

Re Medhurst and Medhurst (1984), 45 O.R. (2d) 575, 4 Admin. L.R. 126, 7 D.L.R. (4th) 335 (H.C.).

The decision of a hospital therapeutic abortion committee to grant a certificate where life or health is endangered is not the exercise of a statutory power of decision. The onus is on the applicant to demonstrate that the committee lacked any evidence to support its opinion.

Re Head and Ont. Prov. Police Commr. (1981), 40 O.R. (2d) 84, 127 D.L.R. (3d) 366 (C.A.).

The Commissioner of the Ontario Provincial Police does not exercise a statutory power of decision when he accepts the resignation of a police officer not given under duress or coercion.

Paine v. Univ. of Toronto (1981), 34 O.R. (2d) 770, 131 D.L.R. (3d) 325 (C.A.); leave to appeal to Supreme Court of Canada refused (1982), 42 N.R. 270.

The court will be slow to exercise its discretion to review a university's process of appointing teaching staff where the university itself provides adequate internal appeal mechanisms. It is doubtful if the general reference in the *University of Toronto Act* to the power of the governing council to appoint members of faculty is a "statutory power of decision".

Re Hancock and Algonquin College of Applied Arts & Technology Bd. of Governors (1981), 33 O.R. (2d) 257, 124 D.L.R. (3d) 148 (H.C.).

A board of governors of a community college which recommends annual estimates to the Council of Regents pursuant to the *Ministry of Colleges and Universities Act* does not exercise a statutory power of decision. The duty imposed by the Act is distinct from a power of discretion.

Re Arts and London & Middlesex County R.C. Sep. Sch. Bd. (1979), 27 O.R. (2d) 468, 106 D.L.R. (3d) 683 (H.C.).

A school board which decided to close a school under the *Education Act*, 1974, was not exercising a statutory power of decision within the meaning of s. 1(f)(i).

Re S & M Laboratories Ltd. and Ont. (1979), 24 O.R. (2d) 732, 99 D.L.R. (3d) 160 (C.A.).

The decision by the General Manager of the Ontario Health Insurance Plan under the *Health Insurance Act* that an overpayment has been made to a medical laboratory and that it should be recovered by deductions from future payments is not a statutory power of decision.

Re Dodd and Chiropractic Review Ctee. (1978), 23 O.R. (2d) 423, 3 L. Med. Q.48, 95 D.L.R. (3d) 560 (Div. Ct.).

The referral to a review committee of the practice of a chiropractor because of questioned claims by the General Manager of the Ontario Health Insurance Plan is not a statutory power of decision.

Re Midnorthern Appliances Industs. Corp. and Ont. Housing Corp. (1977), 17 O.R. (2d) 290 (Div. Ct.).

A decision of the Ontario Housing Corporation that it will no longer consider tenders submitted by a former supplier because of threatened legal action is not an exercise of statutory power of decision as defined in s. 1(f), and consequently is not subject to judicial review.

Re Florence Nightingale Home and Scarborough Planning Bd., [1973] 1 O.R. 615, 32 D.L.R. (3d) 17 (Div. Ct.).

A planning board does not exercise a statutory power of decision when it meets to consider whether a proposed change in an official plan and zoning by-law should be recommended to council for enactment.

Re Robertson and Niagara South Bd. of Educ. (1973), 1 O.R. (2d) 548, 41 D.L.R. (3d) 57 (Div. Ct.).

A motion by a board of education purporting to close a school was not an exercise of a statutory power of decision, but was an administrative decision not subject to judicial review.

Re Lamoureux and Reg. of Motor Vehicles, [1973] 2 O.R. 28, 20 C.R.N.S. 254, 10 C.C.C. (2d) 475, 32 D.L.R. (3d) 678 (C.A.).

The automatic suspension of the driver's licence of a person convicted of impaired driving under the *Highway Traffic Act* is not the exercise of a statutory power.

Statutory Power — s. 1

Bezaire v. Windsor Roman Catholic Separate School Board (1992), 9 O.R. (3d) 737, 8 Admin. L.R. (2d) 29, 94 D.L.R. (4th) 310, 57 O.A.C. 39 (Div. Ct.).

Whether a school board's decision to close a school was a "statutory power of decision" as defined in either the J.R.P.A. or the S.P.P.A. did not have to be determined where there was a duty of fairness owed, and that duty had been breached.

Tomen v. O.P.S.T.F. (1986), 55 O.R. (2d) 670, 29 D.L.R. (4th) 638, 17 O.A.C. 189 (Div. Ct.).

A by-law passed under a general statute governing the internal membership of a corporation without share capital is not subordinate legislation, and therefore is not subject to judicial review.

Re McGill and Brantford (1980), 28 O.R. (2d) 721, 12 M.P.L.R. 24, 111 D.L.R. (3d) 405 (Div. Ct.).

A municipal council's decision to close a road pursuant to s. 466 of the *Municipal Act* decides the "legal rights of persons" and is a statutory power "to make ... any by-law ... having force as subordinate legislation."

Mississauga Hydro Electric Comm. v. Mississauga; Re Murray and Mississauga (1975), 13 O.R. (2d) 511, 71 D.L.R. (3d) 475 (Div. Ct.).

A municipal council resolution is a "regulation, rule, by-law or order, or ... any other direction having force as subordinate legislation" within the meaning of s. 1, bringing the power thus conferred within the definition of "statutory power," and subject to judicial review by the Divisional Court.

Section 2

Applications for judicial review

2. (1) On an application by way of originating notice, which may be styled "Notice of Application for Judicial Review", the court may, despite any right of appeal, by order grant any relief that the applicant would be entitled to in any one or more of the following:

1. Proceedings by way of application for an order in the nature of mandamus, prohibition or certiorari.

2. Proceedings by way of an action for a declaration or for an injunction, or both, in relation to the exercise, refusal to exercise or proposed or purported exercise of a statutory power.

Error of law

(2) The power of the court to set aside a decision for error of law on the face of the record on an application for an order in the nature of certiorari is extended so as to apply on an application for judicial review in relation to any decision made in the exercise of any statutory power of decision to the extent it is not limited or precluded by the Act conferring such power of decision.

Lack of evidence

(3) Where the findings of fact of a tribunal made in the exercise of a statutory power of decision are required by any statute or law to be based exclusively on evidence admissible before it and on facts of which it may take notice and there is no such evidence and there are no such facts to support findings of fact made by the tribunal in making a decision in the exercise of such power, the court may set aside the decision on an application for judicial review.

Power to set aside

(4) Where the applicant on an application for judicial review is entitled to a judgment declaring that a decision made in the exercise of a statutory power of decision is unauthorized or otherwise invalid, the court may, in the place of such declaration, set aside the decision.

Power to refuse relief

(5) Where, in any of the proceedings enumerated in subsection (1), the court had before the 17th day of April, 1972 a discretion to refuse to grant relief on any grounds, the court has a like discretion on like grounds to refuse to grant any relief on an application for judicial review.

Where subs. (5) does not apply

(6) Subsection (5) does not apply to the discretion of the court before the 17th day of April, 1972 to refuse to grant relief in any of the proceedings enumerated in subsection (1) on the ground that the relief should have been sought in other proceedings enumerated in subsection (1).

Case Law

Procedural Requirements

Ontario College of Art v. Ontario (Human Rights Commission) (1993), 11 O.R. (3d) 798, 99 D.L.R. (4th) 738, 63 O.A.C. 393, 19 C.H.R.R. D/199 (Div. Ct.).

The court ruled that an application for judicial review was premature where the board of inquiry had not yet commenced proceedings. The court should not fragment proceedings before administrative tribunals, and it is preferable to consider the issues raised against the backdrop of a full record, including a reasoned decision by the board or tribunal.

550551 Ontario Ltd. v. Framingham (1991), 4 O.R. (3d) 571, 4 B.L.R. (2d) 75, 5 C.B.R. (3d) 204, 91 C.L.L.C. 14,031, 49 O.A.C. 376; additional reasons (October 22, 1991), Doc. 29/91 (Div. Ct.).

The court ruled that an application for judicial review was not premature where the parties bringing the application sought review of an order to pay, even though a statutory right of appeal was available. A writ of execution had already been issued against one of the parties, and in order to exercise their right of appeal, the parties were required to pay the amount due under the order.

Peel Condominium Corp. No. 199 v. Ont. New Home Warranties Plan (1989), 69 O.R. (2d) 438, 61 D.L.R. (4th) 351 (Div. Ct.).

The court ruled that an application for judicial review was premature, although the decision in issue had been made without the required notices, as the applicant had an alternative remedy available in the form of a *de novo* hearing. The court also found that the original decision had not involved a jurisdictional error, and noted that affidavit evidence on the issue of jurisdiction should only rarely be permitted.

N. v. D. (1986), 54 O.R. (2d) 550, 16 O.A.C. 75 (*sub. nom. N. (R.) v. D. (M.)*) (Div. Ct.).

The decision of a lower court on a Charter point should not be subject to judicial review until the proceedings in which the point arose have been disposed of by the lower court.

Re Ont. Prov. Police Commr. and Perrier (1983), 41 O.R. (2d) 550, 147 D.L.R. (3d) 157 (Div. Ct.).

Where delay in bringing an application may cause serious prejudice to its resolution and where the relief sought is largely academic, the court may quash the application.

Re Seaway Trust Co. and Ont.; Re Crown Trust Co. and A.G. Ont. (1983), 41 O.R. (2d) 501 at 532, 37 C.P.C. 8 at 50, 6 C.R.R. 365 (C.A.); leave to appeal to Supreme Court of Canada refused 37 C.P.C. 8n, 6 C.R.R. 365n, 52 N.R. 235.

Where an action would be more appropriate than an application for judicial review in terms of the relief sought, the necessity of *viva voce* evidence, and the potential effect of the decision on non-parties, the Divisional Court properly exercises its discretion in refusing to hear the application.

Koumoudouros v. Metro. Toronto (1982), 37 O.R. (2d) 656, 29 C.P.C. 99, 67 C.C.C. (2d) 193, 136 D.L.R. (3d) 373 (H.C.).

A s. 24(1) *Charter of Rights* challenge of a municipal by-law for alleged infringement or denial of guaranteed rights and freedoms is essentially an application for judicial review. The Divisional Court is the "court of competent jurisdiction".

Re Forestell and Niagara College of Applied Arts & Technology (1981), 33 O.R. (2d) 282 (H.C.).

Where an originating notice of motion failed substantially to comply with the former Rules of Practice (Form 39), the application for judicial review was dismissed.

Re Rymal and Niagara Escarpment Comm. (1981), 129 D.L.R. (3d) 363 (Ont. C.A.).

Where notices of appeal were filed one day late due to postal disruptions and the failure of a government employee to pick up a notice of appeal within the time limit, the Divisional Court properly exercised its discretion in dismissing an application to prohibit the Minister of Housing from proceeding with the hearing of an appeal from a decision to grant a development permit.

Re Innisfil and Barrie; Oro v. Barrie (1977), 17 O.R. (2d) 277, 3 M.P.L.R. 47 (Div. Ct.).

During proceedings before an administrative tribunal, an application for judicial review may be brought at any time, and an applicant need not wait until proceedings are concluded.

Where Right of Appeal Available — s. 2(1)

John Doe v. Ontario (Information & Privacy Commissioner) (1993), 13 O.R. (3d) 767, 19 Admin. L.R. (2d) 251, 106 D.L.R. (4th) 140, 64 O.A.C. 248 (Div. Ct.).

The Information and Privacy Commissioner under the *Freedom of Information and Protection of Privacy Act* is required to develop and apply expertise in the management of many kinds of government information, and thereby acquires a unique range of expertise not shared by the courts. Accordingly, the Commissioner's decision, already protected by the lack of any right of appeal, ought to be accorded a strong measure of curial deference even where the legislature has not insulated the tribunal by means of a privative clause.

Kuntz v. W.C.B., Ont. (1985), 56 O.R. (2d) 497, 22 Admin. L.R. 226, 31 D.L.R. (4th) 630, 17 O.A.C. 170 (C.A.).

The privative clause contained in the *Workers' Compensation Act* bars judicial review unless the Board's interpretation of the statutory provision in issue is patently unreasonable.

Williams v. Kemptville Dist. Hospital (1986), 55 O.R. (2d) 633, 29 D.L.R. (4th) 629 (H.C.).

On an application for judicial review of a hospital board decision, it was found that the board's conduct had been contrary to the rules of natural justice. However there was no order for judicial review, as the applicant had a statutory right of appeal pursuant to the *Public Hospitals Act.*

O.P.S.E.U. v. Forer (1985), 52 O.R. (2d) 705, 15 Admin. L.R. 145, 23 D.L.R. (4th) 97, 12 O.A.C. 1 (C.A.).

Where an administrative tribunal is protected from judicial review by a privative clause, the tribunal should be permitted to perform its functions free of judicial interference, unless the tribunal's actions are patently unreasonable.

Re R. and Burns (1983), 41 O.R. (2d) 774, 5 C.C.C. (3d) 381, 5 C.R.R. 215, 148 D.L.R. (3d) 188 (H.C.).

Where an indictment is quashed on substantive grounds, and there is available an ordinary right of appeal, *mandamus* is not an appropriate remedy.

Re Woodglen & Co. and North York (1983), 42 O.R. (2d) 385, 23 M.P.L.R. 13, 149 D.L.R. (3d) 186 (Div. Ct.).

In the absence of exceptional circumstances, and where there exists a specific alternative remedy, the court ought not to exercise its discretion to grant the extraordinary remedy of mandamus.

Re V.S.R. Invts. Ltd. and Laczko (1983), 41 O.R. (2d) 62, 33 C.P.C. 245 (Div. Ct.).

Where particular difficulties might arise in an appeal by way of stated case of a decision by the Residential Tenancies Commission, the appeal should be stayed pending the disposition of an application for judicial review.

Re A.G. Ont. and Rae (1983), 44 O.R. (2d) 493, 40 C.P.C. 68, (sub nom. *Rae v. Rae)* 4 D.L.R. (4th) 465 (H.C.).

Notwithstanding s. 2 of the Act, where an appeal is provided, judicial review or relief in the nature of *certiorari* should be foregone.

Pronto Cabs Ltd. v. Metro. Toronto Licensing Comm. (1982), 39 O.R. (2d) 488 (Div. Ct.).

Where there exists a statutory right of appeal from a decision of the Metropolitan Licensing Commission, judicial review by way of *certiorari* and *mandamus* is not simultaneously available.

Re Reddall and Ont. College of Nurses (1981), 33 O.R. (2d) 129, 123 D.L.R. (3d) 568; reversed in part (1983), 42 O.R. (2d) 412, 1 Admin. L.R. 278, 149 D.L.R. (3d) 60 (C.A.).

Where the Divisional Court has broad review powers under a provision of the *Health Disciplines Act*, an application for judicial review is redundant.

Mississauga v. Dir., Environmental Protection Act (1978), 8 C.P.C. 292, 6 M.P.L.R. 115, 7 C.E.L.R. 139 (H.C.).

A judicial review of a decision by way of prerogative remedies, such as *certiorari*, should not be granted where there exists an express right of appeal from the decision complained of within the Act itself, except in very special circumstances.

Particular Remedies — Mandamus — s. 2(1) para. 1

Re Olympia and York Devs. Ltd. and Toronto (1980), 29 O.R. (2d) 353, 113 D.L.R. (3d) 695 (Div. Ct.).

Where a city has exercised a statutory power of decision under a statute, the court has jurisdiction to consider an application for a declaration if the interpretation of the statute could have been disposed of in an application by way of *mandamus*.

Particular Remedies — Certiorari — s. 2(1) para. 2

St. Lawrence Cement Inc. v. Ontario (Minister of Transportation) (1991), 3 O.R. (3d) 30, 50 B.L.R. 319 (Gen. Div.).

The Minister of Transportation's decision to disqualify a tender for a provincial government contract was not subject to *certiorari*, as the decision concerned a commercial contract that did not affect the public interest.

Re Rees and P.P.F., Loc. 527 (1983), 43 O.R. (2d) 97, 4 Admin. L.R. 179, 83 C.L.L.C. 14,067, 150 D.L.R. (3d) 493 (Div. Ct.).

The decision of a trade union disciplinary committee to suspend and fire a union member is subject to judicial review on application by the member seeking relief that would be available in proceedings in the nature of *certiorari*.

Sabados v. Can. Slovak League (1982), 35 O.R. (2d) 718, 133 D.L.R. (3d) 152 (Div. Ct.).

The Divisional Court, a division of the High Court of Justice, has jurisdiction to review by *certiorari*, *mandamus*, or prohibition the decision of the board of directors of a federally incorporated fraternal benefit society to terminate the membership of one of its members. The powers of the board are analogous to private powers exercisable by an ordinary corporation created under a federal statute.

Pestell v. Kitchener-Waterloo Real Estate Bd. Inc. (1981), 34 O.R. (2d) 476, 131 D.L.R. (3d) 88 (Div. Ct.).

The decision of an appeal board of a private real estate corporation to expel a voluntary member was not an exercise of statutory power and was not subject to review by way of *certiorari* by the Divisional Court.

Re Ont. Prov. Police Assn. and Ont. (1974), 3 O.R. (2d) 698, 46 D.L.R. (3d) 518 (Div. Ct.).

Individual judges of the High Court have a common law jurisdiction to grant a remedy in the nature of *certiorari* in restricted circumstances. This jurisdiction is vested, pursuant to s. 2(1), in the Divisional Court, which can determine whether a consensual board of arbitration has acted illegally in making a decision.

Re S.E.I.U., Loc. 204 and Broadway Manor Nursing Home (1984), 48 O.R. (2d) 225, 13 D.L.R. (4th) 220, (sub nom. *Durham Bd. of Educ. v. O.S.S.T.F. Dist. 17; O.P.S.E.U. v. A.G. Ont.)* 5 O.A.C. 371.

Where the Inflation Restraint Board did not exercise or propose or purport to exercise a statutory power, the Divisional Court was held to lack jurisdiction to hear an application for judicial review or to grant declaratory relief.

Re Selkirk and Schorr (1977), 15 O.R. (2d) 37, 2 C.P.C. 249 (Div. Ct.).

The Divisional Court has jurisdiction pursuant to s. 2 of the *Judicature Act* to superintend the conduct of its own officers including taxing officers, and has jurisdiction pursuant to s. 2 of the *Judicial Review Procedure Act* to control its officers by way of order of prohibition or by declaratory or injunctive order.

Re Maurice Rollins Const. Ltd. and South Fredericksburg (1975), 11 O.R. (2d) 418 (H.C.).

Although a municipal council by-law de-registering a subdivision plan under the *Planning Act* is not an exercise of a statutory power of decision, it is nevertheless an exercise of a statutory power and is subject to judicial review by way of declaratory relief pursuant to s. 2(1)1 of this Act.

Mississauga Hydro Elec. Comm. v. Mississauga; Re Murray and Mississauga (1975), 13 O.R. (2d) 511, 71 D.L.R. (3d) 475 (Div. Ct.).

Where a notice of application for judicial review has been made, the issuance of a concurrent claim by writ is not necessary to invoke the court's power to make a declaration or to grant an injunction.

Error of Law — s. 2(2)

U.S.W.A., Local 14097 v. Franks (1994), 16 O.R. (3d) 620, 19 Admin. L.R. (2d) 165, 2 C.C.E.L. (2d) 23, 94 C.L.L.C. 14,011, 110 D.L.R. (4th) 762, 69 O.A.C. 148 (C.A.); leave to appeal to Supreme Court of Canada refused 19 O.R. (3d) xvi (note), 19 Admin. L.R. (2d) 165n, 7 C.C.E.L. (2d) 41 (note), 114 D.L.R. (4th) vii (note).

Where a referee under the *Employment Standards Act* makes a decision involving the interpretation of the constituent statute, and that decision is within his jurisdiction, the applicable standard of review is one of reasonableness. The presence of a privative clause does not mean the court should mechanically defer to a tribunal. The significance of the privative clause depends on an analysis of the provision in light of the purpose, nature and expertise of the tribunal in relation to the decision in issue.

Re O.P.S.E.U. and Ont. (1984), 45 O.R. (2d) 70, 5 D.L.R. (4th) 651, (sub nom. *O.P.S.E.U. v. Min. of Correctional Services)* 2 O.A.C. 351 (Div. Ct.).

Where a tribunal commits an error of law or mixed law and fact, as where it fails to evaluate a relevant portion of the evidence, its decision is subject to judicial review as a denial of natural justice.

Connie Steel Products Ltd. v. Greater Nat. Building Corp.; Interprice Elec. Ltd. v. Bank of N.S. (1977), 3 C.P.C. 327 (Div. Ct.).

The purpose of s. 2(2) of the Act is to extend the Supreme Court's superintendence over inferior tribunals and it does not permit the review of decisions taken by other divisions or emanations of the Supreme Court.

Absence of Evidence — s. 2(3)

Great Lakes Power Ltd. v. Ontario (Information & Privacy Commissioner) (1996), 48 C.P.C. (3d) 364 (Ont. Div. Ct.).

In respect of the judicial review of a decision reached following an inquisitorial process where the parties were to be heard in the absence of one another, the court refused to strike from the record affidavit material supplementing the text of the decision. The affidavit material would either cause no harm or would avoid difficulties in understanding the applicant's argument based on abuse of process which might arise if based only on the text of the decision.

Re Securicor Investigations & Security Ltd. and O.L.R.B. (1985), 50 O.R. (2d) 570, 10 Admin. L.R. 189, 18 D.L.R. (4th) 151, 8 O.A.C. 372 (Div. Ct.).

On an application for judicial review, affidavit evidence as to what evidence was before the tribunal can only be used to demonstrate complete absence of evidence on an essential point.

Re Keeprite Workers Independent Union and Keeprite Products Ltd. (1980), 29 O.R. (2d) 513, 114 D.L.R. (3d) 162 (C.A.); leave to appeal to Supreme Court of Canada refused 35 N.R. 85.

Affidavit evidence can only be used to demonstrate the complete absence of evidence on an essential point to augment the record on an application for judicial review of an arbitration award under s. 2(3).

Unauthorized Decision* — *s. 2(4)

Godfrey v. Ontario Police Commission (1991), 5 O.R. (3d) 163, 7 Admin. L.R. (2d) 9, 83 D.L.R. (4th) 501, 53 O.A.C. 338 (Div. Ct.).

The court set aside an order of the Ontario Police Commission where the Commission made a jurisdictional error in construing the scope of its dispositive powers under regulations made pursuant to the *Police Services Act.*

O.S.S.T.F., District 53 v. Haldimand Board of Education (1991), 5 O.R. (3d) 21, 6 Admin. L.R. (2d) 177, 15 C.H.R.R.D./475, 83 D.L.R. (4th) 762, 52 O.A.C. 15 (Div. Ct.).

The court set aside the finding of an arbitration board where the board failed to interpret a collective agreement in accordance with the *Human Rights Code*. That constituted an error in law, as the governing legislation expressly provided that, where there was a conflict between a collective agreement and a provision in an Act, the Act governed.

Biscotti v. Ontario (Securities Commission) (1991), 1 O.R. (3d) 409, 76 D.L.R. (4th) 762, 45 O.A.C. 293 (C.A.); leave to appeal to Supreme Court of Canada refused 3 O.R. (3d) xii, 136 N.R. 407 (note), 50 O.A.C. 160 (note).

The court set aside an interlocutory ruling of the Ontario Securities Commission, where it had made a jurisdictional error by making a blanket ruling, in advance of the calling of any witnesses, that it would not consent to the production of any transcripts supplied under s. 11 of the *Securities Act*, R.S.O. 1980, c. 466 for the purpose of cross-examinations.

Ontario (Employment Standards Officer) v. Equitable Management Ltd. (1990), 75 O.R. (2d) 506, 47 Admin. L.R. 75, 33 C.C.E.L. 114, 90 C.L.L.C. 14,044, 74 D.L.R. (4th) 422, 40 O.A.C. 384 (Div. Ct.).

The court set aside the decision of a referee appointed under the *Employment Standards Act*, R.S.O. 1980, c. 137 where the referee misinterpreted the meaning of s. 13(2) of that Act.

Re Hussey and A.G.Ont. (1984), 46 O.R. (2d) 554, 4 Admin. L.R. 147, 43 C.P.C. 230, 13 C.C.C. (3d) 81, 14 C.R.R. 369, 9 D.L.R. (4th) 696, 3 O.A.C. 166 (Div. Ct.).

Where superintendents of correctional institutions exercise or purport to exercise statutory powers, the court has jurisdiction to review possible violations of prisoners' rights under the *Charter of Rights.*

Re Milstein and Ont. College of Pharmacy (1978), 20 O.R. (2d) 283, 87 D.L.R. (3d) 392, 2 L. Med. Q. 297 (C.A.).

On an application for judicial review of a decision of a disciplinary tribunal, the court may interfere with an improper penalty imposed by the tribunal, as where the penalty is beyond the jurisdiction of the tribunal or demonstrates an error of law.

Parties

Re Ronark Devs. and Hamilton (1974), 4 O.R. (2d) 195 (Div. Ct.); leave to appeal to Ont. C.A. granted without written reasons, appeal dismissed on consent 5 O.R. (2d) 136n (C.A.).

Where a municipality strenuously resists the application by a development corporation for a *mandamus* compelling the issuance of a building permit, a ratepayers' association ought not to be added as a party to the proceedings.

Noddle v. Toronto (1982), 37 O.R. (2d) 421 (H.C.).

Because an application seeking judicial review of a decision by a municipality to issue a building permit to a bus company contained allegations with respect to employee rights, the applicant, a union representative and employee of the company, was permitted to make the application.

Re Metro. Toronto and Bremner (No. 1) (1980), 29 O.R. (2d) 531, 114 D.L.R. (3d) 224 (H.C.).

In an application for judicial review of an order directing that writs of possession be executed against homes on Toronto Island, the court added the residents of the homes as "interested parties" but refused to add the City of Toronto.

Re Durham and A.G Ont. (1978), 23 O.R. (2d) 279, 95 D.L.R. (3d) 327 (H.C.).

In an application for judicial review of a regulation closing a registry office, affected individuals and municipalities have a greater interest than the general public and thus have standing. As the decision to close for reasons of fiscal restraint was a policy decision, no hearing was necessary.

Re Kingston and Mining & Lands Commr. (1977), 18 O.R. (2d) 166 (Div. Ct.).

Where a tribunal's order inaccurately embodies a settlement agreement, an affected party may bring an application for judicial review.

McDonald's Restaurants of Can. Ltd. v. Etobicoke (1977), 5 C.P.C. 55 (Ont. Div. Ct.).

The court refused to add as a party a ratepayer who sought to intervene in an application for judicial review for a building permit, on the ground that his interests were already adequately represented by the municipality.

Re Starr and Puslinch (1976), 12 O.R. (2d) 40 (Div. Ct.).

Two companies whose legal rights and financial positions would be directly affected by the determination of a ratepayer's challenge of a designation in a township's official plan were added as respondents to the application for judicial review.

Re Multi-Malls Inc. and Min. of Transportation & Communications (1975), 7 O.R. (2d) 717 (Div. Ct.).

Where an adjoining municipality has a conflicting interest in a proposed scheme for land development, it should be added as a party respondent to the application for judicial review.

Re Orangeville Highlands Ltd. and Mono; Re Orangeville Highlands Ltd. and A.G. Ont. (1974), 5 O.R. (2d) 266 (Div. Ct.).

A neighbouring municipality, whose interest is the protection of ratepayers and the business community, is not a proper party to an application for a *mandamus* order in a judicial review concerning the granting of a building permit.

Section 3

Defects in form, technical irregularities

3. On an application for judicial review in relation to a statutory power of decision, where the sole ground for relief established is a defect in form or a technical irregularity, if the court finds that no substantial wrong or miscarriage of justice has occurred, the court may refuse relief and, where the decision has already been made, may make an order validating the decision, despite such defect, to have effect from such time and on such terms as the court considers proper.

Case Law

Ellis-Don Ltd. v. Ontario (Labour Relations Board), 10 O.R. (3d) 729, 6 Admin. L.R. (2d) 314, [1992] O.L.R.B. Rep. 764, 57 O.A.C. 11 (Div. Ct.).

The court dismissed a motion to stay a decision of the Ontario Labour Relations Board pending adjudication of an application for judicial review, as the applicant had failed to establish a strong *prima facie* case.

Sobeys Inc. v. U.F.C.W., Local 1000A (1993), 12 O.R. (3d) 157, 93 C.L.L.C. 14,041, 62 O.A.C. 78 (Div. Ct.).

An application to stay the implementation of a decision of the Ontario Labour Relations Board should not be allowed unless a strong *prima facie* case is established that the decision in question is patently unreasonable.

University of Toronto v. C.U.E.W., Local 2 (1988), 65 O.R. (2d) 268, 30 Admin. L.R. 310, 52 D.L.R. (4th) 128, 28 O.A.C. 295 (Div. Ct.).

The court should discourage the interruption of labour relations hearings by declining to decide judicial review applications from interim awards, and by imposing appropriate costs orders, unless the proceeding arises out of exceptional circumstances.

Gardner v. Cornwall Bd. of Commrs. of Police (1986), 56 O.R. (2d) 189, 13 C.C.E.L. 143, 16 O.A.C. 238 (Div. Ct.).

An interim order was granted staying appeal to the Police Commission, pending final determination of a judicial review.

Metro. Toronto School Bd. v. Ontario (Min. of Education) (1985), 53 O.R. (2d) 70, 6 C.P.C. (2d) 281, 23 D.L.R. (4th) 303, 13 O.A.C. 113 (Div. Ct.).

Where a regulation is the subject of an application for judicial review, the regulation should be presumed valid until the application is heard, particularly where the applicants will not suffer irreparable harm if there is no interim order made.

Re United Headwear, Optical & Allied Workers Union of Can., Loc. 3 and Biltmore/Stetson (Can.) Inc. (1983), 41 O.R. (2d) 287, 83 C.L.L.C. 14,037; reversed on other grounds 43 O.R. (2d) 243, (sub nom. *Employees of Biltmore/Stetson (Can.) Inc. v. H.C.M.W., Hat Workers Union, Loc. 82)* 6 Admin. L.R. 281, (sub nom. *Hat Workers Union, H.C.M.W., Loc. 82 v. United Headwear, Optical & Allied Workers Union of Can., Loc. 3)* 83 C.L.L.C. 14,062, 150 D.L.R. (3d) 577 (C.A.).

Notice to bargain given by a trade union to a successor employer before the sale of the business is not effective as a certification. A motions court judge has jurisdiction to hear an application under this section.

Wells Fargo Armcar Inc. v. O.L.R.B. (1981), 34 O.R. (2d) 99 (H.C.).

The High Court has the power, using the criteria applicable to injunctions, to stay a decision of the Ontario Labour Relations Board. However, a strong *prima facie* case of entitlement to relief is not established where the actions of the board do not appear to involve an improper construction of s. 12 of the *Labour Relations Act.*

Re Hayles and Sproule (1980), 29 O.R. (2d) 500 (Div. Ct.).

Pending a judicial review of a disciplinary decision made under the *Police Act*, the court may order a stay of the hearing of the appeal pursuant to s. 4 of this Act.

Re Dylex Ltd. and A.C.T.W. Union Toronto Joint Bd. (1977), 17 O.R. (2d) 488, 77 C.L.L.C. 14,105 (H.C.).

Where a negative vote in a certification drive provides a *prima facie* case for an employer, and if irreparable harm would otherwise result, the court has inherent jurisdiction to stay an order for certification, despite a finding of no urgency and a lack of such express provision in the Rules of Practice or in the Act.

Re I.W.A. and Patchogue Plymouth, Hawkesbury Mills (1976), 14 O.R. (2d) 118, 2 C.P.C. 98 (H.C.).

An application for judicial review of an arbitration award does not effect an automatic stay of its operation. A stay may be obtained by interim order of the Divisional Court under s. 4 of this Act.

Section 4

Interim order

4. On an application for judicial review, the court may make such interim order as it considers proper pending the final determination of the application.

Section 5

Extension of time for bringing application

5. Despite any limitation of time for the bringing of an application for judicial review fixed by or under any Act, the court may extend the time for making the application, either before or after expiration of the time so limited, on such terms as it considers proper, where it is satisfied that there are apparent grounds for relief and that no substantial prejudice or hardship will result to any person affected by reason of the delay.

Case Law

Re Cessland Corp. and Fort Norman Explorations Inc. (1979), 25 O.R. (2d) 69, 100 D.L.R. (3d) 378 (H.C.).

Where a specific provision of the *Mining Act* precluded an extension of the time for bringing an application for judicial review, an application received after the expiry of the statutory 30-day period was dismissed.

Section 6

Application to Divisional Court

6. (1) Subject to subsection (2), an application for judicial review shall be made to the Divisional Court.

Application to judge of Superior Court of Justice

(2) An application for judicial review may be made to the Superior Court of Justice with leave of a judge thereof, which may be granted at the hearing of the application, where it is made to appear to the judge that the case is one of urgency and that the delay required for an application to the Divisional Court is likely to involve a failure of justice.

Transfer to Divisional Court

(3) Where a judge refuses leave for an application under subsection (2), he or she may order that the application be transferred to the Divisional Court.

Appeal to Court of Appeal

(4) An appeal lies to the Court of Appeal, with leave of the Court of Appeal, from a final order of the Superior Court of Justice disposing of an application for judicial review pursuant to leave granted under subsection (2).

2006, c. 19, Sched. C, s. 1(1)

Case Law

Granting of Leave for Hearing by a Judge — s. 6(2)

Provan v. Ontario (Registrar of Gaming Control) (1994), 20 O.R. (3d) 632 (Div. Ct.).

Where the applicant would suffer substantial and irreparable pecuniary loss as a result of delay, leave was granted as the case was one of sufficient urgency that any delay would involve a failure of justice.

Jafine v. College of Veterinarians (Ontario) (1991), 5 O.R. (3d) 439, 6 Admin. L.R. (2d) 147 (Gen. Div.).

The court dismissed an application for judicial review to be heard by a single judge, where the apprehension of the consequences of a negative result from a discipline committee hearing did not form the basis of a valid argument of urgency, or establish that the delay was likely to involve a failure of justice. It was also inappropriate to refer the matter to Divisional Court until after a decision had been rendered by the committee.

Re Passmore and St. Marys (1984), 47 O.R. (2d) 262 (H.C.).

A municipality was granted leave to apply for judicial review, to be heard by a single judge, of a board's decision approving a dump site where the present site was fully used and the municipality intended to start construction on a new site in the near future.

Re T and Western Region Bd. of Review (1983), 44 O.R. (2d) 153, 3 D.L.R. (4th) 442 (H.C.).

Leave was granted as a matter of urgency for judicial review of a decision of a board authorizing electroconvulsive therapy for an involuntary, unconsenting patient.

Re Emerson and L.S.U.C. (1983), 44 O.R. (2d) 729, 41 C.P.C. 7, 5 D.L.R. (4th) 294 (H.C.).

In a case of urgency and likely failure of justice, the court will grant leave for judicial review of the decisions of the discipline committee of the Law Society before consideration by convocation.

Re United Headwear, Optical & Allied Workers Union of Can., Loc. 3 and Biltmore/Stetson (Can.) Inc. (1983), 41 O.R. (2d) 287, 83 C.L.L.C. 14,037; reversed on other grounds 43 O.R. (2d) 243, (sub nom. *Employees of Biltmore/Stetson (Can.) Inc. v. H.C.M.W., Hat Workers Union, Loc. 82)* 6 Admin. L.R. 281, (sub nom. *Hat Workers Union, H.C.M.W., Loc. 82 v. United Headwear, Optical & Allied Workers Union of Can., Loc. 3)* 83 C.L.L.C. 14,062, 150 D.L.R. (3d) 577 (C.A.).

Where a board's decision wrongly caused substantial delay to an application for certification as a bargaining agent, leave to apply for judicial review to a High Court judge was granted.

Wells Fargo Armcar Inc. v. O.L.R.B. (1981), 34 O.R. (2d) 99 (H.C.).

Where delay does not emasculate the certification of a trade union or place the parties in an irredeemably adversarial position, neither urgency nor a failure of justice has been established so as to justify leave under subs. (2) for judicial review of a decision certifying a trade union.

Re Clarke Institute of Psychiatry and C.C.A.S. of Metro. Toronto (1981), 31 O.R. (2d) 486, 20 C.P.C. 46, 119 D.L.R. (3d) 247 (H.C.).

A determination of whether a ten-month-old child was in need of protection or should be returned to his mother, where the Children's Aid Society was planning to put the child up for adoption, presented a matter of urgency and leave was granted for a hearing before a High Court judge.

Re C.P. Express Ltd. and Snow (1980), 31 O.R. (2d) 120, (sub nom. *C.P. Express Ltd. v. Min. of Transportation & Communications)* 19 C.P.C. 16, 118 D.L.R. (3d) 148; affirmed 32 O.R. (2d) 45, 121 D.L.R. (3d) 511 (C.A.).

Leave to apply for judicial review was granted where the delay in answering the question of whether a petition to the Lieutenant-Governor in Council operates as a stay of proceedings was likely to involve a failure of justice.

Re Metro. Toronto and Bremner (No. 1) (1980), 29 O.R. (2d) 531, 114 D.L.R. (3d) 224 (H.C.).

Where the delay in placing an application for judicial review before the Divisional Court calls into question the integrity, wholeness, adequacy, and validity of the judicial process, a failure of justice has occurred so as to justify a hearing of the application by a judge of the High Court.

Re Chapples Ltd. and Thunder Bay (1980), 27 O.R. (2d) 444, 106 D.L.R. (3d) 707; reversed on other grounds 29 O.R. (2d) 522 (C.A.).

Where the status of a nearly completed construction work was questioned, leave to make an application for judicial review to a judge of the High Court was granted, as the delay required for an application to the Divisional Court was likely to involve a failure of justice.

Re Bennett and Belleville (1979), 24 O.R. (2d) 121 (H.C.).

Where there is urgency and where the delay involved in an application for judicial review to the Divisional Court is likely to involve a failure of justice, an application may be heard by a single judge.

Smith v. Zeiger (1978), 2 R.F.L. (2d) 324 (Ont. H.C.).

Due to the protracted nature of an affiliation proceeding, sufficient urgency and potential failure of justice were established to justify an application for judicial review to the High Court.

Re Brendon and Univ. of Western Ont. Bd. of Governors (1977), 17 O.R. (2d) 721, 81 D.L.R. (3d) 260 (H.C.).

When an application for judicial review by a dismissed university teacher could not be heard by the Divisional Court before the start of a new academic year, it was held to be a case of such urgency and possible failure of justice as to justify judicial review by the High Court.

Bay Charles Centre v. Toronto (1977), 3 C.P.C. 343 (Ont. H.C.).

Prospective financial loss and delay are normally insufficient to constitute urgency within the meaning of subs. (2) and do not justify judicial review by a single judge when the Divisional Court is sitting.

Re Simpson and Henderson (1976), 13 O.R. (2d) 322, 71 D.L.R. (3d) 24 (H.C.).

The mere fact that an application to the Divisional Court will cause some delay is not *per se* a matter of emergency. Where, however, an application concerns an upcoming election and requires speedy disposition in the public interest, leave should be granted.

Re Taller and Assessment Commr. (1974), 7 O.R. (2d) 501 (H.C.).

Where the matter is urgent and the delay required for an application to the Divisional Court is likely to involve a failure of justice, the application may be heard in Weekly Court — but the mere consent of counsel is not sufficient for such change in jurisdiction.

Section 7

Summary disposition of mandamus, etc.

7. An application for an order in the nature of mandamus, prohibition or certiorari shall be deemed to be an application for judicial review and shall be made, treated and disposed of as if it were an application for judicial review.

Case Law

Re Beke and R. (1977), 15 O.R. (2d) 603, 34 C.C.C. (2d) 548 (Div. Ct.).

Applications for prohibition in relation to quasi-criminal matters (provincial offences) are governed by this Act and are heard by the Divisional Court; whereas applications for *certiorari, mandamus*, and prohibition in relation to criminal matters are heard by a single judge.

Re Brown and R. (1975), 11 O.R. (2d) 7, 30 C.C.C. (2d) 300, 64 D.L.R. (3d) 605 (H.C.).

An application by motion pursuant to s. 69 of the former *Judicature Act* was not an application for an order in the nature of *certiorari* within the meaning of s. 7.

Section 8

Summary disposition of actions

8. Where an action for a declaration or injunction, or both, whether with or without a claim for other relief, is brought and the exercise, refusal to exercise or proposed or purported exercise of a statutory power is an issue in the action, a judge of the Superior Court of Justice may on the application of any party to the action, if he or she considers it appropriate, direct that the action be treated and disposed of summarily, in so far as it relates to the exercise, refusal to exercise or proposed or purported exercise of such power, as if it were an application for judicial review and may order that the hearing on such issue be transferred to the Divisional Court or may grant leave for it to be disposed of in accordance with subsection 6(2).

2006, c. 19, Sched. C, s. 1(1)

Case Law

South-West Oxford v. A.G. Ont. (1983), 44 O.R. (2d) 376, 40 C.P.C. 86, 8 Admin. L.R. 30 (H.C.).

The burden of proving grounds for transfer of an action to the Divisional Court to be dealt with as an application for judicial review rests with the party making the application. Where the applicant fails to establish sufficient grounds, the matter should proceed as an action.

Loblaws Ltd. v. Gloucester (1979), 25 O.R. (2d) 225, 10 C.P.C. 232, 100 D.L.R. (3d) 536 (Div. Ct.).

An application for summary judicial review under this section should not be made before the pleadings are completed. The onus is on the party seeking s. 8 review to establish that the case is an appropriate one for review by the Divisional Court.

Section 9

Sufficiency of application

9. (1) It is sufficient in an application for judicial review if an applicant sets out in the notice the grounds upon which he is seeking relief and the nature of the relief that he seeks without specifying the proceedings enumerated in subsection 2(1) in which the claim would have been made before the 17th day of April, 1972.

Exerciser of power may be a party

(2) For the purposes of an application for judicial review in relation to the exercise, refusal to exercise or proposed or purported exercise of a statutory power, the person who is authorized to exercise the power may be a party to the application.

Idem

(3) For the purposes of subsection (2), any two or more persons who, acting together, may exercise a statutory power, whether styled a board or commission or by any other collective title, shall be deemed to be a person under such collective title.

Notice to Attorney General

(4) Notice of an application for judicial review shall be served upon the Attorney General who is entitled as of right to be heard in person or by counsel on the application.

Case Law

Re Consolidated Bathurst Packaging Ltd. and I.W.A., Loc. 2-69 (1985), 51 O.R. (2d) 481, 16 Admin. L.R. 37, 14 C.L.L.C. 14,031, 20 D.L.R. (4th) 84, 10 O.A.C. 34 (Div. Ct.); reversed on other grounds (1986), 56 O.R. (2d) 513, 21 Admin. L.R. 180, 31 D.L.R. (4th) 444, 15 O.A.C. 398 (C.A.); affirmed (1990), 73 O.R. (2d) 676 (S.C.C.).

In s. 9(2), the word "may" confers on the person who is authorized to exercise the statutory power the right, but not the obligation, to be a party. Once a tribunal is properly a party to the proceedings, it becomes a rule of court, rather than a rule of law, to decide the extent to which it will be entitled to participate in the argument.

Section 10

Record to be filed in Ontario Court (General Division)

10. When notice of an application for judicial review of a decision made in the exercise or purported exercise of a statutory power of decision has been served on the person making the decision, such person shall forthwith file in the court for use on the application, the record of the proceedings in which the decision was made.

Section 11

References in other Acts, etc.

11. (1) Subject to subsection (2), where reference is made in any other Act or in any regulation, rule or by-law to any of the proceedings enumerated in subsection 2(1), such reference shall be read and construed to include a reference to an application for judicial review.

Proceeding under Habeas Corpus Act

(2) Nothing in this Act affects proceedings under the *Habeas Corpus Act* or the issue of a writ of certiorari thereunder or proceedings pursuant thereto, but an application for judicial review may be brought in aid of an application for a writ of *habeas corpus*.

Case Law

Re Brown and R. (1975), 11 O.R. (2d) 7, 30 C.C.C. (2d) 300, 64 D.L.R. (3d) 605 (H.C.).

Since an application pursuant to s. 69 of the former *Judicature Act* was not an application for an order in the nature of *certiorari*, s. 12 did not apply.

STATUTORY POWERS PROCEDURE ACT

R.S.O. 1990, c. S.22

as am. S.O. 1993, c. 27, Sched.; 1994, c. 27, s. 56; 1997, c. 23, s. 13; 1999, c. 12, Sched. B, s. 16; 2002, c. 17, Sched. F, s. 1; 2006, c. 19, Sched. B, s. 21, Sched. C, s. 1(1), (2), (4); 2006, c. 21, Sched. C, s. 134, Sched. F, s. 136(1), Table 1; 2009, c. 33, Sched. 6, s. 87 [Not in force at date of publication.].

Section 1

Definitions

1. (1) In this Act,

"Committee" [Repealed 1994, c. 27, s. 56.]

"electronic hearing" means a hearing held by conference telephone or some other form of electronic technology allowing persons to hear one another;

"hearing" means a hearing in any proceeding;

"licence" includes any permit, certificate, approval, registration or similar form of permission required by law;

"municipality" has the same meaning as in the *Municipal Affairs Act*;

"oral hearing" means a hearing at which the parties or their representatives attend before the tribunal in person;

"proceeding" means a proceeding to which this Act applies;

"representative" means, in respect of a proceeding to which this Act applies, a person authorized under the *Law Society Act* to represent a person in that proceeding;

"statutory power of decision" means a power or right, conferred by or under a statute, to make a decision deciding or prescribing,

(a) the legal rights, powers, privileges, immunities, duties or liabilities of any person or party, or

(b) the eligibility of any person or party to receive, or to the continuation of, a benefit or licence, whether the person is legally entitled thereto or not;

"tribunal" means one or more persons, whether or not incorporated and however described, upon which a statutory power of decision is conferred by or under a statute;

"written hearing" means a hearing held by means of the exchange of documents, whether in written form or by electronic means.

Meaning of "person" extended

(2) A municipality, an unincorporated association of employers, a trade union or council of trade unions who may be a party to a proceeding in the exercise of a statutory power of decision under the statute conferring the pow-

ers, shall be deemed to be a person for the purpose of any provision of this Act or of any rule made under this Act that applies to parties.

1994, c. 27, s. 56; 2002, c. 17, Sched. F, s. 1; 2006, c. 21, Sched. C, s. 134(1), (2)

Case Law

Statutory Power of Decision — Not Being Exercised — s. 1(1)

B. v. W. (1985), 52 O.R. (2d) 738, (sub nom. *B. (Y.) v. W. (R.))* 16 Admin. L.R. 99, 23 D.L.R. (4th) 248 (H.C.).

When a university decides to suspend a student, the *Statutory Powers Procedure Act* does not apply as such a decision is not made in the exercise of a specific power conferred by statute.

Re Hancock and Algonquin College of Applied Arts and Technology Bd. of Governors (1981), 33 O.R. (2d) 257, 124 D.L.R. (3d) 148 (H.C.).

A college board of governors in carrying out its duty under the *Ministry of Colleges and Universities Act* to recommend annual budget estimates to the Council of Regents exercises an administrative duty and hence does not exercise a statutory power of decision.

Re Weston and Chiropody (Podiatry) Review Ctee. (1980), 29 O.R. (2d) 129, 112 D.L.R. (3d) 343 (C.A.).

Where a review committee considers claims referred to it by the General Manager of the Ontario Health Insurance Plan, its function is purely administrative and thus it does not exercise a statutory power of decision.

Re McGill and Brantford (1980), 28 O.R. (2d) 721, 12 M.P.L.R. 24, 111 D.L.R. (3d) 405 (Div. Ct.).

The function of closing a road is not a statutory power of decision. The power to do so by by-law is a "statutory power" reviewable under the *Judicial Review Procedure Act*, s. 1(g)(i), but that does not attract the application of the *Statutory Powers Procedure Act*.

Re All Ont. Tpt. Ltd. and Ont. Highway Tpt. Bd. (1979), 26 O.R. (2d) 202 (Div. Ct.).

The Board does not exercise a statutory power of decision with regard to an intervenor. A decision would not affect an intervenor's eligibility to receive any benefit nor would a decision from the Board be deciding an intervenor's legal rights.

Re O.S.S.T.F. and Shelton (1979), 28 O.R. (2d) 218, 109 D.L.R. (3d) 59 (Div. Ct.).

The Relations and Discipline Committee of the O.S.S.T.F. does not exercise a statutory power of decision as it only recommends courses of action to the Federation.

Re Webb and Ont. Housing Corp. (1977), 18 O.R. (2d) 427; affirmed 22 O.R. (2d) 257, 93 D.L.R. (3d) 187 (C.A.).

A decision by the Ontario Housing Corporation to terminate a tenancy is not a statutory power of decision.

Re Polten and Univ. of Toronto Governing Council (1975), 8 O.R. (2d) 749, 59 D.L.R. (3d) 197 (Div. Ct.).

The determination of academic appeals by a university faculty committee, where permitted by statute, is not the exercise of statutory power of decision unless the committee was specifically required by law to permit the applicant to be heard before reaching a decision.

Re Raney and Ont. (1974), 4 O.R. (2d) 249, 47 D.L.R. (3d) 533 (C.A.).

The Ministry of Transportation and Communications Qualification Committee is an internal administrative body without statutory existence, thus it cannot be said to be exercising a statutory power of decision.

Re Lamoureux and Reg. of Motor Vehicles, [1973] 2 O.R. 28, 20 C.R.N.S. 254, 10 C.C.C. (2d) 475, 32 D.L.R. (3d) 678 (C.A.).

The automatic suspension of a driver's licence of an individual convicted of impaired driving does not involve any decision-making. Thus, the suspension is not a result of a statutory power of decision.

Re Robertson and Niagara South Bd. of Educ. (1973), 1 O.R. (2d) 548, 41 D.L.R. (3d) 57 (Div. Ct.).

The power exercised by the Board of Education to order the closing of a particular school is not a statutory power of decision. Furthermore, the decision to close a particular school does not affect the rights or privileges of children attending the school as there is no legal right or privilege to have one's children attend a particular school.

Re Florence Nightingale Home and Scarborough Planning Bd., [1973] 1 O.R. 615, 32 D.L.R. (3d) 17 (Div. Ct.).

The conducting of a meeting by a planning board to determine whether or not to recommend changes in zoning by-laws to a council is not an exercise of a statutory power of decision.

Re Thomas and Ctee. of College Presidents, [1973] 3 O.R. 404, 37 D.L.R. (3d) 69 (Div. Ct.).

Where a university committee has decision-making functions transferred to it by a university, this is not a statutory power of decision as the enabling legislation does not impose any duty upon the committee to make decisions.

Statutory Power of Decision — Being Exercised — s. 1(1)

Re Temple and Liquor Licence Bd. of Ont. (1982), 41 O.R. (2d) 214, 145 D.L.R. (3d) 480 (Div. Ct.).

In deciding whether or not to issue a liquor licence to an applicant, the Liquor Licence Board exercises a statutory power of decision.

Re Grant Bus Lines Ltd. and Pension Comm. of Ont. (1980), 30 O.R. (2d) 180, 116 D.L.R. (3d) 336; affirmed (1981), 33 O.R. (2d) 652, 125 D.L.R. (3d) 325 (C.A.); leave to appeal to Supreme Court of Canada refused (1981), 41 N.R. 374.

The Pension Commission of Ontario in making its decisions under the *Pension Benefits Act* affects the legal rights and the eligibility of a person to receive a benefit. Hence, the commission exercises a statutory power of decision.

Re Forde and O.S.S.T.F. (1980), 30 O.R. (2d) 169, 115 D.L.R. (3d) 673 (Div. Ct.).

A statutory obligation to belong to the Federation means that decisions regarding a member's conduct will affect his rights and privileges. Thus the Federation when deciding these matters is exercising a statutory power of decision.

Re Paine and Univ. of Toronto (1980), 30 O.R. (2d) 69, 115 D.L.R. (3d) 461; reversed on other grounds (1981), 34 O.R. (2d) 770, 131 D.L.R. (3d) 325 (C.A.); leave to appeal to Supreme Court of Canada refused (1982), 42 N.R. 270.

The awarding of tenured appointments by a university president, where such power is conferred on that individual by the governing council, is an exercise of a statutory power of decision.

Re Stone and L.S.U.C. (1979), 26 O.R. (2d) 166, 102 D.L.R. (3d) 176 (Div. Ct.).

The Discipline Committee of the Law Society of Upper Canada exercises a quasi-judicial function and its proceedings involve a "statutory power of decision" within s. 1 of the Act.

Re Grant and Metro. Toronto (1978), 21 O.R. (2d) 282 (Div. Ct.).

The discretionary power of a municipal council to pay the legal costs incurred by police officers in defending themselves against charges is a statutory power of decision.

Re Windsor and I.A.F.F. Loc. 455 (1974), 5 O.R. (2d) 690, 51 D.L.R. (3d) 346 (Div. Ct.).

In carrying out its functions, an arbitration board acting under s. 6 of the *Fire Departments Act* exercises a statutory power of decision.

Re Thompson and Lambton Bd. of Educ., [1972] 3 O.R. 889, 30 D.L.R. (3d) 32 (H.C.).

A board of reference convened and acting under the *Schools Administration Act* exercises a statutory power of decision. Despite the fact that the board reports to the Minister of Education, the function of the Minister is purely mandatory — to "direct the implementation of the direction of the board of reference".

Tribunal — s. 1(1)

Re Windsor and I.A.F.F. Loc. 455 (1974), 5 O.R. (2d) 690, 51 D.L.R. (3d) 346 (Div. Ct.).

A board of arbitration acting under s. 6 of the *Fire Departments Act* is a tribunal as defined in the *Statutory Powers Procedure Act*. [*cf. s. 1(1)(d), s. 15.*]

Re Raney and Ont. (1974), 4 O.R. (2d) 249, 47 D.L.R. (3d) 533 (C.A.).

The Ministry of Transportation and Communications Qualification Committee is an internal administrative body without statutory existence, thus it cannot be said to be exercising a statutory power of decision.

Section 2

Interpretation

2. This Act, and any rule made by a tribunal under subsection 17.1(4) or section 25.1, shall be liberally construed to secure the just, most expeditious and cost-effective determination of every proceeding on its merits.

1999, c. 12, Sched. B, s. 16(1); 2006, c. 19, Sched. B, s. 21(1)

Section 3

Application of Act

3. (1) Subject to subsection (2), this Act applies to a proceeding by a tribunal in the exercise of a statutory power of decision conferred by or under an Act of the Legislature, where the tribunal is required by or under such Act or otherwise by law to hold or to afford to the parties to the proceeding an opportunity for a hearing before making a decision.

Where Act does not apply

(2) This Act does not apply to a proceeding,

(a) before the Assembly or any committee of the Assembly;

(b) in or before,

(i) the Court of Appeal,

(ii) the Superior Court of Justice,

(iii) the Ontario Court of Justice,

(iv) the Family Court of the Superior Court of Justice,

(v) the Small Claims Court, or

(vi) a justice of the peace;

(c) to which the Rules of Civil Procedure apply;

(d) before an arbitrator to which the *Arbitrations Act* or the *Labour Relations Act* applies;

(e) at a coroner's inquest;

(f) of a commission appointed under the *Public Inquiries Act*;

Proposed Amendment — 3(2)(f)

(f) of a commission appointed under the *Public Inquiries Act, 2009*;

2009, c. 33, Sched. 6, s. 87 [Not in force at date of publication.]

(g) of one or more persons required to make an investigation and to make a report, with or without recommendations, where the report is for the information or advice of the person to whom it is made and does not in any way legally bind or limit that person in any decision he or she may have power to make; or

(h) of a tribunal empowered to make regulations, rules or by-laws in so far as its power to make regulations, rules or by-laws is concerned.

1994, c. 27, s. 56; 2006, c. 19, Sched. C, s. 1(1), (2), (4)

Case Law

Application of Act — s. 3(1)

Masters v. Ontario (1994), 18 O.R. (3d) 551, 27 Admin. L.R. (2d) 152, 115 D.L.R. (4th) 319, 72 O.A.C. 1 (Div. Ct.).

The government retained outside counsel to investigate and report on allegations of sexual harassment made against the Agent General for Ontario in New York. The Agent subsequently resigned, but brought an application for judicial review, and an order in the nature of *certiorari* quashing the report. It was held that the Act had no application to the original investigation nor to the preparation of the report in the circumstances of the case. No statutory power of decision had been exercised within the meaning of the Act; no hearing was required either by statute or "otherwise by law".

Re Grant and Metro. Toronto (1978), 21 O.R. (2d) 282 (Div. Ct.).

As the *Police Act* imposes no requirement that a trial-type hearing be held, the only other requirement would be "otherwise by law". As the Metropolitan Council makes administrative type decisions, it is not bound in law to provide the trial-type hearing and is not subject to the *Statutory Powers Procedure Act*.

Re Krofchick and Prov. Ins. Co. (1978), 21 O.R. (2d) 805, 91 D.L.R. (3d) 744 (Div. Ct.).

Insurance appraisers are not required by the *Insurance Act* or "otherwise by law" to provide the parties with an opportunity to be heard. Therefore the *Statutory Powers Procedure Act* does not apply to the appraisers.

Re Doctors Hosp. and Min. of Health (1976), 12 O.R. (2d) 164, 1 C.P.C. 232, 68 D.L.R. (3d) 220 (Div. Ct.).

The *Statutory Powers Procedure Act* is not binding on the Crown. However, where the Lieutenant Governor in Council decides to revoke the approval of certain hospitals as public hospitals no right of the Crown is affected by the proceedings.

Exceptions — s. 3(2)(d) — Before an Arbitrator

Re H.F.I.A. and Master Insulators Assn. of Ont. (1979), 25 O.R. (2d) 8, 99 D.L.R. (3d) 757 (Div. Ct.).

The Ontario Labour Relations Board in hearing a grievance regarding a collective agreement comes to a final binding result. The board sits as an arbitrator and decides as an arbitrator. Thus, the *Statutory Powers Procedure Act* does not apply to the board.

Where There is an Investigation and Report — s. 3(2)(g)

Hryciuk v. Ontario (Lieutenant Governor) (1994), 18 O.R. (3d) 695, 115 D.L.R. (4th) 227, 71 O.A.C. 289 (Div. Ct.).

A Commissioner appointed under s. 50 of the *Courts of Justice Act* to determine whether a Provincial Court Judge should be removed from office exercised a statutory power of decision, but s. 3(2)(g) removed the proceeding from the application of Part I.

Re Emerson and L.S.U.C. (1984), 44 O.R. (2d) 729, 41 C.P.C. 7, 5 D.L.R. (4th) 294 (H.C.).

Since the Discipline Committee of the Law Society is the first stage of a single disciplinary proceeding, it does not come within the hearing exemption of s. 3(2)(g).

Re Abel and Dir., Penetanguishene Mental Health Centre; Re Abel and Advisory Review Bd. (1979), 24 O.R. (2d) 279, 46 C.C.C. (2d) 342, 97 D.L.R. (3d) 304; affirmed (1980), 31 O.R. (2d) 520, 56 C.C.C. (2d) 153, 119 D.L.R. (3d) 101 (C.A.).

The Advisory Review Board created under the *Mental Health Act* annually reviews applicants' cases and makes recommendations to the Lieutenant Governor. As the board's report is not binding on the Lieutenant Governor, the board comes within the exception in s. 3(2)(g)(i) therefore the *Statutory Powers Procedure Act* does not apply to the board.

Re Peterson and Atkinson (1978), 23 O.R. (2d) 266, 95 D.L.R. (3d) 349 (Div. Ct.).

A hospital selection committee does not come within the s. 3(2)(g) exception. The committee does much more than recommend, and its recommendations "amount to executive action".

Section 4

Waiver of procedural requirement

4. (1) Any procedural requirement of this Act, or of another Act or a regulation that applies to a proceeding, may be waived with the consent of the parties and the tribunal.

Same, rules

(2) Any provision of a tribunal's rules made under section 25.1 may be waived in accordance with the rules.

1994, c. 27, s. 56; 1997, c. 23, s. 13

Case Law

MacCosham Van Lines (Can.) Co. v. Ontario (Minister of Transportation & Communications) (1988), 66 O.R. (2d) 198, 30 O.A.C. 124 (Div. Ct.).

Where the Ontario Highway Transport Board and a party applying for a rewritten certificate under the *Public Commercial Vehicles Act* both waived a hearing of the board, a third party could not require the board to hold a hearing before rewriting the certificate.

Section 4.1

Disposition without hearing

4.1 If the parties consent, a proceeding may be disposed of by a decision of the tribunal given without a hearing, unless another Act or a regulation that applies to the proceeding provides otherwise.

1994, c. 27, s. 56; 1997, c. 23, s. 13

Section 4.2

Panels, certain matters

4.2 (1) A procedural or interlocutory matter in a proceeding may be heard and determined by a panel consisting of one or more members of the tribunal, as assigned by the chair of the tribunal.

Assignments

(2) In assigning members of the tribunal to a panel, the chair shall take into consideration any requirement imposed by another Act or a regulatoin that applies to the proceeding that the tribunal be representative of specific interests.

Decision of panel

(3) The decision of a majority of the members of a panel, or their unanimous decision in the case of a two-member panel, is the tribunal's decision.

1994, c. 27, s. 56; 1997, c. 23, s. 13

Section 4.2.1

Panel of one

4.2.1 (1) The chair of a tribunal may decide that a proceeding be heard by a panel of one person and assign the person to hear the proceeding unless there is a statutory requirement in another Act that the proceeding be heard by a panel of more than one person.

Reduction in number of panel members

(2) Where there is a statutory requirement in another Act that a proceeding be heard by a panel of a specified number of persons, the chair of the tribunal may assign to the panel one person or any lesser number of persons than the number specified in the other Act if all parties to the proceeding consent.

1999, c. 12, Sched. B, s. 16(2)

Section 4.3

Expiry of term

4.3 If the term of office of a member of a tribunal who has participated in a hearing expires before a decision is given, the term shall be deemed to continue, but only for the purpose of participating in the decision and for no other purpose.

1994, c. 27, s. 56; 1997, c. 23, s. 13

Section 4.4

Incapacity of member

4.4 (1) If a member of a tribunal who has participated in a hearing becomes unable, for any reason, to complete the hearing or to participate in the decision, the remaining member or members may complete the hearing and give a decision.

Other Acts and regulations

(2) Subsection (1) does not apply if another Act or a regulation specifically deals with the issue of what takes place in the circumstances described in subsection (1).

1994, c. 27, s. 56; 1997, c. 23, s. 13

Section 4.5

Decision not to process commencement of proceeding

4.5 (1) Subject to subsection (3), upon receiving documents relating to the commencement of a proceeding, a tribunal or its administrative staff may decide not to process the documents relating to the commencement of the proceeding if,

(a) the documents are incomplete;

(b) the documents are received after the time required for commencing the proceeding has elapsed;

(c) the fee required for commencing the proceeding is not paid; or

(d) there is some other technical defect in the commencement of the proceeding.

Notice

(2) A tribunal or its administrative staff shall give the party who commences a proceeding notice of its decision under subsection (1) and shall set out in the notice the reasons for the decision and the requirements for resuming the processing of the documents.

Rules under s. 25.1

(3) A tribunal or its administrative staff shall not make a decision under subsection (1) unless the tribunal has made rules under section 25.1 respecting the making of such decisions and those rules shall set out,

(a) any of the grounds referred to in subsection (1) upon which the tribunal or its administrative staff may decide not to process the documents relating to the commencement of a proceeding; and

(b) the requirements for the processing of the documents to be resumed.

Continuance of provisions in other statutes

(4) Despite section 32, nothing in this section shall prevent a tribunal or its administrative staff from deciding not to process documents relating to the commencement of a proceeding on grounds that differ from those referred to in subsection (1) or without complying with subsection (2) or (3) if the tribunal or its staff does so in accordance with the provisions of an Act that are in force on the day this section comes into force.

1999, c. 12, Sched. B, s. 16(3)

Section 4.6

Dismissal of proceeding without hearing

4.6 (1) Subject to subsections (5) and (6), a tribunal may dismiss a proceeding without a hearing if,

(a) the proceeding is frivolous, vexatious or is commenced in bad faith;

(b) the proceeding relates to matters that are outside the jurisdiction of the tribunal; or

(c) some aspect of the statutory requirements for bringing the proceeding has not been met.

Notice

(2) Before dismissing a proceeding under this section, a tribunal shall give notice of its intention to dismiss the proceeding to,

(a) all parties to the proceeding if the proceeding is being dismissed for reasons referred to in clause (1)(b); or

(b) the party who commences the proceeding if the proceeding is being dismissed for any other reason.

Same

(3) The notice of intention to dismiss a proceeding shall set out the reasons for the dismissal and inform the parties of their right to make written submissions to the tribunal with respect to the dismissal within the time specified in the notice.

Right to make submissions

(4) A party who receives a notice under subsection (2) may make written submissions to the tribunal with respect to the dismissal within the time specified in the notice.

Dismissal

(5) A tribunal shall not dismiss a proceeding under this section until it has given notice under subsection (2) and considered any submissions made under subsection (4).

Rules

(6) A tribunal shall not dismiss a proceeding under this section 25.1 respecting the early dismissal of proceedings and those rules shall include,

(a) any of the grounds referred to in subsection (1) upon which a proceeding may be dismissed;

(b) the right of the parties who are entitled to receive notice under subsection (2) to make submissions with respect to the dismissal; and

(c) the time within which the submissions must be made.

Continuance of provisions in other statutes

(7) Despite section 32, nothing in this section shall prevent a tribunal from dismissing a proceeding on grounds other than those referred to in subsection (1) or without complying with subsections (2) to (6) if the tribunal dismisses the proceeding in accordance with the provisions of an Act that are in force on the day this section comes into force.

1999, c. 12, Sched. B, s. 16(3)

Section 4.7

Classifying proceedings

4.7 A tribunal may make rules under section 25.1 classifying the types of proceedings that come before it and setting guidelines as to the procedural steps or processes (such as preliminary motions, pre-hearing conferences, alternative dispute resolution mechanisms, expedited hearings) that apply to

each type of proceeding and the circumstances in which other procedures may apply.

1999, c. 12, Sched. B, s. 16(3)

Section 4.8

Alternative dispute resolution

4.8 (1) A tribunal may direct the parties to a proceeding to participate in an alternative dispute resolution mechanism for the purposes of resolving the proceeding or an issue arising in the proceeding if,

(a) it has made rules under section 25.1 respecting the use of alternative dispute resolution mechanisms; and

(b) all parties consent to participating in the alternative dispute resolution mechanism.

Definition

(2) In this section,

"alternative dispute resolution mechanism" includes mediation, conciliation, negotiation or any other means of facilitating the resolution of issues in dispute.

Rules

(3) A rule under section 25.1 respecting the use of alternative dispute resolution mechanisms shall include procedural guidelines to deal with the following:

1. The circumstances in which a settlement achieved by means of an alternative dispute resolution mechanism must be reviewed and approved by the tribunal.

2. Any requirement, statutory or otherwise, that there be an order by the tribunal.

Mandatory alternative dispute resolution

(4) A rule under subsection (3) may provide that participation in an alternative dispute resolution mechanism is mandatory or that it is mandatory in certain specified circumstances.

Person appointed to mediate, etc.

(5) A rule under subsection (3) may provide that a person appointed to mediate, conciliate, negotiate or help resolve a matter by means of an alternative dispute resolution mechanism be a member of the tribunal or a person independent of the tribunal. However, a member of the tribunal who is so appointed with respect to a matter in a proceeding shall not subsequently hear the matter if it comes before the tribunal unless the parties consent.

Continuance of provisions in other statutes

(6) Despite section 32, nothing in this section shall prevent a tribunal from directing parties to a proceeding to participate in an alternative dispute resolution mechanism even though the requirements of subsections (1) to (5) have not been met if the tribunal does so in accordance with the provisions of an Act that are in force on the day this section comes into force.

1999, c. 12, Sched. B, s. 16(3)

Section 4.9

Mediators, etc., not compellable

4.9 (1) No person employed as a mediator, conciliator or negotiator or otherwise appointed to facilitate the resolution of a matter before a tribunal by means of an alternative dispute resolution mechanism shall be compelled to give testimony or produce documents in a proceeding before the tribunal or in a civil proceeding with respect to matters that come to his or her knowledge in the course of exercising his or her duties under this or any other Act.

Evidence in civil proceedings

(2) No notes or records kept by a mediator, conciliator or negotiator or by any other person appointed to facilitate the resolution of a matter before a tribunal by means of an alternative dispute resolution mechanism under this or any other Act are admissible in a civil proceeding.

1999, c. 12, Sched. B, s. 16(3)

Section 5

Parties

5. The parties to a proceeding shall be the persons specified as parties by or under the statute under which the proceeding arises or, if not so specified, persons entitled by law to be parties to the proceeding.

Case Law

Re Temple and Ont. Liquor Licence Bd. (1982), 41 O.R. (2d) 214, 145 D.L.R. (3d) 480 (Div. Ct.).

Where an individual is permitted to make representations before the Liquor Licence Board with regard to an application for a liquor licence, that individual is a party within the meaning of s. 5 of the *Statutory Powers Procedure Act.*

Section 5.1

Written hearings

5.1 (1) A tribunal whose rules made under section 25.1 deal with written hearing may hold a written hearing in a proceeding.

Exception

(2) The tribunal shall not hold a written hearing if a party satisfies the tribunal that there is good reason for not doing so.

Same

(2.1) Subsection (2) does not apply if the only purpose of the hearing is to deal with procedural matters.

Documents

(3) In a written hearing, all the parties are entitled to receive every document that the tribunal receives in the proceeding.

1994, c. 27, s. 56; 1997, c. 23, s. 13; 1999, c. 12, Sched. B, s. 16(4)

Section 5.2

Electronic hearings

5.2 (1) A tribunal whose rules made under section 25.1 deal with electronic hearings may hold an electronic hearing in a proceeding.

Exception

(2) The tribunal shall not hold an electronic hearing if a party satisfies the tribunal that holding an electronic rather than an oral hearing is likely to cause the party significant prejudice.

Same

(3) Subsection (2) does not apply if the only purpose of the hearing is to deal with procedural matters.

Participants to be able to hear one another

(4) In an electronic hearing, all the parties and the members of the tribunal participating in the hearing must be able to hear one another and any witnesses throughout the hearing.

1994, c. 27, s. 56; 1997, c. 23, s. 13

Section 5.2.1

Different kinds of hearings in one proceeding

5.2.1 A tribunal may, in a proceeding, hold any combination of written, electronic and oral hearings.

1997, c. 23, s. 13

Section 5.3

Pre-hearing conferences

5.3 (1) If the tribunal's rules made under section 25.1 deal with pre-hearing conferences, the tribunal may direct the parties to participate in a pre-hearing conference to consider,

(a) the settlement of any or all of the issues;

(b) the simplification of the issues;

(c) facts or evidence that may be agreed upon;

(d) the dates by which any steps in the proceeding are to be taken or begun;

(e) the estimated duration of the hearing; and

(f) any other matter that may assist in the just and most expeditious disposition of the proceeding.

Other Acts and regulations

(1.1) The tribunal's power to direct the parties to participate in a pre-hearing conference is subject to any other Act or regulation that applies to the proceeding.

Who presides

(2) The chair of the tribunal may designate a member of the tribunal or any other person to preside at the pre-hearing conference.

Orders

(3) A member who presides at a pre-hearing conference may make such orders as he or she considers necessary or advisable with respect to the conduct of the proceeding, including adding parties.

Disqualification

(4) A member who presides at a pre-hearing conference at which the parties attempt to settle issues shall not preside at the hearing of the proceeding unless the parties consent.

Application of s. 5.2

(5) Section 5.2 applies to a pre-hearing conference, with necessary modifications.

1994, c. 27, s. 56; 1997, c. 23, s. 13

Section 5.4

Disclosure

5.4 (1) If the tribunal's rules made under section 25.1 deal with disclosure, the tribunal may, at any stage of the proceeding before all hearings are complete, make orders for,

(a) the exchange of documents;

(b) the oral or written examination of a party;

(c) the exchange of witness statements and reports of expert witnesses;

(d) the provision of particulars;

(e) any other form of disclosure.

Other Acts and regulations

(1.1) The tribunal's power to make orders for disclosure is subject to any other Act or regulation that applies to the proceeding.

Exception, privileged information

(2) Subsection (1) does not authorize the making of an order requiring disclosure of privileged information.

1994, c. 27, s. 56(12); 1997, c. 23, s. 13(11)

Section 6

Notice of hearing

6. (1) The parties to a proceeding shall be given reasonable notice of the hearing by the tribunal.

Statutory authority

(2) A notice of a hearing shall include a reference to the statutory authority under which the hearing will be held.

Oral hearing

(3) A notice of an oral hearing shall include,

(a) a statement of the time, place and purpose of the hearing; and

(b) a statement that if the party notified does not attend at the hearing, the tribunal may proceed in the party's absence and the party will not be entitled to any further notice in the proceeding.

Written hearing

(4) A notice of a written hearing shall include,

(a) a statement of the time and purpose of the hearing, and details about the manner in which the hearing will be held;

(b) a statement that the hearing shall not be held as a written hearing if the party satisfies the tribunal that there is good reason for not holding a written hearing (in which case the tribunal is required to hold it as an electronic or oral hearing) and an indication of the procedure to be followed for that purpose.

(c) a statement that if the party notified neither acts under clause (b) nor participates in the hearing in accordance with the notice, the tribunal may proceed without the party's participation and the party will not be entitled to any further notice in the proceeding.

Electronic hearing

(5) A notice of an electronic hearing shall include,

(a) a statement of the time and purpose of the hearing, and details about the manner in which the hearing will be held;

(b) a statement that the only purpose of the hearing is to deal with procedural matters, if that is the case;

(c) if clause (b) does not apply, a statement that the party notified may, by satisfying the tribunal that holding the hearing as an electronic hearing is likely to cause the party significant prejudice, require the tribunal to hold the hearing as an oral hearing, and an indication of the procedure to be followed for that purpose; and

(d) a statement that if the party notified neither acts under clause (c), if applicable, nor participates in the hearing in accordance with the notice, the tribunal may proceed without the party's participation and the party will not be entitled to any further notice in the proceeding.

1994, c. 27, s. 56; 1997, c. 23, s. 13; 1999, c. 12, Sched. B, s. 16(5)

Case Law

Re Central Ont. Coalition Concerning Hydro Transmission Systems and Ont. Hydro (1984), 46 O.R. (2d) 715, 8 Admin. L.R. 81, 27 M.P.L.R. 165, 10 D.L.R (4th) 341, 4 O.A.C. 249, 16 O.M.B.R. 172 (Div. Ct.).

Where a new Ontario Hydro "system plan" is proposed, individuals affected by the proposals are entitled to notice of any hearing. The notice must be reasonable, such that the individual may know the case to be met.

Re Seven-Eleven Taxi Co. and Brampton (1975), 10 O.R. (2d) 677, 64 D.L.R. (3d) 401 (Div. Ct.).

Reasonable notice entails notice sufficient to give an individual whose rights are "in jeopardy" an opportunity to meet the case against him.

Section 7

Effect of non-attendance at hearing after due notice

7. (1) Where notice of an oral hearing has been given to a party to a proceeding in accordance with this Act and the party does not attend at the hearing, the tribunal may proceed in the absence of the party and the party will not be entitled to any further notice in the proceeding.

Same, written hearings

(2) Where notice of a written hearing has been given to a party to a proceeding in accordance with this Act and the party neither acts under clause 6(4)(b) nor participates in the hearing in accordance with the notice, the tribunal may proceed without the party's participation and the party is not entitled to any further notice in the proceeding.

Same, electronic hearings

(3) Where notice of an electronic hearing has been given to a party to a proceeding in accordance with this Act and the party neither acts under clause 6(5)(c), if applicable, nor participates in the hearing in accordance with the notice, the tribunal may proceed without the party's participation and the party is not entitled to any further notice in the proceeding.

1994, c. 27, s. 56

Section 8

Where character, etc. of a party is in issue

8. Where the good character, propriety of conduct or competence of a party is an issue in a proceeding, the party is entitled to be furnished prior to the hearing with reasonable information of any allegations with respect thereto.

Case Law

Re Commodore Bus. Machines Ltd. and Ont. Min. of Labour (1984), 49 O.R. (2d) 17, 10 Admin. L.R. 130, 84 C.L.L.C. 17,028, 14 D.L.R. (4th) 118, (sub nom. *Olarte v. Commodore Bus. Machines Ltd.)* 6 O.A.C. 176 (Div. Ct.).

Section 8 is not intended to preclude the introduction of evidence arising from issues raised by an opposing party at a hearing.

Re Cwinn and L.S.U.C. (1980), 28 O.R. (2d) 61, 108 D.L.R. (3d) 381, 33 N.R. 358n (Div. Ct.).

It is not a denial of natural justice for the Law Society to present evidence at a hearing before the Discipline Committee, though not specified in the complaint, if full particulars of this evidence are provided to the affected member prior to the hearing.

Re All Ont. Tpt. Ltd. and Ont. Highway Tpt. Bd. (1979), 26 O.R. (2d) 202 (Div. Ct.).

The section does not apply to intervenors because, though there may be allegations made challenging their competence, their legal rights are not affected by the immediate proceedings.

Re Don Howson Chevrolet Oldsmobile Ltd. and Reg. of Motor Vehicle Dealers & Salesmen (1974), 6 O.R. (2d) 39, 51 D.L.R. (3d) 683 (Div. Ct.).

The section is not intended to limit cross-examination. Rather it is to permit the person against whom the allegations are made the opportunity of preparing an answer.

Re DiNardo and Ont. Liquor Licence Bd. (1974), 5 O.R. (2d) 124, 49 D.L.R. (3d) 537 (H.C.).

Where the Liquor Licence Board decides to suspend an individual's licence, the combination of the board's "show cause" letter and police and fire department reports is sufficient to satisfy the requirements of s. 8.

Section 9

Hearings to be public, exceptions

9. (1) An oral hearing shall be open to the public except where the tribunal is of the opinion that,

(a) matters involving public security may be disclosed; or

(b) intimate financial or personal matters or other matters may be disclosed at the hearing of such a nature, having regard to the circumstances, that the desirability of avoiding disclosure thereof in the interests of any person affected or in the public interest outweighs the desirability of adhering to the principle that hearings be open to the public,

in which case the tribunal may hold the hearing in the absence of the public.

Written hearings

(1.1) In a written hearing, members of the public are entitled to reasonable access to the documents submitted, unless the tribunal is of the opinion that clause (1)(a) or (b) applies.

Electronic hearings

(1.2) An electronic hearing shall be open to the public unless the tribunal is of the opinion that,

(a) it is not practical to hold the hearing in a manner that is open to the public; or

(b) clause (1)(a) or (b) applies.

Maintenance of order at hearings

(2) A tribunal may make such orders or give such directions at an oral or electronic hearing as it considers necessary for the maintenance of order at the hearing, and, if any person disobeys or fails to comply with any such order or direction, the tribunal or a member thereof may call for the assistance of any peace officer to enforce the order or direction, and every peace officer so called upon shall take such action as is necessary to enforce the order or direction and may use such force as is reasonably required for that purpose.

1994, c. 27, s. 56; 1997, c. 23, s. 13

Case Law

Pilzmaker v. Law Society of Upper Can. (1989), 70 O.R. (2d) 126 (Div. Ct.).

A discipline committee's decision to conduct a hearing in public was made within its jurisdiction. The committee had heard argument on the point, and concluded that the matter was not within the exceptions enumerated in s. 9(1)(b). There was not a strong *prima facie* case that the committee's decision in this regard was wrong.

Ottawa Police Force v. Lalande (1986), 57 O.R. (2d) 509 (Dist. Ct.).

A hearing that affects the public should not be heard *in camera*, unless there are compelling reasons which outweigh the desirability of an open hearing.

Section 9.1

Proceedings involving similar questions

9.1 (1) If two or more proceedings before a tribunal involve the same or similar questions of fact, law or policy, the tribunal may,

(a) combine the proceedings or any part of them, with the consent of the parties;

(b) hear the proceedings at the same time, with the consent of the parties;

(c) hear the proceedings one immediately after the other; or

(d) stay one or more of the proceedings until after the determination of another one of them.

Exception

(2) Subsection (1) does not apply to proceedings to which the *Consolidated Hearings Act* applies.

Same

(3) Clauses (1)(a) and (b) do not apply to a proceeding if,

(a) any other Act or regulation that applies to the proceeding requires that it be heard in private;

(b) the tribunal is of the opinion that clause 9(1)(a) or (b) applies to the proceeding.

Conflict, consent requirements

(4) The consent requirements of clauses (1)(a) and (b) do not apply if another Act or a regulation that applies to the proceedings allows the tribunal to combine them or hear them at the same time without the consent of the parties.

Use of same evidence

(5) If the parties to the second-named proceeding consent, the tribunal may treat evidence that is admitted in a proceeding as if it were also admitted in another proceeding that is heard at the same time under clause (1)(b).

1994, c. 27, s. 56; 1997, c. 23, s. 13

Section 10

Right to representation

10. A party to a proceeding may be represented by a representative.

1994, c. 27, s. 56; 2006, c. 21, Sched. C, s. 134(3)

Case Law

B. v. W. (1985), 52 O.R. (2d) 738, (sub nom. *B. (Y.) v. W. (R.))* 16 Admin. L.R. 99, 23 D.L.R. (4th) 248 (H.C.).

Where there is no issue of credibility in a proceeding, there is a discretion to prohibit cross-examination.

Re Merrick and Dir. of Vocational Rehabilitation Services Branch of Ont. Ministry of Community and Social Services (1985), 49 O.R. (2d) 675, 7 O.A.C. 255 (Div. Ct.).

Where a statute permits a document to be filed, there are no grounds to complain of lack of procedural fairness because the author could not be cross-examined.

Re Ladney and Moore (1984), 46 O.R. (2d) 586, 26 M.P.L.R. 140, 10 D.L.R. (4th) 612, 5 O.A.C. 390, 16 O.M.B.R. 70 (Div. Ct.).

Generally, a party should be permitted to make submissions and adduce evidence before the tribunal reaches its decision.

Re Ellis and Min. of Community & Social Services (1980), 28 O.R. (2d) 385, 110 D.L.R. (3d) 414 (Div. Ct.).

The right to conduct cross-examinations of witnesses, provided for in s. 10(c), does not include the right to require the calling of these witnesses. Specifically, where a statute permits an individual to make his submissions in writing, there is no obligation for that individual to appear as a witness.

Re Henderson and Ont. Securities Comm. (1976), 14 O.R. (2d) 498, 74 D.L.R. (3d) 165 (H.C.).

Any person who has been made a party to the proceedings is entitled to all the rights specified in the section.

Section 10.1

Examination of witnesses

10.1 A party to a proceeding may, at an oral or electronic hearing,

(a) call and examine witnesses and present evidence and submissions; and

(b) conduct cross-examinations of witnesses at the hearing reasonably required for a full and fair disclosure of all matters relevant to the issues in the proceeding.

1994, c. 27, s. 56

Section 11

Rights of witnesses to representation

11. (1) A witness at an oral or electronic hearing is entitled to be advised by a representative as to his or her rights, but such representative may take no other part in the hearing without leave of the tribunal.

Idem

(2) Where an oral hearing is closed to the public, the witness's representative is not entitled to be present except when that witness is giving evidence.

1994, c. 27, s. 56; 2006, c. 21, Sched. C, s. 134(4), (5)

Section 12

Summonses

12. (1) A tribunal may require any person, including a party, by summons,

(a) to give evidence on oath or affirmation at an oral or electronic hearing; and

(b) to produce in evidence at an oral or electronic hearing documents and things specified by the tribunal,

relevant to the subject-matter of the proceeding and admissible at a hearing.

Form and service of summons

(2) A summons issued under subsection (1) shall be in the prescribed form (in English or French) and,

(a) where the tribunal consists of one person, shall be signed by him or her;

(b) where the tribunal consists of more than one person, shall be signed by the chair of the tribunal or in such other manner as documents on behalf of the tribunal may be signed under the statute constituting the tribunal.

Same

(3) The summons shall be served personally on the person summoned.

Fees and allowances

(3.1) The person summoned is entitled to receive the same fees or allowances for attending at or otherwise participating in the hearing as are paid to a person summoned to attend before the Superior Court of Justice.

Bench warrant

(4) A judge of the Superior Court of Justice may issue a warrant against a person if the judge is satisfied that,

(a) a summons was served on the person under this section;

(b) the person has failed to attend or to remain in attendance at the hearing (in the case of an oral hearing) or has failed otherwise to participate in the hearing (in the case of an electronic hearing) in accordance with the summons; and

(c) the person's attendance or participation is material to the ends of justice.

Same

(4.1) The warrant shall be in the prescribed form (in English or French), directed to any police officer, and shall require the person to be apprehended anywhere within Ontario, brought before the tribunal forthwith and,

(a) detained in custody as the judge may order until the person's presence as a witness is no longer required; or

(b) in the judge's discretion, released on a recognizance, with or without sureties, conditioned for attendance or participation to give evidence.

Proof of service

(5) Service of a summons may be proved by affidavit in an application to have a warrant issued under subsection (4).

Certificate of facts

(6) Where an application to have a warrant issued is made on behalf of a tribunal, the person constituting the tribunal or, if the tribunal consists of more than one person, the chair of the tribunal may certify to the judge the facts relied on to establish that the attendance or other participation of the person summoned is material to the ends of justice, and the judge may accept the certificate as proof of the facts.

Same

(7) Where the application is made by a party to the proceeding, the facts relied on to establish that the attendance or other participation of the person is material to the ends of justice may be proved by the party's affidavit.

1994, c. 27, s. 56; 2006, c. 19, Sched. C, s. 1(1)

Case Law

Carter v. Phillips (1988), 66 O.R. (2d) 293 (C.A.).

A commissioner proceeding pursuant to s. 105(1) of the *Residential Tenancies Act* has jurisdiction to order production of records pursuant to s. 12 of the *Statutory Powers Procedure Act*.

Section 13

Contempt proceedings

13. (1) Where any person without lawful excuse,

(a) on being duly summoned under section 12 as a witness at a hearing makes default in attending at the hearing; or

(b) being in attendance as a witness at an oral hearing or otherwise participating as a witness at an electronic hearing, refuses to take an oath or to make an affirmation legally required by the tribunal to be taken or made, or to produce any document or thing in his or her power or control legally required by the tribunal to be produced by him or her or to answer any question to which the tribunal may legally require an answer; or

(c) does any other thing that would, if the tribunal had been a court of law having power to commit for contempt, have been contempt of that court,

the tribunal may, of its own motion or on the motion of a party to the proceeding, state a case to the Divisional Court setting out the facts and that court may inquire into the matter and, after hearing any witnesses who may be produced against or on behalf of that person and after hearing any statement that may be offered in defence, punish or take steps for the punishment of that person in like manner as if he or she had been guilty of contempt of the court.

Same

(2) Subsection (1) also applies to a person who,

(a) having objected under clause 6(4)(b) to a hearing being held as a written hearing, fails without lawful excuse to participate in the oral or electronic hearing of the matter; or

(b) being a party, fails without lawful excuse to attend a pre-hearing conference when so directed by the tribunal.

1994, c. 27, s. 56; 1997, c. 23, s. 13

Case Law

Re Ajax & Pickering Gen. Hosp. and C.U.P.E. (1981), 32 O.R. (2d) 492, 81 C.L.L.C. 14,102, 122 D.L.R. (3d) 109; reversed on other grounds (1982), 35 O.R. (2d) 293, 82 C.L.L.C. 14,164, 132 D.L.R. (3d) 270 (C.A.); leave to appeal to Supreme Court of Canada refused 35 O.R. (2d) 293n, 132 D.L.R. (3d) 270n, 42 N.R. 353.

The section is one of general application and exists as a remedy for contempt in spite of compliance.

Section 14

Protection for witnesses

14. (1) A witness at an oral or electronic hearing shall be deemed to have objected to answer any question asked him or her upon the ground that the answer may tend to criminate him or her or may tend to establish his or her liability to civil proceedings at the instance of the Crown, or of any person, and no answer given by a witness at a hearing shall be used or be receivable in evidence against the witness in any trial or other proceeding against him or her thereafter taking place, other than a prosecution for perjury in giving such evidence.

(2) [Repealed 1994, c. 27, s. 56(29).]

1994, c. 27, s. 56

Case Law

Re O.S.S.T.F. and Shelton (1979), 28 O.R. (2d) 218, 109 D.L.R. (3d) 59 (Div. Ct.).

In deciding that Part I of the *Statutory Powers Procedure Act* does not apply to the Relations and Discipline Committee of the Ontario Teachers' Federation, a committee that merely recommends, the court also decided that s. 14 of the Act does not apply to the above committee.

Section 15

What is admissible in evidence at a hearing

15. (1) Subject to subsections (2) and (3), a tribunal may admit as evidence at a hearing, whether or not given or proven under oath or affirmation or admissible as evidence in a court,

(a) any oral testimony; and

(b) any document or other thing,

relevant to the subject-matter of the proceeding and may act on such evidence, but the tribunal may exclude anything unduly repetitious.

What is inadmissible in evidence at a hearing

(2) Nothing is admissible in evidence at a hearing,

(a) that would be inadmissible in a court by reason of any privilege under the law of evidence; or

(b) that is inadmissible by the statute under which the proceeding arises or any other statute.

Conflicts

(3) Nothing in subsection (1) overrides the provisions of any Act expressly limiting the extent to or purposes for which any oral testimony, documents or things may be admitted or used in evidence in any proceeding.

Copies

(4) Where a tribunal is satisfied as to its authenticity, a copy of a document or other thing may be admitted as evidence at a hearing.

Photocopies

(5) Where a document has been filed in evidence at a hearing, the tribunal may, or the person producing it or entitled to it may with the leave of the tribunal, cause the document to be photocopied and the tribunal may authorize the photocopy to be filed in evidence in the place of the document filed and release the document filed, or may furnish to the person producing it or the person entitled to it a photocopy of the document filed certified by a member of the tribunal.

Certified copy admissible in evidence

(6) A document purporting to be a copy of a document filed in evidence at a hearing, certified to be a copy thereof by a member of the tribunal, is admissible in evidence in proceedings in which the document is admissible as evidence of the document.

Case Law

B. v. Catholic Children's Aid Society (Metropolitan Toronto) (1987), 59 O.R. (2d) 417, (sub nom. *B. (J.) v. Catholic Children's Aid Society (Metropolitan Toronto))* 27 Admin. L.R. 295, 7 R.F.L. (3d) 441, 38 D.L.R. (4th) 106 (Div. Ct.).

A party applying to have his name expunged from the Child Abuse Register was denied natural justice when hearsay evidence of the alleged abuse was admitted on the hearing. The admission of the evidence had precluded the appellant from cross-examining the alleged victim.

Re Commodore Bus. Machines Ltd. and Ont. Min. of Labour (1984), 49 O.R. (2d) 17, 10 Admin. L.R. 130, 84 C.L.L.C. 17,028, 14 D.L.R. (4th) 118, (sub nom. *Olarte v. Commodore Bus. Machines Ltd.*) 6 O.A.C. 176 (Div. Ct.).

A board of inquiry of the Human Rights Commission is within the jurisdiction of the *Statutory Powers Procedure Act*, and therefore the board is entitled to admit and base its decision on similar fact evidence and hearsay evidence.

Lischka v. Criminal Injuries Comp. Bd. (1982), 37 O.R. (2d) 134 (Div. Ct.).

Section 15(1) permits the admission of hearsay and opinion evidence, though in some cases the admission of such evidence could amount to a denial of natural justice.

Lynch v. Ottawa (1974), 7 L.C.R. 7 (Land Compensation Bd.).

In proceedings before the board, hearsay evidence in appraisal reports of sales and offers to purchase is admissible as relevant.

Re Windsor and I.A.F.F. Loc. 455 (1974), 5 O.R. (2d) 690, 51 D.L.R. (3d) 346 (Div. Ct.).

A brief prepared by a union is not evidence. The contents of the brief are representations by the union and, thus, should not be relied upon by the Labour Relations Board in reaching its decision.

Section 15.1

Use of previously admitted evidence

15.1 (1) The tribunal may treat previously admitted evidence as if it had been admitted in a proceeding before the tribunal, if the parties to the proceeding consent.

Definition

(2) In subsection (1),

"previously admitted evidence" means evidence that was admitted, before the hearing of the proceeding referred to in that subsection, in any other proceeding before a court or tribunal, whether in or outside Ontario.

Additional power

(3) This power conferred by this section is in addition to the tribunal's power to admit evidence under section 15.

1994, c. 27, s. 56; 1997, c. 23, s. 13

Section 15.2

Witness panels

15.2 A tribunal may receive evidence from panels of witnesses composed of two or more persons, if the parties have first had an opportunity to make submissions in that regard.

1994, c. 27, s. 56

Section 16

Notice of facts and opinions

16. A tribunal may, in making its decision in any proceeding,

(a) take notice of facts that may be judicially noticed; and

(b) take notice of any generally recognized scientific or technical facts, information or opinions within its scientific or specialized knowledge.

Section 16.1

Interim decisions and orders

16.1 (1) A tribunal may make interim decisions and orders.

Conditions

(2) A tribunal may impose conditions on an interim decision or order.

Reasons

(3) An interim decision or order need not be accompanied by reasons.

1994, c. 27, s. 56

Section 16.2

Time frames

16.2 A tribunal shall establish guidelines setting out the usual time frame for completing proceedings that come before the tribunal and for completing the procedural steps within those proceedings.

1999, c. 12, Sched. B, s. 16(6)

Section 17

Decision

17. (1) A tribunal shall give its final decision and order, if any, in any proceeding in writing and shall give reasons in writing therefor if requested by a party.

Interest

(2) A tribunal that makes an order for the payment of money shall set out in the order the principal sum, and if interest is payable, the rate of interest and the date from which it is to be calculated.

1993, c. 27, Sched.; 1994, c. 27, s. 56

Case Law

Leung v. Ontario (Criminal Injuries Compensation Board) (1995), 24 O.R. (3d) 530, (sub nom. *So v. Criminal Injuries Compensation Board (Ont.))* 82 O.A.C. 43 (Div. Ct.).

On an appeal from a decision of the Criminal Injuries Compensation Board, the appellant argued that the Board had erred in applying Board policy guidelines with respect to, *inter alia*, wage laws. The Board had given no reasons for its decision but on appeal it was found that it could not be said that the Board exercised its discretion unreasonably. While it would have been desirable for the Board to have given reasons, there was no evidence to suggest that the appellant had requested that the Board give reasons, and accordingly s. 17 of the Act did not apply.

Re Temple and Ont. Liquor Licence Bd. (1982), 41 O.R. (2d) 214, 145 D.L.R. (3d) 480 (Div. Ct.).

Because a member of the public making representations before the Liquor Licence Board is a party to the proceedings, that person is entitled to reasons from the board concerning the decision reached.

Re DiNardo and Ont. Liquor Licence Bd. (1974), 5 O.R. (2d) 124, 49 D.L.R. (3d) 537 (H.C.).

Where in response to a request for reasons for their decision the Liquor Licence Board furnished the party with a summary of the proceedings, it was held that this was not sufficient to satisfy the written reasons requirement of the section.

Section 17.1

Costs

17.1 (1) Subject to subsection (2), a tribunal may, in the circumstances set out in rules made under subsection (4), order a party to pay all or part of another party's costs in a proceeding.

Exception

(2) A tribunal shall not make an order to pay costs under this section unless,

(a) the conduct or course of conduct of a party has been unreasonable, frivolous or vexatious or a party has acted in bad faith; and

(b) the tribunal has made rules under subsection (4).

Amount of costs

(3) The amount of the costs ordered under this section shall be determined in accordance with the rules made under subsection (4).

Rules

(4) A tribunal may make rules with respect to,

(a) the ordering of costs;

(b) the circumstances in which costs may be ordered; and

(c) the amount of costs or the manner in which the amount of costs is to be determined.

Same

(5) Subsections 25.1(3), (4), (5) and (6) apply with respect to rules made under subsection (4).

Continuance of provisions in other statutes

(6) Despite section 32, nothing in this section shall prevent a tribunal from ordering a party to pay all or part of another party's costs in a proceeding in circumstances other than those set out in, and without complying with, subsections (1) to (3) if the tribunal makes the order in accordance with the provisions of an Act that are in force on February 14, 2000.

Transition

(7) This section, as it read on the day before the effective date, continues to apply to proceedings commenced before the effective date.

Same

(8) Rules that are made under section 25.1 before the effective date and comply with subsection (4) are deemed to be rules made under subsection (4) until the earlier of the following days:

1. The first anniversary of the effective date.

2. The day on which the tribunal makes rules under subsection (4).

Definition

(9) In subsections (7) and (8),

"effective date" means the day on which section 21 of Schedule B to the *Good Government Act, 2006* comes into force.

1999, c. 12, Sched. B, s. 16(7); 2006, c. 19, Sched. B, s. 21(2)

Section 18

Notice of decision

18. (1) The tribunal shall send each party who participated in the proceeding, or the party's representative, a copy of its final decision or order, including the reasons if any have been given,

(a) by regular lettermail;

(b) by electronic transmission;

(c) by telephone transmission of a facsimile; or

(d) by some other method that allows proof of receipt, if the tribunal's rules made under section 25.1 deal with the matter.

Use of mail

(2) If the copy is sent by regular lettermail, it shall be sent to the most recent addresses known to the tribunal and shall be deemed to be received by the party on the fifth day after the day it is mailed.

Use of electronic or telephone transmission

(3) If the copy is sent by electronic transmission or by telephone transmission of a facsimile, it shall be deemed to be received on the day after it was sent, unless that day is a holiday, in which case the copy shall be deemed to be received on the next day that is not a holiday.

Use of other method

(4) If the copy is sent by a method referred to in clause (1)(d), the tribunal's rules made under section 25.1 govern its deemed day of receipt.

Failure to receive copy

(5) If a party that acts in good faith does not, through absence, illness or other cause beyond the party's control, receive the copy until a later date than the deemed day of receipt, subsection (2), (3) or (4), as the case may be, does not apply.

1994, c. 27, s. 56; 1997, c. 23, s. 13; 2006, c. 21, Sched. C, s. 134(6)

Case Law

Re Powell and Min. of Justice (1980), 31 O.R. (2d) 111, 118 D.L.R. (3d) 158, (sub nom. *Re Powell and A.G. Ont.)* 11 O.M.B.R. 193 (Div. Ct.).

A decision of the Ontario Municipal Board was quashed when an interested party did not receive notice of the decision until after the time for petitioning the Lieutenant Governor in Council had expired.

Section 19

Enforcement of orders

19. (1) A certified copy of a tribunal's decision or order in a proceeding may be filed in the Superior Court of Justice by the tribunal or by a party and

on filing shall be deemed to be an order of that court and is enforceable as such.

Notice of filing

(2) A party who files an order under subsection (1) shall notify the tribunal within 10 days after the filing.

Order for payment of money

(3) On receiving a certified copy of a tribunal's order for the payment of money, the sheriff shall enforce the order as if it were an execution issued by the Superior Court of Justice.

1994, c. 27, s. 56; 2006, c. 19, Sched. C, s. 1(1)

Case Law

WMI Waste Mgmt. of Can. Inc. v. Metro. Toronto (1981), 34 O.R. (2d) 708, 23 R.P.R. 257, 24 L.C.R. 204 (H.C.).

Filing under the section does not incorporate a substantive right to interest on taxed costs. The right to interest in respect of an expropriation claim is a substantive right that must be found in the legislation governing the claim.

Section 20

Record of proceeding

20. A tribunal shall compile a record of any proceeding in which a hearing has been held which shall include,

(a) any application, complaint, reference or other document, if any, by which the proceeding was commenced;

(b) the notice of any hearing;

(c) any interlocutory orders made by the tribunal;

(d) all documentary evidence filed with the tribunal, subject to any limitation expressly imposed by any other Act on the extent to or the purposes for which any such documents may be used in evidence in any proceeding;

(e) the transcript, if any, of the oral evidence given at the hearing; and

(f) the decision of the tribunal and the reasons therefor, where reasons have been given.

Section 21

Adjournments

21. A hearing may be adjourned from time to time by a tribunal of its own motion or where it is shown to the satisfaction of the tribunal that the adjournment is required to permit an adequate hearing to be held.

Section 21.1

Corrections of errors

21.1 A tribunal may at any time correct a typographical error, error of calculation or similar error made in its decision or order.

1994, c. 27, s. 56

Section 21.2

Power to review

21.2 (1) A tribunal may, if it considers it advisable and if its rules made under section 25.1 deal with the matter, review all or part of its own decision or order, and may confirm, vary, suspend or cancel the decision or order.

Time for review

(2) The review shall take place within a reasonable time after the decision or order is made.

Conflict

(3) In the event of a conflict between this section and any other Act, the other Act prevails.

1994, c. 27, s. 56; 1997, c. 23, s. 13

Section 22

Administration of oaths

22. A member of a tribunal has power to administer oaths and affirmations for the purpose of any of its proceedings and the tribunal may require evidence before it to be given under oath or affirmation.

Section 23

Abuse of processes

23. (1) A tribunal may make such orders or give such directions in proceedings before it as it considers proper to prevent abuse of its processes.

Limitation on examination

(2) A tribunal may reasonably limit further examination or cross-examination of a witness where it is satisfied that the examination or cross-examination has been sufficient to disclose fully and fairly all matters relevant to the issues in the proceeding.

Exclusion of representatives

(3) A tribunal may exclude from a hearing anyone, other than a person licensed under the *Law Society Act*, appearing on behalf of a party or as an adviser to a witness if it finds that such person is not competent properly to represent or to advise the party or witness, or does not understand and comply at the hearing with the duties and responsibilities of an advocate or adviser.

1994, c. 27, s. 56; 2006, c. 21, Sched. C, s. 134(7)

Case Law

L.I.U.N.A., Local 183 v. L.I.U.N.A., Locals 506, 527, 837, (sub nom. *Universal Workers' Union, Labourers' International Union of North America, Local 183 v. Laborers' International Union of North America)* 70 O.R. (3d) 435, [2004] O.L.R.B. Rep. 471 (S.C.J.)

The Ontario Labour Relations Board has jurisdiction under ss. 23(1) and 25.0.1 of the *Statutory Powers Procedure Act* as to whether there is a conflict of interest which justifies the disqualification of solicitors representing a party involved in proceedings before the Board.

Re Stone and L.S.U.C. (1979), 26 O.R. (2d) 166, 102 D.L.R. (3d) 176 (Div. Ct.).

The procedure to be followed on a motion for severance of charges before the Discipline Committee of the Law Society of Upper Canada is the same as the procedure to be followed on an application to sever counts on a multiple count indictment against an individual accused of committing a crime.

Re Henderson and Ont. Securities Comm. (1976), 14 O.R. (2d) 498, 74 D.L.R. (3d) 165 (H.C.).

Where an individual has been made a party to the proceedings, a board may not refuse the individual's counsel the right to cross-examine.

Section 24

Notice, etc.

24. (1) Where a tribunal is of opinion that because the parties to any proceeding before it are so numerous or for any other reason, it is impracticable,

(a) to give notice of the hearing; or

(b) to send its decision and the material mentioned in section 18,

to all or any of the parties individually, the tribunal may, instead of doing so, cause reasonable notice of the hearing or of its decision to be given to such parties by public advertisement or otherwise as the tribunal may direct.

Contents of notice

(2) A notice of a decision given by a tribunal under clause (1)(b) shall inform the parties of the place where copies of the decision and the reasons therefor, if reasons were given, may be obtained.

Case Law

Re Rose (1982), 38 O.R. (2d) 162, 29 C.P.C. 235, (sub nom. *Re Rose and Reg. of Collection Agencies)* 137 D.L.R. (3d) 365 (Div. Ct.).

In seeking a stay of execution of a tribunal's decision, absent special circumstances, an applicant ought to apply to the tribunal before making application to the Divisional Court.

Re C.P. Express Ltd. and Snow (1980), 31 O.R. (2d) 120, (sub nom. *C.P. Express Ltd. v. Min. of Transportation & Communications)* 19 C.P.C. 16, 118 D.L.R. (3d) 148; affirmed 32 O.R. (2d) 45, 121 D.L.R. (3d) 511 (C.A.).

A petition to the Lieutenant Governor in Council does not operate as an automatic stay of a decision of the Ontario Highway Transport Board because (1) it does not qualify as "an appeal ... to a court or other appellate tribunal" within the meaning of s. 25 of the *Statutory Powers Procedure Act*, and (2) pursuant to s. 18(a) of the *Ontario Highway Transport Board Act*, only ss. 2-24 of the *Statutory Powers Procedure Act* apply.

Re Schiller and Scarborough Gen. Hosp. (1973), 2 O.R. (2d) 324 (Div. Ct.).

Where an applicant seeks an order removing a stay arising from an appeal, the onus is on the applicant to convince the court that in light of all relevant circumstances the stay should be removed.

Section 25

Appeal operates as stay, exception

25. (1) An appeal from a decision of a tribunal to a court or other appellate body operates as a stay in the matter unless,

(a) another Act or regulation that applies to the proceeding expressly provides to the contrary; or

(b) the tribunal or the court or other appellate body orders otherwise.

Idem

(2) An application for judicial review under the *Judicial Review Procedure Act*, or the bringing of proceedings specified in subsection 2(1) of that Act is not an appeal within the meaning of subsection (1).

1997, c. 23, s. 13

Section 25.0.1

Control of process

25.0.1 A tribunal has the power to determine its own procedures and practices and may for that purpose,

(a) make orders with respect to the procedures and practices that apply in any particular proceeding; and

(b) establish rules under section 25.1.

1999, c. 12, Sched. B, s. 16(8)

Section 25.1

Rules

25.1 (1) A tribunal may make rules governing the practice and procedure before it.

Application

(2) The rules may be of general or particular application.

Consistency with Acts

(3) The rules shall be consistent with this Act and with the other Acts to which they relate.

Public access

(4) The tribunal shall make the rules available to the public in English and in French.

Part III (Regulations) of the Legislation Act, 2006

(5) Rules adopted under this section are not regulations as defined in Part III (Regulations) of the *Legislation Act, 2006*.

Additional power

(6) The power conferred by this section is in addition to any power to adopt rules that the tribunal may have under another Act.

1994, c. 27, s. 56; 2006, c. 21, Sched. F, s. 136(1), Table 1

Section 26

Regulations

26. The Lieutenant Governor in Council may make regulations prescribing forms for the purpose of section 12.

1994, c. 27, s. 56

Section 27

Rules, etc., available to public

27. A tribunal shall make any rules or guidelines established under this or any other Act available for examination by the public.

1999, c. 12, Sched. B, s. 16(9)

Section 28

Substantial compliance

28. Substantial compliance with requirements respecting the content of forms, notices or documents under this Act or any rule made under this or any other Act is sufficient.

1999, c. 12, Sched. B, s. 16(9)

Section 29

29. [Repealed 1994, c. 27, s. 56.]

Section 30

30. [Repealed 1994, c. 27, s. 56.]

Section 31

31. [Repealed 1994, c. 27, s. 56.]

Section 32

Conflict

32. Unless it is expressly provided in any other Act that its provisions and regulations, rules or by-laws made under it apply despite anything in this Act, the provisions of this Act prevail over the provisions of such other Act and over regulations, rules or by-laws made under such other Act which conflict therewith.

1994, c. 27, s. 56

Case Law

Re Thompson and Lambton Bd. of Educ., [1972] 3 O.R. 889, 30 D.L.R. (3d) 32 (H.C.).

As Part I of the *Statutory Powers Procedure Act* applies to a board of reference under the *Schools Administration Act*, where a section of the *Schools Administration Act* is found to be in conflict with the *Statutory Powers Procedure Act*, the latter prevails.

Section 33

33. [Repealed 1994, c. 27, s. 56.]

Section 34

34. [Repealed 1994, c. 27, s. 56.]

Forms 1 and 2 [Repealed 1994, c. 27, s. 56.]. ***See now O. Reg. 116/95.***

FORMS

Made under the *Statutory Powers Procedure Act*

O. Reg. 116/95

1. A summons issued under subsection 12(1) of the Act shall be in Form 1.

2. A warrant issued under subsection 12(4) of the Act shall be in Form 2.

3. This Regulation comes into force on April 1, 1995.

FORM 1 — SUMMONS

Summons To A Witness Before (name of tribunal)

(Name of Act under which proceeding arises)

TO: (*name and address of witness*)

(*For oral hearing*)

YOU ARE REQUIRED TO ATTEND TO GIVE EVIDENCE at the hearing of this proceeding on (*day*), (*date*), at (*time*), at (*place*), and to remain until your attendance is no longer required.

YOU ARE REQUIRED TO BRING WITH YOU and produce at the hearing the following documents and things: (*Set out the nature and date of each document and give sufficient particulars to identify each document and thing.*)

IF YOU FAIL TO ATTEND OR TO REMAIN IN ATTENDANCE AS THIS SUMMONS REQUIRES, THE ONTARIO COURT (GENERAL DIVISION) MAY ORDER THAT A WARRANT FOR YOUR ARREST BE ISSUED, OR THAT YOU BE PUNISHED IN THAT SAME WAY AS FOR CONTEMPT OF THAT COURT.

(*For electronic hearing*)

YOU ARE REQUIRED TO PARTICIPATE IN AN ELECTRONIC HEARING on (*day*), (*date*), at (*time*), in the following manner: (*Give sufficient particulars to enable witness to participate.*)

IF YOU FAIL TO PARTICIPATE IN THE HEARING IN ACCORDANCE WITH THE SUMMONS, THE ONTARIO COURT (GENERAL DIVISION) MAY ORDER THAT A WARRANT FOR YOUR ARREST BE ISSUED, OR THAT YOU BE PUNISHED IN THE SAME WAY AS FOR CONTEMPT OF THAT COURT.

Date .... (*Name of tribunal*)

.... (*Signature by or on behalf of tribunal*)

NOTE: You are entitled to be paid the same fees or allowances for attending at or otherwise participating in the hearing as are paid to a person summoned to attend before the Ontario Court (General Division).

FORM 2 — WARRANT FOR ARREST (DEFAULTING WITNESS)

Ontario Court (General Division)

(***Name of judge***)
(***Day and date***)
(***Court seal***)
(***Title of proceeding***)

Warrant For Arrest

TO ALL police officers in Ontario

AND TO the officers of all correctional institutions in Ontario

WHEREAS the witness (*name*), of (*address*), was served under section 12 of the *Statutory Powers Procedure Act* with a summons to witness to give evidence at the hearing of (*title of proceeding*) before (*name of tribunal*) on (*day*), (*date*) at (*time*),

AND WHEREAS the witness failed to attend or to remain in attendance at the hearing (*or, in the case of an electronic hearing* to participate in the hearing in accordance with the summons),

AND WHEREAS I am satisfied that the witness' attendance or participation is material to the ends of justice,

YOU ARE ORDERED TO ARREST and bring the witness (*name*) before (*name of tribunal*) to give evidence in the proceeding, and if the tribunal is not then sitting or if the witness cannot be brought forthwith before the tribunal, to deliver the witness to a provincial correctional institution or other secure facility, to be admitted and detained there until his or her presence as a witness is no longer required, or until otherwise ordered.

.... (*Signature of judge*)